John Bagnell Bury

A History
of the
Later Roman Empire

from Arcadius to Irene
(395 A.D. to 800 A.D.)

Volume II

D1720277

Elibron Classics
www.elibron.com

A HISTORY

OF THE

LATER ROMAN EMPIRE

A HISTORY

OF THE

LATER ROMAN EMPIRE

FROM ARCADIUS TO IRENE

(395 A.D. TO 800 A.D.)

BY

J. B. BURY, M.A.

FELLOW AND TUTOR OF TRINITY COLLEGE, DUBLIN

VOL. II

London

MACMILLAN AND CO.

AND NEW YORK

1889

LIST OF CALIPHS (632-800 A.D.)

		A.D.
Abu Bekr	. . . . .	632
Omar I	. . . . .	634
Othman	. . . . .	644
Muaviah I } Ali }	. . . . .	656
Muaviah I	. . . . .	661
Yezid I	. . . . .	680
Muaviah II	. . . . .	683
Mervan I	. . . . .	683
Abd Almalik	. . . . .	685
Welid I	. . . . .	705
Suleiman	. . . . .	715
Omar II	. . . . .	717
Yezid II	. . . . .	720
Hischam	. . . . .	724
Welid II	. . . . .	743
Yezid III	. . . . .	744
Mervan II	. . . . .	744

End of Omeyyad dynasty in 750.

ABBASID DYNASTY.

Abd Allah (Abu-l-Abbas)	. . .	750
Abu Djafar Manssur	. . .	754
Mahdi .	. . . .	775
Hadi .	. . . .	785
Harun Arraschid	. . .	786

GENEALOGICAL TABLE OF THE HOUSE OF HERACLIUS

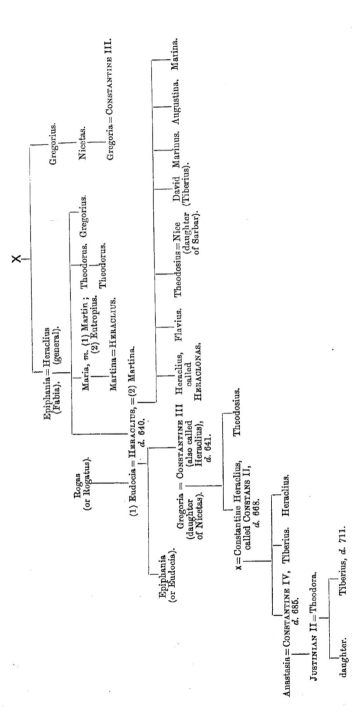

CHRONOLOGICAL TABLE FROM THE ACCESSION OF JUSTIN II, 565, TO THE DEATH OF IRENE, 802

A.D.	INDICTION.	A.M.	IMPERIAL ACCESSIONS.	EVENTS.
565	13–14	6057–8	Justin II.	Embassy of Avars arrives at Constantinople.
567	15–1	6059–60		Lombards and Avars overthrow Gepid kingdom.
568	1–2	6060–1		Lombards enter Italy.
569	2–3	6061–2		Embassy of Turks to Constantinople.
571	4–5	6063–4		Duchy of Beneventum founded.
572	5–6	6064–5		War with Persia begins. Campaign of Marcian.
573	6–7	6065–6		Roman victory at Sargathon. Persians invade Syria. Death of Alboin.
574	7–8	6066–7		Daras taken by Persians. Tiberius defeated by Avars. Tiberius made Caesar and regent.
575	8–9	6067–8		Peace for three years with Persia (except in Persarmenia).
576	9–10	6068–9		Chosroes defeated near Melitene.
577	10–11	6069–70		Slaves invade Illyricum and Thrace, and settle in Roman territory. Maurice invades Arzanene and Cordyene (date uncertain).
578	11–12	6070–1	Tiberius II.	
579	12–13	6071–2		Death of Chosroes Nushirvan.
581	14–15	6073–4		Sirmium lost to the Avars. Treaty with Avars. Roman victory at Constantina.
582	15–1	6074–5	Maurice.	

A.D.	INDICTION.	A.M.	IMPERIAL ACCESSIONS.	EVENTS.
583	1–2	6075–6		Avars seize Singidunum, etc. Battle of the Nymphius.
584	2–3	6076–7		Treaty with Avars. Autharis, king of Lombards. Death of Chilperic. Revolt of Hermenigild against Leovigild.
585	3–4	6077–8		Birth of the prince Theodosius.
586	4–5	6078–9		Victory of Romans (under Philippicus) at Solachon. Avars harry Moesia.
587	5–6	6079–80		Campaign of Comentiolus against Avars.
588	6–7	6080–1		Disaffection in eastern army.
589	7–8	6081–2		Martyropolis taken by Persians. Comentiolus wins a battle near Nisibis.
590	8–9	6082–3		Varahran rebels and becomes king of Persia. Monte Cassino rendered desolate. Agilulf king of Lombards. Gregory (the Great) becomes Pope.
591	9–10	6083–4		Maurice restores Chosroes II to the Persian throne. Peace with Persia. Avars invade Thrace.
592	10–11	6084–5		Expedition of Priscus against the Slaves.
593	11–12	6085–6		Campaign of Peter.
596	14–15	6088–9		Mission of St. Augustine to Britain.
597	15–1	6089–90		Peter's expedition against Slaves. Avars besiege Thessalonica.
598	1–2	6090–1		Avars besiege Singidunum and invade Dalmatia.
599	2–3	6091–2		Avars invade Moesia. Peace between Lombards and exarchate.
600	3–4	6092–3		Great victories of Priscus over the Avars.
602	5–6	6094–5	Phocas.	Gudwin's campaign against Slaves. Revolution, and overthrow of Maurice.
603	6–7	6095–6		Revolt of Narses.
604	7–8	6096–7		Death of Pope Gregory. Treaty with Avars.
605	8–9	6097–8		Conspiracy against Phocas.
606	9–10	6098–9		Daras taken by Persians. Invasion of Syria.
607	10–11	6099–100		Persians invade the Empire.
608	11–12	6100–1		Persians advance to Chalcedon.
609	12–13	6101–2		Revolt of Africa and of Alexandria.

A.D.	INDICTION.	A.M.	IMPERIAL ACCESSIONS.	EVENTS.
610	13–14	6102–3	Heraclius.	Revolt of Jews in Antioch. Phocas overthrown by Heraclius.
611	14–15	6103–4		Birth of Epiphania.
612	15–1	6104–5		Birth of Constantine.
614	2–3	6106–7		Persians invade Syria and take Damascus. Treaty of Heraclius with Sisibut of Spain.
615	3–4	6107–8		Palestine invaded; Jerusalem taken.
616	4–5	6108–9		Egypt lost to the Persians (date uncertain).
617	5–6	6109–10		Persians take Chalcedon.
618	6–7	6110–11		Heraclius thinks of migrating to Carthage.
619	7–8	6111–12		Heraclius flees from Avars.
620	8–9	6112–13		Peace with Avars.
622	10–11	6114–15		Heraclius sets out for the Persian war. (1) Campaign of Cappadocia and Pontus. (16th July, era of the Hegira.)
623	11–12	6115–16		End of first campaign.
624	12–13	6116–17		(2) First campaign of Azerbiyan. Last imperial towns in Spain taken by Svinthila. (3) Campaign of Albania and Armenia.
625	13–14	6117–18		(4) Campaign of Cilicia.
626	14–15	6118–19		(5) Second campaign of Azerbiyan. Great siege of Constantinople by Avars and Persians.
627	15–1	6119–20		(6) Campaign of Assyria. Mohammed writes to Heraclius.
628	1–2	6120–1		
629	2–3	6121–2		Battle of Muta. Heraclius restores cross to Jerusalem.
632	5–6	6124–5		Death of Mohammed. Abu Bekr first caliph.
634	7–8	6126–7		Battle of Adjnadein (July). Omar becomes caliph. Battle of Yermuk (August).
635	8–9	6127–8		Saracens take Damascus.
636	9–10	6128–9		Capture of Emesa and Heliopolis. "Farewell" of Heraclius. Conquest of Antioch, Chalcis, Beroea, Edessa, etc. Battle of Cadesia.
637	10–11	6129–30		Jerusalem taken. Battle of Yalulah.
638	11–12	6130–1		Ecthesis published. Constantine attempts to recover Syria. Muaviah becomes emir of Syria. Conquest of Mesopotamia.

A.D.	INDICTION.	A.M.	IMPERIAL ACCESSIONS.	EVENTS.
639	12–13	6131–2		Amru invades Egypt.
641	14–15	6133–4	Constantine III. Heraclonas.	Death of Heraclius. Death of Constantine III. Fall of Alexandria. Battle of Nehavend.
642	15–1	6134–5	Constans II.	Fall of Heraclonas and Martina. Battle of Scultenna, and conquest of Liguria by Lombards.
644	2–3	6136–7		Othman becomes caliph.
646	4–5	6138–9		Foundation of Cairo (Fostât). Manifesto of Africa against monotheletism.
647	5–6	6139–40		Revolt in Africa.
648	6–7	6140–1		Type of Constans issued.
649	7–8	6141–2		Saracen expedition against Cyprus. Lateran Council condemns the Type.
650	8–9	6142–3		Aradus conquered.
651	9–10	6143–4		Saracens invade Asia Minor.
652	10–11	6144–5		Armenia lost.
654	12–13	6146–7		Saracens take Rhodes. Pope Martin at New Rome.
655	13–14	6147–8		Naval battle of Phoenix. Pope Martin banished to Cherson.
656	14–15	6148–9		Murder of Caliph Othman. Double caliphate.
658	1–2	6150–1		Expedition of Constans against Slaves.
659	2–3	6151–2		Treaty with Saracens.
660	3–4	6152–3		Sylvanus founds a Paulician community.
661	4–5	6153–4		Death of Ali.
662	5–6	6154–5		Constans sets out for Italy.
663	6–7	6155–6		Saracens invade Romania in this and following years.
668	11–12	6160–1	Constantine IV.	Constans assassinated. Revolt of Saborios on Armenian frontier.
669	12–13	6161–2		Saracens attack Sicily.
670	13–14	6162–3		Foundation of Kairowan.
673	1–2	6165–6		Expedition of Muaviah against Constantinople.
674	2–3	6166–7		Siege of Constantinople continued until 677.
675	3–4	6167–8		Slaves besiege Salonica.
676	4–5	6168–9		Capture of Kairowan by Christians, but soon recovered.
677	5–6	6169–70		Siege of Constantinople raised. Slaves again besiege Salonica.
678	6–7	6170–1		Peace with the caliphate. Embassies of western nations to Constantinople. Slaves besiege Salonica.
679	7–8	6171–2		Foundation of Bulgarian kingdom.

A.D.	INDICTION.	A.M.	IMPERIAL ACCESSIONS.	EVENTS.
680	8–9	6172–3		Death of Muaviah. Sixth Ecumenical Council begins.
683	11–12	6175–6		Kairowan taken by Christians.
685	13–14	6177–8	Justinian II.	Treaty with Abd Almalik. Death of Constantine.
687	15–1	6179–80		Transmigration of Mardaites.
688	1–2	6180–1		Slaves settled in *Opsikion.*
690	3–4	6182–3		Expedition of Justinian against Bulgarians and Slaves.
692	5–6	6184–5		Quinisext Council.
693	6–7	6185–6		Battle of Sebastopolis. Revolt of Symbatius. Armenia finally subjected to the Arabs.
695	8–9	6187–8	Leontius.	Fall and banishment of Justinian.
697	10–11	6189–90		Lazica revolts. Asia Minor invaded by Saracens. Hassan's expedition against Africa. Takes Carthage and recovers Kairowan. John retakes Carthage. Election of first doge of Venice.
698	11–12	6190–1	Tiberius III.	John driven from Carthage. Leontius overthrown.
700	13–14	6192–3		Romans invade Syria.
701	14–15	6193–4		Mopsuestia taken by Saracens.
702	15–1	6194–5		Loss of Fourth Armenia.
703	1–2	6195–6		Victory of Heraclius over Saracens in Cilicia.
704	2–3	6196–7		Another victory of Heraclius.
705	3–4	6197–8	Justinian (II) Rhinotmetos.	Fall of Tiberius.
709	7–8	6201–2		Tyana destroyed by Saracens.
710	8–9	6202–3		Expeditions against Cherson and Ravenna.
711	9–10	6203–4	Philippicus.	Fall of Justinian. Saracens cross to Spain.
712	10–11	6204–5		Bulgarians invade Thrace. Amasea taken by Saracens.
713	11–12	6205–6	Anastasius II.	Saracens take Pisidian Antioch. Fall of Philippicus.
714	12–13	6206–7		Roman embassy sent to Damascus.
715	13–14	6207–8	Theodosius III.	Fall of Anastasius (near the end of 715). Gregory II becomes Pope.
716	14–15	6208–9		Saracens invade Asia Minor; besiege Amorium. Leo the Isaurian defeats the son of Theodosius.
717	15–1	6209–10	Leo III.	Fall of Theodosius. Saracens besiege Pergamus. Siege of Constantinople begins (August).

A.D.	INDICTION.	A.M.	IMPERIAL ACCESSIONS.	EVENTS.
718	1–2	6210–11		Siege of Constantinople raised (August). Birth of Constantine V.
720	3–4	6212–13		Constantine crowned. Death of King Terbel.
724	7–8	6216–17		Hischam becomes caliph.
726	9–10	6218–19		First decree against image-worship. Cappadocia invaded by Saracens.
727	10–11–12[1]	6219–20		Revolt in Greece. John of Damascus writes first oration against iconoclasm. Council at Rome against iconoclasm.
728	12–13	6220–1		Revolt in Italy.
729	13–14	6221–2		*Silentium* against image-worship. Deposition of Germanus.
730	14–15	6222–3		Gregory III becomes Pope. Council at Rome against iconoclasm.
731	15–1	6223–4		Leo separates Churches of Sicily, Calabria, and Illyricum from Rome.
732	1–2	6224–5		Census of births proclaimed. Heavy taxation in Sicily.
734	3–4	6226–7		Saracens invade Asia Minor.
739	8–9	6231–2		Saracen invasion. Battle of Acroinon.
740	9–10	6232–3	Constantine V.	*Ecloga* published. Death of Leo. Zacharias becomes Pope.
741	10–11	6233–4		Revolt of Artavasdos.
742	11–12	6234–5		Artavasdos suppressed.
743	12–13	6235–6		Death of Liutprand.
744	13–14	6236–7		Great Plague begins, and lasts till 747.
746	15–1	6238–9		Saracens attack Cyprus.
748	2–3	6240–1		Aistulf king of Lombards.
750	4–5	6242–3		Fall of Omeyyad dynasty. Lombards take Ravenna.
751	5–6	6243–4		Constantine takes Melitene and Theodosiopolis. Stephen II Pope.
753	7–8	6245–6		Council at Constantinople in favour of iconoclasm. Pipin invades Italy.
755	9–10	6247–8		Bulgarians invade Thrace. Pipin again in Italy.
756	10–11	6248–9		Paul I. Pope.
758	12–13	6250–1		Constantine's expedition against the Sclavinias.
759	13–14	6251–2		Bulgarian victory at Berégaba.
760	14–15	6252–3		Eclipse of sun (15th August).
761	15–1	6253–4		Execution of Peter Kalybites and John of Monagria.

[1] For the suppression of an indiction and my revision of the chronology, *see* Note on Bk. vi cap. ii. (vol. ii. p. 425).

A.D.	INDICTION.	A.M.	IMPERIAL ACCESSIONS.	EVENTS.
762	1–2	6254–5		Roman victory over Bulgarians at Anchialus.
764	3–4	6256–7		" Martyrdom " of Stephanus (date uncertain).
765	4–5	6257–8		Unsuccessful campaign in Bulgaria. Conspiracy against Emperor.
766	5–6	6258–9		Aqueduct of Valens restored. Executions of Paul and Andreas of Crete. Execution of Patriarch Constantinos. Constantine Anti-pope.
767	6–7	6259–60		Stephen III Pope.
771	10–11	6263–4		Hadrian I. becomes Pope.
773	12–12¹	6265–6		Victory over Bulgarians at Lithosoria.
774	12–13	6266–7		
775	13–14	6267–8	Leo IV.	Expedition against Bulgaria. Death of Constantine.
778	1–2	6270–1		Successes against Saracens.
780	3–4	6272–3	Constantine VI and Irene.	Harun takes Sêmalûos. Death of Leo IV.
781	4–5	6273–4		Revolt of Elpidius in Sicily.
782	5–6	6274–5		Harun invades Asia Minor.
783	6–7	6275–6		Reduction of Slaves of Macedonia and Greece.
784	7–8	6276–7		Tarasius becomes Patriarch.
786	9–10	6278–9		Harun becomes caliph.
787	10–11	6279–80		Seventh Ecumenical Council (at Nicaea).
788	11–12	6280–1		Bulgarian victory on the Strymon.
789	12–13	6281–2		Romania invaded by Arabs.
790	13–14	6282–3		Struggle of Irene and Constantine begins.
791	14–15	6283–4		Expedition against Bulgarians.
792	15–1	6284–5		Conspiracy in favour of the Caesars. Irene restored to dignity. Second Bulgarian campaign of Constantine VI.
793	1–2	6285–6		Revolt of Armeniac theme.
794	2–3	6286–7		Council of Frankfurt.
795	3–4	6287–8		Constantine divorces Maria, and leads a campaign in Asia. Leo III Pope.
796	4–5	6288–9		Third Bulgarian campaign of Constantine.
797	5–6	6289–90		Constantine blinded and deposed. Conspiracy in favour of the Caesars.
798	6–7	6290–1		Peace with Saracens.
799	7–8	6291–2		Revolt in Hellas.
800	8–9	6292–3		Coronation of Charles the Great.
802	10–11	6294–5		Fall of Irene.

¹ Here one indiction has been extended over two years in order to rectify the chronology.

TABLE OF CONTENTS

BOOK IV

THE HOUSE OF JUSTIN

PART I

THE AGE OF JUSTINIAN

CHAPTER VII

THE LANGUAGE OF THE ROMAIOI IN THE SIXTH CENTURY

CHAPTER VIII

LITERATURE OF THE SIXTH CENTURY

BOOK V

THE HOUSE OF HERACLIUS

CHAPTER I

PHOCAS

CHAPTER II

HERACLIUS (610-622 A.D.)

CHAPTER II

THE ADMINISTRATION OF LEO III

CHAPTER III

THE ICONOCLASTIC MOVEMENT

CHAPTER IV

IMPERIAL ITALY IN THE EIGHTH CENTURY

CHAPTER V

CONSTANTINE V

CHAPTER VI

ICONOCLASTIC POLICY OF CONSTANTINE

CHAPTER VII

BULGARIA

CHAPTER VIII

LEO IV

CHAPTER IX

CONSTANTINE VI AND IRENE

CHAPTER X

THE REACTION AGAINST ICONOCLASM

CHAPTER XI

THE POPES, THE LOMBARDS, AND THE FRANKS

CHAPTER XII

THE GEOGRAPHICAL ASPECT OF EUROPE AT THE END OF THE EIGHTH CENTURY

CHAPTER XIII

SOCIETY IN THE EIGHTH CENTURY

CHAPTER XIV

CONCLUSION

CHAPTER XI

JUSTINIAN'S CAESAROPAPISM

THE absolutism of Justinian extended to the ecclesiastical world, and in church as well as in state history he occupies a position of ecumenical importance. He was a sort of imperial pontiff, and this Caesaropapism, as it has been called, represents the fulfilment of the policy which Constantius tried and failed to realise.

Justinian's ecclesiastical policy rested on his support of the council of Chalcedon, and thus accorded in principle with the policy by which his uncle Justin had restored unity to Christendom. But this unity was only a unity of the western Church with the chief Church in the East; whereas the East itself was divided. The monophysites were a large and important body, and the Emperor was not content not to make an effort to reconcile this difference, especially as the Empress Theodora was an adherent of the heretical creed. His object was to secure a unity in the Church, which should exclude all sectarianism, and embrace both East and West. Consequently he did not rest in the policy of his uncle Justin; he tried to accomplish what Zeno and Anastasius had failed to accomplish, a conciliation of the Chalcedonians and monophysites.

One of his first acts was to deal a final blow to paganism. He shut up the philosophical schools at Athens, with which Theodosius II had not interfered when he founded the university of Constantinople. The abolition of the Athenian university has two aspects. In the first place, it was the last blow dealt by Christianity to the ancient philosophers and their doctrines, and was one of the acts which mark the reign

B

of Justinian as the terminus of the ancient world. In the second place, it was a measure in which Justinian's design of establishing a unity of belief and thought in the Empire was manifested; and it is to be taken closely with the law that pagans and heretical Christians were not to hold office in either the civil service or the army. His general principle is laid down clearly in a constitution (published shortly before his uncle's death)[1]: " All will be able to perceive that from those who do not worship God rightly, human goods also are withheld,"—a most concise expression of religious intolerance. It may be observed that in this constitution the Manichaeans are mentioned with special acrimony, and rendered liable to the extreme penalties of the law. It was the instinct of Christianity, which was essentially monistic, though not with Semitic monism, to fight against all forms of dualism as the most odious kind of heresy.

The monophysites held a peculiar position. They were very numerous, and they were supported by the sympathy of the Empress Theodora, who shared their creed. Justinian considered it an important political object to unite them with the orthodox Church, and it was a theological problem to accomplish this—to make concessions to the heretics without abandoning the basis of Chalcedon.

Justinian might have carried this out in the East without much difficulty, if he had been content to sacrifice union with the western Church. But that would have been to undo what Justin had done and he himself had confirmed; and the union of the eastern and western Churches was of primary importance for the restorer of Roman rule in Italy and Africa. His political designs exercised a perceptible control on his ecclesiastical measures.

This was the dilemma that beset every Roman Emperor—quite apart from his personal opinions—ever since the council of Chalcedon. If he chose to attempt to establish unity in the East, he must sacrifice unity with the West, as Zeno and Anastasius had done. If he chose to seek unity with the West, like Justin, he must be satisfied to see his dominions distracted by the bitter opposition of synodites and monophysites. The imperial throne shared by the orthodox Justinian and the

---

[1] *Cod. Just.* i. 5, 12.   Compare the other laws under the same title.

Eutychian Theodora was symbolic of the division of the Empire in the matter of theological beliefs.

Justinian's achievement was to overcome this dilemma.[1] He was powerful enough to carry a measure which tended to unity by modifying the synod of Chalcedon without breaking with the Church of Rome.

Apart from their personal opinions—which, while we admit that they co-operated, we must set aside in order to observe the influence of circumstances—the policies of Zeno, Anastasius, and Justin in regard to this problem were natural. To Zeno and Anastasius, who had no thought of recovering power in Italy, the opposition of the bishop of Rome was a matter of smaller importance than division in the Empire. Justin's policy was naturally anti-monophysitic, because it was a reaction against Anastasius; and such a policy implied a renewal of relations with Rome. Justinian's intervention in the political world of western Europe altered the position of the bishop of Rome, and in the fifth Council of Constantinople the Emperor exercised an unprecedented authority, which would have pleased Constantius II.

In 536 A.D., by the influence of Theodora, Anthimus, a man of monophysitic opinions, was appointed Patriarch of Constantinople. In the following year Pope Agapetus visited that city on political business, to treat for peace on behalf of Theodahad; it was the second time that an Ostrogothic king had despatched a Pope on a message to an Emperor. Agapetus succeeded in obtaining the deposition of Anthimus, and the election of an orthodox successor, Mennas. That Justinian was not aware of the real opinions of Anthimus, before Agapetus unveiled his heterodoxy, is unlikely, but the supporter of orthodoxy could not refuse to oppose him, once it was made public, and that by the bishop of Rome. Dante represents Justinian as originally holding monophysitic opinions, and owing his conversion to Agapetus.[2]

> E prima ch' io all' opra fossi attento,
> Una natura in Cristo esser, non piue
> Credeva, e di tal fede era contento.

---

[1] Procopius (*de Aed.* i. 1) says of the Emperor's ecclesiastical policy, συντρίψας ἁπάσας τὰς ἐπὶ τὰς πλάνας φερούσας ὁδοὺς διεπράξατο ἐν τῷ βεβαίῳ τῆς πίστεως ἐπὶ μιᾶς ἐστάναι κρηπῖδος.

[2] *Paradiso,* cant. vi. 13 *sqq.*

> Ma il benedetto Agapito, che fue
> Sommo pastore, alla fede sincera
> Mi dirizzò con le parole sue.

The controversy of the "three articles," a long chapter in the ecclesiastical history of the sixth century, began in 544, and lasted for eight years. We need not follow its details, but the elements that were involved in it as well as its consequences must be briefly explained. Three points to be noticed are—(1) that it was externally connected with an Origenistic controversy which had disturbed Palestine for some years past; (2) that the difficulty of concluding the question depended on the wavering position of Pope Vigilius; (3) that Justinian's desire to carry his point was at first quickened by the monophysitic leanings of his consort, who died before the dispute was decided.

At Justinian's desire the Patriarch Mennas held a local synod, at which the writings of Origen were condemned. Theodore Ascidas, bishop of Caesarea, a monophysite who believed in the Origenistic theology, did not oppose this sentence, but made a fruitful suggestion to Justinian, of which the apparently exclusive aim was to reunite the monophysites, but which really contained a blow at a prominent opponent of Origen's methods, Theodore of Mopsuestia. The import of this suggestion was that what really repelled the monophysites was not any point of doctrine, but the countenance given by the council of Chalcedon to certain Nestorians.

Accordingly in 544 Justinian promulgated an edict,[1] wherein the Three Articles (κεφάλαια), which gave the name to the controversy, were enunciated—(1) Theodore of Mopsuestia and his works were condemned; (2) certain writings of Theodoret against Cyril were condemned; and (3) a letter of Ibas, addressed to a Persian and censuring Cyril, was condemned. The council of Chalcedon had expressly acknowledged the orthodoxy of these writings and their authors, and thus the authority of that council seemed called in question, though the edict expressly professed to respect it.

The bishops of the East, including Mennas, signed the

---

[1] This determination of ecclesiastical matters by imperial edicts is the key-note of Caesaropapism. Basiliscus had attempted this policy in his brief reign.

edict; but Mennas made his adhesion conditional on the approval of the bishop of Rome, and it is just the attitude of the bishop of Rome that lends an interest to the controversy.

Vigilius had been elevated to the papal see of Rome under circumstances which appear at least unusual. He was at Constantinople when Agapetus died in 537, and his election rested on the support of Theodora, with whom he is said to have made a sort of bargain not to act against the monophysite Anthimus, the deposed Patriarch. Before he arrived at Rome, Silverius had been elected Pope in Italy, and the deposition and banishment of the latter, on the charge of treason, by Belisarius,[1] give room for suspicion that corrupt dealings were practised for the benefit of Vigilius.

When Vigilius was called upon to sign the edict of the "three articles" he felt himself in a dilemma. The western Church, especially the Church of Africa, cried out loudly against the document, while Vigilius felt himself under obligations to Theodora and the Emperor. A synod at Carthage went so far as to excommunicate the Pope (549).

At first he refused to sign. When he was at Rome, at a safe distance from the Caesar-Pope, resistance did not seem hard. But Justinian summoned him to Constantinople, where he remained until 554. During this time he wavered between the two forces in whose conflict he was involved—the ecclesiastical opinion of the West and the imperial authority. The latter finally conquered, but not until the Pope had been condemned in the fifth general Council, held at Constantinople in 553, after which he retracted his condemnation of the articles,[2] attributing it to the arts of the devil.

The fifth general Council, it should be observed, has an importance beyond the rather trivial subjects discussed. Its basis—its agenda—was an edict drawn up by the Emperor; it adopted theological tenets formulated by the Emperor. This is the most characteristic manifestation of Justinianean Caesaropapism.

[1] *See* Liberatus, *Brev.* 22; Anastasius, *Vita Silverii.* Liberatus wrote his *Breviarium causae Nestorianorum et Eutychianorum*, about 560, against Justinian's Articles.

[2] The "Condemnation of the Three Articles" is ambiguous. I use the expression in its proper sense, as the condemnation of the three proposals of Justinian's edict. But in popular usage the Three Articles meant the opinions which the edict condemned, and thus one who opposed the edict was said to defend the Articles.

The election of Pelagius as the successor of Vigilius[1] to the see of Rome is noteworthy, because the Roman Emperor exercised the right of confirming the election, which had belonged to the Ostrogothic monarch. This right gave Justinian an ecclesiastical power of European extent, and introduced an important theory into Christendom. "According to the *Liber Diurnus* (a collection of forms which represents the state of things in those days or shortly after), the death of a Roman bishop was to be notified to the exarch of Ravenna; the successor was to be chosen by the clergy, the nobles of Rome, the soldiery, and the citizens; and the ratification of the election was to be requested in very submissive terms both of the Emperor and of his deputy the exarch." [2]

Pelagius upheld the three articles of the council, but the unity of the East and the consent of the Pope were purchased at the expense of the unity of the West. Milan and Aquileia would know nothing of the fifth Council, and although the invasion of the Lombards soon drove Milan into the arms of Rome, the see of Aquileia and the bishop of Istria seceded from the Roman Church for more than a hundred and forty years.

In Egypt monophysitism was ineradicable. Alexandria "the Great" was a scene of continual religious quarrels between the Eutychians and the Melchites, as they called the orthodox Catholics. In Syria monophysitism continued under the name of Jacobitism—a name derived from its propagator in the sixth century, Jacob al Baradai, a travelling monk.

The Armenian Church also adopted the Eutychian heresy, and in the ultra-Eutychian form of aphthartodocetism, the doctrine that Christ's body was incorruptible. It is curious that the same cause favoured the survival of the two opposite doctrines, Eutychianism and Nestorianism, in Armenia and Persia respectively. The Persian government tolerated Nestorian Christianity in its dominions, and looked with favour on a monophysitic Armenian Church, because both creeds were opposed to the State religion of Byzantium.

---

[1] Vigilius died at Syracuse on his way back to Rome in June 555. Those who are curious about the details of these transactions may be referred to a chapter in Mr. Hodgkin's *Italy and her Invaders*, vol. iv., entitled "The Sorrows of Vigilius," as well as to ecclesiastical histories.

[2] Robertson, *History of the Christian Church*, vol. ii. p. 334.

I have mentioned aphthartodocetism. It obtained a certain notoriety in the last years of Justinian's reign, for the old Emperor adopted the doctrine himself, and enforced it on his subjects by an edict. His death cut short the full execution of his last and least Caesaropapistic undertaking.

Among his acts of ecclesiastical autocracy we must mention the edict which raised the see of Prima Justiniana, in his own native province of Dacia Mediterranea, to the rank of an archbishopric (535 A.D.) "Desiring," this document begins, "to increase in many and divers ways our native land, in which God first granted us to come into this world, which He himself founded, we wish to augment it and make it very great in ecclesiastical rank."[1] This decree was confirmed in another decree ten years later (545 A.D.) I do not consider it justifiable to say, as ecclesiastical historians sometimes do,[2] that Justinian desired to found a sixth patriarchate; on the contrary, the new archbishop, as I understand the second edict, was to depend on the Pope of Rome, and to hold the same position, for example, as the archbishop of Ravenna.

In regard to the missionary activity which Justinian encouraged for the conversion of heathen nations, I cannot do

---

[1] Novel xix. (ed. Zachariä von Lingenthal, 1881). Below, the imperial style speaks of Dacia Mediterranea as *nostra felicissima patria*. For the confirmation of the privilege, *see* Nov. cli. The old idea that Tauresium, which Justinian restored because it was his birthplace, and called by the name of Justiniana Prima, was identical with Achrida, arose from the circumstance that the title of the archbishop was "Archbishop of Justiniana and Achrida." *See* Appendix E in vol. ii. of Mr. Tozer's delightful book on the highlands of Turkey. "The explanation of the double title is, that while Justinian had established the metropolitan see at the place on which he bestowed his name, it was transferred to Ochrida when that place was made the capital of the Bulgarian kingdom." Mr. Tozer agrees with Mannert in identifying Uskiub with Justiniana. "It fell within the district of Dardania, and was situated at a moderate distance from Ochrida; it was also the most important position in that neighbour-

hood, and from having been the leading city, would be most naturally pointed out for restoration and decoration." "Von Hahn [the Austrian traveller], who passed by here in 1858, has shown that the names Tauresium and Bederiana may be traced in those of Taor and Bader," two villages hard by.

[2] Robertson, ii. 333, "to erect a sixth patriarchate." The express words of Justinian are (Nov. cli. γ´)— καὶ ἐν αὐταῖς ταῖς ὑποκειμέναις αὐτῷ ἐπαρχίαις [Dacia M., Dacia Ripensis, Prevalitana (Πρεβαλέα), Dardania, Upper Moesia, Pannonia] τὸν τόπον ἐπέχειν αὐτὸν τοῦ ἀποστολικοῦ Ῥώμης θρόνου κατὰ τὰ ὁρισθέντα ἀπὸ τοῦ ἁγίου πάπα Βιγιλίου. That is, the archbishop was to hold the place of, or be the representative of, the Pope in these provinces. The Patriarchs did not "hold the place" of the Pope. This disposes of Robertson's remark that Justinian's design "proved abortive." Robertson is also wrong in the date, which he gives as 541.

better than quote the following little-known account of the conversion of the Nobadae [1] :—

" Among the clergy in attendance on the Patriarch Theodosius was a proselyte named Julianus, an old man of great worth, who conceived an earnest spiritual desire to christianise the wandering people who dwell on the eastern borders of the Thebais beyond Egypt, and who are not only not subject to the authority of the Roman Empire, but even receive a subsidy on condition that they do not enter nor pillage Egypt. The blessed Julianus, therefore, being full of anxiety for this people, went and spoke about them to the late Queen Theodora, in the hope of awakening in her a similar desire for their conversion ; and as the queen was fervent in zeal for God, she received the proposal with joy, and promised to do everything in her power for the conversion of these tribes from the errors of idolatry. In her joy, therefore, she informed the victorious King Justinian of the purposed undertaking, and promised and anxiously desired to send the blessed Julian thither. But when the king [Emperor] heard that the person she intended to send was opposed to the council of Chalcedon, he was not pleased, and determined to write to the bishops of his own side in the Thebais, with orders for them to proceed thither and instruct the Nobadae, and plant among them the name of synod. And as he entered upon the matter with great zeal, he sent thither, without a moment's delay, ambassadors with gold and baptismal robes, and gifts of honour for the king of that people, and letters for the duke of the Thebais, enjoining him to take every care of the embassy and escort them to the territories of the Nobadae. When, however, the queen learnt these things, she quickly, with much cunning, wrote letters to the duke of the Thebais, and sent a mandatory of her court to carry them to him ; and which were as follows : 'Inasmuch as both his majesty and myself have purposed to send an embassy to the people of the Nobadae, and I am now despatching a blessed man named Julian ; and further my will is that my ambassador should arrive at the aforesaid people before his majesty's ; be warned, that if you permit his ambassador to arrive there before mine, and do not hinder him by various pretexts until mine shall have reached you and shall have passed through your province and arrived at his destination, your life shall answer for it ; for I shall immediately send and take off your head.' Soon after the receipt of this letter the king's ambassador also came, and the duke said to him, 'You must wait a little while we look out and procure beasts of burden and men who know the deserts, and then you will be able to proceed.' And thus he delayed him until the arrival of the merciful queen's embassy, who found horses and guides in waiting, and the same day, without loss of time, under a show of doing it by violence, they laid hands upon him, and were the first to proceed. As for the duke, he made his excuses to the king's ambassador, saying, 'Lo ! when I had

---

[1] I have extracted this curious narrative from R. Payne Smith's translation of the ecclesiastical history, written in Syriac, of the monophysite John of Ephesus. On missions M. Gasquet (*L'empire byzantin*, p. 75) remarks : " Les missions voilà donc l'élément nouveau qui donne à la politique byzantine son caractère distinctif."

made my preparations and was desirous of sending you onward, ambassadors from the queen arrived and fell upon me with violence, and took away the beasts of burden I had got ready, and have passed onward ; and I am too well acquainted with the fear in which the queen is held to venture to oppose them. But abide still with me until I can make fresh preparations for you, and then you also shall go in peace.' And when he heard these things he rent his garments, and threatened him terribly and reviled him ; and after some time he also was able to proceed, and followed the other's track without being aware of the fraud which had been practised upon him.

" The blessed Julian meanwhile and the ambassadors who accompanied him had arrived at the confines of the Nobadae, whence they sent to the king and his princes informing him of their coming ; upon which an armed escort set out, who received them joyfully, and brought them into their land unto the king. And he too received them with pleasure, and her majesty's letter was presented and read to him, and the purport of it explained. They accepted also the magnificent honours sent them, and the numerous baptismal robes, and everything else richly provided for their use. And immediately with joy they yielded themselves up and utterly abjured the errors of their forefathers, and confessed the God of the Christians, saying, ' He is the one true God, and there is no other beside Him.' And after Julian had given them much instruction, and taught them, he further told them about the council of Chalcedon, saying that ' inasmuch as certain disputes had sprung up among Christians touching the faith, and the blessed Theodosius being required to receive the council and having refused was ejected by the king [Emperor] from his throne, whereas the queen received him and rejoiced in him because he stood firm in the right faith and left his throne for its sake, on this account her majesty has sent us to you, that ye also may walk in the ways of Pope Theodosius, and stand in his faith and imitate his constancy. And moreover the king has sent unto you ambassadors, who are already on their way, in our footsteps.' "

The Emperor's emissaries arrived soon afterwards, and were dismissed by the king of the Nobadae, who told them that if his people embraced Christianity at all it would be the doctrine of the holy Theodosius of Alexandria, and not the " wicked faith " of the Emperor.

In his own dominions too the activity of christian missionaries was necessary, for in the devious recesses of Asia Minor there were many spots, *pagi*, where heathenism survived. It is remarkable that for the conversion of his heathen subjects Justinian employed a monophysitic priest, John of Ephesus, who afterwards wrote an ecclesiastical history in Syriac from the monophysitic point of view. We shall see how the monophysites were persecuted by a zealous Patriarch and an unwise Emperor after Justinian's death. Towards the close of the century, when the heresy was almost exterminated from the Empire, it was revived, as has been already mentioned, by one Jacob al Baradai, who, dressed as a beggar—hence his name "the Ragged"—travelled about in the provinces of Syria and Mesopotamia and organised anew the monophysitic Church.   To the renascent monophysites was attached the name of the second founder of the sect; they were called Jacobites.

CHAPTER XII

THE SLAVES

IN one respect the history of Byzantium, as the capital of the Roman world, differed little from its history as a Greek republic. Both as the mercantile commonwealth and as the imperial city, it was exposed, with its adjoining territory, to the hostilities of the barbarians of various races who infested the wild and ill-known lands of the Balkan mountains or dwelled on the shores of the Danube. In fact, Polybius' remarks on the favourable site of Byzantium seawards and its unfavourable aspect landwards hold good of its subsequent experiences, and the following passage might be taken as a short summary of one side of Byzantine history [1] :—

"As Thrace surrounds the territory of the Byzantines on all sides, reaching from sea to sea, they are involved in an endless and troublesome war against the Thracians, for it is not feasible, by making preparations on a grand scale and winning one decisive victory over them, to get rid once for all of their hostilities; the barbarous nations and dynasts are too numerous. If they overcome one, three more worse than the first arise and advance against their country. Nor can they gain any advantage by submitting to pay tribute and making definite contracts; for if they make any concession to one prince, such a concession raises up against them five times as many foes. For these reasons they are involved in a never-ending and troublesome war. For what is more dangerous than a bad neighbour, and what more dreadful than a war with barbarians? And besides the other evils that attend on war, they have to undergo (to speak poetically) a sort of Tantalean punishment, for when they have diligently tilled their land, which is very fertile, and have been rewarded by the production of an abundant and surpassingly fine crop, then come the

---

[1] Polybius, iv. 45.

barbarians, and having reaped part of the fruits to carry off with them, destroy what they cannot take away. The Byzantines can only murmur indignantly, and endure."

This passage might have been written of the depredations of the Huns, the Ostrogoths, the Avars, or the Slaves.

Of these four peoples, the first three were only comets of ruin in the Balkan peninsula, while the Slavonic peoples, to whose early history this chapter is devoted, probably began to filter into the provinces of Illyricum and Thrace as settlers before the invasions of Attila, and in later times pouring in as formidable invaders, gradually converted those provinces into Slavonic principalities, which, according to the tide of war, were sometimes dependent on, sometimes independent of, the government of Constantinople.

To understand the history of the Haemus countries, the extension of the Slavonic races there, and the campaigns of the Roman armies against the invaders, a general notion of the very difficult and still imperfectly explored geography of Thrace is indispensable.[1]

We may consider Mount Vitoš, and the town of Sardica, now Sofia, which lies at its base as the central point of the peninsula. Rising in the shape of an immense cone to a height of 2300 metres, Vitoš affords to the climber who ascends it a splendid view of the various complicated mountain chains which diversify the surrounding lands—a view which has been pronounced finer than that at Tempe or that at Vodena. In the group of which this mountain and another named Ryl, to southward, are the highest peaks, two rivers of the lower Danube system, the Oescus (Isker) and the Nišava have their sources, as well as the two chief rivers of the Aegean system, the Hebrus (Maritsa) and the Strymon (Struma).

From this central region stretches in a south-easterly direction the double chain of Rhodope, cleft in twain by the valley

---

[1] In the geography, as throughout this chapter, the invaluable work of C. Jiriček, *Die Geschichte der Bulgaren*, has been my guide. I have also consulted the famous *Slawische Alterthümer* (ed. Wuttke) of P. J. Safarik, esp. vol. ii. p. 152 *sqq.* ("Uebersicht der Geschichte der bulgarischen Slawen"). Drinov's *Zaselenie balkanskago poluostrova Sla-* vanyami is unfortunately out of print. A lucid account of the divisions of the Slavonic race will be found in Mr. Morfill's article "Slavs" in the *Ency. Brit.*, an article which is not only very learned but very readable. In the present chapter we have only to do with the south-eastern Slaves (chiefly Slovenes).

of the Nestos (Mesta). The easterly range, Rhodope proper, forms the western boundary of the great plain of Thrace, while the range of Orbelos separates the Nestos valley from the Strymon valley.

The great Haemus or Balkan chain which runs from east to west is also double, like Rhodope, but is not in the same way divided by a large river. The Haemus mountains begin near the sources of the Timacus and Margus, from which they stretch to the shores of the Euxine. To a traveller approaching them from the northern or Danubian side they do not present an impressive appearance, for the ascent is very gradual; plateau rises above plateau, or the transition is accomplished by gentle slopes, and the height of the highest parts is lost by the number of intervening degrees. But on the southern side the descent is precipitous, and the aspect is imposing and sublime. This capital difference between the two sides of the Haemus range is closely connected with the existence of the second and lower parallel range, called the Srêdna Gora, which runs through Roumelia from Sofia to Sliven. It seems as if a convulsion of the earth had cloven asunder an original and large chain by a sudden rent, which gave its abrupt and sheer character to the southern side of the Haemus mountains, and interrupted the gradual incline upwards from the low plain of Thrace.

The important chain of Srêdna Gora, which is often confounded with the northern chain of Haemus, is divided into three parts, which, following Hochstetter, we may call the Karadža Dagh, the Srêdna Gora, and the Ichtimaner. The Karadža Dagh mountains are the most easterly, and are separated from Srêdna Gora by the river Strêma (a tributary of the Maritsa), while the valley of the Tundža (Τα$ίναρος$), with its fields of roses and pleasantly situated towns, divides it from Mount Haemus. Srêdna Gora reaches a greater height than the mountains to east or to west, and is separated by the river Topolnitsa from the most westerly portion, the Ichtimaner mountains, which form a sort of transition connecting the Balkan system with the Rhodope system, whilst at the same time they are the watershed between the tributaries of the Hebrus and those of the Danube. It is in this range too that the important pass of Succi is situated, through which the road led from Constantinople to Singidunum, Sirmium, and Italy.

The river Isker divides the Balkan chain into a western and an eastern half. Of the western mountains, which command a view of the middle Danube, we need only mention the strange region which Kanitz, the Austrian traveller, discovered near the fort of Bêlgradčîk. " Gigantic pillars of dark red sandstone, crowned by groups of trees, rise in fantastic shapes to heights above 200 metres, and, separated by rivulets and surrounded by luxuriant green, they form remarkable groups and alleys, as it were a city changed to stone, with towers, burgs, houses, bridges, obelisks, and ships, men and beasts." [1]

In the central part of the eastern Haemus mountains is the now celebrated pass of Šipka, which connects the valley of the Tundža with the valley of the Jantra (Jatrus), and is the chief route from Thrace into Lower Moesia. Between this spot and the pass of Sliven farther east extend the wildest and most impervious regions of the Balkans, regions which have always been the favourite homes of scamars and klephts, who could defy the justice of civilisation in thick forests and inaccessible ravines—regions echoing with the wild songs and romances of outlaw life. Beyond the pass of the Iron Gates (Πύλαι Σιδηραῖ, Demir Kapu), connecting Sliven with Trnovo, the range splits itself into three prongs ; the north prong touching the river of the Great Kamčija, the middle touching the meeting of the Great and the Little Kamčija, and the southern touching the sea. In this part there are three passes, one of which is reached from Sliven, the other two from Karnabad.

The east side of the great Thracian plain is bounded by the Strandža range, which separates it from the Euxine, and throws out in a south-westerly direction the Tekir Dagh, which stretches along the west of the Propontis, shooting into the Thracian Chersonese and extending along the north Aegean coast as far as the Strymon. The Thracian plain is a flat wilderness, only good for poor pasture.

The oldest inhabitants, of whose existence in the peninsula we know, were a branch of the Indo-European family, which is generally called the Thraco-Illyrian branch, falling as it does

---

[1] I translate from Jiriček, *op: cit.* p. 8.

into two main divisions, the Thracian and the Illyrian.   The Thracians occupied the eastern, the Illyrians the western, side of the peninsula, the boundary between them being roughly the courses of the Drave and the Strymon.   Any descendants of the Thracians who still survive are to be found among the Roumanians, while the Albanians [1] represent the Illyrians and Epirotes.   The Epirotes stood in much the same relation to the Illyrians as the Macedonians stood to the Thracians.   Of the numerous Thracian tribes (Odrysians, Triballi, Getae, Mysians, Bessi, etc.), the Bessi or Satri, in the region of Rhodope, remained longest a corporate nation in the presence of Roman influences ; they were converted to Christianity [2] in the fourth century, and in the fifth century they still held the church service in their own tongue.   The Noropians, a subdivision of the Paeonians, whose lake dwellings are described by Herodotus, deserve mention, because the name survived in the Middle Ages (nerop'ch, mêrop'ch) as the name of a class .of serfs in the Serbian kingdom.   Of the Illyrian tribes the most important were the Autariats, Dardanians, Dalmatians, Istrians, Liburnians.   As to the Thracian and Illyrian languages, a general but vague idea can be formed of them by the help of modern Albanese, whence Dalmatia has been explained to mean " shepherd land " ; Skodra, " hill " ; Bora, " snow " (a mountain in Macedonia) ; Bessi, " the faithful " (originally the name of priests) ; Dardania, " land of pears," etc.   The difficulty experienced by the Romans in subduing and incorporating in their Empire all these brave mountain tribes is well known.

It must be clearly understood that Latin became the general language of the peninsula when the Roman conquests were consolidated, except on the south and east coastlines of the Aegean, Propontis, and Euxine, where the towns, many of them Greek colonies and all long familiar with Greek, continued to speak that language.   That Latin was the language of the greater part of the peninsula there are many proofs.   Priscus tells us expressly, in speaking of his expedition to the country of the Huns, that Latin was the language everywhere.   The bishops of Marcianopolis used Latin in their

---

[1] Hahn finds the descendants of the Illyrians in the Gegi of north Albania, those of the Epirotes in the Toski of south Albania, the river Škumli separating them.

[2] By Nicetas, bishop of Remesiana.

correspondence with the council of Chalcedon. At the end of the sixth century words used by a peasant are recorded, which are the first trace of the Roumanian language, which developed in these regions and was born of the union of Latin with old Thracian.[1] The Emperor Justinian, a native of Dardania, speaks of Latin as his own language.

We need not discuss here the wild theories, resting chiefly on accidental similarity of names which may be made to prove anything, that Slavonic races dwelled along with the Thraco-Illyrian from time immemorial; they have been refuted by Jiriček. The pedantic Byzantine custom of calling contemporary peoples by the name of ancient peoples who had dwelt in the same lands led to a misunderstanding, and originated the idea that the Slavonic races were autochthonous.[2]

But if this theory assigns to the presence of the Slaves a too early period, we must beware of falling into the opposite mistake of setting their advent too late. The arguments of Drinov, which are accepted by the historian of the Bulgarians, make it possible that the infiltration of Slavonic elements into the cis-Danubian lands began about 300 A.D., before the so-called wandering of the nations.

It is probable enough that there were Slaves in the great Dacian kingdom of Decebalus, which was subverted by Trajan. At all events, the Roman occupation of Dacia beyond the Danube for a century and a half between Trajan and Aurelian, left its traces in that country, and also among Slavonic races ; for Trajan or Trojan figured prominently in Slavonic legend as the deliverer from the Dacian oppressor, and was even deified. " Bulgarian songs at the present day celebrate the Tzar Trojan, the lord of inexhaustible treasures, for whom burning gold and pure silver flow from seventy wells."[3] Slavonic tradition called the Romans Vlachians, and the first appearance of the Vlachians beyond the Danube was long remembered.

The Slaves doubtless played a considerable part in the frontier wars of the third century, but whether the Carpi, whom

---

[1] *See* Jiriček, p. 66, where he collects these points. Nicetas, bishop of Remesiana (fourth century), who converted the Bessi, was a Latin writer.

[2] Thus the Servians are called *Tri-*

balli, the Albanese *Acarnanians,* the Hungarians *Pannonians,* etc.

[3] Trajan is a usual name among the Bulgarians. The name of the old Slavonic feast day, Koleda, is said to be derived from Kalendae.

Galerius settled along with the Bastarnae in the provinces of
Moesia and Thrace (298) were a Slavonic race, as some
authorities believe, we cannot be certain. It is possible,
however, that Slaves formed part of the large mass of barbarians—200,000—to whom the Emperor Carus assigned habitations in the peninsula; and there are certainly distinct traces
of the existence of Slavonic communities in itineraries composed in the fourth century.[1] There were many generals
of Slavonic origin in Roman service in the fifth century,
and in the sixth century Procopius has preserved to us
many names of Slavonic towns.

We are then, I think, justified in assuming that in the
fifth century there was a considerable Slavonic element in
the lands south of the Ister, holding the position of Roman
coloni. They formed a layer of population which would give
security and permanence to the settlements of future invaders
of kindred race. And here we touch upon what seems a
strong confirmation of the conclusion to which stray
vestiges lead us, regarding an early Slavonic colonisation.
The Ostrogoths, who invaded and settled in Italy, held
out there but a short time; the duration of Lombard influence
in Italy was longer, but not long; the Vandals were soon dis-
lodged from Africa. On the other hand, the Franks held permanent sway in the lands in which they settled, just as Slavonic
nations still dominate the countries between the Adriatic and
the Euxine. Now the main difference between the conquest
of Gaul by the Franks and the conquest of Italy by the Ostrogoths was, that the former had been preceded by centuries
of gradual infiltration of Frank elements in the countries to
the west of the Rhine, whereas for Theodoric there was no
such basis on which to consolidate a Gothic kingdom. The
natural induction is that the cause whose presence secured
the permanence of the Frank kingdom in Gaul, and whose
absence facilitated the disappearance of the Gothic race from

---

[1] The credit of pointing out this belongs to Drinov. Zemae = modern
Tzema, on the Hebrus; Beodizum =
Voditza, in the *Itiner. Hieron.* and
Itiner. Anton. Safarik (ii. 159) places
the first Slavonic settlements south of
Danube at the end of the fifth century.
Mr. Bryce's researches have discredited
the Slavonic origin of Justinian (*Uprav-
da*), which was often adduced in proof
of early Slave settlements. But this
piece of evidence may be replaced by
another, if my explanation of the name
Belisarius as Slavonic (White Dawn)
is correct; *see* above, vol. i. p. 341

Italy, co-operated to render permanent the Slavonic conquests. This induction, of course, is not strict; we have not excluded the possibility of like effects resulting from different causes, and the case of the Visigoths in Spain is an obvious, though explicable, exception. But the fact that we have distinct traces of early Slavonic settlements supplements the defect of the *a priori* induction. The circumstance that there is no direct mention of such settlements by writers of the time can have little weight in the opposite scale; such things often escape the notice of contemporaries.[1]

The great political characteristic of the Slavonic races was their independence, in which they resembled the Arabs. They could not endure the idea of a monarch, and the communes, independent of, and constantly at discord with, one another, united only in the presence of a dangerous enemy. Owing to this characteristic their invasions cannot have been efficiently organised, and an able general should have been able to cut them off in detachments. The family, governed and represented by the oldest member, was the unit of the commune or tribe; the chiefs of the community, whose territory was called a *župa*, were selected from certain leading families which thus formed an aristocracy.

The character of the Slaves is described by a Greek Emperor as artless and hospitable; but it was often, no doubt, the artlessness of a heathen barbarian. They practised both agriculture and pasture. Physically they were tall and strong, and of blond complexion. Women occupied an honourable position, and the patriarchal character of their social life, by which the family was the proprietor and every individual belonged to a family, excluded poverty. Only an excommunicated person could be poor, and therefore to be poor meant to be bad, and was expressed by the same word.[2] In the sixth century their abodes were wretched hovels, and their chief food was millet.

The Emperor Maurice, in his treatise on the art of war,[3]

---

[1] Jiriček mentions a similar case in the seventeenth century, when the great migration of Serbs from Servia to the Banat and south Russia took place without being mentioned by a historian of the time.

[2] Jiriček, p. 97.

[3] Μαυρικίου στρατηγικόν, published at Upsala, 1664, by J. Scheffer, along with Arrian's *Tactics*. This is the only existing edition, and is very rare. The imperial treatise is divided into Twelve Books, and the subject of the eleventh is the customs and tactics of various

gives us an account of the Slavonic methods of warfare. They were unable to fight well in regular battle on open ground, and thus they were fain to choose mountains and morasses, ravines and thickets, in which they could arrange ambuscades and surprises, and bring into play their experience of forest and mountain life. In this kind of warfare skill in archery was serviceable, and they used poisoned arrows. Their weapons in hand-to-hand fight were battle-axes and battle-mallets. Maurice advises that campaigns against them should be undertaken in the winter, because then the trees are leafless and the forests less impenetrable to the view, while the snow betrays the steps of the foe, and the frozen rivers give no advantage to their swimming powers. It was a common device of a hard-pressed Slovene to dive into a river and not emerge, breathing through a reed whose extremity was just above the surface. It required long experience and sharp eyes to see the end of the reed and detect the fugitive.

The Slaves believed in a supreme God, Svarog, the lord of lightning, who created the world out of the sand of the sea; in lesser gods, among whom was reckoned Trajan; and in all sorts of supernatural beings, good and bad (Bogy and Besy); for instance, in *vlkodlaks* or vampires, from which the modern Greek βρουκόλακας is borrowed, in lake nymphs (*judi*) a sort of long-haired mermaids who draw down fishermen entangled in their locks to the depths below. The most interesting of these beings are the Samovili or Samodivi, who live and dance in the mountains. "They hasten swiftly through the air; they ride on earth on stags, using adders as bridles and yellow snakes as girdles. Their hair is of light colour. They are generally hostile to men, whose black eyes they blind and quaff," but they are friends of great heroes, and live with them as sworn sisters.[1]

Until the last years of the fourth century, when the Visigothic soldiers took up their quarters in the land and exhausted it, the Balkan peninsula had enjoyed a long peace; and after the

foreign nations. He groups Teutonic peoples together as ξανθὰ ἔθνη. In Bk. vii. cap. 1, he says that Huns and Scythians should be attacked in February or March, because their horses are then in bad condition on account of winter hardships (p. 137).

[1] *Posestrinnen,* that is in the relation of *Povratimstvo,* a sworn brotherhood of young men like that of Orestes and Pylades, or Amis and Amile.

final departure of Alaric for Italy, it was allowed almost forty years of comparative freedom from the invasions of foes to recover its prosperity. But the rise of the Hunnic monarchy under Attila in the countries north of the Danube meant that evil days were in store for it; and the invasions of the barbarian Attila, a scourge far worse than the raids of Alaric, reduced the plains and valleys of Thrace and Illyricum to uncultivated and desert solitudes, the inhabitants fleeing to the mountains. And when the Hunnic empire, that transitory phenomenon which united many nations loosely for a moment without any real bonds of law or interest, was dissipated, the races which had belonged to it, Germans and Slaves and Huns, hovered on the Danube watching their chance of plunder. The chief of these were the Ostrogoths, who, while they were a check on the Huns and on Germans more uncivilised than themselves, infested the lands of the Haemus, Illyria, and Epirus, until in 588 Theodoric, like Alaric, went westwards to a new home. The departure of the Ostrogoths was like the opening of a sluice; the Slaves and Bulgarians, whom their presence had kept back, were let loose on the Empire, and began periodical invasions. It must be noted that, beside the Ostrogoths, some non-German nations had settled in corners; the Satages[1] and Alans in Lower Moesia, and Huns in the Dobrudža.

I have already mentioned what is known of these invasions in the reign of Anastasius, and how that Emperor built the Long Wall to protect the capital. The invasions continued in the reign of Justinian and throughout the sixth century, but the Bulgarians soon cease to be mentioned, and it appears probable that they were subjugated by the neighbouring Slaves.

No real opposition was offered to the invasions of the barbarians, until Mundus the Gepid, who afterwards assisted in quelling the Nika insurgents, defeated and repelled the Bulgarians in 530. For the following years, until 534, the Haemus provinces enjoyed immunity from the plunderers, owing to the ability of Chilbudius, master of soldiers in Thrace, who was appointed to defend the Danube frontier, and to the measures which were taken for strengthening the fortifications.

---

[1] They were perhaps Slaves, as Šafařik conjectures; cf. Sotáks in north Hungary.

Besides the outer line of strong places on the river, an inner line
of defence was made in 530, connecting Ulpiana and Sardica.
But, in 534 the death of Chilbudius in a battle with the Slaves
left the frontier without a capable defender, and the old ravages
were renewed.[1] A grand expedition in 540 penetrated to
Greece, but the Peloponnesus was saved by the fortifications
of the isthmus.   Cassandrea, however, was taken, and the invaders crossed from Sestos to the coast of Asia Minor.   The
havoc wrought in this year throughout Thrace, Illyricum, and
northern Greece was so serious that Justinian set about making
new lines of defence on an extensive scale, which will presently
be described.

Two Slavonic tribes are mentioned at this period, the
Slovenes[2] and the Antai or Wends.   They did not differ from
each other in either language or physical traits[3]; both enjoyed
kingless government of a popular nature, both worshipped one
God, both were intolerant of the Greek and oriental conception of
fate.   Procopius relates that about this time hostilities arose
between the two tribes, and the Slovenes conquered the Antai ;
but it has been conjectured that this is an ill-informed
foreigner's account of a totally different transaction, namely the
reduction of the Slavonic tribes by the Bulgarians.   However
this may be, it is certain that the Bulgarians (whom Procopius
calls Huns), the Slovenes, and the Antai were in the habit of
invading the Empire together, and that some bond must have
united the two different races.   It is to be observed, however,
that it is the Slaves who are always in the foreground from this
time forth, and that the Bulgarians are almost never mentioned ;
whence the reverse relation, namely the conquest of the Bulgarians by the Slaves, might seem more probable.   Those
Bulgarians of the sixth century had, it must be remembered,

---

[1] An account of the impostor who
pretended to be Chilbudius, and the
offer made by Justinian to the Antai
that they should settle in Turris (perhaps Turnu Magurel, as Safarik, ii. 153,
and Jiriček suggest) will be found in Procopius, *B. G.* iii. 14.   Theophanes records
an expedition of two Bulgarian princes
(ῥῆγες) in 6031 A.M. = 538-539 A.D.,
against Moesia and Scythia.   Justin,
the commander in Moesia, was slain (cf.
Malalas, p. 437, 19, ed. Bonn).

[2] The settlements of the Slovenes
were probably in the old trans-Istrian
province of Dacia.   It is said that
their descendants in this country were
incorporated among the Roumanians,
who migrated from the south in the
Middle Ages.

[3] According to Procopius, *B. G.* iii.
14.   The Wends of Lausitz belong to
the "western" division of the Slavonic
family.

nothing to do with the foundation of the Bulgarian kingdom, which took place in the seventh century.

In 546 another Slavonic incursion took place, but on this occasion Justinian's principle of " barbarian cut barbarian " came into operation, and they were repulsed by the Heruls.   Two years later the Slaves overran Illyricum with a numerous army, and appeared before Dyrrhachium, and in 551 a band of three thousand crossed the Danube unopposed and divided into two parties, of which one ravaged Thrace and the other Illyricum. Both were victorious over Roman generals ; the maritime city of Toperus was taken ; and the massacres and cruelties committed by the barbarians make the readers of Procopius shudder.[1]   In 552 the Slaves crossed the Danube again, intent on attacking Thessalonica, but the terror of the name of Germanus, who was then at Sardica preparing for an expedition to Italy, caused them to abandon the project and invade Dalmatia.   At the beginning of Justinian's reign Germanus had inflicted such an annihilating defeat on the Antai that the Slaves looked upon him with fear and awe.[2]   The great expedition of Zabergan and the Cotrigur Huns (whom Roesler calls Bulgarians) in 558 was probably accompanied by Slavonic forces.

It is at this point that the Avars, whose empire considerably influenced the fortunes of the Slaves, appear on the political horizon of the West.   But as their presence did not affect the Roman Empire until after the death of Justinian, we may reserve what is to be said of them for a future chapter.

The wall of Anastasius had been the first step to a system of fortifications for defending the peninsula.   Justinian carried out the idea on an extensive scale by strengthening old and building new forts in Thrace, Epirus, Dardania, Macedonia, Thessaly, and southern Greece.

To protect Thrace there was first of all a line of fifty-two fortresses along the Danube, of which Securisma (or Securisca) and others were founded by Justinian, while the rest were strengthened and improved.   South of the Danube, in Moesia, there were twenty-seven strong fortresses.   On the Sea of Marmora Rhoedestus was built, a steep and large sea-washed town, while Perinthus (Heraclea) was provided with new walls.

---

[1] See *B. G.* iii. 38 ; for the incursion of the preceding year, *see* iii. 33.
[2] *Ib.* 40.

The walls that hedged in the Thracian Chersonese were restored. Sestos was made impregnable, and a high tower was erected at Elaiûs. Further west Aenus, near the mouth of the Hebrus, was surrounded with walls ; while north-westward, in the regions of Rhodope and the Thracian plain, one hundred and three castles were restored. Trajanopolis (on Hebrus), Maximianopolis, and Doriscus were secured with new walls ; Ballurus was converted into a fortified town ; Philippopolis and Plotinopolis, on the Hebrus, were restored and strengthened ; while Anastasiopolis was secured by a cross wall ($\delta\iota\alpha\tau\epsilon\acute{\iota}\chi\iota\sigma\mu\alpha$).

The middle Danube was in the same way lined with castles and fortified towns, protecting the frontier of Illyricum; the most important were Singidon (Singidunum, now Belgrade), Octavum, eight miles to the west, Pincum, Margus, Viminacium, Capus, and Novae. In Dardania, Justinian's native province, eight new castles were built, and sixty-one of older date restored. When invaders had penetrated this second line of fortresses they entered Macedonia, where a third system of strong defences obstructed their path. We are told that forty-six forts and towers were restored or built in this district. Among those which were restored may be mentioned Cassandrea, which had been taken by the Slovenes, and among those which were newly built we may note Artemisium in the neighbourhood of Thessalonica.

From Macedonia an invader might pass either southwards into Thessaly or westwards into Epirus. In Thessaly the fortified towns of Demetrias—the " fetter of Greece "—Thebae, Pharsalus, Metropolis, Gomphi, and Tricca formed a line of works across the country. The walls of Larissa were restored by Justinian, and new towns, Centauropolis, on Mount Pelion, Eurymene, and Caesarea (probably new), testified to the Emperor's anxiety to protect his subjects. If an enemy wished to proceed into Greece—supposing that he had succeeded in entering the Thessalian plains—it was necessary for him to overpower or elude the garrison of two thousand men who were stationed in the fortresses that guarded the memorable defile of Thermopylae. These fortresses were restored and strengthened, the walls were made higher and more solid, the bastions and battlements were doubled, and cisterns were provided for the use of the garrison. The town of Heraclea, not far from Thermopylae, was also the object of imperial solicitude; the Euripus was protected by castles; the walls of Plataea, Athens, and Corinth were renewed, and the wall across the isthmus was solidified and improved by watch-towers (φυλακτήρια). If, on the other hand, the foe turned his course westward, Justinian had secured those regions by erecting thirty-two new forts in the New Epirus, twelve new forts in the Old Epirus, and rehabilitating about twenty-five in each province.

In regard to this elaborate system of fortification, which was a conspicuous and not dishonourable feature of Justinian's reign, we must notice that he adopted an architectural innovation.[1] Old-fashioned fortresses had been content with single towers, and were hence called μονοπύργια : the new erections of Justinian were on a larger scale, and were crowned with many towers. It was probably found that the barbarians, who had learned a little about the art of besieging since they came into contact with the Empire, were not baffled by the one-towered battlements, and that stronger forts were necessary.

We cannot hesitate to assume that these measures of Justinian were of great service for resisting the Slavonic and subsequent Avaric invasions. But it must be observed that some of them were intended as barriers not only against external invaders, but also against barbarians who had settled within the boundaries of the Empire. This, we are told expressly,[2] was the case with the renovation of Philippopolis and Plotinopolis. We cannot doubt that these barbarian settlers were Slaves.

---

[1] ᾠκοδόμησατο καινουργήσας is an expression often employed. Procopius' work "on Edifices" is our source for these fortifications.

[2] Proc. *de Aed.* iv. 5.

CHAPTER XIII

CHANGES IN THE PROVINCIAL ADMINISTRATION

THE changes which were made by Justinian in the provincial administration were only of a partial nature, but they are nevertheless important, because they form a stage of transition between the arrangement of Diocletian and the later Thematic system which was developed in the seventh and eighth centuries.

In the earlier system, instituted by Diocletian and Constantine, three points are especially prominent—(1) the separation of the civil from the military administration; (2) the hierarchical or ladder-like principle by which not only the praetorian prefect intervened between the Emperor and the provincial governors, but *vicarii* or diocesan presidents intervened between the provincial governors and the praetorian prefect; (3) the tendency to break up provinces into smaller divisions.

On the other hand, the Thematic system, of which I shall speak in a future chapter, was characterised by features exactly the reverse. Civil and military administration are combined in the hands of the same governor; the principle of intermediate dioceses has disappeared, as well as the principle of praetorian prefectures; and the districts of the governors are comparatively large.

It is then instructive to observe that, though Justinian made no thoroughgoing change in the system that had prevailed during the fourth and fifth centuries, almost all the particular changes which he did introduce tended in the direction of the later system. In certain provinces he invested the same persons with military, civil, and fiscal powers; he did away with some of the diocesan governors, and he combined some of the small divisions to form larger provinces. These changes were made in the years 535 and 536 A.D.

(1.) " In certain of our provinces, in which both a civil and a military governor are stationed, they are continually conflicting and quarrelling with each other, not with a view to the benefit, but with a view to the greater oppression of the subjects; so we have thought it right in these cases to combine the two separate charges to form one office, and to give the old name of praetor to the new governor." [1]

This principle was applied in three cases at the same time (18th May 535). The *praeses* of Pisidia was invested with authority over the military forces stationed in the province, and so likewise the *praeses* of Lycaonia. Each of these officers ceased to be called *praeses*, and assumed the more glorious title of *praetor Justinianus*, which was accompanied with the rank of *spectabilis*. The *vicarius Thraciarum*, or governor of the Thracian diocese, and the master of soldiers in Thrace—officers whose spheres, as experience proved, tended to conflict—were abolished and superseded by a praetor Justinianus *per Thraciam* invested with civil, military, and fiscal powers.

The same principle had been adopted just a month before in the case of the new Justinianean counts of Phrygia Pacatiana and First Galatia. It was adopted two months later in the case of the new Justinianean moderator of Helenopontus and the new Justinianean praetor of Paphlagonia; and in the following year (536) it was applied to the new proconsul of Cappadocia and the proconsul of the recently formed province of Third Armenia.

In Egypt this principle had been practically operative under the old system; in the turbulent district of Isauria the governor (count of Isauria) was invested with both military and civil powers; the duke of Arabia also held the double office. But the point is that these exceptions were recognised as opposed to the general principle, and it was attempted to bring them into accordance with that general principle by the fiction that the count of Isauria, for example, represented two separate persons; he held, as it were, the civil power in his right hand and the military power in his left, and his right

---

[1] Justinian, Nov. xxiii. (ed. Zachariä von Lingenthal). Cf. xxiv. and xxv.

hand was not supposed to know what his left hand was doing. Justinian introduced a new principle and a new kind of governor, in whose hands the two functions were not merely put side by side but were organically united. The truth of this is distinctly demonstrated by the fact that he was obliged to reorganise the office of count of Isauria so that the military and civil powers should cohere.[1] It should be noticed that the epithet *Justinianus* is only connected with the titles of such new governors as were vested with the double function. The new *moderator* of Arabia, who was purely a civil officer, did not receive the imperial name.

(2.) In 535 A.D. (15th April) three diocesan governors were abolished. The vicar of Asiana became the *comes Justinianus* of Phrygia Pacatiana, invested with civil and military powers and enjoying the rank of a " respectable." On the same conditions the vicar of the Pontic diocese became the *comes Justinianus* of Galatia Prima. The count of the East was deprived of his authority over the Orient diocese and, retaining his " respectable " rank, became the civil governor of Syria Prima.[2]

The first change and the third change were permanent, but the abolition of the vicar of Pontica was revoked in 548 A.D.[3]

(3.) Justinian united the praesidial provinces of Helenopontus and Pontus Polemoniacus to form one large province, under the command of a governor entitled *moderator Justinianus*. The new province was called Helenopontus, in preference to the other name, because it seemed fitter to continue to commemorate the name of St. Helen than to adopt a title which not only preserved the memory of a " tyrant " but also suggested war ($\pi\acute{o}\lambda\epsilon\mu os$).[4]

In the same way the province of Honorias, which had obeyed a praeses, and the province of Paphlagonia, which had

---

[1] Justinian confesses that his new principle was suggested by the arrangement already existing in Isauria ($\acute{o}\pi\epsilon\rho$ $\tau\iota\sigma\grave{\iota}$ $\tau\hat{\omega}\nu$ $\pi\rho\grave{o}$ $\dot{\eta}\mu\hat{\omega}\nu$ $a\dot{\upsilon}\tau o\kappa\rho a\tau\acute{o}\rho\omega\nu$ $\dot{\epsilon}\nu$ $\epsilon\grave{\iota}\kappa\acute{o}\nu\iota$ $\kappa a\grave{\iota}$ $\sigma\chi\acute{\eta}\mu a\tau\iota$ $\kappa a\tau\grave{a}$ $\tau\grave{\eta}\nu$ $\grave{I}\sigma a\acute{\upsilon}\rho\omega\nu$ $\chi\acute{\omega}\rho a\nu$ $\mathring{\eta}\lambda\theta\epsilon\nu$ $\dot{\epsilon}\pi\grave{\iota}$ $\nu o\hat{\upsilon}\nu$ $\pi\rho\hat{a}\xi a\iota$ $\tau o\hat{\upsilon}\tau o$ $\dot{\eta}\mu\epsilon\hat{\iota}s$, $\kappa.\tau.\lambda.$ Nov. xxvi.) But he has to apply it in the very province whose administration gave him the suggestion : $o\dot{\upsilon}$ $\gamma\grave{a}\rho$ $\mathring{\epsilon}\tau\iota$ $\beta o\upsilon\lambda\acute{o}\mu\epsilon\theta a$ $\tau\grave{o}\nu$ $\dot{\epsilon}\pi\grave{\iota}$ $\tau a\acute{\upsilon}\tau\eta s$ $\gamma\iota\nu\acute{o}\mu\epsilon\nu o\nu$ $\tau\hat{\eta}s$ $\dot{a}\rho\chi\hat{\eta}s$ $\delta\iota\pi\lambda o\hat{\iota}s$ $\chi\rho\hat{\eta}\sigma\theta a\iota$ $\sigma\upsilon\mu\beta\acute{o}\lambda o\iota s$ $\kappa a\grave{\iota}$ $\lambda a\mu\beta\acute{a}\nu\epsilon\iota\nu$ $\mu\grave{\epsilon}\nu$ $\kappa a\grave{\iota}$ $\tau\grave{\eta}\nu$ $\tau\hat{\eta}s$ $\pi o\lambda\iota\tau\iota\kappa\hat{\eta}s$ $\dot{a}\rho\chi\hat{\eta}s$ $\pi\rho o\sigma\eta\gamma o\rho\acute{\iota}a\nu$, $\lambda a\mu\beta\acute{a}\nu\epsilon\iota\nu$ $\delta\grave{\epsilon}$ $\kappa a\grave{\iota}$ $\tau\grave{a}$ $\tau\hat{\eta}s$ $\sigma\tau\rho a\tau\iota\omega\tau\iota\kappa\hat{\eta}s$ $\dot{\epsilon}\xi o\upsilon\sigma\acute{\iota}a s$ $\sigma\eta\mu\epsilon\hat{\iota}a$ $\kappa a\grave{\iota}$ $\check{o}\nu o\mu a$ $\tau\epsilon\rho\iota\phi\acute{\epsilon}\rho\epsilon\iota\nu$ $\delta\iota\pi\lambda o\hat{\upsilon}\nu$ $\pi\rho\acute{a}\gamma\mu a\tau os$ $\check{o}\nu\tau os$ $\dot{\epsilon}\nu\acute{o}s$, $\kappa.\tau.\lambda.$ The last clause seems sufficient to explain the fact that Hierocles speaks of a *praeses* of Isauria, whence some have assumed that sometimes a *praeses* was appointed side by side with the count.

[2] Nov. xvi.

[3] Nov. clviii.

[4] Nov. xxxi.

obeyed a corrector, were welded together; the new province was called Paphlagonia, and the new governor was a *praetor Justinianus*.[1]

These changes were made 16th July 535. In the following year, 18th March, the two provinces of Cappadocia (prima and secunda) were incorporated under the rule of a proconsul (ἀνθύπατος) entrusted with the civil, fiscal, and military. administration.[2]

A curious combination of provinces under a single governor was the so-called prefecture of the Five Provinces. Cyprus and Rhodes, the Cyclades, Caria, Moesia, and Scythia were placed under the administration of a *quaestor exercitui*, who resided at Odessus. It would be very interesting to know the reasons for this strange arrangement, but unfortunately we do not possess an original document on the subject.[3]

In 535 Justinian made a redistribution of the most easterly districts of the old diocese of Pontica.[4] No change had taken place in the two provinces of Armenia, which were marked in the *Notitia* up to this year, except that First Armenia, which had been a praesidial, had become a consular province. Justinian formed four provinces in Armenia, partly by rearranging the two old provinces, partly by mutilating the province of Helenopontus, partly by incorporating new territory in the provincial system.

The new First Armenia, which had the privilege of being governed by a proconsul, included four towns of the old First Armenia, namely Theodosiopolis, Satala, Nicopolis, and Colonea, and two towns of the old Pontus Polemoniacus, Trapezus and Cerasus. The once important town of Bazanis or Leontopolis received the name of the Emperor, and was elevated to the rank of the metropolis.

The new Second Armenia, placed under a *praeses*, corresponded to the old First Armenia, and included its towns Sebastea and Sebastopolis. But in lieu of the towns which had been handed over to the new First Armenia, it received Komana, Zela, and Brisa from the new province of Helenopontus.

[1] Nov. xxxii.
[2] Nov. xliv.
[3] *See* the comments of Julian, Athanasius, and Theodorus on the lost *Lex ut Bonus*, etc., Nov. lii. John Lydus calls this quaestor the ἔπαρχος (prefect or governor) of Scythia, and says that Justinian gave him three provinces, Scythia, Cyprus, and Caria with the islands, of which he deprived the praetorian prefect of the East. Cf. Nov. lxvii.   [4] Nov. xlv.

The province of Third Armenia, governed by a *comes Justinianus* with military as well as civil authority, corresponded to the old Second Armenia, and included Melitene, Arca, Arabissus, Cucusus, Ariarathea, and Comana (Chryse).

Fourth Armenia was a province new in fact as well as in name; it consisted of the Roman district beyond the Euphrates to the east of Third Armenia. It was governed by a consular, and the metropolis was Martyropolis.

One may at first think that Justinian unnecessarily altered the names, and that he might have continued to call the old Second Armenia, whose form he did not change, by the same name. His principle was geographical order. The new trans-Euphratesian province went naturally with the district of Melitene, and therefore the Second Armenia became the Third, because it was connected with what it was most natural to call the Fourth. This connection was real, because the consular of Fourth Armenia was to be in a certain way dependent on the count of Third Armenia, who was to hear appeals from the less important province. In the same way the new First and Second Armenias naturally went together, and therefore it was convenient that the numbers should be consecutive. The *praeses* of Second was dependent to a certain extent on the proconsul of First Armenia.

The elevation of the *praeses* of Phoenicia Libanesia to the rank of a moderator (*spectabilis*),[1] and that of the *praeses* of Palestine Salutaris to the rank of a proconsul, with authority to supervise and intervene in the affairs of Second Palestine,[2] illustrate the tendency, which is apparent in most of Justinian's innovations, to raise the rank and powers of minor governments. This went along with the tendency to detract from the powers of the greater governors, like the praetorian prefect of the East, whose office was destined before long to die a natural death, or the count of the East, who had already been degraded to the position of a provincial governor.

In all these reforms the double aspect of Justinian's policy strikes us. He is a great innovator, and yet throughout he professes to revoke ancient names and restore ancient offices. In his constitution on the new praetor of Pisidia he appeals

[1] Nov. lv.   [2] Nov. liv.

to the existence of the old praetors under the Roman Republic, of Sicily, Sardinia, Spain, etc., and asserts that he is " introducing antiquity with greater splendour into the Republic, and venerating the name of the Romans." He discourses on the antiquity of the Pisidian and Paphlagonian peoples, and does not disdain to introduce mythical traditions. And when he establishes a proconsul in Palestine he defends his constitution not only by the fact that this land was in early time a proconsular province, but by the circumstance that it had ancient memories. Reference is made to the connection of Vespasian and Titus with it, and above all to the fact that there " the Creator of the universe, our Lord Jesus Christ, the Word of God and salvation of the human race, was seen on earth and deigned to dwell in our lands."

The general import of the details which I have given in this chapter is sufficiently clear. From the beginning of the Empire up to the sixth century the tendencies had been to differentiate the civil from the military administration, to break up large into lesser provinces, and to create an official hierarchy. These three tendencies might all be considered modes of a more general tendency to decrease the power and dignity of the individual provincial governor ; and though, as a matter of fact, this motive did not historically determine them, yet such was their effect. The reaction began in the reign of Justinian, and an opposite movement set in to integrate the provinces and increase the powers of the governors. The organisation of the newly recovered provinces in the West conformed to this principle ; the praetor of Sicily and the exarch of Italy were invested with military as well as civil and fiscal powers, and were directly responsible to the Emperor ; and the principle was also, though not at first, adopted in Africa. This tendency continued till about the ninth century, about which time some of the large districts, which had been formed in the meantime, began to break up into smaller unities.

CHAPTER XIV

THE GEOGRAPHY OF EUROPE AT THE END OF
JUSTINIAN'S REIGN

THE events which occurred in the reign of Justinian produced considerable changes in the map of Europe. The kingdom of the Ostrogoths in Italy disappeared, and the kingdom of the Vandals in northern Africa, which though not strictly European was distinctly within the sphere of European politics and may be regarded as European, had also disappeared; Africa and Italy were once more provinces of the Roman Empire. In Spain too the Romans had again set foot, and some cities both east and west of the Straits of Gibraltar, including Malaga, Carthago, and Corduba, acknowledged the sovereignty of Justinian and his successors.

This phenomenon, the recovery by the Roman Empire of lands which it had lost, was repeated again in later times. In each case we may observe three stages. At the beginning of the fifth century, under the dynasty of Theodosius, the Empire was weakened and lost half its territory to Teutonic nations; then under the dynasty of Leo I. the reduced Empire strengthened itself internally; and this consolidation was followed by a period of expansion under the dynasty of Justin. Again, in the seventh century the limits of the Empire were further reduced by Saracens and Bulgarians under the dynasty of Heraclius, and internally its strength became enfeebled; then under the house of the Isaurian Leo it regained its vigour in the eighth century; and in the ninth and tenth centuries, under the Macedonian dynasty of Basil, lost territory was reconquered and the Empire expanded. In neither case were all the lost provinces won back, and in both cases the new limits very soon began to retreat again.

If we compare the map of Europe in 565 with the map of Europe in 395 we see that the Romans may be said to have won back the lands which constituted the prefecture of Italy; but this general statement requires two modifications. In the north-east corner provinces which had been included in that prefecture, Pannonia, Noricum, and Rhaetia, remained practically in the possession of barbarians; and in the south-east districts were recovered which had belonged, not to the prefecture of Italy, but to the prefecture of Gaul, namely south-eastern Spain, the province of Tingitana which faces it, and the Balearic islands. It might have seemed that the charm of the Roman name and the might of Roman arms, issuing no longer from the city of the Tuscan Tiber but from the city of the Thracian Bosphorus, were destined to enthral Europe again, and that the career of conquest begun by Belisarius would be continued by his successors in the lands once known as "the Gauls" against the Visigoths, the Suevi, the Franks, and the Saxons; but Belisarius and Justinian had no successors. North-western Europe was destined, indeed, to become part once more of a Roman Empire, but a bishop of Old Rome, not an Emperor of New Rome, was to bring this about, two hundred and thirty-five years hence.

The new acquisitions of the Roman Empire were not the only new facts which appear on the face of a historical map. There were other new acquisitions made by the Frank kingdom, the very power which was in future years to erect a rival Roman Empire. During the reign of Justinian the kingdom of the Thuringians, the kingdom of the Burgundians, and the kingdom of the Bavarians were incorporated in the kingdom of the Franks. The once Roman island of Britain, now the scene of wars between its Anglo-Saxon conquerors and the old Britons, had so completely passed out of the sphere of the Empire's consciousness, if I may use the expression, that Procopius relates a supernatural legend of it, as of a mystic land. He calls it Brittia, reserving the old name Britannia for Brittany,[1] and mentions that the king of the Franks claimed

---

[1] Thus the appellation Brittia was intermediate between the old Roman name Britannia and the name Anglia. When the Goths offered to surrender

some sort of suzerainty over it, and on one occasion attached
Angles to an embassy which he sent to Byzantium, in order to
show that he was lord of the island. According to the strange
and picturesque legend, which Procopius records but does not
believe, the fishermen and farmers who live on the northern
coast of Gaul pay no tribute to the Frank kings, because
they have another service to perform. At the door of each in
turn, when he has lain down to sleep, a knock is heard, and the
voice of an unseen visitant summons him to a nocturnal labour.
He goes down to the beach, as in the constraint of a dream,
and finds boats heavily laden with invisible forms, wherein he
and those others who have received the supernatural summons
embark and ply the oars. The voyage to the shore of Brittia
is accomplished in the space of an hour in these ghostly skiffs,
though the boats of mortals hardly reach it by force of both
sailing and rowing in a day and a night. The unseen pas-
sengers disembark in Brittia, and the oarsmen return in the
lightened boats, hearing as they depart a voice speaking to the
souls.

Two other changes must be noticed which took place in
that region of wandering and shifting barbarians on the banks of
the Ister. The Lombards dwelled on the left bank of the Ister
when Justinian ascended the throne ; when Justin II acceded
their habitations were in Pannonia, the land of the Drave and
the Save. The kingdom of the Gepids, which was bounded on
both the south and the west side by the Ister, remained tolerably stationary during the whole reign. But in the latter
years of Justinian a new people had established itself to the
east of the Gepids, on the lower Ister—the Avars, a Hunnic
people who were destined to influence the fortunes of the
Balkan peninsula and the Danube countries for the space of less
than a hundred years, then to sink into insignificance, and finally
to disappear. Their arrival was fatal for the short-lived kingdom of the Gepids, which was crushed, two years after Justinian's
death, by the united forces of the Lombards and the Avars.

We may now consider some special points respecting the
western conquests of Justinian.

Sicily to the Romans, who had already
conquered it, Belisarius replied by offering to bestow Brittia, once an imperial
possession, on the Goths.

Immediately after the overthrow of the Vandal kingdom Africa was placed under the jurisdiction of a praetorian prefect, and thus rendered co-ordinate with Illyricum and the Orient. The act by which this administrative arrangement was made is preserved in the Codex,[1] and possesses extreme importance for students of the history of the Roman civil service.

The new prefecture included the four provinces[2] which composed the vicariate of Africa in the fourth century, and the privileged province, which was governed then by a proconsul. But in addition to these five provinces it comprised Tingitana, which in old days belonged to the vicariate of Spain, and Sardinia, which belonged to the vicariate of Urbs Roma. Of the seven provinces four were governed by consulars by the new arrangement, Byzacium, Tripolis, Carthago (that is Africa), and Tingitana; of these Tripolis and Tingitana had formerly been under *praesides*, while Africa had been governed by a proconsul who was independent of the vicarius. The other three provinces were placed under *praesides*; for Numidia, formerly a consular province, this was a degradation in rank.

The praetorian prefect, whose residence was fixed at Carthago, was to have a bureau of 396 officials. Another constitution which was passed at the same time established military dukes in various provinces.[3]

When the troubles which immediately resulted from the circumstances attending the conquest of Africa had been allayed, the prosperity of the Libyan provinces seems to have revived. The praetorian prefects were endowed with military authority, contrary to the original intention, and afterwards received, vulgarly if not officially, the appellation of exarch; and they were successful in defending their territory against the inroads of the Moors. John, the brother of Pappus, gained such brilliant victories over the Moorish chiefs,[4] two of whom were compelled to attend on him as slaves, that the African poet of the imperial restoration, Flavius Cresconius Corippus,

---

[1] *Cod. Just.* i. 27, 1 (534 A.D.) The first praetorian prefect of Africa was Archelaus.

[2] In the *Notitia*, Mauretania was bi-partite, under two praesides, Mauretania Sitifensis (eastern part) and Mauretania Caesariensis (western part).

[3] *Cod. Just.* i. 27, 2. Five *duces*

were appointed, namely in Tripolis, Byzacena, Numidia, Mauretania, and Sardinia. The coast opposite to Spain was placed under the military control of a tribune subject to the duke of Mauretania.

[4] *See* Procopius, *B. G.* iv. 17 *ad fin.*, and the *Johannis* of Corippus. The date of these events was 546.

thought himself justified in making him the hero of an eponymous poem, the *Johannis*. Paulus was praetorian prefect of
Africa in 552, John (presumably the brother of Pappus) in
558, and Areobindus in 563,[1] but we hear little more of Africa
until the reign of Maurice, when the Exarch Gennadius dealt
treacherously with the Moors, who had been harassing the provinces, and paralysed their hostilities.

The new connection of Sardinia with Africa was not
unnatural. Like Sicily, it had generally played a part in the
dealings of Rome with her enemies in Africa. It had played
a part seven hundred and fifty years ago in the Punic wars; it
had been connected with the war against the Moor Gildo in the
reign of Honorius; recently it had been involved in the fortunes or misfortunes of Africa, and included in the kingdom of
the Vandals. It was therefore natural to include it in the new
prefecture which was raised on the ruins of that kingdom.

The German power which had established itself in northern
Africa had passed away, as the German power which had
established itself on the middle Danube was soon to pass away,
without leaving any permanent trace of its existence; neither
the Gepids nor the Vandals left a historical name or monument
behind them,[2] except indeed the old and improbable derivation
of Andalusia from Vandalusia prove to be really correct. In
this respect the Gepids and the Vandals contrast with the
Burgundians and the Thuringians, whose kingdoms were overthrown, but whose names still survive.

It is a common remark that the extermination of the Vandal
power by the Romans is a thing to be regretted rather than
rejoiced in, and that Justinian removed what might have
proved a barrier to the westward advance of the Saracens at
the end of the seventh century.[3] I think that this view can
be shown to rest on a misconception. In the first place, it is

---

[1] I mention this to show that the
office of praetorian prefect had not been
abolished in Africa, as Mr. Hodgkin
seems to suppose (*Italy and her
Invaders*, iv. p. 45). *See* Novels clx.
clxix. clxxiii. (ed. Zachariä). I assume
in the text that the prefects were invested with military authority; it is
possible, however, that in Justinian's
reign there may have been both a prefect and a magister militum (στρατηγός), and that both functions may

have been afterwards combined in the
office of the exarch; but this does not
seem so probable. When Solomon was
praetorian prefect he seems to have been
in command of the soldiers.

[2] Their name, however, has been perpetuated in the opprobrious word *vandalism*. Transdanubian Dacia was called
Gepidia for a time. There was a remnant of the Gepids in the ninth century
(Roesler, *Romänische Studien*, p. 77).

[3] Cf. Mr. Hodgkin, *op. cit.* iii. 695.

hard to believe that the Vandals would have been able to present any serious resistance to the Arabs; at the end of the fifth century their kingdom was in a state of decline, and it seems probable that it could never have lasted until the end of the seventh century. It seems more probable that if it had not fallen a prey to the Romans it would have fallen a prey to a worse enemy, the Moors; and it seems certain that, even had it escaped Moors as well as Romans, it would have collapsed when the first Saracens set foot on the land. For the domestic condition of the Vandal state must have absolutely precluded all chance of a revival of strength. The kingdom was divided against itself, the native provincials hated their conquerors, who were daily growing more supine and less war-like, and there is no likelihood that an amalgamation would ever have taken place. And, secondly, even granting—what seems utterly improbable—that the Vandals could have held Africa even as effectually as the Romans, it was far more in the interests of European civilisation that the Romans should occupy it, for Africa proved the safety of the Empire at one of its most critical moments—the occasion of the dethronement of Phocas; and on the Empire mainly depended the cause of European civilisation. But, thirdly, if we entertain the still wilder supposition that the Vandals would really have been able to stem the tide of the Asiatic wave which rolled through Africa to Spain, it is very doubtful whether that would have promoted the interests of Europe; for though the Saracen lords of Cordova were Mohammedans and Asiatics, it cannot be denied that their sojourn in Spain was conducive in a marked degree to the spread of culture in the West.

If we are to indulge in speculations of what might have been had something else not been, we might suppose that no Imperial revival of an expansive nature took place, that the Vandals continued to live at their ease and persecute the Catholics in Africa, and that Ostrogothic kings continued to be the "lords of things," *domini rerum,* in Italy. Starting with this supposition, it would be natural enough to imagine further that the events of the Punic wars might be repeated; that the Goths of Italy might invade Africa and overthrow the effete Vandal kingdom just as the Romans had overthrown the Carthaginian republic; and that so the Ostrogoths, who were already in southern Gaul neighbours of their kinsmen the Visigoths, might become their neighbours also at the Pillars of Hercules. And thus,—Italy, Sicily, Africa, Spain, and southern Gaul belonging to Visigoths and Ostrogoths,—we can form the conception of a Gothic empire round the western Mediterranean basin, an empire which might have spread northward and eastward like the Roman Empire of old. Such imaginary displacements of fact sometimes serve to illustrate the import of the events which actually took place.

Sicily, which performed the double function of being a stepping-stone to Africa and a stepping-stone to Italy for the " Roman " invaders, was placed soon after its conquest under the government of a praetor ($\sigma\tau\rho\alpha\tau\eta\gamma\acute{o}\varsigma$), who was endowed with both civil and military authority.[1] Its administration remained, even after the conquest of Italy, independent of the governor, who resided at Ravenna. According to the old order which existed in the fifth century before the reign of Odovacar, Sicily was governed by a consular who was responsible to the vicar of Urbs Roma.

After the partial conquest of Italy by Belisarius the new acquisitions seem to have been placed under a praetorian prefect,[2] on the same basis as Africa, the military and the civil functions being kept distinct. But this arrangement was only temporary, and after the complete and final conquest of the land by Narses the system was adopted of combining the controls of civil, fiscal, and military affairs in the hands of one supreme governor. This principle had already been introduced in many provinces in the East, and had been adopted in Sicily. It is a little strange that it was not immediately adopted in Africa, where, however, the disturbed state of the country soon led to its introduction.

It is evident that a new name was required for the new governor. The title prefect, $\ddot{\epsilon}\pi\alpha\rho\chi o\varsigma$, from being originally

---

[1] The appointment of the praetor seems to have escaped the notice of Mr. Hodgkin. It is proved by the 79th Novel (ed. Zachariä), which was issued before the end of 537.

[2] Maximin was appointed praetorian prefect of Italy in the latter part of 542, see Procopius, *B. G.* iii. 6; but this does not warrant the assertion

of L. Armbrust in his dissertation on *Die territoriale Politik der Päpste von 500 bis 800:* "neben ihm [the exarch] fungirte ein Präfectus Prätorio." If there was an officer called *prefect* at Ravenna, as some passages in Gregory's letters seem to prove, he was not a praetorian prefect of Italy.

purely military, had come to be associated with purely civil functions, while the title *magister militum* was, on the face of it, purely military. The new, or revived, names which Justinian had given to the governors of provinces in whose hands he united the two authorities, praetor, proconsul or moderator, were manifestly unsuitable for the governor-general of Italy. Italy was a large aggregate of provinces, as large as the prefecture of Illyricum, and it would have been absurd to place its governor on a level in point of title with the praetor of Sicily, the proconsul of Cappadocia, or the moderator of Helenopontus. It was eminently a case for a new name, and accordingly a nondescript Greek name, which was applied to various kinds of officers,[1] was chosen, and the governor of Italy was called the *exarch;* but as he was always a patrician, it was common to speak of him in Italy as the Patrician.

We are not informed into what provinces the exarchate of Italy was divided during the fifteen years of its existence before the Lombard invasion. The praetor of Sicily probably remained independent of the exarch, while on the other hand it is possible that the administration of Sardinia may have been separated from Africa, and, like her sister island Corsica, connected with Italy. We may say that the district governed by the exarch corresponded very closely to the joint dioceses of Italy and Illyricum; and we may suppose that, as in Africa, the old distribution of provinces was in the main adopted. In regard to these provinces, it is important to observe that the signification of the word Campania had altered as long ago as the fourth century, and now comprised Latium. Rome herself, however, was perhaps even at this time, as she certainly was in the eighth century, included not in Campania, but in Tuscia, as Etruria was now called. In old days men spoke of the Tuscan Tiber; in the Middle Ages men could speak of Tuscan Rome.

The circumstance that Romans not living at Latin Rome and regarded by the Italians as strangers should have conquered Italy is one of the curiosities of history. The Romans, Romaioi, who came with Belisarius were looked upon as Greeks,

---

[1] Some of the subordinates of the praefectus urbi of Constantinople are called ἔξαρχοι by Constantine Porphyrogennetos.

and spoken of with a certain contempt by the provincials as well as by the Goths. They were not, however, all Greek-speaking soldiers, a very large number were barbarians; but it is probable that very few spoke Latin. Nevertheless it might be said that they represented a Latin power, for the native language of the Emperor Justinian was Latin. He often opposes "our native tongue" to the "common Hellenic speech," and laws were promulgated in Latin as well as in Greek. Latin Italy was not yet out of touch with the Roman Empire. Yet nothing illustrates more clearly the fact that the Empire was becoming every year more Greek in character than the history of its Italian dependencies. It succeeded in Hellenising the southern provinces, and it was just these provinces that remained longest subject to its authority.

The Greek characteristics of the Empire under Justinian are calculated to suggest vividly the process of ebb and flow which is always going on in the course of history. Just ten centuries before, Greek Athens was the bright centre of European civilisation. Then the torch was passed westward from the cities of Hellenism, where it had burned for a while, to shine in Latin Rome; soon the rivers of the world, to adapt an expression of Juvenal, poured into the Tiber. Once more the brand changed hands; it was transmitted from the temple of Capitoline Jupiter, once more eastward, to a city of the Greek world—a world, however, which now disdained the impious name "Hellenic," and was called "Romaic." By the shores of the Bosphorus, on the acropolis of Graeco - Roman Constantinople, the light of civilisation lived, pale but steady, for many hundred years, longer than it had shone by the Ilissus, longer than it had gleamed by the Nile or the Orontes, longer than it had blazed by the Tiber; and the church of St. Sophia was the visible symbol of as great a historical idea as those which the Parthenon and the temple of Jupiter had represented, the idea of European Christendom. The Empire, at once Greek and Roman, the ultimate result to which ancient history, both Greek history and Roman, had been leading up, was for nine centuries to be the bulwark of Europe against Asia, and to render possible the growth of the nascent civilisation of the Teutonic nations in the West by preserving the heritage of the old world.

CHAPTER XV

AN account of the reign of Justinian would be incomplete
without a chapter on the architectural works of his reign and
the school of the christian Ictinus, Anthemius of Tralles; and
this leads us to speak of "Byzantine" art in general.
"Romaic" art, one might think, would be a more suitable
name to distinguish it from "Romanesque," which developed
in the West on parallel lines and out of the same elements;
for so-called Byzantine art was not confined to Byzantium,
and "Byzantine" has no right to a wider signification.

In the first place, it may be observed that the antagonism
of Christians to ancient art has often been misrepresented.
Christians, like pagans, loved to decorate their houses with
statues; the christian city of Constantine was a museum of
Greek art. In the fourth century, at all events, little trace is left
of the earlier prejudice against pictures and images which was
derived from the Semitic cradle of the new religion. Christians adopted old mythological ideas, and gave them an interpretation agreeing with the conceptions of their creed. The
representations of Christ as the Good Shepherd, which were
so common, were closely connected with the Greek type of
Hermes Kriophoros; and in the catacombs we find an
Orpheus-Christ.[1] The nimbus[2] that surrounds the head of
a saint in christian paintings was derived from the pictures
of heathen gods of light; the rape of Proserpine is portrayed

---

[1] *See* the beautiful plate "Orphée
jouant du luth" in Perret's *Catacombes
de Rome*, vol. i. pl. 20.

[2] For the nimbus, *see* Didron's *Christian Iconography* (Bohn series), vol. i.
p. 34. The subject of Byzantine ty-
pology is too technical to be entered
upon here.

on the tomb of Vibia. With such symbolism we may compare
the habit of dedicating churches on the sites of temples to
some christian saint who offered some similitude in name or
attribute to the god who had been worshipped in the old temple.[1]
A church of St. Elias often replaced a sanctuary of Apollo the
sun-god, on account of the Greek name Helios; and temples
of Pallas Athene might be converted into shrines of the Virgin.
It was the same clinging to old forms, in spite of their incon-
sistency with the new faith, that induced the Phrygians to
call themselves Chrestianoi instead of Christianoi, and to
speak of Chrestos instead of Christos.[2] In architecture and all
branches of art the Christians had to accept and modify pagan
forms; just as they employed the materials of Greek and Roman
temples, especially the columns, in building their churches.

The two kinds of art which come before us at this period
are architecture and mosaic. Sculpture had practically
died out with the old Greek spirit itself. For in the first
place there was no longer any comprehension of the beauty
of the human form; the days of the gymnasia had passed
away; and in the second place taste had degenerated, and
men sought and admired splendour of effect rather than
beauty of form. So it was that colossal pillars like that of
Marcian, which seem imposing because they are monstrous,
had become popular; and for the statues of Emperors and
others, which were still executed, precious metals or showy
substances like porphyry were selected in preference to marble.
In addition to these circumstances there was another reason
which tended to render sculpture obsolete. Christians had
adopted the basilica as the most usual form of their places
of worship, and it was evident that plaques or mosaics could
fill the walls better. Work in mosaic was more permanent,
more costly, and more brilliant than painting, and many splendid specimens are still preserved, especially in the churches of
Ravenna and Thessalonica.[3]

[1] *See* Mr. Tozer's note, Finlay's
History of Greece, vol. i. p. 424, in
which he refers to a paper of M. de
Julleville, *Sur l'emplacement et le
vocable des Églises chrétiennes en Grèce.*
"The altar of the twelve gods is replaced by a church of the twelve
apostles. . . . Where there stood two
temples of Demeter there are now two

churches of St. Demetrius. On the
site of a temple of Asclepius is a
church of the Hag. Anargyri, *i.e.* the
unpaid physicians SS. Cosmas and
Damian."

[2] *See* Prof. Ramsay, *Journal of
Hellenic Studies*, iii. 349.

[3] As the scope of this chapter does
not extend beyond the sixth century,

The basilica and the rotunda were the chief forms of christian churches in the fourth and fifth centuries. In each case there were problems to be solved. In the basilica the architect was met by the difficulty of combining the Roman arch with the Greek column. In the case of the rotunda it seemed desirable to associate the dome with other than circular buildings; and of this problem two solutions were attempted. In the tomb of Galla Placidia at Ravenna we see the circular surrendered for a cruciform plan, and the cupola rising from the four corners. On the other hand the Byzantines enclosed the circular building in a square one, leaving a recess in each of the four angles, as in the church of SS. Sergius and Bacchus in Constantinople, and the church of San Vitale at Ravenna.[1] The dome was ultimately to be united with rectangular buildings, but this union was peculiarly Byzantine. The practice of placing a dome over part of a rectangular edifice was seldom adopted in the western architecture of those days.

The problem of uniting the arch with the column weighed especially upon the architect of basilicas. It was solved first at Salona in the peristyle of Diocletian's palace, as has been shown by Mr. Freeman, whose own words it will be well to quote. " To reach anything like a really consistent and harmonious style the problem was to find some means by which the real Roman system of construction might be preserved and made prominent, without casting aside a feature of such exquisite beauty as the Greek column, especially in the stately and sumptuous form into which it had grown in Roman hands. The problem was to bring the arch and column into union— in other words, to teach the column to support the arch. It strikes us that in the palace at Spalato we may see a series of attempts at so doing, a series of strivings, of experiments, one of which was at last crowned with complete success. Of these experiments some would seem to have been already tried else-

---

no reference is made to the churches of Athens, whose dates are uncertain, nor to later buildings of ascertained date like St. Mark's at Venice, which, it need hardly be remarked, is in every sense a Byzantine church.

[1] At Bosra there is a temple externally square, internally circular.

The church of SS. Sergius and Bacchus, now known as the little Aja Sofia, was erected by Justinian near the palace of Hormisdas, south-west of the hippodrome. St. George's at Salonica is an instance of a circular church with a dome.

where; of the successful one we know of no example earlier than Diocletian. . . . The arch was set over the column, but it was made to spring from the continuous entablature or from the broken entablature, or, as in the case of the Venetian windows, the entablature itself was made to take the form of an arch. All these attempts were more or less awkward . . . but in the peristyle the right thing was hit upon; the arch was made to spring bodily from the capital of the column, and was moulded, not with the fine mouldings of the entablature, but with those of the architrave only. . . . The germ of Pisa and Durham and Westminster had been called into life." [1]

The method by which the architects at Ravenna endeavoured to mediate between the column and the arch constitutes a special feature of early Byzantine architecture. It was evident that the entablature was but an awkward link between arch and capital, and the Ravennate architects relinquished it for a new form, a kind of super-capital called by the French *dosseret*. This is a reversed blunted pyramid with sides either convex or concave, the decoration generally consisting of monograms, crosses, or acanthus leaves in very low relief. It is seldom found as a plain block. In Ravenna one pillar in the church of Sta. Agatha has a plain square block between arch and capital, and we find similar blocks represented in the mosaics of San Apollinare Nuovo on the pillars of the palace of Theodoric. This new feature is a distinct step in the development of art called Byzantine; the horizontal structure and all its connections are being abandoned in favour of arches. This link between arch and column is a special feature of Ravenna, but we find it in the churches of St. Demetrius, the Holy Apostles, and Eski Djouma at Thessalonica, and elsewhere. [2]

The architecture of Ravenna [3] falls naturally into three periods, the age of Galla Placidia, the age of Theodoric the Ostrogoth, and the age of Justinian. San Giovanni in

[1] *Historical Essays*, 3d series, p. 61, note on "Diocletian's place in architectural history."

[2] We may perhaps attribute to Ravennate influence the appearance of the "dosseret" (German *Polster*) in a few churches at Rome (Sta. Agatha in Suburra, San Stefano Rotondo, San Lorenzo fuori le mura, SS. Quattro Coronati), and in the crypts of some churches in southern Italy. *See* F. W. Unger, *Griechische Kunst*, p. 342, 346 in Brockhaus, *Griechenland*.

[3] There is a special work on the churches of Ravenna by Quast, *Die altchristlichen Bauwerke von Ravenna*.

Fonte remains as an exquisite relic of the *Ecclesia Ursiana* built before the age of Placidia. Two churches built by Placidia herself were San Giovanni Evangelista and Sta. Croce. The former building now consists almost entirely of restorations; of the original work, executed to fulfil a vow made by the Empress when saved from a storm at sea, nothing remains but the pillars in the nave. Opposite Sta. Croce is the small dark church of SS. Nazario e Celso, built as a mausoleum by Placidia, and containing her own tomb. This building is in the form of a cross with neither nave nor pillars, adorned with arches and cylindrical vaults, and lined with mosaics. The walls outside are crowned by pediments with antique horizontal cornices. We see here an interesting example of the antique and Byzantine styles blended, and for the first time a cupola placed upon a four-cornered building. The palace of the Laurelwood (*Lauretum*), built by Placidia and her son Valentinian, in which Theodoric slew Odovacar, no longer exists.

In the second period, the reign of Theodoric, was built one of the finest Byzantine basilicas, San Martino in Caelo Aureo, now called San Apollinare Nuovo. The date of the "Rotunda of Theodoric" is not unchallenged, and the remains of his palace, now the front of the Franciscan cloister, have perhaps some claim to be considered genuine,[1] although the palace represented in the mosaics of San Apollinare points to a more antique style. Of the original San Martino only the nave remains, and in its gorgeous mosaics may be seen a further development of Byzantine art. Traces of the antique survive in some parts of the ornamentation and in the quasi-Corinthian capitals. No entirely new type of capital is seen in Byzantine architecture before the reign of Justinian; and until then the new art continued to use with more or less modification the old forms. In San Martino the Corinthian form is changed by a considerable widening at the top, and resembles the funnel shape of later Byzantine

---

[1] Low down in the wall of the façade is set a porphyry basin, purporting to contain the ashes of Theodoric, formerly placed in his mausoleum. The tomb still remains, but is called the church of Sta. Maria della Rotonda. See *Anonymus Valesii*, 16, 96: *se autem vivo fecit sibi monimentum ex lapide quadrato mirae magnitudinis opus et saxum in- gens quod superponeret inquisivit.* It has been supposed that this anonymous writer is no other than archbishop Maximian, represented in the mosaics of San Vitale (cf. vol. i. p. 253).

capitals. The wall veil of both sides of the nave is covered with mosaics; on one side is represented a line of martyrs going forth from Ravenna to the presence of Christ, and on the other a procession of virgins, clad in white, with palms in their hands, issuing from Classis, to offer adoration to the Virgin, who is waiting to receive them. In the representation of Ravenna the palace of Theodoric is conspicuous.[1]

Two large and beautiful buildings erected in the reign of Justinian make that period remarkable in Ravennate architecture, the famous octagon San Vitale, the model of Charles the Great for the cathedral of Aachen,[2] and San Apollinare in Classe, one of the most important basilicas in existence. The church of San Vitale was begun under the archbishop Ecclesius before Italy had been reconquered by the Romans; the building was executed by Julian Argentarius,[3] the Anthemius of Ravenna; and the church, completed after the imperial restoration, was dedicated by bishop Maximianus in 546. It is octagon in shape, and covered with a dome. To the east stretches a long choir, and seven semicircular niches break the walls of the seven other sides. A large portion of the interior is cased in slabs of veined marble of various colours. The apse, which is adorned with fine mosaics, is Byzantine in shape, semicircular within and three-sided without, and on either side is a semicircular chapel. The central mosaic represents the sacrifice of Isaac, while on either side is a picture, most suitable to decorate a building which may be considered the monument of the imperial restoration in Italy. On one side is represented Justinian in gorgeous apparel accompanied by the archbishop Maximianus, and attended by priests and officers; and on the opposite side another mosaic shows the Empress Theodora, also in magnificent attire, glittering with pearls and gems, and surrounded by her maidens. Justinian carries a casket and Theodora a goblet, probably containing thank-offerings to be placed on the altar. The original entrance to

---

[1] *See* Agnellus, *Lib. Pont.* p. 113 (*ap.* Muratori, *S. R. I.* vol. ii.), who relates that among other churches used by the Arian Ostrogoths and adapted by Justinian for Catholic use, St. Martinus, called *caelum aureum*, was embellished by mosaics "of the martyrs and virgins walking," *utrasque parietes de imaginibus martyrum virginumque incedentium tessellis decoravit.*

[2] There appears to be an erroneous notion current that San Vitale was copied from St. Sophia at Constantinople, but the two buildings have no resemblance.

[3] *See* Agnellus, *ib.* pp. 95, 107.

the building was on the west, but is now walled up, and the narthex, or, as it was called in Ravenna, the "ardica,"[1] is enclosed in the cloister. The columns have capitals of a new form, some funnel shaped, resembling the impost blocks, others basket shaped and adorned with network.

San Apollinare in Classe was begun under bishop Ursicinus, 534 A.D., and completed and consecrated by Maximian in 549. In plan this great church is like the other basilicas of Ravenna. It has three naves, spanned on each side by arches supported by twelve columns. The pillars, now deep sunken in the floor, many standing in water, rest on Attic bases, very various in form. Their basket-shaped capitals are decorated with acanthus. The narthex is a striking feature of the building, being remarkably high and broad. On the wall veil of the naves above the arches are mosaic medallions representing the archbishops of Ravenna.

A few years before the foundations of the church of San Vitale were laid, a cathedral was built at Parentium, on the peninsula of Pola, by Euphrasius. To the artistic interest of this edifice is joined an historical association, derived from the fact that Euphrasius was appointed bishop of Parentium by Theodoric but built his cathedral after the city had passed into the hands of the Romans. Thus the stately building and its founder suggest the transition from the Ostrogothic to the Justinianean period. The cathedral is thus described by Mr. Jackson[2]: "The church of Euphrasius is a specimen of the Byzantine style at its best. Classic tradition survives in the basilica plan, the long drawn ranks of serried marble pillars, and in the horizontal direction of the leading lines. But the capitals with their crisply raffled foliage, emphasised by dark holes pierced with a drill which recall the fragility and brilliance of the shell of the sea echinus, belong to a new school of sculpture, and the massive basket capitals which are found among them as well as the second capital or impost block which surmounts them all, were novelties in architecture at the time of their erection. These buildings[3] belong to the best school of By-

---

[1] *See* Agnellus, *Lib. Pont.* p. 107, *in ardica.* It seems evident that the collocation of the preposition led to the omission of the initial *n* of a Latinised form of νάρθηξ. *In nardica* became *in*

ardica, somewhat as *a natter* became *an adder.*

[2] *See* Mr. Jackson's *Dalmatia,* vol. i.

[3] St. Euphrasius and the duomo of Elias at Grado, 571-586.

zantine art, and were erected at the same period as those at Ravenna and Constantinople, which they resemble in every detail; and in the church of Parenzo especially one might imagine oneself in the ancient capital of the exarchs."

In the churches of Thessalonica[1] we find the new art in its perfection, especially in its most original and peculiar development, the adorning of the domes with mosaic. The date of many of the churches of Thessalonica is uncertain, and modern specialists are much at variance on the subject. In some cases the buildings themselves afford evidence of great antiquity; for example, the atrium in the nave of St. Demetrius once contained a fountain, which points to the custom of ablution practised by Christians only in the earliest times, and the mosaic pictures in St. George's church of saints who lived before the time of Constantine suggest an early period. The theory, too easily adopted by travellers, that many of these churches were built on the sites of heathen temples has been contradicted and almost disproved by recent research.

Of the more ancient buildings in Thessalonica the churches of St. Demetrius and St. George are the most remarkable. The church of St. Demetrius is a basilica (or *dromikon*) erected in honour of the saint early in the fifth century. The columns of the nave, of *verde antico* marble, are Ionic, and the carefully executed capitals might be called Corinthian but for the eagles with which they are adorned. The *dosserets*, which surmount the capitals, are marked with crosses, sometimes in the middle of foliage.[2] The only decoration of this church consists of coloured marbles, and the effect is more temperate than if it were also embellished with mosaics.

The ancient church of St. George belongs to the class of circular buildings called "tholi," most of which are supposed to have been erected in the early part of the fourth century.[3] It is probable that the dome, which even in the time of

---

[1] For the churches of Thessalonica, *see* the work of Texier and Pullan, *Byzantine Architecture*, in which there are splendid reproductions of the mosaics. [Mr. Mahaffy however communicates the following note: "The colours of the mosaics, as reproduced in Texier, are too bright and staring, nor are they even a fair representation of the newest and brightest condition of the originals."]

[2] Texier and Pullan, *op. cit.* p. 128.

[3] Leo Allatius distinguishes five kinds of churches—1. τρουλλωτά, or θολωτά (tholi); 2. καμαρωτά (vaulted buildings); 3. σταυρωτά (cruciform); 4. δρομικά; 5. *mixta* (mixed style).—*De templis Graecorum recentioribus, Ep.* ii. (ed. 1645).

Constantine was used in christian architecture, was adopted from Persian and other oriental buildings. The opening at the top of the dome was convenient as an issue for the smoke of the fire-worshippers, while the followers of a mystic cult appreciated the gloom[1]; for originally the cupola was lit from the top, as in the Pantheon at Rome. The octagon built by Constantine at Antioch was the model for numerous churches in the East. The entire decoration of the church of St. George consists of mosaics, and the eight pictures in the dome are perhaps the greatest work of the kind in existence. In these eight pictures are represented "rich palaces, in a fantastic style, resembling those painted on the walls of Pompeii; columns ornamented with precious stones; pavilions closed by purple curtains floating in the wind, upheld by rods and rings; arcades without number, friezes decorated with dolphins, birds, palm-trees; and modillions supporting cornices of azure and emerald. In the centre of each of these compositions is a little octagonal or circular house, surrounded by columns and covered by a cupola; it is screened off by low barriers, and veils conceal the interior. A lamp suspended from the ceiling indicates its character; it is the new tabernacle or *sanctum sanctorum* of the Christians."[2] A remarkable feature of this church are the eight quadrilateral chapels formed in the thickness of the walls at equal distances from one another. Some of these niches are ornamented with mosaic pictures of birds, flowers, and baskets of fruit.

The era of Justinian was the golden age of christian art, and St. Sophia, its most perfect achievement, still remains, a wonder displaying all the resources of the new art, and a perpetual monument of the greatness of the Emperor and of the genius of Anthemius of Tralles. Of this master Agathias gives the following account:—

"The city of Tralles was the birthplace of Anthemius, and he practised the art of inventions, by which mechanicians, applying the abstract theory of lines to materials, fabricate imitations and, as it were, images of real things.[3] In this art he excelled greatly and reached the highest point of

---

[1] Compare Unger, *Griechische Kunst*, p. 354. Unger, however, seems to press too far the theory that the chief features of christian art came from the East.

[2] Texier and Pullan, *op. cit.* p. 136.

[3] The ingenious contrivances of this Archimedes of the sixth century for tormenting his neighbours are related by Agathias and reproduced by Gibbon.

mathematical science,[1] even as his brother Metrodorus in so-called philology (γραμματικὰ). I would certainly felicitate their mother on having brought into the world a progeny replete with such various learning, for she was also the mother of Olympius, who studied law and practised in the courts, and of Dioscorus and Alexander, both skilful physicians. Dioscorus lived in his native city, where he gave many remarkable proofs of his skill, and Alexander dwelt in Rome, having received an honourable call thither. But the fame of Anthemius and Metrodorus spread everywhere and reached the Emperor himself, on whose invitation they came to Byzantium and spent the rest of their lives there, and gave remarkable proofs of their respective talents. Metrodorus educated many noble youths, instructing them in his honourable branch of learning, and instilling diligently a love of literature in all. But Anthemius contrived wonderful works both in the city and in many other places which, I think, even if nothing were said about them, would suffice of themselves to win for him an everlasting glory in the memory of man as long as they stand and endure." [2]

The church dedicated by Constantine to the Divine Wisdom (Ἁγία Σοφία) was twice burnt down, first in the reign of Arcadius, and again in the reign of Justinian during the Nika revolt. Forty days after the tumult had subsided the ruins were cleared away by order of the Emperor, and space was provided for a new church to be built on a much larger scale than the old. To Anthemius was entrusted the great work, and Isidore of Miletus and Ignatius were his assistants. The ancient temples of Asia and Greece were robbed of their most beautiful columns, and costly marbles, granite, and porphyry were brought from distant places, from Egypt, Athens, and the Cyclades, as well as from Proconnesus, Cyzicus, and the Troad.[3] The length of the building is 241 feet, the breadth 224 feet; the ground plan represents a Greek cross, and the crowning glory of the work, the aerial dome, rises 179 feet above the floor of the church. Thus here, for the first time, the cupola is united on a large scale with a cruciform building.[4] The dome is lit by forty windows built into the hemisphere itself, and rests lightly on four strong arches supported by massive pillars; its weight is lessened as much as possible by the use of light materials. On the east

[1] δεινὸς ἀνὴρ καὶ κέντρον ἑλεῖν καὶ σχῆμα χαράξαι (Paulus Silentiarius, *Descr. S. Sophiae*, l. 271).
[2] Agathias, v. 8.
[3] These marbles are mentioned in the *Descriptio S. Sophiae* of Paul the Silentiary. This poem and Salzenberg's

splendid work, *Altchristliche Baudenkmale von Constantinopel vom 5 bis 12 Jahrhundert*, are both indispensable and sufficient for the study of St. Sophia.
[4] Thus St. Sophia belongs to the fifth class of Leo Allatius; it is both σταυρωτόν and τρουλλωτόν.

and west are two large half-domes (*conchae*), each lit by five windows. The oval shape of the nave is determined by these half-domes. At either side of the apse there is a smaller side-apse,[1] and on the west, where the narthex corresponds to the apse, there are similar recesses. Two contemporary writers, Paul the Silentiary and Procopius the historian, were impressed with the marvellous brilliance of the interior owing to the skilful arrangement of the windows. "It is wonderfully filled with light and sun rays, you would say the sunlight grew in it" (τὴν αἴγλην ἐν αὐτῷ φύεσθαι).[2] The enclosing walls of the building are built of brick concealed under a coating of marble, and the interior presents a brilliant spectacle of costly marbles, porphyry, jasper, and mosaics, which adorn the walls and cupolas.

In the apse, between four silver columns, were placed the seats of the Patriarch and the priests, also of silver, and a barrier (κιγκλίδες), 14 feet high, of the same metal, separated the bema from the nave of the church. This barrier contained the three sacred doors, and, resting on twelve columns, was a frieze, with medallions, on which amidst adoring angels were represented the Virgin, the Apostles, and the Prophets. A circular shield in the centre bore a cross and the united monograms of the Emperor and Empress. Before the barrier stood the golden altar supported by golden pillars, and over it the silver ciborium. The solea, immediately in front of the bema, and occupying the eastern extremity of the nave, contained seats for the lesser clergy; and in front of the solea was the ambo, a semicircular tribune approached by marble steps and covered with a pyramidal roof, borne by eight pillars and decorated with gems and precious metals. This tribune, under the eastern side of the central dome, was reserved for the singers and readers, and contained the coronation chair of the Emperor.

The aisles are separated from the nave and the four side-apses by arcades of pillars, and the upper rooms are domed. Of the hundred columns which adorn St. Sophia and form its stately arcades, the greater number are of green Thessalian marble[3] (*verde antico*), and were the spoil of pagan

---

[1] Salzenberg calls them Exedrae, but Unger adopts the more convenient name *Nebenapsis*.

[2] Proc. *de Aed.* i. 1.

[3] For Thessalian columns, cp. Paulus Sil. 545, 568.

temples. The eight large green columns in the nave were taken from the temple of Diana at Ephesus, and the eight columns of dark red Theban porphyry in the four side-apses originally stood in the temple at Heliopolis, whence Aurelian brought them to Rome; but, as the gift of a Roman lady, they were destined, with other spoils of paganism, to adorn a christian church. Their capitals present an infinite variety of form. They are of Proconnesian marble, and were manufactured in Byzantine workshops; they transgress in shape and execution the traditions of classic art. They lack, however, a characteristic feature of earlier christian architecture, the *dosseret* or impost block; Anthemius discarded the stilt. The larger and richer capitals are decorated with acanthus, palm leaves, or monograms, deeply cut,[1] and, like the marble friezes, are generally gilt; the smaller capitals are plain, and in shape like a die blunted at the corners. The bases of the pillars [2] (of the usual Attic form) the capitals and the cornices are of marble, chiefly white, but sometimes light gray. The pavement is of dark gray veined marble, chosen no doubt by the architect in pleasing contrast to the rich and varied colour of the interior, with its slabs of many-tinted marbles, its profuse gilding, and brilliant mosaics.[3]

There are nine entrances to the body of the church from the narthex, a narrow hall running across the whole extent of the building, and having at each end lofty vaulted halls. The space under the western semicupola communicates with the narthex by three doors, of which the largest in the centre was called the "king's door"; the west front of the narthex is coated with Proconnesian marble, and its upper story, connected with the rooms above the broad side-aisles, forms the *gynaikitis*, or women's gallery. Seven doors lead from the narthex into the outer narthex (exonarthex), a space enclosed by halls open from within, and vaulted and adorned with mosaic. In this court, where now stands a Turkish fountain and marble basin, stood a covered phiale (fountain),

[1] Salzenberg, p. 77, "tief unterarbeitet, fast frei auf dem Grunde liegend." The effect of this delicate carving, with the detached appearance of the ornamentation, suggests work in ivory.

[2] The eight pillars of Theban porphyry were not long enough, and were eked out by "eine Art Säulenstuhl" (*ib.* p. 78).

[3] Cp. Paul. Sil. 606.

and in the niches of the walls were twelve lions' heads from which flowed a continuous stream of pure water.

Five years and eleven months after the laying of the foundations, St. Sophia was completed and consecrated by the Patriarch (26th December 237). Procopius thus describes it: " The church turned out a beautiful sight, colossal to spectators, and quite incredible to hearers; it was raised to a heavenly altitude, and like a ship at anchor, was eminent above the other edifices, overhanging the city." [1]

When Anthemius saw his own handiwork in its stately strength towering over the city, or lingered under the mysterious firmament of the dome, he may have gloried in the success of his labours.   One would think that the words used of Giotto in the cathedral at Florence might well have been said of Anthemius by a Politian of the Justinianean age: " His name shall be as a song in the mouths of men " *(hoc nomen longi carminis instar erit)* ; and yet how unfamiliar nowadays is the name of Anthemius.

St. Sophia became a model for the whole christian world, and was copied in all large towns during the sixth and following centuries.   Among these lesser churches dedicated to the Divine Wisdom the cathedral of Thessalonica holds the first rank.   It is certainly of the school of Anthemius, and was probably contemporary with the great St. Sophia.   The mosaics in the dome are of the very best school, and preserve to some extent the traditions of Roman art.   The hemisphere of the apse is adorned with a mosaic picture of the Virgin, seated and holding the infant Christ.   Either this design or a colossal figure of Christ [2] was invariably chosen to decorate the hemisphere of Byzantine apses.

It has been already mentioned that sculpture in its classical form had died out, but smaller branches of the art were practised by the Byzantines.   The reliefs on the Golden Gate and on the Pillars of Theodosius and Arcadius [3] were not contemptible, and until the end of the fourth century gems were carved and coins struck in the antique style.   After

---

[1] Procopius, *de Aed.* i. 1.

[2] As for example in the Greek mosaic in the church of San Miniato at Florence, and in the church of William the Good at Monreale near Palermo.

[3] The reliefs on the pillar of Ar-cadius and the frieze of the staircase leading up to it were copied by Gentile Bellini, who was sent to Constantinople in 1479 by the republic of Venice.   The designs are now in the Royal Academy at Paris.

that period the workmanship of coins is inartistic and roughly executed, and the art of carving gems declines.   Chief among the smaller branches of sculpture was ivory carving, especially in the form of diptychs, which it was customary to present to the senate and the consuls, also to churches, and they were much used as new year's gifts.   Their value was sometimes increased by the name of some celebrated divine carved upon them, or by the consecration of an inscribed prayer.   The bishop's chair in the cathedral at Ravenna is a beautiful example of carved ivory.

Painting, however, had superseded all other forms of decorative art, and even in the sculptured adornments and reliefs of the new style the influence and features of painting may be traced in the grouping and general execution of the designs. The writers of this period make frequent mention of paintings in molten wax, κηρόχυτος γραφή,[1] a method described in the famous handbook of Mount Athos.[2]

The illumination of manuscripts was a branch of art much cultivated by the Byzantines.   M. Lenormant thus describes the famous *Codex Rossanensis* :—

" Rossano possesses in the archives of its cathedral one of the most precious and incontestably genuine monuments of Byzantine art of the period before the Iconoclasts, and probably of the age of Justinian. I mean the manuscript known to the learned by the name of *Codex Rossanensis*, and whose existence MM. Oscar von Gebhardt and Adolf Harnack have recently been the first to discover. It is a magnificent volume, composed of 188 leaves of purple-tinted vellum, a foot long, on which the gospels of St. Matthew and St. Mark are written in large silver letters in the form of rounded uncials. . . . But what lends to the Greek gospels of Rossano such great interest is the twelve large miniatures, which are still preserved, a last relic of rich illustrations which have been for the most part unhappily destroyed. Each of these miniatures occupies a whole page and is divided in two parts, the upper containing a subject from the gospels, and the lower four half-length figures of the prophets who foretold the event, each accompanied by the words of his prophecy. The paintings are certainly of the same date as the text, namely the sixth century. The execution is remarkable, the drawing compact, the composition clear and simple, the design exquisite, and the style antique."[3]

---

[1] Two old Greek paintings in wax are found in the MS. of Dioscorides dedicated to Anicia, daughter of Olybrius, and in a MS. of the book of Genesis. *See* Unger, *op. cit.* p. 361.

[2] ἑρμηνεία τῆς ζωγραφικῆς.   Didron obtained a copy on Mount Athos. It is a manual for the technique of painting as well as for the iconography. It has been translated into French by Durand and into German by Schäfer.

[3] *La Grande-Grèce,* i. 347.

In the use of symbols, a striking feature in christian art, we observe the most frequent blending of pagan and christian ideas. The Byzantines adopted the Greek custom of personifying nature, and in many instances classical forms were introduced, even in church paintings. In a Ravenna mosaic of the baptism of Christ, the Jordan is personified, and Theodoric represented himself on the gate of his palace, standing between two figures symbolising Ravenna and Rome. The personifications of Victory and Fortune, Nike and Tyche, are frequent and familiar, and the gnostic sects employed a more intricate symbolism of abstract ideas on their engraved gems and inscriptions on metal.[1] Numerous symbols were used for Christ and God the Father, and display a curious adoption of antique forms; and the resemblance borne by the representations of Christ on early christian tombs to *Sol Invictus* and Serapis is remarkable. On christian gravestones we find the letters D. M., D. M. S., and Θ. K., which suggest the *Dis manibus sacrum* and the θεοῖς καταχθονίοις of the ancients. Perhaps the consecrated ground hallowed the pagan words, just as gems with images of heathen gods were sanctified by a christian inscription or the monogram of Christ, and were countenanced by the Church.

Thus in the development of christian art the old classic traditions had been gradually abandoned, or remained only in allegory and mixed symbolism. The models of Greece and Rome became relics of the old world, curiosities to adorn museums. A new religion had displaced pagan mythology and philosophy, and naturally found an expression in new forms of art. And this new art, born in the atmosphere of triumphant Christianity, reached its perfection in Justinian's church of the Divine Wisdom, which still looks across the Bosphorus upon the sands of Chalcedon.[2]

[1] For example the curious symbol used by the followers of Basilides for the highest Being, called Abrasax, a form with serpents for feet, the body and arms of a man, the head of a cock, and holding in one hand a circle and in the other a whip. These represent the five emanations of Abrasax, φρόνησις, νοῦς, λόγος, δύναμις, σοφία, and the letters of his name, taken numerically, are the number 365.

[2] *Chalcedonias contra despectat arenas* (Claudian, *in Rufinum*, Lib. ii. 55).

CHAPTER XVI

NOTES ON THE MANNERS, INDUSTRIES, AND COMMERCE
IN THE AGE OF JUSTINIAN

THE population of Constantinople at the beginning of the sixth century has been calculated at about a million.[1] The greatest city in Europe, as it continued to be throughout the Middle Ages, and at the same time situated on the borders of Asia, it was full of Gepids, Goths, Lombards, Slaves, and Huns, as well as orientals; Abasgian eunuchs and Colchian guards might be seen in the streets. The money-changers in this mercantile metropolis were numerous, and probably lived in the Chalkoprateia, which in later times at least was a Jews' quarter. But the provincial subjects were not encouraged to repair to the capital except for strict purposes of business; and their visits were looked upon with such jealous eyes that as soon as their business was completed they were obliged to return home with all haste.

In the urban arrangements of Constantinople, for the comfort of whose inhabitants the Emperors were always solicitous, the law of Zeno, which provided for a sea prospect, is noteworthy.[2] The height of the houses built on the hills overlooking the sea was regulated in such a way that the buildings in front should not interfere with the view from the houses behind. Besides the corn, imported from Egypt, which was publicly distributed to the citizens in the form of bread,

---

[1] Krause, *Die Byzantiner des Mittelalters*, p. 17. As the book deals almost exclusively with the later Byzantines (eleventh to fifteenth century), it is of little use for the period with which we are here concerned.

[2] *Cod. Just.* viii. 10, 12.

the chief food of the Byzantines was salted provisions of various kinds (ταρίχη)—fish, cheese, or ham. Wine was grown in the surrounding district, and there was a good vegetable market. Of public amusements there was no lack.[1] As well as the horse-races in the hippodrome, there were theatrical representations and ballets; and it is probable that troupes of acrobats and tight-rope dancers often came from Asia. A theatre, called by the suggestive name of "Harlots," is mentioned and recognised by the pious Justinian without a censure or a blush. Combats of men with wild animals, which had been abolished by the mild and heterodox Anastasius, were once more permitted under the orthodox and severer dynasty of Justin. Curious animals and prodigies were exhibited and attracted crowds; we hear, for example, of a wonderful dog which had the power of distinguishing the characters and conditions of human beings. This animal, whose inspiration was more formidable than if it had been mad with hydrophobia, singled out the courtesan, the adulterer, the miser, or the woman with child; and when the rings of a multitude of spectators were collected and cast before it in a heap, it returned each to the owner without making a mistake.

The conversation which took place in the hippodrome on the eve of the Nika sedition, while it illustrates the political life of the time, is also interesting and important as an example of the language then spoken at Byzantium, and altogether is sufficiently noteworthy and curious to deserve reproduction.[2] In many places, however, the meaning is obscure. It was customary to permit the factions on special occasions to state their grievances to the Emperor. The demarch was the mouthpiece of the deme, and a *mandator* or herald replied for the sovereign.

---

[1] The programme for the consular shows, which lasted seven days, will be found in the 81st Novel of Justinian (ed. Zachariä). On the first day (1st January) the new consul was invested; second day, *mappa*, horse-races in the hippodrome; third day, the *theatro-cynegion*, or combats with beasts; fourth day, *monemerion*, beast-baiting; fifth day, scenic and musical performances at the theatre called "Harlots" (πόρναι); sixth, another *mappa*, or horse-races; seventh, the consul laid down his office. Justinian speaks, in a tone of approval and satisfaction, of the exquisite delight which beast-baiting afforded to the populace.

[2] Theophanes, *Chron.* 6024 A.M. (ed. de Boor, p. 181). The heading is ἄκτα διὰ Καλοπόδιον τὸν κουβικουλάριον καὶ σπαθάριον, and Theophanes probably copied the conversation from a document in the archives of the green deme.

Demarch of Greens. Long may you live, Justinian Augustus! *Tu vincas.* I am aggrieved, fair lord (μόνε ἀγαθέ), and cannot endure the oppression, God knows. I fear to name the oppressor, lest he be increased and I endanger my own safety.

Mandator. Who is he? I know him not.

Demarch of Greens. My oppressor, O thrice august! is to be found in the quarter of the shoemakers.[1]

Mandator. No one does you wrong.

Demarch of Greens. One man and one only does me wrong. Mother of God, let him never raise his head (μὴ ἀνακεφαλίσῃ)!

Mandator. Who is he? We know him not.

Demarch of Greens. Nay, you know best, O thrice august! who it is that oppresses me this day.

Mandator. We know not that any one oppresses you.

Demarch of Greens. It is Calapodius, the spathar (guardsman), who wrongs me, O lord of all!

Mandator. Calapodius is not in power.[2]

Demarch of Greens. My oppressor will perish like Judas; God will requite him quickly.

Mandator. You come, not to see the games, but to insult your rulers.

Demarch of Greens. My oppressor shall perish like Judas.

Mandator. Silence, Jews, Manichaeans, and Samaritans!

Demarch of Greens. Do you disparage us with the name of Jews and Samaritans. The Mother of God is with all of us.

Mandator. When will ye cease cursing yourselves.

Demarch of Greens. If any one denies that our lord the Emperor is orthodox, let him be anathema, as Judas.

Mandator. I would have you all baptized in the name of one God.

The Greens (tumultuously). I am baptized in One God.[3]

Mandator. Really, if you won't be silent, I shall have you beheaded.

Demarch of Greens. Every person is anxious to be in authority, to secure his personal safety. Your Majesty must not be indignant at what we say in our tribulation, for the Deity listens to all complaints. We have good reason, O Emperor! to mention all things *now*.[4] For we do not even know where the palace is, nor where to find any public office. I come into the city by one street only, sitting on a mule[5]; and I wish I had not to come then, your Majesty.[6]

---

[1] εἰς τὰ τζαγγαρεῖα εὑρίσκεται.

[2] οὐκ ἔχει πρᾶγμα.

[3] The Greens apparently take up the words of the mandator, εἰς ἕνα βαπτίζεσθαι, in a monophysitic sense. The words ὡς ἐκέλευσεν Ἄντλας are obscure. Ἄντλας can hardly be the name of the mandator. If it is correct, we may assume it to be a nickname of Anastasius. ἄντλει or ἀντλησον has been suggested in the sense of "fetch water" for the baptismal rite.

[4] ὀνομάζομεν ἄρτι πάντα. The sense demands that ἄρτι should be the emphatic word.

[5] ὅταν εἰς βορδώνην καθέζομαι. Prisoners were drawn by mules to execution or punishment, and perhaps there is some such reference here. One might conclude from this that members of the green faction were not allowed to reside in the city, and were confined to quarters in Pera and Galata, on the other side of the Golden Horn.

[6] εἴθαις μηδὲ τότε, τρισαύγουστε.

Mandator. Every one is free to move in public, where he wishes, without danger.

Demarch of Greens. I am told I am free, yet I am not allowed to exhibit my freedom. If a man is free but is suspected as a Green, he is sure to be publicly punished.

Mandator. Have ye no care for your lives that ye thus brave death ?

Demarch of Greens. Let this (green) colour be once uplifted[1]—then justice disappears. Put an end to the scenes of murder, and let us be lawfully punished. Behold, the fountain is overflowing ; punish as many as you like. Verily, human nature cannot tolerate the two things together (to be murdered by the Blues and to be punished by the laws). Would that Sabbates had never been born, to have a son who is a murderer. The sixth murder has taken place in the Zeugma[2]; the victim was a spectator in the morning, in the afternoon, O lord of all ! he was butchered.

Demarch of Blues. Yourselves are the only party in the hippodrome that has murderers among their number.

Demarch of Greens. When ye commit murder[3] ye leave the city in flight.

Demarch of Blues. Ye shed blood for no reason. Ye are the only party here with murderers among them.

Demarch of Greens. O lord Justinian ! they challenge us and yet no one slays them. Who slew the woodseller in the Zeugma, O Emperor ?

Mandator. Ye slew him.

Demarch of Greens. Who slew the son of Epagathus, Emperor ?

Mandator. Ye slew him too, and ye throw the blame[4] on the Blues.

Demarch of Greens. Now have pity, O Lord God ! The truth is in jeopardy. I should like to argue with them who say that affairs are managed by God. Whence comes this misery ?

Mandator. God is incapable of causing evils.

Demarch of Greens. God, you say, is incapable of causing evils ? Who is it then who wrongs me ? Let some philosopher or hermit explain the distinction.

Mandator. Accursed blasphemers, when will ye hold your peace ?

Demarch of Greens. If it is the pleasure of your Majesty, I am content, albeit unwillingly. I know all—all, but I say nothing. Goodbye, Justice ! you are no longer in fashion.[5] I shall turn and become a Jew. Better to be a " Greek " than a Blue, God knows.

---

[1] ἐπαρθῇ τὸ χρῶμα τοῦτο καὶ ἡ δίκη οὐ χρηματίζει. It seems to me that this admits only of the rendering I have given. Marrast translates " Nos couleurs sont proscrites. Plus de justice pour nous dans l'empire." Mr. Hodgkin, "'Take off that colour [the emblem of the Blues], and do not let justice seem to take sides."

[2] "It is twenty years since [one of our party] was murdered at the Yoking-place" (Mr. Hodgkin) ; but this is pointless. De Boor prints εἰκότως ἕκτος.

[3] πότε σφάξεις καὶ ἀποδημεῖς, Mr. Hodgkin translates "'Sometimes you murder and run away," but that would be ποτέ. πότε is vulgar for ὅτε.

[4] τοὺς Βενέτους πλέκετε. πλέκω, a word of the common language not used in good prose, is evidently related to the Latin *plecto*, which, as is well known, is used of vicarious punishment.

[5] σώζου, δίκη, οὐκέτι χρηματίζεις· μεταβαίνω καὶ τότε 'Ιουδαίζω.

Demarch of Blues. I hate you, I can't abide the sight of you,—your enmity harasses me.

Demarch of Greens. Let the bones of the spectators be exhumed ! [1]

[*Exeunt the Greens.*

It will be noticed that in this dialogue the spokesman of the oppressed faction began with humble complaints; and the scene ended with open defiance. When the Greens marched out of the hippodrome, the Emperor sitting in the cathisma was left for a few moments alone with the Blues; but they quickly followed their enemies, and street conflicts ensued.[2]

If we pass from these stray details of external life to consider the morality of the age, we are confronted on the one hand by the stern laws of Justinian for the repression of what he considered immorality, and his clement laws for the encouragement of reformation; on the other hand by a remarkable picture, painted by a secret hand, of the vice that prevailed in all classes of society. These data are not in opposition, for moral legislation presupposes the prevalence of immorality.

Two laws testify to the solicitude of Justinian for the liberty and protection of women. The earliest of them,[3] issued in 534, made it illegitimate for any person to constrain a female, whether a freewoman or a slave, to appear against her will in a dramatic or orchestric performance. By the same act it was illegal for a lessee to prevent an actress from throwing up her theatrical engagement at any moment she pleased, and he was not even entitled to demand from her securities the money pledged for the fulfilment of her broken engagement. The duty or privilege of seeing that this law was carried out was assigned to the bishops as well as to the civil governors, against whose collusion with the managers of theatres episcopal protests may have been often necessary. It was also enacted that the profession of the stage, which in this age was almost synonymous with the trade of prostitution, should form no let or hindrance to the contraction of a legal marriage with the highest in the land. This liberation from disabilities of a degraded but necessary class is generally

---

[1] ἀνασκαφῇ τὰ ὀστέα τῶν θεωρούντων —implying "let them be murdered and . . ." This expression came into special use for the deposition of a monarch.

[2] *See* vol. i. p. 340.

[3] *Cod. Just.* i. 4, 33 ; compare v. 4, 29.

supposed to have been prompted by a personal episode in the life of the Emperor himself, whose wife Theodora seems to have been once an actress at Antioch.

The other law was published in the following year, and addressed to the citizens of Constantinople. It deals with the practice of enticing young girls away from their homes in order to hire them out for immoral purposes. It is best to quote a portion of Justinian's constitution on the subject[1] :—

" The ancient laws and former Emperors have regarded with extreme abhorrence the name and the trade of a brothel-keeper, and many laws have consequently been enacted against such. We have increased the penalties already defined, and in other laws have supplied the omissions of our predecessors. But we have been lately informed of iniquities of this kind which are being carried on in this great city, and we have not overlooked the matter. For we discovered that some persons live and maintain themselves in an outrageous manner, making accursed gain by abominable means. They travel about many countries and districts, and entice poor young girls by promising them shoes and clothes, and thus entrapping them, carry them off to this fortunate city, where they keep them shut up in their dens, supplying them with a miserable allowance of food and raiment, and place their bodies at the service of the public and keep the wretched fees themselves. And they draw up bonds by which girls bind themselves to this occupation for a specified time, nay, they even sometimes ask the money back from the securities [if a girl escapes]. This practice has become so outrageous, that throughout almost the whole of this imperial city and its suburbs over the water[2] [at Chalcedon and Pera], and, worst of all, in close proximity to churches and saintly houses, dens of such a kind exist ; and acts so iniquitous and illegal are perpetrated in our times that some persons, pitying the girls, desired to deliver them from this occupation and place them in a position of legal cohabitation, but the procurers did not permit it. Some of these men are so unholy as to corrupt girls under ten years old, and large sums of money have been given to buy off the unfortunate children and unite them in a respectable marriage. This evil, which was formerly confined to a small part of the city, has spread throughout its whole extent and the circumjacent regions. We were secretly informed of this some time ago, and as our most magnificent praetors, whom we commissioned to investigate the matter, confirmed the information, we immediately determined to deliver the city from such pollution."

This preamble is followed by prohibition of these abuses ; procurers are banished from the Empire, and especially from the imperial city. It would appear from this law that all

---

[1] Novel xxxix. (ed. Zachariä) : περὶ τοῦ μὴ εἶναι πορνοβοσκοὺς ἐν μηδενὶ τόπῳ τῆς Ῥωμαίων πολιτείας.

[2] ἐν τοῖς περάμασιν αὐτῆς.

disorderly houses were rendered absolutely illegal, and that the only form of prostitution countenanced by law was that of women who practised it on their own account.

Another constitution of the same year,[1] also addressed to the people of Constantinople, deals with the "heavier" or "diabolical" forms of licentiousness, and with the crime of blasphemy. Two bishops who rashly tasted of the Dead Sea fruit were subjected to a painful and shameful punishment by the inexorable Justinian, who adopted the principle that according to the scriptures whole cities as well as guilty individuals were reduced to ruin by the wrath of God in consequence of similar transgressions. The use of blasphemous expressions and imprecations is forbidden with equal severity, and the imperial notion of the law of causation is illustrated by the remark that on account of crimes of this kind "famines and earthquakes and plagues" visit mankind. We may finally mention the enactment of Justinian which suppressed gambling with dice, and other games of hazard.[2]

It is hardly possible to say much here of the curious evidence afforded by the *Secret History* on the subject of contemporary morals. The delicacy or affectation of the present age would refuse to admit the authority and example of Gibbon as a sufficient reason or valid excuse for rehearsing the licentious vagaries ascribed to Theodora in the indecent pages of an audacious and libellous pamphlet. If the words and acts which the writer attributes to Theodora were drawn, as doubtless is the case, from real life—from the green-rooms of Antioch or the bagnios of Byzantium—it can only be remarked that the morals of those cities in the sixth century did not differ very much from the morals of Paris, Vienna, Naples, or London at the present day. The story of Antonina's intrigue with Theodosius, which is quite credible and was probably derived from backstair gossip, contains nothing more enormous than might be told of exalted personages in any court at any period of history.

There is no side of the history of societies in the remote past on which we are left so much in the dark by extant records as their industry, their commerce, and their economy;

---

[1] Novel xxviii.   [2] *Cod. Just.* iii. 43.

and as these departments of life were continually affecting politics, their neglect by contemporary writers renders a reconstruction of political history always defective and often impossible. The chief technical industries carried on at Constantinople seem to have been as follows[1] :—(1) The manufacture of silk fabrics was practised on a large scale before the production of the material was introduced by the two monks, as narrated in a previous chapter. Once the Romans were no longer dependent on the oriental nations for its production and importation, it is to be presumed that the manufacture of the fabric, which must have become considerably cheaper, was carried on on a much more extensive scale.[2] (2) The domestic utensils used by the Byzantine citizens were of glazed pottery, of black or gray colour, and were made at Byzantium. Glass was imported from Egypt, which in old days used to supply Rome. (3) The extensive use of mosaics in the decoration of christian churches and rich men's palaces made the manufacture of the coloured pebbles ($\psi\eta\phi\hat{\iota}\delta\epsilon\varsigma$) quite a lucrative trade. (4) The symbolism of the christian religion gave rise to a new art, and the shops of crucifix-makers were probably a feature of Constantinople. Crosses were made of all sorts of materials, gold, silver, precious stones, lychnites, or ivory. The carving of religious subjects in ivory was an associated branch of this trade. (5) The art of the jeweller was doubtless in great requisition in the luxurious capital, and the pearls which decorate Theodora in the mosaic portrait in San Vitale at Ravenna indicate the style of the imperial court. (6) The implements of war, the arms of the soldiers, and the engines used in siege warfare were manufactured at Constantinople, and stored in a public building called the Mangana.

All these arts flourished in the imperial city, and made it an active industrial centre. In regard to the commercial relations of the Empire, it will be well to quote the words of Finlay, who made a special study of this side of its history[3] :—

[1] *See* Krause, *Die Byzantiner des Mittelalters*, p. 47 *sqq.*

[2] "It would not be just," writes Finlay, "to deny to Justinian some share in the merit of having founded a flourishing branch of trade, which tended very materially to support the resources of the Eastern Empire, and to enrich the Greek nation for several centuries" (*Hist. of Greece*, i. 270).

[3] *History of Greece* (ed. Tozer), vol. i. p. 267 *sq.*

" Several circumstances, however, during the reign of Justinian contributed to augment the commercial transactions of the Greeks, and to give them a decided preponderance in the Eastern trade. The long war with Persia cut off all those routes by which the Syrian and Egyptian population had maintained their ordinary communications with Persia ; and it was from Persia that they had always drawn their silk and great part of their Indian commodities, such as muslins and jewels. This trade now began to seek two different channels, by both of which it avoided the dominions of Chosroes ; the one was to the north of the Caspian Sea, and the other by the Red Sea. This ancient route through Egypt still continued to be that of the ordinary trade. But the importance of the northern route, and the extent of the trade carried on by it through different ports on the Black Sea are authenticated by the numerous colony of the inhabitants of central Asia established at Constantinople in the reign of Justin II. Six hundred Turks availed themselves, at one time, of the security offered by the journey of a Roman ambassador to the Great Khan of the Turks, and joined his train. This fact affords the strongest evidence of the great importance of this route, as there can be no question that the great number of the inhabitants of central Asia who visited Constantinople were attracted to it by their commercial occupations.

" The Indian commerce through Arabia and by the Red Sea was still more important ; much more so, indeed, than the mere mention of Justinian's failure to establish a regular importation of silk by this route might lead us to suppose. The immense number of trading vessels which habitually frequented the Red Sea shows that it was very great."

Finlay goes on to make some instructive observations on the decline of Egypt and the importance of the Jews. " In the reign of Augustus, Egypt furnished Rome with a tribute of twenty millions of modii of grain annually, and it was garrisoned by a force rather exceeding twelve thousand regular troops. Under Justinian the tribute in grain was reduced to about five millions and a half modii, that is eight hundred thousand artabas ; and the Roman troops, to a cohort of six hundred men. Egypt was prevented from sinking still lower by the exportation of its grain to supply the trading population on the shores of the Red Sea. The canal connecting the Nile with the Red Sea afforded the means of exporting an immense quantity of inferior grain to the arid coasts of Arabia, and formed a great artery for civilisation and commerce." The Jews seem to have increased in numbers about the beginning of the sixth century. Finlay accounts for this increase " by the decline of the rest of the population in the countries round the Mediterranean, and by the general decay of civilisation in consequence of the severity of the Roman fiscal system, which trammelled every class of society with regulations restricting the industry of the people. . . . The Jews, too, at this period, were the only neutral nation who could carry on their trade equally with the Persians, Ethiopians, Arabs, and Goths ; for, though they were hated everywhere, the universal dislike was a reason for tolerating a people never likely to form common cause with any other."[1]

As for the Greeks, they "maintained their superiority over the other people in the Empire only by their commercial enterprise, which preserved that civilisation in the trading cities which was rapidly disappearing among the agricultural population." Barbarian monarchs, like Theodoric, used often to support the Jews in order to "render their country independent of the wealth and commerce of the Greeks."[2]

A writer at the beginning of the seventh century, Theophylactus Simocatta, gives a description of the empire of Taugast,[3] which has been identified with China ; the intercourse with the Turks, which began in the reign of Justin II, brought the far East closer to the Roman Empire. He praises the wise laws which prevail in Taugast, and mentally contrasts the luxury of Byzantium with the law which forbids the Taugastians to wear silver or gold, while he attributes to Alexander the Great the foundation of the two chief towns of their realm. Syrian missionaries seem also to have kept up a connection between China and the West ; we read[4] that "in the seventeenth year of the period Chêng kuan (= 643) the king of Fulin, Po-to-li [Po-to-li = the Nestorian Patriarch of Syria, Fulin = the countries in the East once under Roman sway], sent an embassy offering red glass . . . and other articles. T'ai-tsung favoured them with a message under his imperial seal, and graciously granted them presents of silk."

---

[1] The flourishing condition of the Jews in the reign of Heraclius indicates the prosperity they had enjoyed in the preceding century.

[2] See *Edict. Theod.* 143.

[3] *Ecumenical History*, vii. 9. See R. von Scala, *Über die wichtigsten Beziehungen des Orients zum Occidente*, p. 33.

[4] Hirth, *China and the Roman Orient*, *ap.* Scala, *ib.* p. 35.

BOOK IV

THE HOUSE OF JUSTIN

PART II

THE COLLAPSE OF JUSTINIAN'S SYSTEM

CHAPTER I

JUSTIN II AND TIBERIUS II

WE have seen that the Roman Imperium under Justinian reached the absolutism to which it had always tended, and Justinian realised that Caesaropapism at which the christian Emperors had been continually aiming. It has been pointed out that Justinian accomplished his great achievements by means of an artificial State system, which maintained the Empire in equilibrium for the time; but it was only for the time. At his death the winds were loosed from prison; the disintegrating elements began to operate with full force; the artificial system collapsed; and the metamorphosis in the character of the Empire, which had been surely progressing for a long time past, though one is apt to overlook it amid the striking events of Justinian's busy reign, now began to work rapidly and perceptibly.

Things which seemed of comparatively secondary importance under the enterprising government of Justinian, engage the whole attention of his successors. The Persian war assumes a serious aspect, and soon culminates in a struggle for life or death; the Balkan peninsula is overrun by Avars and Slaves; and consequently the Empire cannot retain any real hold on its recent conquests in Italy and Spain. Thus the chief features of the reigns of Justin, Tiberius,[1] and

[1] Our contemporary sources for Justin and Tiberius are the fragments of Menander; the Ecclesiastical History of Evagrius (from an orthodox point of view); the Ecclesiastical History of John of Ephesus (from a monophysitic point of view); a few fragments of Theophanes of Byzantium (see *F. H. G.* iv. pp. 270, 271); a few Novels of Justin and Tiberius; some notices in the *Historia Francorum* of Gregory of Tours. Besides these, we have for the first year of Justin's reign Corippus (of whom more will be said presently).

Maurice are: the struggle against the Persians, with whom the Romans become less and less able to cope, the sufferings of Illyricum and Thrace at the hands of Hunnic and Slavonic barbarians, the conquests of the Lombards in Italy, and the change in the political position of the Emperor, whose power sensibly declines. The general disintegration of the Empire reaches a climax in the reign of Phocas (602-610), and the State is with difficulty rescued from destruction and revived by the energy and ability of Heraclius.

In reading the history of the later years of Justinian we are conscious of a darkness creeping over the sky; the light that had illuminated the early part of his reign is waning. This change had become perceptible after the great plague. But after the death of Justinian the darkness is imminent; the Empire is stricken as it were with paralysis, and a feeling of despondency prevails; the Emperors are like men grappling with hopeless tasks. We are not surprised that an idea possessed men's minds that the end of the world or some great change was at hand[1]; it expressed the feeling that the spiritual atmosphere was dark, and the prospect comfortless. " He that is giddy thinks the world turns round."

I. *Justin II.*

A struggle for the succession between the relations of Justin and those of Theodora had at one time seemed probable, but it had been forestalled by the alliance of the two families in the person of Justin, a nephew of the Emperor, and Sophia, a niece of the Empress. Justin held the position of *curopalates*, which we might translate " mayor of the palace," and on his uncle's death was at once recognised by the senate.[2]   The panegyric of the African poet Corippus,[3] written in four books

Theophylactus, who wrote his History of Maurice in the reign of Heraclius, has a valuable digression on the reign of Maurice's predecessor.

[1] John of Ephesus believed that Christ was coming very soon. Chosroes professed to know more precisely what would happen (Zon. iii. 295). Gregory the Great, *Ep.* v. 21, says that the claim of John Jejunator to the title *ecumenical* indicates the proximity of the time of Antichrist. Tiberius was warned by an angel that he would be spared the spectacle of the approaching times of anarchy (Theophylact. i. 1, 2). Finlay speaks of the time as one of a " universal political palsy."

[2] The succession, however, seems to have been somewhat doubtful beforehand, for it apparently took the *demes* by surprise; cf. Evagrius, v. 1.

[3] Flavius Cresconius Corippus, the author of the *Johannis*. His verses sometimes run smoothly enough, but are

of Latin hexameters, *de laudibus Justini Augusti minoris*, giving a coloured account of the circumstances of the Emperor's accession, had probably a political intention. Justin required a trumpet.

According to the narrative in the poem of Corippus, which we may assume to represent, with sufficient accuracy, what actually happened, Justin was wakened before daybreak by the Patrician Callinicus, who announced that Justinian was dead. At the same time the senate entered the palace buildings, and proceeding to a beautiful room overlooking the sea, whither Justin had already repaired, found him conversing with his wife Sophia. Callinicus, as the spokesman of the senate, greeted Justin as the new Augustus, virtually designated by the late Emperor as his successor. All then repaired to the imperial chambers, and gazed on the corpse of the deceased sovereign, who lay on a golden bier. Justin is represented as apostrophising the dead, and complaining that his uncle left the world at a critical moment: " Behold the Avars and the fierce Franks, and the Gepids and the Goths (Getae, probably meaning the Slaves), and so many other nations encompass us with wars." Sophia ordered an embroidered cloth to be brought, on which the whole series of Justinian's labours was wrought in gold and brilliant colours, the Emperor himself in the midst with his foot resting on the neck of the Vandal tyrant.[1]

In the morning Justin and his wife proceeded to the church of St. Sophia, and made a public declaration of the orthodox

very poor compared with the poetry of Claudian. In the *praefatio* he apostrophises Justin thus—

. . . tu quoque justitiae nomen de nomine sumens,
frena regendorum retinens firmissima regum.
numinibus tribus his regitur quodcumque movetur.

(The three divinities are Vigilantia, Justin's mother, who was still alive, Sophia, and Justin.)

certatim gentes Romana ad foedera currunt.
principe pro justo Romanum nomen amatur
subque pio domino cuncti bene vivere quaerunt.

In the *dedicatio* the praises of the quaestor Anastasius are sung ; he is said to have spurned money, and is compared to a tree, while the Emperor is the fountain which waters it. The general tone is concentrated in the line

felix est totus Justino principe mundus.

In iii. 132 there is an allusion to the name of Justin's father,

ante oculos geniti genitor *dulcissimus* omni tempore erit.

Throughout the poem Corippus plays on the names Justinus, Vigilantia, and Sapientia (Σοφία).

In giving a sketch of Corippus' outline of the proceedings which followed Justinian's death I have taken a hint from Ranke (see *Weltgeschichte*, iv. 2, p. 127).

[1] I doubt whether Corippus had any authority in fact for this incident. The circumstance that the African poet chose the Vandal monarch as the type of the foes vanquished by Justinian makes us suspicious that it is entirely a poetical invention.

faith. Returning to the palace, Justin assumed the royal robes and ornaments, and was raised on a shield lifted by four guardsmen,[1] after which ceremony the Patriarch blessed him and placed the diadem on his head. The Emperor then delivered an inaugural speech from the throne, in which he enunciated his intention to pursue the principles of piety and justice, and regretted that important departments of the administration had been neglected or mismanaged in the last years of Justinian, who in his old age was careless of such matters, and cold to the things of this life.[2] After this oration, the senate in due form adored the new Emperor.

Then, attended by the senators and court, Justin proceeded to the hippodrome, and took his seat in the cathisma. When the jubilant greetings of the people, who had taken no part in his actual elevation, had subsided, the Emperor delivered another oration, exhorting the populace to be peaceable and orderly, and announcing his intention to assume the consulship and honour the following year with his name.[3]

Suddenly the benches which lined each side of the hippodrome were emptied, and crowds of people made their way to the space in front of the cathisma. They presented to the Emperor bonds for loans which his uncle had contracted, and implored or demanded to be repaid. Justin in his speech to the senators had signified his purpose of liquidating these debts,[4] and he now commanded that the money should be paid on the spot. The scene is graphically described by the obsequious pen of Corippus. This popular act was followed by another example of clemency, and many prisoners were released at the prayers of their kinsfolk. Corippus seems to imply

---

[1] The Emperor, of course, *stood* on the shield, which was raised : *stetit ut sua rectus littera*, his own letter being the initial of Justinus, I, which is also referred to in i. 353, *sanctum sic Iota resurgens*, an expression which does not necessarily support the allegation of the *Secret History* that Justin the elder could not write.

[2] ii. 265—

nulla fuit jam cura seni : jam frigidus omnis
alterius vitae solo fervebat amore.

In this speech Justin speaks of himself, the Emperor, as the head (representing the Deity), giving directions to the members of the State body. The treasury, *fiscus*, is compared to the belly.

[3] The inauguration of Justin as consul (1st January 566) is described in the fourth book of Corippus.

[4] We cannot, of course, put much trust in the colouring which Corippus gives to this transaction. It is likely enough that he inserted in Justin's throne-speech the line which expresses an intention to pay the *debita* in order to make it appear that the payment was not extorted from the Emperor by a threatening demonstration ; and it is quite possible that in the hippodrome Justin was confronted, not by tearful suppliants, but by clamorous creditors.

that the prisons were entirely emptied, and takes pains to justify a hardly justifiable act.

The poet goes on to describe the obsequies of Justinian, the beauties of the imperial palace, and the reception of the Avaric ambassadors, but we need not follow him further. The Emperor appointed his son-in-law Baduarius, who had married his daughter Arabia, to the post of curopalates, which his own accession had rendered vacant.[1]

The accession of Justin was not wholly unendangered or unstained with blood. A conspiracy of two senators [2] was detected and punished, and the Emperor's namesake Justin, the son of his cousin Germanus, was put to death in Alexandria as a dangerous and perhaps designing relation. The influence of Sophia may have been operative here, for enmity and jealousy had always prevailed between her aunt Theodora and the family of Germanus.

Sophia had the ambition, without the genius, of her aunt Theodora. Like her, she had been originally a monophysite. But a bishop had suggested that the heretical opinions of her husband and herself stood in the way of his promotion to the rank of Caesar; and accordingly the pair found it convenient to join the ranks of the orthodox, on whom they had before looked down as "synodites." It is perhaps to be regretted that Sophia was not content to induce her husband to alter his opinions and to retain her own faith. The administration of an orthodox Emperor and a monophysitic Empress had worked well in the case of Justinian and Theodora; the balance of religious parties had been maintained, so that neither was alienated from the crown. It is probable that if Sophia had remained satisfied with One Nature, the persecution of monophysitic heretics, which disgraced the latter half of Justin's reign, would not have taken place, and the eastern provinces would have been less estranged from the central power.

When Justin came to the throne he decided to make a fresh start and abandon the unpopular system of his uncle, as is clearly indicated in the poem of Corippus. An opportunity

---

[1] Justin and Sophia had one son, who died early.

[2] Aetherius and Addaeus (Evagr. v. 3).

of taking a first step in this direction was offered almost immediately by the arrival of an embassy of Avars to demand the payments which Justinian's policy was accustomed to grant.[1] Justin boldly refused to concede these payments any longer, and his refusal was the signal for a series of ruinous depredations, which prepared the way for a complete change in the population of the Illyrian provinces. This resolution of Justin was a direct break with a vital part of the Justinianean system, and was perhaps not unwise, for money payments could have hardly restrained the Avars and Slaves much longer from invading the cis-Danubian countries. It was a popular act, because it seemed brave, and might lead to the possibility of lightening the burden of taxation.

Justinian's religious doctrines in his last years had been erratic, and he was stigmatised as a heretic. In this respect, too, Justin's accession signalised a reaction. He published a manifesto ($\pi\rho\delta\gamma\rho\alpha\mu\mu\alpha$)[2] to all Christians strictly orthodox, from whom he expressly excluded the friends of one nature. But at this time he did not purpose to do more than withdraw the light of his countenance from the party which had, in recent years at least, been contented with Justinian. A monophysite expressly acknowledges that for the first six years of his reign Justin was mild and peaceable in his religious policy.[3]

Circumstances necessitated the reaction which Justin's

---

[1] Corippus gives an account of the embassy in the third book of his *de laudibus Justini*. In his reply to the ambassador Targites, Justin is made to say (l. 333)—

res Romana dei est, terrenis non eget armis.

The reception of the embassy took place seven days (l. 151) after Justin's accession, namely on 20th November. The amazement of the barbarians at the splendour of the court is thus described (l. 237 *sqq.*)—

miratur barbara pubes
ingressus primos immensaque [atque ?] atria lustrans.
ingentes adstare viros. scuta aurea cernunt
pilaque suspiciunt alto splendentia ferro
aurea et auratos conos cristasque rubentes.
horrescunt lanceas saevasque instare secures;
ceteraque egregiae spectant miracula pompae
et credunt aliud Romana palatia caelum.

[2] Quoted by Evagrius, v. 4.

[3] John of Ephesus, iii. 1 ; this statement agrees with the date of the Novel concerning the Samaritans, 572 A.D. John of Ephesus is the author of an ecclesiastical history in Syriac, which has been partly translated and partly analysed by Dr. Payne Smith, the well-known Syriac scholar. Many details are to be found in it not only respecting the persecution of the monophysites, through which the writer himself was a sufferer, but also respecting the courts of Justin, Tiberius, and Maurice, and the Persian wars. This history seems to be known to comparatively few writers, and has been strangely neglected by Professor Rawlinson in his work on the Sassanids. It is especially interesting as a history written from the monophysitic point of view. I have used Smith's translation.

reign inaugurated, but they equally necessitated the failure of this attempt at a new policy. Justin was not a strong man, and the circumstances of the time were strong and inexorable. He was completely unsuccessful, as he owned before he died, and his mind was probably diseased long before he became undoubtedly insane. We can measure his want of success by the fact that even the orthodox did not approve of him; and ecclesiastical historians are prepared to forgive much for the grace of the two natures. Evagrius speaks of him in harsh terms, charging him with avarice and profligacy, and with trafficking in ecclesiastical offices. And he seems to have resorted to many modes of raising money which were not calculated to make his rule beloved; for though he wisely remitted[1] a burden of arrears which could not be profitably exacted, he levied on ship-cargoes taxes, which brought in large sums, and also taxed the bread[2] which was publicly distributed in the capital and called " political (or civil) loaves."

But the state of the Empire was such that popularity could only have been obtained by an almost unwise generosity, such as that by which Tiberius afterwards won general affection; and such a policy would have ultimately aided rather than arrested the forces of disintegration. The disintegration took place in two different ways.

(1) On the one hand the imperial power was no longer absolute. The Emperor found himself face to face with a number of wealthy and influential aristocrats, whose power had increased so much in the declining years of Justinian that they were almost able to assume an independent attitude.

---

[1] Novel i. Imp. Justini (566 A.D.) περὶ συγχωρήσεως λοιπάδων δημοσίων (in vol. iii. of Zachariä von Lingenthal's *Jus Graeco-Romanum*). Arrears were remitted by this edict up to the eighth indiction (ἐπινέμησις), that is up to 560 A.D. In this Novel the decline of the army is noticed. The second Novel permits the dissolutions of matrimony if both parties consent (*consensu*); it enunciates the principle that γάμου σεμνότερον ἀνθρώποις οὐδέν ἐστιν. On this subject something will be said when we come to the legislation of the Isaurian Emperors in the eighth century. We may notice here that Justin built the Χρυσοτρίκλινος, " golden chamber," a splendid room in the palace, adjoin-

ing the sleeping apartments of the Emperor and Empress. M. Paspatis has shown that it was situated to the west of the Pharos, which he has identified. *See* Τὰ Βυζαντινὰ ἀνάκτορα, p. 167 *sqq.*

[2] The tax on cargoes was a flagon on a cask of wine. The tax on the " civil loaves " was four darics. *See* John Eph. iii. 11. The flights of stairs, 107 in number, from which the distributions of bread (*panis gradilis*, as it was called in Latin) were made, were a feature of Constantinople. The tally which every householder had to show in order to receive his share was called *calamus*.

History shows us that the maintenance of law is least secure when aristocratic classes become predominant; turbulence waxes rife, attempts to override the rights of inferiors are sure to take place, and the only safeguard is a strong monarchical authority. Now this evil prevailed in the days of Justin. The noble lords were turbulent and licentious, and while Justin made praiseworthy efforts to enforce the law at all costs, there was, doubtless, a constant struggle, in which Justin was generally obliged to compromise; and we can thus understand a bitter allusion in a speech which he delivered on the occasion of Tiberius' elevation to the rank of Caesar.[1] He bade Tiberius beware of the lords, who were present at the ceremony, as of men who had led himself into an evil plight.[2]

Justin's desire to enforce the maintenance of justice, and the corruption with which he had to contend, are illustrated by an anecdote.[3] The prefect of the city was a man who, knowing Justin's anxiety to protect the oppressed, had proposed himself for the post, and had promised that if he received for a certain time full powers, unrestricted by any privilege of class, the wronged individuals who were always addressing appeals to the throne would soon cease to trouble the sovereign. One day a man appeared before the prefect and accused a person of senatorial rank. The accused noble did not vouchsafe to notice the prefect's summons, and, on receiving a second citation, attended a banquet of the Emperor instead of appearing in court. During the feast the prefect entered the banqueting-hall of the palace, and addressed the Emperor: "I promised your Majesty to leave not a single oppressed person in the city within a certain time, and I shall succeed perfectly in my engagement if your authority come to my aid.

---

[1] See *post*, p. 78. God put it in his heart, says Evagrius (v. 13), to record his own errors and give good advice. Compare the account in Theophylactus, iii. 11, 4. Evagrius gives an unfavourable account of Justin's moral character (v. 1): "he wallowed in luxury and unnatural pleasures" (ἡδοναῖς ἐκτόποις); and he also dwells on his greed of money.

[2] The general feeling of the Empire's misfortunes in Justin's reign is reflected in the doggerel epigram written by some of the city wits and

fixed upon a tablet (John Eph. iii. 24)—

" Build, build aloft thy pillar,
And raise it vast and high;
Then mount and stand upon it,
Soaring proudly in the sky:
Eastward, south and north and westward,
Wherever thou shalt gaze,
Nought thou'lt see but desolations,
The work of thy own days."

(This is the translation of Dr. Payne Smith.)

[3] *See* the account in Zonaras, Bk. xiv. cap. 10 (vol. iii. p. 286, ed. Dindorf), and Cedrenus, i. 681 *sqq.* (Bonn).

But if you shelter and patronise wrongdoers, and entertain them at your table, I shall fail. Either allow me to resign or do not recognise the wrongdoers." The Emperor replied : " If I am the man, take me." The prefect, thus reassured, arrested the criminal, tried him, found him guilty, and flogged him. The plaintiff was recompensed amply. It is said that people were so terrified by this example of strictness that for thirty days no accusations were lodged with the prefect.

(2) At the same time the bonds which attached the provinces of the Empire to the centre, and thereby to each other, were being loosened ; and it is important to notice and easy to apprehend that this change was closely connected with the diminution of the imperial authority. For that authority held the heterogeneous elements together in one whole ; and if the position of the Emperor became insecure or his hand weak, the centrifugal forces immediately began to operate. Now, it is to be noted that certain changes introduced by Justinian, which from one point of view might seem to make for absolutism, were calculated to further the progress of the centrifugal tendency if it once began to set in. I refer to the removal of some important rungs in the ladder of the administrative hierarchy ; the abolition of the count of the East and the vicarius of Asiana.[1] These smaller centres had helped to preserve the compactness of the Empire, and their abolition operated in the reverse direction.

A remarkable law of Justin [2] (568 A.D.) is preserved, in which he yields to the separatist tendencies of the provinces to a certain extent. This law provided that the governor of each province should be appointed without cost at the request of the bishops, landowners, and inhabitants of the province. It was a considerable concession in the direction of local government, and its importance will be more fully recognised if it is remembered that Justinian had introduced in some provinces the practice of investing the civil governor, who held judicial as well as administrative power, with military authority also. It is a measure which sheds much light on the state of the Empire, and reminds us of that attempt of Honorius to give representative local government to the cities

---

[1] *See* above, Bk. iv. pt. i. cap. xii.
[2] Novel v. (ed. Żachariä).

in the south of Gaul, a measure which came too late to cure the political lethargy which prevailed.

The estrangement of the eastern provinces from the crown was further increased by the persecutions of heretics, which began about the year 572. The Emperor fell under the influence of the Patriarch, John of Sirimis (a place near Antioch), and to have been induced by him to make a new attempt at unifying the Church by means of persecution.[1] The procedure against the Samaritans[2] (572 A.D.) was so effective that that important people became quite insignificant. The monophysitic monks and nuns were expelled from their monasteries and convents, fleeing " like birds before the hawk." John of Ephesus, a monophysite, describes in his ecclesiastical history the details of this persecution. We may take as an example the case of Antipatra and Juliana,[3] two noble ladies attached to the monophysitic faith. They were confined in a monastery at Chalcedon, and, because they would not accept the formula of the orthodox, were obliged to wear the dress of nuns, were shorn of their hair, and were " made to sweep the convent, and carry away the dirt, and scrub and wash out the latrinae, and serve in the kitchen, and wash the candlesticks and dishes, and perform other similar duties." Unable to endure these hardships, they submitted in form to the Chalcedonian communion. This, however, is said to have been a very mild case. The measure which the monophysites most resented was the annulling of the orders of their clergy. The Patriarch of Constantinople had hereby a welcome opportunity for interfering with the dioceses of Antioch, Alexandria, and Cyprus, over which he desired to exercise a jurisdiction like that which the bishop of Rome possessed over the see of Thessalonica, for example, or the see of Ravenna.

In the year 574 the Emperor became a hopeless and even

---

[1] It is perhaps doubtful whether Justin was personally a fervent believer. He introduced in the coinage of his solidi "a female figure which was generally compared to Venus." Tiberius discontinued this, and had a cross struck upon the reverse of his coins. It is remarkable that this act of Tiberius is regarded by John of Ephesus (iii. 14) as a public profession of Christianity. A coin of Justin with such a figure is given in Ducange's *Familiae Augustae Byzantinae,* p. 70.

[2] Novel vii. (ed. Zachariä).

[3] Juliana belonged to the house of Anastasius the Emperor ; her father was the consul Magnes. She became the sister-in-law of Justin by marrying his brother. *See* John Eph. ii. 12.

dangerous lunatic, and his vagaries were the talk of Constantinople.[1] It was necessary to place bars on his windows to prevent him from hurling himself down, and in his fits he used to bite his chamberlains. The only charm by which they could then quiet his fury was the words, "The son of Gabolo is coming"—a reference to Harith, king of a tribe of Arabs.[2] When he heard this exclamation he was cowed at once. His favourite amusement was to sit in a little waggon, which his attendants used to draw about in the palace chambers, and a musical instrument was constantly played in his presence to calm his temper.

Sophia did not feel equal to carrying on the government without male assistance, especially as the Persian war was pressing the realm hard. Her representations of the unfortunate state of things in the capital had, it is said, induced Chosroes to grant a temporary peace, but the renewal of the war was certain at a near date, while the Avars were unceasing in their hostilities. A firm hand at the reins was indispensable. Accordingly, in the last month of 574, in one of his sane intervals, Justin, at her instance, created Tiberius,[3] the count of the excubiti, a Caesar. On this occasion he delivered an unexpectedly candid and repentant speech, which made a deep impression on contemporaries.[4]

"'Know,' he said, 'that it is God who blesses you and confers this dignity and its symbols upon you, not I. Honour it, that you may be honoured by it. Honour your mother, who was hitherto your queen; you do not forget that formerly you were her slave, now you are her son.

---

[1] Our authority for Justin's madness is John of Ephesus, and the details he gives are quite credible. He professes to conceal some of the worst features of Justin's case. John, although he is a monophysite and detested Justin's later policy, is generally sufficiently moderate. In regard to these details, which orthodox writers suppress, he says (iii. 2): "The whole senate and city, natives as well as foreigners, bear witness to the truth and exactness of our details."

[2] Chorth, the son of Gabolo, was the Syriac equivalent of Harith, the son of Jabal.

[3] For Tiberius, *see* Corippus, *de laudibus Justini*, i. 212 *sq.*—
omnia disponens munivit providus arcem
Tiberius, domini semper cui maxima cura

utilitatis erat: namque illum maximus orbis communis benefactor alens et ab ubere matris suscipiens primis puerum praelegit ab annis utque pater genitum nutrivit, fovit, amavit, paulatimque virum summa in fastigia duxit.

Notice the quantity of *Tiberius*.

[4] I translate from Theophylactus (iii. 11), who professes to quote the unadorned and unadulterated words of Justin (cf. Evagrius, v. 13, and Theophanes *ad ann.* 6070, who places this speech at the time of Tiberius' elevation to the rank of Augustus). I have translated very literally, to reproduce the effect of the disjointed sentences of the feeble speaker. John of Ephesus states (iii. 4) that scribes took down the speech in shorthand, and so it was preserved.

Delight not in the shedding of blood ; take no share in murder ; do not return evil for evil, that you may become like unto me in unpopularity. I have been called to account as a man, for I fell, and I received according to my sins ; but I shall sue those who caused me to err at the throne of Christ. Let not this imperial garb elate thee as it elated me. Act to all men as you would act to yourself, remembering what you were before and what you are now. Be not arrogant, and you will not go wrong : you know what I was, what I became, and what I am. All these are your children and servants—you know that I preferred you to my own blood ; you see them here before you, you see all the persons of the administration. Pay attention to the army ; do not encourage informers, and let not men say of thee, " His predecessor was such and such " ; for I speak from my own experience. Permit those who possess to enjoy their property in peace ; and give unto those who possess not.' "

The Patriarch then pronounced a prayer, and when all had said Amen, and the new Caesar had fallen at the feet of the Augustus, Justin said, " If you will, I live ; if you will not, I die. May God, who made heaven and earth, place in your heart all that I have forgotten to tell you."

But although Sophia approved and promoted the elevation of Tiberius to the rank of Caesar and the position of regent, she was determined to retain all her authority and sovereignty as Augusta, and above all she would not consent to the presence of another queen in the palace. Justin, with the good-nature of a man, suggested that Ino the wife of Tiberius should reside with him, for " he is a young man, and the flesh is hard to rule " ; but Sophia would not hear of it. " As long as I live," she said, " I will never give my kingdom to another," words that breathe the spirit of the great Theodora. Accordingly, during Justin's lifetime Ino and her two daughters lived in a house near the palace in complete retirement. The wives of noblemen and senators were much exercised in their minds whether they should call upon the wife of the Caesar or not. They met together to consider the important question, but were afraid to decide to visit Ino without consulting the wishes of Sophia. When they asked the Empress, she scolded them sharply ; " Go, and be quiet," she said, " it is no business of yours." [1]   But when Tiberius was inaugurated Emperor in September 578, a few days before Justin's death, he installed

---

[1] I have inserted these details because they are almost unknown to historians, although they rest on contemporary authority (John Eph. iii. 7), and be- cause Theophanes relates a discordant story, that on Tiberius' accession in 578 Sophia was ignorant of his wife's existence.

his wife in the palace, to the chagrin of Sophia, and caused the new Augusta to be recognised by the factions of the circus. It is said that a riot took place in the hippodrome, as the Blues wished to change her pagan name to "Anastasia," while the Greens proposed "Helena." Anastasia was adopted as her imperial name.

II. *Tiberius II.*

The independent reign of Tiberius Constantine (for he had assumed with the purple a new name) lasted only four years. Although during his regency the administration was in his hands, yet the influence of Sophia over the occasionally sane Justin had been a considerable limit on his powers and scope of action; for the Empress was determined to be queen in more than name. The limitation of the powers of Tiberius when he was only Caesar are fully apparent from the mere fact that Sophia and Justin retained the management of the exchequer in their own hands. Sophia judged, and not without reason, that the young Caesar was inclined to be too lavish with money; and her prudence withheld from him the keys of the treasury, while he was granted a fixed allowance. After the death of Justin, he did not delay to emancipate himself from her dictation, and she is said to have set afoot several conspiracies to dethrone him. It is related that she suborned Justinian, the son of Germanus, who had won laurels in the East, to join in a plot against Tiberius; but this treason was discovered in time. The clemency of the Emperor pardoned Justinian, but his "mother" was deprived of her retinue and subjected to a strict supervision.

It was thought that of all men Tiberius was the man, had he lived longer, to have checked the forces of dissolution that were at work, and placed the Empire on a new basis. Yet what we know of him hardly justifies such a conclusion. The fact that he was thoroughly well intentioned, and the fact that he was very popular, combined with the circumstance that his reign was prematurely ended by death, have prepossessed men strongly in his favour. No charges can be brought against him like those that have been brought against his predecessor Justin or his successor Maurice. But, notwithstanding, I think it may be shown that he did as much

harm as good to the Empire, and that he was not in any way
the man to stem the tide.

The chief services rendered to the State by Tiberius consisted in the care which he bestowed upon strengthening the
army and his attention to military matters.   In this important
department he had able supporters in Justinian, the son of
Germanus, who is recorded to have revived the discipline of
the army, which was beginning to relax, and in Maurice, who
became Emperor afterwards.   We are told that Tiberius ex-
pended large sums of money in collecting troops,[1] and it
deserves to be specially noticed[2] that in the last year of his
reign he organised a body of 15,000 foederati, which may be
perhaps looked upon as the original nucleus or form of the
bodyguard which in later centuries was called Varangian.
Maurice was appointed general of this company, with the title
" Count of the Federates."

But though he might have made a very good minister of
war, Tiberius did not make a good Emperor.   It was natural
that his first acts should be reactionary, as Justin's government had been extremely unpopular.   He removed the duty
on the " political bread," and remitted a fourth part of the
taxes throughout the Empire.[3]   Had he been contented with
this he might deserve praise, but he began a system of most
injudicious extravagance.   He gratified the soldiers with large
and frequent *Augustatica*, and he granted donations to members
of all the professions—scholastics or jurists (" a very numerous
profession "), physicians, silversmiths, bankers.[4]   This liberality
soon emptied the treasury of its wealth.   " What use," cried
Tiberius, " is this hoarded gold, when all the world is choking
with hunger ? " a sentiment which was hardly relevant, as his
generosity benefited the rich and not the hungry.   The result
was that by the end of the first year of his reign he had spent
7200 lbs. of gold, beside silver and silk in abundance ; and

[1] Theophyl. iii. 12.
[2] Theophanes *ad ann.* 6074 (cf. Zonaras, iii. p. 290).
[3] Novel xi. (ed. Zachariä), 575 A.D.,
περὶ κουφισμῶν πολιτικῶν. One year's
tribute, or *canon*, was remitted to farmers
and proprietors (συντελεσταί), but this
year was distributed over four ; *i.e.* ¼ of

the *canon* of 575-576 was remitted, ¼ of
576-577, etc. · Arrears were remitted up
to the end of the last (fifth) indiction.
[4] John Eph. iii. 11.   He sent to the
army in Asia 800 lbs. of gold to be distributed.   In ordinary times the Augus-
taticum was never higher than nine
darics.

before he died he was obliged to have recourse to the reserve fund which the prudent economy of Anastasius had laid by, to be used in the case of an extreme emergency.[1] And, notwithstanding these financial difficulties, he laid out money on new buildings in the palace.

The consequence of this recklessness was that when Maurice came to the throne he found the exchequer empty and the State bankrupt. He was thus, by no fault of his own, compelled to be extremely parsimonious; and his scrupulous economy rendered him unpopular, while it endeared, by the force of contrast, the memory of the deceased, who had been really the cause of the perplexing situation. There is considerable reason, I think, to remove Tiberius from his pedestal.

Nor did his reign lack the distinction of a persecution of heretics; and yet his pleasant and easy fiscal system secured him such general popularity that even the monophysites were disposed to excuse him from the blame of the persecution, "because he was so much occupied with wars." [2] But his persecution of the Arians will perhaps reflect little credit on him in the eyes of humanity. When he enlisted Goths to compose his corps of foederati, they urged the modest demand that a church for holding Arian services should be granted to them. The bigots of Constantinople were furious at this impious prayer, and there arose a sedition of such formidable aspect [3] that Tiberius, in order to quell it, resorted to the device of commanding or permitting a general persecution of the Arians, that he might thereby be acquitted of having entertained any intention of granting such an outrageous request.

Theophylactus, the historian of Maurice,[4] remarked in praise of Tiberius that " he preferred that his subjects should share the imperial authority with him to their being tyrannically governed like slaves." The natural comment is that these two modes of State economy do not exhaust the alternative courses open to Tiberius; but this remark has a deeper

---

[1] *See* John of Ephesus, v. 20. This statement is inconsistent with the assertion of the writer of the *Secret History* that the hoard of Anastasius was spent during the reign of Justin I. (*see* vol. i. Appendix to cap. ii. of Bk. iv. pt. ii.) It is hardly to be supposed that this reserve fund was distinct from the immense sum mentioned in the *Anecdota*.

[2] John Eph. iii. 21. Eutychius the Patriarch urged him to this course.

[3] The cry of the people was, "Out with the bones of the Arians!" (John Eph. iii. 13).

[4] Theophyl. iii. 16.

historical significance.   The point is not the preference of Tiberius; the point is that the imperial power was drifting away from its old moorings at the promontory of absolutism.

Maurice returned from Persia in the summer of 582, to find the Emperor sick unto death, and to be elected by him to reign in his stead.   The ceremony was performed on the 5th of August.[1]   There were present not only the Patriarch (John the Faster) and the chief ecclesiastics, the guards of the palace, the aulic officials and senators, as in the case of Justin's accession, but also the "more distinguished men of the people," by which must be meant the demarchs and prominent persons in the circus factions.[2]   In his oration on this occasion Tiberius expressed a hope that his fairest funeral monument might be the reign of his successor.   A marriage was arranged between Maurice and Constantina, Tiberius' younger daughter[3]; and thus Maurice, as being the son-in-law of Tiberius, who was the adopted son of Justin and Sophia, may be regarded as belonging to the dynasty of Justinian.   Eight days later Tiberius expired in the palace of Hebdomon, outside the walls.[4]

---

[1] So John of Ephesus, v. 13. The usual date given is 13th August; *see* Clinton, *F. R. ad ann.*

[2] Theophyl. i. 1 : τοὺς ἐπισημοτέρους τοῦ δήμου. Tiberius renamed Maurice by his own name Tiberius, but Maurice did not adopt it in practice. Paul, the historian of the Lombards, remarks that Maurice was *primus ex Graecorum genere in imperio constitutus*, but Maurice traced his origin to Old Rome, though he was a native of Arabissus.

[3] Clinton places the marriage on the same day as the investiture, but this is very improbable. The account of Theo-

phylactus, who places it after Tiberius' death, is more credible.   The unusual splendour of the marriage festivities is noted by Evagrius, who describes the Emperor's gold-embroidered dress, trimmed with purple and decked with precious gems from the Orient.   Religion and Royalty (θεοσέβεια and βασιλεία) presided jointly over the festival.

[4] Theophylactus assigns the death of Tiberius to the day after the investiture of Maurice.   I follow John of Ephesus (v. 13).   Theodosius of Melitene states that Tiberius died of poison taken in a dish of mulberries.

CHAPTER II

MAURICE

Two years after his accession, a son was born to Maurice (4th August 584), whom he named Theodosius, in memory of Theodosius II, the last Emperor who had been born in the purple.[1] This event is said to have been the cause of great rejoicing, and when Maurice appeared in the hippodrome the people shouted, "God grant thee well, for thou hast freed us from subjection to many." This illustrates the fact that a feeling of uncertainty and apprehension always prevailed in the Roman Empire when there was no apparent heir marked out by birth; men dreaded a struggle for sovereignty. In regard to the question how far the principle of heredity was acknowledged, it is important to observe that there is no case of a difficulty arising as to the accession of an Emperor's legitimate son; he was always acknowledged to be the rightful successor.

Maurice occupied the throne for twenty years. During all that time the Empire was harassed by the troublesome hostilities of the Avars and Slaves, and for the first ten years of his reign the wearisome war with Persia was protracted. His great difficulty was want of money, which produced want of

---

[1] John of Ephesus, v. 14. For the reign of Maurice our contemporary authorities are Evagrius' *Ecclesiastical History*; a few fragments of John of Epiphania (*F. H. G.* iv. p. 272 *sqq.*); John of Ephesus for first two years. A semi-contemporary, if I may use the expression, is our most important source, Theophylactus Simocatta, who was born in the reign of Maurice, but must have been young when Maurice died. For the Persian wars he drew upon John of Epiphania. For an account of Theophylactus, *see* below, p. 254. Maurice's own treatise on Strategic does not throw much light on actual historical events. For relations with the Franks we have some original documents in Bouquet's collection (vol. iv.) and notices in Gregory of Tours; for Italian affairs the works of Pope Gregory.

public confidence; and the unavoidable parsimony, which he was forced to practise, naturally won for him the repute of avarice and meanness; he was said to have a diseased appetite for gold. Soon after his accession he was obliged to purchase a temporary peace from the Avars, whom he was not prepared to oppose, by paying a considerable sum from the almost exhausted treasury. Perhaps the impecuniousness which pressed hard on him during the first years of his reign habituated him to a spirit of parsimony, which he continued to exhibit when circumstances both admitted and demanded a less scrupulous economy. It is certain that he attempted several times to retrench in the pay or commissariat of the army; serious mutinies were the consequence; and this unwise policy was one of the chief causes of his fall.

Evagrius, a contemporary ecclesiastical historian, says that Maurice was moderate, self-willed, and keen-witted.[1] He showed his self-will in his operations at Arabissus, which by no means tended to increase his popularity. Though a Roman by descent, he was born at Arabissus in Cappadocia, and he cherished such a curious love for this insignificant place (as Justinian had done for his birthplace in Dardania) that he determined to convert it into a splendid city, and began elaborate buildings, in spite of his parsimonious proclivities. When the buildings were considerably advanced, an earthquake destroyed them, and the self-will of Maurice, who had a touch of the Roman passion for building, caused them to be begun all over again.[2] To this strange affection of Maurice for his remote birthplace was joined a strong attachment to his kinsmen, whom he was anxious to advance into high places.[3] He made his father Paul president of the senate, he gave all his relations rich palaces, and he divided the large property of Justin's brother Marcellus between Paul his father and Peter his brother.

He was also "moderate." His moderation appears especially in his ecclesiastical policy, for he completely rejected the prac-

---

[1] v. 19.

[2] John Eph. v. 22, 23.

[3] *Ib.* 18. Maurice also "gave his sister and her husband Philippicus a large and strong-built house, on the western side of the city, in the suburb called Zeugma; while his other sister, the widow, received a new and well-built mansion, lately erected by the Patrician Peter, and which is almost as large as a city. He also gave to his other relatives large and noble houses."

tice of persecution adopted by his two predecessors, and passed
a law that schismatics should not be compelled to conform. It
is hard to say, however, whether the credit of this ought not
to be ascribed to the Patriarch Johannes rather than to Maurice ;
we cannot be sure that if the former had urged persecution, the
latter would not have acquiesced. For it is worthy of note that
at this period the Emperors, feeling that their authority rested on
an insecure footing, formed close alliances with the Patriarchs,
who possessed immense influence with the people. Justin
was prepared to adopt the ecclesiastical policy of John of
Sirimis, Tiberius was ready to support Eutychius, and now we
find Maurice standing fast by John Nesteutes in his contest
with the see of Rome. It was the aim of the patriarchs of
Constantinople to hold the same position in eastern Christendom that the bishop of Rome was acknowledged to hold in
universal Christendom. In order to accomplish this aim they
had two problems to solve. One problem was to reduce the
large independent sees of the East, Antioch, Alexandria, Jerusalem, under the jurisdiction of Byzantium ; the other problem
was to prevent the interference of the Pope in the affairs of
the East and thereby induce him to acknowledge the Patriarch
of Constantinople as a pontiff of ecumenical position like his own.
The first of these objects was directly aimed at, as we are expressly told, in the persecutions organised by John of Sirimis ;
the second was essayed by John the Faster, who assumed the
title of " Ecumenical bishop." Gregory the Great, who occupied
the chair of St. Peter from 590 to 604, was horrified and grieved
at such presumption. He wrote a friendly letter of expostu-
lation on the subject to Maurice, in which he said that he was
" compelled to cry aloud and say, *O tempora ! O mores !* " He
also wrote a letter to the Empress Constantina, for he understood the art, which popes, bishops, and priests so easily
learn, of bringing female influence into play. To the Empress
he expressed his conviction that John's assumption of the title
universal was a clear indication that the times of Antichrist
were at hand.[1] His argument that Maurice ought to interfere
in the matter is impressive. No one, he says, can govern on
earth (*terrena regere*) rightly except he knows how to handle
divine things ; and the peace of the State depends on the peace

[1] *Epist.* v. 8, 20 and 21. Indict. xiii.

of the whole Church.[1] It is this peace, not any personal interest, that he himself is defending; it is this peace that John is troubling, by interfering with the established economy of Christendom. It consequently behoves Maurice, in the interests of the State, to inhibit the proceedings of his Patriarch. Maurice, however, was not convinced by the reasons of the Pope, but sympathised thoroughly with John's claims to ecumenical dignity. Hence a breach ensued between the Emperor and the Pope, and the latter complains that Maurice, touching another matter, had the indecency to call him "fatuous."

We may date the long struggle between the sees of Rome and Constantinople, which culminated in the final schism of 1055, from the reign of Maurice and the pontificate of Gregory I.

Maurice gives us the melancholy impression of a prince who, possessing many good qualities and cherishing many good purposes, was almost completely ineffectual. The army detested, and pretended to despise him, and the disaffection prevalent in the capital presented a favourable opportunity for revolution. In the year 599 he refused to ransom 12,000 captives from the chagan of the Avars, who consequently put them to death; and this refusal, which perhaps seems inhuman, increased the detestation in which he was held. Theophylactus, in his panegyrical history of the reign of Maurice, does not mention the matter, and his silence suggests that he did not feel able to palliate the act; but it has been conjectured that many of the prisoners were probably deserters,[2] and in any case it is evident that it was not to save money, but to punish soldiers who had been mutinous and intractable, that Maurice acted as he did. It was an impolitic measure, and two years later he attempted another measure, which under the circumstances was equally impolitic, and illustrates that self-will which Evagrius ascribes to him. He issued commands that the army which was defending the Balkan provinces should winter in the trans-Danubian lands of the Slovenes, in order to save supplies. This led to a rebellion. Peter, the general, was placed in a disagreeable predicament between the peremptory behests of his brother the Emperor and the undisguised dissatisfaction of the army. When the matter came to a crisis

---

[1] *Pacem Reipublicae ex universae eccl. pace pendere.* This expresses a principle   which underlies all medieval history.
[2] Finlay, i. 105. See *post*, p. 139.

at Securisca, the soldiers positively refused to cross the river, and raising the centurion Phocas on a shield, they conferred on him the title of captain (exarch).

When the news of the revolt reached Maurice he did not allow it to be published, but with an air of security which he was far from feeling he celebrated a series of equestrian contests in the hippodrome, and made light of the rumours which had reached the city concerning the military insurrection. His heralds or *mandatores* bade the demes not to be alarmed or excited by an unreasonable and unimportant disorder in the camp; at which proclamation the Blues shouted, "God, O Emperor! who raised you to the throne, will subdue unto you every conspirator against your authority. But if the offender is a Roman, ungrateful to his benefactor, God will subject him unto you without shedding of blood."

Three days later Maurice summoned to the palace Sergius and Cosmas, the demarchs of the green and blue factions respectively, and inquired the numbers of the members of their demes. Sergius counted fifteen hundred Greens, while on the list of Cosmas there were only nine hundred Blues. The object of Maurice's inquiries was to form the demesmen into a garrison for the protection of the city against the army, which was already advancing under the leadership of Phocas. They were set to guard the walls of Theodosius.

It is difficult to grasp the exact cause of this revolution and the intrigues which underlay it; but the following points may be emphasised. In the first place, there was not at the outset any intention of elevating Phocas to the throne; he was merely elected general of the rebellious army. In the second place, it was the purpose of the army to depose Maurice and elect a new Emperor, perhaps Theodosius, the son of Maurice, or Germanus, Theodosius' father-in-law. In the third place, the declaration of disloyalty on the part of the army was followed up in Constantinople by the movement of a disaffected party, on whose co-operation the military ringleaders had probably calculated. In the fourth place, the demes play an important part in this movement, and Maurice seems to have acted imprudently in arming them.[1]

---

[1] In the preceding year they had shown a refractory and disloyal spirit, and even thrown stones at the Emperor, on account of scarcity of food; Maurice and Theodosius with difficulty escaped (Theophyl. viii. 5).

While the citizens and the sovereign were in a state of expectancy and anxiety as to the events which a few days might bring about, it happened that the young Emperor Theodosius and his father-in-law Germanus were hunting outside the walls of the city, near a place called Callicratea. A messenger suddenly accosted Theodosius and gave him a letter, purporting to come from the army. The contents of the letter were a request that either he or Germanus should assume the reins of government; " the forces of the Romaioi will no longer have Maurice to reign over them." The sportsmen were accompanied by an imperial retinue, and the incident of the letter soon reached the ears of Maurice, who immediately summoned his son. On the morning of the second day after this occurrence [1] Germanus was admitted to the presence of the Emperor, who, with tears in his eyes, charged him with being the prime promoter of the whole movement. Not only the letter, but the ambiguous fact that the ravages of the mutineers in the neighbourhood of the city had diligently spared the horses of Germanus, seemed to the suspicious monarch sure proofs of guilt. The accused indignantly denied the charge, but the Emperor either was not or feigned not to be convinced. Theodosius, who had been present at the interview, secretly admonished his father-in-law that his life was in danger, and Germanus betook himself to the asylum of the church erected by Cyrus [2] to the Mother of God. Towards sunset the Emperor sent the eunuch Stephanus, the tutor of the young princes, to persuade the suppliant to leave the altar, but members of the household of Germanus, who had attended him to the church, drove the tutor forth ignominiously. Under the cover of night Germanus stole to the surer refuge of the altar of the great church. In the meantime Maurice flogged his son, whom he accused of also tampering with treason. He then sent a body of guards to drag Germanus from St. Sophia, and a large multitude of indignant citizens gathered round the portals of the church. Germanus was at length persuaded to leave the altar, but as he approached the door a man named Andrew cried out,

[1] On the day following (τῇ ὑστεραίᾳ) the incident of the letter, Maurice appointed Comentiolus commander of the garrison ; on the next day (τῇ ἐπαύριον), very early (ὑπὸ πρώτην ἔω), he summoned Germanus.

[2] Prefect of the city in the reign of Theodosius II.

" Back to the shrine, Germanus, save thy life ! An thou goest, death is in store for thee." These ominous words arrested the steps of Germanus, and repenting of his imprudent submission, he returned to the safety of the altar. The populace meanwhile loaded the name of the Emperor with execrations and abuse, calling him a *Marcionist*, a term which implied not only impiety but folly.[1] As the uproar increased, the demesmen, who were stationed on the walls under the command of Comentiolus, were excited by the significant sounds of tumult and sedition ; they left their posts, and soon gave the menaces of the crowd a definite direction. The object of their fury was the house of Constantine Lardys, the praetorian prefect of the East, one of the most illustrious senators in the Empire and a trusted friend of the Emperor ; it was burned down.

When the revolt had reached this point, Maurice dressed himself in the apparel of a private individual, and along with his wife Constantina, his children, and the faithful minister, whose house was even then in flames, embarked in a vessel which lay moored by the private stairs of the palace. The imperial fugitives reached the church of Autonomos the Martyr, on the bay of Nicomedia,[2] and the distress of a nocturnal flight was aggravated for Maurice by a severe attack of gout, a disease to which the luxurious inhabitants of Constantinople were peculiarly liable.[3] As soon as they reached the shore of Asia, Theodosius was despatched to Persia to supplicate the assistance of Chosroes II for the Emperor, who had assisted that monarch in his own hour of necessity.[4]

It seemed possible that Germanus might be raised to the throne, and in that case the revolution might have been bloodless ; but the rivalry of the factions decided that it was not to be so. He had always been a partisan and patron of the Blues, but it was now important for him to gain the united support of both factions, especially as the Greens were numerically stronger. Accordingly he opened negotiations with

---

[1] τῷ τε τῶν Μαρκιανιστῶν καταλόγῳ συνέταττον· αἵρεσις δὲ αὕτη μετά τινος μωρᾶς εὐλαβείας εὐήθης τε καὶ καταγέλαστος (Theophyl. viii. 9). Marcion was a dualist who believed in two Gods, one *good*, the other *just*.

[2] Nicephorus Callistus, *Hist. Ecc.* 18, 40.

[3] νόσοι ἀρθρίτιδες. ταύτης δὲ τῆς νόσου εὐθένεια καθέστηκε δυστυχὴς τοῖς τὸ βασίλειον ἄστυ κατοικοῦσι διὰ παντὸς (Theophyl. viii. 9). The writer hints that he knows the causes, but declines to digress.

[4] See *post*, p. 112.

Sergius, the demarch of the Greens, and promised to favour them in case he were elected. The demarch communicated this proposal to the managing committee of his party, but they met it with a decided refusal. The Greens were convinced that Germanus would never really abandon the Blues. Recognising, then, that he had no chance of realising his ambitious aspiration, Germanus embraced the party of the winner, the centurion Phocas, to whom members of the green faction were already hastening to present their allegiance.

The question arises whether Germanus cherished any treasonable ambition before the suspicion of the Emperor fell on him, or did this suspicion first arouse in him the hope as well as the fears of a conspirator. The narrative of Theophylactus naturally suggests the latter alternative, but does not exclude the former. Another point, which must remain obscure, is whether the letter received by Theodosius really expressed the wishes of the army, or was a device of Phocas, intended to awaken the suspicions of Maurice. The fact that the news of its arrival reached the ears of Maurice so soon, coupled with the probability that Theodosius did not communicate its contents to any one save Germanus, suggests that the intention of the epistle was not what it seemed. If this conjecture is right, it will go far to establish the innocence of Germanus; for the object of Phocas must have been to divide the camp of his opponents by sowing discord between Germanus and Maurice.

The Greens, who had gone forth from the city to meet Phocas, found him at Rhegium, " and persuaded him to advance to Hebdomon." Theodore, one of the imperial secretaries, whose presence at Rhegium is not explained by our authorities, was sent to the city to bid the senate and the Patriarch [1] proceed to Hebdomon for the purpose of crowning Germanus, in whose interests Phocas still pretended to be acting. The name of Germanus moved the senators and the Patriarch Cyriacus; they hastened to the designated spot, only to see the diadem placed on the head of Phocas, amidst the acclamations of the demes, in the church of St. John the Baptist. On the morrow the new Emperor entered the city, carried in an im-

---

[1] On the preceding night the name of Cyriacus, as well as that of Maurice, had been abused by the rioters: ἐπέσκωπτόν τε καὶ τὸν ἱεράρχην, κ.τ.λ.

perial litter drawn by four white horses, and his progress was marked by showers of golden coins among the people.[1] Horse-races celebrated his entry; on the following day he bestowed the usual donations on the soldiers, and his wife Leontia was crowned Augusta.[2]

On the occasion of the coronation of Leontia an incident occurred which indicated that the seat of Phocas was not yet secure. An important part of these ceremonies consisted in the procession from the palace to the great church, and it was customary for the various demes to post themselves at certain stages in the course of the processions, and to utter certain formulae or exclamations as the Emperor or imperial party passed. In certain cases the Emperor used to stop and receive the homage of the demes.[3] The station of each deme was prescribed by custom, but on this occasion a dispute arose between the Greens and the Blues. The Greens desired to make their station in the portal of the palace called Ampelios, and there receive the Empress with the appropriate shouts of applause, but their jealous rivals objected to this arrangement as contrary to precedent. A tumult ensued,[4] and Phocas sent out Alexander, who had made himself conspicuous in the revolt against Maurice, to calm the strife. Cosmas, the demarch of the Blues, entered into argument with the imperial emissary, and Alexander, with the insolence of an Emperor's friend, heaped abuse on the demarch, and even pushed him aside so roughly that he fell. Thereupon the insulted Blues gave vent to their wrath in ominous words, " Begone ! understand the situation, Maurice is not yet dead ! "[5]

The appearance of the usurper quieted the dispute of the

---

[1] οἷα νεφέλην χρυσῆν ὑετίζουσαν τῶν βασιλικῶν θησαυρῶν ἐκπομπὴν τοῖς ἐν-τυγχάνουσι κατωμβρίσατο, a good example of the style of Theophylactus (viii. 10).

[2] According to Chron. Pasch., Maurice fled on 22d November; Phocas was crowned 23d November, entered the capital 25th November, slew Maurice 27th November. Theophylactus does not allow a day to intervene between the coronation and the entry of the usurper (see viii. 10, p. 303, ed. de Boor, where, having mentioned the coronation, he proceeds with τῇ ὑστε-ραίᾳ). If Theophylactus is right, and the

revolt broke out on the 22d, Maurice's death took place on the 26th. Maurice was sixty-three years old when he died.

[3] See the de Caerimoniis of Constantine VII passim.

[4] The narrative of Gibbon is inaccurate, and seems to imply that the dispute took place in the hippodrome on the day before the coronation of Leontia.

[5] ὕπαγε, μάθε τὴν κατάστασιν· ὁ Μαυ-ρίκιος οὐκ ἀπέθανεν. Theophylactus has not changed the actual words, in the ἰδιωτὶς φωνή, as he calls it (viii. 10 ad fin.)

factions, but the words that the Blues had spoken sank into the heart of Phocas, and he decided that the death of Maurice and the extinction of Maurice's children were necessary to his own safety. Accordingly, on the morrow he sent Lilius over to Chalcedon to carry out this decision. In the harbour of Eutropius the four sons of Maurice were first slain, in their father's presence, and the Emperor, adopting the attitude of a philosopher or of a resigned Christian, is reported to have said, " Thou art just, Lord, and just is thy judgment." An incident took place which illustrates the faithfulness of a nurse and the steadfastness of an Emperor. The nurse concealed one of the imperial infants, and presented a child of her own to the sword of the executioner; but the sovereign was as superior as the servant to the promptings of nature[1] and declared the fraud.

Theodosius, the eldest son, did not escape the fate of his father and brothers. He had only reached Nicaea when Maurice, assuming a temper of dignified resignation, gave up all thoughts of struggling, and, disdaining to beg for the assistance of Chosroes, recalled his son. But the report gained ground and was afterwards made use of by the enemies of Phocas, that Theodosius, having reached Persia safely, had wandered to Colchis and ended his life in desert places. This report seemed to have some basis from the fact that Theodosius was not slain at the same time as his father. Phocas had entrusted his creature Alexander with the task of removing both the prince and Constantine Lardys, who had taken refuge in churches, and it was said that Alexander was bribed by Germanus not to slay his son-in-law.[2] Three distinguished men are mentioned as having shared the fate of their august master; Comentiolus "the general of Europe," George the lieutenant of Philippicus, and Praesentinus the *domesticus* of Peter.[3]

It is important to notice the part that the factions of the hippodrome played in this revolution; they strike us as suddenly reasserting a suppressed existence. There was still a strong spirit of rivalry; and although the Blues were obliged to acquiesce in the coronation of Phocas, they were

---

[1] νόμων φύσεως ὑψηλότερος.
[2] Theophyl. viii. 13. Alexander was slain by Phocas on account of this suspicion.

[3] Constantina the Empress and her three daughters were placed in confinement in "the house of Leo" (Theophyl. iii. 15).

not friendly to him. Both parties were opposed to the
government of Maurice, but they were not at one touching the
question who should be his successor.

Here a conjecture may be put forward as to the significance of this opposition of the demes to Maurice. Finlay
acutely suggested that the observation of Evagrius, that
Maurice installed an aristocracy of reason in his breast and
expelled the democracy of the passions,[1] contains a significance
below the surface, and was intended as a hint at the circumstance that Maurice had allied himself with that aristocracy,
which, as I said before, was endangering and limiting the
extent of the imperial power. However this may be, there is
no doubt that Maurice maintained his position as long as he
did through the support of those men, of whose pernicious
influence Justin had bitterly complained. Now, it seems
almost certain that in this respect the attitude of Tiberius
differed from that of Justin and from that of Maurice.
Tiberius took Justin's advice to heart and assumed a position
independent, as far as was possible, of the nobles, whose
power was dangerously and unhealthily increasing. But in
order to render himself independent of this class he was
obliged to depend on another; and the organised demes of the
hippodrome were an obvious resort. I conjecture, therefore,
that he gave them and their leaders a political influence which
they had not possessed since the revolt of 532.

Thus Tiberius and Maurice tried to meet the danger which
was threatening the imperial power in divergent ways.
Tiberius opposed the influence of the aristocrats by making an
alliance with the demes, while Maurice tried to overcome the
peril by an unnatural bond with the forces that were tending
to undermine the throne, and thereby placed himself in opposition to both the army and the people. This difference
partly explains the popularity of Tiberius and the unpopularity
of Maurice, who seems to have been by temperament inclined
to a certain aristocratic exclusiveness.[2]

---

[1] Evagrius, vi. 1 : καὶ αὐτοκράτωρ
ὄντως γενόμενος τὴν μὲν ὀχλοκράτειαν
τῶν παθῶν ἐκ τῆς οἰκείας ἐξεπηλάτησε
ψυχῆς· ἀριστοκράτειαν δὲ ἐν τοῖς ἑαυτοῦ
λογισμοῖς καταστησάμενος ζῶν ἀρετῆς
ἄγαλμα ἑαυτοῦ παρέσχετο, πρὸς μίμησιν
ἐκπαιδεύων τὸ ὑπήκοον. The historian

adds, "These things are not said for
flattery, as the fact that the Emperor
knows not of them sufficiently proves."
[2] It is worth noticing that the only
popular acts of Maurice which his admirer Theophylactus can cite are his
remitting on one occasion a third of

In support of these remarks I may add that in their light
the observation of Theophylactus that Tiberius desired that
his subjects should rule along with him, has a special point;
the expression is strong and must mean more than the influence of court officials.   Moreover, as a matter of fact,
Tiberius recognised the demarchs and others as possessing
political status.[1]   Further, the words of Evagrius about
Maurice, in accordance with Finlay's explanation, will be still
more speaking; the expulsion of the democracy of passions
will have the definite meaning that Maurice abandoned the
democratic policy of Tiberius.   Moreover, the important part
that the factions played in the revolt of 602 seems to pre-
suppose a considerable revival of their political power and
almost a reorganisation since they had been crushed under
the rule of Justinian; and this reorganisation I would attribute
to the policy of Tiberius.

The testament of Maurice, which he had drawn up in the
fifteenth year of his reign, on the occasion of a severe illness,
was found more than eight years after. his death, at the
beginning of the reign of Heraclius.   The document possessed
considerable interest, for Maurice had conceived the design of
adopting the Constantinian policy of dividing the Empire
among his children.   The fatal results to which this had led
in the case of the sons of Constantine did not deter him.   He
assigned New Rome and "the East" to his eldest son Theodosius;   Old Rome, Italy, and the western islands to his
second son Tiberius; while the remaining provinces were to
be sliced up among his other sons,[2] and Domitian of Melitene
was appointed their guardian.   This intention to recur to a
fourth-century practice is worthy of note; and but for the
revolution it might have been carried out.

the taxes, and his laying out 30 lbs.
of gold ("talents") = £1350, on an
aqueduct at Byzantium.   As to the
remission of the taxes, it is to be presumed it was only for a year; otherwise Theophylactus would have said
so; and we do not know whether it
was a spontaneous act of Maurice or
exacted by a popular demonstration.
I shall speak of Maurice's patronage of
learning in another place.

[1] The presence of the demarchs at

Maurice's coronation shows this.   Theophylactus, iii. 16, says of Tiberius,
εἵλετο συμβασιλεύειν αὐτῷ τὸ ὑπήκοον
(iii. 16).

[2] In the fifteenth year of his reign
he had, I presume, only two other
sons; of these, one would naturally
receive Illyricum, including Greece,
the other Africa.   The words of Theophylactus are, τὰ δ' ἄλλα τῆς Ῥωμαίων
πολιτείας τοῖς ἑτέροις παισὶ κατετεμαχί-
σατο.

CHAPTER III

THE PERSIAN WAR (572-591 A.D.)

THE peace which Justinian and Chosroes had ratified in 562, although the long term of fifty years was fixed for its duration, was of necessity doomed to be short-lived, because its basis was a payment of money,[1] and neither party had entertained any expectation that it would last long. The Roman government was fully determined to renew the war, when the first ten years, for which term they made the stipulated payment in two sums, had expired; and Chosroes, though he would have been glad to protract the peace, was indisposed to make any concessions.

And so, as we might expect, the relations between the empires during the first seven years of Justin are strained; they collide in numerous ways, and causes for hostility accumulate. During the first few years fruitless negotiations[2] are carried on, in regard (1) to the cession of Suania to Rome, and (2) to the claims of the Persophil Saracens of Hirah to subsidies from the Roman Emperor, and these haggling negotiations tended to produce ill feeling and dissatisfaction which more important circumstances soon brought to a crisis.

One of these circumstances was the interference of Persia in the affairs of the kingdom of Yemen, in south Arabia. Yemen had been reduced under the sway of an Abyssinian

---

[1] This principle was apprehended and laid down by the Emperor Tiberius II, who said he would not purchase peace like an article for sale, as a bought peace cannot be permanent and firm (Men. fr. 47, F. H. G. iv. 249).

[2] It is to these embassies that Theophanes of Byzantium, the contemporary historian, must refer when he says that the peace was broken in the second year of Justin. They were certainly the first stage in the breach.

dynasty, with which the Roman Emperor was always on friendly terms. Saif, a descendant of the native Homerite kings, intolerant of the yoke of the strangers, sought refuge at the court of Chosroes, and by Persian assistance Yemen was conquered and the Homerite dynasty, in the person of Saif, restored. But Saif reigned only for a short time ; his government was a failure ; and Chosroes set a Persian marzpan (or margrave) over the country, which was placed in somewhat the same relation to Persia as the exarchate of Ravenna to Constantinople. But the Homerites found that the little finger of the marzpan was thicker than the loins of an Abyssinian prince, and sent an embassy to New Rome to beg for assistance.

In 571-572, when the term of ten years was approaching its close and a new payment would soon be due, another appeal to the Emperor, which he was only too ready to entertain, rendered an outbreak of war with Persia probable. Persarmenia, which was in a constant state of actual or intermittent rebellion, as the christian population could not remain happy under Persian domination, appealed to the Emperor of the Romans in the name of their common religion[1]; he accepted their allegiance, and, when Chosroes remonstrated, replied that Christians could not reject Christians.

These relations with two peoples over which Chosroes exercised jurisdiction, and especially the protection accorded by the Emperor to the Persarmenian, were important causes of the ensuing war. But with these yet another cause concurred in producing the result. This was a newly formed relation of alliance with the Turks, who now for the first time appear in the West.[2] They were gradually taking the place of the Ephthalite Huns, whom they had made their tributaries,— those Huns who had been such formidable neighbours to Persia. The Chinese silk commerce and the trade on the Caspian, which had been hitherto monopolised by the Huns, were passing into their hands.

The Turks sent an embassy to the Byzantine court at the end of 568 or early in 569. They had previously tried to enter into commercial relations with Persia, but the Persian

---

[1] Evagr. v. 7.[1]
[2] Formerly called Sacae (Men. fr. 19).

king had a wholesome horror of Turks, and did not wish his subjects to have any dealings with them. He poisoned some of their ambassadors,[1] so that they should not come again. Then Dizabul, khan of the Turks, determined to seek an alliance with the Roman Empire, which seemed to offer special advantages, as its inhabitants used more silk than any other nation.[2] Justin received the embassy kindly, and sent back Roman ambassadors in the autumn to see the Turkish chagan and conclude a treaty. These negotiations did not please Persia, and attempts were made by that power to waylay the ambassadors on their journey back to Byzantium.[3]

The dominion of Dizabul was not a kingdom; it was an empire whose sovereign held sway over four subject kingdoms and received tribute from other peoples, as for instance from the Ephthalites. This empire threatened now to become formidable to Persia, just as the Avars (who, once the subject of these very Turks, had revolted and migrated to the West) had become formidable to the Romans. In fact the Roman Empire and the Persian kingdom were in very similar circumstances. The former was placed between the Avars and the Persians, just as the latter was placed between the Turks (on the north) and the Romans.

The new allies of Justin were anxious that the forces of Persia should be occupied with a war on the western frontier, and did all they could to induce Justin to renounce the peace of fifty years.[4]

Any one of the causes mentioned might have been insufficient to produce a rupture, but all together were irresistible, and accordingly, when the time came for paying the stipulated annuity, Justin refused (572). The war which ensued lasted for twenty years; and its conclusion was due to the outbreak of a civil war in Persia. We may conveniently divide it into two parts, the death of Chosroes Nushirvan in 579 forming the point of division. The meagre accounts of the operations which we possess present little interest and much difficulty.

---

[1] In the case of the first embassy that was sent, he bought the silk and burnt it.

[2] He was not aware that they possessed the secret of its production.

[3] Menander has given us the details of these embassies, which will be found reproduced in Gibbon.

[4] Menander, p. 236, 7 (ed. Müller).

(1) Marcian, a senator and patrician, perhaps a cousin of Justinian, was appointed general in 572, and arrived in Osroene at the end of summer. Nothing took place in this year except an incursion of three thousand Roman hoplites into Arzanene. In 573 Marcian gained a great victory at Sargathon, but failed to take Nisibis, which he had blockaded. It was not for this failure alone that Marcian was deposed and Acacius appointed in his stead; a curious complication with the Saracens of Ghassan seems to have led to the recall of the general.[1]   Harith, king of Ghassan, died and was succeeded by Mondir; and Kabus, king of the rival Saracens of Hirah, seized the opportunity to invade the Ghassanid dominion. But Mondir, having collected an army, defeated the invader, and followed up his success by invading the territories of Kabus, over whom he gained yet another victory. After these successes he ventured to address a letter to the Roman Emperor, with a request for money, and this presumption inflamed the indignation of Justin. The Emperor indited two letters, one to Mondir full of soft words and promises, the other to Marcian ordering him to assassinate the king of Ghassan. Through some mistake the missives were interchanged, and Mondir read with surprise and consternation the warrant for his own destruction. " This is my desert," he said bitterly. Full of resentment, he vowed vengeance against the Romans. At this juncture the Persians and Persophil Saracens invaded Syria and laid it waste as far as Antioch; but Mondir stood aloof, like Achilles, and retired into the desert. Justin bade the generals try to conciliate him, but he would not receive them. He held aloof for three years, at the end of which term he entered into communication with Justinian, the son of Germanus, whose honourable character had won men's confidence ; and by his means a reconciliation was effected.[2]

The invasion of Syria just referred to took place under

---

[1] The affair of Mondir is related by John of Ephesus (vi. 3, 4), and may have been one cause of Marcian's deposition. It is not inconsistent with Theophylactus' expression (iii. 11), ἀσχάλλων τε ἐπὶ τοῖς ἐξ ἀβουλίας περιστοιχίσασιν αὐτὸν ἀτυχήμασιν, κ.τ.λ. The name Mondir was common to the dynasty of Ghassan and the dynasty of Hirah, and hence mistakes have arisen. I have used *Alamundar* to designate the kings of Hirah, cf. vol. i. p. 373.

[2] After this reconciliation Mondir made a sudden attack on Hirah, the capital of Noman (son of Alamundar), and surprised it. This led to the union of the two realms under Mondir.

the leadership of Adormahun (Adarmanes), and the country, as has been said, was devastated up to the walls of Antioch. The city of Apamea was committed to the flames. Syria seems to have been entirely undefended; for thirty years the inhabitants had been exempt from hostile attacks, and had consequently become so unmanly and unaccustomed to the sights of war that they were unable to take measures for their own defence.[1] The captives who were led away to Persia are said to have numbered two hundred and ninety-two thousand.

From these captives Chosroes is recorded to have selected two thousand beautiful virgins, and ordered them to be handsomely adorned like brides and sent as a present to the chagan of the Turks. Two marzpans and a body of troops were appointed to escort them to the land of the barbarians, and received express orders to travel at a leisurely pace. The virgins were dejected for their souls' sakes, because they could no longer hope to receive religious instruction, and they revealed their longings for death to other Syrian captives. When they had arrived within fifty leagues of the Turkish frontier, they came to a great river, and agreed among themselves to die rather than to pollute themselves with heathen ways and lose their Christianity. "Before our bodies are defiled by the barbarians and our souls polluted and death finally overtake us, let us now, while our bodies are still pure, and our souls free from heathendom, in the name and trusting to the name of our Lord Jesus Christ, offer unto him in purity both our souls and bodies by yielding ourselves up now to death, that we may be saved from our enemies and live for evermore. For it is but the pain of a moment which we have to endure in defence of our Christianity and for the preservation of our purity in body and soul." As the virgins were never allowed to be alone, they asked their conductors for permission to bathe in the river: "We are ashamed to bathe

---

[1] John of Epiphania (Müller, *F. H. G.* iv. 275), ὑπὸ γὰρ τῆς προλαβούσης εἰρήνης καὶ ἡσυχίας ἧς ἱκανῶς ἐπὶ τῆς Ἰουστινιανοῦ βασιλείας ἀπολελαύκασιν ἐξελήλυντο μὲν αὐτοῖς ἡ τῶν πολεμικῶν παρασκευή τὸ δὲ ἀνδρεῖον τελέως διέφθαρτο. This evidence regarding the state of Syria in the second half of Justinian's reign is noteworthy. Only short fragments remain of the history of the contemporary John of Epiphania, but Theophylactus, in his digressive resumption of the earlier portion of the Persian war in Bk. iii., follows John Epiph., as is quite clear from a comparison of his text with the extant fragments of John; so that for these years the authority of Theophylactus is perhaps nearly equivalent to the authority of the earlier writer.

if you stand by and look on." The permission to bathe and the seclusion which they requested were granted, and the whole company of virgins rushed suddenly into the water and were drowned. The Persians saw them floating and sinking, but were unable to rescue them.

This example of christian martyrdom, as it may be called, and of overpowering dread of the Turkish minotaur, so many centuries before he had set foot in Europe, is recorded only by John of Ephesus.[1]

It seems that Marcian was recalled and Acacius sent to the East at the beginning of 574. When the Romans abandoned the siege of Nisibis, Chosroes swooped down upon Daras and besieged it, using against its walls the engines which the Romans had left behind them at Nisibis. But it was not easily taken, and the Persians almost despaired. Finally, overconfidence produced remissness in the garrison, and after a siege of six months the city passed into the hands of the Persians, about seventy years after its foundation by Anastasius. Thus Chosroes now held the two great fortresses of eastern Mesopotamia, Nisibis and Daras.

Besides these disasters, other difficulties beset the Roman government. It was perplexed by the hostilities of the Avars on the Danube and it was embarrassed by the mental aberration of the Emperor. Sophia was driven to write a letter of entreaty to Chosroes, and as her request was supported by a sum of 45,000 pieces of gold, she obtained the respite of a year's truce (spring 574 to spring 575).[2] As Justin's malady increased, Tiberius was made regent, or rather subordinate

---

[1] vi. 7.

[2] It is remarkable that Theophylactus, *who had John of Epiphania before him*, places the date of Tiberius' investiture with the insignia of a Caesar in December 575 instead of December 574. Observe that the seventh year of Justin (572) is marked by Theophylactus (iii. 9), who places the incursion into Arzanene in the autumn (iii. 10) of the same year, and the battle of Sargathon and the invasion of Syria and the siege of Nisibis in the following year, τοῦ ἐπιόντος ἐνιαυτοῦ (573). The transition from 573 to 574 is not distinctly mentioned, but is naturally implied at the

beginning of cap. 11, when the appointment of Acacius and the recall of Marcian are stated. The siege of Daras occupies 574, and is followed by the ἀνακωχὴ τοῦ ἐνεστῶτος ἔτους, which must be 575, as the last words of the chapter show. The expression τοῦ ἐνεστῶτος ἔτους is intelligible, as Daras may have been taken in September or later, and this ἔτος may mean the period 1st September 574 to 1st September 575. But for the decisive authority of the contemporary John of Ephesus (iii. 5 and v. 13), I should be disposed to accept the date of Theophylactus for Tiberius' elevation to the rank of Caesar.

co-regent with Sophia, and although the new caesar had no intention of bringing the war to a conclusion, he saw that it was absolutely necessary to gain time and prolong the cessation of hostilities. Accordingly, when the truce had expired, a peace was made for three years,[1] not applying, however, to the war in Persarmenia, on condition that the Romans paid 30,000 pieces of gold annually.[2] For the following three years (576, 577, 578) therefore the war was confined to Persarmenia.[3]

Justinian, the son of Germanus, was appointed commander of the armies and repaired to Armenia (576). Chosroes advanced in person, intending to invest Theodosiopolis, but finding that it was too strong he proceeded westward, and, entering the Roman provinces, marched in the direction of Caesarea in Cappadocia through the country included between the Euphrates and the Lycus. The Romans marched to obstruct his advance in the Antitaurus mountains, in the north-east corner of Cappadocia, but when they approached Chosroes made a northward movement against Sebaste, which he took and burned. But he obtained no captives in that town, for when the rumour spread that the Persians were coming, all the inhabitants of those districts fled. Finding himself in serious difficulties in a hostile and mountainous country, and apparently not supported in the rear, Chosroes began to retreat. But he was not allowed by Justinian to depart with impunity; the Romans pressed on, and the Persians were forced to fight against their will. The battle was fought somewhere between Sebaste and Melitene, probably in the valley of the river Melas, and its details are described or invented by a rhetorical historian.[4] It resulted in a complete victory for Justinian; Chosroes was forced to flee from his camp to the mountains,

---

[1] Chosroes took the first step in bringing about the peace by sending Jacobus. Sophia sent the physician Zacharias to negotiate at Ctesiphon. The Persians were very anxious that the duration of the peace should be for five years.

[2] John of Ephesus mentions these payments (vi. 8). Menander is not our only authority, as Prof. Rawlinson thought.

[3] At this time Tiberius endeavoured to effect the recuperation of Syria by

remitting a year's tribute.

[4] Theophylactus, iii. 14. It is worth noticing that the speech, which he puts in the mouth of Justinian before the battle began, contains a reference to the religious side of these wars—a side which was always becoming more prominent, and afterwards gave a crusade-like complexion to the wars of Heraclius. *See* iii. 13 (p. 137, ed. de Boor), οὐκ ἔστιν ἡμῖν Θεὸς μαστιζόμενος· οὐ γὰρ ἵππον χειροτονοῦμεν εἰς λάτρευμα, κ.τ.λ.

and leave his tent furniture, with all the gold, the silver, and the pearls which an oriental monarch required even in his campaigns, a prey to the conqueror. The booty, it is said, was immense.

The routed Persians grumbled at their lord for conducting them into this hole in the mountains, and Chosroes with difficulty mollified their indignation by an appeal to his gray hairs. Then the Sassanid descended into the plain of Melitene and burned that city, which had no means of resisting his attack. In the meantime, it may be asked, how was the Roman army occupied? It would seem that there was nothing to prevent the Romans from following the defeated and demoralised Persians, and at least hindering the destruction of Melitene, if they did not annihilate the host. This loss of opportunity is ascribed by a contemporary to the envy and divisions that prevailed among the Roman officers.[1]

After the conflagration of Melitene, Chosroes retired towards the Euphrates, but he received a letter from the Roman general, reproaching him for being guilty of an unkingly act in robbing and then running away like a thief. The great king consented to accept offer of battle, and awaited the arrival of the Romans. The adversaries faced one another until the hour of noon; then three Romans rode forth, three times successively, close to the Persian ranks, but no Persian moved to answer the challenge.[2] At length Chosroes sent a message to the Roman generals that there could be "no battle to-day," and took advantage of the fall of night to flee to the river. The Romans pursued and drove the fugitives into the waters of the Euphrates. More than half of the Persian army was drowned; the rest escaped to the mountains. It is said by Roman historians that Chosroes signalised these reverses by passing a law that no Persian king should ever go forth to battle in person.

Thus the campaign of 576 was attended with good fortune for the Romans, notwithstanding the destruction of Sebaste and Melitene. Nor were the events to the west of the Euphrates the only successes. Roman troops penetrated into

---

[1] John of Ephesus (vi. 8), who gives the best account of this campaign.

[2] The account of this affair is given by John of Ephesus, who states that he derived his information directly from the persons who acted as interpreters between the armies (vi. 9).

Babylonia,[1] and came within a hundred miles of the royal capital; the elephants which they carried off were sent to Byzantium.

The following year, 577, opened with negotiations for peace, which Chosroes, dispirited by his unlucky campaign, was anxious to procure. His general, Tamchosro, however, gained a victory over Justinian in Armenia. The Romans, in consequence of their successes, had become elated and incautious, and the Persians suddenly approached, surprised, and routed them. The victors, it is said, lost 30,000 men, the vanquished four times as many, so that the battle must have been an important affair.[2] Encouraged by the change of fortune, Chosroes no longer desired peace, and the negotiations led to no result.

A pious historian[3] considers that this reverse was a retribution on the Roman soldiers for their irreligious behaviour in Persarmenia, a district where there were many christian settlers. When the Roman army invaded it, christian priests came out to meet them with the holy Gospels in their hands, but no reverence was shown to their pious supplications. The worst outrages were committed, without distinction of creed. The soldiers seized infants, two at a time, by their legs, and tossing them up in the air caught the falling bodies on the points of their spears; monks were plundered, hermits and nuns were tortured, if they could not or would not produce gold and silver to satisfy the greed of the depredators. This imprudent behaviour produced a reaction against Roman rule among the Christians of Persarmenia; twenty thousand immediately went over to the Persians,—all in fact except the princes, who escaped to Byzantium.

After this defeat Maurice, who held the office of *comes excubitorum* which Tiberius had filled before his investiture as Caesar, was sent to the East with full powers, and Gregory, the praetorian prefect, accompanied him to administer the military fiscus. Having collected troops in Cappadocia, his native province, Maurice assembled the generals and captains at Kitharizon, a fortress near Martyropolis, and assigned to

---

[1] This invasion is mentioned by both Theophylactus and John of Ephesus.

[2] The numbers are given by John of Ephesus. It is characteristic that

Theophylactus passes over this Roman defeat lightly (iii. 15), mentioning it in words which do not suggest that it was really serious.

[3] John of Ephesus, vi. 10.

each his part. Tamchosro, the Persian general in Armenia, employed a stratagem to put the Romans off their guard. He wrote to the troops at Theodosiopolis, bidding them prepare for battle on a certain day, and in the meantime he left Armenia and invaded Sophene, devastating the country about Amida and thus violating the peace, which had not yet expired. Maurice retaliated by carrying his arms into Persian territory; he overran Arzanene, and penetrated into the province of Corduene, which no Roman army had entered since the days of Jovian. He did not, however, occupy any country except Arzanene; his invasion was the same sort of blow to Persia that the expedition of Adormahun in 573 had been to the Empire. More than ten thousand captives were taken, of whom most were christian Armenians, and a large number were located in Cyprus, where lands were allotted to them. Thus the current of Persian success has now been finally stopped.[1]

There is no doubt that the successes of Chosroes had been due to the bad condition and the disorganisation of the Roman army, and the tide began to change when the generals Justinian and Maurice assumed the command in the East. Justinian reformed the degenerate discipline of the soldiers, and Maurice, who, though he had not enjoyed the advantage of a military training, had made a special study of warfare and afterwards wrote a book on Strategic, did much for the reorganisation of the army. As an example of the kind of reform which Maurice found necessary, I may notice that he was obliged to re-introduce the custom of entrenching a camp; the laziness and negligence of soldiers and officers had, it seems, come to such a pass that they dispensed with the foss as a useless expenditure of labour.

(2) The turn which affairs had taken would certainly, as Menander remarks, have led to a peace, and that on terms tolerably favourable to the Romans, but for the death of the

---

[1] These events are placed by John of Ephesus (vi. 13) in the same year as the defeat of Justinian, 577 (=888 of Alexandria). John of Ephesus has not left an account of the campaign of 578 and 579. Theophylactus does not mark the transition from 577 to 578; he marks the spring of 577 (cap. 15, p. 140, ed. de Boor), and the winter of 578 (cap. 16, p. 143). The question arises whether Maurice's invasion took place in 577 or 578; the latter date is indicated rather than the former by the narrative of Theophylactus, and I am inclined to accept it.

aged Chosroes in spring 579, a few months after the death of Justin (December 578). His son and successor Hormisdas, whose character has been painted in dark colours,[1] rejected the proposals which Tiberius made, and Maurice continued a career of partial success, which culminated in the important victory of Constantina in 581. It must be also observed that Tiberius purchased peace from the Avars for 80,000 aurei (£41,000), in order to throw all the energies of the Empire into the Persian war. Events on the Ister and events on the Euphrates constantly exerted a mutual influence.

The year 579 was marked by the invasion of Media by a portion of the Roman army.[2] In the following year, 580, Maurice combined forces with the Saracen king Mondir (Alamundar) for a grand invasion; but disputes arose between the Roman and the Saracen leaders in the neighbourhood of Callinicum; Mondir is said to have acted treacherously, and the expedition failed. Adormahun had harried Osroene, leaving not so much as a house standing, and had written to Maurice and Mondir, " Ye are exhausted with the fatigue of your march; don't trouble yourselves to advance against me. Rest a little, and I shall come to you." And he was allowed to retreat, says the historian,[3] although 200,000 men were eating at the Emperor's expense. In 581 the Romans gained a great victory at Constantina.

When Maurice became Emperor, in the following year, he adopted the precedent of his predecessors and ceased to be a general. He appointed John Mystacon ("the Moustachioed") commander of the eastern armies, and the year 583 was marked by a defeat of the Romans in a battle on the river Nymphius, the Persians being led by a general entitled the kardarigan.[4] The defeat was mainly due to enmity between John and a captain named Kurs, who was appointed to command the right wing, and disloyally took no part in the engagement.

At the beginning of 584 John Mystacon was deposed from his command as not sufficiently energetic, and was succeeded by Philippicus, the husband of Gordia the Emperor's

[1] Theophyl. iii. 16 (p. 144).
[2] *Ib.* (p. 145).
[3] John of Ephesus, vi. 17.

[4] Παρθικὸν τοῦτο ἀξίωμα, φίλον δὲ Πέρσαις ἐκ τῶν ἀξιωμάτων προσαγορεύεσθαι (Theophyl. i. cap. 9).

sister. In autumn Persia was invaded and the pursuit of the kardarigan was eluded, but nothing of consequence occurred. Early in 585 Philippicus invaded Arzanene, but he was soon obliged by sickness to retire to Martyropolis and entrust the command temporarily to a captain named Stephanus; but this year, like the preceding, was unmarked by any important event.

In the spring of 586 Philippicus, who had visited Byzantium during the winter, was met at Amida by Persian ambassadors, who had come to urge the conclusion of a peace, for which they expected the Romans to pay money. But the Romans had lately experienced no reverses, and therefore disdained the offer. The operations of this year took place in the neighbourhood of the river of Arzamon and the mountain of Izal. The Romans commanded the banks of the river, and as water was procurable from no other source in these regions, it was expected that, if the Persians advanced to the attack, thirst would be a powerful ally. But the Persians loaded camels with skins of water and advanced confidently, intending to attack the Romans on Sunday. Philippicus, informed on Saturday of their approach, suspected their design and drew up his army in array for fighting in the plain of Solachon. The right wing was commanded by Vitalius; the left wing by Wilfred (Iliphredas), governor of Emesa; the centre by Philippicus and his lieutenant Heraclius, the father of that Heraclius who was afterwards Emperor. On the Persian side, the centre was commanded by the kardarigan; Mebodes faced Wilfred; and Aphraates, a nephew of the kardarigan, opposed Vitalius. The Roman troops were encouraged by the elevation of a flag adorned with a picture of Christ, which was believed not to have been made by hands; it was known as a "theandric image." On the other hand the Persian general resorted to the desperate measure of destroying the water supply, in order that his soldiers might feel that life depended on success.

The battle was begun by the advance of the right Roman wing, which forced back the Persian left and fell on the baggage in the rear. But, occupying themselves with the plunder, the victors allowed the fugitives to turn and unite themselves with the Persian centre, so that the Roman centre had to deal with a very formidable mass. Philippicus, who had retired a little from the immediate scene of conflict, resorted to a device to divert the troops of Vitalius from their untimely occupation with the baggage. He gave his helmet to Theodore Ilibinus, his spear-bearer, and ordered him to strike the plunderers with his sword. This device produced the desired effect; the soldiers thought that Philippicus himself was riding about the field, and returned to the business of battle. The left wing of the Romans was completely successful, and the routed Persians fled as far as Daras. But in the centre the conflict raged hotly for a long time, and it was believed by the Christians that a divine interposition took place to decide the result in their favour. The kardarigan fled to an adjacent hill, where he starved for a few days, and then hastened to Daras, whose inhabitants refused to receive a fugitive.

After the victory of Solachon, Philippicus invaded Arzanene. The inhabitants of that district concealed themselves in underground dwellings, and were dug out like rats by the Romans, who discovered them by the tell-tale subterranean sounds. Here Heraclius, who had been sent with a small force in the company of two Persian deserters, who undertook to point out a locality favourable for establishing a fortress, fell in with the kardarigan, but succeeded in eluding his superior forces by a dexterous retreat. A messenger was sent to Philippicus, who was besieging the fortress of Chlomari,[1] to apprise him of the approach of the enemy; and he ordered the trumpet to be sounded, to recall all the troops who were scouring the surrounding country. The kardarigan soon arrived, and the Persians and Romans found themselves separated by a large ravine, which prevented an immediate battle. At night the Persians, marching round this ravine, encamped behind the Romans, and apparently occupied such a dominant position on the hill that it would have been impossible to continue the siege of Chlomari.[2] On the following night in the first watch the Roman camp was suddenly alarmed by the departure of the general, whose conduct seems quite inexplicable, as the Persian forces led by the kardarigan were no match for his own, and there appears to have been no im-

[1] This word occurs only in genitive plural, so it may be Chlomari or Chlomara.

[2] I confess that I do not clearly comprehend the exact details which Theophylactus attempts to describe in ii. 8.

minent danger. The soldiers followed him in confusion, with difficulty finding their way through the darkness of a moonless night; and if the enemy had known the actual state of the case the army might have easily been annihilated. But the movement was so unaccountable that the Persians suspected a stratagem, and did not leave their camp during the night. The fortress of Aphumon, whither Philippicus had made his way, received the Romans, who, harassed by the arrows of the slowly following Persians, arrived during the forenoon, and consoled themselves by deriding the general. The whole army retreated to Amida, the Persians still following and harassing, but not venturing on a general battle.

Philippicus did not carry on in person any further operations during this year, but his second in command, the able officer Heraclius, invaded and wasted the southern regions of Media.

In the spring of 587 Philippicus consigned two-thirds of his forces to Heraclius, and the remaining third to Theodorus of Rabdis[1] and Andreas, a Saracen interpreter, with instructions to harass the territory of the enemy by incursions. The general himself again suffered from illness, and was unable to take the field. Both Heraclius and Theodorus were successful; each of them laid siege to a strong fortress, and both fortresses were stormed.[2]

In winter Philippicus set out for Constantinople, leaving Heraclius in charge of the army, but before he reached Tarsus he learned that the Emperor had signified his intention of appointing Priscus commander-in-chief instead of himself.[3] In spring, accompanied by Germanus the bishop of Damascus, Priscus arrived at Monokarton, where the army was stationed. It was usual for a new general on his arrival to descend from his horse, and, walking between the rows of the marshalled army, honour them with a salutation. Priscus neglected this ceremony; and a dissatisfaction which had been

---

[1] I adopt M. de Boor's suggestion that ὁ ἐκ τοῦ ʻΡάβδιος ὁρμώμενος, or something of the kind, underlies τῷ Τουραβδηνῷ. It is even possible that Του- may be due to a dittography of τῷ.

[2] The fortress taken by Theodorus was named Beiudaes.

[3] Philippicus wrote from Tarsus to Heraclius, ordering him (1) to inform the army of Maurice's ordinance touching the diminution of the rations, (2) to retire himself to Armenia and leave the command of the army to Narses, commandant of Constantina. Hence Heraclius was not present at the time of the mutiny, which his influence might have been able to prevent.

long brewing among the soldiers burst out into open mutiny. This dissatisfaction was caused, not only by the deposition of Philippicus, who was popular among the troops, notwithstanding his strange flight in 586, but by an unpopular innovation of Maurice, who ordained that the rations of the soldiers should be reduced by one-quarter. The injudicious haughtiness or indifference of Priscus offended the soldiers, already disposed to murmur ; and the camp became a scene of disorder. Priscus was thoroughly frightened, and resorted to the expedient of sending Wilfred to march through the camp with the holy "theandric" standard in his hands ; but such was the excitement that the mystic symbol was received with contumely and stones. The general escaped, not unwounded, to the city of Constantina, where he had recourse to the services of a physician ; and he despatched letters to the governors of the surrounding cities and forts, with reassurances that the soldiers would not be deprived of any portion of what they were in the habit of receiving. He likewise sent a messenger to the camp at Monokarton, to announce that the Emperor had changed his mind and that the rations would not be diminished. The old bishop Germanus went on this mission, but the soldiers meanwhile had elected an officer named Germanus,[1] not to be confounded with the bishop, as their general. The representations of the prelate were not listened to, and the soldiers urged the inhabitants of Constantina to expel Priscus.

Informed of these events, Maurice recalled Priscus and reappointed Philippicus, but the mutineers were not satisfied, and refused to submit to the command of their former general. The Persians meanwhile attacked Constantina ; but the provincial commander Germanus, who seems to have acted through constraint rather than inclination, induced a thousand men to accompany him, and relieved the menaced city. He then restored order so far as to enable him to organise a company of four thousand for the invasion of Persia, and at the same time Aristobulus, an emissary of Maurice, succeeded by

---

[1] This Germanus was the duke of Phoenicia Libanesia, *see* Evagr. vi. 5. Besides him and the bishop of Damascus, two other persons of the same name occur in the history of the time ; Germanus, whose daughter was married by Theodosius, the son of Maurice, and Germanus, who was commander of the eastern army at the time of Maurice's death (Theophyl. viii. 15).

gifts and promises in mollifying the exasperated troops. While Philippicus, diffident and uncertain, was still at Hierapolis, a battle was fought at the " City of the Witnesses "[1]—to adopt the style of our historian Theophylactus—and the Romans obtained a brilliant victory.

Early in 589 the Persians captured Martyropolis by the treachery of a certain Sittas, who introduced four hundred Persians into the city on the plea that they were deserters to the Romans, while the truth was that he was himself a deserter to the barbarians. Philippicus surrounded the city, but Mebodes and Aphraates arrived with considerable forces, and the Romans were defeated. Thus Martyropolis passed into the hands of the Persians.

At this juncture Comentiolus succeeded Philippicus, and almost immediately after his assumption of the command he worsted the enemy in an important battle near Nisibis, which was fatal to the general Aphraates, and it is specially mentioned that Heraclius performed signal acts of valour. In the Persian camp rich spoils were obtained.

In the same year[2] the Roman arms won minor successes in the northern regions of Albania. Persia had been encompassed by several dangers at the same time. Arabs invaded Mesopotamia from the south, the Turks threatened in the north, and in the north-west the Chazars poured into Armenia and penetrated to Azerbiyan. The general Varahran was victorious in an expedition against the Turks, and was then sent to Suania, but as he returned thence he was twice defeated by Romanus in Albania on the banks of the Araxes.

But now the course of events in Persia took a turn which proved decidedly favourable to the Romans, and led to a conclusion of the war. Hormisdas deposed Varahran from the command in consequence of his ill success in Albania, and is said to have insulted him by sending him the garment of a woman and a distaff. This story may be true, but we cannot help remembering that it was told long ago of a Cypriote king and a queen of Cyrene, and in recent years of Sophia and Narses.[3] Varahran revolted against the unpopular monarch,

---

[1] Martyropolis.

[2] In the last five months of 589 ; for Theophylactus marks the eighth year of Maurice, which began in August.

[3] *See* below, p. 146. For the king of Cyprian Salamis, Euelthon, who sent a distaff and wool to Pheretima, queen of Cyrene, *see* Herodotus, Bk. iv. 162.

and the result of the civil war was that (September 590) Hormisdas was slain, and the rebel was proclaimed king. The second act of the drama was the contest between Chosroes Eberwiz,[1] a son of Hormisdas, and the usurper, which by the help of Roman arms was decided in favour of the legitimate heir. Chosroes fled for refuge to Roman territory, and sent an appeal for help to the Roman Emperor. The difficulties in which Persia was involved offered an excellent opportunity to New Rome, and Chosroes was fully conscious of this fact. We are informed that the ambassadors who bore Chosroes' letter used thirteen arguments to persuade Maurice ; and especially worthy of notice, even if it be due, not to the brain of Chosroes, but to the pen of Theophylactus, is the argument drawn from the example of Alexander the Great. The Persian empire was at this moment implicated in such serious difficulties that it seemed by no means a chimerical idea or an impossible undertaking for the Roman " Republic," in spite of its de- generate condition, to make an attempt to reduce the Persian kingdom beneath its sway. Consequently the envoys of Chosroes are represented as being at pains to point out that while Alexander had subdued Persia, he had not succeeded in forming a lasting empire ; his vast dominion had been broken up among his successors. The nature of men, the ambassadors are reported to have observed, makes it impossible that a single universal kingdom, reflecting the unity of the divine government, should exist on earth.[2]

This contemporary comparison of a possible undertaking on the part of the Emperor Maurice with the actual under- taking of Alexander more than nine centuries before is interesting. We pause, as we read Theophylactus, and reflect that this " Romaic " Empire, ruling chiefly over lands which had submitted to the sway of Alexander—Macedonia, Thrace, Asia Minor, Syria, Egypt,—and Greek not Latin in its speech, was in a stricter sense the successor of Alexander's empire than the Roman Empire had been when it reached to the northern seas. It was as if the spirit of Alexander had lain dissolved in the universal spirit of Rome for seven hundred

---

[1] The title Eberwiz or Parwiz is explained by Mirkhond as either "powerful king" or "victorious."

See Rawlinson, *Seventh Oriental Mon- archy*, p. 493.
[2] Theophyl. iv. 11.

years, and were now once more precipitated in its old place, changed but recognisable.

Maurice was not emulous of Alexander's glories and dangers ; the Roman Empire at that moment had not the heart to aspire to new conquests. He undertook to restore Chosroes to the throne of the Sassanids, on condition that Persarmenia and eastern Mesopotamia, with the cities of Daras and Martyropolis, should be ceded to the Romans. The terms were readily accepted, and two victories gained at Ganzaca and Adiabene sufficed to overthrow the usurper and place Chosroes II on the throne (591). The peace was concluded, Maurice withdrew his troops from Asia to act against the Avars in Thrace, and for ten years, as long as Maurice was alive, the old enmity between Rome and Persia slept.

A word must be said of the state of Persia under the rule of Chosroes Nushirvan, whose reign extends over nearly half of the sixth century, and may be called the golden or at least the gilded period of the monarchy of the Sassanids.[1] It was a period of reforms, of which most seem to have been salutary. In order to prevent the local tyranny or mismanagement of satraps, who were too far from the centre to be always under the " king's eye," he adopted a new administrative division, which was perhaps suggested to him by the Roman system of prefectures. He divided Persia into four parts, over which he placed four governors, whose duty was to keep diligent watch over the transactions of the provincial rulers. And for greater security he adopted the practice of periodically making progresses himself through his dominions. He was greatly concerned for the maintenance of the population, which seems to have been declining, and he employed two methods to meet the difficulty ; he settled captives in his dominions, and he enforced marriages. He introduced a new land system, which was found to work so well that after the fall of the Sassanid monarchy the Saracen caliphs adopted it unaltered. But perhaps his most anxious pains were spent on the state of the army, and it is said that when he reviewed it he used to inspect each individual soldier. He succeeded in reducing its cost and increasing its efficiency. Like Peter Alexiovitch or Frederick

---

[1] Here I have availed myself of Prof. Rawlinson's account of the reign of   Chosroes in the *Seventh Oriental Monarchy.*

the Great, he encouraged foreign culture at his court, he patronised the study of Persian history, and caused a Shah nameh (Book of the kings) to be composed. Of his personal culture, however, the envy or impartiality of Agathias speaks with contempt, as narrow and superficial[1]; on the other hand, he has received the praises of an ecclesiastical historian. "He was a prudent and wise man," writes John of Ephesus,[2] "and all his lifetime he assiduously devoted himself to the perusal of philosophical works. And, as was said, he took pains to collect the religious books of all creeds, and read and studied them, that he might learn which were true and wise and which were foolish. . . . He praised the books of the Christians above all others, and said, 'These are true and wise above those of any other religion.'"

---

[1] Agathias, ii. 28. Agathias asks how one brought up in the luxury of an oriental barbarian could be a philosopher or a scholar.

[2] vi. 20. John apologises for thus eulogising a Magian and an enemy. What he says about Chosroes' christian proclivities is more edifying than probable.

CHAPTER IV

THE great Slavonic movement of the sixth and seventh centuries was similar in its general course to the great German movement of the fourth and fifth. The barbarians who are at first hostile invaders become afterwards dependent, at least nominally dependent, and christianised settlers in the Empire; and as they always tend to become altogether independent, they introduce into it an element of dissolution. Slaves too are employed by the Romans for military service, though not to such an extent as were the Germans at an earlier date.

This resemblance is not accidental; it is due to the natural relations of things. But it is curiously enhanced by the circumstance that just as the course of the German movement had been interrupted or modified by the rise of the Hun empire of Attila in the plains which are now called Hungary, so the course of the Slavonic movement was modified by the establishment of the Avar empire, in the latter half of the sixth century, in the same regions. And as the power of the Huns, after a brief life, vanished completely, having received its death-blow mainly from Germans, so the power of the Avars, after a short and formidable existence, was overthrown early in the seventh century by the Slaves, for whom the field was then clear. The remnant of the Avars survived in obscure regions of Pannonia until the days of Charles the Great.

The Avars probably belonged to the same Tartaric group as the Huns of Attila. In the last years of Justinian's reign, about the time of the invasion of the Cotrigurs, they first appeared on

the political horizon of the West. They had once been tributaries of the Turk in Asia, and having thrown off his authority had
travelled westward; but we are assured that they had no right
to the name of Avars, and that they were really only Wars or
Huns, who called themselves Avars, a name of repute and dread,
in order to frighten the world.[1]   These pseudo-Avars persuaded
Justinian to grant them subsidies,[2] in return for which they
performed the service of making war on the Utrigurs, the Zali,
and the Sabiri.   But while Justinian paid them, and they
professed to keep off all enemies from Roman territory, their
treacherous designs soon became apparent; they invaded
Thrace (562), and refused to accept the home which the
Emperor offered them in Pannonia Secunda.   In this year
Bonus was stationed to protect the Danube against them, as
Chilbudius in former times had protected it against the Slaves.

At first the Avars were not so formidable as they afterwards
became.   They harried the lands of the Slaves (Antae) who
dwelled beyond the Danube,[3] but they did not venture at first
to harry the lands of the Romans.   When Justin refused to
continue to pay the subsidy granted by Justinian,[4] they took
no steps for redress, and, turning away from the Empire,
directed their arms against the Franks and invaded Thuringia,
a diversion which had no consequences.

But now a critical moment came, and a very curious transaction took place which had two important results.   The
Lombard king Alboin made a proposal to Baian, the chagan or
king of the Avars, that the two nations should combine to
overthrow the kingdom of the Gepids, over whom Cunimund
then reigned.   The conditions were that the Avars should
receive half the spoil and all the territory of the Gepids, and
also, in case the Lombards secured a footing in Italy, the land
of Pannonia, which the Lombards then occupied.   The last
condition is curious, and, if it was more than a matter of form,
remarkably naïve; the Lombards must have known that, in
the event of their returning, they would be obliged to recover

---

[1] Theophylactus, vii. 8; he calls
them Ψευδαβάρεις.

[2] Sarosius, the lord of the Alans, "introduced" the Avars to Justin, who was
stationed as general in Lazica; and
Justin introduced them to his uncle.
The ambassador of the Avars on this
occasion was Kandich. *See* Menander,
frags. 4, 5.

[3] *See* Menander, fr. 6, who relates
the murder of the Antic ambassador
Mezamer by the Avars.

[4] For Justin's refusal, *see* above, p.
72.

their country by the sword. The character of the Gepids seems to have been faithless; but the diplomacy of Justinian had succeeded in rendering them comparatively innocuous to the Empire. Justin now gave them some half-hearted assistance; but they succumbed before the momentary combination of Avars and Lombards in the year 567.

The two results which followed this occurrence were of ecumenical importance: the movement of the Lombards into Italy (568), and the establishment of the Avars in the extensive countries of the Gepids and Lombards, where their power became really great and formidable, and the Roman Empire had for neighbours a Hunnic instead of a German people,—*colubrimodis Abarum gens nexa capillis.*

The chagan, Baian, was now in a position to face the Roman power and punish Justin for the contemptuous rejection of his demands. From this time forward until the fall of the Avar kingdom there is an alternation of hostilities, and treaties, for which the Romans have to pay. At the same time the Balkan lands are condemned to suffer from constant invasions of the Slaves, over whom the Avars acquire an ascendency, though the relation of dependence is a very loose one. At one time the Avars join the Romans in making war on the Slaves, at another time they instigate the Slaves to make war on the Romans; while some Slavonic tribes appear to have been occasionally Roman allies.[1] The Slaves inhabited the larger part of the broad tract of land which corresponds to modern Walachia[2]; while the Avar kingdom probably embraced most of the regions which are now included in Hungary.

The great object of the Avars was to strengthen their new dominions by gaining possession of the stronghold of Sirmium, an invaluable post for operations against the Roman provinces. As, however, Bonus held it with a strong garrison, they could not think of attacking it, and were obliged to begin hostilities by ravaging Dalmatia. An embassy was then sent to Justin, demanding the cession of Sirmium, and also the pay that Justinian used formerly to grant to the Cotrigur and Utrigur Huns, whom they had subdued. It is to be observed that they claimed to be looked upon as the successors of the Gepids.

---

[1] The Antae or Wends, *see* Theophylactus, viii. 5, 13. (602 A.D.)
[2] *See* Roesler, *Rom. Stud.* p. 323.

Their demands were refused; but when Tiberius, who afterwards became Emperor, was sent against them and suffered a defeat, the disaster led to the conclusion of a treaty, which seems to have been preserved for the next few years, and the Romans paid 80,000 pieces of gold.

We may notice that in these transactions a difference is manifest between the policy of Justin and the would-be policy of Tiberius. Justin is bellicose, and refuses to yield to the Avars, whereas his general is inclined to adopt the old system of Justinian and keep them quiet by paying them a fixed sum. We may also notice a circumstance, which we might have inferred without a record, that the Haemus provinces, over which a year seldom passed without invasions and devastations, were completely disorganised and infested by highwaymen. These highwaymen were called *scamars*, a name which attached to them for many centuries; and shortly after the peace of 570 they were bold enough to waylay a party of Avars.[1]

For the next four years we hear nothing of Avar incursions, nor is anything recorded of the general Tiberius. We may suppose that he resided at Constantinople, ready to take the field in case of need; and in 574, when the enemy renewed their importunities for the cession of Sirmium, he went forth against them, and was a second time defeated. Before the end of the year he was created Caesar, and, as he determined to throw all the forces of the realm into the Persian war, he agreed to pay the Avars a yearly tribute of 80,000 pieces of gold.

But now the Slaves, who for many years seem to have caused no trouble to the Romans, began to move again, and in 577 no less than a hundred thousand poured into Thrace and Illyricum. Cities were plundered by the invaders and left desolate. As there were no forces to oppose them, a considerable number took up their abode in the land and lived at their pleasure there for many years.[2]   It is from this time that we

---

[1] Σκαμάρεις (Menander, fr. 35). The earliest instance of the word, as far as I know, is in Eugippius' *Life of Severinus*. *See* vol. i. Bk. iii. p. 286. In the seventh century the word occurs in the Lombard laws; in the eighth century we shall hear of the scamars in the reign of Constantine V.

On this occasion Tiberius forced the robbers to give some satisfaction to the Avars.

[2] John of Ephesus, vi. cap. 25; cf. Menander, fr. 47 *ad fin.*, where Thrace is said to have been ravaged, and the number of Slaves is stated to have been 100,000; and fr. 48: κεραϊζομένης τῆς

must date the first intrusion of a Slavonic element on a considerable scale into the Balkan peninsula.

It was a critical moment for the government, and the old policy of Justinian, which consisted in stirring up one barbarian people against another, was reverted to. An appeal for assistance was made by John the prefect of Illyricum to the chagan of the Avars, who had his own reasons for hostility towards the unruly Slaves, and he consented to invade their territory.[1] The Romans provided ships to carry the Avar host across the Ister, and the chagan burned the villages and ravaged the lands of the Slaves, who skulked in the woods and did not venture to oppose him.

But Baian had not ceased to covet the city of Sirmium, and the absence of all the Roman forces in the East was too good an opportunity to lose. In 579 he encamped with a large army between Singidunum (Belgrade) and Sirmium, pretending that he was organising an expedition against the Slaves, and swearing by the Bible as well as by his own gods that he entertained no hostile intention against Sirmium. But he succeeded in throwing a bridge over the Save and came upon Sirmium unexpectedly ; and as there were no provisions in the place, and no relief could be sent, the city was reduced to such extremities that Tiberius was compelled to agree to its surrender (581). A peace was then made, on condition that the Avars should receive 80,000 aurei annually.

The loss of Sirmium is a turning-point in the history of the peninsula, as it was the most important defence possessed by the Romans against the barbarians in western Illyricum.

'Ελλάδος ὑπὸ Σκλαβηνῶν καὶ ἀπανταχόσε ἀλλεπαλλήλων αὐτῇ ἐπηρτημένων τῶν κινδύνων, on which account Tiberius, not having sufficient forces at his disposal, applied to Baian. The words of John of Ephesus are : "The same year (581) was famous also for the invasion of an accursed people called Slavonians, who overran the whole of Greece and the country of the Thessalonians and all Thrace, and captured the cities and took numerous forts, and devastated and burnt, and reduced the people to slavery, and made themselves masters of the whole country, and settled in it by main force, and dwelt in it as though it had been their own without fear.

And four years have now elapsed and still . . . they live at their ease in the land, and dwell in it, and spread themselves far and wide, as far as God permits them, and ravage and burn and take captive. . . . And even still (584) they encamp and dwell there."

[1] The chief of the Slaves was Daurentius, that is Dovrat, Menander, fr. 48. He had put to death the ambassadors of the Avars, and thus Baian had a private reason for his expedition. There was another invasion of the Slaves in 579, *see* Johannes Biclarensis, *Chronicon* in Roncalli's collection, ii. p. 389.

The shamelessness of the Avaric demands now surpassed all
bounds. When Maurice came to the throne he consented to
increase the tribute by 20,000 pieces of gold, but in a few
months the chagan demanded a further increase of the same
amount, and this was refused.[1] Thereupon (in summer 583)
the Avars seized Singidunum, Viminacium, and other places
on the Danube, which were ill defended, and harried Thrace,
where the inhabitants, under the impression that a secure peace
had been established, were negligently gathering in their harvest.
Elpidius, a former praetor of Sicily, and Comentiolus, one of
the bodyguard, were then sent as ambassadors to the chagan,
and it is recorded that Comentiolus spoke such "holy words"
to the Lord Baian [2] that he was put in chains and barely
escaped with his life. In the following year (584) a treaty
was concluded, Maurice consenting to pay the additional sum
which he had before refused.

It was, however, now plain to the Emperor that the
Avars had become so petulant that payments of gold
would no longer suffice to repress their hostile propensities,
and he therefore considered it necessary to keep a military
contingent in Thrace and modify the arrangement of Tiberius,
by which all the army, except garrison soldiers, were stationed
in Asia. Accordingly, when the Slaves, instigated by the
Avars, invaded Thrace soon after the treaty, and penetrated as
far as the Long Wall, Comentiolus had forces at his disposal,
and gained some victories over the invaders, first at the river
Erginia, and afterwards close to the fortress of Ansinon in
the neighbourhood of Hadrianople.[3] The barbarians were
driven from Astica, as the region was called which extends between Hadrianople and Philippopolis, and the captives were
rescued from their hands.

The general tenor of the historian's account of these Slavonic depredations in 584 or 585 implies that the depredators were not Slaves who lived beyond the Danube and
returned thither after the invasion, but Slaves who were

[1] The Emperor sent the chagan, at
his own request, an elephant and a
golden bed, but both were sent back
disdainfully to the donor (Theophyl. i.
3).

[2] I adopt this expression, used of
Marina and the Lord Lysimachus in

Pericles, as a sort of modern parallel to
the curious expression of Theophylactus, who says that Comentiolus spake
boldly, "θαλαμευόων the Romaic freedom like a chaste wife."

[3] Ardagast was the leader of the
Slovenes.

already settled in Roman territory. Comentiolus' work consisted in clearing Astica of these lawless settlers.[1] It is a vexed question whether the Slaves also settled in northern Greece and the Peloponnesus as early as the reign of Maurice. There is evidence to show that the city of Monembasia, so important in the Middle Ages, was founded at this time on the coast of Laconia, and it seems probable that its foundation was due to Greek fugitives from the Slaves, just as Venice is said to have been founded by fugitives from the Huns.[2]

In autumn (apparently 585) the peace was violated. The chagan took advantage of the pretext that a Scythian magician,[3] who had indulged in carnal intercourse with one of his wives and was fleeing from his wrath, had been received by Maurice in Constantinople. The Emperor replied to the Avar demonstrations by imprisoning the chagan's ambassador Targitios[4] in Chalcis, an island in the Propontis, for a space of six months, because he presumed to ask for the payment of money while his master was behaving as an enemy.

The provinces beyond the Haemus, Lower Moesia, and Scythia, were harried by the Avars, indignant at the treatment of their ambassador (586). The towns of Ratiaria, Dorostolon, Zaldapa, Bononia,—there was a Bononia on the Danube as well as in Italy and on the English Channel,—Marcianopolis, and others[5] were taken, but the enterprise cost the enemy much trouble and occupied a considerable time.[6]

Comentiolus was then appointed general, perhaps *magister militum per Illyricum*, to conduct the war against the Avars.

CAMPAIGN OF 587.—The nominal number of the forces under the command of Comentiolus was 10,000 ; but of these only 6000 were capable soldiers. Accordingly he left 4000 to guard the camp near Anchialus, and divided the

---

[1] Compare especially Theophylactus' expression, τῆς Ἀστικῆς αὐτῆς ἀπελαύνεται (i. 8, p. 53).

[2] *See* Phrantzes, p. 398 (ed. Bonn). *See* Note at the end of this chapter.

[3] He was called *bookolabras* = magician. He seems to have been a Turk by race.

[4] Targites was the name of the Avaric ambassador who visited Byzantium

after Justin's accession.

[5] The others were Akys, Pannasa, and Tropaeum. It is impossible to identify all the small places in the highlands of Moesia and Thrace.

[6] Hopf refers the notice of Evagrius, vi. 10—a passage much discussed in the Fallmerayer controversy — to the Avar expeditions of 583 and 586 (587). *See* Note at the end of this chapter.

fighting men into three bands, of which the first was consigned to Martin, the second to Castus, and the third he led himself.

Castus proceeded westward towards the Haemus mountains and the city of Zaldapa, and falling in with a division of the barbarian army, cut it to pieces. Martin directed his course northwards to Tomi, in the province of Scythia, where he found the chagan and the main body of the enemy encamped on the shore of a lake. The Romans surprised the chagan's camp, but he and most of the Avars escaped to the shelter of an island. Comentiolus himself accomplished nothing; he merely proceeded to Marcianopolis, which had been fixed on as the place of rendezvous for the three divisions. When the six thousand were reunited they returned to the camp, and taking with them the four thousand men who had been left there, proceeded to a place called Sabulente Canalin, whose natural charms are described by Theophylactus, in the high dells of Mount Haemus.[1] Here they awaited for the approach of the chagan, who, as they knew, intended to come southwards and invade Thrace. It would appear that the spot in which the Romans encamped was close to the most easterly pass of Mount Haemus.

In the neighbourhood of Sabulente there was a river which could be crossed in two ways, by a wooden bridge, or, apparently higher up the stream, by a stone bridge.[2] Martin was sent to the vicinity of the bridge to discover whether the Avars had already crossed, while Castus was stationed at the other passage to reconnoitre, and, in case the enemy had crossed, to observe their movements. Martin soon ascertained that the barbarian host was on the point of crossing, and immediately returned to Comentiolus with the news. Castus, having

---

[1] Somewhere in the vicinity of Anchialus. The passage in Theophylactus does not state directly, but leads us to suppose that Sabulente Canalin was in the most easterly extremities of the Haemus range, near Anchialus (vi. 5, *ad init.* γίνεται οὖν ἡμέρᾳ τρίτῃ εἰς τὸ λεγόμενον Σαβουλέντε Κανάλιν εἶτα τῇ Ἀγχιάλῳ προσέμιξεν). Otherwise one might identify it with the region of Kazanlyk, in the neighbourhood of the Sipka pass. Perhaps the Avars crossed the Balkan range by the pass of Luda Kamčija. It would be interesting to know whence Theophylactus derived his description of the amenities of Sabulente. Did he visit it himself? was it described to him by another? or is it merely a rhetorical description, such as might have been written as an exercise (μελετή) by Choricius, and equally applicable to any other spot! Evagrius, whose later years were contemporary with the youth of Theophylactus, has left us a picturesque description of Chalcedon.

[2] τὴν λιθίνην διάβασιν; this can hardly mean stepping-stones.

crossed to the ulterior bank, met some outrunners of the
Avars, and cut them to pieces; but instead of returning to
the camp by the way he had come, he pressed on in the
direction of the bridge, where he expected to fall in with
Martin. He was not aware that the foe were already there.
But the distance was too long to permit of his reaching the
bridge before nightfall, and at sunset he was obliged to halt.
Next morning he rode forward and suddenly came upon the
Avar army, which was defiling across the bridge. To escape
or avoid observation seemed wellnigh impossible, but the members of the little band instinctively separated and sought shelter
in the surrounding thickets. Some of the Roman soldiers were
detected and were cruelly tortured by their captors until they
pointed out where the captain himself was concealed in the
midst of a grove.[1] Thus Castus was taken prisoner by the
enemy.

The want of precision in the narrative of the historian and
the difficulty of the topography of the Thracian highlands
make it impossible to follow with anything like certainty the
details of these Avaric and Slavonic invasions. The chagan,
after he had crossed the river, divided his army into two
parts, one of which he sent forward to enter eastern Thrace
by a pass near Mesembria.[2] This pass was guarded by 500
Romans, who resisted bravely, but were overcome. Thrace
was defended only by some infantry forces under the command of Ansimuth, who, instead of opposing the invaders,
retreated to the Long Wall, closely followed by the foe; the
captain himself, who brought up the rear, was captured by the
pursuers.

The other division of the Avars, which was led by the
chagan himself, probably advanced westward along that intermediate region which lies between the Haemus range and the
Srêdna Gora, and crossed one of the passes leading into
western Thrace.

Comentiolus, who had perhaps also moved westward after
the chagan along Mount Haemus, descended by Calvomonte and
Libidourgon to the region of Astica. It was on this occasion,
perhaps as they were defiling along mountain passes, that the

---

[1] οἷά πως ἐπιφυλλίδα τινὰ ἐν μέσῳ τῆς
ὕλης ἀποκρυπτόμενον.

[2] Probably the pass of Nadir Derbend
or Boghazdere.

baggage fell from one of the beasts of burden, and the words, " torna torna fratre " (turn back, brother),[1] addressed by those in the rear to the owner of the beast, who was walking in front, were taken up along the line of march and interpreted in the sense of an exhortation to flee from an approaching enemy.   But for this false alarm the chagan might have been surprised and captured, for he had retained with himself only a few guards, all the rest of his forces being dispersed throughout Thrace.   Even as it was, the Avars who were with him fell in unexpectedly with the Roman army, and most of them were slain.

After this the forces of the Avars were recalled and collected by their monarch, who for the second time had barely escaped an imminent danger.   They now set themselves to besiege the most important Thracian cities.   They took Moesian Appiaria, but Diocletianopolis, Philippopolis, and Hadrianopolis withstood their assaults.[2]

An incident characteristic of those days determined the capture of Appiaria.   A soldier named Busas, who happened to be staying in the fortress, had gone out to hunt, and " the huntsman became himself a prey."   The Avars were on the point of putting him to death, but his arguments induced them to prefer the receipt of a rich ransom.   Standing in front of the walls, the captive exhausted the resources of persuasion and entreaty, enumerating his services in warfare, and appealing to the compassion of his fellow-countrymen to redeem him from death; but the garrison of the town, under the influence of a man whose wife was reputed to have been unduly intimate with Busas, were deaf to his prayers.   Indignant at their callousness, the captive did not hesitate to rescue his own life by enabling the Avars to capture the town, and at the same time he had the gratification of avenging himself on the unfeeling defenders of Appiaria.   He instructed the ignorant barbarians how to construct a siege-engine, and by this means the fortress was taken.

While the enemy were besieging Hadrianople, Maurice

---

[1] Theophylactus only mentions τόρνα, Theophanes adds φράτερ or φράτρε. The words possess considerable interest, as the earliest extant specimen of the Roumanian or Walachian language, the eastern daughter of Latin ; cf. Roesler, *Romänische Studien*, p. 106.

[2] Evag. vi. 4; Theophyl. ii. 15, 16, 17. Theophylactus apparently thought that Appiaria was south of Mount Haemus.

appointed to the post of general in Thrace John Mystacon, who had formerly commanded in the Persian war; and Mystacon was assisted by the ability and valour of a captain named Drocton, of Lombard origin. In a battle at Hadrianople the Avars were routed, and compelled to retreat to their own country. Shortly before this event Castus had been ransomed.

The misfortunes of the army of Comentiolus and the capture of Castus seem to have produced a spirit of insubordination in the capital, and increased the unpopularity of Maurice. Abusive songs were circulated, and though the writer of the panegyrical history of this reign makes light of the persons who murmured, and takes the opportunity of praising the Emperor's mildness in feeling, or at least showing, no resentment, yet the mere fact that Theophylactus mentions the murmurs proves that they were a notable signification of the Emperor's unpopularity, especially as the events which caused the discontent were not directly his fault.

During 588 the provinces of Europe seem to have enjoyed rest from the invaders, but in 589 Thrace was harried by Slaves, and apparently Slaves who lived permanently on Roman soil.[1]

The position of affairs was considerably changed when in the year 591 peace was made with Persia, and Maurice was able to employ the greater part of the forces of the Empire in defending the European provinces. He astonished the court by preparing to take the field himself, for an Emperor militant had not been seen since the days of Theodosius the Great. The nobles, the Patriarch, his own wife and children, assiduously supplicated him to give up his rash resolve; but Maurice was firm in his determination. His progress as far as Anchialus is described by the historian of his reign[2]; but

---

[1] Theoph. iii. 4: τὸ δὲ Γετικόν, ταὐτὸν δ'εἰπεῖν αἱ τῶν Σκλαυηνῶν ἀγέλαι τὰ περὶ τὴν Θρᾴκην ἐς τὸ κάρτερον ἐλυμαίνοντο. We are told by Evagrius that the mutiny of the soldiers in the East against Priscus seemed a favourable opportunity for incursions.

[2] We may note the stages of Maurice's journey to Anchialus: (1) Hebdomon; (2) Selymbria, where he took ship for

Heraclea, but was driven by a storm into port at (3) Daonion, where he spent the night. Thence he rode to Heraclea (Perinthus), where he visited the church of the Martyr Glyceria; and advancing four parasangs northwards he encamped at (4) a pleasant and populous place, not named. The next halting-place was in the neighbourhood of (5) Enaton, where the

when he arrived there the tidings that a Persian embassy was awaiting him recalled him to the capital, and his speedy return seems to have been also caused by signs and portents. This ineffectual performance of Maurice, who had never been popular with the army, discredited him still more in the eyes of the troops; they had now a plausible pretext for regarding him with contempt. He was skilled in military science, and wrote a treatise on tactics; but henceforward the soldiers doubtless thought that he might be indeed a grand militarist " who had the whole theoric of war in the knot of his scarf," but that certainly his " mystery in stratagem " was limited to theory.

I may mention an incident which occurred in the progress of Maurice, and which transports us for a moment to the habitations of a curious, if not fabulous, people on the Baltic Sea. The attendants of the Emperor captured three men who bore no weapons, but carried in their hands musical instruments. Being questioned by their captors, they stated that they were Slaves who dwelled by the " western ocean." [1] The chagan of the Avars had requested their people to help him in his wars, and these three men had been sent as envoys by the ethnarchs or chiefs of their tribes, bearing a message of refusal. Their journey had occupied the almost incredible period of fifteen months. The chagan had prevented them from returning home, and they had resolved to seek refuge with the Roman Emperor. They had no arms, because the territory in which they lived did not produce iron; hence their occupation was music, which, they said, was much more agreeable, and they lived in a state of continual peace. We are not told what subsequently became of these extraordinary Slaves, except that Maurice, struck with admiration at their splendid stature, caused them to be conveyed to Heraclea.

Emperor remained for three days and nights. While he was there the three musical Slaves were captured. On the fourth day he advanced, and while the retinue was crossing a narrow bridge over the stream of Xerogypson, in a marshy place, a confusion arose which forced the Emperor to dismount and preserve order with a staff. Two stadia ($\sigma\eta\mu\epsilon\hat{\imath}\alpha$) beyond this bridge (6) he encamped for the night; and on the following day reached (7) Anchialus, where he abode a fortnight. It appears, then, that the journey from Heraclea to Anchialus was equivalent to a four days' leisurely march for cavalry. It is evident that Maurice did not follow the high road, which ran by Drizipera, Hadrianople, and Tarpodizus, but marched due north from Heraclea, crossing the Strandža range probably somewhere near Bizya.

[1] This name was applied to the northern as well to the western seas of Europe.

When Maurice returned to Byzantium he was waited on not only by a Persian embassy but by two envoys, Bosos and Bettos, of a king of the Franks,[1] who proposed that the Emperor should purchase his assistance against the Avars by paying subsidies. Maurice consented to an alliance, but refused to pay for it.

During the last ten years of Maurice's reign hostilities were carried on both with the Avars and with the Slaves. As the narrative of our original authority, Theophylactus, is in some points chronologically obscure,[2] it will be most convenient to treat it in annual divisions.

(1) 591 A.D.—The operations of the Avars began at Singidon, as the Greeks called Singidunum, on the Danube. Having crossed the river in boats constructed by the labour of subject Slaves, the host of the barbarians laid siege to the city, but when a week had passed and Singidon still held out, the chagan consented to retire on the receipt of two thousand aurei, a gilt table, and rich apparel. It will be remembered that the capital of Upper Moesia had been captured by the Avars in 583; we must presume that they did not occupy it, for in that case its recapture by the Romans would certainly have been mentioned by the historian.

The chagan then directed his course to the region of Sirmium, where, with the help of his Slavonic boatbuilders, he crossed the Save; thence marching eastwards he approached Bononia on the fifth day. The chief passage of the Timavus (Timok) was at a place called Procliana, and here the advance guard of the Avars was met by the Roman captain Salvian with a thousand cavalry. Maurice had appointed Priscus " General of Europe," and Priscus had selected Salvian as his captain or " under-general." A severe engagement took place,

---

[1] Called Theodoric by Theophylactus. One of Childebert's sons was really named Theoderic, but Childebert did not die till 596, and so there must be a mistake either in the name or in the date. It seems easier to assume that Theophylactus erred in the name, but as far as we know from our other sources (Gregory of Tours and the letters in Bouquet, vol. iv.), the embassies between Childebert and Maurice related only to co-operation against the Lombards and the restoration of Athanagild (*see* below, cap. vi.) M. Gasquet, assuming a double mistake, refers the embassy to 599 A.D., and supposes that by Theoderic (then king of Burgundia) his brother Theodebert, king of Austrasia, is meant (*L'empire byzantin*, p. 203).

[2] *See* a note by the author on the "Chronology of Theophylaktos Simokatta" in the *English Historical Review*, April 1888.

in which the Romans were victorious; and when on the following morning eight thousand of the enemy advanced under Samur to crush the small body of Salvian, the Avars were again defeated. The chagan then moved forward with his whole army, and Salvian prudently retreated to the camp of Priscus, of whose movements we are not informed.

Having remained some time at Procliana,[1] the Avars came to Sabulente Canalin,[2] and thence, having burnt down a church in the vicinity of Anchialus, entered Thrace, about a month after they had crossed the Danube. Drizipera, the first town they besieged in Thrace, is said to have been saved by a miracle, and, having failed here, the enemy marched to Heraclea, where the general of Europe was stationed. Priscus seems to have gradually fallen back before the advancing enemy, and now, when an engagement at length took place, he was routed. Retreating with the infantry to Didymoteichon, he soon shut himself up in the securer refuge of Tzurulon, where he was besieged by the chagan. In order to drive away the barbarians, the Emperor adopted an ingenious and successful stratagem. A letter was written, purporting to come from the Emperor and addressed to Priscus, in which the general was informed that a large force had been embarked and sent round by the Black Sea to carry captive the families of the Avars left unprotected in their habitations beyond the Danube. This letter was consigned to a messenger, who was instructed to allow himself to be captured by the enemy. When the alarming contents of the letter, whose genuineness he did not suspect, became known to the chagan, he raised the siege and returned as speedily as possible to defend his country, having made a treaty with Priscus, and received, for the sake of appearance, a small sum of money. In autumn Priscus retired to Byzantium, and the troops took up their winter quarters in Thracian villages.

(2) 592 A.D.—This year was remarkable for a successful

---

[1] Four days were spent at Procliana; three days were occupied with the march to Sabulente; and four days with the march to Drizipera, which was besieged for seven days. On the fifth day after the siege was abandoned, Heraclea was reached. The siege of Tzurulon lasted either seven or eleven days (according as we interpret ἑβδόμη ἡμέρα καί, Theophylactus, vi. 5 *ad fin.*) Thus the whole campaign lasted about two months, probably August and September.

[2] Canalion, shortened colloquially to Canalin (ο for ω is a feature of modern Greek).

expedition against the Slaves beyond the Ister, who, under the
leadership of Ardagast, had been harrying Thrace. The Emperor had at length come to the conclusion that the invaders
should be opposed at the Danube, and not, as the practice had
been for the last few years, at the Haemus. Priscus, who
continued to hold the position of commander-in-chief, and
Gentzon, who had the special command of the infantry, collected
the army at Heraclea and marched to Dorostolon,[1] or Durostorum, which is now Silistria, with the intention of crossing
the river and punishing the Slaves in their own country. At
Dorostolon, Koch, an ambassador of the Avars, arrived in the
Roman camp, and remonstrated with Priscus on the appearance of an army on the Danube after the treaty which had
been made at Tzurulon. It was explained that the expedition
was against the Slaves, not against the Avars, and that the
Slaves had not been included in the treaty. Having crossed
the Ister, Priscus surprised the camp of Ardagast at midnight,
and the barbarians fled in confusion. Ardagast himself was
almost captured, for in his flight he was tripped up by the
stump of a tree; but, fortunately for him, the accident occurred
not far from the bank of a river. Plunging in its waves,
perhaps remaining under water and breathing through a
reed as the amphibious Slaves were wont to do, he eluded
pursuit.

This victory was somewhat clouded by a mutiny in the
army. When Priscus declared his intention of reserving the
best of the spoils for the Emperor, his eldest son, and the rest
of the imperial family, the soldiers openly showed their displeasure and disappointment at being put off with the refuse
of the booty, or perhaps receiving none at all. Priscus, however, succeeded in soothing them, and three hundred soldiers,
under the command of Tatimer, were sent with the spoils to
Byzantium. On their way, probably in Thrace, they were
assailed by a band of Slaves as they were enjoying the relaxa-
tion of a noonday rest. The plunderers were with some
difficulty repulsed, and fifty were taken alive. It is plain that

---

[1] The march from Heraclea to Drizipera (Drusipara) occupied four days
(τέσσαρας χάρακας), just the time in
which the severe march was accomplished by the Avars in the preceding
year. Ten days were spent at Drizipera, and the journey thence to Dorostolon was performed in fifteen days.
Thus the Danube was reached a month
after the army had left Heraclea.

these marauders belonged to the Slaves who had permanently settled in Roman territory.

Priscus meanwhile sent his lieutenant Alexander across the river Helibakias to discover where the Slaves were hiding. At his approach the barbarians fled to a safe retreat in a difficult morass, where they could defy the Roman troops, who were almost lost in attempting to penetrate the marsh. The device of setting fire to the woody covert in which the fugitives were concealed failed on account of the dampness of the wood. But a Gepid Christian, who had associated himself with the Slaves, opportunely deserted and came to the aid of the foiled Alexander. He pointed out the secret passage which led into the hiding-place of the barbarians, who were then easily captured by the Romans. The obliging Gepid informed his new friends that these Slaves were a party of spies sent out by the King Musokios,[1] who had just learned the news of the defeat of Ardagast; and when Alexander returned triumphantly with his captives to Priscus, the crafty deserter, who was honoured with handsome presents, arranged a stratagem for delivering Musokios and his army into the hands of the Romans. The Gepid proceeded to the presence of the unsuspecting Musokios and asked him for a supply of boats to transport the remnant of the Slavonic army of Ardagast across the river Paspirion. Musokios readily placed at his disposal 150 monoxyles and thirty oarsmen, and he crossed the river. Meanwhile Priscus, according to the preconcerted arrangement, was approaching the banks, and at midnight the Gepid stole away from the boatmen to meet the Roman army, and returned to the river with Alexander and two hundred soldiers. At a little distance from the bank he placed them in an ambush, and on the following night, when the time was ripe, and the barbarians, heavy with wine, were sunk in slumber, the Romans issued from their hiding-place, under the conduct of the Gepid. The signal agreed on was an Avaric song, and the soldiers halted at a little distance till their guide had made sure that all was safe. The signal was given, the boatmen were slaughtered as they slept, and the boats were in the possession of the Romans. Priscus transported three thousand

---

[1] τὸν λεγόμενον ῥῆγα τῇ τῶν βαρβάρων φωνῇ (Theophyl. vi. 9 *ad init.*) The   writer seems to be ignorant that *rex* is a Latin word.

men across the river, and at midnight Musokios, who, like his boatmen, was heavy with the fumes of wine—he had the excuse of celebrating the obsequies of a brother—was surprised and taken alive. The massacre of the Slaves lasted till the morning. But for the energy of the second officer, Gentzon, this success might have been followed by a reverse ; the sentinels were careless, and some of the Slaves who escaped rallied and attacked the victors. Priscus gibbeted the negligent guards.

At this juncture Tatimer arrived with an imperative message from the Emperor, that the army should remain during the winter in the Slavonic territory. The unwelcome mandate would certainly have been followed by a mutiny on this occasion, and perhaps the events of 602 would have been anticipated by ten years, if the commander had been another than Priscus, who had always shown dexterity in managing intractable soldiers. Priscus did not comply with the wishes of Maurice ; he broke up his camp and crossed the Ister. Hearing that the chagan of the Avars, indignant at the successes of the Romans, was meditating hostilities, he sent Theodore, a physician, as an envoy to the court of the barbarian. Theodore is said to have reduced to a lower key the arrogant tone of the chagan by relating to him an anecdote about Sesostris, and the barbarian said that all he asked was a share in the spoil which had been won from the Slaves. Priscus, in spite of the protests of the army, complied with the demand and sent him five thousand captives. For this " folly " he incurred the resentment of the Emperor, who some time previously had determined to depose Priscus and appoint his own brother Peter to the command in Europe.

(3) 593 A.D.[1]—The new general, Peter, proceeded by Heraclea and Drizipera (Drusipara) to Odessus, where the army

---

[1] "Turning to Theophanes, whose sole authority for these wars was Theophylactus, we find that he has hammered out the metal thin, so as to make it extend over the years which are not accounted for. The first campaign of Priscus and the battle of Heraclea took place in 6084, that is 592 ; the expedition against the Slaves is placed in 593, the mission of Tatimer and the recall of Priscus in 594. The campaign of Peter is drawn out to extend over three years—595, 596, 597—and thus the deposition of Peter at the end of 597 agrees with the date of Theophylactus, assuming that he assigned the decease of Johannes Jejunator to 594." *See* the author's note on the chronology of Theophylactus in the *English Historical Review*, April 1888, p. 312. The implication made in that article that Priscus spent the winter 592-593 beyond the Danube I believe, on second thoughts, to be erroneous.

accorded him a kind reception. But unfortunately he was the bearer of an imperial mandate, containing new dispensations, highly unwelcome to the soldiers, concerning the mode in which they were to be paid. The whole amount of the stipend was to be divided into three portions, of which one was to be delivered in clothes, another in arms, and the third in money. When the general read aloud the new ordinance all the soldiers with one accord marched out of the camp, leaving the general alone with the paper in his hands, and took up their quarters at a distance of about half a mile. But Peter was the bearer of other imperial commands also, which were of a more acceptable character, and he decided, by communicating these immediately, to calm the wrath of the soldiers at this attempt to cheat them of their pay. The angry troops were holding a seditious assembly, and loading the name of Maurice with objurgations, when Peter appeared and, procuring silence, informed them from an elevated platform, that the Emperor whom they reviled had resolved to release from service and to support at the public expense those soldiers who had exhibited special bravery and conspicuously endangered life and limb in the recent campaigns; and that he had also decreed that the sons of those who had fallen in battle were to be enrolled in the army list instead of their parents. At these tidings resentment was turned into gratitude, and the Emperor was extolled to the heavens. It is not stated, but it seems highly probable, that the new arrangement in regard to the mode of payment was not pressed; we are only told that Peter sent an official account of these occurrences to the Emperor.

Three days later the army moved westward to Marcianopolis, and on reaching that city Peter sent forward a reconnoitring body of one thousand cavalry under Alexander. These soon fell in with a company of six hundred Slaves, driving waggons piled up with the booty which they had won in depredations at the Moesian towns of Akys, Zaldapa, and Scopis. As soon as they saw the Romans, their first care was to put to death the male prisoners of military age; then, making a barricade of the waggons, they set the women and children in the enclosed space, and themselves stood on the carts brandishing their javelins. The Roman cavalry feared to approach, lest the darts of the enemy should kill the horses under them; but their captain Alexander gave the command to dismount. The engagement which ensued was decided by the valour of a Roman soldier who, leaping up on one of the waggons, felled with his sword the Slaves who were nearest him. The barricade was then dissolved, but the barbarians were not destroyed themselves until they had slain the rest of their captives.

About a week later Peter, who lingered in this region perhaps for the pleasures of the chase, met with an accident in a boar hunt. The furious animal suddenly rushed upon him from a thicket, and in turning his horse he sprained his left foot, which collided with the trunk of a tree. The severe sprain compelled him to remain for a considerable time longer in the same place, to the disgust and indignation of Maurice, who seems to have regarded the cause as a pretext, and wrote chiding letters to his brother. Stung by the imperial taunts, Peter ordered the army to move forward, intending to cross the Danube and invade the territory of the Slaves, even as Priscus had invaded it in the preceding year. But two weeks later a letter from Maurice enjoined on him not to leave Thrace —Thrace is here used in the sense of the Thracian diocese, including Lower Moesia and Scythia—because it was reported that the Slaves were contemplating an expedition against Byzantium itself. Peter accordingly proceeded to Novae, passing on his way the cities of Zaldapa and Iatrus and the fortress of Latarkion. The inhabitants of Novae gave the general a cordial reception, and induced him to take part in the feast of the Martyr Lupus, which was celebrated on the day after his arrival.

On quitting Novae, Peter advanced along the Danube by Theodoropolis and Securisca—or, as it was generally called, Curisca—to Asemus, a city which had been always especially exposed to the incursions of the barbarians from beyond the river, and had therefore been provided with a strong garrison. A circumstance occurred here, which illustrates the quarrels that probably often arose between cities and generals, and which also shows that the firm temper of the men of Asemus had not changed since the days when they defended their city with triumphant valour against the Scythian host of Attila. Observing the splendid men who composed the garrison of Asemus, Peter determined to draft them off for his own army. The citizens

protested, and showed Peter a copy of the privilege which
had been granted to them by the Emperor Justin. Peter,
bent on carrying his point, cared little for the imperial document, and the soldiers of the garrison prudently took refuge
in a church. Peter commanded the bishop to conduct them
from the altar, and when the bishop declined to execute the
invidious task, Gentzon, the captain of the infantry, was sent
with soldiers to force the suppliants from the holy place. But
the solemnity of the church presented so forcibly the de-
formity of the act which he was commanded to commit,
that the captain made no attempt to obey the order, and
Peter deposed him from his office. On the morrow a guardsman was sent to hale the disobedient bishop to the camp, but
the indignant citizens assembled and drove the officer out.
Then, shutting the gates, they extolled Maurice and reviled
Peter, who deemed it best to leave the scene of his discomfiture
without delay.

It is to be presumed that the army advanced westward;
but we are merely told that a few days later a thousand
horsemen were sent forward to reconnoitre. They fell in with
a party of Bulgarians [1] equal in number to themselves. These
Bulgarians, subjects of the Avars, were advancing carelessly,
confiding in the peace which existed between the chagan and
the Emperor. But the Romans assumed a hostile attitude,
and when the Bulgarians sent heralds to deprecate a violation
of the peace, the commander sent them to appeal to Peter, who
was still about a mile behind the reconnoitring party.

Peter brooked as little the protest of the Bulgarians as he
had brooked the protest of the men of Asemus, and sent word
that they should be cut to pieces. But, though the barbarians
had been unwilling to fight, they defended themselves successfully and forced the aggressors to flee; in consequence of which
defeat the Roman captain was stripped and scourged like a
slave. When the chagan heard of this occurrence he sent
ambassadors to remonstrate with Peter, but the Roman general

---

[1] οὗτοι ἑκατοντάσι δέκα Βουλγάροις
προσπίπτουσιν (Theophyl. vii. 4, 1).
This passage is important; it shows
that the Bulgarians maintained
throughout the sixth century a distinct,
though subordinate and dependent,
existence in the neighbourhood of the
Danube, and upsets the theory, which
Hopf affirms with certainty, that the
Bulgarians who harried the Thracian
provinces in the reign of Anastasius
became completely amalgamated with
the Slaves.

feigned complete ignorance of the matter and cajoled the Avars by plausible words.

At this point the narrative of the historian who has preserved the memory of these events suddenly transports us, without a word of notice, into a totally different region,—into the country beyond the Danube, where Priscus had operated successfully in 592. And he transports us not only to a different place, but to a different time; for, having recorded the ill success of Peter and his deposition from the command, he makes it appear, by a chronological remark, that these events took place at the end, not of 593, but of 597.[1]

We are thus left in the dark concerning the events of 594, 595, and 596; while as to 597, we know that Peter was commander of the army, we know some of the details of an expedition against the Slaves beyond the Danube, and it appears probable that in this year the Avars invaded the Empire and besieged Thessalonica. From a Latin source we know that in 596 the Avars made an expedition against Thuringia.

(4) 597 A.D.—At the point where we are first permitted to catch sight of the operations of Peter in Sclavinia, as we may call the territory of the Slaves, he is sending twenty men across an unnamed river to spy the movements of the enemy. A long march on the preceding day had wearied the soldiers, and towards morning the twenty reconnoitrers lay down to rest in the concealment of a thicket and fell asleep. Unluckily Peiragast, the chief of a Slavonic tribe, came up with a party of riders and dismounted hard by the grove. The Romans were discovered and taken, and compelled to reveal the intentions of their general as far as they knew them. Peiragast then advanced to the ford of the river and concealed his men in the woods which overhung the banks. Peter, ignorant of their proximity, prepared to cross, and a thousand soldiers, who had reached the other side, were surprised and hewn in pieces by the enemy, who rushed forth from their lurking-places. The general then determined that the rest of the army should cross, not in detachments, but in a united body, in the face of the

---

[1] Theophylactus, vii. 6, *ad init.* αὖθις γινόμεθα) Ἰωάννης (the Patriarch) πρὸ τεττάρων τοίνυν τούτων ἐνιαυτῶν . . . τὸν τῇδε βίον ἀπέλιπεν. (πρὸς γὰρ τὰ πρεσβύτερα τῆς ἱστορίας

barbarians who lined the opposite bank. Standing on their rafts in mid-stream, the Roman soldiers received and returned a brisk discharge of missiles, and their superior numbers enabled them to clear the bank of the Slaves, whose chief, Peiragast, was mortally wounded. As soon as they landed they completely routed the retreating adversaries, but want of cavalry rendered them unable to continue the pursuit. To explain this circumstance, we may conjecture that the thousand men who had crossed first and were slain by the Slaves were a body of horse.

On the next day the guides lost their way, and the army wandered about unable to obtain water. They were obliged to appease their thirst with wine, and on the third day the evil was aggravated. The army would have been reduced to extreme straits if they had not captured a barbarian, who conducted them to the river Helibakias, which was not far off. The soldiers reached the bank in the morning and stooping down drank the welcome element. The opposite bank was covered with an impenetrable wood, and suddenly, as the soldiers were sprawling on the river margin, a cloud of darts sped from its fallacious recesses and dealt death among the helpless drinkers. Retreating from the immediate danger, the Romans manufactured rafts and crossed the river to detect the enemy, but in the battle which took place on the other side they were defeated.

In consequence of this defeat Peter was deposed and Priscus appointed commander in his stead.

Of the circumstances which led to the attack of the Avars on Thessalonica in this year we are left in ignorance. For the fact itself our only authority is a life of St. Demetrius, the patron saint of Thessalonica, who on this occasion is said to have protected his city with a strong arm.[1] As this work is, like most lives of saints, written rather for edification than as a record of historical fact, we are not justified in using it further than to establish that the Avars besieged the city and were not successful, and that the ordinary evils of a siege were aggravated by the fact that the inhabitants had recently been afflicted by a plague.

---

[1] *Acta Sanctorum*, Oct. iv. p. 13.

In the period of history with which we are dealing we are not often brought into contact with the rich and flourishing city of Thessalonica, the residence of the praetorian prefect of Illyricum. It is not that Thessalonica has been always exempt from sieges and disasters, but it so happens that during the period from the death of Theodosius to the end of the eighth century it enjoyed a remarkably untroubled existence. Just before the beginning of this period its streets were the scenes of the great massacre for which Ambrose constrained Theodosius the Great to do penance at Milan,—an event of which a memorial remained till recently in Salonica, a white marble portico supported by caryatids, called by the Jews of the place "Las incantadas," the enchanted women. And a century after the close of this period, in the year 904, the city endured a celebrated siege by the Saracens; while in later times it was destined to suffer sorely from the hostilities of Normans (1185) and of Turks (1430), under whose rule it passed. In the seventh and eighth centuries the surrounding districts were frequently harried by the Slaves who had settled in Macedonia, but with the exception of the siege in 597 and three successive sieges in the seventh century (675-680 A.D.), the city of Demetrius was exempted from the evils of warfare. Its prosperity is indicated by the fact that it was always a head-quarters for Jews, and at the present day Jews are said to form two-thirds of the population.[1]

(5) 598 A.D.—The two chief events of this year were the relief of Singidunum, which was once more besieged by the Avars, and their invasion of Dalmatia.

Priscus collected his army in the region of Astica in Thrace, and discovered that the soldiers had become demoralised under the ungenial command of Peter; but his friends dissuaded him from reporting the matter to the Emperor. Having crossed the Danube, he proceeded to a town known as Upper Novae, and was met by ambassadors from the chagan, to whom he explained his presence in those regions by the circumstance that they were good for hunting. Ten days later news arrived that the Avars were besieging Singidunum, with the intention

---

[1] *See* Mr. Tozer's book on the *Highlands of Turkey*, vol. i. p. 146. It is worth noticing that the fortifications round Salonica are dated in a brick inscription as belonging to the pontificate of Hormisdas (514 A.D.), a fact which Mr. Mahaffy has recently communicated to me.

of transporting the inhabitants beyond the Ister, and Priscus hastened to its relief. Encamping provisionally in the river-island of Singa, from which the adjacent town derives its name, the general sailed in a fast dromon to Constantiola, where he had an unsatisfactory interview with the chagan.[1] Returning to Singa, Priscus ordered his forces to advance against the besiegers of Singidunum, who speedily retired. The walls of the city, which were unfit to stand a serious siege, were strengthened.

About ten days after this the chagan proceeded to invade the country of Dalmatia. He reduced the town of Bonkeis, and captured no less than forty forts. Priscus despatched a captain named Gudwin, whose German nationality is indicated by his name, with two thousand infantry, to follow the Avaric army. Gudwin chose bypaths and unknown difficult routes, that he might avoid inconvenient collisions with the vast numbers of the invaders. A company of thirty men, whom he sent forward to observe the movements of the enemy, were fortunate enough, as they lay hidden in ambush at night, to capture three drunken barbarians, from whom they learned something of the dispositions of the hostile army, and especially the fact that two thousand men had been placed in charge of the booty. Gudwin, delighted at obtaining this information, concealed his men in a ravine, and as the day dawned suddenly fell upon the guardians of the spoils from the rear. The Avars were cut to pieces, and Gudwin returned triumphantly with the recovered booty to Priscus.

We are told that after these events the chagan desponded,[2] and that for more than eighteen months, from about the early summer 598 to the late autumn of 599, no hostilities were carried on in the Illyrian and Thracian lands.

(6) 599 A.D.—The chagan invaded Lower (or Thracian) Moesia and Scythia, and Priscus, learning that he intended to besiege the maritime town of Tomi, hastened to occupy it. The siege began at the end of autumn and lasted throughout the winter.

(7) 600 A.D.—In spring the Roman garrison began to

---

[1] The historian, Theophylactus, delights to couch the speeches both of the barbarian and the Roman in impossibly grandiloquent language. Pris-

cus speaks of τὴν ἡμέραν . . . ῥοδοειδῆ τε καὶ κροκυνίζουσαν.
[2] ἀθυμίᾳ πολλῇ κατεβέβλητο (vii. 12).

feel the hardships of famine. When Easter approached, Priscus was surprised at receiving a kind message from the chagan, who offered to grant a truce of five days and to supply them with provisions.[1] This unexampled humanity on the part of an Avar was long remembered as a curiosity. On the fourth day of the truce a messenger from the chagan requested Priscus to send his master some Indian spices and perfumes. Priscus willingly sent him pepper, which was still as great a delicacy to the barbarians as it had been in the days of Alaric and Attila, Indian leaf, cassia, and spikenard; "and the barbarian, when he received the Roman gifts, perfumed himself, and was highly delighted." The cessation of hostilities was protracted until the Easter festivities were over, and then the chagan raised the siege.

Meanwhile, as Priscus was shut up in the chief town of Scythia, the Emperor had commissioned Comentiolus to take the field in Moesia. The chagan advanced against him and approached the city Iatrus, on the river of the same name, where the general had taken up his quarters. In the depth of night Comentiolus sent a message to his adversary, challenging him to battle on the following day, and at the same time commanded his own army to assemble in fighting array early in the morning. But the soldiers did not comprehend that this order signified a real battle, and, under the false impression that their commander's purpose was merely to hold a review, they appeared in disorder and defectively equipped. Their surprise and indignation were great when, as the rising sun illumined the scene, they beheld the army of the Avars drawn up in martial order. The enemy, however, did not advance, and they had time to curse their general and form in orderly array. But Comentiolus created further confusion by a series of apparently unnecessary permutations; changing one corps from the left wing to the right, and removing some other battalion from the right wing to the left. The right wing fled, and there was a general flight, but the Avars did not pursue. During the following night Comentiolus made provision for his own escape, and next morning left the camp on the pretext of hunting. At noon the army discovered that

---

[1] 10th April. Theophylactus, vii. 13, 1: πενθημέρους σπονδὰς συστησάμενοι, which Hopf mistranslates (*Griechische* *Geschichte*, p. 91) ". . . schliesst Priscus . . . einen 50 tägigen Waffenstillstand."

their general had deserted them, and hastened to follow him.
But they were pursued by the Avars, who occupied a mountain pass or *cleisura*, — perhaps the Šipka pass, — and the
Romans, now leaderless, were not able to force a passage until
many were slain. When Comentiolus appeared before the
walls of Drizipera he was driven away with stones and taunts,
and was obliged to pass on to Byzantium. The fugitive troops,
with the barbarians close at their heels, arrived soon afterwards
at Drizipera, and the Avars sacked the city.

But the triumph of the chagan was soon turned into
mourning. A plague broke out in his army, the plague of
the *bubo*, and seven of his sons who had accompanied the
expedition died on the same day. Meanwhile the citizens of
Byzantium were so much alarmed at the menacing proximity
of the Avar army, before which Comentiolus had fled, that
they entertained serious thoughts of migrating in a body to
Chalcedon. Maurice first manned the Long Wall with infantry
and with companies formed of members of the blue and green
factions, and then, by the advice of the senate, sent an ambassador to the chagan. When Harmaton arrived at Drizipera
he found the great barbarian in the throes of parental grief,
and was obliged to wait ten days ere he could obtain an
audience in the tent of mourning. Soothing words with
difficulty induced the Avar to accept the gifts of an enemy,
but on the following day he consented to make peace, as his
family affliction had rendered him indisposed for further operations. He bitterly accused Maurice of being the peacebreaker,
and the Roman historian admits the charge.

The terms of the peace were these: the Ister was acknowledged by both parties as the frontier between their dominions,
but the Romans had the privilege of crossing it for the
purpose of operating against the Slaves[1]; twenty thousand
aurei were to be paid by the Romans to the Avars.

It was on this occasion that Maurice refused to ransom
twelve thousand captives from the chagan, who consequently
executed them all. The author of the panegyrical history of
Maurice makes no reference to the matter, and his silence is
remarkable.[2] He would certainly have mentioned it if he

[1] The Slaves were not inactive in the
year 600; we learn from a letter of
Pope Gregory (x. 36) that they plundered Istria, Dalmatia, and even Italy.
[2] Our authority is Theophanes *ad
ann. See* above, p. 86.

could have made any apology for this unpopular act of Maurice.

The Emperor had no intention of preserving the peace, and unblushingly commanded his generals, Priscus and Comentiolus, to violate it. Comentiolus had been reappointed commander, notwithstanding the complaints of the soldiers concerning his recent behaviour. The generals joined their forces at Singidunum, whither Priscus seems to have proceeded after the siege of Tomi, and advanced together down the river to Viminacium (Kastolatz). The chagan meanwhile,. learning that the Romans had determined to violate the peace, crossed the Ister at Viminacium and invaded Upper Moesia, while he entrusted a large force to four of his sons, who were directed to guard the river and prevent the Romans from crossing over to the left bank. In spite of the barbarians, however, the Roman army crossed on rafts and pitched a camp on the left side, while the two commanders sojourned in the town of Viminacium, which stood on an island in the river. Here Comentiolus is said to have acted the part of a *poltroon*, according to a now exploded derivation of the word (*pollice truncus*). He employed a surgeon's lancet to mutilate his hand, and thereby incapacitated himself for action. His poltroonery was probably conducive to the success of Roman arms, for Priscus, untrammelled by an incompetent colleague, was able to win a series of signal triumphs.

Unwilling at first to leave the city without Comentiolus, Priscus was soon forced to appear in the camp, as the Avars were harassing it in the absence of the generals. A battle was fought which cost the Romans only three hundred men, while the ground was strewn with the corpses of four thousand Avars. This engagement was followed by two other great battles, in which the strategy of Priscus and the tactics of the Roman army were brilliantly successful. In the first, nine thousand of the enemy fell, while the second was fatal to fifteen thousand, of whom the greater part, and among them the four sons of the chagan, perished in the waters of a lake, into which they were driven by the Roman swords and spears.

Such were the three battles of Viminacium, fought on the left bank of the Danube. But Priscus was destined to win yet greater victories and to vanquish the chagan himself, who,

unable to recross the river at Viminacium, had returned to his
country by the region of the Theiss (Tissos). Thither Priscus
proceeded, and, a month after his latest victory at Viminacium,
he defeated the forces of the barbarians on the banks of the
Theiss. He then sent four thousand men to the right bank
of that river to reconnoitre the movements of the enemy. This
was the territory in which the kingdom of the Gepids had once
flourished, and certain regions of it were still inhabited by
people of that nation, living in a state of vassalage under the
Avars. The reconnoitring party came upon three of their towns,
and found the inhabitants engaged in celebrating a feast. Before
the dawn of day, when the barbarians were overcome by their
debauch, the Romans fell upon and slew thirty thousand; it
seems, however, doubtful whether all these were Gepids.[1] A
few days later the energy of the chagan had assembled another
army, and another battle was fought on the banks of the Theiss.
Three thousand Avars, a large number of Slaves, and other
barbarians were taken alive; an immense number were slain
by the sword ; many were drowned in the river. The captives
were sent to Tomi, but Maurice was weak enough to restore
them to the chagan without a ransom.

When winter approached, Comentiolus proceeded to Novae,
and thence, having with considerable difficulty procured a
guide, followed the road, or rather the path, of Trajan to
Philippopolis.

(8) 601 A.D.—Comentiolus, who had wintered at Philippopolis and proceeded to Byzantium in spring, was again
appointed commander, but the summer was marked by no
hostilities.   In August, Peter the Emperor's brother was
created "General of Europe." Having remained for some time
at Palastolon on the Danube, he proceeded to Dardania, for he
heard that an army of Avars, under a captain named Apsich,

---

[1] Hopf has reproduced these events
in a strangely confused manner for so
careful a writer ; he seems to have been
unable to follow with ease the Greek of
Theophylactus.   He utterly neglects
the chronology, placing the defeat and
flight of Comentiolus after the success
of Priscus, but that is of small consequence when we compare it with his
account of the operations on the Theiss.
"Das kaiserliche Heer, aufgehetzt von
dem ehrgeizigen Phokas, bedrohte den
Kaiser mit Rebellion.   Dies war in-
soweit günstig für die Avaren, als die
Söhne des Khagans mit 13,000 Mann 601
einen Streifzug nach der Theiss unter-
nahmen und gegen 30,000 'Gepiden'
niedermachten. Allein Priscus vernich-
tete sie und besiegte selbst den zu Hilfe
eilenden Khagan." Even Carl Hopf
is not infallible in using his authorities.

was encamped at a place in that province called the Cataracts. After an ineffectual interview between the Avar commander and the Roman general, the former retreated to Constantiola and the latter withdrew to Thrace for the winter.

(9) 602 A.D.—No martial operations took place during spring, but in summer Gudwin, the officer second in command to Peter, invaded the land of the Slaves beyond the Ister and inflicted terrible slaughter upon them. One Slavonic tribe, the Antae (or Wends), were allies of the Romans, and the chagan accordingly sent Apsich against them by way of a reply to the invasion of Gudwin. We are not informed whether Apsich was successful, but it is recorded that about the same time a large number of Avars revolted from their lord and sought the protection of Maurice.

The last scene in the reign of Maurice has been related in a previous chapter; and at this point our historian, Theophylactus, concludes his work. As no other writer continued where he left off, we hear no more of the Avars and Slaves for sixteen years. Of their doings during the reign of Phocas and the first eight years of the reign of Heraclius our scanty authorities are silent, with the exception of the single notice that in the second year of Phocas the tribute to the Avars was raised. We can, however, entertain no doubt that the Balkan provinces were subjected to sad ravages during the disorganisation which prevailed in the reign of Phocas and the consequent paralysis from which the Empire suffered in the first years of Heraclius. The hostilities of Asiatic enemies were generally wont to have an effect on events in the vicinity of the Danube, and the barbarians can hardly have been disposed to miss such an unrivalled opportunity as was offered to them when Asia Minor was overrun by the Persians.

NOTE ON SLAVONIC SETTLEMENTS IN GREECE

THE groundlessness of Fallmerayer's famous theory that "not a drop of genuine and unmixed Hellenic blood flows in the veins of the christian population of modern Greece" has been shown by Hopf in his *Griechische Geschichte*. One of the passages on which Fallmerayer throws especial weight is Evagrius, vi. 10. It will be advisable to quote it in full:—

οἱ Ἄβαρες δὶς μέχρι τοῦ καλουμένου μακρου τείχους διελάσαντες Σιγγιδόνα Ἀγχίαλόν τε καὶ τὴν Ἑλλάδα πᾶσαν καὶ ἑτέρας πόλεις τε καὶ φρούρια ἐξεπολιόρκησαν καὶ ἠνδραποδίσαντο ἀπόλλυντες ἅπαντα καὶ πυρπολοῦντες, τῶν πολλῶν στρατευμάτων κατὰ τὴν ἑῴαν ἐνδιατρι-βόντων.

Now, in the first place, the Avars, not the Slaves, are the in-vaders mentioned by Evagrius, and therefore the passage does not support Fallmerayer's Slavonic theory. The Avaric invasions of 583 and 587 seem to be referred to. In the second place, the verbs ἀπόλλυντες and πυρπολοῦντες cannot fairly be taken in the sense (which Fallmerayer assigns to them) of extermination. Similar expressions were used long before of Visigothic and Hunnic de-vastations.

Another comment of Hopf is not so convincing. By Hellas, Fall-merayer naturally understood Thessaly and Greece north of the Isthmus. Hopf says (p. 91): "Nur Unkenntniss der Geographie konnte den Syrer Evagrios veranlassen nächst den bekannten Städten Singidon und Anchialos noch 'von ganz Hellas und andern Städten und Burgen zu reden'; entweder dachte er sich unter Hellas eine Stadt oder Burg, was am wahrscheinlichsten, oder er übertrug den antiken Namen des eigentlichen Griechenlands auch auf die thrakisch-makedonischen Provinzen des Römerreichs." Hellas was a division of ecclesiastical geography, and it is almost impos-sible to believe that a man like Evagrius, Syrian though he was, did not know what it meant. ἑτέρας either refers loosely back to Singidunum and Anchialus, or is used, like ἄλλος in classical Greek, in the sense "besides." It is quite possible that in one of these years the Avaric ravages extended south of Mount Olympus; the alternative being that Evagrius recorded an exaggerated rumour.

The passage in John of Ephesus, quoted above, p. 118, is not so easily disposed of, and Hopf, though he shows that it may not necessarily imply Slavonic settlements in *Greece* between 577 and 584, hardly succeeds in proving that such settlements were not made. The most natural interpretation of the passage in John is that the Slaves settled in Hellas as well as in the northern provinces; and as there is no proof to the contrary, we are bound to accept it? Hopf says (p. 104): "Dass die Slawinen, die 577 auch in Hellas plündern, mit denselben Slawen identisch sind, die unter Ardagast, 584-597 die Reichslande verheeren, kann keinem Zweifel unterliegen; wo sie sich sesshaft gemacht hatten, geht aus dem gesagten hinlänglich hervor, nämlich in den Nordprovinzen, zumeist an der Donau." This is a very weak argument. Probably the Slaves who plundered Greece in 577 belonged to the same tribes as those led by Ardagast (though this assumption is not certain); but why should not some of them have settled in Greece? Unless Hopf means by *identisch* individually the same, his argument falls to the ground; and identity in that sense is certainly a gratuitous assumption.

If there is no evidence to support, there is none to contradict Phrantzes' statement that Monembasia was founded in the reign of Maurice, and this may have some slight weight (*see* above, p. 120) in corroborating the statement of John of Ephesus, according to its simplest interpretation. But we may admit Slavonic settlements in Greece before 600 and yet be very far from accepting Fallmerayer's theory. It may be considered certain that these settlements were only in the open country and not in the cities.

CHAPTER V

THE LOMBARDS IN ITALY

THE character of the medieval history of Italy was decided in the sixth century. We can hardly overrate too highly the importance of its reconquest by Justinian, which brought it into contact again with the centre of Graeco-Roman civilisation. The tender hotbed plant of Theodoric's Ostrogothic *civilitas*, which had never looked really promising, had perished before a bud was formed; the thing intermediate between barbarism and high civilisation was put away; and the future development of Italy was to result from the mixture of centuries between the most rude and the most refined peoples dwelling side by side.

The extirpation of the Ostrogoths was almost immediately followed by the invasion of the Lombards; the whole land was imperial for a space of but fifteen years (553-568). These two events, the imperial conquest and the Lombard conquest, possessed a high importance not merely for Italy but for the whole western world. The first secured more constant intercourse between East and West, the second promoted the rise of the papal power.

After the battle in which the allied Avars and Lombards destroyed the monarchy of the Gepids (567 A.D.), Alboin, the Lombard king, with an innumerable host, including many nationalities, even Saxons, advanced from Pannonia to the subjugation of Italy (568 A.D.)[1] The greater part of northern

[1] The story that Narses, the exarch (who had been lately superseded), enraged at an insulting message from the Empress Sophia, revenged himself by inviting the Lombards to invade, may be rejected as a fable. Sophia is said to have sent him a distaff, suggesting that he was not a *man* (Paulus, *Historia*

Italy, Venetia,[1] and Gallia Cisalpina, of which a large region was afterwards to be called permanently by the name of the new conquerors, had no means of defence. Milan was occupied without resistance; and in these regions the invaders were perhaps supported by a remnant of the Ostrogoths. Pavia, the ancient Ticinum, destined to be the capital of the new Teutonic kingdom, held out. The exarch Longinus, who had succeeded Narses, could do little more than make Ravenna and the Aemilia secure. The bishop of Aquileia had fled to Grado,[2] and Honoratus, the bishop of Milan,[3] to Genoa, but Ticinum defended itself so long and so firmly that the irritated Lombard is said to have vowed that he would massacre all the inhabitants. But when the place was taken after a siege of three years, he relented and chose it for his capital. Milan and Ticinum were the cities which Alboin was destined to possess; Ravenna, the Aemilia, and the Pentapolis[4] stood out against the invaders, and Ravenna was probably not even attacked by them. Alboin himself did not penetrate farther south than Tuscany,[5] but his nobles, with bands of followers, pressed forward and formed the duchies of Spoletium and Beneventum. Most of the towns in these districts were totally undefended[6]; the walls of Beneventum

Langobardorum, ii. 5). The same story is told of Hormisdas and Varahran; it was told in ancient times of a king of Cyprus and a queen of Cyrene (Herodotus, iv. 162). *See* above, p. 110.

[1] These districts were in ecclesiastical opposition to Justinian and the Roman see, a circumstance which probably favoured the conquest of Alboin. At this time the Franks were allies of the Lombards and Avars. Cf. Menander, fr. 24. Alboin married Chlotsuinda, a daughter of Chlotar I. (Paul, i. 27).

[2] *Ib.* ii. 10.

[3] Alboin entered Liguria *indictione ingrediente tertia* = September 569 (*ib.* 25).

[4] *Ib.* 14. A difficulty has been felt as to the identity of the cities of the Pentapolis and the Decapolis (so often mentioned in eighth-century history). I believe it has been finally solved by L. Armbrust in his neat little essay, *Die territoriale Politik der Päpste von 500 bis 800* (pp. 54, 55). The Pentapolis = Ariminum, Pisaurum,

Fanum, Senegallia, Ancona; the Decapolis = Auximum (Osimo), Humana (Umana), Aesis (Jesi), Forumsempronii (Fossombrone), Montemferetrum (Montefeltro), Urbinum, Territorium Valvense, Callis (Cagli), Luceoli, and Eugubium. The Aemilia contained the *civitates* of Ferrara, Bologna, Cesena, Imola, etc.

[5] According to Paul (ii. 26), he subjugated all the land *usque ad Tusciam* during the siege of Ticinum; and Paul attributes this celerity to the exhaustion of the inhabitants by the recent plague and a famine. It is doubtful, however, whether the conquest was really so soon accomplished. Alboin captured Verona and Vincentia, but Patavium and Cremona were not taken till the days of Agilulf.

[6] The undefended state of the towns of southern Italy in the time of the Gothic war is proved by the notices of Procopius. The only fortified town in Lucania was Acerenza, on the Calabrian borders (ὅπερ Ἀχεροντίδα καλοῦσι Ῥωμαῖοι, *B. G.* iii. 23); Rossano

had been destroyed by Totila; and thus the conquests were effected without difficulty. The name Zotto, and he is little more than a name, is well known as that of the first duke of Beneventum; he ruled for twenty years, and as his successor Arichis was appointed in 591, the foundation of the duchy of Beneventum is fixed to 571.[1] At first small, the duchies of Spoletium and Beneventum soon expanded at the expense of their Roman neighbours, and the dukes were afterwards able to maintain a position independent of the Lombard kings, in consequence of their geographical separation from the northern duchies by the strip of Roman territory which extended from Rome to the lands of the Pentapolis.

King Alboin was slain in 573. Fate is said to have overtaken him by the hands of his second wife Rosamund, the Gepid princess, who cherished feelings of revenge towards her lord on account of the death of her father Cunimund, and a dark legend has associated itself with her name. The existence of a king was not a necessary element in a Lombard's political vision; royalty could easily be dispensed with. Accordingly, after the short reign of Clepho, Alboin's successor, the dukes did not elect a new sovereign, and for about eleven years there was no central Lombard power.[2] But in 584 the invasions of the Franks compelled the dukedoms[3] to form a united resistance, and necessitated the renewal of the kingly office for the purpose of this unity. Autharis, Clepho's son, was elected king. At the same time the Emperor Maurice appointed a new exarch, Smaragdus, to succeed Longinus.

For a moment it seemed possible that the Lombard power in Italy might be extinguished in the cradle. The activity of Smaragdus succeeded in forming a great coalition against the invaders (588 A.D.); the Franks and the Avars united with the Romans for their destruction. But the Franks were not really earnest supporters of the Roman cause; and the enter-

---

('Ρουσκία) was the chief fort in Bruttii; on Naples and Cumae the whole defence of Campania devolved.

[1] Compare F. Hirsch, *Das Herzogthum Benevent*, p. 3.

[2] Paul, ii. 32: *per annos decem.* During this interregnum the Lombards were active in devastating and conquering. The Benedictine monks of Monte Cassino were forced to flee from their monastery, which was pulled down (590 A.D.) and remained desolate for more than a hundred years. Cf. Paul. Diac. iv. 18. It was rebuilt about 720 by the abbot Petronax in the days of Pope Gregory II.

[3] Apparently thirty-five in number (Paul, ii. 32).

prise came to nothing.[1]   A year or two later we find the ambassadors of the Franks at Constantinople, attempting to induce
Maurice to make them grants of money.

In 590 Agilulf succeeded Autharis.   He conquered the
eastern parts of northern Italy which were still ruled by the
exarch ; especially the cities of Patavium and Cremona, in
the east.   The Lombard conquests were not accomplished as
rapidly as is sometimes represented, not as rapidly by any
means as the conquest of the Vandals in Africa.   It was not
till the reign of Rotharis (636-652) that the coast of Liguria
and the city of Genoa were won.   The conqueror of Liguria
is now celebrated as the compiler of the Lombard code of laws ;
but he also deserves to be remembered as the victorious combatant on the banks of the Scultenna (Tanaro), where the exarch
and the Romans suffered a great defeat (642 A.D.)[2]   After this
the geographical limits of the Romans and Lombards altered
but little ; towns were taken and retaken, but the general outline of the territories remained the same.

The exarchate of Ravenna, including · the Pentapolis and
the Aemilia, naturally maintained itself, as the imperial power
was concentrated there.   Rome, although in a state of sad decline and often hard pressed, was able to keep the Lombards at
bay, chiefly through the exertions of the Popes, who possessed
influence over the Lombards themselves.   Naples and Amalfi
also remained imperial, and the land of Bruttii, for a moment
occupied by the Teutons, was soon won back by the Empire.
In the north, Venice and Istria were under the immediate jurisdiction of the exarch of Ravenna.

It is apparent that the imperial possessions tended to break
up into three groups.   Venice, Grado, and Istria, the nucleus
of the future sovereignty of Venice, formed a group by themselves in the north ; the exarchate of Ravenna, with which
Rome was both administratively and territorially connected,
formed a group in the centre, although Rome tended to become independent of the exarch ; Naples sometimes seemed to
belong to this group, and at other times to fall in with the
southern group, which comprised Sicily, Calabria, and Bruttii.

The distribution of the Lombards corresponds, and each group

---

[1] *See* von Ranke, *Weltgeschichte*, iv. 2, p. 156.
[2] Paul, iv. 45.

fulfils its special function. (1) The northern group includes Pavia, the royal residence, the duchies of Bergamo, Brescia, Friuli, Trient, etc., and Tuscany : this group was associated more especially with the Lombard kings, for in it they possessed a real as well as a nominal jurisdiction. Its function was to oppose the Frank invasions in the north-west and to threaten the exarchate, while on the dukes of Friuli in their march-land devolved the defence of Lombardy against the Slaves and Avars, who pressed on the frontier. (2) The Lombard territory in central Italy was the duchy of Spoletium, which endeavoured to extend its limits to the north at the expense of the Pentapolis and to the west at the expense of Rome. This duchy tended to join Tuscany and include the isthmus of land which lay along the Flaminian road between Rome and the Adriatic. (3) In the south, the duchy of Beneventum included almost all the territory east of Naples and north of Consentia.

But this description of the geographical demarcation of Lombard and Roman territory is not sufficient to explain the relations of the powers. There are two facts which should be emphasised, as having exercised a decisive influence on the development of Italy. The first is, that the Lombards were a military nation with no aptitude for cultivating the soil. They consequently at first left the landowners in possession of their land, exacting from them a tribute of one-third of the produce, but afterwards occupied a third of the land themselves, employing of course slave labour. The result was that no violent change was produced in the character of the population. The other fact was the wide extent of the possessions of the Church, the patrimony of St. Peter ; but to understand the importance of this we must consider the development of the papal power, which the kingdom of the Lombards largely effected, and become acquainted with Pope Gregory I., the greatest figure in Europe at the end of the sixth century.

The greatness of Gregory I.[1] is due to the fact that he

[1] For the study of Gregory's letters, so important for the condition of Italy at this time, a new foundation has been laid by the work of the late Paul Ewald in his "Studien zur Ausgabe des Registers Gregor's I." (in the *Neues Archiv*). Ewald's great discovery was that our present collection of the letters is the result of three different collections, which were welded together. Ewald also showed that the earliest Life of Pope Gregory was that in a St. Gall Codex, composed by an Englishman.

gathered up and presented in a new form and with new emphasis the most lively religious influences that had operated in
the Latin world, namely the theological system of St Augustine and the monastic ideal of St. Benedict ; and that, on the
other hand, he seized and made the most of the gracious
opportunities which the time offered for increasing and extending the influence of the Roman see.

The events of his life peculiarly fitted him for achieving these
results. From the diverse characters of his parents he inherited both a capacity for worldly success and a spiritual
temperament ; his father was a civil magistrate in Rome and
his mother Silvia was a saint. He studied law with a view to
a secular career, but his leisure hours were spent in reading
Jerome and Augustine. The inner voice triumphed in the
end, for, when he attained the high dignity of prefect of the city
(574), the circumstances of state and the gilded pomp which
surrounded him struck him with a sort of terror ; he felt that
the temptations lurking in them might assail and win ; and he
fled, as if from foes, to the shelter of cloister life, having broken
with the world by spending the patrimony of his father on the
foundation of seven monasteries. But the ascetic rigours to
which he zealously submitted himself began to harm his health,
and Pope Pelagius, kindly interfering, caused him to leave
his cell and enter the ranks of the clergy, and sent him as
an *apocrisiarius*, or nuncio, to Constantinople, where he remained for six years (579-585). On his return to Rome he
became abbot of the monastery which he had himself founded
there, and it was at this time that he observed the Anglo-
Saxon slaves in the market-place and conceived the idea of a
mission for the conversion of Britain. He had made all the
necessary preparations to set out for that obscure island, which
had already become a land of fable to the inhabitants of the
Empire, but was prevented from carrying out his intention
by Pope Pelagius, to whom he was far too useful to be lost.
Pelagius died in 590, and Gregory was unanimously elected
to succeed him, but sorely, it appears, against his own will. It is
a remarkable coincidence that the contemporary Patriarch of
Constantinople was also forced unwillingly to accept his chair,
and that he also, like Gregory, practised the most rigorous
asceticism ; and yet that John Jejunator tenaciously clung to

the title "Ecumenical," while Gregory won for the Roman bishop a more ecumenical position than he had ever held before. In these men there seems to have been a real union of pride in their office with personal humility.

From this sketch it will be seen that Gregory had three different experiences. He had the experience of civil affairs, he had the experience of monastic life, he had the experience of ecclesiastical diplomacy. Thus he was peculiarly fitted to carry on the various forms of activity which the papal dignity and the difficult circumstances of Italy rendered possible; and his strong nature, of somewhat coarse fibre, was well adapted to contend with and take advantage of the troubled times. We may consider, in order, his relation to the Lombards, his position in western Christendom, his relation to the Emperor, his theological and literary work.

The hands of the Roman Emperors, Justin, Tiberius, and Maurice, were so full with the wearisome Persian and Avaric wars that they had no money or men to send to the relief of Italy. The exarch could do little, for though he was invested with military as well as civil authority, his attention was chiefly confined to the collection of taxes. While the Pope was naturally concerned for the defence of Rome in the first place, his concern extended also to the rest of Italy, especially to the southern provinces. It was Pelagius, and not the exarch of Ravenna, who sent entreaties for assistance to the Emperors. One of the missions assigned to Gregory when he was apocrisiarius was to obtain aid against the Lombards; but Tiberius was unable to send succour, and advised the Pope either to buy off the enemy, or by a bribe to persuade the Franks to invade Cisalpine Gaul.[1] Shortly after this the Franks were induced to undertake three successive invasions; but these came to nothing, as no intelligent co-operation was carried out between the invaders and the military forces of the exarchate.

In the year in which Gregory became Pope, Autharis died, and his widow, the Bavarian Theudelinda, married Agilulf, who became the new king. Agilulf was an Arian, but Theudelinda was a Catholic, and Gregory possessed so much influence over her that her husband allowed their son to be baptized into the

---

[1] Tiberius, however, relieved the famine which affected Rome in his reign.

Catholic faith and ceased to place the Catholics in his realm under any disabilities. Thus in Gregory's time the see of Rome and the Lombard court were generally on very good terms, although on one occasion (593) Agilulf threatened Rome, and it was necessary to buy him off. The Pope was the mediator of a peace between Pavia and Ravenna in 599.[1]

Thus it was not the king of Lombardy who was a thorn in the side of the Pope, but the dukes of Beneventum and Spoletium. The former pressed on the Roman territory in the south, the latter pressed on it in the east. Now, while it was of course necessary to defend Rome and other important cities against Lombard aggressions, it was also extremely desirable for the Popes to be at peace with the Lombard rulers, as the lands of the Church were scattered through their dominions. Thus the Pope had a far greater interest in maintaining peace than the exarchs, who had no pledges in the hands of the enemy. This circumstance was apparent when, in 592, Gregory concluded a peace with the duke of Spoleto, who was threatening Rome ; and the Emperor Maurice called him " fatuous " for so doing.

Gregory practically managed all the political and military affairs in the south of Italy, though this was strictly the duty of the exarch. He appointed the commanders of garrisons and provided for the defence of cities ; and in this activity not only were his early secular training, and his experience in public affairs, of service, but the fact that he had been a civil functionary in Rome must have secured for him considerably greater power and influence with the people than he could otherwise have possessed. The Pope's practical experience aided him in administering " the patrimony of Peter," to which I have already referred. This was an important matter, as the large possessions of the Church were one of the chief means of supporting and extending the papal power. Nor were these possessions confined to Italy ; the Church owned property in north Africa, in Gaul, and in Dalmatia. The income from these lands enabled Gregory to take measures for the defence of Rome, to give the monthly distributions of bread and money to the poor, to ransom captives taken in war. He was therefore extremely careful in watching over the

---

[1] *See* Paul, iv. 8. Callinicus was the exarch who concluded this peace.

economy of the Patrimony, which was placed in the hands of ordained clergy called *rectores* or *defensores*; and he used to inquire into the minutest details.

In Spain, in Gaul, and in Africa the influence of Rome was considerably increased under Gregory, while the conversion of Britain extended the limits of western Christendom.[1] Leander, the bishop of Seville, who was a warm supporter of Gregory, induced Reccared, the Visigothic king, whom he had converted from Arianism to Catholicism, to send to the bishop of Rome an announcement of his conversion, accompanied by the guerdon of a gold cup, as an offering to St. Peter.[2] In Gaul Gregory exercised considerable indirect influence, and the bishop of Arles acted as a sort of vicar or unofficial representative. The exertions of the Pope were successful in suppressing or lessening many abuses, such as simony and persecution of the Jews; and he maintained a correspondence with the celebrated Queen-mother Brunhilda. Brunhilda's acts are supposed to have secured her an honourable place among the Jezebels of history, but Pope Gregory felt great joy over her "christian spirit." It is certainly futile to assume, with Gregory's defenders, that he was ignorant of the contemporary history of the courts of Paris and Soissons, because very small connection subsisted then between Italy and France; nor, on the other hand, can the correspondence be regarded as either surprising or damning. Brunhilda was liberal in endowing churches and religious institutions; she was sympathetic and helpful in Gregory's missionary enterprises; she was Roman in her ideas. If her political conduct was not irreproachable, she had thrown much in the counter scale; if she was a fiend, she was certainly a fiend angelical. When we take into account the ideas of that age, in which heresy was looked on as the deadliest sin and religious zeal as efficient to cancel many crimes, it is hardly to be wondered that Gregory treated Brunhilda with respect.

In Africa Gregory had far greater authority than in Gaul, where he had no official position. Not only were the bishops of Carthage and Numidia his ardent supporters and useful

---

[1] 596 was the date of the mission of St. Augustine. Ten thousand Anglo-Saxons were converted, but with the Britons he was not successful.

[2] Gregory conciliated Reccared with the Empire. The Visigothic king adopted the imperial name of Flavius. Cf. Greg. *Ep.* ix. 122 and xiii. 47.

instruments, but the exarch Gennadius, who had earned a fair fame by delivering his provinces from the Moorish hordes who vexed it, favoured and encouraged the increase of the Pope's influence. A regular system was introduced of appealing to the see of Rome as the supreme ecclesiastical court.

The relations of Gregory to the Emperor Maurice, whose subject he was, were not untroubled by discord, and in the extension of his ecclesiastical jurisdiction the Pope sometimes came into collision with the Emperor. In Dalmatia, for example, a certain Maximus was elected bishop of Salona. Gregory forbade his consecration, and Maximus appealed to Maurice, who espoused his cause. Then Gregory forbade him to perform the episcopal offices, but Maurice continued to support Maximus in his contempt of the papal commands. As Gregory had no means of enforcing his will, he consulted his dignity by transferring the matter to Maximian, the bishop of Ravenna, and Maximus, as directed, betook himself thither. He was there convinced of his fault and confessed that he had "sinned against God and against Pope Gregory."

Gregory's quarrel with the Patriarch of Constantinople has been already referred to, and in this affair too the Pope came into collision with the Emperor. It has also been mentioned that there was discord between them on the matter of Gregory's relations to the Lombards. A law of Maurice which prevented soldiers from shirking service by entering monasteries was yet another cause of dispute.

The consequence was that the relations between Gregory and Maurice were strained; Gregory was inclined to attribute all the evils which beset the Empire to the iniquity of the Emperor, and he was so unspeakably relieved by the death of Maurice that he could not restrain the voice of jubilation. He looked upon Phocas, whose name became in the eastern part of the Empire a "common nayword and recreation" for all that is abominable, as a public deliverer to whom the thanksgiving of the world was due; and his congratulatory letter to Phocas, wherein he says that "in heaven choirs of angels would sing a gloria to the Creator," may still be read.

This is a page in Gregory's correspondence which, like his letters to Brunhilda, has been made a subject for sectarian controversy. Protestants seize hold of it as a glaring blot in the Pope's character, while Catholics are at pains to defend him on the plea that he knew nothing either of Phocas personally or of the circumstances under which he had assumed the crown.   It has been especially urged that there was no apocrisiarius at Constantinople at the time to inform him of the details, and that he had merely heard the bare fact that Phocas had succeeded Maurice.   Here again we have no proof of the extent of the Pope's information; but it seems gratuitous to assume that he knew nothing of the details.   Such an assumption would not be made in the case of any one but a saint; the ground for the exception being that the character of a saint is inconsistent with the authorship of a letter in which the perpetrator of such acts as those of Phocas is not merely acknowledged but eulogised.   But we must remember the ideas which were prevalent at the time; when we are at a house of entertainment in the sixth or seventh century we must be particularly careful not to reckon without our host. Maurice was, in the eyes of Gregory, a pestilence to the Empire and a foe to the Church; his death was a consummation eminently to be desired; and he who should achieve such a consummation was a person devoutly to be blessed.   There seems therefore no reason to suppose that Gregory was not aware that the feet of Phocas, as he ascended the throne, were stained with innocent blood; he looked upon the acts as a political necessity, for which it would have been hardly fair to condemn the new Emperor.[1]   On the other hand, we need not suppose that Gregory was influenced by any ulterior motive to speak insincerely in his letter, or that he aimed at flattering Phocas into commanding the Patriarch of Constantinople to discard the obnoxious ecumenical title.   This ensued; but we need not assume that it was compassed by insincerity on the part of the Pope.

Thus Gregory with consummate dexterity took advantage of all the means that presented themselves to put the papal power on an independent footing, and win for it universal recognition in the West.   But it is especially important to observe

---

[1] It may be noted that the correspondence with Brunhilda and that with Phocas, taken together, make the case against the assumption of ignorance stronger.   If we assume knowledge in one case we may assume it in the other, and it is gratuitous to assume ignorance in both cases.

how the double rule in Italy contributed to the realisation of the Pope's ambition. If there had been no Lombard invasion, if Italy had been the secure possession of the Roman Empire, Gregory would have been at the mercy of the Augustus of Byzantium and would have had no power to act independently. On the other hand, the presence of the imperial power was equally important; it would have been still more disastrous to become the subject of the Lombard king. Thus the independence of the Popes was struck like a spark between the rival temporal powers that divided Italy.

If we turn to his more specially religious work, we find that Gregory exerted a far-reaching influence over the future life of the Church. He had himself been deeply moved by the monastic ideal of St. Benedict, of whom he wrote a biography; and he assiduously endeavoured to make salutary reforms in cloister life. He firmly suppressed those vagrant monks, whom the sanctity of a religious dress could not always shield from the obnoxious name of *beggars*. He forbade youths under eighteen years to take the vows, nor would he permit a married man to enter a monastery without his wife's express consent. He relieved monks of all mundane cares by instituting laymen to look after the secular interests of the religious establishments.

The clergy (*clerus*), whom he was careful to dissociate completely from the monastic profession, were the object of still more solicitous attention. His *Regula pastoralis*, or manual of duties for a bishop, became and remained for centuries an authority in the Church and an indispensable guide for bishops.[1] The celibacy of the clergy was his favourite and most important reform, and even in Gaul he was able to exert influence in that direction. The reforms in the liturgy which have been attributed to him are doubtful; but the introduction of the solemn Gregorian chant instead of the older less uniform Ambrosian music has rendered his name more popularly known than any of his other achievements.

In doctrine he followed the respectable authority of the founder of Latin theology, St. Augustine. But theology was

---

[1] Hinkmar of Reims (870) says every Frankish bishop was bound to it at his consecration.

the Pope's weak point; here the coarse fibres of his nature are
apparent, his want of philosophy, his want of taste. Take,
for example, his theory of the redemption. Influenced by
familiarity with the ideas of Roman law, men were prone
to look on the redemption as a sort of legal transaction between God and the devil, in which the devil is overreached.
Gregory, true to the piscatorial associations of the first bishop
of Rome, presents this idea in a new, definite, and original
form.[1] It is easy to identify leviathan in Job with the Evil
One; and once this identification is made, it is obvious that
the redemption must have been a halieutic transaction, in
which God is evidently the fisherman. On his hook he places
the humanity of Jesus as a bait, and when the devil swallows
it the hook pierces his jaws.

Consistent with the coarseness displayed in this grotesque
conception, which is put forward earnestly, not as a mere play
of imagination, was his unenlightened attitude to literature and
classical learning, in which he went so far as to despise
grammar[2]; and this trait of his character is brought out in the
twelfth-century legends, which ascribe to him the destruction
of the Palatine library and other acts of vandalism. The
superstitious love of miracles and legends, exhibited in every
page of his works, may be added to complete a superficial
sketch.[3]

The great historical importance of the pontificate of
Gregory I. consists in the fact that he placed the Roman see
in a new position and advanced it to a far higher dignity than
it had previously enjoyed. The germ of the papal power,
which so many circumstances combined to foster and increase,
lay in the position of the Pope as a defender of the people
against temporal injustice and misery. This idea is expressly
recognised by Cassiodorus, the secretary of Theodoric, in a
letter to Pope John: *securitas ergo plebis ad vestram respicit
famam, cui divinitus est commissa custodia.*[4] It was on the

---

[1] *Homiliae in Evangelia,* Lib. 1,
Hom. 25 (ed. Migne, vol. ii. p. 1194).
[2] In a letter to Desiderius of Vienna
—the true Vienna, as Mr. Freeman
calls it.
[3] For this account of Gregory I have
been assisted by the able article of R.

Zoepffel in Herzog and Pfitt's *Ency-
clopädie für protestantische Theologie.*
Gass has some good remarks on
Gregory's *Moralia* (a commentary on
Job in 35 books), *Gesch. der christlichen
Ethik,* i. 181.
[4] *Variae,* xi. 2.

same principle that the bishops influenced the election of the *defensores civitatis* and co-operated with them. Justinian in 554 sent standards of coins, measures, and weights to the Pope and the senate, thus recognising that the activity of the bishop of Rome was not limited to affairs of religion and morals. But Gregory the Great was the first pontiff who made temporal power an object of aspiration, and took full advantage of the opportunities which were offered. Pope Pelagius (555-560) had called in the assistance of military officers against bishops who resisted his authority, but Gregory appointed civil and military officers himself. He nominated Constantius tribune of Naples when that city was hard pressed by the Lombards, and entrusted the administration of Nepi, in southern Tuscany, to Leontius, a *vir clarissimus*. He made peace on his own account with the Lombards when they were at war with the imperial representative, and asserted that his own station was higher than that of the exarch.[1] At the same time he would not tolerate interference in temporal affairs on the part of any subordinate dignitary of the Church, whether bishop or priest, and, like Pelagius, he used the arm of lay authority to suppress recalcitrant clergy.

During the seventh century, for it is convenient to antici-pate here the only remarks that have to be made on the subject, no great Pope arose, no Pope of the same power as Gregory I.; yet his example was not forgotten. Honorius (625-638), the *dux plebis* as he is called in an inscription, consigned the government of Naples to the notary Gaudiosus and the master of soldiers Anatolius, and instructed them in what manner they were to govern.[2] We shall see that during the disputes with the monotheletic Emperors of Constantinople the soldiers at Rome always espoused the cause of the Popes against the exarchs.

---

[1] *Ep.* ii. 46: "eum loco et ordine praeimus."

[2] See L. Armbrust, *Die territoriale Politik der Päpste von 500 bis 800* (in which useful information is conveni-ently collected), note 5, p. 31: "idem in eodem Gaudioso notario et Anatholio magistro militum Neapolitanam civi-tatem regendam committit cum omnibus ei pertinentibus et qualiter debent regi scriptis informat. Diese Nachricht verdanken wir der Kanonsammlung des Kardinals Deusdedit der sie aus dem Registrum Honorii geschöpft hat, liii. c. 149, ed. Martinucci, p. 322."

CHAPTER VI

THE EMPIRE AND THE FRANKS

WE have become acquainted with the internal decline of the Empire from the death of Justinian to the fall of Maurice, we have followed the course of the wars with Persia and witnessed the depredations of the Avars and Slaves in the Balkan peninsula, and we have seen how the Lombards wrested half of the Italian peninsula from its Roman lords. We must now learn the little that is to be known of the relations of the Empire to the Merovingian kings of Gaul; and our evidence, although fragmentary, is quite sufficient to show not only that the Roman Empire still maintained its position as the first state in Europe, and that New Rome was regarded as the centre of civilisation, but that the Merovingians still acknowledged a sort of theoretical relation of dependence on the Emperors.

Chlotar, son of Chlodwig, survived his brothers, and was sole king of Gaul for a short time before his death. He died in 561, and his four sons, Sigibert, Chilperic, Charibert, and Gunthramn, divided Gaul into four kingdoms,[1] even as their father and uncles had divided it fifty years before after the death of Chlodwig. In 574 Sigibert, who ruled in Austrasia (formerly the kingdom of Theoderic), sent an embassy to Justin.[2] The two envoys, Warmar a Frank and Firminus a Gallo-Roman

---

[1] Chilperic was allotted the north-eastern kingdom of Soissons (the original kingdom of his father Chlotar I.); Sigibert received Austrasia (chief towns, Remi and Mettis); Charibert received Neustria, the kingdom of Paris (including Aquitania); while Gunthramn ruled in Burgundia. Sigibert's kingdom also included Provincia and some territory (especially the city of Arverni) between Aquitaine and Burgundy (Gregory of Tours, *Hist. Franc.* iv. 22).

[2] Gregory of Tours, iv. 40. Sigibert died in 575. Charibert had died in 567 or 570.

of Auvergne, sailed to Constantinople, and were successful in obtaining from Justin what their master sought; what this was we are not informed. In the following year they returned to Gaul.

Some years later, probably at the end of 578 after the death of Justin, Chilperic sent ambassadors to New Rome. The object of this embassy was, I conjecture, to congratulate the new Emperor Tiberius on his accession. The ambassadors did not return to the court of Chilperic until the year 581; the delay seems to have been partly due to a shipwreck which they suffered near Agatha, on the coast of Spain. They brought back gold coins, each weighing no less than a pound, sent by the munificent Tiberius as a present to Chilperic. On the obverse was an image of the Emperor with the legend, round the edge, TIBERII CONSTANTINI PERPETVI AVGVSTI, while on the reverse were represented a chariot and charioteer, with GLORIA ROMANORVM. These coins and many other ornaments, which the envoys had brought, were shown by Chilperic to the historian Gregory of Tours.[1]

It is remarkable that, while Chilperic and Sigibert thus maintained friendly relations with the Empire, we never hear of Gunthramn sending embassies to Constantinople. Now, the interests of Gunthramn and the interests of the lords of Austrasia collided. When Sigibert died, his son Childebert was a mere child, and his widow Brunhilda carried on the government. Brunhilda was a Visigothic princess, and had received a Roman education; she had, therefore, a leaning towards the Roman Empire, and maintained a friendly intercourse both with New Rome and with Old Rome. Gunthramn was not on good terms with his sister-in-law; presuming on the youth of his nephew and the rule of a woman, he had seized cities which had belonged to Sigibert, and was determined to retain them.

This then is the situation at the accession of Maurice. Brunhilda, the queen of Austrasia, is friendly to the Empire and at enmity with Gunthramn, the king of Burgundia, who maintains apparently no relations with the Empire. It is plain that it would be advantageous for Maurice to have a friend or a vassal in the south of Gaul instead of Gunthramn, and that such a change would also please Brunhilda. Accord-

---

[1] Gregory of Tours, vi. 2. The ambassadors returned in 581, and had been sent *ante triennium ad Tiberium imperatorem.*

ingly, we are not surprised to find that both Maurice and Brunhilda support the enterprise of a pretender to wrest Burgundy from Gunthramn.

This pretender was named Gundovald, and he fancied himself, whether truly or not, to be the son of Chlotar I. He had been born in Gaul, carefully nurtured, and received a liberal education[1]; his hair fell in tresses down his back, as it was worn by sons of kings; and he was presented by his mother to Childebert as the son of Chlotar, and therefore Childebert's nephew; "His father hates him," she said, "so do you take him, because he is your flesh." Then Chlotar sent a message to his brother demanding the boy, and Childebert did not refuse to send him. Gundovald's hair was shorn by the order of his reputed father, who repudiated the relationship. From this time until the death of Chlotar he supported himself by painting the walls and domes of sacred buildings.[2] After the death of Chlotar he found a refuge with Charibert, whom he regarded as his brother. His hair grew long again, but, probably after Charibert's death, Sigibert summoned him to his court, and having caused him to be tonsured,[3] sent him to Köln. Gundovald fled from Köln to Italy, where he was received by the exarch Narses,[4] and married a wife, by whom he had two sons. From Italy he proceeded to Constantinople, where the Emperors Justin and Tiberius accorded him a kind welcome,[5] and he abode there for several years, treated as a royal refugee.

Gunthramn Boso, a general of Gunthramn, king of Burgundy, arrived at Constantinople and informed Gundovald of the situation in Gaul. The only representatives of the house of Chlodwig were the childless Gunthramn, the child Childebert, and Chilperic, whose family was dying out. It seemed an excellent opportunity for Gundovald to claim a share in the heritage of his father Chlotar, and Boso invited him to return

---

[1] Gregory of Tours, vi. 24.

[2] *Ib.* vii. 36 : *Tunc es pictur ille, qui tempore Chlotarii regis per oraturia parietes adque cameras caraxabas ? Caraxare = χαράσσω* here means to paint, in which sense it is used in ix. 5 ; but in viii. 29 it is used in the sense *cavare*. Gundovald went in Gaul by the nickname Ballomer, *see* vii. 14, 36, 38.

[3] I apologise for this barbarous but useful verb.

[4] *Ib.* vi. 24 and vii. 36 (*Narsiti praefecto Italiae*).

[5] *Ib.* vii. 36, *ab imperatoribus susceptus benignissime*,—I presume Justin and Tiberius. The dates of these events are uncertain, and it is possible that Gundovald may not have reached Byzantium until after Justin's death, and that *ab imperatoribus* may refer to the kind reception of Tiberius and subsequent favour shown by Maurice.

to Gaul: "Come," he said, "for all the chief men of the kingdom of King Childebert invite you, and no one has dared to breathe a word against you. For we know that you are the son of Chlotar, and there is left in Gaul none able to rule his kingdom, unless you come." Having assured himself of the good faith of Boso by exacting oaths from him in twelve different sanctuaries,[1] and having bestowed gifts upon him, Gundovald set sail for Massilia, where he was received by the bishop Theodorus.[2] Massilia nominally belonged to both Burgundy and Austrasia, but at this time Gunthramn's power was preponderant there. The sympathies of the bishop, however, were with Brunhilda and Childebert, and he therefore welcomed Gundovald, whom they had invited.

Although no Roman ships or Roman soldiers had accompanied Gundovald from Constantinople to support him in his attempt to establish himself on a throne in Gaul, yet there is no doubt that Maurice looked with favour on his enterprise, and assisted him with ample sums of money. He arrived at Massilia with large treasures,[3] of which the perfidious Boso robbed him. Gunthramn of Burgundy considered the arrival of Boso due to a definite scheme on the part of the Roman Emperor to reduce the kingdom of the Franks under the imperial sway [4]; and he arrested bishop Theodorus on the charge

[1] Gregory of Tours, vii. 36.
[2] *Ib.* and vi. 24.
[3] *Ib.* vii. 36, *thesauros meos abstulit*; vii. 24, "Guntchramnus vero dux cum duce Guntchramni regis res Gundovaldi divisit et secum Arverno detulit inmensum ut ferunt argenti pondus et auri vel reliquarum rerum."
[4] *Ib.* vi. 24: *repotans eum, cur hominem extraneum intromisisset in Galleis, voluisset Francorum regnum imperialibus per haec subdere ditionibus.* See M. Gasquet, *L'empire byzantin et la monarchie franque*, pp. 187, 188. In proof of the connection of Maurice with the expedition of Gundovald, M. Gasquet cites a passage in viii. 2, where Palladius, bishop of Saintes, charged with having taken part in the consecration of the bishop of Dax by the orders of Gundovald, replied, *Non potui aliud facere nisi quae ille qui omnem principatum Galliarum se testabatur accipere imperabat*; which M. Gasquet ingeniously and probably explains of a com-

mission given by Maurice to Gundovald. M. Gasquet also discusses the numerous coins of Maurice which have been found in the cities of the Rhone. It was usual to coin money with the image of the Emperor in Gaul under the Merovingians, but it is remarkable that while no coins of Tiberius have been found, only one of Justin, only one of Heraclius, and three of Phocas, we should have more than thirty of Maurice (from Marseilles, Arles, Vienne, Viviers, Valence, Uzès). M. Gasquet thinks that these were coined by Gundovald; his Austrasian allies allowed him to have them struck in their mints at Viviers and Uzès, while at the other towns he compelled the officials of Gunthramn's mints to work for him (p. 191). The abundance of these coins M. Gasquet explains by Gundovald's finding it necessary to coin immediately some of the nuggets which he had brought from Constantinople.

that he co-operated in this scheme by receiving the "stranger" Gundovald.

From Marseilles Gundovald proceeded to Avignon, where he was received by the Patrician Mummolus, who embraced his cause. But Boso, having betrayed the man whom he had invited to Gaul, and robbed him of his treasures, returned to his loyalty to Gunthramn, and led an army against Mummolus. The Burgundians, however, were vanquished, and Gundovald, who had withdrawn to an island on the sea-coast, returned to the city of Avignon. Two important dukes, Desiderius and Bladastes, embraced the pretender's cause; and after Chilperic's death, in 584, the arms of Gundovald and his supporters won many important towns in south-western Gaul, including Tolosa and Burdigala. But his success depended ultimately upon the support of Austrasia, and when Childebert made peace with Gunthramn the cause of Gundovald was lost. He was deserted by his adherents, and delivered by Mummolus into the hands of Gunthramn's army. Boso killed him by hurling a stone at his head, and his corpse was treated with contumely by the soldiers.[1] Such was the end of the pretender Gundovald, who seems to have been commissioned by the Emperor Maurice to wrest southern Gaul from Gunthramn in somewhat the same way as the great Theodoric was commissioned by Zeno to wrest Italy from Odovacar.

The peace between Gunthramn and Childebert did not interfere with the relations between the court of Metz and the court of Byzantium. Maurice sought the help of the Austrasian forces against the Lombards of Italy, and for that purpose sent fifty thousand solidi to Childebert or Brunhilda.[2] He also adopted Childebert as a son, even as Justinian had adopted Theudebert. Childebert crossed the Alps with a large army, but the Lombards hastened to submit themselves before he had time to strike a blow, and induced him with gifts and promises of loyalty to return to his kingdom. When Maurice heard that he had made peace with the Lombards he sent

---

[1] At Convenae (Comminges), where he was besieged. Count Ollo of Bourges called out, "Behold your Ballomer, who says he is the brother and the son of a king" (Greg. Tur. vii. 38). The sons of Gundovald were in Spain, cf. ix. 28.

[2] *Ib.* vi. 42 : *Ab imperatore autem Mauricio ante hos annos quinquaginta milia soledorum acceperat, ut Langobardus de Italia extruderit.* As *ante hos annos* means before 584, Maurice's communication with Childebert must have been very soon after his accession.

ambassadors to demand back the money from Childebert, who had not fulfilled his part of the bargain; but Childebert, confiding in his strength, did not even deign to reply.[1]

No less than four times did the king of Austrasia, urged by the importunities of his "father" the Emperor Maurice, set forth against the lords of northern Italy, but each time he accomplished nothing. In the year 586, two years after his first expedition, the incessant demands of the imperial envoys[2] that he should either perform his promise or repay the money, induced him to lead an army against Italy; but dissensions among the generals compelled him to return, probably before he had reached the Alps, and he made peace with Autharis, king of the Lombards, to whom he also promised his sister Chlotsuinda in marriage. But in 588 he promised the same lady to Reccared, king of the Goths, who had been converted recently to the Catholic faith, and determined once more to cross the Alps and co-operate with the exarch of Ravenna in driving the Lombards from Italy.[3] This time the Lombards and Franks met in battle, and the forces of Childebert suffered a terrible defeat.[4]

The letter of Maurice, in which he reproaches Childebert for his half-heartedness after this failure, is preserved,[5] and Childebert again crossed the Alps in 590 with an army commanded by no fewer than twenty dukes.[6] The fourth expedition was little more successful than the other three. The Romans failed to co-operate with the Franks; the Lombards diligently avoided hazarding a battle; and ultimately disease broke out in the army of Childebert, and compelled him to return to Transalpine Gaul.

But the question of warring together against the Lombards was not the only cause of the embassies which passed between the courts of New Rome and Austrasia. Childebert had a sister, Ingundis, who married Hermenigild, son of Leovigild, king of the Visigoths. Ingundis and her husband were adherents of the Catholic faith, and they both endured persecu-

---

[1] Gregory of Tours, "nec responsum quidem pro hac re voluit reddere."

[2] *Ib.* viii. 18: "compellentibus missis imperialibus, qui aurum quod anno superiore datum fuerat requirebat." See Johannes Biclarensis, *Chron.* 586 A.D.

[3] Greg. ix. 25 : *cum ejus consilio eos*

ab Italia removerit.

[4] *Ib. tantaque ibi fuit stragis de Francorum exercitu ut olim simile non recolatur.*

[5] Bouquet, *Historiens des Gaules et de la France,* iv. p. 86 (lxiii.)

[6] Gregory, x. 3.

tion at the hands of the Arian king. It was in vain that they
placed themselves under the protection of the " Republic " in
southern Spain; Leovigild captured Hermenigild and threw
him into prison.[1] Ingundis, with her infant son Athanagild,
resolved to seek at New Rome[2] the protection which the Republic
could not afford her at Seville (Hispalis). She died on her
journey, but Athanagild reached Byzantium and was reared
as a Roman by the care of Maurice. What ultimately became
of this Visigothic prince is not known, but in the year 590
we find his grandmother Brunhilda, herself originally a Visigothic princess, and his uncle Childebert begging Maurice to
send the boy to Gaul. Maurice probably regarded him as a
useful hostage for the loyalty of the Austrasian king; but
though we have the letters of Brunhilda and Childebert concerning the restitution of Athanagild, the reply of Maurice has
not been preserved. Childebert left no stone unturned to
induce Maurice to comply with his wish. He wrote not only
to Maurice himself, but to all the persons at Constantinople
who possessed influence at court, including Paul the Emperor's
father,[3] Theodore the master of offices, John the quaestor,
Magnus the curator (of the palace), Italica a patrician lady,
Venantius a patrician. Moreover, Brunhilda wrote both to
Maurice and to the Empress Anastasia.[4] We have also the
letters of Brunhilda and Childebert to Athanagild. All these
epistles were carried to New Rome by ambassadors, of whom
the spatharius Gripo seems to have been the chief,[5] and the
tone of this correspondence illustrates the lofty position
which the Roman Emperor held in the eyes of the western
nations. The majesty of the Imperator was still considered
something far higher than all German royalties. Childebert's
letter to Maurice begins thus: " The King Childebert to the
glorious pious perpetual renowned triumphant Lord, ever
Augustus, my father Maurice, Imperator." [6] The Emperor, on

---

[1] *See* vol. i. Bk. iv. pt. i. cap. vii.
ad fin.

[2] So Gregory of Tours, viii. 28, *ad
ipsum principem.* He also states that
Ingundis died in Africa. The notice
of Paul the Deacon (*Hist. Lang.* iii. 21)
is discordant. According to Paul, she
was on her way to Gaul and on the
Spanish march fell in with soldiers,

who took her to Sicily, where she died.

[3] Bouquet, iv. p. 83 *sqq.*

[4] *Ib.* p. 83, liii.

[5] *See* Gregory of Tours, x. 2, but
the names of the ambassadors in
Gregory and those mentioned in Childebert's letter are different, except that of
Gripo.

[6] Bouquet, p. 82, xlix.

the other hand, adopts the following form of address, which may be given in the original Latin [1] :—

"In nomine Domini nostri Dei Jesu Christi Imperator Caesar Flavius Mauricius Tiberius fidelis in Christo mansuetus maximus beneficus pacificus Alamannicus Goticus Anticus Alanicus Wandalicus Herulicus Gypedicus [Gepaedicus] Africus pius felix inclytus victor ac triumphator semper Augustus Childeberto viro glorioso regi Francorum."

Like Justin II, Maurice adopts all the pompous titles of his great predecessor Justinian ; they were part of the inheritance. He is fully conscious that he is the greatest sovereign in Europe, or even in the world, and the kings of the West acknowledge that they owe him homage and deference as Roman Emperor. In the economy of the Empire the king of the Franks is only a *vir gloriosus.*

[1] Bouquet, p. 88, lxv.

CHAPTER VII

IT will not be inappropriate to give some account of the Greek language as it was spoken by the Romans of the fifth and sixth centuries and written by their historians. It is to be observed that in the year 400, when Gaul and Spain were still Roman, the Greek-speaking people in the Empire were in a minority, and the official language of the Empire was still purely Latin. In the year 500, when not only Gaul and Spain, but Africa and even Italy (practically if not theoretically) had been lost, the Empire was a realm of Hellenic speech with the exception of Illyricum, and though Latin was still the official language, the Emperors often issued their constitutions in Greek. When Africa, Italy, and the western islands were recovered, the Latin element was once more considerable, but not so considerable as the Greek. Justinian, although Latin was his native tongue, as he often states with a certain pride, issued most of his constitutions, which were to have effect in the Greek-speaking part of the Empire, in the Greek language. An official of the civil service in the sixth century complains that a knowledge of Latin is no longer as valuable as it used to be, inasmuch as it is being superseded by Greek in official documents. By the end of the sixth century Latin had ceased to be the imperial tongue.

This disuse of Latin had a considerable effect on the vocabulary of the Greek language. Official or technical Latin terms, for which there were no equivalents ready to hand, had already made their way into Greek speech, but no one would have ventured to use them in writing without an apology. But once they were regularly employed in the imperial constitutions, they became as it were accredited; they began to lose their foreign savour, and were no longer looked on as strangers; prose-writers no.longer scrupled to use them.

But we must carefully distinguish between three kinds of Greek. There was (1) the vulgar spoken language, from which modern Greek is derived. Its idiom varied in different places; the Greek spoken in Antioch, for example, differed to some extent from that spoken in Byzantium or that spoken in Alexandria. Antiochian Greek may have been influenced by Syriac, as Syriac was certainly influenced by Greek. There was (2) the spoken language of the educated, which, under the influence of the vulgar tongue, tended to degenerate. There was (3) the conventional written language, which endeavoured to preserve the traditions of Hellenistic prose from the changes which affected the oral "common dialect." We may take these three kinds of Greek in order.

(1) Of the vulgar dialect, such as it was spoken at Byzantium in the sixth century, a specimen has been preserved in the dialogue which took place in the hippodrome between the Emperor and the green faction shortly before the revolt of Nika.[1] From this and from stray words which are preserved by historians or inscriptions, we see that it is already far on its way to becoming what is called Romaic; in fact it was already called Romaic. A sixth-century inscription in Nubia proves that the word νηρόν was then used for "water," whence comes the modern Greek νερό. A mule is βορδώνης instead of ἡμίονος, and σγανδάριν or γανδάριν is apparently used for an ass. A standard is βάνδον, an iron-headed club is δίστριν, baggage is τοῦλδον, and σκούλκα is used for a guard or watch. Besides the strange vocabulary, derived partly from Latin and partly from local Greek words, changes are taking place in the grammar and syntax. Terminations in -ιον, for example, are becoming corrupted to -ιν: the perfect tense and many prepositions and particles are falling into disuse.

---

[1] Another specimen is found in Theophanes, 6093 A.M. The Greens and Blues arrayed a man resembling Maurice in a black cloak (σαγίον μαῦρον), and having crowned him with a crown of onions (ἀπὸ σκόρδων), set him on an ass and mocked him thus: εὔρηκε τὴν δαμαλίδα ἀπαλήν καὶ ὡς τὸ καινὸν ἀλεκτόριν ταύτῃ πεπήδηκεν καὶ ἐποίησε παιδία ὡς τὰ ξυλοκούκουδα· καὶ οὐδεὶς τολμᾷ λαλῆσαι ἀλλ' ὅλους ἐφίμωσεν· ἅγιέ μου, ἅγιε φοβερὲ καὶ δυνατέ, δὸς αὐτῷ κατὰ κρανίου, ἵνα μὴ ὑπεραίρεται· κἀγώ σοι τὸν βοῦν τὸν μέγαν προσαγάγω εἰς εὐχήν.

(2) That the language of educated people was different from that of the vulgar, and approximated to the written language, is proved by a passage in Menander.[1] It was, nevertheless, subject to the same tendencies, as is fully demonstrated by the fact that these very tendencies soon affected written prose and changed Hellenistic into Byzantine literature. Graecised Latin words must have been used even more by the higher classes than by the lower; a superelegant writer at the beginning of the seventh century employs φαμιλία (*familia*) without a line of apology. These Latinisms were chiefly adopted in matters appertaining to Roman law, to the imperial administration, or to warfare. There were also many new colloquial usages of old words, which the purism of Procopius or Agathias would not have countenanced. The adjective ὡραῖος, for instance, meant nothing more than "fair" or "pretty"; πονῶ meant "I am ill," and κινδυνεύω was used in the special sense of being sick unto death; κινῆσαι had the intransitive signification of breaking up or moving on; ἐθεραπεύθην meant "I was pleased."[2] It was some time, doubtless, before unsightly forms like ἔβαλα were adopted from the mouths of the common people, but the perfect and pluperfect tenses were soon relegated to the speech of the pedant and the prose of the man of letters; the old variety of particles and prepositions was replaced by a baldness and monotony of expression which correspond to the more simple constructions that came into use; ἐάν was used with the indicative mood.

(3) It has been already pointed out that the Greek historians of the fifth and sixth centuries wrote in a traditional prose style, handed down by an unbroken series of Hellenistic writers from Polybius, and, although it underwent some modifications, differing less from the style of Polybius than the style of Polybius differs from the style of Xenophon. Olympiodorus seems to have been the only writer who ventured to introduce words and phrases from the spoken language, and thus his writings may be considered, in point of style, a mild anticipation of the chronicles of Malalas and Theophanes.

---

[1] Menander, fr. 12 (*F. H. G.* iv. p. 217); he professes to have given the words of the Roman ambassador as they were spoken, not translated ἐς τὸ Ἀττικώτερον.

[2] *See* the monograph of G. Sotiriadis on *Johannes von Antiochia*, in which the use of phrases like this is applied as a criterion to test the genuine fragments of Johannes.

Procopius and Agathias and Menander could not, indeed, avoid the necessity of sometimes introducing technical or official Latin words which had become current in spoken Greek, but they always considered themselves bound to add an apologetic "so-called" or "to use the Latin expression."[1] As a rule, however, they employ periphrases, and avoid the use of such titles as praetorian prefect, magister militum, or comes largitionum. Even the word "indiction" is considered un-dignified, and rendered by such a circumlocution as "the fifteen-year circuit." It would be interesting, if we had more data, to trace the reciprocal influences exerted on each other by the spoken language of the higher classes and the con-ventional prose.

This conventional prose never ceased to be written until the fifteenth century. Laconicus Chalcocondyles and George Phrantzes are, as far as their Greek is concerned, lineal descendants of Polybius. There was indeed a break from the middle of the seventh century to the end of the eighth, from Theophylactus to Nicephorus the Patriarch, but even during this period of historiographical inactivity the conventional Greek was employed by theological writers.[2]

It is natural that in the sixth century, when the Roman Empire was losing its Latin appearance and assuming a Greek complexion in language, and in other respects too, the word "Roman" should have become elastic and ambiguous. In Greek writers 'Ρωμαῖοι generally means all the subjects of the Empire; but it is also used of the inhabitants of Old Rome; and it is even used of the ancient Romans as opposed to the "modern" Romans of the Empire. All these usages will be found in Procopius. Again, the expression "Romaic lan-guage" may signify one of two things. It sometimes means Latin and sometimes it means Greek. In the former case it

---

[1] For example, ῥαιφερενδάριον τῇ Λατίνων φωνῇ τὴν τιμὴν ταύτην καλοῦσι Ρωμαῖοι (Procopius, i. 256, ed. Bonn). Heaps of examples may be found in turning over the pages of Procopius. He uses, however, a few words, for example πατρίκιος, without deeming it necessary to explain. Olympiodorus had used δισιγνάτος and ῥήξ without ceremony.

[2] *E.g.* John of Damascus. *See* Mr. Freeman's very interesting article in the *Hellenic Journal* (vol. iii.), "On some Points in the later History of the Greek Language." He has not, I think, sufficiently realised that the conven-tional prose style continued to be written by people like Theodore Studita, Ignatius, etc., during the period be-tween Menander and Leo Diaconus. The chief inaugurator of the Renaissance of Hellenism in the eleventh century was Michael Psellus, the stylistic father of Anna Comnena and Zonaras.

is opposed to Greek, whether spoken or written; in the latter
case it is spoken Greek opposed to written Greek. Written
Greek is called the "language of the Hellenes"; and, as applied
to language, the word "Hellenic" has escaped the opprobrious
religious meaning which had become attached to the name
"Hellên." Procopius for the most part speaks of "Latin" and
not of "Romaic"; the latter term was fast becoming fixed in
its application to the language which was spoken at New
Rome. It should be noticed that Romaic never came to be
synonymous with Hellenic; writers could never lose the consciousness of the vast gulf which separated the conventional
language of written prose, which they often fondly imagined
to be Attic, from the language of daily life. By the end of the
sixth century Romaic has become equivalent to the language
of the *Romaioi*; it is no longer used for the language of
the *Romani*. This is apparent from its use in Theophylactus Simocatta. We are often startled in the pages of this
writer by meeting the word Λατῖνοι, and reading that the
Latins were carrying on operations in Mesopotamia or Thrace.
The affected historian uses the word as synonymous with
'Ρωμαῖοι. The Latin name had once meant the *populus
Romanus*; in Theophylactus it meant the λαὸς 'Ρωμαϊκός.[1]
Virgil or Livy might have spoken of Latins warring on the
Euphrates or the Danube; at a much later time we are accus-
tomed to speak of the Latins at Constantinople or in Palestine;
but it is strange to find the "Latins" commanded by Priscus
and Philippicus—names indeed that suggest Old Rome—at
the end of the sixth century. But if Theophylactus uses
Latin in a forced sense as the equivalent of Romaic, he uses
Romaic in its natural sense and not as an equivalent of Latin.
And when a word which he calls Romaic happens to be of
Latin origin, he does not desire to convey that fact to the
reader, but only to indicate that it is a word of the vulgar
language, which cannot be introduced into prose by a dignified
writer without an apologetic explanation.[2]

[1] I use λαός, not δῆμος: because
λαός is the Romaic word which was
used of the army, and when Theophylactus speaks of *Latins* he always refers
to the soldiers.

[2] For example, τοῦλδον, baggage, the
old French *toudis*, is thus explained:

ἀποσκευὴ ἦν σύνηθες 'Ρωμαίοις τῇ
ἐπιχωρίῳ φωνῇ τοῦλδον ἀποκαλεῖν (ii. 4,
1); we read of the διαφρουρά, ἣν σκούλκαν
σύνηθες τῇ πατρίῳ φωνῇ 'Ρωμαίοις ἀποκαλεῖν (vi. 9, 14); so βάνδον (*bandum*, a
standard), iii. 4, 4. When Procopius
spoke of the standard which Romaioi

It is interesting to observe how, while Greek words were told off to serve as the equivalents for Latin words con-noting purely Roman things or relations, in other cases the Latin words were naturalised and assumed a Greek garb. Thus at a very early stage of the relations between Rome and Greece ὕπατος became the technical word for consul, and ἀνθύπατος for proconsul. ἔπαρχος was adopted to express prefect, and ἐπαρχία was used in the double meaning of pro-vince or prefecture; praeses was officially rendered by ἡγεμών. On the other hand, comes was introduced as κόμης, and de-clined as a Greek noun (gen. κόμητος); the comes sacrarum largitionum was called at Constantinople ὁ κόμης τῶν σακρῶν

call βάνδον (vol. i. p. 415, ed. Bonn) he probably meant to say that bandum was a Latin word; but Theophylactus, when he says the same thing, means that it was a Romaic word, a word of the spoken language, perhaps of non-Hellenic derivation. Similar explana-tions are given by Theophylactus in similar formulae of δίστριον "an iron club," σκρίβων "a scribe." We read of Musokios "the rex, as he is called in the language of the barbarians"; Theophy-lactus did not even know that rex was a Latin word (vi. 9, 1, τὸν λεγόμενον ῥῆγα τῇ τῶν βαρβάρων φωνῇ); we also hear of τὸν λεγόμενον κόστον (costum, spikenard, vii.13, 6). He does not, however, scruple to use πραίτωρ (i. 4, 6), φαμιλία (vi. 5, 15); the use of καβαλάριος in the letter of Chosroes is not remarkable, as it was the composition of Chosroes (who wrote it Ἑλληνικοῖς γράμμασιν), not of the historian. The only place where he talks of the Latin tongue is i. 3, 7, when he is explaining σκρίβων ὃν σκρίβωνα τῇ Λατινίδι φωνῇ Ῥωμαῖοι κατο-νομάζουσιν, but I question whether Λατινίδι means more than Ῥωμαϊκῇ: for Theophylactus was evidently ignorant of Latin, and in viii. 5, 10 he speaks of ὃν σκρίβωνα εἴωθε τὰ πλήθη ἀποκαλεῖν. This is the key to his use of the ex-pression "Romaic language"; it is the language of τὰ πλήθη, to whom he applies the name Λατῖνοι as well as Ῥωμαῖοι: cf. ii. 2, 5, οὓς Σαρακηνοὺς εἴθιστο Λατίνοις ἀποκαλεῖν.

If any further proofs are needed of what Theophylactus meant by Romaic, it may be noticed that when Priscus addressed the army (τοῖς Ῥωμαίοις) in their native tongue (vi. 7, 9), he spoke

in Romaic, not in Latin; and when we read of him as τὰ Θεμιστοκλέους Ῥωμαϊκῶς ἀττικίζοντος, the phrase seems to mean that he avoided colloquial ex-pressions and grammar,—he made a dignified speech.

In Maurice's Strategic (Στρατηγικόν, often wrongly called Tactics; see above, Bk. iv. pt. i. cap. xii. p. 18) we meet with an immense number of Latin mili-tary terms slightly altered to suit the Greek language, or not altered at all. For example, ἀκίαι, acies (i. cap. 5); δηποτάτοι (who follow the army and re-move the wounded), ἀντικένσωρες (pre-cede in marches, select routes, etc.), μίνσωρες (mensores), καντάτωρ, etc. (i. 3); ὀπισθοτελίνων, ἀντελίνων (i. 2), etc. ῥόγα=pay, occurs in Maurice (i. 2, χρυσικῆς ῥόγας), and he tells us that τοῦλδον (see above) includes slaves. Latin was still used in words of com-mand (iii. caps. 2 and 4), such as largiter ambula, ad latus stringe, silentium, move! sta! cede! transmuta! also torna! and the curious mina! to which ἔλα corresponds in the treatise on tactics of Leo VI (cf. Festus, Aga-sones, equos agentes, id est minantes).

Maurice expressly says in his preface (which he begins by asking the blessing of the Holy Trinity) that he has no concern for κόμπος ῥημάτων.

[σκοῦλκα "a watch" (σκουλκάτωρ "a spy") is Latin (= ex-*culca); we can trace the original in Walachian a se culca and Italian coricarsi "to lie down" (perhaps from collocare se). It is perhaps worth conjecturing that τοῦλδον came from *tullum, a possible past part. of tollo, tuli, in the sense portatum.]

λαργιτιώνων : and as for the *comes rerum privatarum* he received the name κόμης τῶν πριβάτων. *Dux* became δούξ, and a secretary was called by a word of curious aspect, ἀσηκρῆτις, which is merely the familiar *a secretis*. The *magister officiorum* is ὁ μάγιστρος τῶν ὀφφικίων : but στρατηγός is commonly used for *magister militum*.[1] *Castrum, castellum, velum, familia, follis* had become thoroughly naturalised words in the " Romaic " vocabulary of the sixth century, κάστρον, κάστελλον, βῆλον, φαμιλία, φόλλις : μάππα (*mappa*) as a technical word in the hippodrome, ἰνδικτιών (*indictio*) for the official chronological reckoning, σκρίβων for scribe, φόρον for *forum*, were equally familiar. The Latin words *tu vincas!* (τού βίγκας) were an exclamation equivalent to " God save the king ! " in Constantinople. These are a few examples taken at random to illustrate how Latin words made their way into the Greek tongue.

The treatment of Latin verbs in *-ari* (*-ari*) deserves to be specially noticed. They were adopted with the Greek termination *-εύω* : thus *praedari* appears as πραιδεύω, *ordinare* as ὀρδινεύω, *applicare* as ἀπλικεύω.[2] This reminds us of the German termination *-iren*, by which French and Latin verbs are Germanised (*imponiren, frisiren,* etc.) ; in fact, Latin *dirigere* produces in German *dirigiren*, just as it produced in Romaic δηριγεύω.

The Greek adjective Ῥωμαῖος was never replaced by the Latin adjective *Romanus* ; in fact, in later times Ῥωμανός was used in a special sense to denote the Romans who lived on the coasts of Dalmatia and maintained their independence against the Slaves. The Greek βασιλεύς was adopted as the equivalent of *Imperator*, and became confined to this sense, at all events after the overthrow of the Persian monarchy in the seventh century ; and the Latin *rex* (ῥήξ) was the word applied to barbarian monarchs. But αὐτοκράτωρ was also used as an official title of the Emperor ; while the Persian king and other foreign powers generally called him " Caesar." At the foundation of the Empire the appellation Augustus was rendered in

---

[1] στρατηγός, also translated *praetor*. When Justinian set a praetor over reconquered Sicily, his Greek name was στρατηγός.

[2] The aspirate seems to have come

from some connection with ἁπλούς, but it must have soon fallen off, as there are no (pronounced) aspirates in modern Greek. ὀρδινεύω occurs in Maurice's *Strategic,* i. cap. 5.

Greek by Σεβαστός, but in later times Αὔγουστος appears to have become the current term; Justinian uses Αὔγουστος ἀεισέβαστος in official documents. The Empress was always called Αὔγουστα.

The fates of the words Hellene (῞Ελλην) and barbarian (βάρβαρος) are extremely curious. Originally they were conjugate terms; the world was divided into Hellenes and barbarians. The course of history, the diffusion of Christianity, and the influence of the Roman Empire brought it about that each became the conjugate of something quite different. ῞Ελλην came to mean a non-christian or a pagan, and thus was opposed to Χριστιανός : while βάρβαρος came to be opposed to ῾Ρωμαῖος. It will be remembered that in the plays of Plautus, taken from Greek originals, a Roman was spoken of as a barbarian. It may be noticed, as a curious freak of usage, that the Latin word for pagan, *paganus*, made its way into the Greek language, but in a different sense; παγανικός was used of secular as opposed to sacred or holyday things, and especially of everyday as opposed to festal apparel.[1]

When ῞Ελλην received its new theological meaning, what word, it may be asked, was used to denote the Greeks as opposed to the Latins? The answer seems to be that the need of such a word was not much felt, and whenever occasion demanded there was the word Γραῖκος (*Graecus*) to fall back on. But all the Greeks were ῾Ρωμαῖοι, they formed no nation; and no subject of the Empire belonged to a class called "Greek"; he belonged to such and such a province, or to such and such a city.

After Justinian the Roman Emperors ceased to speak either in private or in public life the tongue that was spoken at Old Rome. The official language had already become practically Greek; we can trace this tendency in the Code of Theodosius, where we find no vestige of the purism of Claudius, who would not admit a Greek word in an edict; but in the Code of Justinian it is no longer a mere tendency. Yet this official Greek is full of Latinisms, and until the last day of the Roman or Romaic Empire memories of its origin from Latin Rome survived in its language.

---

[1] It often occurs in Constantine Porphyrogennetos, *de Caerimoniis*. Maurice (*Strategic*, i. cap. 6) uses παγανός in the sense of *civilian*. He uses the Greek συντελεστής in much the same sense—a rustic or colon, opposed to στρατιώτης. συντελεσταί is used in laws for landed proprietors (χωρίων κύριοι).

CHAPTER VIII

LITERATURE OF THE SIXTH CENTURY

WHEN the gods of Greece were hurled from heaven by the God of Christianity, Athens was left for two hundred years as a " hill retired " on which their votaries could stand apart " in high thoughts elevate," reasoning of Providence and fate. But this inner circle could not resist for ever the atmosphere that encompassed it; this quietistic negation of the prevailing spirit could not last. And so, when Justinian in 529 A.D. commanded that the schools of Athens should be closed, we can hardly suppose that he anticipated by many years their natural death.

Proclus must be looked on as the last link in the chain of Greek philosophy; he was the last philosophical genius, the last originator of a system. But the seven professors who were ranged round the deathbed of philosophy, and who, despairing of pursuing their studies conveniently within the Empire, betook themselves to Persia, have won a place in the recollection of posterity by their curious and somewhat pathetic experiences. All seven were Asiatics, and had a high reputation; the most celebrated were Simplicius of Cilicia and Damascius of Syria, a Neoplatonist.[1] Exaggerated rumours had represented to them Chosroes as a sort of royal philosopher, if not the ideal of Plato, yet equal at least to Julian or Marcus Aurelius, and they formed golden dreams of living in an enlightened kingdom, a place like heaven, in which thieves do

---

[1] Agath. ii. 30 : οὗτοι δὴ οὖν ἄπαντες τὸ ἄκρον ἄωτον κατὰ τὴν ποίησιν τῶν ἐν τῷ καθ' ἡμᾶς χρόνῳ φιλοσοφησάντων. The other philosophers were Isidorus of Gaza, Eulampius of Phrygia, Priscian of Lydia, Hermeias, and Diogenes of Phoenicia.

not break through and steal.[1]   They were disappointed.   Among
the subjects of Chosroes they found human nature as near the
ground as in the lands which they had left, and on the throne
they found a man who affected higher culture, but was really
ignorant.[2]   Disillusionised, they returned to the Roman Empire;
it was more tolerable to them to be put to death among Roman
christians than to be lords among the Persian fire-worshippers.[3]
Chosroes, however, rendered them a service.   In the peace of
532 A.D. he bargained with Justinian for the personal safety
of the seven philosophers, whom he could not persuade to
remain at his court.

A thinker who deserves the name of a philosopher, although
he wrote professedly in the interests of christian theology, was
Johannes Philoponus, who lived in the sixth century and was
a contemporary of Simplicius.[4]   In his early years he wrote a
book against Aristotle's doctrine that the world is eternal, to
which attack Simplicius wrote a reply.   He also composed a
work, still extant, on the eternity of the world, arguing against
the demonstrations of Proclus.   The noteworthy point is that
he met the pagan theories on their own ground, and attempted
to construct the world from the indications of reason alone,
without help from revelation.   His position was that reason
of itself leads to the doctrines of Christianity.   In another
direction, however, he propagated nominalistic opinions which
endangered a cardinal dogma of the Church.   His logical
theories may be considered as a sort of link between the
nominalism of Antisthenes the Cynic and the nominalism of
the medieval school of Roscelin; and he consistently applied
his logic to the Trinity in a way that threatened the divine
unity.   He may be looked upon as a forerunner of the christian philosophers of the Middle Ages, such as Michael
Psellus in the East and the schoolmen in the West.   He
introduced the application of Aristotelianism to Christianity.

The *Christian Topography* of Cosmas Indicopleustes, an
Egyptian monk who visited the East at the beginning of

---

[1] καὶ οὔτε φῶρες χρημάτων οὔτε ἁρπα-
γες ἀναφύονται.

[2] Chosroes was afterwards the dupe
of an ignorant impostor, Uranius (554
A.D.), who pretended to be a philosopher.

[3] One thing to which the philosophers especially objected, according to
Agathias (ii. 31), was τὴν τῶν μίξεων
κακοδαιμονίαν.

[4] His date is often wrongly placed in
the seventh century.

Justinian's reign, is interesting not only for the light which it throws on the state of southern Asia, but also for its cosmological speculations. The problem was to explain the position of the earth in the universe and determine its shape, so as not to conflict with foregone theological suppositions. The rising and setting of the sun were of course the chief difficulties. The notion of Lactantius, Augustine, and Chrysostom touching the Antipodes was that it was a place where the grass grew downwards and the rain fell up. Cosmas looked on the earth as a flat parallelogram whose length from east to west was twice as great as its breadth from north to south. This parallelogram, according to his view, is enclosed by walls on which the firmament rests, and the sun and the moon and the stars move underneath this firmament. In the northern part of the earth there is a very high mountain, round which the sun and other heavenly bodies move; this explains day and night, as the mountain conceals the sun and stars from view when they are on the other side.[1] In the same plane as the earth, but beyond its confines, lies the place where man dwelled before the Deluge.[2]

The difference in spirit between the fifth century and the sixth is perhaps most evident in the sphere of history.[3] As a rule, the historians of the fifth century are either pronounced christians or pronounced pagans; as a rule the historians of the sixth century are neither pronounced christians nor pronounced pagans. Procopius and Agathias, nominally Christians, allow christian conceptions to have no influence over

---

[1] This theory is taken from Patrinius.

[2] Cosmas begins his work, which consists of twelve books, in true monkish style: "I, the sinner and wretch, open my stammering stuttering lips" . . . ἀνοίγω τὰ μογιλάλα καὶ βραδύγλωσσα χείλη ὁ ἁμαρτωλὸς καὶ τάλας ἐγώ. Students of the history of the Epigoni owe a debt of gratitude to Cosmas for having copied and inserted in his work part of a Greek inscription on a marble throne at Adule, set up by Ptolemy III after his great eastern expedition (cf. Mahaffy, *Greek Life and Thought*, p. 320).

[3] Between Malchus and Procopius intervened three historians, of whose works fragments remain; Eustathius of Epiphania (who carried his history down to 502, and was utilised afterwards by Evagrius); Hesychius of Miletus, and John of Antioch, both of whom likewise carried down their histories to the reign of Anastasius. On John of Antioch's date, see the work of G. Sotiriadis, *Zur Kritik des Johannes von Antiochia*. These historians fill a gap in the εἱρμός (as Evagrius would say) from Olympiodorus to Theophylactus. Peter of Thessalonica, the patrician whom Justinian employed on embassies to the Ostrogothic and Persian courts, wrote a history of the Roman Empire from the time of Augustus till the time of Julian (or perhaps later). He seems to have been an able and cultured man.

their historical views, and Menander writes in the same spirit.[1]

Procopius of Caesarea,[2] the secretary of Belisarius and the historian of his campaigns, wrote a history of the Persian, Vandalic, and Gothic wars, which, while it is arranged in geographical divisions after the fashion of Appian, has its unity in a central figure, the hero Belisarius. Procopius has been compared both to Herodotus and to Polybius. He has been compared to Herodotus on account of his love of the marvellous, which, however, did not eliminate his love of historical truth, such as he conceived it; and if Herodotus' care for truth can be called in question, that of Procopius can certainly not be doubted, notwithstanding the fact that his friendship with Belisarius has often biassed him. Like Herodotus also, he gives us much ethnographical information. He has been compared to Polybius because he explains the course of history by reference to *Tyche,* Fortune, or to the divinity ($\tau\grave{o}$ $\theta\varepsilon\hat{\iota}o\nu$) that shapes our ends. Tyche continually interferes with the plans of men, and the final cause of their foolish acts is " to prepare the way for Tyche."[3] He attributes envy ($\phi\theta\acute{o}\nu o\varsigma$) to this deity.[4] It would be interesting to know how he conceived the relation of Tyche to the divine principle, and whether he was a sceptic in regard to a scheme or a final cause of the universe. Did he believe that chance corrects chance ?

And yet he professes faith in Christianity. He tells us that he believes that Jesus was the Son of God for two reasons, because he committed no sins, and on account of the miracles which he performed. The second reason is characteristic of a lover of the marvellous. He does not think of questioning the truth of the record; the only question for him is whether the miracles as recorded point to the divinity of the operator. But this acceptance of the christian creed does not affect his views of history. He practically permits the Father, the Son, and the Holy Ghost to rest idly like the gods of Epicurus, careless of mankind; he is not influenced by the christian views of history introduced by Eusebius. In fact Procopius was at

---

[1] Malchus had written in this way. *See* vol. i. p. 328.

[2] The best modern work on Procopius is the monograph of Dahn; the historian of the *Kings of the Germans,* entitled *Procopius von Cäsarea.*

[3] *B. V.* i. 18.

[4] *B. G.* ii. 8.

core, in the essence of his spirit, a pagan; Christianity, assented
to by his lips and his understanding, was alien to his soul, like
a half-known foreign language. He could not think in christian terms; he was not able to handle the new religious
conceptions; he probably felt wonder, rather than satisfaction,
at the joys that come from Nazareth. And we may safely
say that it was just this pagan nature, deeper perhaps than
that of the aggressive Zosimus, that made him such a good
historian. He is almost worthy to be placed beside Ammianus.

He attended Belisarius in his campaigns and kept a diary, from
which he afterwards composed the eight books of his History.
He adopted a geographical arrangement, and so placed the two
Persian wars together, although the Vandalic war and the first
period of the Gothic war intervened. We have thus the record
of an eye-witness who kept a diary, as is especially plain in his
description of the sailing of the expedition against the Vandals.[1]
Of the history of events in which he did not himself assist as
a spectator or actor he gives us scant information. He is not
satisfactory as to the causes of the Gothic war or as to the
intrigues in Constantinople which affected the career of
Belisarius. But these are just the deficiencies to be expected
in an eye-witness who concentrates all his interest on the part
of the drama which he sees himself, and in a contemporary
who is unable to obtain a complete view of the situation.

Procopius is not out of touch with his own age, like Tacitus
or Zosimus; although, on the other hand, he is not enthusiastic
about it, like Polybius or Virgil. He is able to appreciate the
greatness of Justinian, and his ardent admiration of Belisarius
sometimes damages the credit of his statements. The book
on Edifices, which he wrote later than his history, is a monument in honour of Justinian's vast activity, and there is no
reason to consider it an insincere work, although it was
perhaps written to order.

The History of Procopius, which closes with 550 A.D., was
continued by Agathias of Myrrina, a *scholasticus* or lawyer, who
wrote five books embracing the history of seven years (552-
558). They contain an account of the end of the Gothic war

---

[1] Ranke has brought out this very clearly and convincingly. (*Weltgeschichte,*
iv. 2, essay on Procopius.) .

and describe the invasion of Zabergan, but are mainly occupied with the Perso-Colchian wars, and supply us with some important details about early Sassanid history, which the writer obtained from Persian records through the medium of his friend Sergius, who, as an interpreter, was skilled in the Persian language.

Like Procopius, Agathias was a Christian, and, like Procopius, he did not permit his professed religion to influence his historical conceptions. We should never have known from his history that he was not a pagan[1]; but some of his epigrams apprise us of his Christianity. He does not, however, refer events to the leading of Tyche; he usually speaks of the divine principle, τὸ θεῖον, to which he attributes the exercise of retribution. In telling of the plague which destroyed the army of Leutharis in Italy, he observes that some wrongly ascribe it to the corruption of the atmosphere; others, also erroneously, placed its cause in a sudden change from the hardships of war to the luxury of rest and pleasure. The real cause, according to him, was the unrighteousness of the victims, which brought down divine wrath upon their heads.

He has a firm belief in free will, and this is a point of difference between his view and that of Procopius. Procopius emphasises Tyche; Agathias emphasises free will. Speaking of wars, he will ascribe them neither to the divine principle, which is in its nature good and not a friend of wars, nor yet to fate or blind astral influences. "For," he says, "if the power of fate prevail, and men be deprived of the power of volition and free will, we shall have to consider all advice, all arts, all instruction as idle and useless, and the hopes of men who live most righteously will vanish and bear no fruit." He therefore attributes wars to the nature of men, and believes that they will continue to occur as long as the congenital nature of men remains the same.[2]

He professes to have a strict ideal of what history should be. It should be useful for human life, and not merely a bare uncritical (ἀνεξέταστος) relation of events, which would be little

---

[1] An echo of scripture is put in the mouth of Phartazes the Colchian (p. 165, ed. Bonn), "What shall we gain if we annex the whole of Persia and lose our own souls?"

[2] Agathias was a sceptic on the matter of investigating natural phenomena; an interesting subject of research, he says, but it is vain to suppose that we ever get at the truth; it is enough to believe in a divine arrangement.

better than the fables told by women in their bowers over their spinning. It should be true, irrespective of persons. Both he and Procopius are distinctly conscious of the obligation to truth. Agathias blames previous historians for their careless inaccuracy, for their distortion of facts to flatter kings and lords, as if history were not different from an encomium, and for their tendency to revile or disparage the dead.

Agathias, like Thucydides, has a high idea of the vast importance of the age in which he lived. " It happened in my time that great wars broke out unexpectedly in many parts of the world, that movements and migrations of many barbarous nations took place. There have been strange issues to obscure and incredible actions, random turns of the scales of fortune. Races of men have been overthrown, cities enslaved and their inhabitants changed. In a word, all human things have been set in motion. In view of this, it occurred to me that it would not be quite pardonable to leave these mighty and wonderful events, which might prove of profit and use to posterity, unrecorded."

He was not content with his profession. He describes himself, in accents of complaint, sitting from early morn to sunset in the " Imperial Porch" poring over his briefs and legal documents, feeling a grudge against his clients for disturbing him, and still more vexed if clients did not appear, as he depended on the emoluments of his profession for the necessaries of life. He had thus little leisure to devote to literary pursuits, such as writing epigrams or making researches in Persian history ; and literary composition, he tells us, was his favourite occupation.

Menander of Constantinople studied for the bar, but he had as little taste as Agathias—whom he admired and probably knew —for spending his days in the Imperial Porch. As however, unlike Agathias, he had money at his disposal, a profession was not inevitable ; so he cast aside his law books and adopted the idle life of a " man about town."[1] He took an interest in horse-races and the excitement of " the colours," that is the blue and green factions. He was fond of theatrical ballet-dancing, and

---

[1] κεχηνὼς περιενόστουν (*F. H. G.* iv. p. 201). He belonged to the *protectores* or guards, a nominal honour.

he confesses that in the wrestling schools he often stripped off all sense and all sense of decency along with his dress. After this candid confession of wickedness and " wild oats," he informs us that the taste for letters displayed by the Emperor Maurice, who used often to spend a great part of the night in discussing or meditating on questions in poetry and history, infected himself, and caused him to reflect that he might do something better than loiter about. Thus Maurice appears as a lover of literature who not only patronised but stimulated; and this character is confirmed by the testimony of Theophylactus.[1] The only work which the Emperor is known to have composed is the treatise in twelve books on military science. Accordingly, Menander determined to continue the history of Agathias cut short by that writer's death. He carried it down to the last year of Tiberius, 582 A.D., and he formed his style on the model of Agathias. Only fragments of his history remain, but they give us a favourable impression of the writer.

Almost the same period as that covered by Menander was dealt with in the history, also lost, of Theophanes of Byzantium, who began with the year 566 and ended with 581. He wrote in the last years of the sixth century.[2]

Justinian himself was a man of culture, who occupied himself with profound studies without allowing them to relax his firm grip of the helm of State. He presents an example of the polymathy which was characteristic of the sixth and the two preceding centuries, and of which Boethius, as we shall see, was a typical example in the West. He composed treatises on theological controversies[3] which are still extant, but we must suppose that he also patronised literature in general, even

---

[1] viii. 13, 16 : μενοῦνγε λέγεται τὸν Μαυρίκιον φιλοτίμως ἔχειν περὶ τὴν τῶν λόγων μεγαλοπρέπειαν τιμᾶν τε λίαν λαμπρῶς τοὺς ἐνηθληκότας περὶ τὰ κάλλιστα τῶν μαθημάτων.

[2] John of Epiphania, a townsman and relation of the ecclesiastical historian Evagrius, also continued the history of Agathias, and carried his narrative down to the restoration of Chosroes in 591. Fragments of his history remain (Müller, *F. H. G.* iv. p. 272) ; it was utilised by Theophylactus Simocatta. Evagrius, born in 535 or 536 at Epiphania, lived in Antioch as

a lawyer (*scholasticus*), was elevated to the rank of quaestor by Tiberius, and received the δέλτους ὑπάρχων, appointment to a prefecture, from Maurice. His works were (1) panegyric on Maurice, unluckily lost ; (2) a collection of *acta ;* and (3) a collection of letters and decrees, which are no longer extant ; (4) an Ecclesiastical History from 431 to reign of Maurice, which has been preserved and is a valuable source.

[3] He wrote a treatise against the monophysites, and many official letters and manifestos on the "Three Chapter" question (*see* Migne, *Patrol. Gr.* vol. 86).

though on religious grounds he shut up the schools of Athens, whose open paganism was a manifest scandal in the christian world. We know that he engaged the services of writers to compose poems or histories in praise of his own deeds.[1] The book on edifices of Procopius is a work of this kind, and it is possible that the book on offices (περὶ ἀρχῶν) written by Johannes Lydus was partly inspired by Justinian.

As most of the literary men of the time were educated for the legal profession and many of them entered the civil service, it is worth while to give a short biographical account of Johannes (known as *Lydus*, the Lydian), from whose pen three treatises [2] are wholly or partially extant. Born at Philadelphia of noble provincials in easy circumstances, he went to Constantinople in his youth for the purpose of making a career. He learned philosophy, and read Aristotle and Plato under the direction of a pupil of the great Proclus named Agapius, of whom a versifier said in an unmetrical line, " Agapius is the last, but yet the first of all."[3]

He had been for a year a clerk in a civil service office, when he obtained the post of shorthand writer in the staff of his townsman Zoticus of Philadelphia, who had been appointed praetorian prefect. This post proved lucrative. He won 1000 gold solidi (£625) in a single year. A relation, who was in the same office as he, and Zoticus the prefect were useful friends, and did him a good office in procuring him a rich wife, who had a dowry of 100 pound weight in gold and was also remarkable among her sex for her modesty. Johannes wrote an encomium on Zoticus for which he received a golden coin (chrusinos) for every line, which seems a liberal reward to literary merit, and indicates that the bad poets of the time might count on distinguished patronage. Having steadily advanced through all the grades of the service (*cursus officiorum*), in which his excellent knowledge of Latin, a rare accomplishment then in Constantinople, must have stood him in some stead, he reached the rank of *cornicularius* at the age of sixty (in 551). But the service was declining owing to a diminution of the tribute received and for other reasons,

---

[1] *See* J. Lydus, περὶ ἀρχῶν, iii. 28.

[2] *De Mensibus ; de Ostentis* (which has been edited by C. Wachsmuth); and *de Magistratibus.*

[3] Ἀγάπιος πύματος μὲν ἀτὰρ πρώτιστος ἁπάντων ; Christodorus, who wrote a poem on the Heavens of Proclus.

and Lydus found that the emoluments long looked forward to with expectant confidence, which should have been at a minimum 1000 solidi, proved absolutely nil.   In bitterness of mind at this disappointment he composed the book *on Offices*, in which he gives an account of the civil service and explains its decline.

Of his personal treatment by the Emperor he could not complain.   Justinian had engaged him, perhaps in the early part of his reign, to compose a panegyric on himself and also a history of the Persian wars.   At the end of John's career Justinian wrote a letter ($\pi\rho\alpha\gamma\mu\alpha\tau\iota\kappa\acute{o}\nu$) to the prefecture, in which he dwelled on his rhetorical excellence, his grammatical accuracy, his poetical grace, his polymathy, and went so far as to say that his labours illuminated the language of the Romaioi.   He praised him for having spent time on study, although a civil servant, and enjoined the prefect to reward him at the public expense, and confer dignities upon him in recognition of his eloquence. The prefect, on receiving the letter, assigned Lydus a place in the Capitolium or Capitoline Aule, that is, a lecture-room in the university buildings, where he might give public instruction, presumably in rhetoric.   Pecuniarily, however, he was passed over as though he had never performed public services [1] ; on the other hand, he received honour and consideration from the Emperor, and enjoyed the leisure of a quiet life. He retired to the peace of his library, having served the State for more than forty years, feeling himself very ill used, and probably soured in temper.   In religion the complexion of Lydus was doubtful ; sometimes he speaks like a pagan, sometimes like a christian, so that one is not quite sure when he is speaking in earnest; but, christian or pagan, he was superstitious.

Poetry was dead; the epigrams of Agathias and the composition in hexameters on the church of St. Sophia do not deserve the name; and few of the verses would satisfy " the scrupulous ear of a well-flogged critic."   We may admit, however, that the iambic lines in the style of late Attic comedy, which

---

[1] He mentions that when he laid down his office, he visited the prefect's tribunal to pay his respects.   Heph- aestus, the prefect, kissed him, and read out a rescript, for which he had to pay a large sum.

Agathias prefixed to this book of epigrams, are not quite un-
worthy of a writer of new comedy,[1] and that the hexameters which
follow, in praise of Justinian's Empire, are written with some
spirit in spite of their affectation. Agathias tells us that in his
boyhood he was chiefly addicted to heroic verse, and " loved the
sweets of poetical refinements." [2] This expression could hardly
apply to Homer; his luscious models must have been the
Alexandrine writers, Theocritus, Callimachus, and the rest, or
recent composers like Nonnus, as may be also inferred from the
works which he wrote under this inspiration, a collection of
short poems in hexameters called Δαφνιακά, consisting of erotic
stories and " other such witcheries." In complete satisfaction
with himself and the poetical flights of his youth, Agathias,
having given an account of his poems, is unable to contain his
enthusiasm, and suddenly breaks out, " For veritably poetry *is*
something divine and holy. Its votaries, as Plato would say,
are in a state of fine frenzy." When we think of the produc-
tions of the fine frenzy of the writer himself, this outburst is
sufficiently amusing.

The description of St. Sophia and the inaugural poem on
the opening of the cathedral, to which the description is
annexed, breathe the enthusiasm of flattery, in which the flat-
terer, Paul the Silentiary,[3] was perhaps himself in earnest.
The first eighty lines, written in iambics and consisting of a
glorification of Justinian, were intended to be recited in the
palace. Then follow more iambics to be recited in the
Patriarch's residence, beginning thus : " We come to you, sirs,
from the home of the Emperor to the home of the Almighty
Emperor, the deviser (νοητής) of the universe, by whose grace
victory cleaves unto our lord " (συμφυὲς τῷ δεσπότῃ). And
this approximation of God to the Emperor, suggesting a comparison between them, occurs frequently. Speaking with conventional modesty of his own verses, the author says that they
will not be judged by " bean-eating Athenians, but by men of
piety and indulgence, in whom God and the Emperor find
pleasure." This contempt for the ancient Athenians is a touch

---

[1] It is interesting to note that it
contains a quotation from Aristophanes'
Peace.

[2] τὰ ἡδύσματα τῶν τῆς ποιητικῆς κομ-
ψευμάτων.

[3] Another poem by Paul, *de Ther-
mis Pythiis* (baths patronised by the
Empress Theodora), will be found in
Migne's edition.

of characteristic christian bigotry, and, if I may hazard the conjecture, is intended as a laudatory allusion to Justinian's measure of sweeping away the decrepit survival of Attic culture and exclusiveness in 529.

The iambics are succeeded by hexameters which begin with the praise of peace and the boast of the superiority of New to Old Rome—

εἴξατέ μοι 'Ρώμης Καπετωλίδες εἴξατε φῆμαι,
τόσσον ἐμὸν βασιλεὺς ὑπερήλατο θάμβος ἐκεῖνο
ὅππoσον εἰδώλοιο θεὸς μέγας ἐστὶν ἀρείων,

where Paul does not lose an opportunity of comparing Justinian to the Deity. It would be wearisome to follow the poem to its close. Its chief interest consists in its architectural information, which has been encased in a metrical dress with some ingenuity.

When we turn to the Latin literature of the sixth century the most prominent figure that meets us is Cassiodorus, the statesman of Theodoric and his successors (born about 480). Starting as an assistant in the bureau of his father, who had served as a finance minister under Odovacar and held the praetorian prefecture under Theodoric, he was fortunate enough to win the Gothic king's notice, while yet a mere subaltern, by a panegyric which he pronounced on him on a public occasion. Theodoric, who immediately recognised and welcomed his talent, appointed him to the post of quaestor, allowing him to dispense with all the grades of the civil service. The quaestorship was an office in which scope was given for literary talents, and Cassiodorus took full advantage of the opportunity. The letters which he wrote for Theodoric, along with those which he composed during subsequent reigns, were collected by him shortly before he retired from public life and published in a still extant collection under the title of *Variae Epistolae.*[1] Under Amalasuntha, Theodoric's daughter, under Theodahad the student of Plato, and Witigis the thorough Goth, Cassiodorus held the exalted post of praetorian prefect. About the year 539, not long before the capture of Ravenna by the Romans, he retired after forty years of public service,

---

[1] Mr. Hodgkin has published a translation of many of the *Variae*, with a valuable introduction.

to his birthplace Squillace in Bruttii, a charming spot for which he entertained a romantic affection. He founded there two monasteries, of which one, up in the hills, was for the men who were uncompromisingly austere, while the other, down below, built beside a fish-pond, and hence called *vivarium*, was for those monks who took that less strict and more cheerful view of the spiritual life of the cloister which characterised western monasticism once it had grown independent of its oriental origin.

Here Cassiodorus made a new departure, which, quiet and unostentatious as it was, has led to incalculably fruitful results for the modern world. This new departure consisted in occupying the abundant leisure of the monks with the labour of multiplying copies of Latin texts. To this simple but brilliant idea of taking advantage of the unemployed energy that ran to seed in monastic society for the spread and transmission of learning, both profane and sacred, we owe the survival of the great bulk of our Latin literature. There was a chamber, called the *scriptorium* or "writing-room," in the monastery, in which the monks used to copy both pagan and christian texts, working by the light of "mechanical lamps," *mechanicas lucernas*, whose peculiarity was that they were self-supplying, and measuring their time by sun-dials or water-clocks.

The style of Cassiodorus accords only too well with the principle stated by himself in the preface to his letters. "It is adornment (*ornatus*) alone," he says there, "that distinguishes the learned from the unlearned." He thus candidly takes pride in what is the characteristic of all ages of decadence, a love of embellishment for its own sake. He finds it impossible to state a simple or trivial fact in simple words. He essays to raise triviality to the sphere of the dignified and solemn; he succeeds in making it appear ridiculous. He will not allow the simple to wear the grace of its own simplicity. Nothing is more curious and amusing, though it soon becomes wearisome, than the correspondence of Theodoric in Cassiodorian dress, each epistle posing as it were in tragic cothurni and trailing a sweeping train.

Thus in the letters which describe the duties of the various ministers of state and other public officers, the quaestor makes it his object to give a tincture of poetry to functions, which in themselves suggest neither very solemn nor very poetical associations. He reminds the prefect of the corn-supplies that Ceres herself discovered corn, and that *panis*, " bread," may be derived from the great god Pan. The prefect of the police he apostrophises thus : " Go forth then under the starry skies, watch diligently with all the birds of night, and as they seek food in the darkness, so do thou hunt therein for fame."   To the count of the port of Rome he cries : " Excellent thought of the men of old to provide two channels by which strangers might enter the Tiber, and to adorn them with two stately cities which shine like lights upon the watery way ! " (vii. 9).

These examples of his manner are more favourable to him than many others that might be selected ; I have purposely avoided quoting passages in which he out-Cassiodores Cassiodorus.   Yet, though this manner has its amusing side, it may be said that Cassiodorus had really that sort of nature which, removing " the veil of familiarity " from common and trivial things, finds in them a certain dignity and feels a reverence for them; and that he unsuccessfully tried to express this feeling by using grandiloquent and embellished language, a feat in which Pindar was successful when, for example, he called a cloak " a healthy remedy against weary cold."

As an instance of the far-fetched and frigid conceits which were popular in that age, I may quote the words used by Cassiodorus of monks engaged in copying the sacred writings : " The fast-travelling reed writes down the holy words, and thus avenges the malice of the wicked one, who caused a reed to be used to smite the head of the Saviour."

It is interesting to record the attention paid by Cassiodorus to the beautiful binding of his books, and the biblical language in which he justifies it is characteristic of his age. It is meet, he says, that a book should be clothed in a fair dress, even as the guests were arrayed in wedding garments in the New Testament parable.

Beside the letters, Cassiodorus wrote (1) a treatise on the soul in which its relation to the body is treated with a delicate touch of paganism that reminds us of Hadrian's *hospes comesque corporis;* (2) the *Historia Tripartita*, a compilation from Socrates, Sozomen, and Theodoret, and a history of the Goths from which Jordanes drew ; (3) various theological works; (4) an educational work "on the Arts and Disciplines of the Liberal Letters"[1]; (5) a treatise, composed in his ninety-third year,[2] on orthography, intended as a guide to the monks at Squillace in their spelling.   Thus the influence of Cassiodorus and the traditions of culture and accuracy which he established at Squillace formed a counterpoise to that spirit, represented by Pope Gregory I., which regarded grammar as trivial and culture as superfluous, or even a temptation ; a spirit which soon launched the Church into the waters of ignorance and barbarism.

Another prominent figure in the reign of Theodoric, but who did not, like Cassiodorus, enjoy a happy old age amid the ruins of his country, was Boethius the Patrician, whose unfortunate end is veiled to a certain degree in obscurity.   We know not what were the real motives for his condemnation, passed formally by the Roman senate, and his subsequent execution (524 A.D.)   Charges were brought against him of astrological magic, stigmatised as a serious crime by the Theodosian Code, but it is evident that these were only pretexts.   He seems to have been suspected of taking part in a conspiracy ; yet the silence of Cassiodorus, as Mr. Hodgkin justly insists, is ominous for the fame of the Gothic king.   The blow seems to have fallen quite unexpectedly on Boethius and his affectionate father-in-law Symmachus, who had the reputation of being a " modern Cato," *Catonis novellus imitator,* and who shared the fate of his son-in-law.

In prison under the pressure of this sudden calamity, which burst like a peal of thunder on the calm course of his life,—justifying the saying of Solon, that the happiness of a man's life must not be asserted till after his death,— Boethius composed the work which has immortalised him, the *Consolation of Philosophy.*   He did not lay the world under such a great obligation of gratitude as Cassiodorus ; and yet this work was better known and more read throughout the Middle Ages, although it completely ignores Christianity, than any of Cassiodorus' writings.   It was translated into Anglo-Saxon by King Alfred, and into English by Chaucer.

---

[1] In this work, grammar, rhetoric, dialectic, arithmetic, music, geometry, and astronomy—the seven liberal arts —are discussed.

[2] 593 A.D.   He had lived to see the Lombard invasion.

Boethius was an Aristotelian, and he employed his leisure in translating works of Aristotle into Latin. It was partly through these translations that Aristotelianism was accessible to the students of the Middle Ages; and thus the two chief literary men at the beginning of the sixth century, Cassiodorus and Boethius, made each in his way contributions of vast importance to the culture of medieval and modern times. Cassiodorus may be considered to have secured the survival of Latin literature, as was explained above, while Boethius laid the foundations for Scholasticism. Boethius and Johannes Philoponus were the realist and the nominalist respectively of the sixth century.

The Latin of Boethius is far superior to the Latin of Cassiodorus. It is elegant, but not exaggerated through an extravagant love of embellishment. In fact he had the faculty of taste, which even in the lowest stages of decadence distinguishes good and bad writers, and of which Cassiodorus was almost destitute.

The *Consolatio Philosophiae* has a considerable charm, which is increased by the recollection of the circumstances under which it was composed. A student who, maintaining indeed a lukewarm connection with politics, had spent most of his days in the calm atmosphere of his library, where he expected to end his life, suddenly found himself in the confinement of a dismal prison with death impending over him. There is thus a reality and earnestness in his philosophical meditations which so many treatises of the kind lack; there is an earnestness born of a real fervent need of consolation, while at the same time there is a pervading calm. The lines of poetry, sometimes lyrical, sometimes elegiac, which break the discussion at intervals, like organ chants in a religious service, serve to render the calmness of the atmosphere distinctly perceptible.

The problem of the treatise [1] is to explain the "unjust confusion" which exists in the world, the eternal question how

---

[1] Book i. contains the story of Boethius' personal wrongs, which he relates to Philosophia; Bk. ii. contains a discussion on Fortune; Bk. iii. passes to the *Summum Bonum*; in Bk. iv. Philosophia justifies God's government; Bk. v. deals with free will. W. Gass, in his *Geschichte der christlichen Ethik*, i. p. 177, says of Boethius that in his *Consolatio* "gleicht er nicht einem Koheleth, weit eher einem Hiob im Platonischen Gewande . . . selbst im Kerker soll ihn sein frommer Optimismus nicht verlassen." On Boethius *see* Ebert, *Allg. Gesch. der Literatur des Mittelalters im Abendlande*, i. 462 *sqq.*

the fact that the evil win often the rewards of virtue (*pretium scleris—diadema*) and the good suffer the penalties of crime, can be reconciled with a " deus, rector mundi." If I could believe, says Boethius, that all things were determined by chance and hazard, I should not be so puzzled. We need not follow him in his discussion of the subject, which of course is unsatisfactory—did it really satisfy him?—and need only observe that in one place he defines the relation of fate to the Deity in the sense that fate is a sort of instrument by which God regulates the world according to fixed rules. In other words, fate is the law of phenomena or nature, under the supreme control of the highest Being, which he identifies with the *Summum Bonum* or highest good.

But the metaphysical discussion does not interest the student of literature so much as the setting of the piece and things said incidentally. Boethius imagines his couch surrounded by the Muses of poetry, who suggest to him accents of lamentation. Suddenly there appears at his head a strange lady of lofty visage. There was marvellous fluidity in her stature; she seemed sometimes of ordinary human height, and at the next moment her head seemed to touch heaven, or penetrated so far into its recesses that her face was lost to the vision. Her eyes too were unnatural, brilliant and transparent beyond the power of human eyes, of fresh colour and unquenchable vigour. And yet at the same time she seemed so ancient of days " that she could not be taken for a woman of our age." Her garments were of the finest threads, woven by some secret art into an indissoluble texture, woven, as Boethius afterwards learned, by her own hands. And on this robe there was a certain mist of neglected antiquity, the sort of colour that statues have which have been exposed to smoke. On the lower edge of the robe there was the Greek letter Π (the initial of Πρακτική, Practical Philosophy), from which stairs were worked leading upwards to the letter Θ (Θεωρητική, Pure Philosophy). And her garment had the marks of violent usage, as though rough persons had tried to rend it from her and carried away shreds in their hands. The lady was Philosophia; she bore a sceptre and parchment rolls. She afterwards explained that the violent persons who had rent her robe were the Epicureans, Stoics, and other late schools; they succeeded in tearing away patches of her dress, fancying severally that they had obtained the whole garment. Philosophia's first act is to drive out the Muses, whom she disdainfully terms "theatrical strumpets," and she makes a remark, with which many perhaps who have sought for consolation in poetry will agree, that it "accustoms the minds of men to the disease but does not set them free."[1]

The description of the lady Philosophia has a considerable aesthetic value. The conception of her robe resembling marble statues discoloured by smoke, is a really happy invention to suggest that antique quaintness which the Greeks expressed by the word εὐπινής.

But the most striking feature of the *Consolatio* is the interspersion of the prose dialogue with poems at certain intervals,[2] which, like choruses in Greek tragedy, appertain, though more closely than they, to the preceding argument. Thus the work resembles in form Dante's *Vita Nuova*, where the sonnets gather up in music the feelings occasioned by the narrated events. These poems, which betray the influence of Seneca's plays,[3] have all a charm of their own, and metres of various kinds are gracefully employed. The second poem, which forms a pause after Philosophia has driven out the Muses and taken her seat, begins thus—

> heu quasi praecipiti mersa profundo
> mens hebet et propria luce relicta
> tendit in externas ire tenebras,
> terrenis quotiens flatibus aucta
> crescit in immensum noxia cura.
> hic quondam caelo liber aperto
> suetus in aetherios ire meatus
> cernebat rosei lumina solis,
> visebat gelidae sidera lunae
> et quaecumque vagos stella recursus
> exercet varios flexa per orbes,
> conprensam numeris victor habebat.

This idea of the mind, vexed by the cares of earth, leaving its own light and passing "into outer darkness," *in externas*

----

[1] Ed. Peiper, p. 5: *hominumque mentes [musae] assuefaciunt morbo, non liberant.*

[2] Varro and Macrobius and Martianus Capella had mixed poetry and prose before, but Boethius was the first to use the artifice with artistic effect.

[3] Peiper in his Teubner edition, 1871, gives a list of passages which contain excerpts from or echoes of Seneca's tragedies.

tenebras, would be a suitable illustration of the spiritual meaning of the outer darkness spoken of in the New Testament.
Another poem, constructed with as much care as a modern
sonnet,[1] sings of the " love that moves the sun and stars,"

> hanc rerum series ligat
> terras ac pelagus regens
> et caelo imperitans amor,

an idea best known to modern readers from the last line of
Dante's *Divina Commedia*, but which is as old as Empedocles.
In another place we have an anticipation of Shelley's " nought
may endure but mutability,"—

> constat aeterna positumque lege est
> ut constet genitum nihil.

As an example of poetical tenderness, quite Virgilian, I may
quote two lines of a stanza, where the author is illustrating
the return of nature to itself by a caged bird, which, when it
beholds the greenwood once more, spurns the sprinkled crumbs—

> silvas tantum maesta requirit,
> silvas tantum voce susurrat.

Immediately after this poem Boethius proceeds thus: " Ye
too, O creatures of earth! albeit in a vague image, yet do ye
dream of your origin," vos quoque, O terrena animalia! tenui
licet imagine vestrum tamen principium somniatis,—a felicitous
expression of pantheism.

I must not omit to notice the delicate feeling for metrical
effect which Boethius displays in the poem on the protracted
toils of the siege of Troy and the labours of Hercules.   It is
written in Sapphic metre, but the short fourth lines are omitted
until the end.   The effect of this device is that the mind and
voice of the reader continue to travel without relief or metrical
resting-place until all the labours are over and heavenly rest
succeeds in the stars of the concluding and only Adonius—

> superata tellus
> sidera donat.

The age was so poor in works of pure literary interest that
I have gladly lingered a little over the *Consolatio* of Boethius.

---

[1] ii. viii. p. 48; it consists of thirty lines thus arranged, 4+4+4+3=
4+4+4+3.

It remains to add that he wrote short books on christian theology, and must therefore have been professedly a Christian. This religion, however, did not influence his pagan spirit, just as it left Procopius untouched; and it was probably the theological subtleties that interested him and not the spirit of the faith. He was a very accomplished man, acquainted with a diversity of subjects; polymathy, as I said before, was a characteristic of the time. As well as a philosopher and a poet, he was a musician, he was learned in astronomy, he was fond of inventive science, like the Greek architect Anthemius. It would appear, indeed, that scientific studies were fashionable in the sixth century; natural science was a favourite subject of Cassiodorus.

If the church of San Vitale at Ravenna is the great monument of the imperial restoration in Italy, the poems of Flavius Cresconius Corippus may be considered the monument of the imperial restoration in Africa. He is not known, indeed, to have chosen the victories of Belisarius as the subject of a special work, but in his *Johannis* and in his *de laudibus Justini*, which have been mentioned in previous chapters, joy over the fall of the Vandal and the restoration of Africa to the Empire is expressed in strong and sometimes effective language.[1]

---

[1] It would take us too far away from our subject, "the Roman Empire," to enter upon the important works of Gregory of Tours or the interesting poems of Venantius Fortunatus, the court poet of the Frank kings and the friend of St. Radegundis who founded the monastery at Poictiers. Of both these writers excellent editions have recently been published in the *Monumenta Germaniae Historica*.

BOOK V

THE HOUSE OF HERACLIUS

CHAPTER I

PHOCAS [1]

THE reign of Phocas the Thracian, which lasted for eight years, was the realisation of that dreaded something whose approach had long been felt. The calamities which Tiberius and Maurice had been spared closed in round the throne of Phocas, who is himself represented to have been the most baleful calamity of all. The Empire sank into the lowest depths of degradation and misery, and it seemed that nothing short of some divine miracle could restore it to wellbeing.

By contemporaries Phocas was regarded [2] as a fell monster,

---

[1] Our chief authorities for the reign of Phocas are the *Paschal Chronicle* and Theophanes. Of these the former perhaps possesses the value of a contemporary source, as it is generally supposed to have been composed (at Alexandria) soon after 630 A.D. In that case its author (not authors, *vide* Clinton, *F. R.*) would have witnessed, unless he were very young when he wrote, the calamities of the first decade of the seventh century, just like Theophylactus, who wrote about 628-630, and has some notices bearing on the reign of Phocas. We have, moreover, a few fragments of a John of Antioch (published in Müller's *Fragmenta*, vol. v.), who is doubtless the same as John Malalas, and lived about 700. He, I believe, was the chief source of Theophanes. Of the fall of Phocas we have an account in the *Brief History* of Nicephorus, a contemporary of Theophanes (about 800). For western affairs we have Isidore of Seville and Paul the Deacon, and some letters of Gregory I. who died in 604. No laws or letters of Phocas have survived.

The chronology of Theophanes becomes at this point a little confusing, because he inadvertently ran two indictions into one *annus mundi*, and thus apparently assigns seven (instead of eight years) to Phocas. The consequence is that throughout the seventh century his Years of the World and his indictions do not correspond. But his chronology is really correct; his indictions are always right, and whenever he mentions the *annus domini* (τῆς θείας σαρκώσεως), it always corresponds to the indiction. *E.g.* 6133 A.M. really corresponds to 640-641 A.D. and the fourteenth indiction; but Theophanes equates it with the fifteenth indiction, and equates the following year 6134 with A.D. (634, Alexandrine=) 642-643. The mistake is not corrected until the year 6197, where the events of one indiction are spread over two Years of the World.

[2] He was called the New Gorgon. For strong words about him, *see* George of Pisidia, *Bell. Avar.* 49 *sqq.* and *Heracl.* ii. 6 *sqq.* The intestine tumults which prevailed everywhere after the death of

without a palliating virtue or a redeeming grace, and the character which he has transmitted to history is that of a " remorseless, treacherous, lecherous, kindless villain." The abnormal wickedness of his mind is said to have been reflected in a peculiarly repulsive exterior, and he produces the impression of a hideous nightmare brooding over an exhausted and weary realm.

Whatever may have been his character, the short chronicle of his reign is a chronicle of misfortunes, anarchy within and hostility without; and we never feel quite sure that we have fathomed the depth or measured the breadth of these misfortunes, for the chroniclers seem to have avoided dwelling on the reign as if it were a sort of plague spot.

Chosroes made the dethronement and death of Maurice a pretext for declaring war; he posed as the avenger of his friend and benefactor. But it must not be imagined that this was anything more than a pretext. The renewal of the old quarrel between East and West must not be laid to the charge of Phocas, though we hold him answerable, at least partially, for the inadequate defence of the Empire. That the acts of Phocas were not the real cause of the war is proved by two things,— by the express statement of a contemporary historian, hostile to Phocas, that Chosroes' holy plea was hypocritical,[1] and by the fact that, some time before the death of Maurice, the Sassanid had become restless and an outbreak of war had been with difficulty avoided.[2]

To meet the threatened Persian invasion the hopes of the Romans rested on the able general Narses, whose name was so much dreaded or respected by the enemy that Persian children trembled when they heard it pronounced. But not only to the enemy was he an object of terror; his ability and reputation awakened the suspicion and fears of Phocas. He revolted and occupied Edessa; he even urged the Persians to begin hostilities[3]; and the Emperor was obliged to divide his

Maurice—in Thessalonica, in the East (Cilicia, Asia, Palestine)—are noticed by the author of the Life of St. Demetrius (*Acta Sanctorum*, Oct. iv., p. 132).

[1] Theophylactus, viii. 15, κατειρωνευόμενος.

[2] *Ib.* Maurice found it necessary to

appoint a new commander at Daras, as Narses and Chosroes did not like each other; but hostility to Phocas afterwards induced them to act together.

[3] Theophanes, 6095 A.M.   ὁ δὲ Ναρσῆς γράφει πρὸς Χωσρόην τὸν βασιλέα

forces to contend against two foes (603 A.D.) Narses was finally lured by false promises of reconciliation to present himself in Byzantium, and Phocas was not ashamed or afraid of committing him to the flames. This affair was fortunate for Chosroes, as Narses was the only Roman commander at the time who possessed military talent. Both the general Germanus and the general Leontius had been severely defeated by the Persians; the former had died of a wound, the latter had been thrown into chains by the indignant Emperor; and the protection of Christendom against the fire-worshippers was consigned to Domentziolus, a nephew of Phocas.[1] If the Emperor had been endowed with any political ability he might have made Narses his friend and thereby saved Syria.

A peace was concluded with the Avars and an increase of the yearly tribute granted (604 A.D.) in order to render the troops of Illyricum and Thrace available for the war in Asia. But the tide of success had set in for the Persians, who after some smaller successes had gained an important victory over Leontius at Arzamon. Their ravages continued during the following year, and in 606 Daras was once more lost to the Romans, western Mesopotamia and Syria were overrun by the enemy in two successive years,[2] and countless Roman captives were scattered among the provinces of Persia. But in 608 the danger was brought nearer to the careless inhabitants of the capital; for, having occupied Armenia and Cappadocia, Paphlagonia and Galatia, the army of the fire-worshippers advanced to the Bosphorus, showing mercy in the march to neither age nor sex,[3] and encamped at Chalcedon, opposite to Constantinople. And thus, says the historian, there was "tyranny" both inside and outside the city.[4]

In the affair of Narses, Phocas had shown political ineptitude. At a later period he showed himself yet more inconceivably inept. In Syria there was always a spirit of disaffection, more or less widely spread, towards the orthodox Byzantine

---

Περσῶν ἀθροῖσαι δυνάμεις, κ.τ.λ. In 604 Narses fled from Edessa to Hierapolis; at the end of the same year, or perhaps in 605 (6097 A.M.), Domentziolus lured him to Byzantium.

[1] Not to be confounded with Domentziolus, the brother of Phocas. The nephew had been appointed curopalates on the accession of his uncle.

[2] 606 and 607—the dates of Theophanes, but in this reign his dates are not trustworthy, as he loses a year and gives only seven years to Phocas.

[3] λυμαινόμενοι ἀφειδῶς πᾶσαν ἡλικίαν (Theophanes, 6100 A.M.)

[4] *Ib.*; Nicephorus, p. 3 (where παρὰ πολλοῖς ᾄδεσθαι probably refers to George of Pisidia).

government, for Syria was a country full of Jews as well as heretics of divers kinds. This spirit demanded, in time of war, singularly delicate manipulation on the part of the government; but Phocas conceived the ill-timed idea of constraining all the Jews to become Christians. The consequence of this policy was a great revolt of the Hebrews in Antioch ; Christians were massacred, and a cruel and indecent punishment was inflicted on the Patriarch Anastasius.[1]   Bonosus, a creature of Phocas, who was created count of the East and sent to put down the rising, cast out all the Jews from the city (610 A.D.), but the affair shows how favourable was the political situation of the Syrian provinces for the aggressions of the Persians. The Persian general, Shahr Barz, " raged by land and sea " (we are told by the Armenian[2] historian Sepêos) ; " he transported handsome Roman villas, along with their inhabitants, to Persian soil, and commanded his architects to construct towns in Persia on the model of the destroyed cities. He called one of these towns Antioch the Renowned." Both in Syria and in Egypt there seems to have prevailed a chronic anarchy ; all the smouldering feuds of parties had burst into flame ; Blues and Greens made the streets of Alexandria[3] and Antioch the scenes of continual bloodshed.

In Constantinople, to which the activity and apprehensions of the Emperor were chiefly confined, the deepest dissatisfaction had prevailed since the death of Maurice.   Conspiracy followed conspiracy, but Phocas dexterously maintained his seat, equally skilful in detecting and merciless in punishing the conspirators.[4]   The patricians, who were most closely attached

---

[1] Theophanes, 6101 : ἀποσφάττουσιν Ἀναστάσιον . . . βαλόντες τὴν φύσιν αὐτοῦ ἐν τῷ στόματι αὐτοῦ. Cottanas, a *magister militum* (στρατηλάτης), was sent with Bonosus.   The date 610 is fixed by the *Chron. Pasch.*

[2] *See* the *Journal asiatique*, February 1866.   Compare Drapeyron, *L'Empereur Héraclius*, p. 96.   Greek writers call Shahr Barz ("the Royal Boar") Σάρβαρος.   From the Armenian historians we learn that the invader of Cappadocia in 609 (?) was Shahen ; he took Caesarea, which was abandoned by the Christians and only Jews remained in it.   The same historians supposed that Theodosius, the son of

Maurice, was really alive, and state (1) that he accompanied the Persian army under the general Razman to Mesopotamia and Syria in 604 or 605, when Amida, Edessa, and Antioch were taken ; and (2) that he marched with another general against Armenia in 607-608 and reduced Satala and Theodosiopolis (Patcanian, in the *Journal asiatique, ib.* p. 197 *sqq.*)

[3] Revolt of Africa and Alexandria in 609 ; see *Chron. Pasch.*   The Patriarch of Alexandria was slain.

[4] He put to death Alexander, who had been a fellow - conspirator with himself against Maurice.

to Maurice, namely Peter his brother, Comentiolus, and Lardys, were at once executed, while Philippicus (Maurice's brother-in-law) and Germanus were compelled to assume clerical orders. Priscus, on the other hand, the able commander who had conducted the campaigns against the Slaves and Avars, and had been so often superseded by the incapable friends of Maurice, was an adherent of Phocas, who was further supported by his brother Domentziolus [1] and by Bonosus.

During the first three years of this reign the intrigues of the enemies of Phocas revolved round Constantina, the widow of Maurice, who with her three daughters had been placed in strict confinement, while the hopes of the dissatisfied and the fears of the usurper were kept alive by the false and carefully fostered rumour that Theodosius—the Theodosius who should have been Theodosius III—was not dead, but was wandering in the far East. Germanus, the father-in-law, and Constantina, the mother of Theodosius united their energies to set on foot a conspiracy, in which a large number of leading men took part. Two distinct attempts were made to achieve the overthrow of Phocas.[2] The first of these failed, because the Emperor was popular with the more powerful faction, which had helped to set him on the throne. The Greens reviled the name of Constantina in the hippodrome, and the bribes which Germanus offered to their demarchs were rejected. Constantina and her daughters, who were in readiness for the expected insurrection, took refuge in St. Sophia, and the influence of the Patriarch Cyriacus protected them with difficulty from the wrath and violence of Phocas. They were immured in a monastery, and Germanus was compelled to wear the tonsure.[3]

---

[1] This Domentziolus was nicknamed κονδόχειρ, see John Ant. 218 f. In 610 he seems to have been *magister officiorum*.

[2] Theophanes places these attempts in 606 and 607. But the *Paschal Chronicle*, in which the second only is mentioned, places it in June 605. We must accept this date, which seems trustworthy; but a doubt arises whether the author of the *Chron. Pasch.* confounded two distinct occasions, or Theophanes (or his authority) differentiated one occasion. I have supposed that Theophanes is right in distinguishing, but wrong in his dates;

and otherwise it seems likely that the event placed by Theophanes in 606 should have taken place in an earlier year. Phocas would hardly have left these suspicious personages free so long; in fact, according to *Chron. Pasch.*, Constantina was immured, Philippicus and Germanus were tonsured in 603.

[3] These events occurred probably in 604. Philippicus, Maurice's brother-in-law, was perhaps connected with this conspiracy; he became a monk and dwelled in a monastery which he had founded at Chrysopolis. Cf. Theoph. 6098 A.M. But John of Antioch (that is John Malalas), fr.

But the relations of Maurice still maintained their treasonable projects, and after the lapse of more than a year (in 605) organised a plot against the life of Phocas, which would probably have succeeded but for the treachery of one Petronia, who acted as the bearer of the correspondence between Constantina and Germanus. Constantina was put to the torture, and the names of many distinguished patricians, noble lords, and high officials were revealed; chief among whom was Theodorus, the praetorian prefect of the East. He was sentenced to be cudgelled to death, and sundry modes of rendering death hideous were discovered for the other conspirators.[1]   Constantina, her three daughters,[2] and her daughter-in-law were executed, as well as Germanus.

This formidable conspiracy must have tended to make Phocas yet more suspicious, and consequently more tyrannical; while the bloodshed which ensued seemed to stamp him as a sanguinary tyrant, and rendered him far more unpopular than before. An alienation soon came about between him and the *comes excubitorum* Priscus,[3] on whom he had bestowed his daughter Domentzia in marriage; and, strange to say, the origin of this alienation is attributed to an accidental occurrence which took place during the nuptial festivities. The marriage was celebrated in the palace of Marina,[4] and an equestrian contest was held in honour of it. The chiefs of the blue and green factions, supposing that the marriage had a certain political significance and that Priscus might be looked upon as the probable successor to the throne, took upon themselves in a rash moment to place laurelled images of the bride and bridegroom beside those of the Emperor and Empress on pillars in the hippodrome. But the suggestion misliked Phocas; he investigated the matter, and ordered the demarchs to whom it was traced to be put to death. The people, however, begged them off, but Phocas was never satisfied that Priscus had not been privy to the treasonable act. This occurred in 607. In the following year Priscus opened a correspondence

---

218 d (*F. H. G.* vol. v.), states that he embraced the monastic life at the time of Maurice's fall, and this agrees with *Chron. Pasch.*

[1] *Chron. Pasch.* eighth indiction (= 604-605).

[2] Anastasia, Theoctiste, and Cleopatra (*Chron. Pasch.*)

[3] Priscus, whom Nicephorus strangely calls Crispus, was apparently prefect of the city at the time of his marriage; at least the τηνικάδε of Nicephorus seems to mean so (p. 4).

[4] Marina was one of the daughters of Arcadius, each of whom had a palace of her own.

with Heraclius, the exarch or Patrician of Africa [1]; and in the series of circumstances that brought about the fall of Phocas this was the first.

Since Gennadius had quelled the turbulent Moors, Africa had been the most prosperous and favoured spot in the Roman Empire ; and from Africa, if from anywhere, men might expect salvation to come. The arts of peace flourished, and the happiness of peace was experienced under the beneficent rule of the Patrician Heraclius, whom we have already met as a general of Maurice in the East. The exarch, in the security of distant Carthage, was able to defy the Emperor with impunity and to discontinue communications with Constantinople ; and in the meantime, perhaps, he and his brother Gregorius [2] were maturing plans and making preparations for an expedition against the detested tyrant. It was not till two years later that, urged by the importunities of Priscus and the pressing entreaties of the senate, who could tolerate the distempered state of things no longer, and were powerless to change it without help from the provinces, he despatched an armament which at length delivered New Rome from the watchful tyranny of Phocas.

The few notices which have come down to us show clearly the exasperation and despondency which prevailed among residents in the capital. A pestilence and its twin-sister a famine desolated the city during the same year in which the Asiatic enemy was advancing on Chalcedon ; and in connection with this we must remember that no supplies were available from Africa, and that in the following year the disaffection in Egypt may have increased the starvation in Constantinople. The result was a sedition, and the disloyalty of the Byzantines was openly displayed. His own party, the Greens, insulted Phocas at the games, and told him that he had lost his wits.[3] The infuriated monarch commanded Constans, the prefect of the city, to slay or mutilate the contumacious offenders and not to hold his hand. These punishments were the signal for a general

---

[1] John of Antioch, fr. 218 e. It is not quite clear whether the official term was exarch or stratêgos (praetor). In the West the governor of Africa was generally called the Patrician.

[2] Nicephorus, p. 3 (ed. de Boor), οὗτοι κοινῇ βουλευσάμενοι, κ.τ.λ.

[3] Theophanes, 6101 A.M. ; John Ant. 218 e ; πάλιν εἰς τὸν καῦκον ἔπιες πάλιν τὸν νοῦν ἀπώλεκας, (so de Boor) "You have drunk again of the cup ; you have again lost your sense." The allusion is obscure.

riot in the streets; the offices of the prefect and the prisons were burnt down, and the prisoners were loosed from their cells. Then Phocas issued a mandate to the effect that the green faction should no longer have political status.[1]

The deliverance that came from Africa at the end of 610 was perhaps hastened by personal interests of the exarch. Phocas had discovered that Epiphania,[2] the wife of the exarch, and Eudocia, the betrothed of his son, were residing in Constantinople, and he placed them in the monastery of the New Repentance[3] under strict confinement. This was partly an act of vengeance, but partly also a measure of prudence, to secure hostages in case Heraclius should become positively hostile.

The exarch was now old, and had himself no wish to return to the murky Byzantine atmosphere, even for a throne; but he organised an expedition which had a somewhat romantic character. He prepared an armament of "castellated vessels,"[4] manned with Moors, which he consigned to the care of his son Heraclius; and he equipped an army of cavalry to proceed along the coasts of Africa, Egypt, Syria, and Asia, under the command of his nephew Nicetas, the son of Gregorius. The agreement was made that whichever of the two cousins reached Constantinople first and slew Phocas was to be rewarded by the crown. It was plain that, except the elements were adverse to Heraclius, Nicetas had no chance, while on the other hand he ran no risk. There was a certain dramatic appropriateness in this assignation of routes,—that Heraclius, the man of genius, should take the short and perilous way, and that Nicetas, the man of respectability, should plod on the firm earth. The elements conspired to favour the man of genius, who felt confident of success because he possessed a mystical picture of the Virgin, not made with hands, but carried down by angels

[1] Before the final deliverance came, another conspiracy, according to Theophanes, was set on foot by Elpidius and Theodorus, prefect of the East, the project being to make the latter Emperor; but it was betrayed. It seems almost certain, however, that Theophanes has fallen into some confusion, for in the conspiracy of 605 Elpidius and Theodorus, praet. pref. of the East, had been executed.

[2] Theophanes, but John Ant. calls her Fabia, fr. 218 f, and *Chron. Pasch.* (ind. 15) notes that Eudocia was "also called Fabia."

[3] Theoph. 6102, τῆς Νέας Μετανοίας.

[4] *Ib.* πλοῖα καστελλωμένα. For the overthrow of Phocas we have, as well as Theophanes and the *Paschal Chronicle*, the narrative of Nicephorus the Patriarch (a contemporary of Theophanes) in his *Short History*. The Moors are mentioned by John Ant. fr. 218 f, and Nicephorus, p. 3.

from heaven.   On one of the last days of September or one of
the first days of October 610, he cast anchor at Abydos, and
learned from the " count of Abydos " [1] the situation of affairs
in the capital.   Officials who had been banished by the tyrant
flocked to his standard, and with no uncertain hope he continued his course to Heraclea and thence to the island Kalo-
nymos.   The city was defenceless.   The guards and a regiment
of soldiers called Bucellarii were at the disposal of Priscus, who
was eagerly awaiting the African army, and on 3d October
Phocas saw with despair the ships of the deliverer passing
Hebdomon, and slowly approaching the harbour of Sophia.
The Greens set fire to the building of the Caesarian harbour,
which they had been enlisted to defend, and it was plain from
the situation that the knell of Phocas had knolled.   A naval
engagement took place on Sunday, 4th October; the men of
Phocas retreated,[2] and then the Emperor, who had returned
to the palace, was abandoned completely.   The circumstances
of his death are uncertain.   The story is that on Monday a
certain Photius (curator of the palace of Placidia), who owed
Phocas a grudge for having placed him in the ludicrous and
painful position of a deceived husband, rushed into the palace,
and, stripping the victim of his imperial robes, dragged him
from his hiding-place to the presence of Heraclius. [3]   A
short dialogue took place between the fallen and the future
Emperor.

" Is it thus," asked Heraclius, "that you have governed the
Empire ?"

" Will you," replied Phocas, " govern it better ?"[4]

This epigrammatic and pregnant question of Phocas was his
best defence, and there was more than one grain of truth contained in it.   But at the moment it seemed to the conqueror

[1] When was this office introduced?
It was doubtless connected with the
custom dues.   John Ant., 218 f, gives
the best account of the revolution, but
many of the details are obscure.

[2] The Greens threatened Bonosus at
the harbour of Caesarius; οἱ δὲ ἄνθρωποι
τοῦ Φωκᾶ ἀνεχώρησαν (John Ant. 218 f,
5). So Nicephorus, p. 4.   Bonosus cast
himself into the sea (Chron. Pasch.)
Phocas had gone to Byrides (Βυρίδες),
a place which cannot be identified,
situate on the sea between the city and

Hebdomon.   From it he saw the ships
of the foe at Hebdomon.
[3] John Ant., 218 f, 6, who is not followed by Theophanes, but is supported
by the Paschal Chronicle.   From Nicephorus it would appear that Phocas was
taken in a boat to the ship of Heraclius,
and that the dialogue took place there.
Probus, a patrician, helped Photius,
according to Chron. Pasch.
[4] Or, perhaps, "may you be able to
govern it better," σὺ κάλλιον ἔχοις (Müller for ἔχεις) διοικῆσαι (John Ant. 218 f).

merely the sneer of a doomed criminal, though in later years it may have often recurred to him in a new light.

In his wrath, according to one account, he kicked the tyrant and caused him to be hewed in pieces on the spot "as a carcase fit for hounds,"[1] while another record intimates that Phocas fell a victim to the eager vengeance of the circus factions.[2] Domentziolus, Bonosus, and Leontius the treasurer perished with him, and the corpses were burned in a place called Bous.

The impression left by the Emperor Phocas is that of a shapeless monster, a suitable head for the shapeless anarchy that beset the Empire. Yet in Italy a statue was erected (608 A.D.) in his honour by the exarch Smaragdus, and the quiet condition of the Roman provinces there is mentioned with satisfaction in a loyal inscription.[3] It might be said that this honour had a double sense; and that Phocas was really thanked for his inability to interfere.[4]

On the 5th October 610, Heraclius was proclaimed Augustus by the senate and the people, and crowned by the Patriarch Sergius.[5]

---

[1] John Ant. 218 f.

[2] Theophanes. In Nicephorus, Bonosus is called Βονόσσος, and Domentziolus Δομεντίόλος. Leontius (called by John Ant. σακελλάριος, which Nicephorus translates into βασιλικῶν χρημάτων ταμίας) was perhaps the brother or father of the Empress Leontia. He was a Syrian, *Chron. Pasch.* (ὁ ἀπὸ σακελλαρίων). For the name *sacellarius* ("purser"), equivalent to *comes sacri patrimonii, see* below, p. 324.

[3] *Corpus Inscr. Lat.* vi. p. 251, tit. 1200, on the base of a column dug up in March 1813. Smaragdus (*ex praepos. sacri palatii ac patricius et exarchus*

Italiae) dedicates the statue *pro innumerabilibus pietatis ejus beneficiis et pro quiete procurata Ital. ac conservata libertate,* on the 1st of August in the eleventh indiction (fifth year after consulship of Phocas). Smaragdus had been exarch in the reign of Maurice, 583-588; he was again exarch from 602 to 609.

[4] Phocas enlisted the support of Gregory I. by making the Patriarch Cyriacus give up the title *ecumenic*.

[5] Cyriacus died in 606, and was succeeded by Thomas, whom Sergius, the dean of St. Sophia and ptochotrophus, succeeded in 610.

CHAPTER II

HERACLIUS (610-622 A.D.)[1]

THE Roman Empire in the reign of Justinian might be compared to one making ready to set forth on a wild and dangerous night journey. We saw how the shades closed round it, and how it utterly lost itself in marshes and dark woods under Justin, Tiberius, and Maurice. It then falls unawares into the power of a fell giant, and for eight years, under Phocas, languishes in the dungeons of his castle. Heraclius is the knight-errant who slays the giant and delivers the pining captive. Or, to speak in the language of the time, he is the Perseus who cuts off the Gorgon's head.

But the mere death of the oppressor did not dispel the

---

[1] Our contemporary authorities for the reign of Heraclius are George of Pisidia (for whose work *see* below, cap. iv.) and the *Paschal Chronicle* (compiled at Alexandria), which goes down to the year 628. The Ἱστορία σύντομος of Nicephorus the Patriarch (about 800 A.D.), and the Chronicle of his contemporary Theophanes are valuable, though later, sources; both probably derived their information from John Malalas of Antioch, whose date is disputed, but who probably lived about 700. The Armenian history of Sepêos supplies some facts not recorded by the Greek writers, but unfortunately I only know it from an article in the *Journal asiatique* (Feb. 1866), entitled "Essai d'une histoire de la dynastie des Sassanides," and from M. Drapeyron's excellent work, *L'Empereur Héraclius et l'empire byzantin*, as my attempts to obtain a copy of M. Patcanian's Russian trans-

lation of Sepêos were vain.

For western events we have the Chronicle of the contemporary Isidore of Hispalis down to the fifth year of Svinthila (625 A.D.); we have the Chronicle of Fredegarius, who lived under Dagobert, and recounts the marvellous deeds (*miracula*) of Heraclius against the Persians in a somewhat legendary form (cap. 62 *sqq.*) As M. Gasquet remarks (*L'empire byzantin*, p. 205), Fredegarius "has his eyes constantly turned towards Constantinople, which is for him always the capital of the world." Our other Latin sources are the *Liber Pontificalis*, which goes under the name of Anastasius, and the *Historia Langobardorum* of Paul. The anonymous *Gesta Dagoberti* does not concern us. For our authorities for Saracen history and the monotheletic controversy, I may refer the reader to subsequent chapters.

horrors of darkness which encompassed the Empire around, and the deliverer had now a far harder thing to achieve. He must guide the rescued but still forlorn State through the pitfalls and perils of the dolorous fields which lay round about it. He found the sinews of the Empire paralysed, Europe overrun by Slaves, Asia at the mercy of the Persians; he found demoralisation prevailing in every place and in every class.[1] The breath of fresh air which was wafted with him from the healthful provinces of Africa, and gave for a moment a pleasant shock to the distempered city of Byzantium, was soon lost in the close and choking atmosphere; and it was a question whether Heraclius would really be able to govern much better than Phocas.

For the situation was eminently one that demanded a man of strong will more than a man of keen intellect. The first thing was to gain the confidence of the people, and for this purpose sheer strength of character was necessary. Until the physician had won the confidence of the patient, it was impossible for him to minister with efficacy to the distempered frame. Heraclius was in the vigour of his manhood when he came to the throne, about thirty-six years old. But he does not appear to have been endowed with that strength of character which is always masterful and sometimes wilful. A very ingenious psychological analysis of his character was made by a French historian, and is worthy of attention. Starting with the triple division of the mind into will, intellect, and sensibility, M. Drapeyron defines the perfect man, the Greek of the best age, as one in whom these three faculties are in perfect equilibrium. All less favoured ages produce men in whom one or other faculty predominates and upsets the balance; Heraclius, for example, was one in whom sensibility was more powerful than intellect and intellect more powerful than will. He adduces many passages from the contemporary "poet" George of Pisidia, who was an intimate friend of Heraclius, to prove the impressionable temperament (συμπάθεια) of the Emperor.[2] The merit of this analysis is that it seems to explain things apparently inconsistent and unaccountable in

---

[1] George of Pisidia, *Bell. Av.* 62, writes: ὅλον τὸ σῶμα τοῖς πόνοις ἐβόσκετο, cf. Theoph. 6103 A.M. εὗρε παραλελυμένα τὰ τῆς πολιτείας Ῥωμαίων πράγματα.

[2] The personal appearance of Heraclius is described by Cedrenus thus:

"He was of middle stature, strongly built, and broad-chested; his eyes were fine, rather gray in colour; his hair was yellow, his skin white. When he became Emperor he shaved his long bushy beard and shaved his chin." As

his life. Every one who reads the history of Heraclius is met by the problems : how did the great hero of the last Persian war spend the first ten years of his reign ? and why did he relapse into lethargy after his final triumph ? The assumption that his will was naturally weak and his sensibility strong offers a way of explanation. For a strong sensibility under the influence of a powerful impression may become a sort of inspired enthusiasm, and, while it lasts, react upon the will. The inspiration, on this theory, did not move Heraclius for ten years; then it came, and, when the object was attained, passed away again, leaving him exhausted, as if he had been under a mesmeric influence. From this point of view one naturally compares him with his contemporary Mohammed, the difference being that in the Arabian enthusiast the disproportion between the will and the sensibility was less.

That Heraclius had a capacity for enthusiasm, which found vent in the only channel then open to enthusiasm, namely religious exaltation, cannot be questioned; that he had, like most of his contemporaries, a mystical or superstitious belief in portents and signs is most certain; and that he had an excitable temperament is probable enough. But we do not altogether require M. Drapeyron's plausible and subtle analysis to explain the conduct of the Emperor in the early years of his reign. The first absolute condition of success was to gain public confidence. And as he was not a man who could do this by sheer force of character, he could only effect it by tact, wariness, and patience. The machine of the State was out of order, all the bells were jangled, and in the midst of the difficult complications Heraclius was obliged to feel his way slowly. When we read that the Persians were encamped at Chalcedon in 609 and that the first campaign of Heraclius was in 623,[1] we are fain to imagine that he must have gone to sleep for more than ten years " in the lap of a voluptuous carelessness." It seemed as if the new Perseus had been himself gorgonised

John Malalas generally gives short descriptions of the external appearance of the Emperors (which in other cases Cedrenus utilised), I have no doubt that this description comes from a lost book of John Malalas. It is not the wont of Theophanes to reproduce these physical details.

[1] It is worth noticing that, according to the Armenian historian Sepêos (*see* Patcanian in the *Journal asiatique*, Feb. 1866, p. 199), Heraclius took the field against the Persians soon after his accession. Sepêos also differs from Greek chroniclers in regard to the Persian general at Chalcedon in 615 ; according to Sepêos he was Razman, also called Khorheam, not Shahen.

by the face of the dead horror.   But we must glance more closely at the difficulties which surrounded him.

In the first place, a serious limit was imposed on the activity of the Emperor by the power of the aristocracy, which since the last days of Justinian had become a formidable rival to the throne.   Both Maurice and Phocas adopted the plan of attaching a special group of ministers to their persons, and thus forming an imperial party which in case of necessity might act against refractory patricians.   This group would naturally include the Emperor's kinsmen.   Maurice made his father Paulus chief of the senate, and his brother Peter, in spite of military incapacity, general.   Phocas created his brother Domentziolus curopalates and subsequently general; and it may be conjectured that Leontius, the Syrian treasurer, was a relative of his wife Leontia.   Heraclius followed the example of his predecessors.   He too assigned the post of curopalates to his brother Theodorus; and Theodorus and his cousin Nicetas formed the nucleus of an imperial party.   This circumstance aroused an opposition with which it was necessary for the Emperor to deal warily.   He appointed Priscus (the son-in-law of Phocas), who had invited him to Europe, to command the army stationed in Cappadocia.   But Priscus was not content with the new Emperor, nor with his own share in the fruits of the revolution, and his conduct exhibited tokens of dubious loyalty.   Heraclius decided to act with a judicious caution, and proceeded in person to Caesarea, the chief town of Cappadocia, in order to sound the sentiments of the suspected general.   Priscus at first feigned to be ill; but Heraclius saw him before returning to Byzantium, and it is said that, while the Emperor was imperturbably gentle, the general almost openly insulted him.   "The Emperor," he said, "has no business to leave the palace for the camp."   But Heraclius was biding his time.   He asked Priscus to be the godfather of his son Constantine, and the general came to Constantinople.   Before an assembly, in which the Church, the nobility, and the demes were represented, Heraclius judged Priscus from his own lips, and compelled him to take the vows of monasticism.[1]

[1] He is said to have struck him with a book and said, " You were a bad son-in-law, you could not be a good friend."   For the whole story, *see* Nicephorus, pp. 5, 6.

This was a distinct triumph for the Emperor, and an important advantage gained, for the sympathies of all classes seem to have been enlisted on his side. It was to assure himself of this support that he had proceeded in the matter with such diplomatic caution. The possessions of Priscus, it may be added, were divided between Theodorus and Nicetas, a circumstance which, among other indications, shows that they were looked upon as the supports of the throne. Gregoria, the daughter of Nicetas, was betrothed to the infant Constantine.

An incident is recorded which illustrates the general demoralisation, the power of the patricians, and the cautious manner in which the Emperor was obliged to feel his way and gain step by step on the prevailing anarchy. Not far from Constantinople lived two neighbours, a patrician named Vutelinus[1] and a widow with several children. A field on the borders of their lands, which both claimed, gave rise to a dispute, and Vutelinus employed an armed band of servants to assert his rights. The household of the lady offered resistance, and one of her sons was beaten to death with clubs. Then the lady set out for the capital, bearing the bloodstained garment of her son in her hand, and as the Emperor rode forth from the palace she seized the bridle of his horse, and cried out, " If you avenge not this blood, according to the laws, may such a lot befall your own sons." The Emperor concealed the sympathy and indignation which he felt, and dismissed her, merely saying that he would consider the matter at some seasonable time. His apparent indifference seemed to her a refusal to execute justice, and her despairing grief as she was led away moved the Emperor more deeply. In the meantime her appeal frightened Vutelinus, and he concealed himself in Constantinople. But one day Heraclius, who knew his appearance, espied him in the hippodrome, and caused him to be arrested. He was tried, and condemned to be beaten to death by his servants in the same way as the widow's son had been slain; the unwilling executioners were then to suffer death themselves.

We may mention another incident which shows that during the reign of terror a sort of oriental barbarity had crept into

---

[1] Βουτηλῖνος. The story is recorded by Nicephorus, p. 8.

the Roman Empire and demoralised public feeling. Heraclius lost his wife Eudocia two years after his accession, and as the funeral procession passed through the streets, and the inhabitants were watching it from their windows, it happened that a servant-maid spat just as the corpse, carried on an open bier, was passing, and "the superfluity" fell on the robes of the dead Empress. It will hardly be credited that the girl was sacrificed on the tomb.[1] We are not told what Heraclius thought of the matter.

Other difficulties which surrounded Heraclius were the want of money and the want of an efficient army. His close connection with Africa probably assisted him at first and rescued the financial department; but all reserve funds were exhausted; Asia, infested by the enemy, must have been almost unproductive as a source of revenue, and the lands of Illyricum and Thrace, and perhaps Greece, were at the mercy of Slavonic invaders.[2] Africa, the south-west of Asia Minor, Egypt, and Italy must have been the chief sources of income. But the poverty of the treasury is proved by the bankruptcy which prevailed some years later, when Heraclius was preparing for his great expedition.

It is impossible to arrive at a certain conclusion as to the forces which were available when Heraclius came to the throne. We only know that the army was inefficient, and that of the soldiers who had served in the reign of Maurice and revolted against him only two were alive at the time of the death of Phocas.[3] Priscus commanded an army in Cappadocia, and this army seems to have been attached in a special manner to his own person; perhaps he had raised it himself. For when he became a monk by enforced constraint the Emperor showed marked consideration to his soldiers, and said, "You were till now the servants of Priscus, to-day we have made you the servants of the Empire." This army and the troops which Heraclius and Nicetas had brought with them from Africa are the only field forces of whose actual existence we are certain.

Thus difficulties bristled about Heraclius on all sides,—a

---

[1] Her mistress barely escaped with her life. Nicephorus, p. 7.
[2] Cf. Isidore, *Chron.* 120; in the beginning of the reign of Heraclius, *Sclavi Graeciam Romanis tulerunt.* It is hard to say how much this means.
[3] Theoph. 6103 A.M.

corrupt administration of justice, an inadequate army, an ill-filled treasury, which the fresh aggressions of the Persians made annually emptier. These things demanded reform; and the limits impressed on the Emperor by the power of the patricians, as well as the prevalent demoralisation in all classes, made reform necessarily tardy, notwithstanding the best intentions.

Without supposing Heraclius to have been a John-a-dreams, we can well understand how, with such a prospect before him, he may not have been anxious to ascend the throne, and would not have envied Priscus or Nicetas the diadem; we may suspect that, as he reflected on the rottenness of the time, he often regretted deeply that he was " born to set it right."

He seems to have found a compensation in domestic life for the comfortless duties of politics; and, as these personal matters had some important political bearings, we must not omit to notice them. His marriage with the delicate Eudocia was celebrated on the day of his coronation; she bore him two children, Epiphania and Heraclius Constantine, but died herself of epilepsy in August 612.[1] Soon afterwards he celebrated a second marriage with his niece Martina, and this created a great scandal among his orthodox subjects, who considered such an alliance incestuous ($αἱμομιξία$). Their superstitious objections seemed justified by the fact that of her two first children, Flavius and Theodosius, one had a wry neck and the other was deaf and dumb; and the physical sufferings of the Emperor himself, endured in the last years of his life, were looked upon as a retribution of this sin. Martina was a strong and ambitious woman, who seems to have always exercised a potent fascination on her husband; and if Heraclius had not felt that she was a necessity to him, he would hardly have run the risk of giving general offence and creating distrust when all his endeavours were directed to win the confidence of his subjects. It is remarkable that George of Pisidia, the friend of Heraclius, never mentions Martina's name, and some words seem to point to a sore spot. Martina was always looked on as " the accursed thing."

---

[1] Theoph. 6103 A.M., Nicephorus, p. 9. Constantine was crowned 22d January 613 (*Chron. Pasch.*, but 25th December 612 according to Theophanes). Epiphania was crowned in October 612.

Of the operations of Chosroes at this period and the losses of the Romans we know only the most important, and even these in the barest outline; for the historians seem to make a practice of omitting painful details, and George of Pisidia has formulated the principle that it is meet to commit to silence the greater part of our distresses.[1]   Syria was invaded and Damascus taken, in 613 or 614,[2] by the great general Shahr Barz or "Royal Boar." An embassy treating for peace was sent to Chosroes, but without result[3]; and in 614 or 615 Palestine was invaded; Jerusalem was taken; "the wood," as the true cross was called, was carried to Persia; and the Patriarch Zacharias himself was led into captivity.   Concerning the capture of Jerusalem we possess some significant details.[4] At the first appearance of the Persians the inhabitants made little resistance, and were easily persuaded to receive a Persian garrison.   But when the army had retired, the Christians suddenly rose and slaughtered most of the Persians and Jews in the city.   Shahr Barz returned, and having taken the city after a stubborn resistance, which lasted about three weeks, he avenged his countrymen by a massacre of three days.   We are told that 90,000 Christians were handed over to the untender mercies of the Jews; and the Jews had so many accounts to settle that, notwithstanding their careful habits, they ransomed prisoners for the pleasure of butchering them.

The loss of the country and the city with which the religious sentiments of the Byzantines were so closely associated was soon followed by the loss of the country which chiefly supplied the material needs of Constantinople.   Egypt became a Persian province; for ten years a Copt, Mukaukas, administered it for the Persian king, and the centre of his government was not at Alexandria but at Misr (Babylon, near Cairo).   Here, as in Palestine, as in Syria, as in the country about the Euphrates, the efforts of the Persians would never have been attended with such immediate and easy success but for the disaffection of large masses of the population.   This disaffection rested chiefly on the religious differences, which were closely associated

---

[1] *Bell. Avar.* l. 12.
[2] Clinton, following *Chron. Pasch.* 614. Theophanes, 6104 A.M., that is (as Theophanes is a year wrong) 6105 = second indiction = September 613 to September 614.

[3] Chosroes assumed the position of wishing to restore Theodosius, the son of Maurice, who was really dead.
[4] *Chron. Pasch.* and Sepêos.

with differences in nationality.   In Egypt there was bitter
enmity between the Greek Melchites (Royalists) and the native
Jacobites and monophysites[1]; in Palestine the irreconcilable
feud between Christians and Jews determined the fate of the
Holy City; and in Syria Nestorians were not unkindly disposed
to the Sassanid kingdom, which had generally afforded them a
hospitable shelter.

   In regard to the Jews, Heraclius was disposed to follow the
policy of his predecessor.   He seems to have considered that
any attempt at conciliation or tolerance would be wasted, or
perhaps he was influenced by the deadly power of superstition.
This policy appears too in his relations with foreign states ;
he initiated an anti-Jewish movement throughout Europe.
A treaty which he made with Sisibut, the Visigothic king of
Spain, in 614, the year of the massacres of Jerusalem, probably
contained the stipulation that Sisibut should compel the Jews
of Spain to become Christians.[2]   And six years later, in his
negotiations with the Frank king Dagobert, he induced that
monarch to adopt the policy of persecution.   According to
Fredegarius,[3] Heraclius discovered by the aid of astrology
that the Roman Empire was destined to be blotted out by
circumcised peoples, and therefore sent to Dagobert an order or
a request that he should baptize and convert all the Jews in his
kingdom; and Dagobert did this.   Moreover, Heraclius made
the same ordinance in all the provinces of the Empire, for
he knew not whence the disaster was to come.

   Although the Emperor's resources did not avail to save
Syria and Egypt from the invaders, and from themselves, or
even to secure Asia Minor, we cannot argue that he was inactive or that there were not Roman armies in the field.   When
Priscus had withdrawn to lead a holier life in 612, Philippicus,
who had unwillingly abandoned the world at the instance
of Phocas, came forth from his monastery, and was appointed
general instead of Priscus.   At the same time Theodorus, the
Emperor's brother, received a military command.   We may

---

[1] The monophysites, however, were
not unanimously in favour of Persian
rule.   Benjamin left Alexandria and
returned when Egypt was reconquered.

[2] Isidore, *Hist. Goth.* cap. 60 (cf.
cap. 120) blames the persecution of

Sisibut, but does not attribute it to
Heraclius.

[3] Fredegarius, *Chron.* cap. 65. This
policy of Heraclius is noticed by Finlay, i. p. 326.

suppose that Philippicus until his death, which occurred not long after this,[1] protected, like Priscus, the province of Cappadocia; and it is to be presumed that Theodorus was stationed in some other province of Asia Minor, perhaps in Cilicia. For from the situation of affairs it is natural to conclude that Heraclius, despairing of the southern countries, would devote all his resources to the defence of Asia Minor.[2] But even Asia Minor was not to escape the horrors of invasion. After the conquest of Egypt, the general Shahen entered Asia Minor, meeting, as far as we know, no opposition, and advanced to Chalcedon,[3] as another general had done in the last years of Phocas. The blockade of this town lasted a considerable time, and it is said that the Persian general and the Roman Emperor had an interview, in which the former professed himself desirous of bringing about a peace, and sanguine of the success of negotiations. He offered to go himself, along with the Roman ambassadors, to Chosroes, and use his influence with his master. Heraclius readily agreed, and three envoys were nominated : Olympius, praetorian prefect (presumably of the East); Leontius, prefect of the city; and Anastasius, chancellor of St. Sophia. The most important feature of this embassy is that it was sent, not in the name of the Emperor himself, but of the members of the senate, who composed a long letter to Chosroes. The document justifies Heraclius and makes Phocas the scapegoat; moreover, it reflects the general idea of the Romans that the losses of their provinces were ultimately due to their own sins, and not to the powers of the enemy.[4] As soon as the

---

[1] About a year later, Niceph. p. 7.

[2] It is worth noticing that Nicetas, who started along with Heraclius for Africa in autumn of 610, did not arrive in Constantinople till about April 612 (see Nicephorus). We know not what detained him on his journey, but it may be conjectured that he lingered in Syria to operate against the Persians —perhaps to succour Antioch.

[3] Here I follow Nicephorus (p. 9), who calls Shahen Σάϊτος, and the MSS. of Theophanes, 6107, 6108 A.M., where, however, de Boor follows the Latin translator Anastasius and reads Καρχηδόνα and Καρχηδόνος for Χαλκηδόνα and Χαλκηδόνος. Is a fact really preserved in the translation of Anastasius? Is it really true that the Persians antici-

pated the Saracens in wresting Carthage from the Empire as well as in wresting Syria and Egypt ? And if so, had the Persian occupation anything to do with Heraclius' project of making Carthage the imperial capital?

[4] The long document (composed and sent ἀπὸ τῶν ἀρχόντων ἡμῶν) is preserved in *Chron. Pasch.* I follow Theophanes in placing the embassy in the end of 617 or 618. *Chron. Pasch.* places it in 615, but this is inconsistent with Nicephorus, for Shahen had already blockaded Chalcedon for a long time when the interview took place, and he can hardly have reached Chalcedon before end of 615 at earliest, but more probably in 616. Cf. Theophanes (fourth indiction). M. Drapeyron, p. 129, places it

ambassadors passed the frontiers, Shahen placed them in fetters; but worse things awaited Shahen himself. Chosroes, who from this time forth constantly displays a sort of irrational insolence, was so indignant that Shahen had conversed with Heraclius and yet had not brought him bound hand and foot to his feet, caused the general to be flayed alive ; the ambassadors he subjected to a rigorous confinement.

The loss of Egypt, and the loss of Jerusalem and the holy "wood" were disastrous in different ways. The cessation of the corn supply caused a famine at Constantinople, and the famine produced its natural offspring—a pestilence. Pestilence and famine are often called sisters, each is really both a cause and an effect of the other. Famine induces scanty clothing, dirt, overcrowding, huddling together for the sake of warmth ; and thus are formed centres of weak organisms for the germs of the disease to breed in and spread. The plague, on the other hand, involves a cessation of work and production. This calamity must have seriously paralysed the action of the government, which was always to a certain extent unhealthily confined by the paramount importance of everything that affected the imperial city.

The capture of the Holy Rood was equally serious in a moral aspect; it seemed as if the Deity, by permitting the material instrument of redemption to fall into the hand of the adversary, had plainly turned away in anger from the sins of the Christians and withdrawn his favour. To the inhabitants of Constantinople especially it must have been a grievous distress, for, apart from its intrinsic value, the Holy Rood was closely associated with Helena, the sainted mother of Constantine the Great.[1] When she went as a pilgrim to Jerusalem she was seized by a strong desire to find the actual wood on which Christ had been crucified. Inspiring Macarius, the bishop of Jerusalem, with her ardour, she caused Mount Calvary to be excavated, and three crosses were discovered. Then the question was, which of the three was the Holy Cross ? It was soon solved. Held over the face of a lady who was sick unto death, the true cross healed her by the efficacy of its shadow.

after Heraclius' design of going to Carthage was surrendered, and any date in 618 before 1st September is consistent with Theophanes' notice.

[1] The doings of Helena in Palestine are narrated by Eusebius, *Vita Constantini*.

Helena caused it to be divided into two parts, of which one was sent to her son Constantine, while the other, placed in a silver case, of which the bishop of Jerusalem kept the key, was deposited in the church of the Resurrection. The loss of this, the most precious relic of Christendom, seemed a fatal omen and could not but dispirit still more deeply the desponding hearts of the Romans.

It was after the failure of the embassy to Chosroes that Heraclius conceived a remarkable idea, which, if it had been carried out, would have altered the history of the Roman Empire. He felt that amid the prevailing demoralisation and indifference it was utterly impracticable to make any effectual attempt to rescue the Empire from dismemberment. For he was not given free scope or allowed a fair chance. His actions were limited by the aristocracy, which seems to have assumed an independent position ; he was, in point of power, rather the first man of the senate than an Emperor raised above all alike. It seemed as if the imperial dignity were drifting back into its first stage of six centuries ago. The fact that the senate, and not the Emperor, sent the embassy to Chosroes is the clearest indication of the actual tendency of politics at this time. On the other hand, the atmosphere of Constantinople, the imperial city, had been corrupted by three centuries of degrading bounty. The inhabitants were spoiled children; they looked upon the Emperor as their own peculiar property; their mere residence in Constantinople entitled them to the privileges of idleness, of eating bread for nothing, of witnessing games and court pageants. In such an atmosphere, amid such a wicked and adulterous generation, Heraclius despaired of making a fresh start. While he remained there he must necessarily keep up the old palatial traditions, maintain a costly court expenditure with the money which should have supported a campaign. The iron fetters of " damned custom " lay heavy on his soul ; and he concluded that the only chance of breaking with the past and starting afresh on rational principles, and thereby rescuing the Empire, was to go to a new place, and change the capital of the Roman world. Once he had resolved, the most natural place to select was Carthage, the scene where his youth had been spent. It·was the only prosperous city of first-rate importance at this time, and it was the centre of flourishing provinces, which were devoted to the Heraclian family. There he might make a fresh start with hands untied, independent of the Byzantine nobility and unparalysed by Byzantine demoralisation. There he could be as economical as he pleased, his household could be as simple as was necessary, and he could organise a campaign against the Persians in a secure and distant retreat.

Heraclius made up his mind to carry out this revolutionary project, and before he published his intentions he secretly despatched to Africa the treasures of the palace. Fate itself declared against the design, for the larger part of the gold and silver and precious stones was wrecked in a storm. Then the Byzantines learned the resolve of the Emperor, and great was their consternation. They constrained the Emperor to abandon the plan and not desert Constantinople. The Patriarch Sergius bound him with solemn oaths in the church of St. Sophia that he would never leave the queen of cities.[1] This scene must have produced a deep impression on all who took part in or witnessed it.

If I am not mistaken, this was the turning-point of Heraclius' reign. For, although his design of making a new beginning in Africa was frustrated, this very design rendered it possible to make a new beginning in Constantinople, a consummation for which he could hardly have ventured to hope. We may say that the idea, which he wellnigh executed, caused a moral revolution. The possibility of losing the Emperor, of no longer being the privileged imperial city, brought suddenly home to Constantinople the realities of its situation, and awakened it from the false dream of a spoiled child. When the inhabitants saw that they were not indispensable to the Emperor, as the Emperor was to them, and imagined themselves left without protection, they took a different view of the relations of things. And to this awakening we may ascribe the salvation of the Empire.

At the same time a new element began to permeate the air and react against the morbid despondency which possessed men's minds. A religious enthusiasm spread, and the war against the Persians was regarded in a more religious light than

[1] Niceph. p. 12.

it had been conceived before; it was regarded, namely, as a death-struggle between Christendom and heathendom. Perhaps the capture of the Holy Rood more than anything else rendered this aspect of the war visible; the contest became a crusade. This spiritual change is marked politically by the close alliance which was formed at this time between the Emperor and the Patriarch Sergius, who was henceforth not only a spiritual but a temporal adviser.[1] Sergius was a strong energetic prelate who had the power of influencing men and stirring up enthusiasm; and he played as important a part in the last Persian war as the Pope played in the First Crusade. The religious feeling that prevailed was expressed in solemn services; and while the threats of Chosroes, that he would not spare the Christians until they denied the Crucified,[2] stirred up religious fury against the Antichrist, the recovery of two relics,—the Lance which pierced the side and the Sponge which mocked the thirst of Christ,—shed a gleam of hope, as a sort of earnest that the Holy Cross would be ultimately recovered. It was about this time that Chosroes sent a characteristic letter to Heraclius, intended to be a leisurely reply to the embassy of Shahen. The letter ran thus[3]:—

" The noblest of the gods, the king and master of the whole earth, the son of the great Oromazes, Chosroes, to Heraclius his vile and insensate slave.

" Refusing to submit to our rule, you call yourself a lord and sovereign. You detain and disperse our treasures, and deceive our servants. Having gathered together a troop of brigands, you ceaselessly annoy us; have I not then destroyed the Greeks? You say you have trust in God; why then has he not delivered out of my hand Caesarea, Jerusalem, Alexandria? Are you then ignorant that I have subdued land and sea to my laws? And could I not also destroy Constantinople? But not so. I will pardon all your faults if you will come hither with your wife and children. I will give you lands, vines, and olive groves, which will supply you with the necessaries of life; I will look upon you with a kindly glance. Do not deceive yourself with a vain hope in that Christ who was not able to save himself from the Jews, that killed him by nailing him to a cross. If you descend to the depths of the sea I will stretch out my hand and will seize you, and you shall then see me unwillingly."

Such a letter as this was advantageous to the cause of Heraclius.

---

[1] Was it now that he exhorted him to give up Martina? Cf. Niceph. p. 14.

[2] Theophanes, 6109 A.M.

[3] Sepêos, as quoted by M. Drapeyron, *op. cit.* p. 133.

As the loss of the cross, at first depressing, proved subsequently stimulating when the reaction came, so the loss of Egypt, at first disastrous, turned out beneficial in improving the moral tone of the capital. Once Heraclius had won his new position and a certain flame of unselfish enthusiasm had been kindled, he was able to refuse to continue the free distribution of "the political bread," and demand a small payment; and a few months later he could venture to discontinue the practice altogether.[1] This reform had many beneficial effects. In the first place, it was a direct relief to the public purse. In the second place, by rendering idleness less possible and by setting free funds to support labour, it increased labour. And in the third place, the idlers who could not or would not produce became recruits in the army. And, beside these results, the moral tone was raised.

But this relief was not enough to supply Heraclius with the funds necessary for effectual military operations. It was in fact merely a set-off against the loss of Egypt; it was no absolute gain to the exchequer. The financial perplexity was solved by the religious character of the war, which produced a close alliance between Church and State and made Sergius the ardent right-hand man of Heraclius. The Church granted a great loan to the State, which was to be paid back with interest at the end of the war. The immense treasures of the churches of Constantinople were melted and converted into coin; and the political insolvency was rescued by a peculiar form of national debt, which recalls the public loan made by the Romans in the second Punic war.

No event betrays more significantly than this loan that the character of the last Persian war was that of a holy crusade.

Perhaps for no lustrum in the seventh century are exact dates so desirable as for these years (617-622), during which the Roman Empire revived and a new spirit passed into its dry bones. And it is irritating to find that the notices of the chroniclers are vague and contradictory. But without attempting to establish definite dates for everything, I think the

---

[1] *Chron. Pasch.* 618 A.D. ἀπῃτήθησαν οἱ κτήτορες τῶν πολιτικῶν ἄρτων διὰ διαγραφῶν (like a capitation tax) καθ' ἕκαστον ἄρτον νομίσματα γ', which means three *aurei* (£1 : 17 : 6), not per loaf, but for the right of one ticket for receiving loaves daily. διὰ διαγραφῶν implies it was to be a yearly payment.

general nexus of events is plain, and this nexus is important. The design of Heraclius to migrate to Carthage (618) led to the reaction, and this reaction enabled him to incite the citizens to enthusiasm and carry out the needful reforms.[1]

At this juncture another element in the political situation becomes prominent, the dangerous neighbourhood of the Avaric kingdom, of which we have heard nothing since the treaty with Phocas in 604. In the meantime, however, the Avars had not been idle. One year in alliance and the next year at feud with their old allies the Lombards, they were alternately ravaging Istria in conjunction with that people and invading northern Italy. In 619 the chagan proposed to make a treaty with Heraclius, and won the hearts of two Roman ambassadors by his amiable behaviour. He proposed a conference at Heraclea, to which the Emperor eagerly consented, for it was now of the greatest consequence to him to secure for Constantinople immunity from attacks on the Thracian side, while he threw all his forces into the contest in the East. The preparations for the interview made by the Romans and those made by the Avars were of a very different nature. Heraclius made arrangements to entertain the barbarians by a scenic representation, and to dazzle them with all the sumptuousness of imperial splendour and court pageantry. The chagan, on the other hand, despatched a chosen body of troops to conceal themselves on the wooded heights that commanded the Long Wall. But fortunately Heraclius, who was waiting at Selymbria, received intelligence of this suspicious movement, and perceived that the chagan's intention was to seize his person by cutting off his retreat. He did not hesitate to throw off his royal dress and disguise himself in humble raiment; and, with his crown concealed under his arm, the Emperor fled to Constantinople. He arrived just in time to take some measures for the defence of the city. The Avars, baulked in their stratagem, pursued him hotly, and, penetrating into the suburbs of the city, wrecked several churches. Not only did the apparatus which had been provided for the scenic performances, and those who were engaged in the preparations, and the imperial robes, become the

---

[1] The order of events in Nicephorus leads us to refer the Carthage design to 618, and in 618 the *Paschal Chronicle* places the corn reform. The nexus is patent.

booty of the chagan, but men and women to the number of 270,000 were carried away to captivity.[1]

We are not accurately informed what followed this alarming occurrence. It seems that the chagan tried to gloze over the treachery, and it is probable that Heraclius, unlike the unpopular Maurice, ransomed the captives and bought a peace.[2] He had already directed the exarch of Ravenna to make a defensive treaty with the Lombards for operations against the Avars, and this was to a certain extent a check on the hostilities of the heathen.

But before Heraclius set out to conduct the Persian war he conceived the idea of throwing a sop to Cerberus and paying a compliment to the chagan of the Avars. He is said to have appointed that monarch guardian of his son,[3] and he sent as hostages to the Avaric court two Roman nobles, along with a nephew and a son of his own; the latter, who " came saucily into the world before he was sent for," bore the Gothic name Athalaric. By this scheme Heraclius not only conciliated the Avars but possessed spies in the enemy's country, who could give early warning of harm intended to the Empire.

The new spirit of vigour and enthusiasm that prevailed had manifested itself in 618, and yet Heraclius was not ready to set out on his first campaign until 622. The year 619 is accounted for by the affair with the Avars which was so nearly fatal to the Emperor, but by what cares he was occupied during the two ensuing years we are not informed by our Greek authorities. We can hardly assume that all this time was required for the organisation of his army, especially as in 622 he spent several months in drilling his troops in Cilicia.

The solution of this difficulty is that he was engaged in hostilities with the Persians who were stationed at Chalcedon, and that these hostilities have been completely omitted by the Greek historians. That town, taken by the Persians in 617, had become the station of an army which was always watching

---

[1] There was probably a large number of people at Heraclea assembled for the gaieties, and many also at Selymbria with the Emperor. Many too must have been carried off from the immediate vicinity of the capital.

[2] This may be concluded from Niceph.

p. 15: κατὰ δὲ τὸν αὐτὸν καιρὸν, κ.τ.λ.

[3] This guardianship was, of course, only nominal and complimentary. It strongly confirms the often doubted notice of Procopius that Arcadius appointed the king of Persia guardian of his son Theodosius.

for an opportunity to attack the great city across the straits. This solution would be only a probable conjecture but for a record preserved by an Armenian historian of an event which must be placed in one of these years.[1] By the orders of Chosroes the Persians assaulted Constantinople, but the Greek fleet attacked them and utterly discomfited them, with a loss of 4000 men and their ships. This encouraging success indicates to us another preoccupation of Heraclius. It was not only necessary to organise an army; it devolved upon him to organise a navy also, in order to secure the capital during his absence.

By the end of 621 all the preliminaries were over. Friendly relations had been established with the Avars; the imperial city on the Bosphorus had a fleet to protect it against the Persians of Chalcedon; the military chest was well provided, owing to the co-operation of the Church; and an army had been formed, which was to be further increased on its arrival in Asia. There was a deliberation and want of haste about all these preparations which lent them a certain solemnity; and all minds must have been wrought up to form high expectations for the success of this enterprise, which was marked by two novelties. It was a distinctly religious war, in which the worshippers of Christ and the worshippers of fire were fighting to the death; and it was to be conducted by the Emperor in person,[2] an arrangement which to the inhabitants of Byzantium was a new and strange thing, for since Theodosius the Great no Emperor who reigned at New Rome had led an army to victory or defeat. Zeno the Isaurian had indeed proclaimed that he would conduct a campaign against Theodoric, and more recently Maurice had marched as far as Anchialus to take the field against the Avars; yet at the last moment both Maurice and Zeno had abandoned their valorous purposes. But Heraclius was not as Zeno or as Maurice, and the recent naval success in the Bosphorus was an inspiriting omen of victory.

The winter before his departure (621-622) was spent by Heraclius in retirement. He was probably engaged in studying strategy and geography and planning his first campaign. Those

---

[1] Sepêos. *See* Drapeyron, *op. cit.* p. 131, who adopts this theory as to the date. In 620 the Persians took Galatian Ancyra (Theoph. 6111 A.M.)

[2] Some disapproved of this plan and tried to retain him (compare the similar case of Maurice, above, p. 124), George Pis. *Exp. Pers.* i. 120 *sqq.*

who look upon him as an inspired enthusiast would like to see in this retirement the imperative need of communion with his own soul and with God; they suppose that he was like John the Baptist, or that, like Jesus, he retired to a mountain to pray. To support this idea they can appeal to George of Pisidia, who, speaking of this retreat, says that the Emperor "imitated Elias of old," and uses many other expressions which may be interpreted in a similar manner. It is probable that Heraclius was fain to possess his soul in silence for a few months; but it is hazardous to press the theological word-painting of a poetical ecclesiastic into the service of the theory that Heraclius was a semi-prophetic enthusiast with a naturally weak will. When George of Pisidia mentions in another place that the Emperor studied treatises on tactics and rehearsed plans of battle, we feel that we are on surer ground.[1] The *Strategic* of Maurice, doubtless, was constantly in his hands.

Heraclius appointed his son Constantine, now ten years old, regent during his absence. The actual administration was vested in Sergius the Patriarch and Bonus a patrician, who were to act, of course, in concert with the senate. The political position of Sergius is highly significant of the time, and indicates the close bond which was drawing together Church and State, a bond substantially welded by the material sacrifice which the Church had made. It was natural that when the Church had ventured the greater part of her possessions in the enterprise, she should have a representative in the government. Such a colossal shareholder had a claim to appoint a director. But, apart from this consideration, Sergius was the strongest and firmest supporter of the Emperor throughout his reign, quite an invaluable ally.

On the day after Easter 622 Heraclius sailed from Constantinople. His departure was celebrated with religious circumstance, emphasising the religious character of his enterprise, to prevent the infidels from insulting the heritage

---

[1] *Heracliad*, ii. 120 and 136—

οὐκ ἦν γὰρ ἔργον πολεμικῶν συνταγμάτων
ὃ μὴ μετῆλθες τῇ σχολῇ τῶν σκεμμάτων,
τυπῶν, προτάττων, εὐτρεπίζων, προσγράφων

καὶ σχηματουργῶν τῆς μάχης τὰς εἰκόνας, κ.τ.λ.

M. Drapeyron's minute study of George of Pisidia causes him to ascribe an undue importance and a too literal meaning to every word.

of Christ. George of Pisidia delivered an oration on the occasion, and foretold that Heraclius would redden his black leggings in Persian blood.[1]   The Emperor took with him that image of the Virgin not made with hands [2] which had been propitious to him when, almost twelve years before, he sailed against Phocas.

[1] This is recorded by Cedrenus, i. p. 718 (ed. Bonn). Cedrenus had before him a source which we do not possess —the source doubtless which was used by Theophanes. Entering the church with black shoes, Heraclius prayed "Lord God (θεέ, a curious vocative), give us not up for a reproach to our enemies on account of our sins"; and George Pisides said in solemn iambic verses, "O king,

μελαμβαφὲς πέδιλον εἴλιξας πόδα
βάψαις ἐρυθρὸν Περσικῶν ἐξ αἱμάτων."

Did George relate this incident in a lost poem ? or did he really extemporise the iambics ?

[2] George Pis. *Exp. Pers.* i. 140 (a passage which caught the fancy of Theophanes, who quotes part of it, 6113 A.M.)—

μορφὴν ἐκείνην τῆς γραφῆς τῆς ἀγράφου
ἣν χεῖρες οὐκ ἔγραψαν ἀλλ' ἐν εἰκόνι
ὁ πάντα μορφῶν καὶ διαπλάττων Λόγος
ἄνευ γραφῆς μόρφωσιν, ὡς ἄνευ σπορᾶς
κύησιν αὐτὸς, ὡς ἐπίσταται, φέρει.

CHAPTER III

THE Persian campaigns of Heraclius are six in number: (1) the campaign of Cappadocia and Pontus, 622-623; (2) the first campaign of Azerbiyan, 623; (3) the campaign of Albania and Armenia, 624; (4) the campaign of Cilicia, 625; (5) the second campaign of Azerbiyan, 626; (6) the campaign of Assyria, 627-628. The year 626 was also signalised by the joint attack of the Persians and Avars on Constantinople.[1]

I. *Campaign of Cappadocia and Pontus, 622-623 A.D.*

The plan of the first campaign of Heraclius was a distinct surprise. It was probably expected that he would sail up the Black Sea and enter Persia by Armenia. He took a completely different course. He sailed southward through the Hellespont, coasted along Asia Minor, then, bearing eastward, made for the bay of Issus, and landed at those remarkable Gates which form the entrance from Syria to Asia Minor, "the gates of Cilicia and Syria." These Gates are a narrow road between the range of Mount Amanus on the east and the sea on the west, about six days' march from Tarsus. The place played a part of strategic importance both in the expedition of Cyrus the younger and in the Persian expedition of Alexander. Its importance for Heraclius' purposes lay in its geographical advantages. It was a common centre to which

---

[1] The best and fullest account of these campaigns has been written by Drapeyron.

Roman subjects in Syria on the one hand, and in Asia Minor
on the other, who had escaped the sword or chains of Chosroes,
could gather to the standard of the Emperor; and no place
could offer a more secure retreat for organising and drilling
his army at leisure and for assimilating the new recruits
to the troops which he had brought with him.   These preparations occupied the summer and autumn, and Heraclius
showed that both in directing tactics and in inspiring confidence he possessed a rare talent for military command.
He had already, on the voyage, won golden opinions by his
personal energy in a storm which almost wrecked his ship;
and he appears to have adopted a tone of genial comradeship
which infused confidence into his followers and aided his
Roman discipline in holding together the heterogeneous masses
that composed his army.   He did not forget to keep alive the
religious enthusiasm which had inspired the expedition, and
doubtless he sometimes delivered half-religious half-martial
orations, such as became a crusader.[1]   The practical part of
the preparations seems to have been thorough; and he exercised his own generalship and his soldiers' presence of mind
in sham battles.

As winter approached, Heraclius passed from Cilicia into
Cappadocia, and a trifling victory over some Saracen guerilla
bands[2] was hailed as an earnest of a prosperous issue.

In the meantime King Chosroes had sent a mandate to
Shahr Barz,—who, regardless of Heraclius, was still watching
his opportunity at Chalcedon,—to move eastward and oppose
the advance of the Roman army.   This was just what Heraclius
desired.   The Persians entered Pontus, .expecting that the
Romans would remain in the south of Cappadocia until winter
was over; but, finding that Heraclius continued his northward
march, they passed into that country.   The armies met, and
Heraclius found himself in an unfavourable position before he
had time to choose his own ground; moreover, he was threatened with want of supplies.   He extricated himself from
this difficulty by a curious ambiguous movement, a sort of
double-faced march.[3]   To the Persians he seemed to be moving

---

[1] *See* George Pis. *Exp. Pers.* ii. 88 *sqq.*
[2] *Ib.* 218, τὸ Σαρακήνων τάγμα τῶν
πολυτρίχων.

[3] This movement was called the τάξις
πεπλεγμένη.   George Pis. *Exp. Pers.*
261 *sqq.*—

in a southerly direction, whereas he really took a northerly
route, and before they were aware what had taken place he
had crossed the Antitaurus range and entered the region of
Pontus where the Lycus and Halys approach each other.
Shahr Barz now took it for granted that the Romans would
winter in Pontus, but Heraclius soon gave him cause for uneasiness by feigning a movement in the direction of Armenia,
as though he intended to invade Persia on that side. The
Persian general then adopted the curiously infelicitous scheme
of marching southwards to Cilicia, thinking apparently that
Heraclius would follow him to secure the Gates at Issus. But
the Gates had served the Emperor's purpose, and he was now
indifferent in their regard ; so the decoy did not succeed. Then,
weary of this game of hide-and-seek, and uncertain of
Heraclius' design in respect to Armenia, Shahr Barz retraced
his steps and crossed the Antitaurus in the face of the Roman
forces which occupied the passes.

Once more the armies were face to face, but on this occasion
Heraclius had been able to choose his position.[1] The versifier
who celebrated this campaign has left an edifying description
of the contrast between the two camps.[2] Cymbals and all
kinds of music gratified the ears of Shahr Barz, and naked
women danced before him ; while the christian Emperor
sought delight in psalms sung to mystical instruments, which
awoke a divine echo in his soul.

For several days the armies stood opposed in battle array
without venturing on an engagement ; and it is said that
Heraclius employed stratagems to induce his opponent to fight ;
on one occasion, for example, causing a banquet to be prepared
in the open air, to invite a Persian surprise. At last Shahr

ἀντιστροφὴν ἐνταῦθα συντομωτάτην
καὶ σχηματισμὸν αἰνετῆς πλαστουργίας
ἐξεῦρες, ὦ κράτιστε, τοῖς μὲν βαρβάροις
δείξας πρόσωπον ἐκδρομῆς ἐψευσμένης.

To understand clearly in what this
artifice consisted, we should require
some topographical knowledge. Perhaps a few battalions marching slowly
in the false direction concealed from
the eyes of the foe a rapid northward
movement of the main body.

[1] Neither the composition of George
of Pisidia nor the Chronicle of Theophanes gives any preciser information as

to the place of the battle. The time is
determined by an eclipse of the moon,
which took place on 22d January 623,
a day or two before the engagement
(George Pis. *Exp. Pers.* iii. 1).

[2] *Ib.* ii. 240 *sqq.* This description is
given on the occasion of the first meeting in Cappadocia. He mentions the

γυναικῶν ἐκτόπων
ὄρχησιν εἰς γύμνωσιν ἠρεθισμένην

as contrasted with Heraclius'

σεμνὰ ταρθένων σκιρτήματα,
τῶν σῶν λογισμῶν τὰς ἀπόρους ἐλπίδας.

Barz conceived a plan which he thought would ensure success. One night he hid a body of men in a ravine on one side of the plain, and the next day, relying on this ambush, he prepared for action. But the Roman scouts had discovered the stratagem, and Heraclius availed himself of it to hoist the Persians with their own petard. He detached a regiment and sent it in the direction of the ambush, having given instructions to the soldiers that on approaching the spot they were to feign a panic and flee. · The concealed Persians fell into the snare; they rushed out and pursued the simulating fugitives without caring to keep order. Heraclius came quickly up with the rest of his army to overwhelm the pursuers, and then the main body of ·the Persian host approached to assail Heraclius. We cannot clearly determine the course of the action or the causes which threw the Persian army into disorder, but it seems that when the calculation of Shahr Barz had been defeated by the promptitude of the Emperor, and the circumstances of the engagement had been decided for him, and not by him, he was not equal to the occasion, and could not prevent confusion from overwhelming his troops. The Persians were soon in headlong flight, stumbling among rocks and falling over precipices, where the pursuers easily cut them down. The pursuit was compared to the hunting of wild goats.

After the first great victory which established the reputation of Heraclius as a competent general and restored the lustre of Roman arms, the triumphant army established its quarters for the end of winter and the early spring in Pontus, while the Emperor, accompanied by George of Pisidia—his "poet-laureate"—returned to the imperial city to arrange a dispute which had arisen with the chagan of the Avars. Besides his arrival as a victorious hero, one evident fact brought home to the eyes of the Byzantines how much he had already accomplished, the fact, namely, that a Persian army was no longer menacing their city from the opposite shore of the Bosphorus.

II. *First Campaign of Azerbiyan*, 623 A.D.

At the end of March [1] Heraclius returned to the army

[1] The date is fixed by the circumstance that he spent Easter (27th March) at Nicomedia. He left Constantinople on the 15th (Theophanes).

accompanied by the Empress Martina; he had become so popular that he might venture with impunity to take "the accursed thing" into his tent. Now that he had secured Asia Minor, his obvious policy was to carry the war into Persia and attack the lion in his lair. He therefore lost no time in passing through Lazica into Armenia, and, marching eastwards, he crossed first the river Araxes and then the chain of mountains which separates Armenia from Atropatene or Azerbiyan, "the land of fire," the northern district of Media and chief seat of the Zoroastrian fire-worship. He had signified to Chosroes his intention to invade Persia unless that monarch made reasonable offers of peace; and Chosroes, who had already ordered Shahr Barz to return to his familiar quarters at Chalcedon, sent messengers to recall him, and hastened to collect another army under Saes. The king himself took up quarters at Ganzaca,[1] the royal city of Azerbiyan, in which there was a magnificent palace.

Meanwhile the champion of Christendom advanced through this fertile country, laying it waste and destroying the towns,[2] and the visible signs of heathen fire-worship whetted the swords of the Roman fanatics. He advanced directly on Ganzaca, where the great king awaited him with a garrison of forty thousand men. But a slight occurrence sufficed to make Nushirvan turn and flee. Some Saracens attached to the Roman army happened to surprise a company of the Persian royal guard,[3] and Chosroes immediately left Ganzaca, and all that was therein, to his enemy, and fled westward in the direction of Nineveh. Perhaps not "all that was therein," for the Christians had hoped to find the Holy Rood at Ganzaca, and were sorely disappointed to learn that it had been removed. On the other hand, they found a remarkable work of Persian

---

[1] Identified by some with Tauris, by others, including Prof. Rawlinson, with Takht-i-Soleima.

[2] The speech placed by Theophanes in the mouth of Heraclius, and the reply of one who spoke on behalf of the army, are evidently taken from a poem, and doubtless from a lost poem of George of Pisidia; most of the sentences fall into iambic lines. Thus—

τὸ τῶν Ῥωμαίων (sic) αὐτοδέσποτον κράτος.
στῶμεν κατ' ἐχθρῶν δυσσεβῶς ὡπλισμένων
πίστιν λάβωμεν τῶν φόνων φονεύτριαν.

And—

ἥπλωσας ἡμῶν δέσποτα τὰς καρδίας,
τὸ σὸν πλατύνας ἐν παραινέσει στόμα,
ὤξυναν ἡμῶν οἱ λόγοι σου τὰ ξίφη,
κ.τ.λ.

The style of these lines is redolent of the Pisidian, who is always using πλατύνω, ὀξύνω, παραίνεσις, ἁπλόω (or ἐξαπλόω). For αὐτοδέσποτον, see *Hexaemeron*, 348.

[3] τῇ τοῦ Χοσρόου βίγλᾳ (*vigiliae*), Theoph.

"blasphemy," which provoked their religious wrath, and was destroyed with exultant zeal.   This was a statue of Chosroes standing in the temple of the Sun, round which winged images of the sun, the moon, and the stars hovered to receive his adorations.   Thebarmes, the birthplace of Zoroaster—the Jerusalem of Persia—was reduced to ashes, and the Christians felt, when they had destroyed the temple of Fire, that they had retaliated on their enemies for the capture of the Holy City.

The enthusiasm of the troops might have led them on to the consummation of their successes by the capture of Dastagherd and Ctesiphon, but winter was approaching, Shahr Barz would soon arrive with his army from the west, and perhaps other deterrent circumstances, which we cannot guess, now influenced the resolution of Heraclius.   Prudently proof against the lure of a speedy and brilliant termination of the war, he decided to winter in Albania, and by employing the test of a *sors evangelica,* he carried the spirit of his troops with him in a course really dictated by rational considerations. His mercy[1] or policy liberated the 50,000 captives whom he had taken; their sustenance was a burden on the winter march, and at the same time this kindness alienated the loyalty of many Persians from the unpopular Chosroes.

III. *Campaign of Albania and Armenia,* 624 A.D.

Of the three Caucasian countries which border on the north of Armenia—Colchis, Iberia, and Albania,—Albania is the most easterly.   Bounded on the east by the Caspian, on the west by Iberia, it is separated from Armenia on the south by the Cyrus, which, mixing its waters with the great Armenian river Araxes at some distance from its mouth, flows along with it into the Hyrcanian Sea.   In this country Heraclius recruited his army with Colchian, Iberian, and Abasgian allies, and entered into negotiation with the Khazars, a Hunnic people of the trans-Caucasian steppes.

---

[1] Theophanes' εὐσυμπαθήτῳ καρδίᾳ smacks of George of Pisidia, and I have no doubt that he wrote a poem (now lost) describing this campaign. κοσμόλεθρον Χοσρόην, two lines further, sug- gests the same source; and ἡ πλάνη τῶν ἀνθράκων (308, 5, ed. de Boor) of the fire-worship at Ganzaca, reads like the end of a line of George.

The campaign of 624 consisted of a series of movements and counter-movements to and fro between Albania and Armenia, wherein both sides exhibited dexterity, but the Roman Emperor proved himself superior. At first he was opposed by two Persian armies, one commanded by a new general, Sarablagas,[1] the other by the inevitable Shahr Barz. The object of Sarablagas was to prevent the Romans from entering Persia, and accordingly, having garrisoned the passes of Azerbiyan, he stationed himself on the lower Cyrus near its junction with the Araxes. Heraclius, however, marched in a north-westerly direction and crossed the river considerably higher up, but his advance was retarded by a mutiny of his Caucasian allies, and in the meantime Shahr Barz, who had entered Armenia from the south-west, had arrived on the scene of action and effected a junction with his colleague Sarablagas. When these tidings arrived, the obstructives in the Roman camp were pathetically penitent, and bade Heraclius lead them where he would. He then advanced towards the place where the Persians were stationed, defeated some of their outposts, and passing on marched to the Araxes.

But ere he reached the river he suddenly found himself face to face with the Persian army, which, as he thought, he had left behind him; the two generals had hastened to outstrip him by fast marches and cut off his progress towards Persia.[2] Heraclius did not intend to give battle at such a disadvantage, and under the shelter of night he retraced his steps until he reached a plain where he could occupy a favourable position. The Persians imagined that he was fleeing for dread of them, and pursued him with a rash negligence of precautions; but they were calmly received by the Roman army, which was drawn up at the foot of a wooded hill. The victory of the Araxes was as complete as the first victory had been on the confines of Pontus and Cappadocia, and it proved fortunate for the Romans that the enemy were defeated just at that moment, for another army was close at hand under the command of Saes, and arrived almost immediately after the

---

[1] ἄνδρα δραστήριον καὶ τύφῳ πολλῷ ἐπηρμένον, "energetic and conceited," Theoph. 6115 A.M. Sarablagas commanded troops specially named after Persian sovereigns, the "Perozites" (after Perozes) and "Chosroes'

own," Χοσροηγέται.

[2] The decision of the two generals was determined partly by the statement of two deserters that the Romans were fleeing, partly by their wish to gain a victory before the arrival of Saes.

action. The victorious Romans fell upon the new army, which, tired by the march and dispirited by the misfortune, was soon scattered.[1] Sarablagas was among those slain in the first engagement.

Notwithstanding this double victory, the judicious Emperor did not entertain the intention of invading Persia yet. It does not appear that his army was over strong, and the Iberian and Abasgian allies, weary of warfare, signified their determination to return to their habitations. He therefore fell back upon Albania again, and the Persians, observing that he had lost his allies, and thinking that they might even yet crush him, followed on his steps. On one occasion, when a battle seemed imminent, Heraclius is said to have made a brief speech, and if the words which a late chronicler has recorded[2] were not actually uttered by him, they were almost certainly composed by a contemporary.

"Do not be afraid of the number of the enemy, for with God's grace one Roman will turn to flight a thousand Persians. For the safety of our brethren let us sacrifice our own lives unto God, winning thereby the martyr's crown and the praises of future generations."

In this short exhortation, which, if not spoken by the Emperor, is at least a product of the atmosphere of his army, the religious character of the war is manifest; those who perish are *martyrs*.

The battle, however, did not take place; Heraclius again repeated his favourite movement of passing away at night from the presence of the foe and returned to Armenia. Shahr Barz remained, but Saes, following the Romans, found himself involved in difficult morasses; it was already winter, and his troops became disorganised and useless. Having thus dis-

---

[1] παρέλαβε δὲ καὶ τὸ τοῦλδον αὐτῶν (the baggage, including slaves).

[2] Here again we can trace the words of Theophanes to George Pisides with a probability that is almost certainty. The following iambics are patent—

λόγοις ἀνεπτέρωσε καὶ παραινέσει
τούτους λέγων ἤλειφε· μὴ ταραττέτω
ὑμᾶς, ἀδελφοί, πολεμίων πλῆθος [φίλοι]
θεοῦ θέλοντος εἰς διώξει χιλίους
στέφος λάβωμεν μαρτύρων . . .

In the *Heracliad* (ii. 144) George

seems to refer to some other person (ἄλλοι) writing a history of Heraclius' campaigns, and one might imagine that these lines in Theophanes come from the work of a pupil or contemporary imitator ; but it is not likely that there should be no record of his name. The fact that Suidas does not hint at the existence of other poems of George is no objection to my theory, as the list of Suidas does not include all his extant works.

posed of one of the hostile armies, Heraclius retraced his steps once more and found that Shahr Barz had taken up quarters in the strong town of Salban.   But even there he was not safe.   The Roman Emperor surprised the fortress early in the morning, and massacred the people, who offered little resistance, while the Persian general, leaving even his arms behind him, fled for his life.

After this successful and intricate campaign, in which they had defeated three Persian armies, the Romans passed the rest of the winter at Salban, the modern Van.

IV. *Campaign of Cilicia*, 625 A.D.

In drawing up the plan of his next campaign Heraclius may have taken the following points into consideration.   The Persians had had sufficient experience of warfare in the highlands of Armenia to prevent their essaying it again with such an antagonist as the Roman Emperor; so that there was no good reason for him to remain in those regions, especially as he could no longer rely on the useful help of the neighbouring tribes.   It remained for him therefore either to invade Persia again—whether Assyria or Azerbiyan—or to return into Asia Minor, whither Shahr Barz would probably once more betake himself.   The tidings of possible hostilities on the part of the Avars may have decided him to adopt the latter course, as it was desirable that he should in such a contingency be nearer at hand to provide for the protection of the capital of the Empire.

In 623 he had left Asia Minor by the northern route; in 625 he returned thither by a southern route, which involved the labour of crossing Mount Taurus twice.   Marching in a south-westerly direction through Armenia, skirting Mount Ararat on the north, he followed for a while the course of the Murad Tschai, that branch of the river Euphrates which, rising near Ararat, flows between Taurus and Antitaurus.   Before he approached the confluence he turned southwards and, crossing Mount Taurus for the first time, entered Arzanene, where he recovered the Roman cities of Martyropolis and Amida.[1]   When

---

[1] From here he was able to send letters to Byzantium, and thereby fill the city with joy.

he reached the Euphrates [1] he was opposed by Shahr Barz, who destroyed the bridge, but the army gained the right bank by a ford north of Samosata. He then crossed the Taurus for the second time, and, entering Cilicia at the town of Germanicia, arrived at the Sarus. Here the Persian general overtook him. The river separated the two armies, but an engagement soon took place which, owing to the enthusiastic precipitancy of the Romans, proved wellnigh a Persian victory. The presence of mind and personal prowess of Heraclius retrieved the fortunes of the day; he is said to have slain a gigantic warrior and to have performed prodigious deeds of valour, which excited the marvel of Shahr Barz,[2] and which well became a hero who was destined to figure in medieval legend. The defeated army abandoned the idea of contending further with their invincible adversary and retreated to Persia, while Heraclius, following the same route which he had taken in his first campaign, proceeded to Pontus and established his winter quarters on the Black Sea.

V. *The Second Campaign of Azerbiyan; the Victory of Theodorus; the Siege of Constantinople,* 626 A.D.

The Roman Empire was more seriously menaced in 626 than in any of the foregoing years; it was beset with dangers which put the ability of Heraclius in forming combinations to a severe proof, and he was obliged to leave the execution of his arrangements chiefly to others. Not only did Chosroes attempt, as the historian of the Sassanid dynasty tells us, " to bring the war to a close by an effort, the success of which

---

[1] He crossed the Nymphius first. In Theophanes here there is perhaps an echo of a line of George Pisides: ἐκδραμὼν διεξόδους ἀντιπρόσωπος ἤει τῷ Σαρβάρῳ. ἤει has taken the place of a trisyllable. Further on we have μήπως ὁδὸς γένηται τοῖς ἐναντίοις. In the description of the battle it is said that the barbarians, fleeing along the narrow bridge, threw themselves into the water "like frogs"; this simile also suggests George Pisides. The remarks on Heraclius' doughty deeds, which Shahr Barz makes to the renegade Cosmas, point in the same direction; *see* next note.

[2] Shahr Barz is said to have remarked to Cosmas (a Roman who had apostatised) ὁρᾷς τὸν καίσαρα, ὦ Κοσμᾶ, πῶς θρασὺς πρὸς τὴν μάχην ἵσταται | καὶ πρὸς τοσοῦτο πλῆθος μόνος ἀγωνίζεται καὶ ὡς ἄκμων τὰς βολὰς ἀποπτύει. If we write ἵσταται μόνος for μον. ἀγ. and ἀλλ' ὥσπερ for καὶ ὡς we have two iambic lines, which we may assume belonged to a lost poem of George Pisides, whence Theophanes obtained his knowledge of this campaign. Notice that he calls Cosmas a *magarite* instead of a Mediser, by a natural anachronism (*see* below, p. 267).

would have changed the history of the world,"[1] but the chagan of the Avars prepared a gigantic expedition for the capture of Constantinople; and the two dangers were still more formidable from the fact that they were not independent. Movements in the East had often before influenced movements on another frontier of the Empire, the clash of arms in the Euphrates had roused an echo on the Danube; there had even been attempts at joint action between the enemies of the Empire in the East and its enemies in the West; but this was the first time that such an alliance took the form of anything resembling strict co-operation. And it was now carried out in a really alarming manner, as the two foes appeared almost simultaneously on either side of the Bosphorus, leagued for the destruction of the imperial city.

Chosroes levied a new army and appointed Shahr Barz to lead it against Byzantium. His more experienced troops, which had lived through the dangers and defeats of recent years, he placed under the command of Shahen or Saes,[2] whom he ordered to hunt down Heraclius, under pain of an ignominious death.

Heraclius laid his plans with considerable skill. He made no attempt to prevent Shahr Barz from reaching Scutari, nor did he think, as many would have thought, of rushing with all his forces to the protection of the capital and abandoning the ground which he had already gained in the East. He divided his army into three portions. One portion he retained himself to protect Armenia, and, in case he found it advisable, to invade Persia. The second he entrusted to his brother Theodore,[3] to operate against Saes. The third, a corps of veterans, was sent as a reinforcement to Constantinople, with the most minute directions as to the mode of defence which should be adopted.

Of the details of Heraclius' operations we are not informed. He entered into a close alliance with the Khazars, whom he met as they returned from a plundering expedition in Azerbiyan, and won the affections of Ziebil their king, or the brother of their king.[4] Having entertained him sumptuously

---

[1] Rawlinson, p. 516.

[2] He also gave to Saes fifty thousand men from the army of Shahr Barz, and called them "Gold-Lancers," χρυσολόγχεις (Theoph. 6117 A.M.)

[3] It may perhaps be conjectured that during the preceding years Theodore had been stationed in Asia Minor.

[4] Theophanes calls him the brother of the chagan of the Khazars, but in

and bestowed upon him and his attendants rich raiment and pearl earrings, Heraclius confidentially exposed to his view the picture of a maiden in rich costume. "God," said the Emperor, "has united us; he has made thee my son. Behold, this is my daughter, and an Empress of the Romans. An thou assist me against mine enemies, I give her to thee to wife." Impressed by her beauty or her splendour, Ziebil was more ardent than ever in his friendship, and gave the father of his promised bride forty thousand Khazars; and Heraclius, when he had drilled them in the military discipline of a Roman army, proceeded to lay Azerbiyan waste once more.[1]

Ziebil died before the end of the year, and Epiphania Eudocia,[2] almost the victim of a political expediency, happily escaped banishment to the wilds of Scythia and an uncivilised people, to which her father and stepmother would not have hesitated to sacrifice her in the interests of Christendom.[3] Ziebil's death was not so welcome to Heraclius, as it caused the return of his Khazar allies to their homes; and at the end of the year he found himself in Media with a weak army.

Of the collision of Theodore and Saes we know little more than the result. The battle was fought in Mesopotamia, and a great hailstorm, to which the Persians were exposed while the Romans were sheltered, decided the victory for the latter. Saes was the servant of a more than austere taskmaster, and this defeat cast him into such low spirits that his death anticipated the vengeance of Chosroes. But that monarch rivalled Xerxes of old by flogging the dead body in impotent spite, an act which shows that Chosroes was really possessed by a sort of lunacy (*Kaiserwahnsinn*), the madness of a weak

Nicephorus he is apparently the king himself. I suspect that the story which I have reproduced in the text may be half mythical, and perhaps we should rather accept the account of the Armenian writer Sepêos, who says that Heraclius had sent one Andreas to treat with the khan of the Khazars, and the khan aided him with troops under the command of his nephew. See *Journal asiat.* Feb. 1866, p. 207. Ziebil and Heraclius besiege Tiflis together.

[1] Nicephorus the Patriarch confounds this invasion with the invasion of 623.

[2] Then about fifteen years old. Nicephorus calls her Eudocia, but Epiphania of course is meant. I suppose that she had the double name, just as her brother and her stepbrother were called Heraclius Constantine.

[3] In the following century a Khazar princess marries a Roman Emperor (Constantine V). The projected sacrifice of the daughter of Heraclius to political expediency has a parallel in the fourteenth century in the fate of Theodora, the daughter of John Cantacuzenos, whom her father sent to the harem of the Turkish sultan.

man in an irresponsible position. It is remarkable that he never lost faith in Shahr Barz, numerous defeats and failures notwithstanding.

In the end of June (626) the last-named general resumed his old station at Chalcedon, and almost at the same moment (29th June) the vanguard of the Avar army began the blockade of Constantinople on the land side.[1] All the inhabitants of the suburbs fled into the city, and the Bosphorus was illuminated on both shores by the flames of burning churches. When the chagan himself drew near he sent an unexpected embassy,[2] holding out the possibility of peace, which he had before declined to consider, if an adequate offer should be made him. But the citizens—having full confidence in the ability of Bonus the Patrician, relying, moreover, on the valour of the experienced veterans whom their Emperor had sent to them, and wrought up into a state of religious enthusiasm, which Sergius fanned to flame, against the heathen who threatened the very heart and brain of Christendom—unanimously disdained to make terms with the ungodly.

The siege lasted throughout the month of July, and it is noteworthy that the Persians did not attack the city. They hovered, a black threatening mass, on the opposite shore, and laid waste the surrounding districts of Asia, but they left the whole work of the siege to their allies. At one moment, indeed, they seem to have entertained some intentions of joining the Avars in Europe, but these intentions were not realised.

The city was defended by more than 12,000 cavalry. The army of the Avars, on the other hand, numbered 80,000, and consisted of many nations and tongues, Bulgarians, and various tribes of Slaves,[3] and perhaps Teutonic Gepids. From the Golden Gate on the Propontis to the suburb of Sycae on the

---

[1] Attempts had been made in vain to induce the chagan, by offers of money, to desist from the expedition. In the *Bellum Avaricum* of George of Pisidia we have a contemporary, but poetical, source; we have also a full account in the *Chronicon Paschale.*

[2] Athanasius, a patrician of Hadrianople, was his ambassador. He was also one of the five envoys sent to

the chagan during the siege (*Chron. Pasch.*)

[3] Geo. Pis. *Bell. Av.* 197: Σθλάβος γὰρ Οὔννῳ καὶ Σκύθης τῷ Βουλγάρῳ αὖθις τε Μῆδος συμφρονήσας τῷ Σκύθῃ. For the Gepids, *see* Theophanes, Βουλγάροις τε καὶ Σκλάβοις καὶ Γηπαίδαις συμφωνήσας. We met them on the Theiss in the days of Maurice (*see* above, p. 141) as Avaric subjects.

Golden Horn they threatened the walls with all kinds of ingenious machines; while Slavonic sailors, female as well as
male, had small boats ready in the Golden Horn to support the
land operations by attacks on the water side. In the end
of July the chagan himself arrived, and then the most formidable and concentrated assault by land took place, and was
successfully repulsed, partly, it was said, by the potency of a
miraculous image of the Virgin. After this failure the chagan
received (2d August) ambassadors from the Romans and the
Persians at the same hour in his tent, and insulted the former
by constraining them to stand while the latter, who were
dressed in silk, were allowed to sit. High words arose between the Persians and Romans, which edified and delighted
the "abominable chagan," but the incident was not without
its use. For the captains of the Roman ships carefully
watched the straits that night and intercepted the three Persian
envoys. One of these they slew in sight of the Persian camp,
another was mutilated and sent back to the chagan, the third
was beheaded. This interception of intelligence disconcerted
the plan that had been formed for common action; and two
days later the Roman fleet succeeded in destroying a number
of rough transport rafts, which had been launched in the waters
of the Bosphorus to convey some Persian regiments across
the straits (3d August). On the same night a double attack
by land and sea was organised, the arrangement being that
when the Slavonic and Bulgarian marines, who anchored in
the north-western recess of the Golden Horn, saw a signal of
fire rising from a fort in the adjoining quarter of Blachernae,[1]
they should row down the inlet and proceed to Sycae.
Fortunately Bonus received intelligence of this design, and
thwarted it by giving the signal himself before the Avars were
ready. The Slaves saw the fire and acted according to the
arrangement; but they were enclosed and overwhelmed by the
Roman ships, which waited for them like a trap. At this
misfortune the bulk of the Avar army was seized with panic
and began to retire in haste. The chagan himself is said to
have felt superstitious terrors and seen visions of unearthly
beings. It seemed as if the image of the Virgin had really

---

[1] This fort ($\pi\rho\text{ο}\tau\epsilon\acute{\iota}\chi\iota\sigma\mu\alpha$) of Blachernae was called $\Pi\tau\epsilon\rho\acute{o}\nu$, "Wing" (Nicephorus, p. 18).

infected his imagination; he said that he saw a woman richly dressed passing along the fortifications. And some of his soldiers professed to have followed a dame of queenly aspect, who issued from the gate of Blachernae and sped towards rocks on the sea-shore, amid which she vanished away. Such incidents as this are a feature of the stories of sieges of that age.

The chagan retreated to his own kingdom, not without menaces that he would return again ere long, and the Byzantines could rest and give thanks to the Virgin [1] that they had successfully surmounted the first really imminent danger that had threatened their city since its new foundation ; while the good tidings which had reached them of the victory of Theodore and of the alliance of the Emperor with the Khazars,— an alliance which was Heraclius' answer to the combination of Shahr Barz with the Avars,—gave them further cause for jubilation.

VI. *Campaign of Assyria*, 627-628 A.D.

Abandoned by his Khazar allies in December, Heraclius spent the rest of the winter in Azerbiyan. We lose sight of him during the spring and summer of 627, and are unable to determine whether he spent those seasons in Media or in Assyria, where we meet him in autumn.[2] A new Persian general named Razates,[3] to whom Chosroes significantly said, "If you cannot conquer, you can die," was sent out against him. The battle, which decided the war and the fate of Chosroes, was not long delayed, and took place in the auspicious neigh-

---

[1] The repulse of the Avars and Persians was commemorated by a special office of the holy Virgin, performed on the Saturday of the fifth week in Lent. The hymn composed for this occasion, perhaps by George Pisides, is called the ἀκάθιστος ὕμνος, and has twenty-four οἶκοι or stations. The κοντάκιον of the hymn (a sort of prelusive abridgment of the whole ritual) begins thus—

τῇ ὑπερμάχῳ στρατηγῷ τὰ νικητήρια
ὡς λυτρωθεῖσα τῶν δεινῶν εὐχαριστήρια
ἀναγράφω σοι ἡ πόλις σου, θεοτόκε.

The composition of short hymns for ritual (τροπάρια) was initiated by St.

Romanus, who lived in the reign of Anastasius I.

[2] Rawlinson is hardly right in assigning his start from Lazica with the Khazars to September 627. For the final campaign we have the contemporary authority of George of Pisidia in his *Heracliad*, a hymn of jubilation on the theme ὁ πυρσολάτρης ἐξοφώθη Χοσρόης, but we learn from it few details.

[3] So Theophylactus, viii. 12, and Theophanes ; Nicephorus calls him Rizates. Theophanes wrongly places this battle in December of the fifteenth indiction (626-627) ; it really occurred in the first indiction.

bourhood of Nineveh and Gaugamela. Razates, with the words of his sovereign echoing in his ears, challenged Heraclius in the midst of the battle to a single combat; and the Emperor, riding on his steed Dorkon,[1] like Alexander on Bucephalus, eagerly accepted the challenge. The Roman hero was victorious; Razates did not conquer, but he died. Heraclius is said to have slain other Persian warriors also, single-handed. Night terminated the battle, which had resulted in an overwhelming victory for the Romans, and they were fortunate enough to have secured a royal prisoner, the prince of the Iberians.

Heraclius then marched slowly southwards along the eastern bank of the Tigris, crossing the great Zab and the lesser Zab. Having spent Christmas in the " Paradise " of Yesdem, he advanced[2] upon Dastagherd, the residence of Chosroes, built on the river Arba, about seventy miles north of Ctesiphon. In the meantime he had the good fortune to intercept a letter from Chosroes to Shahr Barz, recalling that commander from Chalcedon. Another letter of opposite import was substituted in its place, and the Persian general received a mandate to remain where he was, inasmuch as a brilliant victory had been gained over the Romans.

Chosroes fled to Ctesiphon on the approach of the hostile army, and when he had passed within its gates, remembered too late the vaticinations of the magi, that if he set foot again in that city[3] his destruction was certain. He hastened to leave the fatal spot, and, in the highest compulsion of base fear, fled eastwards, with his favourite wife Schirin, to the district of Susiana. The Romans meanwhile did not spare the magnificent palaces of Dastagherd,[4] and, though they treated the inhabitants with humanity, they were guilty of gross vandalism. The buildings and all the splendours of the place were committed to the flames (January 628).

From this moment the part played by Heraclius became

---

[1] φάλβας,ὁ λεγόμενος Δόρκων (Theoph. 6118 A.M.) φάλβας has generally been taken as the name of the horse, but de Boor prints thus. Tafel conjectured φάλιος (? φαλιός). The ending as suggests that φάλβας denotes some brand (cf. κοππατίας, σαμφόρας). Possibly, as Ducange suggests, it may be connected with Lat. *fulvus*.

[2] The park at Veklal, with ostriches, gazelles, and wild asses, described by Theophanes, calls up reminiscences of Xenophon's *Anabasis*.

[3] He had not set foot in it for twenty-four years; Dastagherd was his residence.

[4] They also destroyed the palaces of Dezeridan, Rusa, Veklal, and Vevdarch.

that of a controlling spectator who allowed events to take
their own course, though his consent or veto was decisive.
He did not wish to abuse his victory; he sent a message to
Chosroes offering peace on reasonable terms; and the Persian
monarch wrote his own death sentence by refusing. For a
long time the grandson of Nushirvan had been unpopular;
his irrational cruelty and his political folly had alienated his
subjects. The madness exhibited by this rejection of the
clement offer of the victor was followed by an edict, ordering
the old men, the women and the children to defend Ctesiphon.
The insanity of a despot could scarce go further, and Heraclius,
willing that the inevitable revolution should take its own
course, retired north-eastward, and crossing Mount Zagros, just
in time to escape a tremendous snow-tempest, established his
quarters at Ganzaca.

The revolution against Chosroes was twofold. Shahr Barz
and the army at Chalcedon threw off their allegiance, while at
the same time Gundarnaspes, the general at Ctesiphon, combined
with Siroes, the king's eldest son, to dethrone his father, who,
under the influence of his seductive wife Schirin, had decided
to leave the throne to a child of hers. Chosroes, who had
lately had the audacity to complain to his courtiers that they
were not all dead in fighting for his cause, was quickly seized
and thrown into the "castle of Forgetfulness," loaded with chains.
He was killed there by a process of slow starvation, which
was varied by the spectacle of his own and Schirin's children
executed before his eyes. His son is said to have taken an
unfilial delight in the tortures of a worthless parent, of whom
he spoke in the most bitter terms in a manifesto which he
indited to Heraclius. Siroes professed a desire to compensate
for all the miseries which his father had inflicted on the
Persian kingdom by a reign of beneficence, and he began the
reaction by opening the prisons and granting an exemption
from taxes for three years. Heraclius, in his letter of con-
gratulation to the new king, addressed him as "my dear son,"
and while he professed that if Chosroes had fallen into his
hands he would have done him no hurt, he admitted that
God had wisely punished the sins of the Persian king for the
sake of the world's peace. He politically treated the parricide

with the greatest friendliness, just as Pope Gregory had treated Phocas.

Shortly before his death Chosroes had taken a step which led to the alienation of Shahr Barz. Indignant at his general's delay in appearing, the true cause whereof, the interception of his own letter, he could not suspect, and full of distrust, he wrote to the kardarigan, who was second in command at Chalce-don, a letter containing instructions to put Shahr Barz to death and hasten back to Persia. The bearer of this letter fell into the hands of the Romans as he travelled through Galatia, and the epistle was forwarded to Constantinople. The authorities there knew how to make the best use of it. They laid it before Shahr Barz himself, and a dexterous artifice was adopted to create general disaffection in the Persian army. The names of four hundred important officers were annexed to the document, which was altered in such a way [1] as to convey an order for their deaths. They were then assembled together, the letter was laid before them, and with one consent they voted that Chosroes had forfeited the crown. Peace was made with the young Emperor Constantine, and the army hastened to Persia to depose an ungrateful tyrant.

The peace made between Heraclius and Siroes forms the conclusion of the Persian war. The restoration of all the Roman provinces, the surrender of all the Roman captives and of the Holy Rood were the main conditions, and the Emperor left his brother Theodore in Persia to make arrangements for their fulfilment. He sent to the imperial city, in announce-ment of his victory, a triumphant manifesto,[2] which opened with the jubilate, "O, be joyful in the Lord,"—a song of exultation over the fall of Chosroes Iscariot, the blasphemer, who has gone to burn for ever in the flames of hell. The same spirit is echoed in the Epinikion, composed for the occasion by the "poet-laureate," George of Pisidia, entitled the *Heracliad*.[3]   A resolution, which was to become law

---

[1] φαλσεύσας τὴν Χοσρόου ἐπιστολὴν (Theoph.) φαλσεύειν is the Graecised form of *falsare*.

[2] Preserved in *Chronicon Paschale*, first indiction. The letter was read out from the ambo of St. Sophia.

[3] George afterwards wrote a poem

called *Hexaemeron*, "the six days," on the creation, but alluding also to the war of six years in which Heraclius had conquered the Persians. Theo-phanes was doubtless thinking of it when he wrote (6119 A.M.): "The Emperor, having subdued Persia in

with the Emperor's consent, was initiated by the Byzantines on this auspicious occasion, that Heraclius should be surnamed *Scipio* and his successors *Scipiones*. The great heroes of the Republic of Old Rome were not yet forgotten by the New Romans of the Bosphorus, and it was recognised that the Imperator who beat back the Asiatic power of the Sassanids was a historical successor of the imperator who overthrew the Asiatic commonwealth of Carthage.

Extremely noteworthy and characteristic is this combination of Roman reminiscences with an intensely christian spirit. Before the end of the same century such combinations have become a thing of the past.

The letter of Heraclius came in May; he did not arrive himself at the palace of Hieria, close to Chalcedon, till some months later. All the inhabitants of Constantinople crossed the Bosphorus to meet him, and received him with taper processions and myrtle branches; but he did not enter the city in triumph until Theodore, his brother, arrived with the precious relic of the Holy Rood. Of the triumphal procession I need only remark that he made his entry by the Golden Gate and was received by Sergius in the church of St. Sophia, where the true cross, solemnly "uplifted," [1] lent a peculiar solemnity to the service of thanksgiving. The ceremony in St. Sophia corresponded to the ceremony in the Capitol at triumphal processions in Old Rome.

The sun of Heraclius' house turned the winter of men's discontent to glorious summer for a moment, and perhaps many fondly imagined that by the battle of Nineveh and the ensuing peace with Persia the clouds which had so long loured over the Roman Empire had been dissipated for ever. But another cloud, yet as small as a man's hand, was even then visible on the southern horizon, and unluckily its import was mistaken. The Persian war was over in 628; the Saracen

---

six years and made peace in the seventh, with great joy returned to Constantinople, having fulfilled thereby a sort of mystic *theoria*. For God created all the world in six days, and called the seventh the day of rest."

[1] Nicephorus makes the "uplifting" take place before the arrival of Heraclius (p. 22 ; ἀνύψωσε is the word), but he is untrustworthy here in his chronological arrangement. He doubtless had authority for placing the ceremony in the second indiction = 628 after 1st September. Heraclius brought four elephants from the East to amuse the Byzantine populace.

conquests in Syria began in 633. In those five intervening years much might have been done to avert the coming storm if the danger could have only been realised, but, as it was, the policy of Heraclius was in every way calculated to ensure success to the new foes.

These five years might be considered the ultimate boundary between the Old and the Middle Ages [1]; the appearance of the Saracen launches us into the medieval high seas, and few vestiges of antiquity remain. The Persian war had the double character of an age of transition. As a war of Romans against Persians it attached itself to the ancient order of things, and this element is not absent from its poet George of Pisidia, while as a religious war it was medieval, an anticipation of the holy wars of the eleventh and twelfth centuries. In short, it was a Roman crusade.

It was unfortunate, from a political and economical point of view, that the Church and State, as creditor and debtor, coincided in the arrangement that the national debt should be liquidated with all possible expedition. For the sources from which it was necessary to raise the payment were the provinces, which had for many years suffered the devastations of a cruel enemy and endured the tyranny of a foreign ruler; and it was desirable that time should be allowed them to recover their old prosperity before a severe tribute was imposed. This was the first mistake, and a serious one. Had the Church been more self-denying or more patient, had Syria and Mesopotamia been left for a few years exempt from the burden of taxes, a firmer resistance might have been offered to the Arabian invader.

The second mistake was the continuation of an unfortunate policy which had already proved disastrous, the persecution of the Jews. They were massacred in Palestine, they were massacred also at Edessa, and were forced to flee to Arabia. We are tempted to think that but for this fatal error events might have taken a different course, for we can hardly overrate the

---

[1] In another place I have spoken of the plague in the reign of Justinian as marking a division between the ancient and medieval worlds. But just as medievalism appears before Justinian, remnants of the ancient spirit linger after Justinian; and if the reign of the great Emperor of the sixth century is the most important epoch of partition, the reign of the great Emperor of the seventh century is a further limit. *See* below, p. 457.

importance of the Hebrews in those countries. Their wealth is illustrated by the princely entertainment with which Benjamin, a Jew of Tiberias, honoured Heraclius and his retinue on their journey to Jerusalem in 629. Benjamin had the reputation of being a persecutor of Christians, and yet he consented, at Heraclius' request, to be baptized a Christian himself. Other Jews would not have been so easily converted, but kindness might have made them loyal.

Heraclius remained no long time in the queen of cities after his triumph.[1] Accompanied by Martina and her son Heraclius Constantine, who had been recently created Caesar, he hastened in spring 629 to restore the cross to its resting-place in Jerusalem and to set in order the affairs of his eastern provinces, where he found much to occupy him. He was obliged to keep a wakeful eye on Persia, which was in a state of political unrest; he was engaged in schemes of religious unity, which always seems so simple and is so impracticable; and he began to direct his attention to the movements in Arabia.

The burden of Persia may be told in a few words. Siroes reigned only eight months, and, after the short reigns of two intervening sovereigns, Shahr Barz ascended the throne with the approval of Heraclius, to whom he showed himself grateful. The protracted residences of that general in the neighbourhood of Byzantium seem to have rendered him a sort of Philhellene, or, as contemporaries might have said, Philoromaic. His son, whom he named Nicetas, received the title of Patrician from the Roman Emperor, who further patronised his Persian friend and former foe by accepting the hand of his daughter Nice for the deaf prince Theodosius.[2] Perhaps we may combine the names of the son and daughter, "Niketas" and "Nike," with the fact that Shahr Barz gave the Holy Sponge and the Holy Spear back to Nicetas, Heraclius' famous cousin, and may draw the conclusion that there existed between the Greek patrician and the Persian general specially friendly relations

---

[1] Heraclius Constantine, the son of Eudocia (generally called Constantine to distinguish him both from his father and from his stepbrother), was instituted consul in 629; Niceph. p. 22.

[2] *See* Nicephorus, p. 21 (ed. de Boor). I cannot hesitate to accept the reading of the Vatican MS. Νικήταν υἱὸν Σαρβάρου. This is the most important correction of a detail of received history which M. de Boor's study of Nicephorus has contributed.

which induced the latter to give his children those Greek names.   But the simplest explanation may be that the children of Shahr Barz were baptized, and that Nicetas stood as sponsor for them.   The cruel policy which Shahr Barz adopted when he became king led to his murder, and with some trouble Heraclius brought it about that his son Isdigerd received the crown.   Isdigerd was the last of the Sassanids.

CHAPTER IV

MONOTHELETISM

WE have often had occasion to notice the heresies that pervaded and divided Egypt, Syria, and Mesopotamia. The heretics were far more numerous than the orthodox, for religion and nationality in general coincided. In Egypt, for example, there were about 30,000 Greek Melchites over against five or six million Coptic monophysites. Syria and Mesopotamia were divided between Nestorianism and Jacobitism, a sort of Neoseverianism, which had spread into Egypt and Ethiopia. And the religion of Armenia was purely and simply monophysitic.

Heraclius dreamed that it might be possible to accomplish what many Emperors before him had essayed in vain, and unite all these heretics with the orthodox Byzantine Church by a new formula more inclusive or more elastic.

A new formula presented itself opportunely, the doctrine of a single energy. It must not, however, be thought that it was discovered for this ecclesiastico-political purpose.[1] On the contrary, it was a natural development of the old christological controversies of the fifth century. Sergius had considered and made up his mind on the question before there was any thought of drawing profit from it in an irenic direction. It was a question, of course, for adherents of the council of Chalcedon, not for monophysites. The latter, holding a

---

[1] Cf. Hefele, *Conciliengeschichte*, iii. p. 111 ; there "kam noch ein irenischer Zweck dazu." Hefele has been my chief guide throughout this chapter. There is a good history of the controversy by Prof. G. T. Stokes in the *Dict. of Christ. Biography* under the heading "Person of Christ."

single nature, necessarily held a single energy and a single will. But it was not clear whether dyophysites should hold a divine and human energy as well as a divine and human nature. It might be questioned whether it was legitimate to ascribe a human energy and a human will to Christ, and the Ecumenical Councils had uttered no opinion on the subject. A decision in favour of monotheletism (as the new doctrine was called) would provide a common ground for monophysites and Chalcedonians to join hands. This fact was perhaps the doctrine's strongest condemnation if we assume that the monophysitic controversy was more than a verbal one, and that the Chalcedonians were right, whereas it was the doctrine's strongest confirmation if we believe that the two parties divided the truth or falsehood between them.

But while the monotheletic controversy was a natural offspring of the ancient conflicts of the fifth century, it must be admitted that the new doctrine would never have led to a conflict in the seventh century but for the irenic advantages which, it was hoped, might be extracted from it.

That Sergius initiated Heraclius in his new doctrine—it could not yet be called a heresy, as no decision of the Church had been pronounced—long before it began to have any political importance, is proved by a conversation which took place in 622 between Heraclius and Paul of Armenia, wherein the former asserted that the energy ($\dot{\epsilon}\nu\dot{\epsilon}\rho\gamma\epsilon\iota\alpha$) of Christ was single. It was probably at this time, when his attention was specially directed to Armenia, that it first occurred to Heraclius to make a political weapon of monotheletism and reconcile the monophysitic Church of Armenia with the orthodox Greek religion; and a synod which was held in the same year at Theodosiopolis, called the synod of Garin, has been rightly brought into connection with this scheme. I have used the convenient word *monotheletism*, but it should be noticed that in the early stage of the controversy *monenergetic* would be a more appropriate adjective than monotheletic, for the singleness of the *energy*, not the simplicity of the *will*, was the point at issue.

His military occupations did not prevent Heraclius from prosecuting this design; and we find that he issued a decree (before 626) to Arcadius, bishop of Cyprus, in which island there was a colony of Armenians,[1] enjoining on him to teach the doctrine of " one hegumenic energy"; and perhaps the success of this attempt at unity on a small scale within the limits of an island encouraged him to apply afterwards the same balm to the wounds of the entire Empire.   In 626, while he was in Lazica, he sounded Cyrus the bishop of Phasis, and, through the influence of Sergius the Patriarch, secured his co-operation.

But after the successful issue of his campaigns Heraclius could devote more assiduous attention to the question ; and the problems connected with the administration of the recovered provinces of Syria and Egypt suggested that the monotheletic talisman might be used with salutary effect.   And hence Greek historians[2] speak as though the doctrine had first emerged in 629 at an interview which took place in that year at Hierapolis between the Emperor and Athanasius the Jacobite.   An agreement was made between them ; the Jacobites were to return to the Church on the basis of the new theory, and Athanasius was to be raised to the patriarchal chair of Antioch.   In the following year Cyrus of Phasis was made Patriarch of Alexandria, and his first act was to win over the important sect of the Theodosians or Phthartolatrai.

So far the policy of unification was successful. Sergius the Patriarch of Constantinople, Athanasius the Jacobite Patriarch of Antioch, Cyrus the monophysite Patriarch of Alexandria were unanimous in teaching " one theandric energy."

But many orthodox Christians felt qualms of distrust touching this new panacea which had been evolved by Sergius and Heraclius.   They did not feel certain of their new bed-fellows—Jacobites and Theodosians and dwellers in Meso-potamia ; they suspected that there was something unsound in the doctrine of the single energy.   They found an able spokesman in a monk of Palestine named Sophronius, who was possessed of considerable dialectical ability and became the champion of dyotheletism, the doctrine of two wills.   He soon became convinced that there was a touch of insincerity in the new movement, that there was at least a readiness to sacrifice complete sincerity to political expediency.   This was

---

[1] These Armenians were settled in Cyprus by Justin II (*see* above, p. 104).

[2] Theophanes, 6021 A.M., *i.e.* 629,

630. He calls Athanasius "a clever villain, with the native unscrupulous-ness of the Syrians."

indicated in the opinion expressed by the Patriarch of Alexandria that for the sake of ecclesiastical unity doctrinal expressions should be " economised," that is, adapted to expediency. The influence of Sergius, however, kept Sophronius dumb for a year or two, but when he was appointed Patriarch of Jerusalem in 634—this appointment was a false step on the part of Heraclius—he refused to keep silence any longer and prepared to forge a thunderbolt. Apprised of this, the Patriarch of Constantinople determined to anticipate him and crush his opposition by the authority of the bishop of Rome. Sergius wrote an account of the controversy to Pope Honorius ; and in this letter his position, which he wished the Pope to endorse, was, that the unity of the Church now restored should not be again endangered by any use of the expressions in dispute; that no person should speak of either two energies or one energy. This evasion of the question by silence had already been enjoined on Sophronius and Cyrus. The reply of Pope Honorius (635) not only endorsed the " just mean" of Sergius, but agreed with the doctrine of monotheletism, and this consenting of the Pope has given rise to much discussion. The most reasonable conclusion[1] is that Honorius, with an occidental distaste for dialectics, did not really apprehend the point at issue. It seemed to him a question of grammar rather than of theology. He uses the expression " one will," and yet we need not regard him as a monothelete, for he places " one energy" and " two energies" on exactly the same footing; and the second letter that he wrote was practically orthodox. Nor, on the other hand, need we reject as not genuine the acts of the sixth Ecumenical Council which condemned Honorius; it was for the "imprudent economy of silence" that he was condemned.

In the meantime the *epistola synodica*[2] of Sophronius appeared, demonstrating that the new doctrine was inconsistent with orthodoxy; but the object of the monotheletes was rather to hush up the controversy, which had already produced a

---

[1] Cf. Hefele, whose discussion of the question is impartial. Dr. Döllinger in his *Papstfabeln des Mittelalters* has a chapter on the Honorius problem (p. 131 *sqq.*), and notices that the Pope used *energy* and *energies* in different senses ; the plural meaning manifestations of energy and not the operations of two distinct faculties.

[2] Hefele designates this as the most important *Urkunde* of the whole controversy.

desirable result, than to argue for their opinion. The Ecthesis, which was composed by Sergius,[1] was promulgated by the Emperor in 638 (639), and may be looked upon as the official answer to Sophronius' letter; it forbids all mention to be made of one energy or two energies, while it proclaims the doctrine of one will. Before the Ecthesis was published Sophronius had died, but he left his controversial zeal as a heritage to a certain Stephen, from whom he exacted a solemn oath that he would proceed to Rome and make war against the monotheletes to the death. The four eastern Patriarchs accepted the Ecthesis, but John IV, who became Pope in 640, condemned it; and thus the attempt at union in the East, a union unstable as water,[2] led to a schism with the West like Zeno's Henotikon in the fifth century. What remains of the history of monotheletism belongs to a future chapter.

In the eleventh indiction, 638, the year of the publication of the Ecthesis, the Patriarch Sergius died, and was succeeded by Pyrrhus, also a monothelete, and a most intimate friend of the Emperor.

---

[1] In a letter to Pope John IV the Emperor explicitly disavows the composition of the Ecthesis and devolves the whole responsibility upon Sergius. The text of the Ecthesis will be found in Mansi, x. 991.

[2] ὑδροβαφῆ ἕνωσιν, a different metaphor (Theophanes).

CHAPTER V

LITERATURE IN THE REIGN OF HERACLIUS

THE works of two authors[1] of this age, a prose-writer and a verse-writer, have come down to us. The Egyptian Theophylactus Simocatta[2] composed a history of the reign of Maurice[3] and a work on natural history[4]; while George of Pisidia celebrated the exploits of Heraclius in verse. Both the verse-writer and the prose-writer are characterised by a painful attention to style and an affected use of far-fetched expressions; in fact they were both, as we say now, euphuists. The development of euphuism at this period is highly remarkable; we can see traces of it in Agathias and other historical writers, but in the works of Theophylactus bombast, in all its frigidity, was carried to an unprecedented extreme.[5]

The *Ecumenical History*—such is the pretentious title—opens with a dialogue between the queen Philosophy and her daughter History, written in a style which the author fondly imagines to be poetical Attic. Philosophy promises to listen to the siren songs of History, and, like the hero of Ithaca, not to

---

[1] The *Chronicon Paschale* is also supposed to have been compiled in the reign of Heraclius, but it does not call for special notice here.

[2] Simocatta (Σιμοκάτος) apparently means "flat-nosed cat." The domestic cat was becoming common at this time. κάτος is used by Evagrius, and Gregory the Great, I believe, had a pet cat. On the word "cat," *see* Lenormant, *La Grande-Grèce*, vol. i. p. 102 *sqq.* Through the Syriac *qatô, catus* and κάτος come from "African languages," cf. Nubian *kadiska.* The Egyptian *mau* and the Coptic *schau* are quite different.

[3] The best edition of Theophylactus is that recently published by C. de Boor (1887), founded on a collation of the Vatican MS. and provided with excellent indices. (*See* my notice in the *Classical Review*, March 1888.) Theophylactus composed his history after the fall of Chosroes, "the Babylonian dragon"; *see* viii. 12, 13.

[4] Letters are also extant, of which some are erotic.

[5] So Photius, πλήν γε δὴ ἡ τῶν τροπικῶν λέξεων καὶ τῆς ἀλληγορικῆς ἐννοίας κατακορὴς χρῆσις εἰς ψυχρολογίαν τινὰ καὶ νεανικὴν ἀπειροκαλίαν ἀποτελευτᾷ.

stuff her ears. They both rejoice that the pollution (of Phocas) has been driven from the palace by the might of the "Heraclidae," and that literature is able to revive. History attributes the new movement especially to the Patriarch Sergius, "the great high priest and president of the world."[1] "He is my oldest friend," replies Philosophy, "and my dearest treasure." "He," says History, "breathed in me the breath of life, lifting me from the tomb of my illiterate plight as though he raised an Alcestis with the strength of a delivering Heracles. And he generously adopted me and clothed me with bright apparel and adorned me with a golden chain."[2] Here we catch a glimpse of Sergius as the centre and patron of a literary revival; and this is confirmed by all that we hear of him in the poems of his friend George the Pisidian.

The opening sentences of the funeral oration which Theophylactus pronounced over the Emperor Maurice eight years after his death (610 A.D.)[3] are preserved, and are a curious specimen of his extraordinary style :—

"Let theatre and platform and freedom of speech mourn with me to-day ; but let tragedy and tear keep holiday. Let dirge dance and leap in delight, being worshipped and honoured by a feast of such dejection. Let words shear themselves of sound, and the Muses shear themselves of fair speech, and Athens put off her white cloak. For the virtues are widowed, and seek for their charioteer, some violent envy having broken his wheel. Spectators, would that ye had not been witnesses of these evils. The subject is an Iliad of evils ; the Furies are the chorus of my discourse ; and the stage of my drama is a conspicuous tomb."

When the Persian war came to an end in 591, Maurice transported the military forces from Asia to Europe to act against the Avars. The historian describes this transaction as follows : " And so, now that day smiled upon the affairs in the East, and made not her progress mythically, in Homeric fashion, from a barbaric couch, but refused to be called ' rosy fingered,' inasmuch as their sword is not crimsoned with blood, the Emperor transfers the forces to Europe."[4] It is hardly credible that a sane man should use such language ; and most pages of

---

[1] τῆς ἀπανταχόθεν οἰκουμένης, reference to the title *œcumenical*.

[2] Philosophy goes on to say: "He philosophises on earth not in the body, or else, speculation herself, being made flesh, moves about as man with men."

[3] Theophyl. viii. 12, 3 : τούτων δῆτα ὑπὸ τοῦ συγγραφέως ᾀδομένων ἐπὶ τοῦ βήματος τῆς τυραννίδος ληξάσης. He calls himself "the father of the history," as he calls an assassin "the father of murder."

[4] v. 16, 1.

the History teem with similar passages. When a general changes his mind, he is said to "obelise" his first plan and "give the prize of victory to his second thoughts."[1]

Four important works[2] of George of Pisidia remain, and of these three celebrate directly the achievements of Heraclius. The *Persian Expedition*, in three acroamata or cantos, comes first, composed after the first campaign of Asia Minor, in 623. The *Avaric War* tells how the combined forces of Avars, Bulgarians, Slaves, and Huns, in league with the Persians, were driven back from the imperial city. The two cantos of the *Heracliad* celebrate the final triumph of Heraclius and the fall of Chosroes—the fall of one whereby all were saved.[3] "Where now is the babble of the ever-erring magi?"[4] George looked on the Persian war as a crusade, and on Heraclius as the champion of Christendom. This note dominates in his compositions; the *Heracliad* open with an invocation to the Trinity. His other work was the *Hexaemeron*, or poem of the six days of the Creation; it suggested too an allegorical application to the six campaigns of Heraclius. Written at the suggestion of the Patriarch Sergius and dedicated to him, it was intended to refute pagans and philosophers, not living philosophers, for there were none, but Aristotle and Plato, Porphyrius and Proclus. Euclid is confounded by the bee and Orpheus by the swan; Procluses are bidden to hold their peace and let the rustics speak—

σιγῶσι Πρόκλοι καὶ λαλῶσιν ἀγρόται.[5]

As in the prose of Theophylactus, we are often offended by bombast and affected expressions in the verses of the Pisidian, but the poet never goes so far as the historian.[6]   It seems probable

---

[1] vi. 7, 7.

[2] Some of his minor works are also extant, for example, a poem against Severus; a poem on the Resurrection; lines on the Vanity of Life; a prose encomium on the Martyr Anastasius. The best complete edition is that of Migne. I have shown above (pp. 231, 232, 234, 236) that it is probable that George wrote other historical poems which have been lost.

[3] ἑνὸς πεσόντος καὶ σεσωσμένων ὅλων (i. 52).

[4] ποῦ νῦν ὁ λῆρος τῶν ἀεισφαλῶν

μάγων (ii. 60).   [5] l. 69.

[6] As an example of his stilted style I may quote (*de Exp. Pers.* ii. 289)—

πολλὴ δὲ φροντὶς τῶν φρενῶν κλονου-
      μένων
κατεῖχεν αὐτὸν καὶ λογισμῶν συγχύσεις
τὸν νοῦν ἐπεγρόφωσαν ἐσκοτισμένον.

He thus describes winter (*Hex.* 295)—

χειμῶνος ὥρα καὶ τὰ δένδρα συντόμως
ἐκ τῆς πυράγρας τοῦ κρύους μαραίνεται.
φθίνει τὸ κάλλος, ἀσθενοῦσιν οἱ κλάδοι,
ἐκρεῖ τὸ φύλλον ὥσπερ ἐκ νεκροῦ τρίχες.

that he was never indifferent to the strict laws of quantity observed by ancient writers of iambic verse; and though the rule of the Cretic ending, which Porson rediscovered, was not known to him, he adopted a harder canon and allowed only barytone words to end his lines.[1]

[1] *See* an article by Hilberg, entitled "Kann Theodoros Prodromos der Verfasser des Χριστὸς Πάσχων sein?" in *Wiener Studien*, vol. viii. Hilberg speaks of "die tadellose Correctheit" of George Pisides, and holds that all false quantities in his poems are due to false readings. In the *Hexaemeron* there are only three cases of more than one trisyllabic foot in a line. Late corrections of proparoxytone verses (by persons accustomed to political verses, which always end with paroxytone words) are, as Hilberg remarks, often to blame for irregularities in our MSS. of George.

CHAPTER VI

THE Roman Empire was delivered for ever from the Persian foe, but, like a ship that "having 'scaped a tempest is straightway calmed and boarded with a pirate," it was almost immediately assailed by a new and more deadly adversary, who displayed the resistless energy and was animated with the uncompromising spirit of a religious enthusiasm.

When Mohammed appeared, Arabia was in a state of decline. The religion of its inhabitants, not very sublime originally—a sort of Sabaeanism derived from Chaldaea [1]—had degenerated into superstition, which attached to every object in nature maleficent and beneficent deities or *ginns*; and superstition was naturally accompanied by religious indifference. "The Arab of Mohammed's time was what the Bedouin of to-day is, indifferent to religion itself," [2] though observing a few rites and muttering a few phrases. Many Jews and Christians resided in Arabia; there was a christian bishopric in Yemen; and thus the monotheistic ideas of those creeds were not unfamiliar to the Arabs, among whom arose a monotheistic sect called the Hânifs. But the Hânifs had no inspiration; Judaism was too worn a thing to attract; while Greek Christianity, with its metaphysical subtlety, could not take hold of the Semitic mind. A new revelation was required; and there was a wide field for social and moral reform, which a new religion would naturally cover; there was the possibility of higher civilisation and of a more advanced form of political existence. For the

---

[1] Seth and Enoch were its prophets.
[2] Palmer, in his interesting Introduction to his translation of the Q'uran.

ordinary occupations of the Arab were murder and highway robbery,[1] and the only checks on the shedding of blood were the fear of certain revenge and the institution of the sacred months, which for a short period of the year secured the sanctity of human life.   It was usual to bury alive superfluous female children, and one of the reforms of Mohammed was the abolition of this custom.   These habits, which transgressed the first conditions of a stable society, rendered political union impossible; and the feeling of devotion to the tribe, which was strongly developed in the Arab—and necessarily developed, for without it life in Arabia would have been impossible—tended in the same direction.   Their pride in birth, the freedom of their life, their passion for poetry, lend a sort of romantic nobility to the children of Hagar, as they were called by the Greeks; but enough has been said to show that there was another and dark side to the picture.

Mohammed the Prophet has been looked upon by some as a hero,[2] by others [3] as literally the emissary of the devil; and less extreme views fall again into the two classes of those who think, like Sprenger, that with the prophet's burning enthusiasm was combined an element of vulgar cunning, and those who, without admiring him, take a more lenient view of his character, as conditioned by a quasi-hysterical organism.   His peculiar sensibility to physical pain, his tendency to fall into profound fits of melancholy indicate the frame, bodily and mental, of one who is always wandering on the borderland between illusion and reality; and "his first revelations," says Palmer, "were the almost natural outcome of his mode of life and habit of thought, and especially of his physical constitution."   The significance of his attachment to Hadiɡah, the widow whom he married, consisted in her ability to charm those demons of unrest and melancholy which afflict too sensitive natures.

Widely as Mohammed is separated from the prophets of the Old Testament, there is a common element which unites the Hebrew and the Arab and separates them from all Aryan thinkers.   An incapacity for consecutive thinking, a directness

[1] Palmer, in his Introduction to his translation of the Q'uran.
[2] Carlyle, *Lectures on Hero-worship*, "The Hero as Prophet."
[3] By Muir. Sprenger in his *Das Leben und die Lehre des Mohammad* says that this theory is the only one which can lay claim to manly seriousness.

which disdains process, a love of antitheses which never seeks contentment in a synthesis, a vagueness which delights to lose itself in metaphor, a freedom which will not be bound in the close but fruitful matrices of logic and which consequently becomes as monotonous as the reaches of the desert in which it was developed,—all these kindred features belong to both Mohammed and the Hebrew prophets; all of them were alien and would have been contemptible to the countrymen of Socrates and Plato. Nor were the Semites lovers of the beautiful, in the true sense, any more than they were philosophers. They were keenly susceptible to grandeur and sublimity and all that suggests the immense or the illimitable, but they were strangers to the beautiful; their love for beauty in women did not advance beyond the limits of the sensual. Their admiration for objects of art or beautiful girls is always linked somehow with luxury or sensuality.

The "Chapter of Unity" in the Koran resumes the central point of the new religion.

> " In the name of the merciful and compassionate God.
> Say, ' He is God alone !
> God the eternal !
> He begets not and is not begotten !
> Nor is there like unto him any one !' "

The doctrine of pure monotheism was Mohammed's great inspiration. To profess belief in God and in Mohammed as his prophet was the first of the five practical duties of a Mussulman.[1] It is not necessary to go here into further details concerning the Islamitic creed; but I must not omit to remind the reader that Mohammed brought it on several sides into historical connection with the past. He did not utterly break with the pre-existing cult of Arabia, for he made the black stone in the wall of the Kaabah at Mecca the most precious object of external veneration to his followers. This stone, which is mentioned by Diodorus Siculus, was originally a white stone in paradise, but it was " blackened by the kisses of sinful but believing lips." [2]   Nor did Mohammed cease to believe in genii (*g*inns); he thought that he himself was sent as an apostle to genii as well as to men.[3]   He also con-

---

[1] The others were prayer, fasting, almsgiving, and pilgrimages—duties which also bound Christians.
[2] Palmer, *op. cit.* p. xiii.   [3] *Ib.*

nected his religion with both Judaism and Christianity, accepting their scriptures and their prophets. He used at first to look on Jerusalem as the holy city and pray with his face turned towards it; and it was not till the Jews had rejected him at Medina that he turned his face to Mecca. He regarded Christ as his own predecessor; and a prophecy of the coming of Mohammed, involving a slight change in reading and a hideous change in sense, was found in that verse of John which promises the coming of a comforter.[1]

The Koran, we are told by a competent authority,[2] derived much of its power, impressiveness, and popularity, less from the original sayings of Mohammed than from the mode in which it introduced "popular sayings, choice pieces of eloquence, and favourite legends current among the tribes for ages before his time." It is important to observe these links which bound Mohammed with the past. He had really no original doctrine; he only taught an old doctrine, of which his countrymen were losing sight, in a new and impressive manner, at the right moment and in the right way. His originality lay in the identification of himself with his doctrine, which went so far that it seemed often mere madness or mere imposture. He contrived to wrap his own personality and his revelation in an atmosphere of magnetic enthusiasm, which is called inspiration.

In 628 Mohammed took the first step in the direction of spreading his religion beyond the confines of Arabia. He wrote letters to the Emperor Heraclius,[3] to the king of Persia, and to the king of Abyssinia (Nuggàsî), exhorting them to embrace the faith of Islam.

The king of Abyssinia accepted the invitation in an enthusiastic and humble letter. Chosroes, transported with fury, characteristically ordered the governor of Yemen to send him the insolent Arab in chains. Heraclius said neither no nor yes, but sent presents to Mohammed in acknowledg-

---

[1] John xvi. 7; περίκλυτος = A'hmed substituted for παράκλητος.

[2] Palmer.

[3] M. Drapeyron draws a parallel between the career of Heraclius and that of Mohammed. From 610 to 622 Mohammed was persecuted by Koreisch-ites, Heraclius was a prey to misfortune; 622, both gird on the sword about the same time; 624, the battle of Beder, contemporaneous with the defeat of Shahr Barz in Albania, etc. This is fanciful.

ment of his communication. Arab writers boast that he was really converted to Islamism; Greek writers affirm that Mohammed came and did homage to him. After this Mohammed entered into correspondence with Mukaukas, the Coptic governor of Egypt, who, though he did not definitely profess belief in the new religion, treated the prophet with profound respect, and sent him among other suitable presents two Egyptian maidens. The first collision between the Romans and the Moslem was at Muta, near the Dead Sea, in 629. The result was a Cadmean victory for the latter, who were considerably inferior in point of numbers; and Khalid, "the Sword of God," won his first laurels in this battle. It was in the following year that Mohammed entered Mecca in triumph and made the Kaabah the central shrine of Islamism. Two years later he died (8th June 632), and for a moment the stability of his work seemed precarious. The Arab tribes fell away; Al Mundar, king of Bahrein, on the west coast of the Persian Gulf, revolted. Abu Bekr, who, along with Omar, had supplemented by practical wisdom the visionary nature of the prophet, was elected the first caliph (*successor*). He saw that the salvation of the cause must be wrought, not by conflicts in Arabia, but by foreign conquest; he apprehended that the prophet must look for honour, not in his own country or in peace, but abroad and by the sword. Accordingly preparations were made for war against both the Persians and the Romans; and while Khalid, son of Welid, was sent against Irak, four generals were commissioned to attack Syria.[1]

The programme of these enthusiasts, inspired with greed and faith, lusting equally after proselytes and riches, was characteristically concise and direct. Three alternatives were offered to the foe—the Koran, tribute, or the sword. Heraclius, who had established his headquarters at Edessa, had made no adequate preparations to oppose them. He foolishly trusted that the Saracens of the deserts which separate Syria from

---

[1] Theophanes places this in 6124 A.M., which should correspond to 631-632 A.D., but, as Theophanes lost a year in the reign of Phocas, it means 632-633. The death of Abu Bekr (Abubachar) is correctly placed in the following year, 6125, but the capture of Bostra, the defeat of Theodore, and the defeat at Gabatha are placed after the accession of Omar. Nicephorus records the fate of Sergius (of whom he enigmatically speaks as ὁ κατὰ Νικήταν, p. 23). The Saracens sewed him up in the skin of a camel newly slain and left him to putrefy.

Arabia would prove a sufficient barrier against the people of the south, whose formidable character he seems to have insufficiently realised. But those Saracens soon showed that they were unwilling to resist the invaders of their own race, and even Roman governors proved recusants to their religion and country. A small army under the general Sergius was defeated, and the Arabs captured Bostra[1] and Gaza.

One who is not an orientalist and cannot consult the Arabic authorities at first hand will be inclined to conclude that it is hardly safe to venture on any but the shortest and barest account of the conquest of Syria. The interesting and romantic details which Ockley took from the dubious Al Wakidi, and which Gibbon took from Ockley, must probably for the most part be relegated to the same room as the story of Regulus. The difficulty of critically testing materials distorted by oriental fancy, Mohammedan orthodoxy, and political party spirit was fully felt by Weil,[2] whom I have followed, while I would refer the reader who wishes for a mixture of legend and history to the pleasant pages of Ockley.

The four generals to whom Abu Bekr had entrusted the war against the Christians were Abu Ubeida, Schurahbil, Amru, and Yezid. It was intended that each should attack a separate part of the Syrian provinces, but the serious resistance which was encountered made a combination of forces necessary, and the caliph therefore recalled Khalid from southern Mesopotamia, where he had enjoyed a career of uninterrupted success.[3] It appears that shortly before the arrival of Khalid a battle was fought at Adjnadein,[4] in which the Saracens were victorious (30th July 634), but it is not clear whether this was the battle in which Theodore, the Emperor's brother, commanded the defeated side.[5] The decisive battle was fought soon afterwards (end of August) on the banks of the Yermuk, or Hieromax, which flows into the Lake of Tiberias.[6] The Roman generals were a Persian named Baanes,

---

[1] Romanus, the governor of Bostra, betrayed it. He was the first *magariser* (see p. 267).

[2] *Geschichte der Chalifen*, 1846.

[3] Six victories are specially mentioned by Weil, i. pp. 32, 36, 37.

[4] *Ib.* p. 40. Muir, *Annals of the Early Caliphate*, p. 206, places the battle of Adjnadein in spring 636.

[5] Theoph. 6125 A.M. mentions that Theodore, being defeated, went to Heraclius at Edessa.

[6] The most important question in the chronology of the Syrian campaigns is the date of the battle of Yermuk. Was it fought in 634 or in 635? Was it the battle of Adjnadein or the battle of Yermuk that imme-

but called by Arabic authorities Vartan,[1] and Theodore Trithy-
rius, the imperial treasurer, who is to be distinguished from
the Emperor's brother of the same name.[2] Khalid on this
occasion was the life and soul of the Saracens; he allayed the
discords of the commanders and won a complete victory.

Great preparations had been made by the Romans, and
60,000 light-armed troops of the Philhellene Arabs of Ghassan
reinforced the army of Baanes.[3] It is difficult to harmonise
the accounts of this fiercely fought battle, and we cannot but
see that the chaff of legend is mixed with the grain of history,
as in the "Homeric" siege of Damascus. The storm of sand,
for example, which blinded the Persians at Cadesia, has been
transferred in one narrative to the banks of the Yermuk. Abu
Ubeida yielded to his more martial captain Khalid the chief
command in the action, and contented himself with the
humble and useful post of standing in the rear and driving
forward the fugitives. The Arabs were fortified for their
toil by the concise and vivid words, "Paradise is before you,
behind you the devil and the fire of hell." In the engagement we can detect that the Moslem were again and again
compelled to retreat, and were exposed to terrible showers
from the bows of Armenian archers. For a long time the
result wavered, and the balance of Mars was equal. It was
perhaps decided by a curious ambush devised by the Arabs,
who placed around the tents of their camp camels with their

diately preceded the advance on Damascus? It is to be observed that
Theophanes, while he places the battle
in 6126 A.M., that is 635 (not, as is
generally stated, 636), makes the attack
on Damascus a consequence of it, and
when we combine this with the circumstances that (1) he places it at the
end of the first year of Omar instead
of at the beginning, and that (2) 23d
August (al. 23d July), the day of the
battle, fell on Tuesday in 634, we may
conclude that it took place in 634;
see Weil, i. p. 45 note, and p. 47 note.
Most historians, however, accept the
date 636, while Finlay holds that there
were two battles of Yermuk, the first
in 634, before the siege of Damascus,
and the second in 636. In any case
the date 636 seems unfounded. Muir
places a battle of Wacûsa or Yermuk
in April 634, and a second greater

battle at the same place in August-
September of the same year, the intervening months having passed away in
skirmishing (p. 98).

[1] Another of the difficult questions
which beset the history of these years
is the identity of Vartan; was he
Baanes (Vahan) or not? Finlay distinguishes two generals (vol. i. p.
360).

[2] This is clear from the narrative
of Theophanes. After the defeat of
Heraclius' brother, Baanes is sent with
Theodore, the sacellarius, against the
Arabs (6125 A.M. = 634); they win a
victory and drive the enemy to Damascus. It is to be observed that Theophanes places the departure of Heraclius
from Syria before the battle of Yermuk.

[3] Weil gives the number of the
Greeks as at least 80,000.

feet bound together.[1] The Romans did not hesitate to attack the camp, and a large company of concealed foes cut them to pieces or put them to flight. A general rout ensued, and many of the Romans were drowned.

The result of this battle decided the fate of Damascus, the stronghold of southern Syria. The small army that hastened to its relief was met and vanquished, and in 635 the city surrendered.[2]

It is not a little surprising how completely this first expedition of the Saracens paralysed an Emperor who had deservedly won a high military reputation. It did not occur to him to lead his army in person, and when we combine this fact with the utter physical prostration and mental derangement from which he suffered in the following year, we cannot avoid the conclusion that his health was already rapidly failing. It is to be further observed that Martina, his constant companion, who possessed the same sort of influence over him that Schirin had possessed over Chosroes, aware of her husband's declining health, was in all probability taking measures to secure her own interests in the case of his possibly approaching decease. The offspring of the intrigues of an ambitious queen is suspicion, distrust, and division ; and not only does the conduct of Martina after her husband's death compel us to entertain the idea that she was an intriguer while he lived, but direct indications of division and distrust in the imperial family are preserved. The relations of an Emperor are often obstacles to the designs of his consort; and Theodore and Martina, though uncle and niece, were antagonists. Accordingly we find that Theodore's defeat at Adjnadein or Gabatha was made a pretext against him ; Heraclius sent him bound as a prisoner to Constantinople, and instructed Constantine to make his disgrace public and keep him in strict confinement. We can hardly avoid suspecting that the disgrace of Theodore was due to the

---

[1] The authority is the Armenian history of Sepêos. *See* Drapeyron, *L'Empereur Héraclius*, p. 367.

[2] According to the romance of Al Wakidi, Damascus was defended with heroism and suffered a cruel vengeance. When the soldiers became weary of slaughter the remainder of the inhabitants received permission to withdraw from the city, and set out in the direction of Laodicea under the conduct of Thomas, the commander of the garrison, and his wife, one of the imperial princesses. But the Saracen general, repenting of his clemency, overtook the fugitives as they rested in a valley and massacred them. The daughter of Heraclius, we are told, was spared and restored to her father, while her husband died fighting.

enmity of Martina, as we hear that he was one of those who condemned her marriage.

After the capture of Damascus the invaders appear to have remained quiet for almost the space of a year, but at the end of 635 or the beginning of 636 the "high roofs of Emesa"— *Emesae fastigia celsa*—or Hims, as it was called by the Arabians, and the city of Heliopolis or Baalbec were taken. Thereupon Heraclius, who was at Edessa or Antioch, forgetful of his ancient valour, despaired of saving the provinces of Syria, and determined to save his own person by flight to Constantinople,[1] even as he had fled on another occasion many years before at Selymbria. He was able, notwithstanding the proximity of the Saracens, to hurry to Jerusalem and seize the cross, which he was resolved to prevent from falling again into the hands of unbelievers. He bade farewell to Syria, and when he arrived at Chalcedon he established his residence in Hieria, his favourite palace, and was seized there by a sort of hydrophobia. He was afraid to go on board a ship for even such a short voyage as the crossing of the Bosphorus, and used to send his sons to represent their father at public ceremonies in the capital. At length some one proposed to make a wide bridge of boats, and by covering it with earth, and hedging it with green branches, lend it the aspect of a hedged lane on dry land. Over such a bridge the Emperor consented to ride. The reception of the cross at St. Sophia was a rite of sad solemnity, contrasting doubtless in the minds of spectators with the glory of its reception six years before.

During these days there was a usurper in Syria, and there were conspiracies in Constantinople. Baanes the Persian, Heraclius' general, took advantage of the Emperor's withdrawal, which he might represent as a shameful desertion, to proclaim himself Augustus; but, under the circumstances, the matter was not of much importance. In the conspiracies the Emperor's love-child Athalaric and his nephew Theo-

---

[1] The farewell of Heraclius to Syria is placed by Ockley and Gibbon in 638; but cf. Weil, p. 79, and Finlay (i. p. 360) who points out that "Ockley's Arabian authorities confounded the young Heraclius with his father." Theophanes is hardly right in placing the event in 634. Muir (*op. cit.* p. 201) places it in 636, after the fall of Aleppo, Hims, and Antioch. The same authority sets the capitulation of Jerusalem at the end of 636, whereas I have accepted the date of Theophanes, 637; Nicephorus (p. 24) implies that Egypt was being conquered while Heraclius was still in Syria.

dore [1] were the chief offenders; they were both banished to islands.

Abu Bekr had died just before the battle of Yermuk was fought, and had been succeeded by the great and austere Omar, for whom the attractions of the future life did not consist in its licensed sensuality. He was sterner than Abu Bekr, and his drastic management soon restored the discipline of the army, which had degenerated after the capture of Damascus. The turbulent and ruthless Khalid was deposed from the chief command and made the lieutenant of Abu Ubeida.

The captures of Emesa and Heliopolis were soon followed by the fall of Tiberias, of Chalcis, of Beroea, of Epiphania, and of Larissa. Edessa agreed to pay tribute; Antioch fell,[2] probably by treachery, for so much credit I am inclined to give to the story of Yukinna, the typical *magariser*. There can be no doubt that the rapid conquest of Syria was facilitated by the apostasy of Christians, as well as by the treachery of Jews; it was expected that the yoke of the Arab might prove lighter than the yoke of the Roman; and there was certainly no lack of magarisers. The very name *magarise*, " to embrace Islam," is a Syriac form which passed into Greek,[3] and proves the frequency of apostasy to Mohammedanism in that country.

The chronological order of the capture of these towns is uncertain, but there is little doubt that after a siege of two years Jerusalem was compelled to surrender in 637. The inhabitants refused, however, to yield to any general save Omar himself.

Accordingly the Caliph Omar came from Arabia to take

---

[1] The implication of Theodore, son of the general of the same name, seems to connect the conspiracy with the imprisonment of his father.

[2] Theoph. places the capture of Antioch in 638 or at earliest in last months of 637 (6129 A.M.)

[3] I conjectured myself that μαγαρίζειν was connected with Ἀγαρηνὸς (Saracen, lit. descendant of Hagar) and had come through the Syriac, whence the initial μ; but I find that Payne Smith had already noticed it in his *Thesaurus*. Dr. Gwynn communicated to me the following note: " From the name ܡܓܪ

are formed the verbs ܡܓܪ and ܡܓܪܬܐ (as if Aphel and Ethpael), both meaning to become Moslem. Their participles are ܡܓܪܐ and ܡܓܪܢܐ. The latter is the form I have met in the continuator of the *Chronicon* of Barhebraeus, but I find in the *Thesaurus* that the Aphel form is more usual. Payne Smith (s.v.) mentions the Greek μαγαρίζω as formed from it, as you supposed."

formal possession of the Holy City,[1] and men wondered at his austere surroundings and his rough dress, which was simple even to ferocity, a much worn and much torn skin. The Patriarch Sophronius, the combatant against monotheletism, acted as a lugubrious guide through the holy sights of the city, and with difficulty persuaded the caliph to array himself in more decent costume to enter the precincts of the church of the Resurrection. The sight of Omar kneeling at the shrine drew from the bishop the exclamation, uttered in Greek, "The abomination of desolation which was spoken of by Daniel the prophet, is in the holy place." A mosque was erected on the site of Solomon's temple, but the Christians were tolerated as subjects of the caliph, on condition that they made no attempt to proselytise the disciples of Mohammed, and paid a tribute.

Heraclius made a last desperate attempt to recover the lost provinces in 638. He sent his son Constantine to Syria, and an army was collected at Diarbekr or Amida, which proceeded to besiege Emesa. Khalid hastened from the north, Abu Ubeida from the south, to relieve it, and a battle was fought in the neighbourhood which decided that Syria was to remain in the hands of the Mohammedans until three centuries hence the valour of imperial successors of Heraclius should set up a christian standard once more in Syrian provinces. In 638 Muaviah was appointed emir of all the Saracen empire from Egypt to the Euphrates. Once Syria was conquered, the Roman possessions in Mesopotamia were an easy prey to the Saracens. Edessa, Constantina, and Daras were taken in 639, and the reduction of these strong places meant the conquest of Mesopotamia.

Meanwhile the Persian kingdom had been overthrown in the great battle of Cadesia (636). That field was the scene of struggles which lasted four days, but ultimately the elements intervened, and a storm of sand contributed to the victory of Said (Sa'ad).[2] Some months later the conqueror entered Ctesiphon, and divided its riches and its marvels. Among the treasures found in the palace Takht-i-Khosru may be mentioned

---

[1] Theophanes places the conquest of Palestine at end of 637 A.D. (see *sub* 6127 A.M.) He describes Omar as ὑπόκρισιν σατανικὴν ἐνδεικνύμενος.

[2] The Persian army numbered 120,000. The great standard of the Persian kingdom, said to be a blacksmith's apron, was captured in this battle.

the golden horse, the silver camel with the golden foal, and the immense carpet of white brocade " with a border worked in precious stones of various hues to represent a garden of all kinds of beautiful flowers."[1]   Sixty thousand soldiers received about £312 apiece.   The battle of Yalulah, fought early in 637, finished the work of Cadesia, and by the end of that year all the land west of Mount Zagrus from Nineveh to Susa was Arabian. The last king, Isdigerd, had sought a refuge in distant mountain fastnesses, and three years later he made a forlorn attempt to recover his kingdom.   But the battle of Nehavend, "the victory of victories" (Fattah-hul-Futtûh), stamped out for ever the dynasty of the Sassanids, which had lasted somewhat more than four hundred years (226-641).[2]

The Arab conquest of Persia was marked by the foundation of Kufa on the ruins of Ctesiphon, and the erection of the city of Bussora, or Bassra, on "the river of the Arabs," as was called the united stream of the Euphrates and Tigris.   Bussora became soon a great mercantile centre.

The Conquest of Egypt by Amru.—The general Amru, who is said to have had previous acquaintance with Egypt, and was doubtless aware of the internal dissensions which prevailed in that land, obtained with difficulty the permission of the caliph to invade it in 639 or 640.   If a foreign invader was welcome to some in Syria, still more was he welcome in Egypt.   The native Copts, who were Jacobites, hated the Greeks, who were Melchites, and this element in the situation was made use of by Amru to effect his conquest.[3]

The conquest of Egypt is somewhat clearer in detail than the conquest of Syria.   Perenum or Farma was taken first,

---

[1] Rawlinson, *op. cit.* p. 566.   Careless of the unity of a work of art, the caliph allowed it to be cut up and divided.

[2] Isdigerd lived for ten years in refuge among the Turks and the Chinese. In 651 he made an attempt with their help to recover his kingdom, but was repulsed and slain.

[3] In 635 Cyrus, Patriarch of Alexandria, had, without consulting the Emperor, agreed with the Saracens to

pay them 120,000 dinars a year.   When Heraclius heard thereof he indignantly sent Manuel, an Armenian, as *præfectus augustalis*, who refused to pay the stipulated money.   Hence the expedition of Amru (Theoph. 6126 A.M.) Nicephorus notices the scheme of Cyrus to marry one of Heraclius' daughters to Amru and convert him to Christianity (p. 24).   But the dealings of Cyrus with the unbelievers drew suspicions of paganism on him (p. 26).

with the help of the Copts; the invader was next opposed at Bilbeis and at Umm Danin by Greek forces, and, having overcome in two battles, he laid siege to Babylon. Here he waited for reinforcements from Omar, who sent him 12,000 men, and after a siege of some months Babylon fell. The capture of this city was as decisive for the fate of Egypt as the capture of Damascus had been for the fate of Syria. It is probable that a great many Syrians were influenced by the latter event to desert the imperial cause; it is certain that the success of Amru at Babylon decided Mukaukas, the Coptic governor, to yield to the Arabs, and exchange the yoke of Constantinople for the yoke of Mecca. The simple life of the Arabs, their religious enthusiasm, and their contempt for death inspired him with reverence; he did not hesitate to make peace, and agree, on behalf of the Copts, to pay a moderate tribute.

The impression made upon him by the followers of Mohammed was thus described by Mukaukas when the Emperor Heraclius upbraided him for submitting to the invader[1]: "It is true," he said, "that the enemy are not nearly so numerous as we, but one Mussulman is equivalent to a hundred of our men. Of the enjoyments of the earth they desire only simple clothing and simple food, and yearn for the death of martyrs because it leads them to paradise; while we cling to life and its joys, and fear death." This illustrates the spirit which enabled the Arabians to carry all before them in the first years of their new greatness; the joys of paradise were before their eyes as they fought. Al Wakidi gave poetical expression to this spirit in the words which he placed in the mouth of a youth fighting under the walls of Emesa: "Methinks I see the black-eyed girls looking upon me; one of whom, should she appear in this world, all mankind would die for love of her. And I see in the hand of one of them an handkerchief of green silk and a cap of precious stones, and she beckons me and calls out, Come hither quickly, for I love thee."[2]

From Memphis and Babylon the Greeks retired to Alexandria, fighting as they went. Four places[3] can be dis-

<hr />

[1] Weil, vol. i. p. 111.
[2] Gibbon, cap. li.
[3] Weil, *ib.* p. 112 *sq.* (1) Terenut,

five days' journey from Alexandria; (2) Kom Scharik; (3) Siltis; (4) Keriun, a day's journey from Alexandria.

tinguished at each of which a stand was made, and at some of these stages more battles than one were fought, in which the Arabs were usually victorious. At length Alexandria was reached. The great Greek city which supplied New Rome with corn might perhaps have been saved and formed the basis for the recovery of Egypt if Heraclius had lived longer. But as he was making preparations to send an armament for its defence he died of a painful disease, which had been long afflicting him (10th February 641), and the intrigues and disturbances which ensued upon his death absorbed the attention of Constantinople. No help was sent to Alexandria; on the contrary, it even seems that troops were withdrawn from it, for selfish purposes, by one of the opposing parties in the capital. The inhabitants ultimately abandoned all thoughts of defence; those who possessed property left the city by sea, carrying off their possessions; and in December 641, after a siege of fourteen months, Amru made his entry.[1]

Egypt was now a possession of the Saracens; and, with the exception of Cyprus, the Roman Empire no longer held any territory in the East south of the Taurus mountains. Omar would not permit Amru to make Alexandria the capital of the new province; it was too far from Medina, and the land about Misr (Babylon) was more fertile. Accordingly a new city was founded on the spot where Amru had encamped when he was besieging Babylon, and was hence called Fostât, "the Tent"; but the town afterwards assumed a more ambitious name and became Cairo, "the City of Victory," and the mosque of Amru commemorates to this day the Saracen conquest of Egypt. To the Egyptian population, whose squalor formed a vivid contrast to the splendour and luxury of Alexandria, the change of masters did not seriously matter. The cultivation of the soil was left in their hands; Egypt was now to be a granary for the Arabs, as it had been formerly a granary for the Romans. The old canal which connected the Nile with the Red Sea was opened up. "The channel followed the most eastern branch of the river as far north as

---

[1] Weil, i. 114. According to Theophanes, Manuel was the general of the Greeks. Nicephorus mentions three generals who were successively sent to defend Egypt (p. 24). John was slain in battle, Marinus was defeated and hardly escaped with his life, and Marianus suffered a great defeat and was himself slain.

Bilbeis, then turned to the right through the vale of Tumlât, and, striking the salt lakes near Timseh, so reached the Red Sea by what is now the lower portion of the Suez Canal." [1]

I may quote part of a letter [2] which the Caliph Omar wrote to the conqueror of Egypt, to illustrate the government of the first caliph and especially the character of Omar. One might imagine that he would have shown respect and honour to the general who had won such an important land for Islam, but his words express the sternness of an austere deity, who is not satisfied with works and reaps where he has not sown :—

" I have reflected on you and your condition ; you are in a great and excellent land, whose inhabitants God blesses by number and might, by land and sea—a land which even the Pharaohs, in spite of their unbelief, brought by useful works into a flourishing condition. I am therefore extremely surprised, that it does not bring in half of what it brought in formerly, although this decrease cannot be excused by famine or a bad year. You wrote to me before of many imposts which you laid on the land. I expected they would pour in ; but instead I receive excuses, which do not please me. I shall not accept a whit less than the former revenue."

The preceding account of the Saracen conquests may appear a dry sketch, because it is barren in details. But this is unavoidable. For in the story of the conquest of Syria legend is so mingled with history, that if we once attempt to choose among the details, which come mainly from oriental sources, we can never be sure with which element we are dealing. No compromise is possible between Weil and Ockley. Again, it may seem to some that the conquest of Syria demands as a sort of due, even in a Roman History, a long disquisition on the Saracens, an elaborate biography of Mohammed, and a collection of anecdotes to illustrate the characters of the caliphs and their emirs. But here, as in the case of the Lombards

[1] Muir, *op. cit.* p. 244. The statistics of the population of Alexandria given by Arabic historians are interesting if true. The male population was 600,000 ; the number of male taxable Jews was probably about 70,000 ; the Greeks numbered 200,000, of whom 30,000 escaped before the siege. In the city were 4000 baths, 400 theatres ; in the harbour 12,000 vessels (?) (p. 240, cf. Weil, i. p. 116). The burning of the library by the Saracens is only a legend (cf. Weil, *ib.*) Weil sketches the history of the canals from the Nile to the Red Sea ; the first was begun and abandoned by Necho, son of Psammetichus, about 615 B.C., but the Persian Darius completed it ; the second was dug by Ptolemy Philadelphus, but fell into neglect, and was opened again by Trajan ; it fell into neglect again under the later Emperors, and was restored by Amru (p. 120 *sqq.*)

[2] Weil, who is more inclined to reject than to accept, concludes that this letter is genuine. I translate from his translation (p. 124).

and the Franks, where the temptation to write episodes is strong, I have diligently avoided Herodotean digressions.

Before we conclude this chapter we must bid a more solemn farewell to Heraclius, whose death has been already casually mentioned. On the 11th of February 641 the saviour of New Rome was laid beside Constantine, her founder, and Justinian, who had made her glorious, in the church of the Holy Apostles, which Constantine's mother had built. For three days the body was exposed to view in an open coffin, watched over by eunuchs, in accordance with the wishes of the dead Emperor.[1]

Heraclius is one of those unfortunate heroes who have outlived their glory, and have thereby won the sympathy as well as the admiration of posterity. Alexander the Great died in the fulness of his prosperity; Constantine the Great did not experience the mortification of seeing his work undone; Justinian passed away before his successes in Italy were half reversed by the Lombard invaders and before his system collapsed. But the Emperor who saved the inheritance of Rome at the time of sorest need, the warrior who, like Alexander, overthrew a Persian sovereign, the champion who maintained the cause of Hellenism as well as the cause of Christendom, was destined to live too long. He was to live to see the provinces which he had won back from the fire-worshipper fall a prey to the Semitic unbeliever; he was to live to behold the Holy City in the power of a more dreadful foe than the Persian; he was to live to hear a new word of more ominous sound than the old and familiar "Medism." And the woes of his latter years were aggravated by a hideous disease.[2] But his name was not forgotten; like Alexander the Great, he passed into medieval legend.[3]

---

[1] Nicephorus, p. 27. He died at the age of sixty-six.

[2] Dropsy, ἡνίκα ἀπουρεῖν ἔμελλε σανίδα κατὰ τοῦ ἥτρου ἐπετίθει· ἐστρέφετο γὰρ αὐτοῦ τὸ αἰδοῖον καὶ κατὰ τοῦ προσώπου αὐτοῦ τὰ οὖρα ἔπεμπεν. To the superstitious mind of a Patriarch the nature of the disease was determined by the nature of the sin which Heraclius had committed in marrying Martina. The member which offended suffered. Niceph. *ib.*

[3] Otto of Freisingen wrote a romance of Heraclius in the twelfth century. M. Drapeyron (*op. cit.* p. 282) notices that there is a colossal statue at Barletta, supposed to be of Heraclius. Heraclius conquering Chosroes was the subject of a painting on enamel at Limoges (*ib.*). Heraclea, a town in Venetia, was founded soon after the victory of 628, commemorating in its name the same hero (*ib.*)

CHAPTER VII

IN the first half of the seventh century important Slavonic migrations took place which affected the future of the Haemus peninsula. The details and the dates of these movements are obscure, but the general outline is sufficiently clear.[1]

In the year 610 we hear of Bavarians in conflict with Slaves (Slovenes) on the upper Drave,[2] and we find the latter taking up a permanent abode in the district of Carniola or Krain. At the same time, farther south, the settlements of the Slovenes in Illyricum, Macedonia, and Moesia were increasing, so that there was a considerable Slovene population extending from the frontiers of Bavaria almost to the Aegean. But this homogeneous population was not destined to become welded together and form one nationality; for a few years later—at what moment cannot exactly be determined, but certainly during the reign of Heraclius—two other peoples, Slavonic but not Slovenic,[3] known as the Croates and the Serbs, pressed into the lands of Upper Moesia, Lower Pannonia, and Dalmatia, which they permanently occupied, thereby cutting off for ever the Slovenes of Carniola and Carinthia from the Slovenes of Macedonia and Lower Moesia. The lot of the north-western Slovenes was to be linked with that of the Franks and the Western Empire; while their south-eastern

---

[1] My chief guide has been Dümmler's excellent article on the history of Dalmatia in the Vienna *Sitzungsberichte* (23d April 1856, p. 353 *sqq.*), to which I may refer the reader who is curious as to the literature of the subject.

[2] Paul, *Hist. Lang.* iv. 39.

[3] I use the adjective Slovenic of those Slaves who were called Σκλαβηνοί or Σθλαβηνοί by Greek writers. Their descendants in Carniola, Carinthia, etc., speak a language closely related to the Serbo-Croatian.

brethren were to be closely connected with the Eastern
Empire.

Dümmler supposes that the Croates and Serbs[1] were
tribes under Avaric suzerainty, and that with the consent of
their lords they crossed the Danube to take possession of
Dalmatia and Upper Moesia, which the Slovenes had laid
waste. The fact that Pope John IV, a Dalmatian by birth,
sent an abbot to Istria and Dalmatia, between 640 and
642 A.D., to collect christian relics and ransom christian
prisoners from the heathen, proves that the newcomers occupied
those provinces in the reign of Heraclius. In later years,
when the power of the Avars had passed away and the Serbs
and Croatians had been converted to Christianity and entered
into connection with Byzantium, the idea arose that they had
been originally invited to settle in their homes by the Emperor
Heraclius, and this idea, accepted and echoed by the Emperor
Constantine Porphyrogennetos, has been generally received.

I have been speaking of the Croatians as an unequivocally
Slavonic people, and this is the generally received doctrine.
I believe, however, that it is not a strictly correct view. Before the tenth century the legend had arisen that the Croatians
came to their new abodes from the land of White Croatia
under the leadership of five brothers, Klukas, Lobel, Cosentzes,
Muchlô, Chrobátos, and two sisters, Buga and Tuga.[2] This
Croatian legend has a strong family resemblance to the Bulgarian legend of Krobat (or Kubrat) and his five sons, which
will be related in another chapter[3]; and I think we can hardly
hesitate to suppose that Krobat and Chrobátos are the same
prehistorical hero of the Hunnic nation to which the various
closely related tribes of the Bulgarians, Cotrigurs, and Onogundurs belonged. If this be a true view, the name *Croatia*
is not Slavonic, and, as a matter of fact, no probable Slavonic

---

[1] Constantine Porphyrogennetos says
that the original home of these peoples
was in White Servia (beyond Hungary),
but he is confusing the Serbs and Serbs.
Dümmler believes that there may be
some foundation for a Great or White
Croatia (Βελοχρωβάτοι) to the north-east
of Bohemia, as the Croatian name
appears in the neighbourhood of Kra-
kau. Constantine thought Σέρβλοι was
a Latin word equivalent to *servi* (*de*

Adm. Imp. iii. 152), whence also the
name σέρβουλα for poor shoes such as
Slaves wear, and τξερβουλιανοί for the
cobblers who make them; the Serbs,
he says, were so called because they
were the δοῦλοι of the Roman Emperor.
Σπόροι in Procopius, *B. G.* iii. 14, has
been identified by Safarik with the
Serbs.

[2] Const. Porph. iii. p. 143 (ed. Bonn).

[3] Below, cap. xi.

explanation of it has ever been suggested. On the other hand, the Hunnic or Bulgaric name leads us to the interesting conclusion that the establishment of the Croatian Slaves as an independent state in Dalmatia was due to the same conditions that established the kingdom of the Bulgarian Slaves in Moesia. The Slaves of Croatia were clearly conquered by a Bulgarian people, just as the Slaves of Moesia were conquered by a Bulgarian people. But when and where the former conquest took place cannot be determined. It does not seem probable that Hunnic Croatians suddenly entered Dalmatia in the seventh century and conquered the Slaves who had been forming settlements there for the past hundred years. Some definite record of such an event would have been preserved, and there would have been most certainly a Croatian kingdom ruled by sovereigns of Hunnic names, instead of a number of practically independent župans. We must therefore suppose that Dalmatia was invaded in the reign of Heraclius, not by Croatian Huns, but by Croatian Slaves, that is to say, Slaves who had been conquered many years before in some country north of the Danube by Bulgarians, and had already absorbed the individuality of their conquerors. Turanian Chrobat or Krobat was associated in the legend with Slavonic names, *Buga* and *Tuga*, Weal and Woe. I may add that this theory is supported by the non-Slavonic name of the Croatian governor, Boanos (βοάνος), which strongly reminds us of the Avar Baian, and of Baian or Batbaian, who in Bulgarian legend was one of the sons of Krobat.

The invasion of Croatians and Serbs caused a general flight coastwards among the Roman inhabitants of Dalmatia, and new towns were founded on islands and promontories, just as Venice is said to have been founded by fugitives from the Huns and as Monembasia was probably founded in the Peloponnesus by fugitives from the Slaves. The inhabitants of the ancient Tragurium (Traü) [1] withdrew to the opposite island of Bua; Rausium,[2] or Ragusa, was founded by the citizens who fled

---

[1] Tragurium is mentioned by Polybius (xxxii. 18). It is called Τετραγγούριον by Const. Porph.

[2] It is hard to decide whether there is anything in the statement of Constantine Porph. (*de Adm. Imp.* iii. 136)

that the original name of the Ῥαουσαῖοι was Λαυσαῖοι, from a "Romaic" word λαῦ = cliff (apparently connected with λᾶας). The change from λ to ρ is highly improbable, as there is no other liquid in the word to cause assimilation or

from the old Greek colony of Epidaurus; and the town of Cattaro (Dekatera) had a similar origin. Salona, the home of Diocletian in his last years, did not escape destruction, and some of its inhabitants founded the town of Spalato,[1] or Spalatro, around the palace of Diocletian, from which it derived its name. Is it fanciful to suppose that, when the people of Salona fled from their city at the approach of the invaders, they made for the Emperor's palace, and that some cried in Greek, *'s palation* ('ς παλάτιον—that is, "to the palace !"), and that hence the name *Spalation*, which became Spalato, was given to the new town? Further north, in the district of Liburnia, the city of Jadera[2] (Zara) defied the Slave, and four islands opposite the mainland — Veglia, Arbe, Cherso, and Lussin, of which the two latter together are called by one name, Opsara — also remained under the supremacy of the Empire. The inhabitants of these cities and islands were called *Romanoi* by the Greeks, and retained the Latin language. A Byzantine stratêgos, in whose hands military and civil powers were combined, resided at Zara, and it may be conjectured that he was responsible to the exarch of Ravenna. The payment of a certain tribute and the contribution of ships and sailors for service in the Adriatic were practically the only link of connection that bound these dependencies with the Empire.

The kingdom of the Croatians was probably much larger from the seventh to the ninth century than in later times; for at first it seems to have included Bosnia, which was afterwards lost to the Serbs.[3] Croatia was divided into four župes, governed by independent princes called župans. There was one great

---

dissimilation (as *e.g.* in *lusciniola*, rossignol). *Argosy* is generally derived from the ship Argo; but it is possible that Ragusan galleys may have been the original argosies, and that the metathesis of the first two letters may have been due to reminiscences of the mythical vessel.

[1] 'Ασπάλαθον, interpreted by Constantine Porph. as παλάτιον μικρόν, a little palace; a derivation which seems in the highest degree doubtful. ἀσπάλαθος is a prickly shrub with a fragrant oil, and this Greek name seems to have been a Volksetymologie.

[2] Const. Porph. says that Diadora was called in "Romaic" *Jam erat* (Romaic in this passage means Latin), in the sense that it was founded before Rome (!) It is not easy to see how he got *jam erat* from Jadera.

[3] Dümmler deduces this from the statement of Const. Porphyr. that Croatia had declined in the middle of the ninth century, and that its military power had once amounted to 60,000 cavalry and 100,000 infantry—numbers incredible from the size of their land in later times—combined with the notice that at first the Croatians spread themselves in Pannonia (evidently Lower Pannonia) and Illyria, *i.e.* Dalmatia and the land north and east towards the Save and Drina.

župan, but his was merely a titular greatness, which, however, afterwards developed into real monarchical power under the external influence of other monarchical constitutions.[1]

South of the Croatians, who had occupied northern Dalmatia as far as the river Cettina, were the four races of maritime Serbians. The Narentanes,[2] who became renowned as pirates, dwelled between the Cettina and the Narenta, and for many generations, living amid inaccessible rocks, resisted the influences of Christianity, whence they were called by their Roman neighbours *Pagans*, a word which a Greek writer of the tenth century supposed to be Slavonic and translated "unbaptized." The district between the river Narenta and the town of Ragusa was occupied by the Zachlums, an important tribe; south of whom dwelled the less considerable Travouni between Ragusa and Cattaro; and the Dukljani[3] between Cattaro and Antivari, in the district corresponding to modern Montenegro.

We seldom meet with the Romans of Dalmatia and their Slavonic neighbours in the general current of Roman history during the seventh and eighth centuries. We may conclude that as the power of the Avars decreased, the power of the Slaves increased; and that when Avaric influence had quite passed away, the Slaves entered into peaceful relations with the Emperor of Constantinople before the end of the seventh century, perhaps in the year 678, when all the powers of the West vied in establishing friendly relations with Constantine IV. Soon afterwards they were converted to Christianity.

We may now turn from the south-western Slaves, who were destined to remain free from Turanian influence, to the south-eastern Slaves, who were soon to pass under a Turanian yoke. The statement of Constantine Porphyrogennetos that Heraclius settled the Slaves in Thrace and Macedonia cannot be accepted without reservation. We have seen how during the last thirty years of the sixth century Thrace and Illyricum were receiving a considerable Slavonic population; the invaders took up their abode in the land, and lived half as peasants half as freebooters. During this time the valiant and experienced Priscus was at

---

[1] Dümmler notices that the court of the great župan bears clear traces of Frank influence.

[2] The islands of south Dalmatia, Lesina, Curzola, Méleda, were colonised by the Narentanes.

[3] So called from the town of Dioclea.

the head of a Roman army in those provinces, and could to a certain extent keep the Slaves in check and prevent the land from being deluged with the strangers. But during the reigns of Phocas and Heraclius the political anarchy and the pressing difficulties of the Persian war rendered the government unable to extend its protection to the Illyrian and Thracian provinces; they were left to shift for themselves. The large fortified towns, Thessalonica, Hadrianople, or Marcianopolis, were able to defy the Avar and the Slave, or to purchase exemption from their hostilities; but there were no forces to hinder the occupation of the land. When the great Scythian destroyer marched against the city of Constantine in 626, to capture it in conjunction with the Persian, it must have been through an almost Slavonic land that his way lay. The connection then of Heraclius with these Slavonic settlers, which had been somehow handed down to the imperial antiquarian, probably consisted in arranging a "mode of living" with them. Heraclius doubtless made compacts with the chiefs of their tribes—even as Constantine and Aetius made compacts with Visigoths and Vandals, and Zeno with the Ostrogoths—that they should inhabit certain limited territories. It cannot be doubted that Heraclius, after his Persian victories, directed his attention to the condition of the Haemus countries, which sorely needed succour after a long neglect; but for us their history is buried in obscurity during this period. At the same time the decline of the Avar monarchy, which set in soon after the failure of the chagan at Constantinople, influenced the political situation, and a general revolt of the subject Slaves and Bulgarians, which drove the Avars westward, may have been attended with new migrations to the lands south of the Danube.[1]

Regions of Lower Moesia and the lands of Macedonia about Thessalonica seem to have been the two chief Slavonic districts, or, as we may call them, the Sclavinias.[2] The action of Heraclius doubtless consisted in recognising these settlements as dependencies on the Empire. Before we reach the end of the

---

[1] Of the fall of the Avar monarchy we hear little. Suidas, *sub voce* Ἄβαρις, has this notice, ὅτι τοὺς Ἀβάρις οἱ Βόλγαροι κατὰ κράτος ἀρδὴν ἠφάνισαν. In late legends the Avars are called Ὄμβροι, and a Russian proverb is preserved by

Nestor—"They have vanished, like the Obri, without posterity, without heir" (*ni plemene ni naslědka*).

[2] *Sclavinia* (Σκλαβινία) is now used of the lands which corresponded to the ancient Pannonia.

seventh century we shall hear of the " seven Slavonic tribes " in Moesia, which were subdued by the Bulgarians, but we know nothing more precise about the Moesian Sclavinia.

Of the Macedonian Sclavinia we know more ; the *Life of St. Demetrius* has preserved some details touching the tribes which, settled in the neighbourhood of Thessalonica, harried its territory and threatened its walls.   Between Thessalonica and Beroea, in the valleys of the Axios and the Haliacmon, abode the tribes of the Drogubites and Sagudates.   South of these, a district on the Gulf of Pagasae (Volo), in Thessaly, was occupied by the Belegezêtes (whose name survives in the modern Velestino), the Berzêtes, and the Bajunêtes.   All these tribes combined to besiege Thessalonica in the episcopate of archbishop John II (675-681), and the city of St. Demetrius was hardly saved by the miraculous protection of its patron. Other Slaves were settled on the Strymon, and the Runchines were among the most formidable neighbours of the cities of Macedonia.   Most of these barbarous tribes infested the sea as well as the land, and penetrated in their light piratical boats into the waters of the Propontis.[1]

We saw reason to suppose that in the reign of Maurice Slaves had begun to settle in the lands south of Mount Olympus.   It is almost certain that the Slavonic element in Greece increased during the reign of Heraclius, while the entire attention of the government was occupied by the struggle with Persia, for we can hardly refuse to allow so much credit to the strong statement of the contemporary Isidore of Seville that " the Slaves took Greece from the Romans," *Sclavi Graeciam Romanis tulerunt.*[2]   But while we infer so much from the words of the Spanish bishop, I think we can hardly infer more.   It is certain at least that the large towns did not fall a prey to the Slaves.   Athens, for example, was still Greek and to some extent still a seat of learning, for the great Theodore of Tarsus, to whom our own England owes so much, was educated there. Nor had the country yet become Slavised, as it is said to have become in the following century.

[1] *Acta Sanctorum*, Oct. iv. pp. 162-174.   *See* Hopf, *Griechische Geschichte*, p. 94, and below, p. 337.   [2] *Chron.* 120.

CHAPTER VIII

CONSTANS II

THE history of the successors of Heraclius is veiled in the most profound obscurity. We have no contemporary historians; the writers on whom we are obliged to rely almost entirely, lived more than a hundred years later,[1] and it is not even certain from what sources they obtained their materials. From the curt and scanty notices of these chronicles it is impossible to obtain a clear or definite idea of the state of the Empire, and

---

[1] Theophanes, confessor, and Nicephorus, Patriarch of Constantinople. Both wrote, the former his *Chronicle* and the latter his *Short History*, at the beginning of the ninth century. The interesting question is, what were their sources for the history of the seventh century. We have seen that Theophanes utilised George of Pisidia for the Persian wars of Heraclius, and up to the year 628 (or perhaps for a few years later) there were the entries of the *Chronicon Paschale*, which was doubtless consulted both by Theophanes and Nicephorus. But these sources (1) do not account for all their notices in the reigns of Phocas and Heraclius, and (2) entirely deserted them for the later part of Heraclius' reign and for the reigns of the Heraclidae. If we compare the two chronicles it is easy to see that the sources used by Nicephorus were also used by Theophanes, and in some cases their very words are the same. But it is also clear that Theophanes had access to earlier writers whose works were not in the hands of Nicephorus; for (1) the sources of Nicephorus deserted him entirely for the reign of Constans, (2)

Nicephorus is not clear, like Theophanes, in the matter of chronology. One of the authorities used by Theophanes was doubtless the Chronicle of John of Antioch, called Malalas, who probably lived about 700. I suspect that for the reign of Constans, Malalas was the chief source. It is worthy of note that in several places Theophanes uses the Macedonian names of the months (6136, 6150, 6164, 6186, 6205 A.M.), generally in recording such occurrences as earthquakes. As this was a characteristic of the *Paschal Chronicle* (not of John Malalas), I would conjecture that he consulted some lost Alexandrine continuation of the *Paschal Chronicle*.

Besides these later writers we have, chiefly for the ecclesiastical history, the *Acta Conciliorum* and the *Liber Pontificalis*. Some chapters in Paul's *Historia Langobardorum* are important for the later years of Constans. The *Vita Scti. Demetrii* has been already referred to. Zonaras and Cedrenus (or rather John Scylitzes) preserve some details unnoticed by Theophanes, which they probably drew directly from Theophanes' sources.

our account of the reigns of Constans II, Constantine IV, and Justinian II must necessarily be defective.

Yielding doubtless to the persuasions of his beloved and ambitious wife and niece Martina, Heraclius had drawn up an impracticable will, in which he enjoined that the administration of the Empire after his death should be carried on jointly by his eldest son and colleague Constantine, by Heraclonas [1] his son by Martina, and by Martina herself. Accordingly, when her husband had closed his eyes, Martina called a conclave, consisting of the senate and the Patriarch Pyrrhus, and laid the testament of the dead Emperor before them. It seems that she then summoned the citizens of Byzantium to the hippodrome, and there, supported by the presence of Pyrrhus and the senate, made known publicly the last injunctions of the great Heraclius. The people demanded with impatient clamours that the two young Emperors should appear, and Martina unwillingly allowed them to come forward. She was determined from the beginning to take the first place, and keep both her august stepson and her own son, also august, in the background. But the public opinion of the Romaioi disapproved of the sovereignty of a woman, and they made her understand that her audacious project would meet with opposition. Some one is said to have cried out to the Augusta, " You are honoured as the mother of the Emperors, but they as our Emperors and lords." A cogent reason too was assigned for her remaining in an honoured obscurity; " When foreign ambassadors come to the court, you cannot receive them or reply to them "; and this decisive objection was thrust home by the rude exclamation, " God forbid that the Roman Empire should fall so low." The people dispersed cheering the Emperors, and the Empress retreated, discomfited but not hopeless, to the imperial palace.

This first scene, in which the schemes of Martina were baffled, was of evil augury for the future, and we shall not be surprised to hear that, failing to accomplish her ambitious

[1] Theophanes calls him Heraclônas, Nicephorus calls him Heraclius. His proper and imperial name was doubtless Heraclius, and he was named popularly Heraclonas to distinguish him from his father. He attended his father in Syria against the Saracens, and was crowned Augustus in 638 (Nicephorus, pp. 23 and 26). He was born in 615, and therefore was about twenty-six years old at his father's death.

purposes by fair means, the stepmother was prepared to resort to more doubtful practices. For not only had she been herself repulsed, but the public voice had unmistakably declared that Constantine, the eldest son, who had held the position of Augustus for many years, should enjoy a greater dignity and authority than his younger stepbrother.

There were two opposite parties now, the party of Martina in close league with the monotheletic Patriarch Pyrrhus, and the party of Constantine, who had faithful adherents in Philagrius the lord treasurer (*comes sacrarum largitionum*), and his squire ($\dot{\upsilon}\pi\alpha\sigma\pi\iota\sigma\tau\dot{\eta}s$) Valentinus. As Constantine was orthodox and believed not, like his father, in One Will,[1] the opposition of Pyrrhus to his government was all the bitterer. If Constantine had been a stronger man he must certainly have prevailed against his enemies, supported as he was by general public opinion. One is tempted to think that he might have safely banished his stepmother. He won at least one success with the help of Philagrius, who revealed to him that Heraclius had consigned to the care of Pyrrhus a sum of money which might serve as an ample reserve store for Martina if she should ever be driven from the court. Constantine forced the reluctant Patriarch to produce the money.

After this, Constantine fell sick, and for change of air crossed over to his palace at Chalcedon. But the salubrious atmosphere of Asia did not avail, and he died, after a reign of three months and a half. It was generally supposed that poison was administered to him by his stepmother, but as one of our authorities, who gives fuller details of these events than the others, does not even hint at such a suspicion,[2] we are not entitled to assert it as a historical fact, though it may seem credible or even probable. When Philagrius, who waited on the Emperor, saw that his master's end was approaching he felt fears for his own safety, and advised Constantine to engage the army to protect the rights of his children to the succession, in case he died.

---

[1] Zonaras, vol. iii. p. 313 (ed. Dindorf).

[2] Nicephorus, from whom the preceding account is derived; as he uses the expression νόσῳ χρονίᾳ συνείχετο, and Constantine seems to have lain ill for some time at Chalcedon, the poison, if there was poison in the case, must have been a slow one. Pyrrhus, according to Theophanes, had something to do with his death; but then Pyrrhus was a monothelete. Martina's guilt was generally believed, and Constans asserted it as a fact in a speech to the senate after his accession.

Constantine gladly accepted the advice, and sent Valentinus with a letter to the army, also entrusting to his care a large sum of money,[1] with which he was to persuade the generals and soldiers to resist the machinations of Martina and her children.

Heraclius was proclaimed in the city successor of Constantine; and the proclamation of her son meant the ascendency of Martina. One of his or her first acts was to banish Philagrius to Septae, a fort in Africa near the Straits of Gibraltar; and other persons attached to Constantine were punished, though not with death. Valentinus meanwhile was not inactive, and he appeared at Chalcedon, with the troops of Asia Minor, as the champion of the children of Constantine. The time of the vintage was approaching, and, as a large number of the inhabitants of Constantinople possessed vineyards on the Asiatic coast round about Chalcedon, the presence of Valentinus there in a hostile attitude threatened to be eminently vexatious. Heraclius, the eldest son of Constantine III, was in Constantinople, and his stepuncle Heraclonas, in order to anticipate, or perhaps repel, the suspicions and murmurs of the people, produced him in public as a proof that he was safe, and embraced him as if he were his own son. This display of affection seemed credible, as he had received Heraclius in his arms after immersion in the baptismal font. He confirmed this demonstration by swearing on the wood of the cross, in the presence of Pyrrhus, that neither from himself nor from others should the children of Constantine receive hurt. The asseverations of his own good faith were accompanied by imputations against the genuineness of the conduct of Valentinus, whom he accused of aiming at the imperial throne. To confirm this charge he crossed over to Chalcedon in the company of the young Heraclius and tried to persuade Valentinus that his intentions towards the princes were friendly and loyal. But the squire of Philagrius refused to accept his suspicious assurances; and when they of the city heard this, they believed the Emperor and reviled Valentinus.

Meanwhile the vintage was ripe, and the soldiers did not spare the grapes; nor were the vintagers from the city allowed

---

[1] Nicephorus, p. 29 : χρήματα συντελοῦντα εἰς τοσότητα ἀριθμοῦ μυριάδων [πέντε] διακοσίων καὶ ἔτι μύρια καὶ ἑξακισχίλια νομίσματα = 2,010,600 aurei = £1,256,625, omitting πέντε which is very doubtful.

to land in Asia. This state of things produced impatience and discontent, which were augmented for the orthodox by the fact that the monotheletic and unpopular Patriarch was closely associated with the Emperor and his mother. Pyrrhus was called upon, perhaps by a deputation, to crown Heraclius, and the importunity of the people was so urgent that the Patriarch communicated it to the Emperor, and the Emperor assented to the coronation. The crown of his father Constantine, which Heraclonas had put away in the sanctuary of the church, was placed on the head of Heraclius,[1] whose name by the will and acclamation of the people was changed to Constans [2] or Constantine.

A strong feeling of odium prevailed against Pyrrhus. The ignorant and superstitious portion of the community thought doubtless that his impious views on the matter of one will were mysteriously connected with the disagreeable state of things that had come about. It appears that on the day of the coronation the rabble proceeded to St. Sophia with intent to lay rude hands on Pyrrhus. When they failed to find him there they entered the thusiasterion, with a crowd of Jews and other " cacodox " persons ; they tore up the sacred robes and defiled the holy place, and then paraded through the city with the keys of the church gates hung on a pole. That night Pyrrhus, seeing that his life was in jeopardy, stealthily entered the great church, and worshipped there for the last time. He laid his cloak ($\dot{\omega}\mu\dot{o}\phi o\rho o\nu$) on the altar and said, " I resign not my sacred office, but I take my leave of a disobedient people." He crept out unobserved and remained concealed in the house of a pious woman until he found an opportunity to sail to Carthage.[3]

---

[1] Nicephorus says that Heraclius (Heraclonas) bade Pyrrhus crown his nephew, " but the people constrained the Emperor to accomplish the work." I suppose the incident indicates the odium that prevailed against Pyrrhus. The crown, valued at 70 lbs. of gold, belonged to Heraclius ; it had been buried with him, but his son Constantine had exhumed it, and, after the death of the latter, Heraclonas dedicated it in St. Sophia.

[2] Theophanes calls him Constans, but on his coins he is called Constantine, and Nicephorus the Patriarch was ignorant of the name Constans. I strongly suspect that Constantine was his imperial name, and Constans only a popular name (a parallel case to Heraclonas). In that case he was the true Constantine IV, and sixteen, not fifteen, Constantines ruled over the Romans.

[3] Nicephorus, p. 31 : $\tau\rho\dot{o}s$ $\tau\dot{\eta}\nu$ $X\alpha\lambda\kappa\eta\delta\dot{o}\nu os$ [sc. $\pi\dot{o}\lambda\iota\nu$] $\dot{a}\pi\dot{\epsilon}\pi\lambda\epsilon\iota$. The editor, de Boor, queries "$K\alpha\rho\chi\eta\delta\dot{o}\nu os$?" in a footnote, and it is almost certain that here (as in other places) there has been a confusion between Chalcedon and Carthage. For the following reference to Maximus and Theodosius, the pillars of orthodoxy in Africa, $\dot{\epsilon}\nu$ $'A\phi\rho\iota\kappa\dot{\eta}$,

The coronation of Constans the Second rendered it practicable to make an arrangement with Valentinus and his soldiers at Chalcedon; and this was really the motive of the popular movement. The terms of the compact were that the Caesar David, the brother of Heraclonas, should be crowned Emperor, and named Tiberius,[1] that Valentinus should be created *comes excubitorum*, that no account of the money which the late Emperor had given him should be demanded, and that the soldiers should receive a largess. These events took place in the month of October (641), and at the same time Paulus, the chancellor of St. Sophia, was elected to the patriarchal chair instead of Pyrrhus, whose theological views he shared.

Thus at the end of the year 641 there were three Emperors, Heraclonas, Constans, and Tiberius; but the mode in which the coronation of Constans had been extorted and the well-known unscrupulousness of Martina precluded the hope of a permanent harmony. Concerning the course of events our authorities fail us; all we know is that before a twelvemonth had elapsed the senate resolved to adopt the violent measure of deposing Heraclonas and banishing him, along with his mother Martina. The sentence of banishment was accompanied by a barbarous act of justice or revenge; the tongue of the Empress was cut out and the nose of her son was slit. We cannot hesitate to suppose that some terrible provocation had been given. It is remarkable that Valentinus was banished at the same time, whence we must conclude that he had

---

is hardly relevant if it was not at Carthage that Pyrrhus was questioned by the curious monks—τίνες τῶν μοναζόντων . . . ἀνερεύνων; and it is not conceivable that monks at Chalcedon would have to seek information from Pyrrhus concerning what must have been perfectly familiar to them, the Ecthesis (τῶν ἐκτεθέντων) of Heraclius.

[1] Niceph. p. 31. (David and Marinus, the sons of Martina, had been created Caesars, and her daughters, Augustina and Martina, had been created Augustas in 639 or 640, *ib.* p. 27.) After this point there is a gap of more than thirty years in the epitomised history of Nicephorus, who proceeds from the election of Paul to the patriarchate in 641 to the death of Constans, whom he calls Constantine, in 668, and having

barely mentioned this event goes on to the year 673. Thus for the reign of Constans we depend chiefly on Theophanes (for other sources, *see* above, p. 281).

There is no reason to ascribe this lacuna to our MSS. and not to Nicephorus himself. It seems to me, as I already stated, to indicate that for the reign of Constans there was extant only one Greek source of any value, and that this source was consulted by Theophanes, while it was not in the hands of Nicephorus. I hold that this source was the Chronicle of John Malalas of Antioch. Theophanes probably also consulted some other meagre chronicle in which the Macedonian months were used. *See* above, p. 281.

changed parties. What became of the Emperor Tiberius we are not informed.

Before September 642 Constans, then a boy of eleven years, was sole sovereign, and not long after that date he made a short statement to the senate [1] which has been preserved and deserves to be quoted :—

> " My father Constantine, in the lifetime of Heraclius, his father and my grandfather, reigned in conjunction with him for a considerable time, but after his death for a very short space of time. For the envy of his stepmother Martina cut off his excellent hopes and deprived him of his life,—and this for the sake of Heraclonas, the son of her incestuous union with Heraclius. Your vote chiefly contributed to the just deposition of her and her son from the imperial dignity, that the Roman Empire should not behold a most illegal thing. Your noble lordships are well aware of this ; and I therefore invite you to assist me by your advice and judgment in providing for the general safety of my subjects."

This short speech is noteworthy in two ways. It shows that a general belief prevailed that Martina had poisoned Constantine ; and it indicates the importance of the senate at this time. By the decision of the senate Martina and Heraclonas had been deposed, and the tender age of Constans obliges us to assume that the administration of the Empire was entirely in the hands of the senate during the next few years.

Two revolts may have alarmed the inexperience of Constans in the early part of his reign. A patrician named Valentinian, who was apparently a general of troops in Asia Minor, rebelled, but Constans caused him to be executed, and recalled the army to the duty of loyalty (645). It is tempting to suppose that Valentinian is a mistake for Valentinus, and that the squire of Philagrius who undertook the cause of the children of Constantine had been made a Patrician ; but the other statement that some one named Valentinus was banished along with Martina makes us hesitate to accept this identification.

Two years later Gregory,[2] the exarch or governor of Africa, revolted " along with the Africans," but was soon afterwards

---

[1] Theoph. 6134 A.M. Κώνστας πρὸς τὴν σύγκλητον ἔλεγεν.

[2] One is fain to conjecture that this Gregory may have belonged to the Heraclian family—may have been a son or grandson of Gregory the uncle of Heraclius.

routed by the Saracens, who invaded those provinces and compelled the people to pay tribute (647-648).

While this tragic drama was being enacted among the children of Heraclius at the court of Byzantium, the Saracens were extending their power. In the year 646 the officer Manuel, who had unsuccessfully defended Alexandria, made an essay to recapture it, with a fleet of 300 ships, but the Greeks were utterly defeated in a battle which was fought close to the city. In consequence of this attack the Arabs razed to the ground the walls of the city of the Ptolemies, and made Fostât, afterwards to become Cairo, the capital of Egypt. To the Egyptian dominion of the caliph, Amru had added the western line of coast, including the town of Barca,[1] as far as Tripolis, and in these regions tribute was paid to the Arabs in the form of African slaves. In 647 Abu Sarh, who had succeeded Amru as governor of Egypt, advanced along the coast in the direction of Carthage, and, as has been already mentioned, defeated the Roman governor Gregory, who opposed him at the head of an army of 120,000 men. The Semites were beginning to reappear in a quarter from which a powerful branch of the same race had been exterminated eight hundred years before.

In the same year which witnessed the failure of the armament of Manuel at Alexandria, another expedition sent by land against Muaviah, the general in Syria, was also repulsed, and the Saracens overran parts of Asia Minor and Armenia, and advanced as far as Tiflis. In the meantime the death of the unbending Omar and the election of the more flexible Othman led to many consequences, good and bad, for the power of the new nation. The chief injurious consequence was that the dissensions and discords, which the strong personality of Omar had firmly suppressed, broke out under the weaker and less unselfish supremacy of Othman. The chief advantage was that Muaviah, the energetic ruler of Syria, was permitted to organise a fleet, which Omar, who had a superstitious distrust of the perfidious sea, had obstinately forbidden.

---

[1] The surrounding district seems to have been called Barkaine, for we read in Nicephorus (p. 24) that John was appointed *stratêgos* (general) of Barkaine, and sent to Egypt against the Saracens.

The first expedition of the new naval power was against Cyprus (649). The armament numbered 1700 ships; Constantia, the capital city, was taken, and the whole island was ravaged. But Muaviah did not attempt to occupy it permanently, and perhaps he was prevented from doing so by the news that the Roman chamberlain Kakorizos was sailing against him with a large force. The emir sailed back to the coast of Syria and turned his attention to the little island of Aradus, lying not far from the mainland between Gabala and Tripolis. But all his endeavours to take the fort were vain; and equally vain was his attempt to induce the inhabitants to surrender by the mediation of a bishop named Thomarichos. The Saracens returned to Damascus, but next year attacked Aradus again with greater success. The city was burnt, the island was left uninhabited, while the people were allowed to depart and settle elsewhere. Aradus had been a flourishing mercantile city for many centuries; it was the Venice of the Syrian coast, secured by its insular position. Strabo the geographer noticed that the Aradians resisted all temptations to follow the example of the Cilicians and adopt the trade of piracy. The destruction of the place by Muaviah is an example of the barbarous and short-sighted policy of Mohammedan conquerors.

In the following year (651) an Arab general marched into the southern provinces of Asia Minor and carried away 5000 captives. Constans, who was hampered by Italian and perhaps by other affairs at this time, sent an ambassador to Muaviah and arranged a peace of two years, for which he was probably obliged to pay a considerable sum. This peace was not actually violated, but in the following year the Romans lost Armenia by the revolt of the Patrician Pasagnathes (a Persian), who made a treaty with Muaviah, delivering up his own son as a pledge. The Emperor, who had proceeded to Caesarea in Cappadocia in order to see what measures could be taken, despaired, we are told, of Armenia, and returned to Byzantium. Nevertheless, two years later he sent forth an army under Maurianus to recover that important country; but Maurianus was driven before the Saracen general Abib to the foot of Mount Caucasus (654 A.D.), and Armenia remained tributary to the caliph.

In the same year (654) the Romans met with another reverse in the loss of the important commercial island of

Rhodes. We are told that the celebrated statue of Helios, called the Colossus of Rhodes, was sold [1] to a Jewish trader of Edessa, who carried off the metal on 900 camels; a notice which shows the wealth and enterprise of the Jewish merchants at this time.

Encouraged by his successes, achieved on an element strange to the children of the desert, against Cyprus, Rhodes, and the little fort of refuge at Aradus, Muaviah ventured to organise a grand expedition against New Rome herself (655 A.D.) Constans, informed of his intention, prepared a fleet, and, sailing to the coast of Lycia, anchored at Phoenix. The events that followed may be told in the words of the chronicler :—

" All the armament of Muaviah was collected at Tripolis in Phoenicia. And having seen this, two brothers, servants of Christ, who abode in Tripolis, the sons of Bucinator, pierced by the zeal of God, rushed to the prison of the city, where there was a multitude of Roman prisoners. Bursting open the gates and loosing the prisoners they rushed to the house of the amêr (emir) of the city and slew him and his staff, and, having burned all the furniture, sailed to Romania. Muaviah, however, did not give up his design. He marched himself on Caesarea in Cappadocia, and made Abulathar captain of the naval armament. The latter sailed to a place in Lycia called Phoenix, where the Emperor Constans was stationed with the Roman fleet, and fought a naval battle with him. And as the Emperor was preparing to fight, on that night he dreamed that he was in Thessalonica, and awaking he related the dream to an interpreter of dreams, who said, ' Emperor, would that you had not slept, nor seen that dream ; for your presence in Thessalonica means, being interpreted, that the victory inclines to your foe.' [2] But the Emperor took no account of this, and drew up his fleet in line-of-battle and challenged an engagement. The ships met, and the Romans were defeated, and the sea was stained with the blood-streams of the Romans. The Emperor changed garments with another; and the son of Bucinator (mentioned

---

[1] Theophanes incorrectly describes it as *now* pulled down. The colossus had been thrown down by an earthquake about 225 B.C. (Polybius, v. 88). Pliny (*Hist. Nat.* 34, 18) writes *sed jacens quoque miraculo est.* It was the work of Chares of Lindus, and either its material or the price thereof was supplied by the siege-engines of Demetrius Poliorcetes. *See* Mahaffy, *Greek Life and Thought*, pp. 334 and 342 *sqq.*

[2] θὲς ἄλλῳ νίκην, " give victory to another."

above), leaping into the imperial vessel, hurried off the Emperor into another vessel and unexpectedly saved him. But he himself, standing bravely in the imperial ship, slew many, this most noble man, and devoted himself to death for the Emperor; for the enemy surrounded him and compassed him about, supposing him to be the Emperor, and, having slain many, he was himself slain by the foe, along with the man who wore the imperial clothes. But the Emperor was thus saved by flight, and having left all he sailed to Constantinople." [1]

After this great reverse an event happened which proved fortunate for the Romans, by preventing Muaviah from following up his success. This event was the murder of Caliph Othman (656 A.D.), which was succeeded by a struggle for the caliphate between Muaviah and Ali. The weak Othman had fallen the victim of a conspiracy, and Muaviah assumed the part of his righteous avenger. On a pulpit in the great mosque of Damascus he hung up the bloody shirt of the slain caliph and the mutilated fingers of Nâila, who had tried to protect him. Ali, the son-in-law of Mohammed, had made the new city of Kufa the capital of his caliphate. Having subdued a revolt at Bussora by the celebrated victory "of the Camel," he invaded northern Syria, and the battle of Siffûn, where the forces of the rival caliphs met, was finally decided by an appeal to the infallible Koran. Having signed a document by which both agreed to accept the arbitration of the sacred book, Muaviah and Ali returned to their respective cities, Kufa and Damascus. The arbitrators appointed were Amru, as the representative of Muaviah, and Abu Mûsa, as the representative of Ali. Abu Mûsa was outwitted by the cunning of Amru, and Muaviah, according to the terms of the contract, was the rightful caliph. But, as Ali declared the arbitration unfair, and would not surrender his claim, the double caliphate lasted until his death in 661 A.D., after which event his son Hassan[2] abdicated in favour of Muaviah.

Occupied with these conflicts and rivalries, Muaviah was obliged to submit to a treaty favourable for the Romans in 659 A.D. The caliph agreed to pay to Constans 1000 nomismata

<hr>

[1] Theophanes *ad* 6146 A.M. He always calls Muaviah *Mavias*. He uses the word ἀμηρεύω, "be ameer," of the caliphs.

[2] Weil, i. 265. Hassan was the hero of no less than seventy divorces.

(£625), and for every day as long as the peace should last, a horse and a slave.

In the preceding year Constans had availed himself of the tranquillity of his neighbours on the south-eastern frontier to make an expedition against the Slaves who were settled in the provinces of the Balkan peninsula, and were manifesting an unruly spirit. The country which these Slaves occupied was called Sclavinia, but we are not informed where this country lay. Thus we cannot decide with certainty whether Constans marched westward to the Macedonian land beyond Mount Rhodope, where, as we know, there were Slavonian settlements, or northward to the Moesian lands beyond Mount Haemus, which were then almost entirely Slavonic ; but the former alternative, which is adopted by the German historian Hopf,[1] seems the more likely. Constans compelled them to pay the tribute which they had refused, and led away many captives.

Constans was a man of strong will and restless energy, and he displayed these qualities in the sphere of religion as well as in other departments. To his ecclesiastical policy we must attribute, in the first instance, his unpopularity with the people of Constantinople, whose detestation he cordially reciprocated ; and this unpopularity, hampering and oppressing him at every step, drove him to make the remarkable resolution of transferring the seat of empire to the West. This then is the most fitting place to give a brief account of the ecclesiastical affairs of his reign, with which his expedition to Italy naturally connects itself.

After the death of Heraclius a monk named Maximus carried on a vigorous campaign in Africa against monotheletism ; and in 646 A.D. the African councils, at his instigation, drew up a manifesto against the heresy, which they forwarded to Pope Theodore, a Greek by birth. In accordance with a suggestion made by the orthodox African bishops, the Pope wrote on the matter to Paul, the monotheletic Patriarch of Constantinople, and Paul replied in a letter professing in the strongest terms adhesion to the doctrine of one will. The Pope decided to excommunicate the heretical Patriarch, and performed the ceremony with the utmost solemnity.

[1] *Griechische Geschichte*, p. 94.

The reply made by New Rome to the deposition of Paul was an edict of the Emperor Constans known as the *Type*.[1] This document is not a declaration of monotheletism, like the Ecthesis of Heraclius, but deals with the question of one will as the Ecthesis had dealt with the question of one energy. Under pain of serious penalties, it is commanded that no one shall speak of either one will or two wills, one energy or two energies; that the whole controversy shall be buried in oblivion, and that "the scheme which existed before the strife arose shall be maintained, as it would have been if no such disputation had arisen."

The spirit of the Type of Constans was similar to the spirit of the Henotikon of Zeno, but was marked by a more absolute and imperial tone. Paul, doubtless, urged Constans to issue an edict establishing the doctrine of one will, but if Constans was not wholly indifferent on the subject, he was certainly not a bigot,[2] and such an edict would have been dangerous, or at least imprudent, in the face of the great body of orthodox opinion in Constantinople. He was only seventeen years old when the Type was promulgated, and we are not informed whether he acted by the advice or against the counsels of the senate. The document certainly displays the true spirit of imperial indifference which cares more for the State than for the Church; and its form, an edict and not a symbolum, distinguishes it essentially from the Ecthesis of Heraclius. The penalties to be incurred by those who disobeyed the decree were, in the case of a bishop or clerk, deposition; in the case of a monk, excommunication; in the case of a public officer in civil or military service, loss of his office; in the case of a private person of senatorial rank,[3] loss of property; in the case of a private person of obscure position,[4] corporal punishment and banishment for life.

The strict or bigoted orthodox adherents of the doctrine of two wills deemed the Laodicean injunction of neutrality no less to be reprobated than a heretical injunction of monotheletism. The Type implied that the one doctrine was at least as good as the other; and in Rome there existed a strong feeling

---

[1] The text of the Type (Τύπος) is preserved among the acts of the Lateran Council of 649; Mansi, *Concil.* x. 1029, 1031. Compare Hefele, *Con-* *ciliengeschichte*, iii. 186 *sqq.*

[2] His father Constantine had not been a monothelete.

[3] τῶν ἐπισήμων.   [4] τῶν ἀφανῶν.

on the matter, which led to the convocation of the Lateran Synod in the following year (649 A.D.)   Pope Theodore had died in the meantime, and his successor, Pope Martin, presided at a council which condemned monotheletism and the Type. Martin was a man of learning and endowed with a fine physical frame, "marked out by providence," says a Catholic historian, "to be the martyr for the dyotheletic faith."   After the synod he wrote to the Emperor, informing his Majesty of its conclusions, and requiring him to condemn the heresy, "for the safety of the State is always wont to flourish along with the orthodox faith, and the Lord, *rightly* believed in by your clemency, will assist your power in making war justly against your enemies."

While the Lateran Synod was sitting, Olympius arrived as the new exarch from Constantinople, with imperial instructions to secure the observance of the Type in Italy and not to respect the person of the Pope.   It is said that Olympius ordered his squire to kill Martin at the communion office, but, though the man constantly watched and waited, by some miraculous accident he was never able to see the Pope. The superstition of Olympius was touched by this evidently supernatural frustration of his impious plans, and he revealed the whole design and the reason of his presence at Rome to the intended victim.   "Having made peace with holy Church, he collected his army and proceeded to Sicily against the Saracens who were dwelling there.   And on account of sin there was a great mortality in the Roman army, and after that the exarch fell ill and died." [1]

But a new exarch, Theodore Calliopas, who did not arrive in Italy until 653 A.D. (15th June), was not of such impressionable stuff.   He was obliged to wait for some days in Rome until he could conveniently arrest the Pope, who happened to be ill; but he soon seized a favourable opportunity and conveyed the holy father to a ship which lay in readiness to bear him to Constantinople, that he might there reply to charges of treason which were alleged against him.   Martin was said to have conspired with Olympius in revolting against the Emperor, and it was on this charge of conspiracy, and not on the ground of ecclesiastical opposition to an imperial edict,

[1] Anastasius, *Vit. Pont.*, *Vit. Mart.*

that it was resolved to condemn him. He was not taken directly to Constantinople, but was detained a prisoner at the island of Naxos for a whole year.[1] He relates himself that he was allowed to enjoy such meagre comforts as an inn could afford, and to refresh himself occasionally with a bath. He arrived at New Rome in September 654, and on the day of his arrival was left from morning until evening on the deck of the ship, exposed to the jeers and scoffs of Byzantine scurrility.[2] At night the weary pontiff was carried from the ship to the prison of Prandearia, where he was obliged to remain for ninety-three days. It is said that during this time he was not permitted to bathe once. It is evident, although not expressly stated, that these long periods of imprisonment antecedent to the trial were adopted in order to break the Pope's firm spirit and torture him into accepting the Type. This treatment was an imitation of the measures that Justinian had employed to tame Pope Vigilius.

At last the unhappy bishop of Rome was brought before the tribunal; a *sacellarius*[3] or private treasurer of the Emperor conducted the proceedings. The illustrious prefect of the city was also present, but not apparently as presiding judge. We need not describe the details of the trial, which seems to have lasted but a short time. The Pope denied all the vain allegations of conspiracy and rebellion, and sometimes retorted on his ignorant or malignant accusers. It appears that the Emperor sat during the proceedings in an adjoining room, for it is related that the sacellarius came forth from the Emperor's chamber and said to Martin: "Thou hast fought against the Emperor—what hast thou to hope? Thou hast abandoned God, and God has abandoned thee." The same minister gave orders that the pontifical robe should be torn from the body of the Pope, and then turning to the prefect of the city, said,

[1] Naxos was reached in three months, but we are not told where they halted *en route*. The Pope was allowed only six servants (*pueruli*) and a *cauculus*, perhaps a personal attendant (Ducange, *Gloss. Med. Lat.*, explains it by *famulus*). According to our notions, this part of the treatment was not too fell. The arrest and voyage of Martin are related by himself in a letter to a friend (Mansi, x. 851-853); of his sufferings at Con-stantinople we have the account of a *quidam Christianissimus* (*ib.* 853 *sqq.*), cf. Hefele, iii. 208 *sqq.*

[2] Martin lay "a spectacle for all angels and men," says our "most christian" informant; he calls the mockers *lupaces* (which is perhaps intended to suggest a *lupanar*), *ib.* 854.

[3] The general name in the seventh century for the count of the sacred patrimony (*see* below, p. 324).

" Take him, and hew him in pieces." He also called upon all those who were present to curse the primate of Christendom. The executioners roughly rent the tunic from neck to skirt and exposed the venerable person of the Pope to the gaze of his enemies or judges. Iron chains were cast upon his neck and he was dragged off to the praetorium, where he was detained for a short time, caged up with common criminals. Thence he was conveyed to the prison of Diomede and thrown with such violence into a cell that his legs were cut and the floor was stained with his blood. It was now midwinter and bitterly cold, so that the Pope, who was in a weak state of health and unable to use his limbs (he had been obliged to assume an erect position at the trial), must have suffered intensely. Two women connected with the prison pitied and were fain to assist him, but fear withheld them.

While the bishop of Old Rome was undergoing these hardships, his rival, Paul the Patriarch of New Rome, was lying sick, nigh unto death. Constans, after the trial of Martin, visited the bedside of Paul and related all that had happened, to cheer the sick man's heart with triumph. But Paul felt no satisfaction. He said, "Woe unto me, that I have this too to answer for," and conjured the Emperor to desist from further cruelty and not to put Martin to death. The Emperor did not indeed relent, but he decided to change the fate of Martin from death to banishment; and, after a space of eighty-five days spent in prison, the fallen Pope was permitted to say farewell to his friends. He was then confined for two days in the house of the secretary Sagoleba, and on the 26th of March 655 was sent to the remote shores of Cherson, where he died before the end of the year (16th September),[1] having endured great privations. In the meantime Paul the Patriarch had died and was succeeded by Pyrrhus, the same who had held the patriarchal chair in the days of Heraclius and Martina, and had relinquished without resigning the office. He had in the meantime visited Carthage and Italy, and at Old Rome had for a while, really or feignedly, acknowledged the error of his ways and confessed the doctrine of the two wills, but afterwards returned, in the choice language of an orthodox

---

[1] Some letters written by Martin at Cherson are preserved, Mansi, x. 861 *sqq.*

writer, "like a dog to his vomit." His second patriarchate lasted for less than five months.

Although Constans was a friend of Paul, and naturally desired to support the Byzantine archbishops, his policy in persecuting Pope Martin was by no means the same as that of Justinian in persecuting Pope Vigilius. The Caesaropapism of Justinian, who composed ecclesiastical works himself, was different from the imperialism of Constans. Both sovereigns wished to make the Church dependent on the State, but to Justinian the ecclesiastical unity was an end in itself, while to Constans it was mainly a means to political unity. Justinian was interested in the nature of the doctrine for its own sake, Constans only desired that the doctrine should be uniform. The eyes of both Justinian and Constans were fixed on Italy ; his Italian policy influenced perceptibly the ecclesiastical measures of Justinian ; but it was solely with a view of drawing Italy closer into the frame of the Roman Empire that Constans was so earnestly concerned for the unity of religious belief.

A great object of Constans was to bring the outlying provinces of the Empire, the exarchate of Africa and the exarchate of Italy, into closer union with the centre, so that the Empire might present a compact resistance to Mohammedan progress. Syria and Egypt had been lost, and Constans could hardly look forward to recovering them in the immediate future ; in Rhodes, Cyprus, and Armenia, however, he might hope to re-establish Roman supremacy. But first of all it was imperative to prevent Saracen aggression in the West, where the fertile provinces of Africa and Sicily [1] were seriously threatened by the unbelievers. At this time the affairs of the Balkan peninsula, already thoroughly penetrated with the Slavonic element, seem to have occasioned little concern. When he had recalled the refractory Slaves to a sense of their obligations to the Empire by his expedition in 658, Constans might feel secure in regard to those provinces ; and as for Asia Minor, it was well garrisoned with soldiers and regularly organised under a military administration. He was free then to fix his

---

[1] The first expedition of the Saracens against Sicily was made from Syria in 652 ; it was against them that Olympius, the exarch, fought. *See* Amari, *Storia dei Musulmani di Sicilia*, i. p. 82 *sqq.* The second expedition was from Alexandria in 669 (*ib.* pp. 98, 99), for which *see* below, p. 310.

attention on the West, and he might dream of recovering the lost lands of Italy from the Lombards and rivalling the fame of Justinian.

Circumstances suggested to his mind a new idea, and carried him further in his occidental policy than he had meditated. He was personally unpopular at Constantinople, and we may suspect that conspiracies sometimes menaced his throne and his life. By the orthodox he was naturally detested. He had followed up the persecution of Pope Martin by the persecution of Maximus and his two disciples,[1] who enjoyed a wide celebrity as champions of the true faith against the monotheletes, and this persecution seems to have created even greater odium than the affliction of the Pope. But an unwise act in the year 660 embittered still more the hatred with which the Emperor was regarded.

Of Theodosius, the brother of Constans, we hear for the first time on the occasion of his death, and we know not whether he held the rank of Caesar or not. He seems to have been orthodox in religion, but we are ignorant in what way he became an object of suspicion to his brother. Constans had compelled him to become a deacon, before the death of the Patriarch Paul, who consecrated him; and it is said that Theodosius often administered to his imperial brother the "undefiled mysteries in the holy cup." In the year 660 the suspicions of the Emperor were again aroused, and he put Theodosius to death. It is said that he repented afterwards of this act. "After his death," we are told, "he (Theodosius) frequently appeared to him (Constans) in his sleep, wearing a deacon's dress and offering him a cup of blood, saying, 'Drink, O brother'; for which reason, overcome by despair and dread of the apparition, he determined to go to Sicily." [2]

It is vain to suppose that we can guess all the motives that may have influenced Constans to bid farewell to the city of the Bosphorus in 662, but we may decidedly reject a sensational story like this, related by a writer of the eleventh century, and evidently emanating from the church party inimical to Constans. It is bound up with other suspicious details. "He left his wife and three sons," proceeds the

---

[1] The Anastasii (Theoph. 6160 A.M.)
[2] This is related only by Cedrenus (Bonn), vol. i. p. 762.

chronicler, "in the city, and embarked in a fast sailer (dromon);
and he turned back and spat at the imperial city.   But even
in Sicily the dream did not leave him," etc.   This attribution
of an act of childish and indecent spite to a man of strength
and ability like Constans, throws suspicion on the whole
narrative.

   The scheme of Constans to transfer the seat of empire from
New Rome back once more to Old Rome [1] was, we may presume, influenced by two chief motives, one negative and one
positive, either of which would alone have hardly been sufficient to determine him to take such a course.   The negative
motive was a desire to leave Byzantium, where he did not feel
at ease and was hampered by his unpopularity.   The positive
motive was a resolve to attempt to reconquer Italy, if not the
whole peninsula at least southern Italy, from the Lombards.
He would at the same time be able to protect Sicily and Africa
from the advance of the Asiatic foe.

   When we remember the scheme entertained by this Emperor's grandfather Heraclius and thwarted by the influence of
the Patriarch Sergius, to transfer the imperial residence from
New Rome to Carthage, we are tempted to draw an analogy,
and conclude that this westward tendency, manifested on two
occasions in the seventh century, was due to the pressure from
the East—a sort of unconscious retreat, in the case of Heraclius
before the Persians, in the case of Constans before the Saracens,
in order to win a breathing space for organising forces and
means of resistance.   This was a direct motive with Heraclius;
it may have been an indirect cause with Constans.   At least
we may be sure that in resolving on the important step, he
took the Saracen problem—the "eternal question"—seriously
into consideration.   But the negative motive, the feeling that
their administration was cramped in the pampered city of
Byzantium, was operative with both Emperors.   The Byzantines would not allow Heraclius to leave them, but they made
no effort to retain his grandson.   Yet afterwards, when Constans sent for his wife and his three sons, they were not permitted to obey the summons.[2]

[1] Constans said it was fitting to pay
higher honour to mothers than to
daughters (Zonaras, vol. iii. p. 316

(ed. Dindorf), Bk. xiv. cap. 19).   This
is not mentioned by Theophanes.
[2] *See* below, p. 305.

On his way to Italy, Constans visited Athens. This mention of Athens as a station of the imperial journey indicates the flourishing condition of the Greek city in the seventh century. Thence he proceeded to Tarentum. An army accompanied him; we are not told of what numbers it consisted, but it was large.[1] A story is narrated that when Constans landed at Tarentum his first act was to consult a hermit whether his project to subdue the Lombards would be successful. The holy man prayed a whole night, and in the morning replied, "No, because a certain queen coming from another province built a basilica of St. John the Baptist in Lombard territory, and therefore they are protected by the saint. The time will come when the *oracle* will be despised, and then the race shall perish." [2]

Notwithstanding the hermit's answer, Constans invaded the territory of the duke of Beneventum and captured almost all the towns that he passed.[3] He razed Luceria to the ground, but failed to take Aventia. Finally, he laid siege to Beneventum. The duke at this time was Romuald, a stripling, the son of Grimuald. Grimuald had seized the Lombard crown when it was disputed by the two sons of Rotharis, and had left the duchy to his son. Romuald despatched his *nutricius*,[4] Sesuald, to the lands beyond the Po, to obtain succour from his father. Constans meanwhile pressed the town hard, but the resistance was brave. At length Sesuald returned, bearing the news that Grimuald was coming to the rescue of his son, but the Romans—or Greeks, as the Latin historian calls them—captured the messenger before he reached the city. The Emperor was frightened at the news, and hastened to make a truce with Romuald, who gave him his sister Gisa as a hostage. Constans then [5] led Sesuald in front of the walls, having instructed him, on pain of death, to announce to the men

[1] *Acta Scti. Barbari; collecta innumera suorum multitudine mare transgressus est.* Cf. F. C. Schlosser, *Geschichte der bilderstürmenden Kaiser des oströmischen Reichs*, p. 80.

[2] We are told that the prophecy was fulfilled by the basilica at Modicia (Monza) becoming the resort of adulterers, etc. Paul the Deacon, the historian of the Lombards, who wrote in the latter part of the eighth century, is the main authority for the proceedings of Constans in Italy and Sicily (Bk. v. cap. 6 *sqq.*)

[3] *omnesque pene per quas venerat Langobardorum civitates cepit* (Paul, v. 7).

[4] A tutor or τροφεύς (*educator*).

[5] This is the order of events in Paul; but, as the editor of the *M. G. H.* edition remarks in a note, the narrative hardly hangs together, and perhaps we should suppose that the episode of Sesuald preceded the peace.

of the city that Grimuald could not come. Sesuald demanded to see Romuald himself, and, when the duke appeared, bade him hold out a little longer with constancy, as the king was approaching, and prayed him in return for his own sacrifice of life to protect his wife and children. By the order of Constans the head of the dauntless Sesuald was hurled by an immense catapult[1] into the town.

Aware of the approach of the Lombard king, Constans abandoned the siege and proceeded in the direction of Naples, but on the way he was harassed by an attack of Mitola, the count of Capua, near the river Calor.[2] Remaining himself at Naples, the Emperor committed 20,000 men to the command of a noble named Saburrus, who boldly promised to subdue to his sway the Lombards of the Beneventan duchy. But Saburrus was ignominiously defeated at Forino by Romuald, who advanced to meet him with part of his father's army.

It appears that, discouraged by this defeat and the unexpected resistance of the Lombards, Constans surrendered his idea of shifting the balance of the empire to the West; he certainly abandoned the project of fixing his capital at Rome. He proceeded thither from Naples, and was met at the sixth milestone from the city by a great procession, led by Pope Vitalian, who presented him with a cloak inwoven with gold. He stayed for twelve days within the walls, the first Emperor of New Rome that had visited Old Rome for wellnigh three centuries. But he showed scant respect for the eternal city, the venerable mother of the Empire. He dismantled her of her bronze ornaments,[3] in order that he might enrich her daughter, the younger Rome.[4] This incident seems to signify that he intended to return to his eastern residence at some future time.

Meanwhile he had resolved to live in the city of Syracuse, whither he proceeded[5] from Rome by Naples and Reggio. A

---

[1] Paul, v. 9, *petrariam*.

[2] Near Beneventum.

[3] He stripped the Pantheon of its bronze tiles, *tegulas aereas*. Phocas had given the Pantheon to the Roman Church, and it had become the basilica of the Blessed Mary (*beatae Mariae*), Paul, v. 11. It is also worthy of note that Maurus, the archbishop of Ravenna, induced Constans to make him independent of Rome, and give the Ravennate archbishops the privilege of receiving the *pallium* directly from the Emperor. The epitaph of Maurus lauds him for having freed Ravenna from the yoke of Roman servitude (Agnellus, *Vita Mauri*, cap. 4).

[4] *easque* [*tegulas*] *simul cum aliis omnibus ornamentis Constantinopolim transmitteret* (*ib.*)

[5] *per indictionem septimam*, 663-664 (*ib.*)

Latin historian complains that he governed with a rod of iron. "He imposed such afflictions on the people, on the inhabitants or proprietors of Calabria, Sicily, Africa, and Sardinia, as were never heard of before, so that even wives were separated from husbands and sons from their parents."[1]   Churches were robbed of their treasures.   The south of Italy belonged, not to the exarchate of Ravenna, but to the government of Sicily and Sardinia; and perhaps the disorganised state of Africa, owing to the attacks of the Saracens, induced Constans to attach its administration also to that of Sicily.   He thus formed a sort of special imperial prefecture or principality, with Syracuse for capital and residence.   How far he directed the administration in the East we are not told, but his son Constantine is represented by the historians as acting irresponsibly at Constantinople, and carrying on negotiations with the court of Damascus.

In his sphere of government, where he presided for about five years, Constans had two enemies, one on either side, the Saracens in Africa and the Lombard duke of Beneventum in southern Italy.   He recovered Carthage and other cities which had fallen into the hands of the Mohammedans, but these successes were obliterated by the great defeat which a Roman army of 30,000 men experienced at Tripolis.   The Saracens, however, did not yet obtain a permanent footing in Africa, and if Constans had not imposed such severe taxation, and thus appeared less a deliverer than an oppressor, it is possible that Africa might have remained a Roman province longer than it did.   In Italy, Romuald gained some successes, but made no considerable addition to Lombard territory.   The presence of Constans in the West seems to have roused some apprehensions in the Frank kingdom; the mayors of the palace may have thought that he cherished the daring design of recovering the long-lost Gallic provinces for the Empire.

In the year 668 Constans was assassinated at Syracuse in the baths called Daphne.   A certain Andreas, the son of Troilus, went into the bath with him to wait upon him.   As the Emperor was preparing to smear himself with Gallic soap,[2] Andreas, seizing the vessel in which the soap was contained,

---

[1] Agnellus, *Vita Mauri*, cap. 4.
[2] γαλλικῷ σμήχεσθαι (Theoph. 6160 A.M.)

struck him on the head with it and fled.   When the Emperor
tarried long in the bath, his attendants, who were waiting outside, rushed in and found him dead.   As soon as he was
buried, unknown persons [1] compelled an Armenian named
Mizizios to assume the purple, "because he was very good-
looking and handsome."   The usurper's reign was short, for
the young Constantine arrived promptly from Constantinople
with a large armament [2] and put both Mizizios and Andreas
to death.   It is possible that Andreas may have been the
instrument of conspirators greater than himself; for a certain
Justinian of high position was executed, and his son Germanus,[3] who was destined in future days to be famous as a
Patriarch of Constantinople and an opponent of iconoclasm,
underwent the indignity of emasculation.   The names Justinian and Germanus remind us of the great imperial house
of the sixth century, and one is tempted to conjecture that
Germanus the Patriarch may have been a descendant of kinsfolk of the Emperor Justinian.

Constans may be considered a typical example of a certain
class of later Roman Emperors.   There is, I apprehend, a
general idea current that the Emperors who reigned at Constantinople were, almost without exception, either weak and
cruel profligates or strong and cruel profligates, and that, if any
were strong, their strength was generally misdirected.   Such
an idea is totally false.   Brought up in an atmosphere of intrigue and danger, calculated to foster the faculty of self-help
in a strong boy and at the same time to produce a spirit of
cynicism, Constans grew up a stern and inflexible man, with
decided opinions on policy and administration, resolved to act
independently and not afraid of innovation, surprisingly free

---

[1] Theoph. (6160 A.M.) does not define
who the persons were. That the elevation
of Mizizios was not the will of the army
is stated by Paul. Diac. v. 12, *regnum
arripuit sed absque orientalis exercitus
voluntate* ; but the editor of Paul (in
M. G. H.) thinks that Paul's only
source was the *Life of Pope Adeodatus*,
and that he misunderstood the words
*Mezezius qui erat in Sicilia cum exercitu
orientale intartizavit et arripuit regnum.*
These words, however, do not justify
us in making the army primarily responsible, though of course it must have
tacitly consented.

[2] Paul does not mention the presence
of Constantine. He says : *contra quem
Italiae milites, alii per Histriam, alii
per partes Campaniae, alii vero a parti-
bus Africae et Sardiniae venientes in
Siracusas eum vita privarunt.* Some
MSS. insert *emiliae* before *milites*, and
I believe it should be retained, as re-
ferring to troops from the exarchate.
I would read *Italiae alii Aemiliae
milites*, alii having fallen out after the
similar letters of *Italiae* ; or perhaps
omit *Italiae*, which is unnecessary.

[3] Zonaras, vol. iii. p. 316 (ed. Dindorf).

from religious bigotry in a bigoted age, an unusually strong
and capable ruler. Although his ecclesiastical attitude drew
upon him the disfavour of orthodox contemporaries and
historians, we hear not a single hint that he was addicted to
sensuality, and this is a testimony to his austere life—negative
indeed, but extremely weighty when we consider what scan-
dalous calumnies it has always been usual to circulate on the
smallest pretext regarding persons of obnoxious religious
opinions. He was never under the influence of ministers, as
far as we know, and his independent self-reliant conduct may
have sometimes seemed obstinacy; but it is hard, on our insufficient data, to judge of individual deeds. In regard to the
act which has excited most odium, the execution of his brother,
we are ignorant of his motives and the circumstances of the
case. It was an unwise act for a prince who was unpopular
with the orthodox; an orthodox prince, like Constantine the
Great, might have done worse things with impunity.

We can, however, form an opinion of the general policy of
Constans, and we must pronounce it to have been perverse,
though not fruitless. In two different ways he opposed the
tendencies of his age.

In the first place, the Roman Empire was becoming every
year more deeply tinged with an ecclesiastical colour. In
this respect a great change had silently taken place during the
last hundred years, since the time of Justinian. The christian
element of the christian Roman Empire has become dominant
in men's minds, the Roman element has fallen into the background. The importance of the Patriarch has increased, and a
close union between him and the Emperor is more than ever
necessary. I do not refer to any change in State mechanism
or in the administration of law, though here too Roman traditions have undergone distinct alterations, but to a change in
the public mind, and the views of people on politics, society,
and life in general. Now when Constans, by the issue of
his Type, asserted, as it were, the insignificance of the burning
theological problem of the day, and, assuming an attitude of
indifference to the doctrinal question, regarded the matter
entirely from a political point of view, he clearly opposed the
tendency of his age to look upon church matters as the vital
interests of the world. In this respect Constans had more

in common with the earlier than with the later Roman Emperors, and so far he was retrograde.

In the second place, ever since Constantine the Great had built his new capital on the Bosphorus, the gravitation of the Empire had tended to centre in New Rome; the Roman Empire had tended to contract itself to south-eastern Europe, while the provinces which it still retained in the West became, as it were, important outposts. The idea of Constans to take the sceptre from the daughter and restore it to the mother was retrograde and unpractical; and he could make no serious attempt to realise the scheme. It would have involved a struggle against the conditions of geography, a struggle wherein only in its best days the Roman Empire could succeed. Since the time of Theodosius the Great, nay since the time of Diocletian and still earlier, we can trace the tendency of south-eastern and south-western Europe to throw off the unnatural unity superinduced by Roman sway. Notwithstanding, Constantinople retained a hold on parts of Italy and Sicily for many centuries, but the bond was always loose. At the same time the influence of Greek civilisation on western Europe through these Italian provinces was of high importance; and thus, although the scheme of Constans to abandon New Rome was perverse, he must have done useful work in consolidating the Roman power in southern Italy, and laying a foundation for its permanence there until the eleventh century.

But if Constans stands condemned in the light of ecumenical tendencies, Demosthenes, Cicero, Julian, and many others stand by his side. It may seem startling to place him among men devoted to an ideal or inspired by enthusiasm; but this severe Emperor of the seventh century, animated with some reflection of the old Roman spirit, and out of touch with his own age, was one of the men in history who have trodden the winepress alone. Of his domestic life we know nothing, not even the name of his wife. The only record on the matter, washed up from the waves of time, is that from Italy or Sicily he summoned his wife and sons, and that two powerful ministers (or, some writers said, the Byzantine people[1]) refused to permit

---

[1] Zonaras, xiv. 19, "Some of his friends prevented this. But others say that the people (τὸ πλῆθος) of the city did not permit them to go." Theo-phanes says in one place (6153 A.M.) that the Byzantines would not let them go, in another place (6160 A.M.) he attributes the intervention to Andreas

306 HISTORY OF THE LATER ROMAN EMPIRE BOOK V

them to obey the summons. The last years of his life at least were not enlivened or encumbered by domestic society.

As to the Saracens, little was added to their previous conquests during the reign of Constans, and therefore we must pronounce that his foreign policy was on the whole successful. They had indeed secured a footing in Armenia, in Cyprus, in Rhodes,[1] even in Africa, but these were small reverses compared with the losses experienced by Heraclius. It may also be said that Muaviah would probably have extended his dominions farther but for the war of succession with Ali ; nevertheless we are only entitled to consider actual results, and we must agree with Finlay when he says of Constans that "the Empire underwent no very sensible diminution of its territory during his reign, and he certainly left its military forces in a more efficient condition than he found them." Nor should I omit to mention that to Constans may have been due a partial reorganisation of the provinces.

The Saracens were not inactive while Constans was in the western regions of the Empire ; they invaded Asia Minor almost every year. In 663 "Romania," as the Roman Empire was called in Asia, was invaded, many captives were led away, and many places rendered desolate. In 664 Abd Errahman repeated the expedition, and this time wintered in Roman territory, where in the following year he was joined by a body of Slaves, who had crossed the Hellespont and preferred to be the slaves of the caliph than the subjects of the Emperor. Five thousand of these Slaves were settled in Syria, at a place called Seleucobolus, in the district of Apamea.[2] The years 666 and 667 were marked by expeditions of Busur against Romania. It does not appear that any permanent injury was inflicted by these incursions.

At this time the troops stationed on the Armenian frontier, and called *Armeniakoi*, were commanded by a general of Persian origin, named Saborios (Sapor). In 668 he revolted against the Emperor and sent his captain [3] Sergius to Muaviah, promising that he would subject Romania to the Saracens if the

the chamberlain and Theodore, ὁ κολω-
velas (*see* below, p. 309). He had evidently two sources before him.
[1] Rhodes was only held for a short

time.
[2] Theoph. 6156 A.M.
[3] στρατηλάτης, apparently used in a general, not a technical sense.

caliph would help him against the Emperor. Constantine, the Emperor's son, who directed the administration at Constantinople, sought to checkmate this movement by sending another ambassador to the court of Damascus, but the diplomacy of Sergius was successful, and Muaviah's general Phadalas was sent to assist Saborios. Then Constantine appointed Nicephorus, a patrician, to lead a Roman force against Saborios, who was stationed at Hadrianopolis in Bithynia, prepared for war. An accident hastened the suppression of the revolt. Saborios was in the habit of taking exercise daily on horseback outside the walls of the town. One day, as he was approaching the gate, he applied the whip to his horse too severely, and the animal disdaining the bridle rushed off at a furious gallop, the head of the rider was dashed against the gate, and death followed.

Meanwhile Phadalas had advanced to Hexapolis, and, seeing that the Romans were united, the Armeniac troops having returned to their allegiance after the death of Saborios, he sent for reinforcements to Muaviah. The caliph sent his son Yezid with an army, and the combined forces proceeded to Chalcedon and captured many prisoners. They also took the important town of Amorium in Phrygia, and, having secured it by a garrison of 5000 men, returned to Syria. Towards the end of the year Constantine commissioned Andreas, the same chamberlain whom he had sent as an ambassador to Muaviah, to recover Amorium. Andreas arrived by night, and the deep snow aided his enterprise by raising the ground and so lowering the height to be scaled. By means of a plank or ladder, he and all his company entered the city, and every Arab in Amorium was slain.

CHAPTER IX

CONSTANTINE IV [1]

WHEN Constantine IV set out from Constantinople at the time of his father's death to arrange the troubled affairs of Sicily, his face was smooth. When he returned, having successfully accomplished his mission, he wore a beard, and the Byzantines gave him the name of Pogonatos or "the Bearded." This circumstance is interesting, because since the fifth century, when Leo was called Makelles and Anastasius Dikoros, there is no record that any Emperor received a nickname, but from the end of the seventh century forward, few Emperors escape unhonoured by some popular appellation, so that the practice of nicknaming sovereigns is one of the minor features of the Byzantine world. Had the imperial residence been Alexandria, not an Emperor from Constantine to Heraclius would have escaped the stinging wit of the Alexandrines, who were notorious for their love of mockery, like the Florentines in later centuries. When Alexandria was lost to the Empire, her mantle, or at least some shreds of it, fell upon Byzantium.

Constantine had no intention of sharing the administration or the imperial title with his two young brothers Heraclius and Tiberius, who had perhaps received the rank of Caesar before their father's death. But the army of the Anatolic district, which embraced the regions of Isauria, Lycaonia, Pisidia, and western Phrygia, suddenly marched to Chrysopolis and sent over the straits to Constantinople a deputation demanding that the two brothers should be crowned Emperors. They

---

[1] For this reign we have the history of Nicephorus as well as the chronography of Theophanes.

based their demand on the ingenious and fanciful idea that, because they believed in the Trinity, it was meet that they should be governed by three Emperors. The assignment of such a reason indicates a religious and theological view of things becoming dominant in men's minds, so as to penetrate other and alien relations of life. Constantine entrusted to Theodore, captain of Coloneia,[1] the delicate task of praising the soldiers for their excellent motives and persuading them to return to their stations, while their leaders visited the capital and consulted with the senate touching the execution of the wishes which they had expressed. When the army had obediently departed, Constantine caused the instigators of the movement, who came at his invitation to Constantinople, to be gibbeted at Sycae. We are also informed, in apparent connection with this affair, that the Emperor slit the noses of his two brothers, but the record is considered somewhat suspicious, as we learn on the same authority that in the year 680 Constantine deprived his brothers Heraclius and Tiberius of the imperial dignity and reigned alone with his son Justinian.[2] If this seems unlikely, we may suppose, with Finlay, that the noses of the two princes were not slit until 680, and that the first notice of the chronicler anticipates the order of events ; or we may suppose that the mutilation took place in 669, but that at some time between that year and 680 Constantine was compelled by political considerations or public opinion to associate his brothers in the Empire again.[3]

The chief events of the reign of Constantine IV were the Saracen war, including the seven years' siege of Constantinople, the establishment of the Bulgarian power on the south side of the Danube, and the sixth Ecumenical Council. Bul-

---

[1] The meaning of this title is not quite clear. Coloneia is of course the town (near the river Lycus, and almost due south of Cerasus), after which the theme Coloneia was called in later times. It can hardly have been formed into a separate district at this time, but perhaps the commandant of the city had an independent and honourable position. Theodore seems to have been an important personage of Byzantium ; but why the captain of Coloneia should be an influential minister in the capital is not clear.

[2] This is confirmed by a letter of Pope Agatho (Mansi, xi. p. 233). Constantine's marriage with Anastasia probably took place about the time of his father's death.

[3] *See* Theophanes, 6161 and 6173 A.M. Perhaps, however, Schlosser's explanation (*Gesch. der bilderstürmenden Kaiser*, p. 89) is the true one. He thinks that, if we find a difficulty in the statements of Theophanes, it is because we forget that the mutilation took place secretly in the recesses of the palace ("dass dies im neuen des Palastes vorging"). It may be observed that Theophanes' dates at this period are rather untrustworthy.

garian and Slavonic affairs will be dealt with in another chapter.

The usual invasions of Asia Minor by Saracen generals continued as before. The severe winter of 669 was spent by Phadalas on the shores of the Propontis at Cyzicus, and in 670 many Roman subjects were led into captivity by Busur. Africa had been attacked in 669, and, after the death of Constans, a formidable descent was made on Sicily by the Saracens of Alexandria, who carried off all the treasures that Constans had collected.[1]

But in 672 [2] Muaviah, who had conceived the ambitious project of conquering the whole Roman Empire, and thought perhaps that the young Constantine would prove a less firm adversary than his father, prepared a great naval expedition. The armament set sail under the command of Abd Errahman before the end of the year; and during the winter months some of the ships anchored at Smyrna, the rest off the coast of Cilicia. The troops of Abd Errahman were reinforced by yet another squadron before they proceeded to the Hellespont, into whose waters they sailed about April. From April to September (673) the fleet lay moored from the promontory of Hebdomon, on the Propontis, as far as the promontory of Kyklobios, near the Golden Gate, and engagements with the Roman fleet which defended the harbour continued from morning to evening. Constantine had made provision in good time to receive the enemy. He constructed a large number of fireships and fast-sailing boats provided with tubes or siphons for squirting fire, of which we do not know the exact nature.[3] These engines were very formidable, and in September the Saracens, having accomplished nothing, sailed to Cyzicus, which they captured and made their winter quarters. The same operations were carried on during the following year with the same result, and were repeated every year until 677.[4] Then

[1] Their leader was Abd Allah Ibn Kais (*see* Amari, *Storia dei Musulmani di Sicilia*, pp. 98, 99; Paul. Warn. *Hist. Lang.* v. 13). This was the second landing of the Saracens in Sicily. After this all their attacks were from Africa.

[2] Elmakin places the expedition in 672, and this agrees with Theophanes. The Arab authorities say very little about it, as it was not an exploit to be proud of. Their silence confirms the Roman accounts. *See* Weil, i. p. 293.

[3] διήρεις εὐμεγέθεις κακκαβοπυρφόρους καὶ δρόμωνας σιφωνοφόρους (Theoph.)

[4] Theophanes says the siege continued for seven years; but this statement is at variance with his own chronology, for while he makes 673 (*i.e.* 674)

at length the Saracens, "put to shame by the help of God and the Mother of God, and having lost many fighting men and received great injury, returned in great grief." This was not the end of their disasters. The unsuccessful fleet was caught in a storm at Syllaeum and dashed to pieces on rocks. All the ships that escaped were attacked by a Byzantine admiral, who commanded the Cibyraiot fleet,[1] and were destroyed. The naval armament in the Hellespont had been doubtless supported every year by a land army on the Asiatic shore[2]; it is at least certain that, concurrently with the rout and destruction of the fleet of Chaleb, the Saracens met with a disaster on land. An army under Sofian was defeated by the Roman generals Florus, Petronas, and Cyprianus, and 30,000 Arabs were killed.[3]

It is not clear from the words of our authorities whether "Romaic (Greek) fire" was actually used during the siege; but at all events the Greeks discovered it about this time. The discovery is attributed to Callinicus, an architect of Heliopolis in Syria, who fled to the Romans, "and having prepared marine fire, burned the ships of the Arabs and their crews alive." *Marine fire* ($\pi\hat{v}\rho\ \theta\alpha\lambda\acute{a}\sigma\sigma\iota o\nu$) is the name by which it was known. It is an obvious supposition that the siphon-boats, mentioned above, were connected with the new discovery, but our best authority mentions the marine fire subsequently, as if it had been introduced after the siege, so that it will be safer to conclude that the siphon-boats and the *caccabopyrphori* were inventions of a simpler and less infernal kind, like the fireships of Gaiseric, or the sulphur-machines said to have been used by Proclus against Vitalian.

---

the first year of the operations, he places the peace with Muaviah in 677 (6169 A.M. = September 676 to September 677) *i.e.* 678. I have no doubt that a siege of *seven* years was a fabulous tradition, and it may be observed that Theophanes makes the siege of Caesarea by the Saracens in the reign of Heraclius last seven years. The tradition can be partly accounted for if we remember that the Saracens set sail in 672, and suppose that the peace may not have been *concluded* until the end of 678; it might be roughly said that seven years had elapsed between these extreme dates, and this very loose statement might have

been transferred to the actual siege.

[1] $\tau o\hat{v}\ \tau\hat{\omega}\nu\ K\iota\beta\upsilon\rho\alpha\iota\omega\tau\hat{\omega}\nu\ \sigma\tau\rho\alpha\tau\eta\gamma o\hat{v}$ (Zonaras, xiv. 20), a detail mentioned neither by Theophanes nor by Nicephorus, which indicates that Zonaras had another source before him.

[2] That the Saracens were not idle in other parts of the Empire is shown by the fact that Phadalas wintered in Crete in 673-674.

[3] The commander, Abd Errahman, was killed during the siege, a victim (say Arab historians) of the envy of Muaviah. He was succeeded by Sofian Ibn Auf. Yezid, Muaviah's son, took part in the expedition.

The utter failure of his ambitious enterprise inclined Muaviah to peace, and another circumstance confirmed his inclination. Bands of freebooters, or *armatoli*, who led an outlaw life in the wild heights of Mount Taurus, had penetrated to the recesses of Mount Lebanon,[1] where they assisted the cause of Christendom by harassing and plundering the unbelievers and affording a safe shelter to christian refugees. The Greeks called these outlaws *apelátai*,[2] but they are more generally known by the name Mardaites (" rebels "), which was applied to them by the Saracens.[3] They increased in number and power, being constantly reinforced by Slaves and Syrian natives, and they soon dominated Palestine "from the Black mountain to Jerusalem."[4] The presence of this hostile mountain population of Christians was a serious danger to the Saracen power in Syria, and a notable advantage to the Roman Emperor. It is not surprising that Muaviah was glad to accept a disadvantageous peace. The Greek chronicler states that he and his counsellors were much afraid, " supposing that the Empire of the Romans is guarded by God." He therefore sent ambassadors to Byzantium, offering to pay a yearly tribute. The Emperor sent back with them to Damascus a patrician named Johannes, and nicknamed Pitzigaudes,[5] as an old and experienced statesman of sound judgment, to arrange the terms of the treaty, and Muaviah, we are told, showed him the most profound respect.

Two instruments were drawn up to the effect that the peace was to last for thirty years, on condition that the Saracens paid the Romans 3000 lbs. of gold, fifty captives,[6] and fifty thoroughbred horses annually.

The repulse of the first great expedition organised by the

---

[1] The clearest account of the origin of the Mardaites is given by Sathas, *Bibl. Graec. Medii Aevi*, ii. Introduction, p. 45 *sqq.*

[2] Equivalent, as Sathas says, to ἀπόβλητοι or ἅρπαγες. They carried great iron clubs, whence ἀπελατικόν "a club."

[3] *Mardaitarum, hoc est rebellium nomen eisdem crearunt* (Edenensis apud Assemanni, *Bibl. Orient.* i. 502). The Turkish equivalent would be ζορμπάδες (Sathas, *loc. cit.*) Cf. the notices in Theophanes *sub annis* 6169, 6176, 6178. The accounts given by Theophanes of the Mardaites are confirmed by Syrian

and Saracen historians (Sathas, *ib.* p. 51). Nicephorus calls the Mardaites ὁπλίτας.

[4] Theophanes, 6169 A.M. In the days of Justinian II they numbered 12,000.

[5] Pitzigaudes, or Pitzigaudios, may perhaps be connected with the word that was used in a diminutive form to revile Justinian (*see* vol. i. p. 343), σγαύδαρι = τζγαυδάριον.

[6] So Nicephorus ; Theophanes gives (absurdly) 8000, a mistake which perhaps arose from a confusion of N´=50 with ͵H = 8000.

Asiatic foe to pull down the bulwark of Europe was a noble triumph for Constantine.   On him devolved the defence of European Christendom and European civilisation against the withering wind which blows from Arabian deserts, against Islam which blights thought and slays freedom; and he conducted the defence well.   And the European nations recognised what he had done, and acknowledged him as the most powerful representative of the great cause of Europe.[1]   We are told that the advantageous peace which Constantine made with the Saracen caliph created a great sensation throughout the West, and redounded to the name and glory of the Roman Emperor.   The chagan of the Avars, and the kings who ruled beyond him, the governors and castaldi, and the greatest chiefs of the western nations sent ambassadors laden with presents to Constantine, and entreated him to confirm peace with them.   The Emperor received the embassies graciously, and there was a universal state of security both in the East and in the West.   It is to be regretted that our historians have not mentioned precisely the names of the nations which desired the friendship of him whom they recognised as a champion against the Moslem.   By the kings who ruled beyond the Avars we may understand the Franks, and perhaps even the Anglo-Saxons, while the governors and castaldi (*κάσταλδοι*) evidently refer to the Lombard duchies and castaldies.   It is possible that the Visigoths may have also sent envoys to the great " Republic."

It is a curious coincidence that it was under an Emperor bearing the name of its founder that the city of Constantine was first to undergo the assault of the Mohammedan destroyer, and that also under an Emperor Constantine it was finally to pass into Mohammedan hands.   We may say that in this siege the keynote was struck of all that New Rome was to

---

[1] It is important to remember, as I have from time to time in the preceding pages observed, that the western sovereigns throughout the sixth and seventh (and eighth) centuries never ceased to regard New Rome as the centre of the civilised world, and to consider themselves, not co-ordinate with, but subordinate to, the Roman Emperors in dignity.   This spirit is reflected in Gregory of Tours, and in John of Biclaro, who cares far more for the *urbs regia*, where he spent many years, than for the Gothic court of Toledo.   But it is equally reflected in Fredegarius and Isidore of Seville.   Isidore writes of the prosperity of the Gothic kingdom : *fruiturque hactenus inter regias infulas et opes largas imperii felicitate secura.*   This is the ideal,—the happiness of the Empire.

perform as the bulwark of Europe while she was still Rome [1] ; and we may regard the embassies of the western nations on this occasion as an unconscious recognition of the fact.

Muaviah died in 680, and his son Yezid, who had succeeded in obtaining his recognition as heir-apparent four years before, reigned in his stead.   Yezid's short reign was disturbed by the opposition of Abd Allah Ibn Zubeir and saddened by the tragedy of Kerbela.   A plague in Syria, the hostile inroads of the Mardaites of Lebanon, and serious agitations in Arabia disposed Abd Almalik to maintain the peace with the Empire, and the treaty was renewed (685) on the slightly altered conditions that the payments were to consist of one pound of gold, one slave, and one horse for every day in the year.[2]

In the reign of Constantine, Crete was the only Roman country that the Arabs succeeded in making tributary, and this success was only temporary.   The christian inhabitants indeed may not have felt much repugnance to the Saracen yoke, for the policy of Muaviah was to make his burden light and to treat with clemency, humanity, and toleration his christian subjects. It is even related that in the year 678, when an earthquake shook Mesopotamia, and the ambo and dome (*batan* and *trullus*) of the church in Edessa fell in, Muaviah, at the request of the Christians of the place, rebuilt the edifice.   ·

Having made a brilliant peace with the caliphate, and having also made a treaty more prudent than honourable with the Bulgarians, as will be related in another chapter, Constantine enjoyed peace until his death, and was at leisure to turn his attention to ecclesiastical affairs.   He did not, like his father, struggle against the current ; he did not think of pressing any measure like the Type of Constans ; but, professing a strict impartiality, which was probably genuine, he was willing to let the monotheletic question be decided entirely by the Church.

After the death of Constans, Pope Vitalian, apprehending

---

[1] For the last four centuries she has been an outpost of Asia instead of a bulwark of Europe ; but it is possible that in the future, when she is no longer Stamboul and neither Turkish nor Greek is spoken by her rulers, she may have to perform the same functions as in the days when she

was called New Rome.
[2] Theoph. places the peace in 6176 A.M., which corresponds (as Theophanes is a year wrong) to 684-685.   Muaviah II succeeded Yezid in 683, Mervan followed in 684, and Abd Almalik (called by Theoph. Abimelech) in April 685 (died 705).

no danger from the young Constantine, whom he had assisted in quelling the usurper Mizizios, was emboldened to declare himself in favour of the two wills.[1] In consequence of this, Theodore, the Patriarch of Constantinople, and Macarius, the Patriarch of Antioch, pressed the Emperor to allow Vitalian's name to be struck off the diptychs of Constantinople (678 A.D.) Constantine refused to act hastily, but, as soon as the peace with the Saracens gave him time for other affairs, he conceived the idea of organising a " Catholic assembly " to decide finally on a controversy, concerning which he had not himself made up his mind. He therefore wrote a letter to Pope Donus, whom he addressed as "Ecumenical Pope" (οἰκουμενικὸς πάπας), and proposed a Catholic congress, to be held in Constantinople, at which the western dioceses should be fully represented. He suggested that the Pope should send three or more deputies connected specially with the Roman curia, twelve archbishops and bishops from other dioceses under his jurisdiction, and four monks from each of the four Greek cloisters at Rome. He also promised that the exarch of Italy should receive commands to assist and further the journey of the delegates by supplying money and ships, even armed vessels—castellated *carabi*—if necessary.

But when Constantine dated this letter (12th August 678), the Pope to whom it was addressed had been already four months dead (since 11th April)—an indication of the rate at which news travelled at this period. Pope Agatho had succeeded Donus, and on receipt of the imperial epistle he determined to hold a preliminary synod at Rome, in order to obtain a consensus of the opinions of western divines touching the matters in dispute. A considerable time intervened before the bishops could be collected, as many came from great distances, and the synod was not held until Easter 680. Bishops from all the " nations " were present—from the Lombards, from the Franks, from the Goths, from the Slaves,[2] from the " Britons," or, as we should say, the Anglo-Saxons. Felix of Arles represented the Gallic Church; Wilfrid of York was present, but by accident and not as a deputy.[3] The synod condemned mono-

---

[1] *See* Hefele, iii. 225. Robertson erroneously ascribes this step to Pope Adeodatus, of Donatist name, Vitalian's successor. [2] That is, Dalmatia.

[3] Other synods were held about the same time, *e.g.* one at Milan, another at Hedtfield convoked by Thomas of Canterbury.

theletism, and a report of its acts was despatched to Constantine, accompanied by a letter from Pope Agatho, intended to be a sort of appendix to the *Epistola dogmatica* of Leo I.[1]   The Pope apologises for the delay in assembling the synod, owing to the great distance of the bishoprics, some of which were at or beyond the northern ocean.   He states that he had hoped for the presence of the archbishop and philosopher of the great island Britannia, Thomas of Canterbury, but that prelate was unable to come.   In compliance with the Emperor's suggestion, he sends three bishops—Abundantius of Palermo, Johannes of Reggio, and Johannes of Porto, with two priests, a deacon and a subdeacon of Rome, along with Theodore, a priest, to represent the Church of Ravenna,—not, however, trusting much to their learning, for people who live among the " nations " and have to win their livelihood by bodily labour cannot acquire much erudition ; they were, however, well grounded and firm in the tenets of the five general councils.   He then proceeds to expound a symbolum of the orthodox faith.   The letter was addressed to Constantine, Heraclius, and Tiberius.

When the Italian delegates arrived at Constantinople they were received with honour and maintained at the Emperor's expense, the palace of Placidia being placed at their disposal. It is related that on a certain Sunday they took part in a solemn procession to the church of St. Mary in the suburbs of Blachernae.   The Emperor meanwhile issued a *sacra* " to the most blessed archbishop and ecumenical patriarch " Georgios, directing him to summon an assembly of metropolitans and archbishops.

The sixth Ecumenical Council [2] met in a domed chamber (*trullus*) in the imperial palace on the 7th of November, and its sittings, eighteen in number, lasted for wellnigh a year, the last being held on the 16th of September 681.   As the Bishop of Rome sent delegates, as the Patriarchs of Constantinople and Antioch were present in person, and as the Patriarchs of Alexandria and Jerusalem were represented by priests, the council was ecumenical.

The holy Gospels were placed in the middle.   The Emperor, surrounded by ministers and officers, presided, but directed

---

[1] " A sort of Seitenstück to the *Epistola* of Leo to Flavian " (Hefele).

[2] For this council, *see* Mansi, xi. p. 208 *sqq.* ; Hefele, iii. 235 *sqq.*

only the formal side of the proceedings, as an impartial and disinterested chairman, and took no share in the theological discussions. He thus followed the example of Marcian, who presided at the council of Chalcedon. To the right of the Emperor sat George the Patriarch of Constantinople, Macarius the Patriarch of Antioch, the representative of the patriarchate of Alexandria, and others; to the left sat the delegates of the Pope, Theodore of Ravenna, Basil of Gortyn, and the representative of Jerusalem. It should be noticed that several of the Greek bishops were really representatives of the Roman Church, namely Johannes, the archbishop of Thessalonica, "vicar (βικάριος) of the apostolic throne of Rome"; Stephanos of Corinth, "legate of the apostolic throne of Rome"; and Basil of Gortyn in Crete, "legate of the holy synod of the apostolic throne of elder Rome." At the first eleven sittings and at the eighteenth the Emperor presided; his presence at the others was prevented by business.[1]

The council unanimously, with the exception of two individuals, condemned the monotheletic doctrine, as savouring of Apollinarianism, in that it diminished the fulness of Christ's humanity, and asserted as the true doctrine that "there are two natural wills and two natural energies, without division, alteration, separation, or confusion." It also anathematised the chief representatives of the false doctrine, including Pope Honorius. The Patriarch George had declared his acceptance of the two wills at the eighth session (7th March), and on the same occasion it was voted that the name of Pope Vitalian should be restored to the diptychs,[2] to which course the Emperor consented, and the members of the synod cried out:

"Long live the preserver of the orthodox faith! Long live the new Constantine the Great, the new Theodosius the Great, the new Marcian, the new Justinian! We are slaves of the Emperor!

"Long live the orthodox Pope Agatho of Rome!

"Long live the orthodox Patriarch George!

"Long live the holy senate!"

At the ninth sitting Macarius of Antioch, who had read a

---

[1] At the last sitting 174 members were present, but the earlier sessions were not so fully attended.

[2] Theodore, the predecessor of George, had struck out his name, apparently in spite of the reluctance of the Emperor.

manifesto of his articles of belief, and Stephanos were deposed
from their offices, and therefore could not attend the succeeding
sessions.[1]   We may observe that Macarius, when he was
pressed concerning his doctrine, had declined to use a numerical
adjective—one or two—and professed to hold simply, with
Dionysius, a theandric energy. This position was perhaps more
philosophical than either of the debated alternatives, but it
tended to coincide with monotheletism.

A curious incident diversified the course of discussion at
the fourteenth sitting. A certain Polychronius, who was a
monothelete, offered to prove the truth of his doctrine by the
performance of a miracle, and the council consented to witness
the experiment.   In the open air outside the palace a corpse
was laid, and Polychronius detained in suspense or amusement
a large crowd, while he endeavoured to resuscitate the dead
body by whispering formulae in its ears.   Doubtless many
who watched his operations were not sure of the event, but,
when all his incantations proved vain, he was hooted as a new
Simon Magus.

The proceedings of the council concluded as usual with an
address to the Emperor, who affixed his signature to the acts,
with the words " we read and approved." [2]

I cannot leave this subject without a word on the delicate problem of the condemnation of Pope Honorius, which
bears directly on the question of papal infallibility, and was
brought up in that connection at the Vatican Council of
1869 and 1870.   It is not of serious consequence whether
Honorius, who was not a strong man, deserves the benefit of a
doubt, though it is plain enough that his own words are not
consistent with the accepted orthodox belief; but it is of great
consequence, from an ecclesiastical point of view, whether the
sixth Ecumenical Council anathematised a Pope as a heretic,
as in that case one Pope at least was not infallible.   Baronius
could not admit such a monstrosity, and resorted to a theory,
—generally rejected as baseless and elaborately refuted by
Hefele,—that the acts of the sixth Council were tampered with
by the Patriarch Theodore, who abandoned his heretical belief

---

[1] Theophanes was appointed to
succeed Macarius and was present at
the fourteenth sitting ; hence Zonaras

mentions him as the Patriarch of
Antioch at the council.
[2] ἀνέγνωμεν καὶ συνῃνέσαμεν.

and was restored to the see of Constantinople after the death of George. As he had been anathematised by the council, it was his interest, says Baronius, to erase his name from the black list; and accordingly he substituted ONOPION for ΘΕΟΔΟΡΟΝ, and also made certain additions and alterations in the order of the acts. For further details on the subject I may refer the curious to Hefele.[1]

Constantine died in the year 685, leaving the Empire, at peace with foreign nations, to his son Justinian. He was buried in the church of the Holy Apostles.

NOTE ON GREEK FIRE

THE invention of Greek fire is attributed to a Syrian named Callinicus. It was preserved for a long time as a secret by the Roman government, but in the tenth century books were written on the subject.

The following receipt for the manufacture of Greek fire is contained in a treatise by a tenth-century writer, known as Marcus Graecus, on the composition of inflammatory powders and liquids for military purposes. "Take pure sulphur, tartar, sarcocolla (Persian gum), pitch, dissolved nitre, petroleum, and huile de gemme (?); boil these ingredients together; saturate tow with the concoction, and set fire to it. The conflagration will spread, and can only be extinguished by urine, vinegar, or sand."[2] Another compound closely resembled gunpowder: a pound of sulphur was pounded in a mortar with two pounds of charcoal and six pounds of nitre; the mixture was poured into long, narrow, and tight envelopes, like cartridges, closed at the ends with iron wire. These shells were ignited and hurled through the air, probably by catapults. The naphtha or fire of Medea mentioned by Procopius seems to have been a simpler form of the later πῦρ θαλάσσιον.

---

[1] *Conciliengeschichte*, vol. iii. 278.
[2] I have taken this from the article   on Marcus Graecus in the *Biographie littéraire*.

JUSTINIAN II, like his father Constantine and his grand-father Constans, was placed in the position of an absolute ruler at a very early age. He was only sixteen when his father died. But, although the energy of the Heraclian family descended to him in sufficiently full measure, he was not endowed with the cool judgment and steady head of his father and grandfather, and he was seduced by a desire of personal glory, which had never misguided them into taking a false step. The conse-quence was that he committed many fatal blunders, and became extremely unpopular. This public odium, however, was in-directly incurred, for it attached primarily to the misconduct of favourite ministers, against whose influence the young monarch was not proof. It is in the days of adversity, after.he has been ignominiously expelled from the throne, that the vigour and spirit of the man are most clearly revealed.

Abd Almalik renewed with Justinian the peace which he had made with Constantine on terms that superficially seemed more favourable.[1] The caliph undertook to pay 1000 nomis-mata and the daily tribute of one horse and one slave, while the Romans and Saracens were to divide between them the revenues of Armenia, Iberia, and Cyprus. Justinian, on the

---

[1] 688 A.D. The date given by Theophanes is 6178 (=685-686, *i.e.* 686-687), but I believe with Weil that this must be wrong. For Theophanes agrees with the Arab sources in placing the peace and the revolt of Said in the same year ; but the Arab sources, whose authority on purely Saracen history is worth more than that of a Greek writer, place the rising of Said not earlier than 688 ; hence we must conclude that Theophanes' date is wrong. *See* Weil, ii. 468. Similarly we must place Justinian's dissolution of the peace in 692 or 693, not, as Theophanes, in 6182.

other hand, undertook to compass the removal of the Mardaites, who were a perpetual thorn in the side of the caliphs, from their homes in Lebanon. These mountaineers "rendered unsafe and uninhabited all the mountain towns of the Saracens from Mopsuestia to the Fourth Armenia." They were, however, monotheletes, and this fact made the Roman government look on them with disfavour, in spite of the services which they rendered in weakening the common enemy. And so Justinian did not demur to a measure, which really meant, in the chronicler's words, a maiming of the Roman power, by removing "the brazen wall," that is the Mardaites. We are not informed how the measure was executed; but it must be remembered that these christian outlaws considered themselves the subjects of the Emperor, and it was perhaps at the instance of Constantine IV that they had entered the highlands of Syria. Certain it is that the Mardaites, to the number of twelve thousand, were transferred to Romania. Of these some were settled in Thrace,[1] others in Asia Minor, while others were enrolled in the army, and Justinian proceeded in person to the Armenian provinces in order to superintend the disposal of the immigrants. In the meantime Leontius, general of the *Anatolic* troops,[2] had subjected Albania and Iberia to the Roman supremacy, and sent a large return of tribute money to the Emperor. This expedition involved direct hostility with the Saracens and was a breach of the peace, but Abd Almalik was then too much hampered by other affairs to retaliate.

During the year 689 or 690 Justinian was occupied by a war with the Bulgarians, provoked by himself, in which he was successful; and the Slavonic captives whom he carried off he established in Asia Minor, near the Hellespont, and formed of them "a supernumerary corps" ($\pi\epsilon\rho\iota o\acute{u}\sigma\iota os$ $\lambda a\acute{o}s$) 30,000 strong. It appears that Justinian by his policy in regard to the Mardaites had lost the support of the soldiers of Mount Taurus and the Anatolic district, and was obliged to have recourse to the Slaves.[3] Trusting to the strength of these new military forces,

---

[1] M. Sathas (*op. cit.* p. 53) says that they were divided into two bodies, of which one was scattered throughout Hellas, especially Epirus, where to the present day their descendants are called Mirdites, Μιρδῖται, while the other division was ultimately settled in the

Cibyraiot theme. *See* Theophanes, 6178, 6179 A.M., and Constantine Porph. *de Adm. Imp.* cap. 50, iii. p. 229.

[2] For the *Anatolic theme*, *see* below, cap. xii.

[3] M. Sathas, *loc. cit.* M. Sathas notices that from Justinian II to 1204

he was not afraid to defy the power of the Saracens and dissolve the peace. In 692[1] he refused to receive a new Saracen coinage, introduced by Abd Almalik, inscribed with verses of the Koran.[2] The payments had been made before in the municipal coins of Syria, on which the effigy of the Roman Emperor was represented. Abd Almalik protested that he had fulfilled his part of the bargain, and that he desired peace. But as he had reduced to his sway Persia, Mesopotamia, and Arabia, his hands were free, and he did not shrink from war; and, as Justinian was obdurate, the Saracens marched to battle with the document on which the terms of the peace were inscribed stuck on the point of a lance, as a standard and a protest. The engagement took place in Cilicia, near Sebastopolis, and victory was ensured to the Saracens by the desertion of the "supernumerary corps" of Slaves, in which the Emperor had too lightly placed his confidence. Two-thirds of these troops joined the enemy and turned upon the Romans.[3] Justinian fled to the Propontis with the remnant of the barbarians, and at Leucata, near Nicomedia, he put to death the Slaves who had been faithful to him in his fury against those who had been false.

The defeat at Sebastopolis led to the revolt of Symbatius (Simpad), a patrician of Armenia holding the same position that Saborios had held in the reign of Constans. He subjected southern Armenia to the Arabs.[4] Soon afterwards the Roman dominions were invaded by the unbelievers, and on this

the question of the imperial succession is solved exclusively by the troops of the Taurus (including the Anatolic theme).

[1] The chronology is extremely uncertain, and I have ventured to depart from Theophanes, for it seems probable that he may have erred in the dates of other events as well as in those of the Saracen wars. I am persuaded that the Bulgarian war followed the peace with the Mohammedans.

[2] *See* Weil, ii. 468 *sq.*

[3] An Armenian historian, according to St. Martin, gives the number of deserters as 7000 horse.

[4] Theophanes places the dissolution of the peace in 6182, the battle of Sebastopolis in 6183, and the revolt of Symbatius in 6185; he mentions no events in 6184. But the revolt of Simpad must have followed hard upon

the affair of Sebastopolis, and it seems probable that Theophanes, led on by the context, anticipates events, as he sometimes does, and that both the battle and the revolt of Armenia took place in 6185, or in 693.

It will be convenient to put together in this place (after St. Martin) the chief facts regarding the relations of the Arabs to Armenia:—

637. First Saracen invasion.
639. Saracens penetrate to Tovin, which, however, is soon afterwards lost.
650. Armenia becomes a Saracen province.
656. Armenians revolt against the Arabs, but in 657 return to their allegiance. The country is ruled by tributary Armenian princes.
686. Romans attempt to recover Armenia, and hostilities continue till
693, when the Arabs subject the land and Arab governors are appointed.

(*see* St. Martin, *Mémoires sur l'Armenie,* i. 340).

occasion the Slavonic refugees proved serviceable, because they were versed in the topography of the country.

Other transplantations and immigrations, as well as those of the Mardaites, took place in the reign of Justinian. A famine in Syria (687) induced a number of the natives to migrate to Romania. I have already mentioned the transportation of the Slaves to Asia Minor, and although most of these were formed into a military body, some were doubtless settled as agriculturists in the north-western provinces on the Propontis. To the same regions the Emperor also designed to transplant part of the population of Cyprus. Cyprus, by the new arrangement which had been made with Abd Almalik, was half-Roman and half-Saracen territory ; and Justinian wished to leave the whole island to the rival power without surrendering the Roman tributaries. As the Cypriotes sailed across to the mainland the ships were caught in a storm, many were drowned, and the rest returned to the island. But the design was carried out notwithstanding this mishap, and the Asiatic residence of the bishop and people of Cyprus was a new city, named Justinianopolis, in the neighbourhood of Cyzicus.[1]

The fact that the north-western provinces, known at this time as the district of Opsikion, were chosen for the transplanted settlers can be explained by historical events. Throughout the entire century they had been continually exposed to the devastations of foes, first the Persians, then the Saracens, who used to establish themselves on the shores of the Propontis or the Bosphorus, to menace the capital of Romania. This circumstance necessarily brought about depopulation in those districts, and there was need of new colonists.

Justinian's foreign policy, including his idea of a supernumerary Slavonic corps, had been eminently unsuccessful ; his domestic policy was also a failure. This was chiefly due to the proceedings of his two notoriously unpopular and unprincipled ministers of finance. The influence of ministers or subordinates had been almost quite inoperative in the reigns of Constans and Constantine, both strong and independent monarchs ; but Justinian was a man of more impulse than

[1] The repopulating of Cyprus is attributed by Constantine Porph. (*de Adm. Imp.* cap. 47) to the same monarch, Justinian, but M. Sathas has shown that the imperial writer was mistaken, and that the act was really due to Tiberius III (Apsimar). *See* below, p. 356.

steadiness, and was amenable to both good and bad influences. He unwisely allowed great latitude to his two favourites, Stephanus and Theodotus, whose cruelty and rapacity covered him with odium and obloquy.

Theodotus, who had been the abbot of a monastery,[1] was general logothete[2] (γενικὸς λογοθέτης), an officer corresponding

[1] A monastery in Thrace, built near the straits called Stenon at the mouth of the Euxine.

[2] The history of the financial bureaux of the Roman Empire is curious. (1) Originally the private property of Augustus and his successors (*patrimonium*) was distinguished from the *fiscus* or property of the *princeps*. (2) But when the Flavians succeeded the Julio-Claudian dynasty they inherited the patrimony, which therefore came to be regarded as crown property instead of family property. Hence arose a second distinction between the *patrimonium* (which soon became merged in the fisc) and the *res privata*, which corresponded to the old *patrimonium*. This *res* (or *ratio*) *privata* branched off in the time of Septimius Severus, and the distinction was between the *fisc* + *patrimonium* and the *res privata* ; and after Caracalla there are no traces of patrimonial officers (procurators) in Italy. (3) The *res privata* in turn travelled along the same path as the *patrimonium*. In the fourth century the fisc is administered by the illustrious count of the sacred largesses, and the private estates by the illustrious *comes rei privatae* ; but the *res privata* ceases to grow, and the personal property of the Emperor is managed (probably) by the grand chamberlain (*praepositus sacri cubiculi*). This was certainly the case in the fifth century, and at length the Emperor Anastasius, finding it an inconvenient system and approving of the principle of division of labour, instituted a new officer, the *comes sacri patrimonii*. And thus *patrimonium* emerges once more as an official term bearing its original significance. At the beginning of the third century the *patrimonium* meant crown property and *res privata* meant personal property ; at the beginning of the sixth century *patrimonium* meant personal property and *res privata* crown property. (*See* O. Hirschfeld, *Untersuchungen auf dem Gebiete der römischen Verwaltungsgeschichte*, i., especially p. 43).

We learn of this measure of Anastasius from John Lydus, ii. 27 : ὁ λεγόμενος πατριμώνιος φύλαξ τῆς ἰδίᾳ πως ἀνηκούσης τῷ βασιλεῖ καὶ τυχὸν ἐκ προγόνων περιουσίας, ὃν καὶ αὐτὸν οὐ πρὶν ἀριθμούμενον Ἀναστάσιος ὁ πάντα ἔμφρων ἀνεστήσατο, διάκρισιν ὥσπερ εἰώθει περινοῶν τοῖς πράγμασιν ὅπως μὴ συγχύσει κάμνοιεν. I think the word ἀνεστήσατο, "re-established," refers to a temporary institution of an office of similar name in the reign of Arcadius (*sacri patrimonii comitiva*, mentioned in an inscription). This notice of Lydus is confirmed by *Basilica*, vi. 1, 102, 103 (ed. Heimbach, i. p. 148), and by certain juristic glosses quoted by Böcking, who has a learned and valuable note on the subject in his *Notitia Dignitatum*, ii. 376 *sqq*. As Böcking says, the names of the three officials *com. sacr. larg.*, *com. rei priv.*, and *com. sacr. patr.* might be translated in German (respectively) by *Finanzminister des Reichsschatzes, F. des Kronschatzes*, and *F. des kaiserlichen Privatvermögens*.

In Greek the *patrimonium* was generally called ἡ ἰδικὴ περιουσία or οὐσία, and thus the *com. patr.* is called in the *Basilica* (*loc. cit.*) κόμης τῆς ἰδικῆς περιουσίας. But in popular speech he was known as the *sacellarius* or purser. The words σακέλλιον and σακελλάριος occur in an *oratio* of Gregory of Nazianzus *in Julianum*, and come from the Latin diminutive *saccellus* (*saccellarius*), a little bag. In later times σακελλάριος passed back into Latin (*sacellarius*, with only one c). In the *Chronicon Paschale*, Leo (or Leontius) the Syrian is called ὁ ἀπὸ σακελλαρίων, and I presume this means that he was once count of the patrimony. In the reign of Heraclius we meet the sacellarius Theodore, whom Nicephorus describes as τῶν βασιλικῶν χρημάτων ταμίαν, and now in the reign of Justinian we meet Stephanus holding the same office. The old Latin name was probably almost obsolete.

As the adjective ἰδικός was applied to the Emperor's private property, it was

to the former count of sacred largesses. A monk who forsook his retreat to become a civil minister would naturally be looked upon in those days with the utmost suspicion. The oppressions which he exercised and the extortions which he practised are reported to have been terrible. But his offences were aggravated by the fact that he went beyond his jurisdiction and succeeded in exacting money with no sufficient reason from men of senatorial rank, on whom the office of the private domains had no legal claim, and confiscating their property; he was able even to put them to death. He was cruel to his victims, we are told, and used to hang them up by ropes and scorch their bodies with a straw fire [1] lit beneath them.

Stephanus, a Persian eunuch, was *sacellarius*, or keeper of the privy purse, and he too by his "bloodthirsty" oppression of the citizens made the Emperor hated. A story is told that once, when the Emperor was absent, "the savage beast" amused himself by administering a whipping to the Empress-mother Anastasia as if she were a little school-girl. Whether it was at the suggestion of one or other of these two men that the prefect of the city was empowered to imprison for years many persons of high rank and position, or whether the prefect was like unto the ministers of the treasuries, we cannot say. The general result was that Justinian's government was detested.

Like his distinguished namesake Justinian I., the Emperor was seized with a passion for building. He erected a new and splendid triklinos [2] in the palace, and appointed Stephanus as a kind of taskmaster to superintend the progress of the building and accelerate its completion. It was a con-

---

natural that men should apply a conjugate adjective to the public treasury. The adjective chosen by the instinct of the Romaioi was γενικός; the exchequer was called τὸ γενικόν; and the count of the sacred largesses came to be called the λογοθέτης τοῦ γενικοῦ or λογ. γενικός, a name which Nicephorus (p. 37) paraphrases as τῶν δημοσίων λογιστήν. In the year 609 we meet with Anastasius, κόμητα τῶν λαργιτιώνων, but in the course of the seventh century the name fell into disuse. I suspect that some changes in the financial administration were made by Constans, who was probably his own chancellor of the exchequer.

Meanwhile we hear nothing more of

the *comes rei privatae* (κόμης τῶν πριβάτων). I conjecture that the same fate that befell the *patrimonium* in the third century befell the *res privata* in the seventh; the private estate was absorbed by the fisc (that is, the *sacrae largitiones* or the γενικόν).

[1] μετεώροις σχοινίοις ἀναρτῶν καὶ ἀχύροις περικαπνίζων (Nicephorus, p. 37), while Theophanes uses the word ὑποκατνίζων. For their accounts of these two ministers, Nicephorus and Theophanes had the same source before them, as is clear from the similarity of their language.

[2] This large hall extended from west to east, and was connected with the Χρυσοτρίκλινος by a long gallery called

genial work to the inhuman sacellarius, who did not content himself with beating the workmen, but used to stone both them and the overseers.

Close to the palace was a church sacred to the Mother of God, whose situation presented an obstacle to new plans of Justinian. He wished to utilise the place partly for a fountain[1] and partly for tiers of benches to accommodate the members of the blue faction when they were receiving the Emperor on public occasions. He therefore begged the Patriarch Callinicus[2] to deconsecrate the church that he might pull it down, but the Patriarch replied, "We have received a form of prayer for the establishment of a church, but for the abolition of a church we have not received such." But when the Emperor pressed him hard, he said evasively, "Glory be to God, who is long-suffering now, always, and for ever and ever, Amen!" This convenient formula was accepted as an adequate prayer of deconsecration; the church was pulled down and the fountain was made; and at Petrion a new church to the Virgin was built to compensate her for the demolition of her house in the Augusteum.

Justinian professed to concern himself for the morals of his subjects. At least he assembled a synod (*in trullo*) in 692,[3]

the Τρίκλινος Λαυσιακός, according to the reconstruction of the palace by M. Paspatis.

George Pachymeres writes thus of Justinian's triklinos (ii. 145, ed. Bonn):
ἔξαιτον ὄντα καὶ μέγαν καὶ θαυμαστόν λέχριον ὄντα τοῖς κατὰ πύλας εἰσιοῦσι πρώτης καὶ ἄνωθεν ἕως κάτω διήκοντα, λαμπρὸν μὲν τοίχοις, λαμπρὸν δ' ἐδάφει καὶ περιττὸν τὸ κάλλος. C. Manasses (l. 3301) calls the room—

δεῖγμα λαμπρότητος αὐτοῦ
καὶ μεγαλοπρεπείας
ὁ χρύσεός τε καὶ τερπνὸς ἐν
ἀνακτόροις οἶκος.

Paspatis conjectures that it was covered

with a roof, partially if not wholly (p. 256).

It is hardly necessary to remark that τρίκλινος means a hall or gallery or large room (roofed or open) provided with seats or couches, and does not, like the Roman *triclinium*, imply a dining-room.

[1] φιάλη, a cascade fountain (like modern fountains in appearance), such as is represented in mosaics in the apse of San Vitale at Ravenna. This church of the Virgin is called τῶν μητροπολίτου, that is one of the churches under the immediate care of the metropolitan.

[2] The form Gallicinus occurs in some MSS. of Paulus Diaconus (vi. 31), apparently a Latin popular etymology. To an Italian, Callinicus meant nothing; the very similar Gallicinus suggested "crowing cock." The mistake is of course due, not to Paul, but to a copyist, and also occurs in the case of Callinicus a patrician.

[3] It was held in the same domed room in the palace as the sixth Council,

of which the object was to consider important matters which had been neglected at previous councils. Amid the excitement of theological discussion, moral life had declined and church discipline had become relaxed; the Emperor desired to reform morals, to bring christian life into order, and to uproot the remains of Jewish and heathen perversity. The acts of this synod are peculiarly interesting to the general historian, as illustrating manners and morals, and we shall return to it in another place. It was called *Quinisextum*, because it was a sort of supplement to the fifth and sixth general Councils and it purposed to be ecumenical, but the Pope, Sergius, refused to sign the acts on account of certain clauses, such as the prohibition of fasting on Saturdays and the permission to priests to marry.[1] Justinian attempted to force the Pope to his will by violence, such as Constans had used to Martin, but the feeling in Italy was strong for the bishop of Rome, and the soldiers of the exarchate supported him against the spatharius whom Justinian had sent to seize him.

At length in 695 the inevitable retribution came, and Justinian suffered the penalty of his unpopular policy and injudicious oppression of the higher classes. His fall came about on this wise.

Leontius, an Isaurian, the general of the Anatolic theme, whom we saw fighting in Armenia and Iberia and gaining repute in war, had incurred the Emperor's suspicions or the enmity of his favourites, and had pined for three years in prison.

---

and is known as the synod *in trullo* (par excellence). Its date has divided historians, but there seems no doubt that 692 is right, as Hefele thinks. Tarasius (at the seventh Council, at Nicaea) said that this synod took place four or five years after the council of 680 - 681, that is in 686; but it took place in the fifth indiction, whereas 686 fell in the fourteenth indiction, and the date is otherwise untenable. Tarasius probably confounded the synod *in trullo* with the synod which met to preserve the acts of the sixth Council from forgery (687). We must read 6199 A.M. ($\varsigma\rho Ϟ\theta'$) instead of 6109 (which on any theory is absurd) in the third canon of the acts of the synod, where the preceding year is referred to and defined as the fourth indiction; whereby,

reckoning according to the Byzantine era of the world, we obtain 691, and therefore the synod met in 692 (or in last four months of 691). It is strange that Hefele makes no reference to the remarkable passage in Theophanes (*ad* 6177 A.M.), who quotes the third canon in full and *gives the correct date*, $\varsigma\rho Ϟ\theta'$, but falls into a mistake through computing by the Alexandrian era, and thus places it in 707, which is impossible.

[1] The four others which they rejected were, the approbation of the eighty-five apostolic canons; the command to abstain from blood and things strangled; the clause against representing Christ as a lamb; and the equality of the bishop of Constantinople with the bishop of Rome.

Perhaps it was in connection with the defeat at Sebastopolis that Justinian placed him in confinement. But at length (in 695) he was suddenly released, and at the same time informed that he had been appointed " General of Hellas " and must without delay set out for his district with three fast sailers. He had two friends who used to visit him in prison, Paulus, a monk and astronomer, and Gregory of Cappadocia, who had once commanded a mountain fort, presumably in Asia Minor, with the title of *kleisuriarch*, and, having since become a monk, was then abbot of the monastery of Florus. These two monks had often averred to Leontius, while he was in prison, that he was destined to become Emperor of the Romans. On the night of his departure for Greece he met them,[1] to say farewell; he reminded them of their prediction, and observed bitterly, " Now my life is ending in misery, for I shall be expecting every moment death to follow me." " Fear not," they replied, "the prophecy will be soon fulfilled. Only listen to us and follow us."

In accordance with the directions of these ecclesiastics, Leontius took his men and his arms and proceeded silently to the praetorium, or residence of the prefect of the city. He knocked at the gate and announced to the porter that the Emperor was waiting without, having come for the purpose of arranging the treatment of some of the prisoners who were incarcerated in the buildings. The prefect, informed of the imperial presence, came hastily down to open the gate; and was immediately overpowered by Leontius, beaten and bound. Then the prisoners, who were numerous and of exalted rank, were set free. Most of them were soldiers, and some had languished in the dungeons for seven or eight years. Leontius, sure of their fidelity, provided them with arms, and then proceeded with his party to the Augusteum, crying aloud, " Ho, all Christians to St. Sophia!" and he sent others to cry the same summons in other regions of the city. A multitude of citizens thronged to the church, and in the meantime the revolutionist, along with the two monks and the most important of the released prisoners, went to the *Patriarcheion*, where they found the Patriarch filled with alarm.

---

[1] In the Julianisian port of Sophia, near the region of Mauron, in the south-west part of the city.

It is stated as the cause of his fear that the Emperor had given orders to a patrician and general named Stephanus, and surnamed Rusius (not to be confounded with Stephanus the sacellarius), to massacre the people of Constantinople by night, beginning with the Patriarch. This mandate would be quite credible if attributed to Justinian after his return from exile, but I feel considerable hesitation in believing that he had at this time reached such a pitch of insanity.

The Patriarch Callinicus not unwillingly accompanied Leontius to the cathedral. There he said to the people, "This is the day which the Lord has made," and all the people cried, "Let the bones of Justinian be dug up," that is : may Justinian be accursed.[1] After this preliminary quasi-religious sanctification of their future acts, all proceeded to the hippodrome. Thither the unfortunate Justinian was led at daybreak ; and in the southern crescent, where such scenes usually took place,[2] his nose and his tongue were slit, after which despiteful usage he was shipped off to the Tauric peninsula, whither his grandfather had banished Pope Martin.

The mutilation which Justinian suffered cannot have been so severe as the terms naturally suggest. The operation performed on his tongue did not deprive him of the power of speaking, and we may assume that the cutting of the nose did not mean its total removal. In fact, it seems probable that the words are more cruel than the acts really were ; and that the *rinokopia* and *glossotomia*, which were ordinary occurrences in Byzantium, and are cited as instances of Byzantine cruelty, were little more than a very severe and indelible brand, which, however, did not materially affect the victim's general wellbeing.[3]

The expulsion of Justinian was accompanied by the execution of the two detested ministers of finance Stephanus and Theodotus, who with their feet tied together were dragged

---

[1] ἀνασκαφῇ τὰ ὀστέα Ἰουστινιανοῦ (Theoph.) This was the regular form of cursing in Byzantium, so that ἀνασκάπτω came to mean "curse."

[2] σφενδόνη.

[3] In regard to Byzantine punishments Zachariä (*Griechisch-römisches Recht*, Pref. p. viii.) remarks : "Freiheits-und Gefängniss-strafen bleiben den Byzan-

tinern fast ganz fremd, weil ihnen, wie allen Orientalen, das *far niente* ein Genuss statt eines Uebels ist, und selbst die freiwillige Absperrung in Klöster und Zellen etwas verlockendes hat : statt der Freiheitsstrafen entwickelt sich vielmehr ein raffinirtes System von Leibes-und Lebensstrafen, welches die Türken nur zu eifrig adoptirt haben."

through the thoroughfare and burned at the place called Bous.

Thus the prediction of the astronomer Paulus came to pass, and Leontius the Patrician, instead of being "General of Hellas," became Emperor of the Romans. And thus too the dynasty of Heraclius, having lasted for eighty-five years, came to an end; for we need hardly reckon to its credit or discredit the few years during which Justinian, having returned from exile, enjoyed the supreme power again and committed acts that were worthy only of a madman.

I may conclude this chapter by putting forward the conjecture that Justinian II. made Justinian I. a model for his own acts. I do not mean that he attempted to adopt the spirit of the great monarch's administration; I mean that he had a fancy for aping his namesake in certain minor matters. In the first place, unlike his immediate predecessors and forefathers, he caused expensive architectural works to be executed; like Justinian I., he desired to be remembered as a builder. In the second place, he intended to force Pope Sergius to comply with his will by violence, as Justinian I. had forced Pope Vigilius. Here of course he had the more recent example of his grandfather Constans. In the third place, when he was in exile he married, as we shall see, the sister of the chagan of the Khazars. As Justinian's wife she was called Theodora, and I conjecture that the banished monarch, when he chose this name for her, thought of Theodora the wife of his great namesake. In the fourth place, he formed designs against Abasgia, as we shall learn in a future chapter, and here too I think he was recurring to the days of Justinian I. Certain it is that from Justinian I. to Justinian II. we hear of few dealings between the Empire and the Abasgians. Again, the foundation of Justinianopolis recalls the eponymous cities of Justinian I. Once more, Stephanus and Theodotus, the instruments of cruelty and extortion, remind us of John the Cappadocian; and since John's prefecture no Emperor is recorded to have employed such notorious oppressors until the monk became logothete and the eunuch *sacellarius* under the second Justinian.

CHAPTER XI

By the middle of the seventh century the Balkan lands were, as we have seen, covered with Slavonic settlements, so that in Moesia, Illyricum, Macedonia the Slaves constituted the bulk of the population. The towns on the sea-coast were still Greek, and the remains of the old Albanese and Thracian nations lingered still among the mountains; but it was evident that destiny had marked out the peninsula north of Mount Olympus for a Slavonic country.

The Slaves, however, were themselves incapable of union; they had no political instinct in that direction; and if a principle of unity had not been induced from without, they might have never become dominant, they might have even been gradually crushed by the Emperors of Constantinople.

The people who supplied the unity, which the Slovenes were by themselves incapable of realising, were the Bulgarians, a non-Aryan race allied with the Khazars, Magyars, etc., and belonging to what is called the Ugro-Finnic branch. We have already met them as early as the end of the fifth century fighting with Theodoric, and defeated by him; we have then seen them invading the Roman Empire in the reigns of Anastasius and Justinian, and afterwards, at the end of the sixth century, reduced to a condition of semi-dependence on the Avar monarchy. These Bulgarians, who dwelled on the Euxine coast north of the Danube in Budžak and Bessarabia, had separated from the great Bulgarian nation, whose home was in the lands between the Don, the Volga, and the Kuban, east of the Sea of Azov.[1]

The Greek historians Theophanes and Nicephorus,[2] living at the end of the eighth century, record a story about the Bulgarians, which they must have drawn from a common source, as not only their facts but their verbal expressions coincide. This story is legendary, but it has a historical foundation. Kobrat, or Kourat, was king of the kindred nations of the Bulgarians and Kotragoi in the reign of Heraclius. He died in the reign of Constans, leaving five sons, whom he exhorted to cling together and not break up the Bulgarian power. As might have been predicted, they did not follow his admonition. The first son, Baian or Batbaian (a name that reminds us of the chagan of the Avars in the reign of Maurice), remained in the territory of his father; the second, whose name was Kotragos, established himself on the right bank of the Don; the third, Asperuch, crossed the Dniepr and Dniestr, and settled near the north bank of the Danube; the fourth migrated to Pannonia, and was subject unto the Avars; the fifth travelled still farther west, and settled in the "pentapolis of Ravenna."

This notice crowds into the reign of Constans the Second events that took place nearly two centuries before. The migration of the third brother, Asperuch (or Isperich, as he is called in the Slavonic record of Bulgarian monarchs[3]), represents a migration that took place before the year 480 A.D. We may further conjecture that the migrations of the fourth

---

[1] περὶ τὴν Μαιῶτιν λίμνην κατὰ τὸν Κώφινα ποταμόν (Nicephorus, ed. de Boor, p. 33).

[2] M. Jiriček, in his excellent chapter on "die Einwanderung der Bulgaren," is not quite accurate in his statement touching the Greek account of the *Vorgeschichte* of this people. In the first place, he speaks as if it were only to be found in the history of Nicephorus, and does not once mention Theophanes; and yet Theophanes is fuller in his details than Nicephorus, although both drew from the same source. But the curious point is that M. Jiriček, while professing to quote from Nicephorus, really quotes Theophanes — *e.g.* the name Batbaian is the form in Theophanes, Baianos the form in Nice-

phorus, and Jiriček gives the former. In the second place, he places Kobrat's death and the division of the kingdom in the reign of Constantine IV; but Nicephorus (like Theophanes) places it in the reign of "the Constantine who died in the West" (*i.e.* Constans II). Apparently M. Jiriček has quoted his authorities here at second hand.

[3] This obscure record (*see* Jiriček, p. 127) contains several inexplicable Bulgarian words, which Hilferding has tried to interpret by the help of Hungarian. According to it, Kurt reigned sixty years. The name of the royal Bulgarian family was *Dulo*. The list begins from the earliest times and goes down to 765 A.D. The first Bulgarian king, Avitochol, reigned 300 years.

and fifth brothers do not represent separations from the mother nation on the bank of the Kuban, but rather offshoots from the daughter nation between the Danube and Dniestr. Both these later settlements of the Bulgarians in Pannonia and in Italy must have taken place in the seventh century; and we must evidently connect the fifth with the notice of Paul, the historian of the Lombards, that King Grimuald settled some Bulgarians, who entered Italy peacefully under the leadership of one Alzeco, in the neighbourhood of Beneventum.[1]

The Bulgarian king[2] who revolted against the Avars and allied himself with Heraclius, Kobrat or Krobat, is called Kurt in the Slavonic list of Bulgarian monarchs to which we have already referred. Nicephorus records that Kubrat, the nephew of Organ and chief of the Onogundurs, revolted against the chagan of the Avars and made a treaty with Heraclius, who conferred on him the title of Patrician; moreover, Kubrat expelled the Avars from his own land. This event was decisive for the history of the Bulgarians, just as the battle of Netad was decisive for the history of the Ostrogoths.

In the reign of Constantine IV the independent Bulgarians began to distress the neighbouring Roman territory by their incursions. The Emperor determined to take vigorous measures immediately, and, instead of merely strengthening the frontier defences, to attack the enemy in their own country and teach them a salutary lesson. He prepared a naval armament as well as a land army, and transported the Asiatic troops to Europe. The territory of the Bulgarians was called Oglos or Onglos (an angle or corner), and corresponds to the district marked Budžak on modern maps. Here they possessed strong

---

[1] Paul. Diac. v. 29. The places conceded to the Bulgarians were Sepinum (Sipicciano), Isernia (Sergna), Bovianum, and other *civitates*. Alzeco's title was changed from *dux* to *gastaldius*. Those who were subjects of the Avars afterwards migrated to the territory of the Franks, who treacherously murdered them all (Fredegarius, cap. 72).

[2] King of the Onogundurs (Nicephorus, p. 24). Nicephorus does not identify the Onogundurs with the Bulgarians, nor Onogunduric Kubrat, of the reign of Heraclius, with Bulgarian Kubrat, of the reign of Constans (as he sup-

poses); but Theophanes, 6171 A.M., makes the former identification, τῶν Οὐννογουνδούρων Βουλγάρων καὶ Κοτράγων. The first Kubrat or Kurt is historical, and really reigned on the Danube, but the second Kubrat is legendary, or at least a personage of remoter antiquity. The actual reign of a famous Kubrat in the seventh century led to the old legends being attached to his name, and it was supposed that it was he who led the Bulgarians from the Caucasus to the Danube. *Organ* (the father of Kubrat) is a Turkish name.

and inaccessible fortresses, secured by precipitous rocks which rose behind and perfidious morasses which stretched in front, so that it was a difficult country for an invader. When they saw the great expeditions by land and sea that had come against them, the Bulgarians, greatly terrified, retreated into their fastnesses, and for four days endured a siege. But unluckily the Emperor, who had accompanied the naval armament in person, fell sick of a pain in his foot, and, commanding his forces to continue the siege, departed with a few ships to Mesembria. Some regiments of cavalry misconstrued the departure of the sovereign as flight, and, seized with a groundless panic, fled themselves. The panic was communicated to the rest of the army, the flight became general, and the Bulgarians, issuing from their retreats, pursued and completely routed the Romans. All whom they captured they put to death. Still pursuing, they crossed the Danube and advanced to Varna, near Odessus. Struck by the natural features of Moesia, which seemed to lend it a peculiar security,—the Haemus on the south, the Danube on the north, the Euxine on the east,— they determined to change their habitation and establish themselves south of the Danube.

Accordingly, the Bulgarians reduced to subjection the seven Slavonic tribes that dwelled in Moesia, experiencing probably little resistance, and disposed them along the frontiers of the new Bulgarian kingdom, to defend it on the west against the Avars and on the south against the Romans.[1] The tribe of the Severs [2] (Σεβέρεις) was placed to guard the pass of Beregaba in the eastern Balkans. The Roman towns and forts were gradually reduced, and Constantine, after the failure of his great expedition, was constrained to make a treaty with the new kingdom that was being founded within Roman territory, and to agree to the payment of a certain sum of money every year to the Bulgarian king, Isperich. The motive of Constantine in paying this tribute seems to have been to save Thrace from immediate invasion, so that he might have time to take measures for its permanent security against " the new and abominable " neighbours.

---

[1] There is a story, resting on Arabian authority, that the entire Bulgarian kingdom was surrounded by a thorn hedge provided with wooden windows (Jireček, p. 133).

[2] Roesler regards them as Huns.

The chief towns of the new kingdom founded by Isperich were Prêslav (Peristhlaba),[1] on the Kamčija (about a degree due west of Varna), and Drster (Durostorum, the modern Silistria), on the Danube; and in these regions the kingdom continued for more than two centuries with little change in its boundaries, nearly corresponding to the modern principality of Bulgaria. It was not till the tenth century that Bulgarian supremacy extended to the south-west, and included the Slaves of Macedonia and Dacia. In the meantime the conquered Slaves were by a gradual process conquering their Tartaric conquerors.[2] The Bulgarian customs had little influence on the Slavonic character; and the Bulgarian language had less influence on the Slavonic language. On the contrary, the Bulgarians were Slavised, and ultimately absorbed among the Slaves, so that the Bulgarian people of the present day is purely Slavonic, with nothing non-Aryan about it except its name and a slight infusion of Tartar blood.

In these events we see two features of Slavonic history prominently marked. We observe on the one hand the inability of the wayward Slavonic tribes to form a political unity, without an alien power to give the initiative by subjecting them to a monarchy. On the other hand we see the assimilative absorbing power of the Slavonic race—herein somewhat resembling the Hellenic—which was able in a short time to obliterate the identity of the conquerors, while it profited by the principles of unity and monarchy which they had introduced. I call these two phenomena features of Slavonic history, because they recurred some centuries later in the more celebrated case of the Russians, and, if my conjecture touching the Croatian Slaves is right, they had occurred in a less pronounced form before.[3] The unity, to which the Slaves of Russia would never have attained of themselves, was superinduced by the Northmen of Scandinavia, who founded a Russian kingdom; but the language, the manners, and the identity of the conquerors were soon absorbed in Slavism.

Thus for the Slaves the way to unity and empire has lain

---

[1] It is uncertain when Peristhlaba was founded. At first Varna was probably the capital.

[2] Noble Slaves were admitted by their conquerors to a share in the administration. As to the Slavonic cultivators of the soil, Jiriček says they were probably reduced to a sort of partial *Leibeigenschaft.*

[3] *See* above, cap. vii.

through acceptance of a foreign yoke; they have lost their life in order to save it.

The khan of the Bulgarians ruled with a council of six *bolyars* (βοῖλάδες, whence the Russian *boyar*), and the constitution rested on an aristocratic basis. The customs of the Bulgarians had an oriental complexion, and differed totally from those of the Slaves. They were polygamists. The women veiled their faces, and the men wore turbans, and both sexes wore loose trousers. The king partook of his meals alone, without the company even of a wife. The Bulgarians cared only for war, and their barbarous manners present no trace of industrial development. In their old homes they did not use coins; cattle were the medium of exchange. They were a superstitious people, and considered magical rites a necessary preliminary to battle.[1]

About ten years after the settlement of Isperich and his Bulgarians in Moesia, the young Emperor Justinian dissolved the peace which his father had made by refusing to pay the stipulated tribute (689 A.D.)[2] He ordered the cavalry regiments stationed in Asia Minor to cross over to Thrace, "desiring to lead captive the Bulgarians and the Sclavinias," that is the Sclavinia which was now included in the Bulgarian kingdom and the Sclavinia to the west of Mount Rhodope, which was nominally part of the Roman Empire, but was constantly rebelling. In the following year (690) Justinian first marched northwards against the Bulgarians, whom he repulsed, and then turned westwards against the Slavonic settlements in the neighbourhood of Thessalonica. He succeeded in collecting a vast number of Slaves, some of whom voluntarily joined him, while others he forcibly constrained; and, having transported them to Asia Minor, settled them in the district of Opsikion. We have already seen how he formed thirty thousand of these captives into a "supernumerary corps" under the command of Nebulus, and how twenty thousand of them deserted to the Saracens.

The Bulgarians enjoyed a slight revenge for their defeat. They waylaid Justinian, "as he was returning," in a mountain pass, and he escaped with difficulty. But it is not clear

---

[1] *See* Jiriček and Roesler, *Rom. Stud.* p. 239. The main source is the *Responsa ad cons. Bulgar.* of Pope Nicolas (Harduin, v. p. 353).   [2] Theoph. 6180 A.M.

whether this took place as he was returning from Thessalonica with his captives or after he had settled them in Opsikion. The Bulgarians, however, seem not to have harassed the Empire again during the reign of Isperich, who died in 700 and was succeeded by Terbel.

I may add a word as to the history of the old Bulgarians who dwelt on the Kuban and Kama. Their kingdom was called Great Bulgaria, and was on friendly terms with the Saracens, who converted it to Mohammedanism in the tenth century. It suffered from the enmity of the Khazars and the Russians, and was finally, in the thirteenth century, exterminated by the Tartars. And thus the only relic of the Bulgarians is their name, which in western Europe[1] has come to be a word of opprobrium, connoting a nameless vice.

I may conclude this chapter by noticing the series of attacks which were made upon Thessalonica by the Macedonian Slaves in the latter part of the seventh century. In 675 or 676 the fierce tribes who dwelled on the coasts of the Thermaic and Pagasaic gulfs blockaded the capital of Illyricum by land and sea. But the ships of the besiegers were scattered by a storm; and, as far as we can determine from the account transmitted by a biographer who writes for edification, a sally of the besiegers put the land army to flight, and Chatzon, the chief of the expedition, was captured, and stoned to death by women. The inhabitants attributed this deliverance to the special intervention of St. Demetrius, whose church still attests the honour in which he was held; just as, nearly a hundred years before, the repulse of the Avars was gratefully set down to his protection.

But the Slaves had not abandoned the idea of obtaining possession of the great capital of Illyricum. In 677 the aid of the holy Demetrius was again needed, when the barbarians returned to the assault, reinforced by Avars and Bulgarians and provided with poliorcetic machines. The blockade lasted for a month, and then the foe retired, the saint having again wrought deliverance for his city. At this time John II was archbishop of Thessalonica, and his activity in providing for the defence of the town is closely connected with the super-

[1] Similarly from the Ugrian (Hungarian) name comes our "ogre."

natural colouring given to the events by the ecclesiastical biographer, in whose pages the praetorian prefect plays a subordinate part. The city suffered from an earthquake soon after this siege, and had the distress of beholding the church of its patron in flames. A greater misfortune befell it in the death of the archbishop. Then we have a glimpse of Perbund (Pervund), " chief " of the Runchines, walking in the streets of the town; but the praetorian prefect suspects him, commits him to irons, and sends him to Constantinople. He attempts to escape from prison and is slain.

In consequence of this dealing with Perbund, his tribe, the Runchines, combine with the Sagudates and march against Thessalonica (678). For two whole years the city is closely blockaded, and endures all the miseries incident to a siege. The Emperor is unable to send more than ten small ships to its relief; and the raising of the siege is finally due to dissensions among the beleaguerers. The Belegezêtes desert to the Romans, and the enemy's camp is broken up (680); but the credit of the deliverance falls to the share of the saint. Once more, in the following year, the city is besieged; and once more the besiegers are repulsed by its protector. In the meantime the waters of the northern Aegean are infested by the Slavonic pirates.[1]

[1] For these events, *see* the " Vita Sancti Demetrii," in the *Acta Sanctorum*, Oct. iv. (162-174). The name of the praetorian prefect is mentioned—Charias.

NOTE

THE question touching an early introduction of Islam among the Bulgarians is discussed by C. M. Fraehn in an essay on "Drei Münzen der Wolga-Bulgaren aus dem x. Jahrhundert n. Chr." (*Mém. de l'acad. imp. des sciences de St. Pétersbourg,* vol. i. 6th series, 1832, p. 171 *sqq.*) Some of the customs of the Moesian Bulgarians (above, p. 336) and the name of one of their kings (Omar, below, p. 473) point this way; but the authority of Ibn Foszlan and others establishes that Great Bulgaria was converted to Mohammedanism in the tenth century. Fraehn accordingly assumes an earlier and a later introduction of Islam, and connects the hostilities of the heathen Khazars with the early conversion (p. 189).

CHAPTER XII

ORIGIN OF THE SYSTEM OF THEMES

ONE of the most obscure and also most interesting problems of seventh-century history is the origin of the "Byzantine themes." In the tenth century the Emperor Constantine Porphyrogennetos wrote a treatise on the themes or districts into which the Empire was at that time divided, and he distinctly assigns their origin to the seventh century. The assertion of the imperial writer would by itself weigh little, because he was lamentably ignorant of history and quite destitute of critical ability, but it is confirmed by the undesigned testimony of the historians Nicephorus and Theophanes, whose narrative of the latter years of the seventh century presupposes at least the beginning of a thematic division, if I may be permitted to use the expression. Nicephorus and Theophanes lived indeed a century later, but they made use of earlier sources. Constantine further fixes the latter part of the reign of Heraclius as the date of the introduction of the theme system. This statement is not contradicted by the scanty records of the history of that time; but it is not necessitated. The passages in Theophanes and Nicephorus which bear on the question prove only that the new division was partially made before the death of Constans (668 A.D.) There are, however, reasons for supposing that Constantine was in a certain sense right.

Many of the themes which existed in the middle of the tenth century had been created recently, within the preceding fifty or sixty years. Such were either smaller districts of subordinate importance, which had previously been subdivisions of large themes, or else new acquisitions won from hostile territory, such as Longobardia and Lycandos. With the origin of these Constantine was of course familiar. But he did not think of applying the facts, which he had heard with his ears and his father had told him, to the course of past history, and concluding by analogy that many other themes were also of later institution; and that the whole Empire had originally been divided into a few large districts, from which the elaborate system of seventeen Asiatic and twelve European themes gradually developed.[1]

For this is the conclusion to which we are led by a careful collection of all the passages bearing on the subject in our two chief sources for Roman history from Constans II to Nicephorus I.

The word *theme* meant properly a military division or regiment, and this fact indicates that the geographical themes had a military origin, and that the new division was due at least primarily and partly to needs of warfare. The language of the historians makes this fact plain, and we can trace in their pages the transition from theme in the sense of troops quartered in a particular district to theme in the sense of the district over which the *stratêgos* or military governor presided. But we can also see their origin clearly stamped on the names of the themes themselves; and here we find an important distinction which helps to elucidate the whole subject. A certain number of the thematic names are of military origin, while the rest are purely geographical. Of military origin, for example, was the Opsikian theme, so called because the Opsikion (*obsequium*) or imperial guard was quartered in that district; the Armeniac theme received its appellation from the Armeniakoi, or troops placed to guard the Armenian frontier; whereas Cappadocia, Paphlagonia, Lycandos are geographical names.

Now a study of our historical authorities shows us that the former class of themes are the most ancient, and that themes with names like Cappadocia and Sebasteia were formed long afterwards. Hence we may draw the general conclusion that the thematic system grew gradually and undesignedly out of military necessities, and was not created

[1] In the eleventh century the number of themes had increased to thirty-eight.

suddenly (like the French departments) by the fiat of one Emperor.

But the military necessities which existed in the reigns of Heraclius and his successors are by no means a complete explanation. It seems to me that we shall miss the import of the new provincial system which developed in the seventh and eighth centuries if we fail to recognise that it was really initiated in the sixth century, and that the administrative changes of Justinian were the link between the system of Diocletian and the medieval system. I showed in a former chapter how Justinian's reforms departed from the principles of Diocletian, and anticipated an arrangement which was elaborated in later times.[1] Thus it would be false to consider that the tendency to supersede the hierarchy of officials and abandon the principle of division of labour—in fact, to recur to the system of the imperial provinces under the early Emperors—appeared first in the seventh century; the new departure was really made by the great Justinian. What was the stratêgia (or *praetura*) of Sicily but a theme founded in the sixth century? But the circumstances of the seventh century, the wars with the Persians and the Saracens, favoured the development of this Justinianean novelty and gave it a particular direction. The absence of definite statements in our meagre sources renders it impossible to trace out in detail the course of this development; nevertheless a careful examination of incidental notices may lead us to some important conclusions. We may first see what intimations our authorities, Theophanes and Nicephorus, give us of the existence of themes (or rather *stratêgiai*) in the seventh century; we may then pass on to consider their origin; and finally we may glance, in anticipation, at the development of the system in the eighth century.

I. The earliest definite notice that concerns us is that of the revolt of Saborius or Sapor, the *general* of the *Armeniakoi*, in

---

[1] I had written this chapter long before I read the excellent Russian work of N. Skabalonovitch, entitled "The Byzantine Empire and Church in the Eleventh Century" (*Vizantyskoe Gosudarstvo i Tserkov v xi. Věkě*). I see that he recognises the Justinianean reforms as an anticipation of the themes (p. 185) in his interesting chapter on the thirty-eight themes in the eleventh century.

the last year of Constans.[1] This entitles us to conclude that at that time the provinces of the Empire bordering on Armenia were under the separate government of a general, and the regiments under his command were called Armeniakoi. Two years later we learn that the soldiers "of the theme of the Anatolikoi" went to Chrysopolis and preferred a curiously expressed request to Constantine IV,[2] and twenty years later Leontius was general of the Anatolikoi (690 or 691). These passages prove the existence of an Armeniac and of an Anatolic district, under separate stratêgoi, in the reign of Constans II.

Two other districts, afterwards called themes, seem to have been under the authority of independent military governors in the latter half of the seventh century; they are first mentioned in the reign of Justinian II.[3] That Emperor settled the Slaves "in the parts of Opsikion" in 687-688, an expression which shows that the troops quartered there had already associated their name with the territory. The commander of the Opsikians was not entitled general, but *count*, and the "county" of Opsikion stretched along the Propontis and reached to a considerable distance inland; it included Dorylaeum, near which city the district of the Anatolics began. Moreover, "Hellas" was under the command of a general, for we hear that Leontius was released from prison and appointed stratêgos of Hellas.

There is no direct evidence that the southern coast of Asia Minor, from near Miletus on the west to near Seleucia on the east, constituted in the seventh century a *Cibyraiot theme*. We hear of no stratêgos of the Cibyraiots until the year 731; but, although we hear of no stratêgos, we hear of a *drungarius*. In 697 Apsimar, who became the Emperor Tiberius III, was drungarius of the Cibyraiots.[4] The words of the chroniclers imply that he was especially connected with the people or soldiers of Corycus (Attalia); but it is not clear whether he was subordinate to some one who bore the title stratêgos of the Cibyraiots, or whether he was himself the sole admiral of

---

[1] Theophanes, 6159 A.M. For an earlier mention of the Armeniakoi, see below, p. 347.

[2] *Ib.* 6161 A.M. Theophanes' expression, τοῦ θέματος τῶν Ἀνατολικῶν, hardly proves that the district of the Anatolics was as yet definitely termed a theme.

[3] *Ib.* 6180 A.M. Cf. 6203, 6205 A.M.

[4] *Ib.* 6190 A.M. δρουγγάριον τῶν Κιβυραιωτῶν εἰς Κουρικιῶτας ὑπάρχοντα. Nicephorus, p. 40: στρατοῦ ἄρχοντα τῶν Κουρικιωτῶν τυγχάνοντα τῆς ὑπὸ Κιβυραιωτῶν χώρας.

the Cibyraiots. It is evident, however, that the little maritime town of Cibyra,[1] between Side and Ptolemais, had already given her name to the naval troops of those regions, a distinction such as her greater namesake, the inland Cibyra of Caria, never achieved; and perhaps this distinction was due to some energetic enterprise against a Saracen fleet. The term drungarius[2] was specially applied to admirals and to commanders of the watch.

In the seventh century then it appears that there were at least three administrative divisions in Asia Minor, the Opsikian, the Anatolic, and the Armeniac, subject respectively to a count and two stratêgoi; and probably a fourth, the Cibyraiot drungariate. The question now arises whether there were not also other independent districts, which do not happen to be mentioned because they played no prominent part in the seventh century. Now in 711 we are told that Justinian II collected the Opsikians and *Thracesians,* and of these Thracesians one Christopher was the *turmarch.*[3] The Thracesians were evidently regiments transferred from Thrace to Asia Minor for military service against Persians or Saracens. They were originally one *turma* or division of the troops commanded by the stratêgos of Thrace, but when they were permanently established in Asia Minor they could no longer obey that general and were under the supreme command of their turmarch. This turmarchy some years later was raised to the dignity of a stratêgia, or theme proper. As for the Bucellarian theme, which included the old provinces of Honorias and First Galatia, we hear nothing of the Bukellarioi[4] until the year 765, and I think we shall be safe in attributing the

---

[1] Constantine Porphyrogennetos calls it a contemptible place (εὐτελοῦς καὶ ἀκατονομάστου πολίσματος), and says the name was given to the theme for insult and not for honour, on account of the rebellious nature of the people of the district (*de Them.* vol. iii. pp. 35, 36). Finlay thinks that the imperial writer was mistaken, and that the theme derived its name from the greater Cibyra. But the greater Cibyra did not belong to this theme.

[2] *Drungus,* "a troop of soldiers," is used in Vopiscus' *Life of Probus,* cap. 19. In the *Strategikon* of Maurice (Bk. i. cap. 3, περὶ ὀνομάτων), a δρούγγος is said

to contain three μοῖραι and be equivalent to a μέρος: thus a drungarius would be much the same as a μεράρχης. Epiphanius (I learn from the notes on Maurice) derived δρούγγος from ῥύγχος, a snout.

[3] Theophanes, 6203 A.M. Θρακήσιος is simply formed from Θράκης, the genitive case by the termination ιος.

[4] We find Roman and foreign troops called Bucellarii at the beginning of the fifth century; *see* Olympiodorus, fr. 7, τὸ Βουκελλάριος ὄνομα ἐν ταῖς ἡμέραις Ὀνωρίου ἐφέρετο κατὰ στρατιωτῶν οὐ μόνων Ῥωμαίων ἀλλὰ καὶ Γότθων τινῶν ὡς δ'αὔτως καὶ τὸ φοιδεράτων κατὰ δια-

origin of the theme to Leo III, who, as we shall see hereafter, probably organised a symmetrical system of thematic divisions. Optimaton,[1] "the poorest of the themes," did not perhaps become a theme until a still later period. Paphlagonia, in the eighth century, though perhaps not in the seventh, was a part of the Armeniac district,[2] and Cappadocia was included in the Anatolic. The parts of Cilicia close to the Saracen frontier were presumably governed by one or more cleisurarchs, perhaps responsible to the Anatolic general.

It is possible that there may have existed in the seventh century an anticipation, in some sort, of a theme which did not exist in the days of Constantine Porphyrogennetos, but existed a little later in the days of Basil II. We read that when Heraclius, sailing from Carthage against Phocas, anchored in the Dardanelles, he received some information from a certain functionary called the count of Abydos. It is tempting to think that he may have had control as a governor over the surrounding districts, and that thus the theme of Abydos, which was formed by splitting up the theme of the Aegean Sea, was anticipated.[3] But perhaps it is safer to attribute only financial offices to this Abydene count, and connect him exclusively with the dues[4] which were exacted from merchants entering the Propontis.

φόρου καὶ συμμιγοῦς ἐφέρετο πλήθους. Cf. fr. 11, in which the derivation of the word is given from βουκέλλατον, "stale bread." Optila, the Hunnic assassin of Valentinian III, was a bucellarius of Aetius (Idatius). In the Strategikon of Maurice (Bk. i. cap. i. p. 20) bucellarii and foederati are mentioned as ἄρχοντες, and again (in cap. 9) bucellarii and spatharii are coupled together. It has been suggested to derive the word from bucula, part of a shield.

[1] The origin of the Optimati is also mentioned by Olympiodorus, fr. 9 : τῶν μετὰ Ῥοδογάϊσον Γότθων οἱ κεφαλαιώτατοι ὀπτίματοι ἐκαλοῦντο, εἰς δώδεκα συντείνοντες χιλιάδας, οὓς καταπολεμήσας Στελίχουν Ῥοδογάϊσον προσηταιρίσατο. The origin of the Optimati in the East was presumably of a similar nature ; it is possible that the Goths led captive by Stilicho may have been settled in Bithynia and other parts of Asia Minor. So at least M. Sathas supposes ; but he adopts the erroneous reading of Zosimus, which places the defeat of Radagaisus on the banks of the Danube (Bibliotheca Graeca Medii Aevi, ii. Preface, p. 36). Greeks from the mountainous regions of Taurus were associated with these Optimati as followers (ὑπασπισταί), and called ἁρμάτοι (Maurice, Strategikon, i. 3) ; they bore the same relation to the Optimati as παῖδες to the foederati. Hence the name Gotho-Graeci was applied to the descendants of these strangers, who became gradually Hellenised, while the name Optimati, as Constantine Porph. remarks, became a name of dishonour. The armati assumed the name ἱκανάτοι, and reduced their former masters to the position of servants (Sathas, loc. cit. p. 38).

[2] Maria of Paphlagonia, to whom Constantine VI was betrothed, was ἐκ τῶν Ἀρμενιακῶν (Theoph. 6274 A.M.)

[3] Compare Skabalonovitch, op. cit. p. 205.

[4] Called κωμέρκια Ἀβύδου.

To sum up, our chronicles prove that there existed in Asia Minor in the seventh century two themes or districts under stratêgoi, or governors in whose hands military and civil authority were combined. These were the Armeniac and the Anatolic themes, and both were much larger [1] then than we afterwards find them in the tenth century. Besides these, there was the Opsikian theme governed by a count, who in dignity and power was on a level with the stratêgoi. There were also the drungariate of the Cibyraiots (at least this seems the most probable theory) and the turmarchy of the Thracesians; and these administrations were probably independent, though not equal in dignity to the stratêgiai. Thus practically the Cibyraiot theme and the Thracesian theme existed in the seventh century. In Europe we find two stratêgiai, Thrace and Sicily, dating from the reign of Justinian, and two stratêgiai of later date, Africa [2] and Hellas. The exarchate of Ravenna was similar in nature though different in title; and the praetorian prefect of Illyricum,[3] who still kept state at Thessalonica, was in some sense a military governor, as the defence of the city devolved upon him. We may tabulate then the following list of military districts for the seventh century :—

ASIA.	EUROPE.
1. County of Opsikion.	1. Stratêgia of Thrace.
2. Stratêgia of the Anatolikoi.	2. Stratêgia of Hellas.
3. Stratêgia of the Armeniakoi.	3. Stratêgia of Sicily.
4. Turmarchy of the Thracesians.	4. Stratêgia of Africa.
5. Drungariate of the Cibyraiots.	5. Exarchate of Ravenna.
6 (?). Stratêgia of Coloneia.[4]	6 (?). Prefecture of Illyricum.

But besides these there were possibly other independent governments in Asia Minor which chance has not recorded. Perhaps we may take it for granted that some of the stratêgiai instituted by Justinian had not yet been superseded. The

---

[1] The Anatolic theme included the later themes of Charsianon and Cappadocia, *see* Const. Porphyr. *de Adm. Imperio*, cap. 50.

[2] In the reign of Justinian, Africa was governed by a praetorian prefect and a magister militum, but it was soon changed to a stratêgia or *praetura*. Cf. Nicephorus, p. 3, τῆς στρατηγίδος ἀρχῆς.

[3] We find him in the reign of Constantine IV operating against the Strymonian Slaves, in the *Life of St. Demetrius*. His existence at the end of the eighth century is attested by a letter of Theodore Studita.

[4] I doubtfully include this on my list on account of Theodore, ὁ τῆς Κολωνείας, who played a part at the Byzantine court in the reign of Constans II and his son, as mentioned above, p. 309.

stratêgos of Lycaonia had probably given way before the jurisdiction of the Anatolic general, and it is possible that the
same fate may have befallen the Justinianean praetor of Pisidia.[1]
But the moderator of Helenopontus was perhaps still in existence, and the region of Paphlagonia may not have yet been
incorporated in the Armeniac theme, but may have enjoyed
the rule of an independent stratêgos, as in the sixth century.
The proconsulate of Cappadocia had certainly ceased, and perhaps the proconsulate of Asia; but Asia is still spoken of as a
separate province, though a governor is not mentioned.   It
may also be noticed that there was a stratêgos of the Roman
cities on the coast of Dalmatia,[2] but it is uncertain whether he
was responsible to the exarch of Ravenna or directly to the
Emperor.

II. Though the mist of ages has obscured the actual circumstances which attended the innovations noticed in the
foregoing pages, we can make some attempt at explaining how
they came about.   First of all, I would once more insist that
the beginning of the changes was prior to the seventh century
—that the change really began with the administrative reforms
of Justinian.   In fact, as I said before, Justinian founded the
theme of Sicily and the theme of Thrace, though they were not
then called themes but *stratêgiai*.   The stratêgos or praetor
who governed in Sicily in the sixth century was the forerunner
of the stratêgos who governed there in the eighth century ;
and the son of Artavasdos, who was stratêgos of Thrace in 740,
was the official descendant of the first stratêgos who was appointed by Justinian, when the vicariate was abolished.

I shall begin with the Armeniac theme, because its origin
admits of a simple explanation.   It will be remembered that
Justinian in the early years of his reign instituted a new
military commander, entitled *magister militum per Armeniam*.
The Greek word *stratêlatês* was almost entirely confined to
express the Latin *magister militum*, while the word *stratêgos*,
which in stricter use corresponded to *praetor*, was also employed
as an equivalent for *magister*.   And thus we find John Mystacon (in the reign of Maurice) at one time described as the

[1] We find an Anatolic general active in Pisidia (Theoph. p. 389, ed. de Boor).
[2] *See* above, p. 277.

stratêgos and at another time as the stratêlatês in Armenia.[1] Some years later, when Asia Minor was overrun by the Persians, and the civil authority of the praetorian prefect of the East or of the governors of the Armenian provinces could not be maintained in the constant presence of the foe, it was natural that the general of the Armeniac armies should extend his control to civil matters and act as a provincial governor. The ambiguity of the word "stratêgos" rendered this change easy and natural.   Men were accustomed to the stratêgoi of Paphlagonia, Lycaonia, Sicily, Thrace; and it was not hard to think of the general of Armenia as a stratêgos in the same sense— a military and civil governor.   It is impossible to determine when this change was officially recognised.   In the last Persian campaign of Heraclius we meet one George, a turmarch of the *Armeniakoi*,[2] and I think we may assume that at that time the name Armeniakoi was the ordinary term for the troops under the stratêgos (or magister) of Armenia.

This theory is illustrated by the parallel case of Africa.   A *magister militum* and a praetorian prefect at first coexist ; the prefect soon disappears ; and the *magister* becomes a stratêgos,[3] in the sense which the word bears in the Novels of Justinian.

The origin of the Anatolic theme is susceptible of a similar explanation.   When the Syrian provinces were lost to the Saracens, the troops of the East, who obeyed the *magister militum per orientem*, retired to Asia Minor, and henceforward the energies of that officer were limited to a narrower scope.   For security against the new lords of Syria it was necessary to place the provinces north of the Taurus under military control; the old office of praetorian prefect of the East[4] fell then, if it had not fallen before, into disuse ; and the supreme military commanders became also the supreme civil governors.   This seemed no great innovation, for the stratêgiai instituted by Justinian had accustomed the government to the idea of combining civil and military functions.   And thus the stratêlatês of the East,[5] or, as he was perhaps usually called, stratêgos,

---

[1] Compare Theophanes (ed. de Boor), p. 253, 14, with 266, 21.

[2] *Ib.* 325, 3.

[3] In the West he was generally called the Patrician of Africa.

[4] The last *praefectus praetorio per or.* (ἔπαρχος) of whom we hear is Theodorus in the reign of Phocas (Theoph. p. 295, 5, ed. de Boor).

[5] Cottanas held this post in the reign of Phocas (*ib.* 296, 22). A στρατηλάτης, Ptolemaeus, is mentioned towards the end of Heraclius' reign (*ib.* 340), and Sergius, a στρατηλάτης, is sent

became stratêgos in a new sense, and the ambiguity of the term facilitated the transition. The adjective *anatolic* (eastern) was the word commonly applied to the army of the general of the Anatolê (East),[1] and so, when certain districts in Asia Minor were consigned to the care of that general, they were known as the districts of the Anatolics. This I believe was the origin of the Anatolic theme.

Thus the governors (stratêgoi) of the two most important provinces or themes of Asia in the seventh century, the Anatolic and the Armeniac, were the descendants of *magistri militum*, who had been instituted respectively by Diocletian and Justinian.

Neither the chroniclers nor George of Pisidia give us information as to the divisions of the armies which followed Heraclius to battle. But we hear of the Armeniakoi, and there were of course the Anatolikoi. Distinct from these were the troops from Thrace and the troops from Greece. May we not assume that Heraclius, reviving the classical name of Hellas, called the latter *Helladikoi*, on the analogy of Anatolikoi and Armeniakoi? The soldiers from Thrace, we may argue from the name of the later theme, were known as Thracesians. Besides these, there were the regiments especially attached to the person of the Emperor; they were named in Latin *obsequentes* or *obsequium*, in Greek the *opsikion* or *opsikians*.

We may assume with tolerable certainty that when Syria was lost, these regiments, with the exception of the Helladikoi, were disposed in various parts of Asia Minor. The Helladikoi returned to Greece to defend it against the inroads of the Slaves; the Opsikian regiments were disposed in the regions adjoining the Propontis; the Thracesians, or at least some of them, occupied parts of Lydia and Phrygia; while the central districts of Cappadocia, Galatia, and Phrygia were assigned to the Anatolics. This accords with the statement of Constantine Porphyrogennetos that the themes were formed in the days of Heraclius on account of the Saracen invasions.

The soldiers of Opsikion were often designated as the *peratic themes* ("the themes over the water"); and some of

by the stratêgos of Armenia to the Saracen caliph in the days of Constans; but I question whether στρατηλάτης has its technical sense in the first case, and I am sure it has not in the second.

[1] τῆς ἑῴας and τῆς ἀνατολῆς are used indifferently.

the Asiatic regiments were specially distinguished as the *cavallaric* or cavalry themes.[1]

The question arises whether the new provincial governors were invested with financial as well as with civil and judicial powers in the seventh century. In later times they did not exercise financial functions, which were assigned to special imperial officers, called *prôtonotarioi* or *dioikêtai*; but it is possible that this arrangement was due to Leo III, who paid special attention to the financial administration, and that at first the stratêgoi superintended the collection of tribute. Justinian certainly had in some instances assigned such functions to his praetors, but it is hardly probable that the Emperors, especially the Emperor Constans, would have long left such extensive powers in the hands of their governors without control. I think we may assume that the tribute was levied by officials not formally dependent on the governors, though dependent on their help in case difficulties arose.[2]

III. ADMINISTRATIVE ORGANISATION UNDER LEO III.—As we are discussing the subject of the themes, it will be convenient to anticipate a little and speak of some further changes which were probably made by Leo, the first Isaurian Emperor. Finlay said that the division into themes, which he supposed to have been made by Heraclius, was reorganised by Leo III, but he has not given any proof of his statement.[3] I have shown in what sense the assertion is true that they were established by Heraclius.

Now there are, I believe, sufficiently clear indications that Leo the Isaurian made certain changes in the administrative divisions of the Empire, which entitle him to be considered the first organiser of a regular system of themes. In the year 731 we find the Cibyraiots under the government, not of a

---

[1] Compare Theophanes, 6206, 6263, 6265 A.M. They were τὰ ἔξω καβαλλαρικὰ θέματα, apparently as opposed to "internal" themes or regiments stationed at Byzantium.

[2] Compare Skabalonovitch, *op. cit.* pp. 189, 190, for the relations of the finance officers with the governors of the themes in the eleventh century. I

may notice that Skabalonovitch designates the tendency to centralisation and the organisation of defences against the Saracens as the two principles (one internal and one external) which concurrently determined the institution of the theme system (p. 184).

[3] *History of Greece*, vol. ii. p. 12.

drungarius, but of a stratêgos.[1]   In 740 we find the Thracesians ruled by a stratêgos, no longer by a turmarch.[2]   A Bucellarian theme[3] under a stratêgos is mentioned first in the reign of Constantine V, Leo's son and successor (765-766).   But when we put these data together, we can hardly avoid drawing the conclusion that Leo III introduced a symmetrical system of stratêgiai or themes, (1) by raising the Thracesian subdivision to be a chief division, independent of the Anatolic general; (2) perhaps by giving the name of stratêgos to the Cibyraiot governor,[4] who was independent before, but was hereby raised to equality with the Anatolic and Armeniac stratêgoi; (3) by constituting the Bucellarian theme out of what was before, perhaps, a minor division of the Opsikian.   The result was that the Anatolic theme was curtailed, and though it continued to be highly important, it no longer overshadowed Asia Minor. These new arrangements were doubtless accompanied by a strict definition of subdivisions,—turms and cleisurae.

In Leo's time then, and throughout the eighth century, the Asiatic themes seem to have been[5]:

1. Opsikian.	4. Armeniac.
2. Anatolic.	5. Cibyraiot.
3. Thracesian.	6. Bucellarian.

7. Coloneia (?).

In regard to the European provinces, Thrace, like Sicily, had been a stratêgia since the days of Justinian.   We find Hellas governed by a stratêgos at the end of the seventh century,[6] and although we meet a turmarch of Hellas in 727,[7] there is no reason to suppose that a stratêgia had been changed into a turmarchy. The general of "Hellas," a name which came to be specially used of northern Greece, doubtless administered the affairs of the Peloponnesus[8]; and thus there would naturally be two

---

[1] Theophanes, 6224 A.M., Manes was the stratêgos.   Cf. 6235, 6237, 6263 A.M.

[2] *Ib.* 6233 A.M., Sisinnakios was the stratêgos.   Cf. 6234, 6235, 6251, 6258, 6262, 6265, 6270 A.M.

[3] *Ib.* 6258 A.M.   Cf. 6263, 6270, 6285 A.M.

[4] It is possible, however, that this change may have been of earlier date and carried out by Tiberius III (Apsimar), who was a native of those regions (perhaps of Attalia) and con-

cerned himself with their organisation. *See* below, p. 356.   The district of Cibyra included the island of Rhodes.

[5] Besides these there was the independent catepanate of the Mardaites of Attalia, instituted by Tiberius III, and there were probably several independent cleisurarchies (*e.g.* of Seleucia).

[6] Theophanes, 6187 A.M.

[7] *Ib.* 6219 A.M.

[8] The Peloponnesus is called in Theophanes (6247 A.M.) τὰ κατωτικὰ μέρη.

turmarchies in his district, a turmarchy of Hellas and a turmarchy of the Peloponnesus; if his sway extended to the
Adriatic, there was a third turmarchy—called perhaps Epirus
or Nicopolis. It is impossible to say whether these turmarchies
existed at the end of the seventh century, when Justinian II
appointed Leontius stratêgos, or were established by Leo III.
In any case there is no reason to suppose that those regions
had ceased to constitute a stratêgia in 727. Agallianus, the
turmarch of Hellas in that year, governed the Helladikoi—the
soldiers and people of northern Greece.[1]

It is not clear whether Macedonia constituted a theme at
this time.[2]   The land was inhabited by Slavonic tribes, and it
seems probable that the sway of the praetorian prefect of
Illyricum was practically limited to Thessalonica. We may
perhaps assume doubtfully a theme of Macedonia.

On the whole then I would set down the European themes
in the eighth century as—

1. Thrace.   3. Hellas (including Peloponnesus).
2. Macedonia (?).   4. Sicily (including Calabria and Bruttii).

To these divisions must be added (5) the government of
the islands, which in later times was called a theme; (6) the
exarchate of Italy; and (7) the free state of Cherson.[3]

---

[1] It is as groundless to say of the name Ἑλλαδικοί that it was contemptuous as it would be to say the same of the name Ἀρμενιακοί; cf. my remarks, p. 437.

[2] There was a general of Macedonia in 801-802; cf. Theophanes, 6294 A.M.

[3] The reader may like to have before him the list of themes in the tenth century enumerated by Constantine Porphyrogennetos in his little work on the themes. I. Seventeen Asiatic: 1. Anatolic; 2. Armeniac; 3. Thracesian; 4. Opsikian; 5. Optimaton; 6. Bucellarian; 7. Paphlagonia; 8. Chaldia (about Trapezus); 9. Mesopotamia; 10. Coloneia; 11. Sebasteia (Second Armenia); 12. Lycandos; 13. Cibyraiot; 14. Cyprus; 15. Samos; 16. Aegean; 17. Cappadocia. II. Twelve European: 1. Thrace; 2. Macedonia; 3. Strymon; 4. Thessalonica; 5. Hellas; 6. Peloponnesus; 7. Cephallenia; 8. Nicopolis; 9. Dyrrhachium; 10. Sicily; 11. Longobardia; 12. Cherson.

There is no evidence to prove that the themes of Strymon, Macedonia, Cephallenia, Nicopolis, the Aegean were or were not established in the eighth century. Cephallenia, like Cherson, was used as a place of exile; Apsimar banished Bardanes thither.

CHAPTER XIII

TWENTY YEARS OF ANARCHY [1]

The twenty years which intervened between the banishment of Justinian in 695 and the accession of Leo the Isaurian in 717 witnessed a rapid succession of monarchs, all of whom were violently deposed. Isaurian Leontius was succeeded by Apsimar, who adopted the name Tiberius, and these two reigns occupied the first ten years. Then Justinian returned from exile, recovered the throne, and "furiously raged" for six years (705-711). He was overthrown by Bardanes, who called himself Philippicus; then came Artemius, whose imperial name was Anastasius; and finally the years 716 and 717 saw the fall of Anastasius, the reign and fall of Theodosius, and the accession of Isaurian Leo, whose strong arm guided the Empire from ways of anarchy into a new path. This period may be most conveniently treated by dividing it into three parts. The more orderly reigns of Leontius and Tiberius III we may associate together; the adventures of Justinian and his acts after his restoration stand by themselves; the

[1] Theophanes and Nicephorus, who are still our main, I may say only, sources, record with considerable fulness the revolutions which overthrew successively Justinian, Leontius, Tiberius, Justinian again, Philippicus, Anastasius, and Theodosius in a period of twenty years. Their accounts completely harmonise and are often verbally identical, so that they must have drawn from the same source. What was this source? May I venture to conjecture that the *demes* of Byzantium preserved official records of events in which they were implicated or interested, and that the historians obtained access to these *acta*? This conjecture I would support by the fact that Theophanes derived the celebrated conversation between the Emperor and the Greens in 532 from certain ἄκτα (at least this seems the natural interpretation of the passage). It seems best to suppose that the ἄκτα were preserved in the archives of the demes, who had organised committees and officers; where else would the conversation in question have been preserved? (*See* above, p. 56 note 2.)

reigns of the three subsequent Emperors form the third group.

I. The Leontius whom Verina crowned at Tarsus and Isaurian rebels acknowledged in the fifth century has never been enrolled on the lists of Roman Emperors, and thus the Isaurian Leontius who overthrew the dynasty of Heraclius is the first and only sovereign of his name. He enjoyed power for three years. His reign began auspiciously with a year of peace, but in 697 troubles threatened him from three quarters. Lazica and "Varnucion" revolted under the Patrician Sergius, who magarised or went over to the Arabs; Asia Minor was overrun by a Saracen army; and the same enemy occupied Africa and placed garrisons in the chief towns. The affairs of Africa led in an unforeseen way to the deposition of the Emperor.

Almost due south of Carthage, the city of Kairowan was founded in the reign of Constantine IV by Okba (670)[1]; six years later it was taken by the Christians, then retaken by the Saracens, and taken yet again by the Christians (683), in whose power it remained until it was recovered by Hassan, whom Abd Almalik sent against Africa at the head of a large army (697). Hassan also conquered Carthage and compelled it to receive a garrison. But before the year was over, Leontius sent an efficient general, John the Patrician, in command of the entire Roman fleet, to rescue Africa from the invader. When John reached Carthage he found that the Saracens had secured the entrance to the port by a strong chain. But, bursting through this obstacle, he expelled the garrison from the city; and then freed all the other fortified towns from their Saracen occupants. Thus in a short space of time the Roman dominion was re-established, and the successful general wintered at Carthage, waiting for imperial behests from Constantinople. In the meantime Abd Almalik prepared a larger fleet than he had sent to the western seas before, and early in 698 his armament arrived at Carthage and drove the Roman vessels from the harbour. Seeing that with his present forces he had no reasonable prospect of holding out against a

---

[1] Amari, *Storia dei Musulmani di Sicilia*, i. p. 113. Okba Ibn Nafi was the founder.

Saracen siege, John returned to the East in order to obtain reinforcements. His fleet put in at the island of Crete, which lay directly in his homeward course; and events took place there which proved important to the whole Empire.

The subordinate generals of the various regiments and themes conspired to throw off their allegiance to Leontius, and incited the army to join in the revolt. It is said that they did not wish to return to the Emperor " for fear and shame "; whence we may perhaps conclude that they had in some way thwarted the commander-in-chief and feared the consequences that might ensue if he should complain to the Emperor. The rebels fixed their hopes and favour on Apsimar,[1] the *drungarius* or admiral of the Cibyraiots, as the inhabitants of the coast countries Pisidia and Pamphylia were officially called, and they gave him a new and august name, Tiberius.

Apsimar and his party sailed directly to Constantinople, and anchored at Sycae. For a time Leontius held out, but his enemies succeeded in bribing certain officers who possessed keys of the gates[2] to admit them near the palace of Blachernae. When the soldiers obtained admission they stripped the inhabitants of their goods and plundered their houses. It was an unfortunate year for the citizens of Constantinople. They had hardly recovered from a deadly plague[3] which had ravaged the city for four months, when they were forced to submit to violence and pillage at the hands of the troops who were paid to defend them. We shall see this occurrence repeated before many years have elapsed.

Tiberius III dealt with Leontius even as Leontius had dealt with Justinian. He mutilated his nose, but, instead of banishing him to Cherson, confined him as a monk in the cloister of Dalmatus. The chief supporters of the deposed monarch were flogged and banished. Having established himself securely on the throne, Tiberius took measures for the safety of the provinces of Asia Minor by entrusting his brother Heraclius with the sole command of all the cavalry regiments

---

[1] Apsimar was doubtless a native of those parts. I conjecture from his name that he was originally one of the Gotho-Graeci, for *mar* is the common ending ("prince") which we meet in Teutonic names—Hinkmar, Gelimer, Billimer, etc.

[2] On receiving the keys these warders

were obliged to take a peculiarly solemn oath of fidelity ($\phi\rho\iota\kappa\tau\grave{o}s$ $\acute{o}\rho\kappa os$,—by the holy table).

[3] A plague of the same nature as that which raged in the days of Justinian, the chief symptom being a swelling in the groin.

(*cavallaric* themes), and charging him to provide by careful personal inspection for the efficient defence of the important passes of Cappadocia. For a short time a revolt in Persia and the outbreak of a plague in Syria staved off an invasion ; and in 700 the usual course of events was reversed, and, instead of finding the Saracens invading Romania, we find the Romans overrunning northern Syria. According to the exaggerated accounts of the Greek historians, they killed two hundred thousand Arabs, besides carrying away immense spoil and many captives. In the following year the caliph retaliated, and Mopsuestia was taken and received a garrison of Mohammedans.

This success was followed up by the acquisition of the Fourth Armenia, the province which had been formed by Justinian I. and included the city of Martyropolis and the fort of Kitharizon. The inhabitants revolted from the Romans under a Persian, Baanes, who was nicknamed " Seven Devils." At this time the Romans seem to have frequently employed Persians as governors of frontier provinces.

Armenia was now vacillating between allegiance to the Romans and allegiance to the Saracens, as it had formerly wavered between the Romans and the Persians. In 703 the Armenian rulers rebelled against the Commander of the Faithful and slew the Mohammedans who were residing or sojourning in Armenia. They then sent a request to Tiberius III that he would occupy the country afresh with Roman troops. But the wrath of the caliph was prompter than the succour of the Emperor, and a Saracen general speedily arrived and quelled the insurrection. The Armenian grandees who had been the leaders of the rebellion were assembled by the stratagem of the relentless captain into one place and burned alive.

The loss of the Fourth Armenia and the subjugation of the Romanising party within Armenia itself were perhaps partially compensated for by a great victory which the Emperor's brother Heraclius gained over Saracen invaders in Cilicia, 703 A.D., and by a second great victory which the same general achieved in the following year over another army in the same district.

Amid the details which historians record of the elevations and falls of the Emperors of this period, who appear and vanish so rapidly in scenes of treason and violence, we are apt to lose sight of the steadfast and successful resistance which the Empire never failed to offer to the Saracens. Outlying provinces indeed, like Africa and Sicily, might be doomed to Mohammedan servitude; but ever since the days of Heraclius the main strength of the curtailed Empire was preserved. Had it not been for the able sovereigns and generals of New Rome, the Saracens might have almost, if I may use the word, Islamised Europe.

To Tiberius III we must doubtless attribute the repopulation of Cyprus,[1] whose inhabitants had been transferred to the shores of the Propontis by the policy of Justinian II. Tiberius sent three noble Cyprians, named Phangumes, to the court of Damascus, bearing to the caliph a request that he would allow the Cyprian captives, whom he retained in bondage, to return to their country. The caliph consented, and thus the island was repopulated. Moreover, at the request of the Cyprians,[2] who were much troubled by Saracen pirates, the same Emperor provided for the defence of the island by placing in it garrisons of the Apelatai or Mardaites of Mount Taurus,[3] who were known as *Stratiotai* (Stradioti). The attention of Tiberius, who was perhaps born and reared in Pamphylia, seems to have been specially directed towards the southern coast lands of Asia Minor, and he placed the rest of the Mardaites in the city of Attaleia under a chief of their own, who was called a *catepan*.[4] It is also possible that he organised the Cibyraiot

---

[1] Constantine Porph., who is our authority, attributes this to Justinian II (*de Adm. Imp.* cap. 47), but M. Sathas (*Bib. G. Med. Aev.* Introd. p. 33 *sqq.*) shows that it must be attributed to Tiberius. According to Constantine himself, the repopulation took place seven years after the evacuation, and this at once brings us to 698.

[2] Sathas, *ib.* p. 55. He quotes from Amadi, *Storia di Cipro*, MS. fol. 7: "Questi [the Cyprians] essendo sta infestati da corsari, et ricordandossi che ·per avanti li corsari presero et ruinorono molte fortezze, li parse richeder al Imperatore, che si trovava in Constantinopoli et pregarlo humilmente volesse mandar uno signore con homini d'arme al governo et custodia del paese a spese de essi habitanti; la qual instantia parendo al Imperator justa

et ragionevole, vi mando un capo con molti homini de arme, molte nobil famiglie, et altri Stradioti."

[3] M. Sathas deduces that the Stradioti came from those regions from three circumstances: (1) the preservation of *Apelatic* songs in Cyprus, where they are more abundant than elsewhere; (2) the notice of Cyprian chronographers that Mamas, the patron saint of the *Apelatai*, was transferred from Mount Taurus to Cyprus; (3) the co-operation of the garrisons in Cyprus and the Mardaites in Attalia against the Saracens (Const. Porph. *de. Caer.* i. p. 660).

[4] κατεπάνω; according to M. Sathas, an Apelatic Hellenising of *capitanus*. See Const. Porph. *de Adm. Imp.* cap. 50, where details are recorded of a dispute between a catepan and an imperial *a secretis*.

district and placed it under the command of an independent stratêgos.

The reign of Tiberius III was by no means discreditable as far as foreign politics were concerned, and the silence of historians leads us to conclude that his subjects were not oppressed by heavy burdens. The only act recorded of him which discloses the apprehensiveness of an illegitimate sovereign is the banishment of Philippicus, the son of a patrician, to the island of Cephallenia. Philippicus had dreamed that his head was overshadowed by an eagle,[1] a dream which, according to the convention of necromancy, betokened future empire, and was likely to awaken the fears even of a legitimate Emperor. The fall of Tiberius was brought about by the banished descendant of Heraclius, the Emperor Justinian, and to him we must now return.

II. Cherson, called in earlier times Chersonesus and built not far from the site of the modern Sebastopol, was a flourishing commercial city[2] which maintained down to this late period and still later its old Hellenic traditions and municipal organisation, little affected by the Roman administration, for though it belonged to the Empire it held a unique, almost independent position. This position was secured by the privileges which were granted to the community by Diocletian and Constantine in return for the assistance which the Chersonite soldiers had rendered to the former against the king of Bosporus, to the latter against the Sarmatians and Goths. A golden statue of the great Constantine, his own gift, was placed in the council hall of the city. The prosperous history of this municipality, a strange survival of old Greek life, was occasionally varied by hostilities with the town of Bosporus, situated on the straits which connect the Euxine Sea with Lake Maeotis, and corresponding to the ancient Panticapaeum, while over against it, embayed on the opposite shore, was the city Phanagoria, dependent on the Khazars. We see in the warfare of these cities the relations of old Greek history repeated; we see the rivalry between a city like Athens, wedded to freedom, and a city prone to submit to the thraldom imposed by despots.

---

[1] Compare the story of the eagles floating over the head of Marcian as he slept.

[2] Cherson imported corn, wine, and oil, and exported hides, salt fish, and probably cattle. Compare Finlay, vol. i. p. 402.

Cherson would have fain made Bosporus a free state like unto herself; Bosporus[1] essayed to inoculate Cherson with the disease of tyranny. But the cause of republicanism prevailed, and while Bosporus was made free for a season, though she afterwards returned to her old ways, Cherson successfully escaped the plots that were laid against her constitution by Bosporite intriguers.

Justinian, who had been condemned to live in this remote corner of the Empire, was not overcome by his misfortunes, and did not despair of recovering his throne. Desire of vengeance was a powerful motive for weaving schemes and cherishing hopes. The magistrates of Cherson, aware of his uneasy spirit and his unconcealed designs, deemed it dangerous to have in their state a plotter against the existing government, and determined either themselves to slay him or to send him to Tiberius. Justinian, learning their intentions, fled to a place called Daras (or Doros), close to the territory of the Tetraxite Goths, a people which we met before in the days of the first Justinian. The banished Emperor then communicated with the chagan of the Khazars, and asked him to accord a refuge to a fallen monarch. The chagan was proud to show him every honour, and to give him his sister in marriage; and Justinian and his wife established their abode in Phanagoria. We are told that this princess was called Theodora, but we cannot suppose that this was her original name. It is clear that she adopted the Greek name at the time of her marriage; and I suspect that Justinian selected "Theodora" because the illustrious wife of his renowned namesake Justinian I. bore that name. In other matters also he seems to have copied the example of the same sovereign,[2] and it was perhaps in memory of the great Emperor that he had been baptized Justinian.

The Emperor Tiberius III was soon informed of these events in the Tauric peninsula, and was seized with alarm. He sent an embassy to Khazaria, and promised money to the chagan if he would send him Justinian alive or dead. These offers tempted the cupidity of the barbarian, and he did not

[1] Bosporus was conquered by the Khazars in the sixth century in the reign of Justin II (Menander, *F. H. G.* iv. p. 247), and, although left to manage its own affairs, it continued to be tributary to the chagan.

[2] I have put forward this conjecture above, p. 330.

scruple to betray his august brother-in-law.   He sent a guard
to Justinian on the pretext of protecting him against violence
on the part of the Khazars themselves, and gave secret orders
to Papatzýs, one of his ministers in Phanagoria, and to Balgitzis,
governor of Bosporus, to kill Justinian.   Bosporus stood in
a sort of dependent relation to the Khazars, resembling the
relation of Cherson to the Romans.   Justinian was apprised
of the danger that menaced him by his wife Theodora, to
whom it was revealed by a servant of her brother.   Justinian
sent for Papatzýs, with whom he had been on terms of personal
friendship, and when he was alone with him strangled him
with a cord.   He then requested a private interview with
Balgitzis, and dealt with the governor of Bosporus as he had
dealt with the governor of Phanagoria.   These two feats show
not only the personal strength, but the energy, resources, and
boldness which seem never to have failed this clever and
eccentric prince.   Having sent Theodora back to her brother,
he secretly embarked in a fishing boat which he found on the
shore, and sailed to a place called Symbolum, near Cherson.
He sent one of his few attendants into the city to fetch some
friends or adherents who had remained there.

The vessel bearing back the exiled Augustus sailed along
the northern coast of the Euxine, and somewhere between the
mouths of the Dniestr and the Dniepr it was caught in a
storm.   The crew despaired.   One of his attendants said to
the Emperor, "Lo now, my lord, we perish.   Make a compact
with God for your safety, that, if he restore your sovereignty,
you will take vengeance on none of your enemies."   But
Justinian answered angrily, "If I spare a single one of them,
may God drown me here."   And they came safely forth from
the storm and reached the Danube.   This incident illustrates the temper of Justinian's metal.   If he was not
great enough to grant a general political pardon, oblivious
of personal wrongs, he was not weak enough to sink, in a
moment of superstitious fear, to the tameness of repentance
or forgiveness.   His courage and indomitable spirit did not
desert him in the imminent peril of a shipwreck.

The rescued mariners sailed up the Danube, and Justinian
sent Stephanus, one of his companions, to Terbel, king of
Bulgaria, who, as the city of Peristhlaba had hardly yet been

built, was probably residing in Varna. Stephanus invited Terbel to assist in the restoration of his master to the imperial throne, and promised in return that Justinian would give his daughter[1] in marriage to the Bulgarian monarch, as well as many gifts. Terbel gladly consented to the proposals, and welcomed Justinian with great honour.

These events took place in 704, and Justinian spent the winter with the Bulgarians. In the following year he marched to Constantinople, accompanied by his host Terbel and a large Bulgarian and Slavonic army. For three days they remained outside the walls, attempting to persuade the citizens to declare for the legitimate monarch, but the citizens only insulted them. At the end of three days, however, Justinian with a few soldiers succeeded in gaining an entrance by a conduit somewhere near the palace of Blachernae, in which he took up his abode for a time. The city was won without a struggle,[2] and Terbel returned to his kingdom laden with gifts, among which royal plate is especially mentioned, and honoured with the dignity of Caesar.

The vengeance of Justinian on his enemies was summary and unsparing. Apsimar, or Tiberius, who fled to Apollonias,[3] was captured ; and Leontius, who for seven years past had lived the religious or innocuous life of a recluse, was dragged from his monastery by the sovereign whom he had mutilated and banished. Both the illegitimate but well-meaning monarchs who had ruled the Roman world during the ten years of Justinian's exile were haled in chains through the streets, and exhibited in the hippodrome. Sitting aloft in the cathisma, the restored Emperor presided at the games with his feet resting on his prostrate fettered rivals ; and the facetious populace shouted a verse from the psalms, "Thou hast trodden on the asp and the basilisk ; the lion and the dragon thou hast trampled under foot."[4] When the spectacle was over they

---

[1] Justinian's daughter must have been an infant. We know not the date of his marriage with Theodora or the length of his residence at Phanagoria ; but the existence of this daughter shows that the marriage took place not later than 703.

[2] The actual capture of the city seems not to have taken place until after 1st September, as Theophanes

places his sojourn in Blachernae in 6197 (704-705), but the recovery of the throne (βασιλείαν ἀπολαμβάνει) in 6198. Here Theophanes rectifies the discrepancy between the A.M. and the indictions by spreading the events of one year over two. *See* above, p. 197.

[3] Thracian or Bithynian Apollonia?

[4] The lion (λέοντα) refers to Leontius, while the asp (ἀσπίδα) is a play on

were taken to the Kynegion and decapitated. Heraclius, the able brother of Apsimar, was brought in chains from Thrace and hanged, with all his captains. The Emperor extended his vengeance even to Apsimar's soldiers, but whether we are to interpret literally the statement that they were all put to death is doubtful. The Patriarch Callinicus was deprived of his eyesight and sent to Old Rome, and Cyrus, a monk of Amastrê, was appointed to succeed him. The restoration of the Heraclian house was in fact succeeded by a reign of terror. Men of civil and military distinction were slain in multitudes, and the manners of their destruction were various. Some were invited by the Emperor to a repast,[1] and as they rose at its conclusion were taken to be gibbeted or decapitated; to others he made death bitter[2] by enclosing them in a sack and casting them into the sea.

The second Justinian did not forget the second Theodora. He sent a large fleet to Khazaria to fetch her, but the ships were wrecked on the way, and the loss of life was considerable. The chagan is said to have thereupon sent a message to Justinian: "Fool, should you not have fetched your wife in two or three vessels and not caused the death of so many? Do you expect that you will have to seize her by force? Learn that a son has been born to you. Send and take both her and him." Accordingly the Emperor sent Theophylactus the chamberlain; and Theodora and her son, having arrived safely at Constantinople, were crowned Augusta and Augustus.

The six years of Justinian's second supremacy were inglorious, yet were not marked by any overwhelming loss. He quarrelled with the royal "Caesar," and made an unsuccessful expedition by land and sea against Bulgaria. Anchialus was blockaded and taken, but the cavalry, who formed the most important part of the army at the time, were not sufficiently wary, and as they straggled about in disorder the enemy attacked and routed them. For three days Justinian remained shut up in Anchialus with a remnant of horse-soldiers who had escaped, and then, having ordered all the horses to be

---

*Aps*imar. Basilisk moreover suggests βασιλεύς (emperor). This verse (Psalm xci. 13) is different in our version ("Thou shalt tread upon the lion and adder: the young lion and the dragon

shalt thou trample under feet") and in the Septuagint.   [1] ἀριστόδειπνον.   [2] πικροθανάτους ἐποίει (Theoph. 6198). Justinian was nicknamed *Rhinotmêtos*, "Nose-mutilated."

houghed and so rendered useless to the enemy, he returned by sea to Byzantium.

The town of Tyana, situated on the road that crossed Asia Minor and connected the Propontis with Syria, was lost to the Saracens after a long siege. Justinian sent two generals at the head of an army, consisting of both untrained husbandmen and regular soldiers, to relieve the place. Here again, as in the Bulgarian expedition, want of discipline proved disastrous, and the Romans were routed. Pressed by hunger, Tyana yielded, and the place was left deserted. The inhabitants had stipulated that they should be allowed to settle elsewhere, but the Saracens perfidiously enslaved some and banished the rest to the desert.[1]

The caliphs were beginning to abandon the clement and enlightened policy of Muaviah, in whose reign the Christians had been treated almost as well as if they had lived under a christian government. Abd Almalik imposed a tax called the Haratch, which fell exclusively on Christians and was a heavy burden. This innovation probably induced many Christians to flee to the refuge of the Empire. Valid took the great church of Damascus, which was famous for its splendour, from the Christians, and converted it into a mosque. He also ordained that the State accounts should no longer be kept in Greek.[2] It appears, however, that the Arabians were not good arithmeticians, and they continued to employ Greek notaries.

The fact that the army of relief which Justinian sent to Tyana was largely composed of peasants seems to confirm the statement that he more than decimated the Roman armies in a spirit of improvident revenge. It is plain at least that after the death of Apsimar there was a decline in the military power of the Empire. The years 710 and 711 were marked by Saracen invasions.

Against Cherson, which had cast him out in his adversity, the Emperor was filled with an animosity which assumed the nature of a monomania. He resolved upon the destruction of its inhabitants. In 710 he prepared for this purpose a large

---

[1] Theoph. 6201 A.M.

[2] Theophanes (6199 A.M.) says that Greek characters were still used for numbers, because the Arabs could not express 1 or 2 or 3 or 8½, ἢ τρία, *i.e.* either τὰ τρία, ⅔, or fractions whose denominator is three. This is a curious record of a nation who in later times were famous for mathematics and invented manipulations with zero (*cipher* = Arab. *sifr*, whence Low Latin *zephyrum*, Ital. *zero* for *zefiro*).

fleet, consisting of all kinds of ships,—fast sailers, triremes, immense convoy vessels, fishing smacks, and even small boats (*chelandia*). These were collected and fitted out at the expense of all the inhabitants of Constantinople, including the guilds of artisans[1] as well as the senators. Maurus and Stephanus Asmictus, who were entrusted with the command of this expedition, apparently received orders to slay or send to Constantinople the members of the chief Chersonite families, and to make Helias, a spatharius, governor of the city. The commands were nearly but not entirely obeyed, for the striplings were reserved for slavery. Tudunus the governor and other men of note were sent to Justinian, who tormented some of them by tying them to spits ($\sigma o \acute{v} \beta \lambda a\iota$) and roasting them before a fire ; while he killed others by binding them to small boats, which were filled with stones and sunk in the sea.

But Justinian was by no means satisfied that the youths had been spared, and he issued commands that they should be conveyed to Constantinople. For this purpose an armament set sail from Cherson in October 710, but one of the fatal storms which so often trouble the treacherous Euxine befell it, and seventy-three thousand persons are said to have been drowned. This misfortune delighted the Emperor, who seems to have become really insane. He despatched another fleet to lay the city of Cherson level with the soil and destroy every human being in the place. Helias, the new governor of Cherson, along with the Armenian Bardanes, also called Philippicus, who, having been exiled to Cephallenia by Apsimar and recalled by Justinian, had accompanied the expedition to Cherson, determined to resist the inhuman project, and they sent for aid to the Khazars. The affair assumed the complexion of a revolt, and the army that had been sent to wreak vengeance on the Chersonites declared against Justinian. When that monarch learned the course that things had taken, he attempted to repair his fatal blunder, and despatched to Cherson George Syrus[2] the general logothete, John the prefect of the city, and Christopher a captain[3] of the Thracesian troops, to retract the imperial orders and restore things to their former position, to send apologies to

---

[1] $\sigma \nu \gamma \kappa \lambda \eta \tau \iota \kappa \hat{\omega} \nu$ $\tau \epsilon$ $\kappa a\grave{\iota}$ $\grave{\epsilon} \rho \gamma a \sigma \tau \eta \rho \iota a \kappa \hat{\omega} \nu$ $\kappa a\grave{\iota}$ $\delta \eta \mu o \tau \hat{\omega} \nu$ $\kappa a\grave{\iota}$ $\pi a \nu \tau \grave{o} s$ $\grave{o} \phi \phi \iota \kappa \acute{\iota} o \nu$ (Theoph. 6203 A.M.)

[2] He was a patrician.

[3] $\tau o \nu \rho \mu \acute{a} \rho \chi \eta s$ $\tau \hat{\omega} \nu$ $\Theta \rho a \kappa \eta \sigma \acute{\iota} \omega \nu$ (Theophanes).

the chagan of the Khazars, and to bring to Constantinople the leaders of the revolt, Helias and Bardanes. He sent with them Tudunus, the former governor, and Zoilus, the " first citizen "[1] of Cherson, who had survived the process of roasting at a slow fire ; he expected that their fellow-citizens, on receiving them back, might be ready to surrender Bardanes and Helias.

The rebels received this company into the city. They put the prefect and the logothete immediately to death, and sent their followers to the land of the Khazars, a bourn from which they never returned. The name of Justinian was then publicly cursed[2] in Cherson and the other towns of the peninsula, and Bardanes, under the more classical name Philippicus, was proclaimed Emperor. When the news of this revolution reached Constantinople, Justinian slew the children of Helias in the arms of their mother, and compelled the unfortunate lady to submit to the embraces of a hideous " Indian " (Ethiopian) who enjoyed the privilege of being the imperial cook.

Then for the third time Justinian prepared an armament for the purpose of abolishing Cherson. He placed it under the command of Maurus[3] the Patrician ; he did not forget to provide a battering-ram, a *helepolis*, and other engines for the destruction of fortresses, and he strictly enjoined the captain to spare not a soul in the doomed city, and to keep him (Justinian) constantly informed by letters touching all that happened. Maurus laid siege to the town, and by means of his engines made some impression on the walls and battlements, but the arrival of the Khazars, to whom Philippicus had fled for refuge and succour, put an end to the siege. The army of Maurus, thus foiled and afraid to return unsuccessful, could hardly choose but embrace the cause of Philippicus, who, still uncertain of his prospects, had remained at the chagan's court. The chagan would not surrender the suppliant until he had exacted a promise from the Roman soldiers that they would not injure him, and received a security in money.

As Justinian gained no tidings of prosperity or adversity from Maurus, he suspected treachery, and took measures for the

---

[1] τὸν ἐκ σειρᾶς καὶ γένους ὄντα πρωτοπολίτην (Theoph.)   [2] ἀνέσκαψαν.
[3] Maurus was the name of one of the generals of the first expedition. I presume that he returned in command of

the ships which conveyed Tudunus and the other prisoners to Constantinople, while Stephanus returned with the main armament which was lost at sea. Maurus was nicknamed Bessus.

defence of his throne. He had recourse once more to Terbel, the Bulgarian king, and obtained from him about three thousand soldiers. With these auxiliaries he crossed over to Asia, and along with the Opsikian and some of the Thracesian troops proceeded along the coast to the plain of Damatrys, where he left the main body of the army, and proceeded himself with a small company as far as Sinope, impatient to receive news from the Tauric peninsula. As he anxiously watched the sea, he saw at length the fleet of the rebels making full sail for Constantinople. "Roaring like a lion," as the chronicler says, Justinian hastened back to Damatrys. But meanwhile Philippicus was received in the capital without striking a blow, and took prompt measures to secure his authority. Helias was sent forth against Justinian, and by promising immunity from punishment to the men at Damatrys, he induced the whole army to desert the Emperor, whom he immediately decapitated with his sword.[1] Philippicus sent the spatharius Helias to Old Rome, to display in its streets the head of the fallen Emperor.

Tiberius, the little son of Justinian, who can have been little more than six years old, took refuge under the guidance of his grandmother in the church of the Virgin, near the palace of Blachernae. Maurus the Patrician and Johannes Struthus, a spatharius, were sent to put him to death, that the lineage of Heraclius might be exterminated. They found him clinging with one hand to the leg of the altar; a fragment of the wood of the cross was clasped in the other, and his neck was hung with holy relics. Hard by, outside the precincts of the altar, sat his grandmother Anastasia,—it seems that his mother Theodora was already dead,—and when the officers entered the old lady fell at their feet and begged them to spare the life of the little boy. She clung to her grandson, but Struthus approached and dragged him away, replacing the holy wood on the table and hanging the sacred charms around his own neck. They took the child to the postern gate of Callinice,[2] stripped

---

[1] Barasbakurios (protopatrician and count of Opsikion), who had accompanied Justinian back from Cherson and remained true to him, was also killed. Theophanes rightly records the second and third expeditions to Cherson and the overthrow of Justinian under the year 6203 (= September 710 to September 711); but he also records (by a natural regression) under the same year the first expedition, which must have been sent before September 710.

[2] ἐπὶ τῷ ἄνω τῶν Καλλινίκης παραπορτίῳ, Theoph., and so Nicephorus, in whose text there is some corruption here.

him naked, and, laying him on the lintel of the gate, "cut his throat like a sheep's."[1]   He was buried in the church of SS. Cosmas and Damian,—the last representative of the house of Heraclius.

Before Justinian was banished in 695 he had made an unsuccessful attempt to compel Pope Sergius to accept the acts of the Trullan Synod.   After his restoration he returned to this question again, and sent a copy of the acts to Pope John VII, requesting him to assemble a council for the purpose of considering them.   As John knew that some of the clauses would be inevitably rejected, he refused to undertake the matter from prudence or timidity (706 A.D.)   Justinian summoned John's successor, Constantine, to the East, and received him at Nicomedia with an honour and respect very different from the usual reception accorded to Popes at New Rome.   It seems probable that Constantine may have partly yielded to Justinian's wishes about the synod of 692; certain it is that he returned to Old Rome, having received from the Emperor a confirmation of the privileges of the Roman see.[2]

The city of Ravenna was unfortunate enough to incur the displeasure of the tyrant who so furiously raged against Cherson.   The men of Ravenna had not deemed it necessary to disguise their delight at the dethronement of a prince whose restoration they could not foresee; and they had also ventured to protect Pope Sergius against the violence with which Justinian threatened him.   The Emperor, we are told, bethought himself how he might best take vengeance on the disobedient city of the exarchs.[3]   He despatched a fleet under a certain Theodore, who faithfully executed the imperial mandates.   The nobles and chief men of Ravenna were invited to a banquet

---

[1] δίκην προβάτου (Theoph.), which Nicephorus expresses by ζῴου ἀλόγου δίκην, a phrase which illustrates the origin of ἄλογον ("horse") in medieval and modern Greek.

[2] In the opinion of J. Langen (*Geschichte der römischen Kirche von Leo I. bis Nikolaus I.*, 1885, pp. 598, 599), we may assume that Justinian and the Pope came to an understanding concerning the Trullan Synod, and that Justinian probably yielded to Constantine in regard to (article 36) the primacy of the Roman see.   It is worth noticing

that at this time the bishops of Rome were generally Greeks, and perhaps, as has been suggested, this indicates the influence of the exarchs of Ravenna.

[3] Our authorities for this episode in the history of Ravenna are *Liber Pontificalis, Vita Constantini I.* (Migne, *Patrol.* 128, p. 947), and Agnellus, *Vita Felicis* (Muratori, *S. R. I.* ii. 1, p. 160), where full details are given.   Compare Muratori, *Annali*, iv. pp. 184, 185.   Gibbon does not mention this act of Justinian.

near Classe, where tents were pitched on a meadow of green grass within sight of the Greek ships. The unsuspicious guests were seized, gagged, and thrown into the holds of the vessels, and then the ministers of vengeance set fire to the city. Among those who were taken to New Rome was the archbishop Felix, and, while the other prisoners were cruelly put to death, Justinian in consequence of a dream allowed him to escape with the loss of his eyes.[1] One of the most notable victims was Johannicis, once a secretary at Byzantium, who was crushed to death between two stones.

The most serious single event in the six years' reign of Justinian Rhinotmetos was the destruction of Tyana, but, as we noticed before, this disaster was only a result of the degeneration in discipline and the decrease in numbers of the military forces. The problem which devolved upon a subsequent Emperor to solve was the reorganisation of the army. As to Justinian himself, our narrative has brought out the salient features of his character, in both prosperity and adversity. It is well worthy of notice that no writers allege any charge of sensuality against him, or even hint that his erratic nature transgressed the bounds of conventional morality in the direction of unchastity. The quality of continence seems to have been hereditary in the race of Heraclius.

III. PHILIPPICUS, ANASTASIUS II, AND THEODOSIUS III.— Armenian Philippicus was not the sort of man to heal the diseases of the Empire or to guide it out of the waves of anarchy into secure roads. He was essentially a man of pleasure, who had no sense of the responsibility of his position, and looked on the imperial throne as a personal prize which the occupant for the time was only called upon to enjoy. The unsettled condition of things and the swift succession of Emperors were well calculated to nourish such agreeable and unprincipled notions. It is said, however, that the sentiments which he judiciously expressed in conversation were sound and laudable, and diametrically opposed to his actual behaviour. He spent large sums of money on luxurious indulgences and frivolous amusements; he was unduly addicted to

---

[1]. Felix was consecrated in 708. Philippicus restored to him his confiscated property. He died in 724, and his sarcophagus may be seen in the church of San Apollinare in Classe.

the pleasures of bed and board; and besides all this he was a monothelete.

The first condition of regenerating the Empire was the reorganisation of the army, and this obvious duty was utterly neglected by Philippicus, whose reign of two years was marked by military disasters on the northern as well as on the south-eastern frontier.

Terbel, on the pretext perhaps of avenging his friend Justinian, as Chosroes II in the days of Phocas professed to avenge his friend Maurice, penetrated with his Bulgarians and Slaves through the pass of Phileas into Thrace and marched to the Bosphorus, plundering and slaying as he went. At the straits they found merry parties of rich people preparing to cross over to the Asiatic suburbs, where they were to celebrate a marriage feast and enjoy sumptuous entertainments. These holiday-makers were provided with the various materials required for the festive celebration, including valuable silver plate. The Bulgarians came upon them as they were on the point of cross-ing, and spoiled and massacred them. The suburbs of the capital up to the Golden Gate were plundered, and no opposition was offered to the enemy, who retreated at their leisure, laden with booty and driving droves of cattle.

At the same time Asia Minor was exposed to the usual Mohammedan invasions. Amasea in Pontus and other strong cities in that district were taken in 712, and in the following year Antioch of Pisidia fell into the hands of the foe. The only act attributed to the inactive Emperor is the removal of the Armenians from their own land to the Fourth Armenia and districts in the neighbourhood of Melitene. This shows that the Saracen occupation of that province was only temporary, and that it had been left by them in a depopulated condition, which Philippicus was induced to remedy by new Armenian settlers.

The fact that Philippicus was a heretic was perhaps more fatal to him than his want of energy and his spendthrift ways. He banished the orthodox Patriarch Cyrus to a monastery and appointed John, a monothelete, in his stead. A monotheletic party was organised at Constantinople, consisting of numerous ecclesias-tics and senators, and led by the new Patriarch; Germanus, bishop of Cyzicus, who afterwards became Patriarch; Andrew, bishop of Crete, who was under the jurisdiction of the Pope; Elpidius, a deacon of St. Sophia; Antiochus, keeper of the records; and the quaestor, Nicolaus, who had at one time been a cupbearer,[1] a man profoundly versed in medicine. The acts of the sixth Council were publicly burnt, and the names of the anathematised monotheletes were again inserted in the diptychs. Old Rome declared herself opposed to this heretical policy by hanging a picture of the sixth Council in one of her churches instead of the Emperor's portrait; and there was a popular insurrection, which Pope Constantine could with difficulty quell, against an officer sent thither by Philippicus. It was said that the cause of Philippicus' repudiation of the sixth Council was the fact that a monk had at one time predicted that Bardanes would possess the throne on the condition that he subverted the acts of that synod.[2]

At Whitsuntide in 713 the reign of this sovereign came to a violent end, owing to the hostility which was felt towards him by the military commanders. After the calamitous inroad of the Bulgarians, the Opsikian troops had been stationed in Thrace to defend the passes of Mount Haemus. Their commander, the Patrician George Buraphos, entitled "the Count of Opsikion," and another patrician, Theodore Myacius, conspired to overthrow the government of Philippicus, and they sent Rufus, the protostrator or colonel of Opsikion, along with some soldiers, to accomplish the deed of violence which was necessary for their purpose.

Philippicus had just celebrated the commemoration of the birthday of the city by the usual spectacles in the hippodrome. We are told that on this occasion the Greens were victorious in the contests. He had made his arrangements for Whitsunday; he was to enter the hippodrome to the sound of music, he was to bathe in the public baths of Zeuxippus, and then to breakfast in the palace with "the citizens of ancient family."[3] As he was enjoying a mid-day siesta on the eve of Pentecost, after a morning banquet with his friends, Rufus and the soldiers who had been chosen for the act of treason traversed the rooms of the palace, entered the sacred bedchamber, and, rousing the Emperor from his sleep, hurried him off to the tiring-room

---

[1] ἀπὸ καυκοδιακόνων (Theoph.)
[2] A similar story is told of Leo III, as the reader will learn below.

[3] Theoph. 6205, μετὰ πολιτῶν ἀρχαιογενῶν ἀριστῆσαι.

(*ornatôrion*) of the green faction in the hippodrome.   No one recognised the Emperor, and the conspirators deprived him of eyesight.

The next day was Whitsunday, and when the people were assembled in the church of St. Sophia, Artemius, the chief secretary of the deposed sovereign, was brought in and crowned by the Patriarch under the name of Anastasius.   It is unfortunate that we are not accurately informed of all that happened in the hours that intervened between the seizure of Philippicus and the coronation of Anastasius, but it is evident that the senate and the people united to determine the election[1] of the new Emperor independently of the Opsikian party, who certainly would not have chosen him ; for immediately after his accession he blinded, and banished to Thessalonica, George the count of Opsikion and Theodore Myacius.

The second Anastasius proved himself, on the whole, equal to the emergencies of the time.   He recognised that the pressing necessity was to regenerate the military power of the Empire, and he set himself with diligence to perform the task.   He promoted the most efficient men to the chief command, paying especial attention to the cavalry regiments, which at this period were of greater importance than the infantry.   His practical knowledge of the details of official work, and his general experience as an important minister, fitted the former chief secretary to direct the general administration of the Empire with ability and skill.   If his reign had not been cut short he might have enabled the State to tide over its perilous season and founded a new dynasty, especially as he was an orthodox adherent of the doctrines of the sixth Council.   But unfortunately there was a fatal circumstance connected with his elevation, which caused his fall ; he had ascended the throne, not as the candidate, but as the opponent of the influential Opsikian theme, whose count he had sent into exile.

Anastasius II reversed the ecclesiastical policy of his predecessor.   He deposed the Patriarch John, and translated Germanus, the bishop of Cyzicus, to the see of Constantinople.[2]

---

[1] So Zonaras, Bk. xiv. 25, "The members of the senate and the mass of the people create Artemius the *proto-asecrêtis* Emperor."

[2] 11th August 715. The *citatorium* of translation has been preserved by Theophanes, and may be cited as a specimen of such formulae.   "By the vote and

Germanus is the same man who had been emasculated by Constantine the Fourth and who had supported the monotheletic tendencies of Philippicus; but he suddenly and opportunely returned to the orthodox faith. It is related that John too professed that he had been really orthodox always, and that he had only consented to the heretical measures of Philippicus in order that a real heretic might not be appointed. This laudable " economy," however, did not enable him to retain the chair.

A report reached Byzantium in 714 A.D. that the Saracens were mustering their forces, and preparing for a grand expedition against the Roman Empire both by land and by sea. In consequence of these tidings, Anastasius sent a deputation of senators to Damascus for the nominal purpose of proposing a peace to Valid, but really in order to spy the extent of the Saracen power and to discover what truth was contained in the alarming rumour. The most prominent member of this embassy was Daniel of Sinope, the prefect of the city, who was entrusted with the secret behests of the Emperor. They went and saw and returned with the news that the report was entirely true. Then the Emperor, with a promptitude similar to that which Constantine IV had exhibited on a like occasion, made preparations to withstand a siege. He issued a proclamation that each inhabitant was to provide himself with means to procure sustenance, sufficient to last for three years, and that all who were too poor to compass this were to leave the city instantly. He filled the royal storehouses and granaries with copious supplies of corn, and carefully provided for their security. He renewed the sea walls, which were showing signs of decay, and built new ships to defend the city against attacks on the sea side; while for the protection of the inland fortifications he erected engines of all kinds for hurling darts and stones.

Anastasius, however, was not destined to win the glory of successfully withstanding a Saracen siege. The death of Valid,

approval of the most religious priests and deacons and all the pure (εὐαγοῦς) clergy, and the sacred Senate and the Christ-loving people of this divinely protected and imperial city, the divine grace, which doth at all times tend that which is weak and fill up that which is deficient, translates Germanus, the most holy metropolitan and president of the metropolis of Cyzicus, to be bishop of this divinely protected and imperial city."

who was succeeded by Suleiman, interrupted the course of the preparations; but Suleiman by no means intended to abandon the project, and in 715 news arrived that a fleet of the Saracens of Alexandria had repaired to Phoenicia, in order to hew cypress wood for ships, and increase the power of their navy. The Emperor, who knew the value of promptitude, conceived the idea of attacking the enemy while they were engaged in this occupation. He appointed Rhodes[1] as the place of meeting for the troops whom he destined for the expedition; and he caused the forces of the Opsikian theme to embark in swift vessels and sail thither, whence, united with the other themes under the general command of John, the general logothete, who was an ordained clergyman,[2] they were to proceed to Phoenicia. At Rhodes, John found the commanders of the various regiments filled with zeal for the expedition, and ready to obey his commands; the Opsikians alone were recalcitrant. They renounced allegiance to the Emperor, whom they had never loved, and, disdaining to obey a general logothete, beat John to death with clubs. The collected forces were immediately dispersed, and returned to their various stations, while the rebellious theme proceeded to Constantinople in order to carry their revolt to its natural conclusion. They desired to subvert Anastasius, and gave no thought to the question of a successor; even as they had overthrown Philippicus without a plan or a thought for the future. It is in the conduct of the Opsikian theme that we see the anarchical complexion of the times most clearly reflected. On the way to Constantinople, however, they actually deigned to reflect that it would be well to choose a head for their enterprise, and to put forward a candidate to replace the sovereign whom they had determined to dethrone. Characteristically they chose at haphazard one who could be nothing more than a figure-head. At Adramyttium, on the sea-coast of Mysia, they picked up a stray tax-gatherer named Theodosius, who, if he had no vestige of those qualities which are generally demanded in an Emperor, bore at least an imperial name. His obscure respectability rendered him inoffensive, and if unwillingness to become an

---

[1] The occupation of Rhodes by Muaviah had been only temporary.

[2] He was deacon of St. Sophia, and popularly called Papa Johanácis. Theophanes (ed. de Boor), p. 385.

Emperor is a token of fitness for occupying a throne, Theodosius was certainly worthy, for he fled from the threatened honour and concealed himself in the mountains. He was found, however, and constrained by force to assume the dignities and incur the dangers of a tyrant.

Thus it came about that the ships and engines and fortifications, which Anastasius had prepared to repel assaults of the unbelievers, were applied to the use of defending his government against a refractory division of the army. The Emperor left his most trusted ministers in charge of the city, and, crossing over to Asia, shut himself up in Nicaea. Meanwhile the Opsikian troops which had rebelled at Rhodes had been reinforced by other regiments which belonged to the Opsikian district, and also by the soldiers called Gotho-Graeci.[1] They marched to Chrysopolis (Scutari), and with an armament of merchantmen which they had collected they carried on an ineffectual warfare for six months with the fleet which defended the city. Then Theodosius crossed over and occupied the Thracian districts to the west and north of the city walls. Treachery, like that which delivered Constantinople into the hands of Apsimar and caused the fall of Leontius, now delivered it into the hands of Theodosius, and caused the dethronement of Anastasius. The officers in whose custody were the keys of the gate of Blachernae proved untrue to their trust, like their predecessors, and Theodosius was admitted. At night the Opsikian soldiers and the Gotho-Graeci entered the city and pillaged it, sparing none. Here again was a repetition of the things which had happened when Leontius was deposed by Apsimar.

Theodosius sent the ministers of Anastasius and the Patriarch Germanus to Nicaea to assure the Emperor that further resistance was vain. Anastasius submitted quietly to the will of fate or providence, and was allowed to live as a monk at Thessalonica without undergoing any ill treatment.

The reign of Anastasius was too brief, notwithstanding his honest endeavours, to restore order to the disordered State, or to wipe away the effects of so many years of " tyranny." " The

---

[1] The origin of the *Gotho-Graeci*, Γοτθογραῖκοι, and *Optimati* has been noticed above, p. 344.

affairs of the Empire and the city," says Nicephorus, "were neglected and decaying, civil education was disappearing, and military discipline dissolved." It was a time for the enemies of the Romans to reap a harvest of prisoners and captured cities. Theodosius had good intentions, but was utterly ignorant of politics, and completely incapable of administration; and during the short period to which he gave the name of Theodosius III he is a lay figure, almost forgotten, in the background. We may occupy the space which should have been devoted to the acts or policy of an Emperor with a digression on the adventures of the man who stood in the foreground and was destined to be Theodosius' successor, Leo the Isaurian, general of the Anatolic troops.

According to some, Leo was a native of Germanicia in Commagene, but the more approved account places his origin in the Isaurian mountains.[1] In the first reign of Justinian II his parents emigrated to Mesembria in Thrace by the orders of that monarch, who, it will be remembered, had a passion for transplanting his subjects. When Justinian returned with the Bulgarians to recover his throne, Leo met him on the way with a gift of five hundred sheep, and this mark of attention pleased the Emperor so much that he made Leo a spatharius (aide-de-camp). A malevolent or premature accusation that the spatharius was plotting to ascend the throne himself, while it was triumphantly repelled, and only brought shame upon the accusers, who could not prove their charge, left a rankling suspicion in the heart of the sovereign, who took an early opportunity to despatch Leo on a commission to Alania—a bourn from which he expected that his ambassador would never return. The purpose of his mission was to provoke the Alans to invade and reduce the Abasgi, a people who, once infamous for their trade in emasculated boys, had been reformed, christianised, and reduced to a sort of dependence by Justinian I. The Roman Emperors used to appoint the

---

[1] Theophanes, 6209 A.M., ἐκ τῆς Γερμανικέων καταγόμενος, τῇ ἀληθείᾳ δὲ ἐκ τῆς Ἰσαυρίας, and he is generally known as "the Isaurian." His family was perhaps transferred to Thrace at the time of the dispersion of the Mardaites, and perhaps his father was one of the "Macedonians," as the Drakoi Hellenes or Armatoli of Mount Taurus were called. Cf. Sathas, *Bib. Gr. Med. Aev.* ii. Introd. p. 43. The name *Macedonian* is a relic of the days of Alexander and his successor, and was used in the sense of *noble*: "it survived up to the last century among the mercenary soldiers in Naples and Venice" (*ib.*)

governors of Abasgia, but this relation can hardly have lasted long, as the Empire in the seventh century was beset by too great dangers and difficulties to retain its grasp on this remote country. We may assume that the Abasgi had been practically independent for more than a century when Justinian II conceived the idea of reducing them to subjection; and here, again, I am inclined to suppose that he was consciously imitating his more glorious namesake. The Alans occupied a wild and spacious territory north of the Caucasian range, but they had no access to the Euxine, from which they were shut off by the Abasgi, who lined its eastern shores.

We are fortunate to possess an account of Leo's adventures, risks, and escapes in these barbarous regions, and the record [1] is apparently genuine, and certainly credible, sounding almost like an excerpt from a diary kept by Leo himself.

From Constantinople the ambassador may have proceeded to Trapezus either by land or by sea, and thence he sailed to Phasis, the important seaport of Lazica. In Phasis he stored the sums of money which the Emperor had given him for the execution of his diplomatic mission, and then proceeded to Apsilia with a few natives who knew the topography of the country. He crossed the Caucasus and entered Alania, where he was received with high honour by Itaxes, lord of the Alans, and his proposals were favourably entertained. But in the meantime Justinian, who desired the final disappearance of Leo, had perfidiously caused the money stored in Phasis to be removed, and had permitted the fact to be so generally known that the news thereof reached the adjacent land of Abasgia. Then, as the Alans were preparing to invade and subject Abasgia, the potentate of the Abasgi addressed the potentates of the Alans thus: " Justinian had at his disposal no other such consummate liar, save only this man, to let loose upon us and to excite us against one another. For as to the money which he promised you, he deceived you,[2] for Justinian sent and took it away. But do ye hand him over to us and we will give you 3000 nomismata; and let our love not be dissolved." But to this remonstrance the Alans replied, " We

---

[1] Theophanes, 6209 A.M. He mentions that Saracen influence was already dominant in Abasgia as well as in Iberia and Lazica.

[2] ἡμᾶς in Theophanes, — but it evidently refers to the Alans.

followed his advice, not for the sake of money, but for the love of the Emperor." The lord of the Abasgi sent once more, doubling his offer; and this time the Alans, conceiving a subtle purpose, consented. They had no intention of betraying their friend Leo, but they deemed it an excellent opportunity to spy out the enemy's country. So they said to Leo, "You see, the road to Romania is shut up, and you cannot pass. Wherefore let us deal subtly and pretend to agree to surrender you, and so discover their passes, and plunder and destroy their country, acting thereby to our own advantage."

Accordingly, ambassadors of the Alans went into Abasgia to arrange the compact, and, having received the usual gifts, returned along with a company of Abasgi, who were to pay the stipulated money and to receive Leo in return. The bargain was faithfully carried out, but the Abasgic captors had hardly departed with their prisoner when they were attacked by a band of Alan soldiers, who, as had been preconcerted, rescued Leo and bound his guards. Then the Alans invaded Abasgia with great effect, owing to the knowledge of its topography which they had acquired through the embassy.

When these events came to the ears of Justinian, and he saw that Leo was inviolable among the Alans, he wrote to the Abasgic monarch: "If you allow Leo to pass safely through your country, I shall condone all your errors." The Abasgi, who entertained a salutary fear of the Roman Empire, were delighted, and offered their children as hostages to the Alans that their guest would receive no harm. But the suspicious Leo refused to avail himself of the opportunity, saying, "The Lord can open me a door to go out."

Some time after this (probably in 712)[1] a joint army of Romans and Armenians invaded Lazica and laid siege to Archaeopolis. Hearing that an army of Saracens was approaching, they retired to Phasis, but a division of about two hundred men was left behind in the Caucasian region of Apsilia, whither they had diverged to plunder. Separated from

---

[1] The only expedition to Armenia that we hear of at this time is that sent by Philippicus, 6204 A.M., 712 A.D. This does not indeed accord with Theophanes' statement that Leo after his final escape returned to Justinian, but it does accord with the direct statement of Zonaras that when he returned both Justinian and Philippicus were Emperors of the past and Anastasius was on the throne. If we assume that Leo was sent in 710 (the latest probable date) and returned in 713, he was three years in Alania.

their companions and cut off from the Empire by the Saracens, who had occupied Lazica, they were obliged to remain in the defiles of the Caucasus, living as desperate brigands. The rumour of their presence reached Alania at the other side of the mountains, and it was suggested to Leo that he should embrace the chance and join them. In the month of May, under the guidance of fifty Alans, he crossed the snows of Caucasus with the help of *cyclopodes* or snow-shoes, and was glad after his long expatriation to come among Romans again. But his return was as yet only half accomplished. It was still a difficult problem how he and the two hundred soldiers were to reach Phasis.

In the Caucasian highlands, not far from the place where Leo joined his countrymen, was a fort called Sidêron, which was then held for the Saracens by a governor named Pharasmanios. As Pharasmanios was at peace with the Armenians, Leo ventured to send a messenger to him with this message: " Make peace with me and become a subject of the Romans. Supply us with the means of reaching the sea and crossing to Trapezus." But Pharasmanios rejected the request.

Then Leo placed some of his men [1] in an ambush at night, directing them, when those in the fort issued forth in the morning to work in the fields, to seize as many as possible, or at least prevent their returning to the gates, until he and the rest of his comrades arrived. The plan was carried out successfully, and Pharasmanios was left with a small number in the fort. Leo approached the gates and repeated his proposals, but the governor again refused. The place, however, was too strong to take.

A circumstance now occurred which converted the obstinacy of the governor into a reluctant compliance. When Marinus, the potentate of the Apsilians, an adjacent and subordinate tribe, heard that Leo was besieging Sidêron, he concluded that the Romans must be numerous, and fearing their hostility, he came with a band of three hundred and offered to conduct Leo to the coast. Then Pharasmanios, perceiving the attitude

---

[1] Theophanes says "some of his men and Armenians." It is not clear whether this means that Armenians had subsequently joined the band, or only refers to Armenians who had ori- ginally formed part of the Roman army. Is this fort (Σιδηρόν) the same as the fort of the Misimiani, called Tzachar or Σιδηροῦν ? *See* vol. i. p. 463.

of Marinus, relented and said, " Take my child as a hostage ;
I agree to serve the Empire." Leo received the child, but
insisted that the father should surrender the fort, and gave him
a safe-conduct, promising to enter the gates with not more
than thirty men. The recent adventures of the spatharius had
trained him in the arts of prudence or perfidy, and he issued
secret commands to his troops to burst into the fortress as
soon as the gates were opened. He burned the place to the
ground, and then paid a visit to ·Apsilia, where he was honourably received. Thence he was escorted to the coast and returned to Constantinople, where great changes had taken place
during his absence. Justinian had been deposed, Philippicus
had reigned, and Anastasius was on the throne (713 A.D.) [1]

This Emperor, who sought out men of merit and ability
for military commands, made Leo general of the Anatolic
theme. The Armeniac regiments, which protected the eastern
provinces, were entrusted to Artavasdos. These two generals,
although they stood aloof when the Opsikians deposed
Anastasius, looked with unveiled hostility and cold derision on
the government of Theodosius. The eyes of Asia were fixed on
Leo as the man who, both by his position as the most powerful
general in the Empire and by his natural talents, was the best
qualified candidate for the imperial diadem.

In the meantime the Caliph Suleiman was preparing to
carry out the projected expedition against the Empire. He
sent two armies into Romania, one under his brother Moslemah
and another under a general named Suleiman. The latter,
advancing through the Anatolic districts, approached Amorium,
—the city which in the days of Constans II had been seized
for a short time by the Saracens and soon recaptured. Suleiman
saw that it was insufficiently defended, and perceived at the
same time that Leo, the Anatolic general, was in opposition to
the government of Theodosius. He also discovered that Leo
was regarded as destined to be the next Emperor, and he
argued that it would be a great blow to the Empire to seize
the person of such an able man. For this purpose he resorted
to stratagems, of which details have been preserved.

[1] So Zonaras distinctly states, and it
is otherwise probable (cf. note p. 383),
Bk. xv. cap. 1. If he had returned in
the days of Justinian, as Theophanes
says, surely that monarch would have
dealt stringently with him as a possible rival whom he had already persecuted.

He wrote a letter to Leo to this effect: "We are aware that the Empire of the Romans devolves upon you. Come then to us that we may discuss the conditions of peace." Meanwhile he blockaded Amorium, awaiting the arrival of Moslemah, who was to join him; and as the Saracens approached the walls of the city, they cried out, according to the directions of their general, "Long live the Emperor Leo!" and exhorted the Amorians to take up the cry. Leo, in reply to the letter which he had received, demanded why Amorium was blockaded if the Saracens desired peace. To which Suleiman said, "Come, and I shall retreat."

Thus assured, but still distrustful, Leo approached Amorium with three hundred cavalry. A company of Saracens clad in complete armour advanced to meet him, and encamped about half a mile from their own army. For three days they met daily and discussed the possibility of arranging a peace. Leo was well aware that his enemies were secretly plotting to capture him, while he was himself scheming to save Amorium, which he knew would surrender when Moslemah arrived. In order either to test their intentions or by some means to communicate with the Amorians while the Saracen officers were engaged,[1] he invited the chief men of the Mohammedan army to a banquet, and while they were enjoying themselves a messenger succeeded in conveying to the besieged a secret message: "Fear God and do not betray yourselves, for lo, Moslemah approaches." Meanwhile Suleiman had also determined to take advantage of the banquet for his own purpose, and had commanded three thousand cavalry to encircle the place. As the company sat at table a sentinel entered and informed Leo that the camp was surrounded by horsemen; but a Saracen cavalier named Zuber immediately stepped forward and explained to the astonished general that a slave had run away from their camp with a large sum of money, and that they had mounted horse to catch him. "Do not put yourselves out, gentlemen," said Leo, who understood the art of dissimulation; "in whatever part of our camp he takes refuge, we shall find him."

[1] It is hard to follow the details of Theophanes' narrative, which is not marked by lucidity. It seems plain to me that the communications with the Amorians took place during the protracted banquet. It would be interesting to know whence Theophanes obtained these details. He does not mention whether Suleiman was at the banquet or not.

Before the banquet was ended, Leo contrived to have an interview with the bishop of Amorium, who stole out of the city to his camp and was introduced to a room in his tent. But the Saracen guests discovered that the bishop had paid the general a visit, and indignantly demanded that Leo should give him up to them. Leo gained time by parleying, while attendants disguised the bishop as a woodman or a water-carrier, and sent him from the dangers of the camp to flee to the security of the mountains. Then Leo asseverated that the bishop was not in the camp, and urged the Saracens to search it. This altercation probably led on to a general discussion of differences and grievances, which Leo at last terminated by offering to go to Moslemah and leave the decision to him. The Saracens agreed to the proposal, and he was allowed to leave the camp with a body of two hundred men, on the pretext of hunting. But he soon abandoned the beaten tracks and diverged to the north. When some Saracens, who had accompanied him for the sport, asked him whither he went, he replied that he intended to change the position of his camp "to the meadows."[1] "Your plea is not good," they said, "and we will not go with you."[2] When they had departed Leo remarked to his men, "They have pledged their faith to us, but nevertheless they wished to seize us and thereby to destroy the Christians of Amorium; yet of our men and beasts which we left behind us they have taken none." He then advanced ten miles farther and encamped. Next day he sent the domesticus of his *strators* or harness-corps to Suleiman, bearing a message of reproach for his treacherous intentions.

These details I have thought it worth while to reproduce fully, often almost in the words of the chronicle in which they are preserved, because, while they are to be found in few

[1] εἰς τὰ λιβάδια θέλω μεταπληκεῦσαι.

[2] It would be interesting to know whether all these conversations were conducted by interpreters. One circumstance suggests the possibility that Leo may have known Arabic. If interpreters (Saracens who knew Greek) were present, he could not so easily during the banquet have given secret orders; if he could converse with his guests in Arabic, he could speak to his attendants in Greek without fear of being understood. Of course this assumption is not necessary, but the various machinations which Leo was obliged to carry on during the banquet would have been more easily practicable if interpreters were not present. The fact that afterwards a Saracen caliph made an attempt to convert Leo to Islam may also point in this direction: if Leo knew Arabic, the caliph would have thought him a specially favourable subject.

modern books on the subject, they seem to have been drawn originally from memoirs of some eye-witness, perhaps of Leo himself, or at least to have been related by an eye-witness to some contemporary writer. Though they are sometimes affected with the incoherence of a chronicle, they exhibit the circumstantiality of memoirs.

The Saracen army soon became weary of their leaguer before the walls of Amorium, and showed signs of mutiny. The soldiers wished to plunder the country, and the generals were obliged to yield and raise the siege. When they had retreated, Leo appeared at Amorium, and having removed the women and children and all valuable property, and placed in the city a garrison of eight hundred men under the command of a turmarch, he proceeded southward to Pisidia.

In the meantime Moslemah had crossed the passes and entered Cappadocia, which was then destitute of defenders. Cappadocia was included in the Anatolic district, and Leo apparently had not a sufficient number of troops at his disposal to defend all points. The chief towns were doubtless garrisoned, and some of his troops may have perhaps been in Cilicia or Pisidia acting against the Saracen general Omar, who had invaded those parts. The Cappadocians went forth from their abodes to meet Moslemah, offering him abject submission. But Moslemah, aware (perhaps from letters of Suleiman) of the relations subsisting between the Emperor Theodosius and Leo, and wishing to catch the latter by a bait and " through him subjugate Romania," asked the Cappadocians whether they were subjects of the general Leo, to which question they replied in the affirmative. " Do ye whatever he does ? " " Yes." " Depart then to your fortresses and fear no one," said the generous or wily Saracen, and he commanded his army to abstain from plundering all the regions which were subject to the administration of Leo.

When Leo heard this, and knew that Suleiman had communicated to Moslemah the events of the camp at Amorium, he wrote to Moslemah that he wished to visit him, but that the treacherous attempts of Suleiman had filled him with apprehension and deterred him from going. The following conversation is recorded to have passed between the Saracen general when he received the letter and the messenger who brought it.

Moslemah. " I see your general mocks me, because I wholly abstained from ravaging his provinces."

Messenger. " Not so, but he really means what he says."

Moslemah. " How is Amorium affected towards him ? "

Messenger. " Well, and is loyally subject unto him."

Moslemah (angrily). " Why do you lie ? "

Messenger. " It is as I say. And he has thrown a garrison into it with a turmarch, and driven out the superfluous families." [1]

Moslemah, whose intentions had been to take Amorium in summer, to wait for the fleet and proceed to the coast of Asia Minor [2] for the winter, was much vexed at the news. He sent back a message to Leo, inviting him to come and make peace. Leo calculated that in the course of five days Moslemah would have passed beyond the limits of the Anatolic district, and he shaped his plans accordingly. He sent two consulars [3] to Moslemah with this message : " I received your letter, and accept your offer and shall come to you. But, as you know, I am a general, and must travel with my appurtenances and silver plate and my retinue. Send me then an assurance for the safety of each of them, so that, if things turn out satisfactorily—well, but if not, I may return without injury or despite." The envoys overtook Moslemah at Theodosiana, and obtained from him the required safe-conduct. But his large army, which soon exhausted the supplies of a district, would not permit him to halt anywhere for long ; he was obliged to be constantly moving to new pastures ; and when the envoys had returned to Leo, Moslemah had already reached Acroinon and was beyond the boundaries of the Anatolic provinces (autumn 716).

While Leo was thus baffling the Saracens in Asia, Theodosius was sitting in the palace on the Byzantine acropolis,

---

[1] φαμιλίας, that is women, children, and non-fighting population, for whom the compound plural substantive γυναικόπαιδα was in use.

[2] ἐπὶ τὴν 'Ασίαν κατελθεῖν (Theoph. p. 389, ed. de Boor). 'Ασία, as opposed to Cappadocia and Phrygia, means the western districts of Asia Minor, κατελθεῖν means to go towards the coast.

[3] I thus translate ὑπάτους, which Ducange (*Gloss. Med. Graec.*) renders *viri primarii.* It was an honorary title.

shrinking under the undesired grandeur that had come upon him but could not make him great. He posted his son, whom he had presumably invested with the imperial title, on the Asiatic side of the Propontis, perhaps in command of the Opsikian troops. Having assured himself that Moslemah had evacuated Romania, Leo advanced to Nicomedia and routed the young prince[1]; but this victory did not immediately secure him the crown. He probably spent the winter at Nicaea or at Nicomedia (716-717),[2] and early in the ensuing year was proclaimed Emperor. The immediate cause of the general consent both of the military commanders and of the civil ministers to the elevation of Leo is represented to have been a well-grounded fear, occasioned by the certainty that a vast Saracen armament would in a few months besiege Constantinople, and the consciousness that Theodosius was devoid of the skill required for its defence, and utterly unfit for the duties of a commander. Otherwise they might perhaps have preferred the inoffensive Theodosius, who could never have attempted to strain the imperial authority against the aristocracy. There was a formal meeting of the Patriarch, the senators, and chief officials to choose an Emperor, and they chose Leo, with the knowledge and consent of Theodosius himself, who, we are told expressly, consulted the senate and the Patriarch touching his own resignation.[3] He received an assurance of personal safety, and was permitted to withdraw to a monastic retreat at Ephesus, where he died and was buried. The word ὑγίεια, "health," was the inscription which the third Theodosius wrote for his tomb.

The twenty-one years of anarchy, which happily came to an end by the accession of Leo the Third, were the direct result

---

[1] He was accompanied by "the officials of the palace" and provided with βασιλικὴ ὑπουργία. It is curious that his name is not preserved.

[2] Philippicus was deposed at Whitsuntide 713; Anastasius reigned more than two and less than three years; Theodosius about one year, until the proclamation of Leo, March 717. Theophanes says Philippicus reigned two years and nine months, and Anastasius one year and three months. But here he is not consistent with himself. Anastasius succeeded at Pentecost 713 and reigned till after August 715 (see Theoph. 6207 A.M.); Theophanes relates his fall under 6207, though it is evident that it really took place in 6208, possibly at the end of 715. It is clear that Nicephorus is not accurate in assigning two years to Anastasius (both in his History and in his Chronography).

[3] Combine the statement of Nicephorus, *Brev.* p. 52 (ed. de Boor), with that of Theophanes.

of the long struggle between the Imperium and the aristocracy,[1] which had been going on ever since the death of the great autocrat Justinian, and was itself an offspring of the original dyarchical nature of the Roman Empire. The senatorial classes, who were now chiefly natives of Asia Minor, did not wish to make any fundamental change in the constitution; they only wished to limit the absolutism of the Emperor and to fetter his hands. Their opposition hampered Constans II and Constantine IV (as it had hampered Justin II and Tiberius II), but did not oppress them; they guided the helm with tact and firmness. But Justinian II, like the Emperor Maurice, had little or no tact, and firmness in him was misapplied and impolitic; he strained the bow too tight and it gave way. The executions and long imprisonments of numerous nobles were an apparently drastic but really inept way of crushing the opposition.

Closely combined with this opposition was a spirit of nationality which had been growing up in Asia Minor, and which could not escape the attention of the Emperors. It was perhaps with a view to keeping this spirit in subjection, as well as with a view to defending the Empire against the Saracens, that the country was organised anew into large districts with separate and independent generals. Justinian's system of transplanting human beings was a line of policy partly directed to the same purpose. The importation of Mardaites, Cypriotes, and Slaves might be expected to assist in denationalising Asia Minor, while a stray notice makes us suspect that he also exported inhabitants of those provinces to Europe. The parents of Leo III were transferred from the regions of Mount Taurus to Thrace, and it is highly improbable that this was an individual case. The Isaurians were peculiarly obstinate in clinging to their nationality.

The year 695 was thus a year of triumph for the anti-imperial aristocratic party. The legitimate and autocratic Justinian was deposed, and one of themselves, an Isaurian and former general of the Anatolic theme, was elevated in his stead.

But it is not long before the inherent elements of the situation display themselves. The illusions of the aristocracy

---

[1] Finlay notices this, vol. i. p. 397.

are exposed, its pretensions are shown to imply anarchy by the logic of facts; and the necessity of a real imperial power is demonstrated. At the same time the far-sightedness of the policy of the Heraclian dynasty in their administrative organisation of Asia Minor is clearly shown.

In the first place, the candidate of the party of opposition finds on his elevation that he must desert his old aristocratical principles and become an autocrat, if his administration is to be really efficient and if he is not to be a mere puppet. This was the first proof of the necessity of imperial autocracy under the given conditions. In the second place, the political differences in the Empire, which had not even in Asia Minor the unity produced by a common nationality, exposed an illegitimate Emperor like Leontius to the jealousy and rivalry of sections other than that to which he belonged. Leontius was the representative of the Anatolic districts; the soldiers of other Asiatic districts combined to overthrow him. This want of national unity made the strong hand of a single individual indispensable to maintain the integrity of the Empire. In the third place, unity, integrity, and common action were of vital importance at this time, when the Moslem were threatening Christendom, and it was a lively consciousness of this fact that caused the senators and military commanders to reject the weak and meek Theodosius, whose character ought to have rendered him the ideal Emperor of the refractory aristocracy, and elect the able Isaurian who made the Empire feel the power of a firm will and obey the constraint of a strong hand.

I may notice here the curious resemblance between the state of affairs that lasted for a considerable time in the Frank kingdom and a political phase which appeared for a moment in the Roman Empire. It is well known how the Merovingian monarchs became finally unburdened of all the duties and attributes of royalty except the name, while the real power centred in the mayors of the palace (*majores domus*).[1] And so, just for a moment, at New Rome it appeared possible that Theodosius might have continued to reign in name, and might have been succeeded by a series of inoperative Emperors, while the actual power might have been invested in some

---

[1] The *taikôs* of Japan are an instance of a similar historical phenomenon.

minister, perhaps the *curopalates*, who was the Byzantine analogue of the mayor of the palace. Yet, though this might have appeared possible, it was really impossible. The feeling for the dignity of the imperial throne was too strong to permit of its ever becoming permanently a political non-entity.

While we followed the events which led to the fall of Leontius we had hardly time to realise the fact that Africa had finally passed away from the hands of her Roman rulers and was once more, after a period of nearly eight hundred and fifty years, subject to a Semitic people. It was decreed that Heraclius and his race should see Roman provinces subdued one after another by the enemies of Christendom; but it might seem a slight concession on the part of inexorable fate that the country which had sent a saviour to New Rome in her great need should not be lost by one of his dynasty, but should remain, at least formally, Roman until the last "Scipiad" had fallen. The retreat of the Romans from Africa was the knell of the greatness of Carthage; her history was now over. The consistent policy of the caliphs dethroned the venerable Phoenician city from her position as the capital of Africa, and the circumstance that she had been originally a Semitic, not a Greek or Roman, foundation did not save her from the lot of Alexandria. It was mortifying enough for Antioch and Toledo to behold the exaltation of Damascus and Cordova; but Cordova and Damascus were ancient and famous cities. The mighty capitals of Persia, Egypt, and Africa had to bear the greater indignity of yielding precedence to upstart rivals with strange names—Kufa, Bagdad, Cairo, and Kairowan.

CHAPTER XIV

THE prevalence of superstition and the decay of culture render the seventh century perhaps the darkest age of Europe within historical times; and the contemporary glory of the Arabs makes Christendom seem all the darker. We may first glance at the superstition which prevailed in the Roman Empire, and then consider the decline of culture and the decay of education; after this we may pass to the moral condition of the clergy, and finally notice the rise of the Paulicians.

When I speak of the deplorable extent of superstition, I do not refer primarily to the lower classes of society, among whom it prevails at all ages. The degrading feature of the end of the seventh century, which the Emperors of the eighth century tried so manfully to reform, was the ignorant credulity of the richer classes; and this credulity was generally accompanied by moral obliquity. Men who professed to be educated believed in the most ridiculous miracles; and the law of natural cause and effect, which however inadequately recognised has generally maintained some sort of ascendency in human reason, became at this period practically obsolete. A Patriarch and a Pope believed in the power of painted virgins to heal the sick and maimed, or to exude unearthly balsams; and no hesitation was felt in accepting the legends, that certain pictures regarded with peculiar veneration were, like manna, manufactured in the workshops of heaven. To this subject I shall have occasion to recur when I come to the war that was waged by the Isaurian sovereigns against the adoration of pictures; and there is no clearer and surer proof of the malignancy of this moral pestilence than the fact that Leo III made an attack upon superstition the basis of his policy of reform. The clergy could not guide mankind to a spiritual apprehension of the great doctrines of Christianity, because they had lost that spiritual apprehension themselves ; they taught the worship of dead symbols and the efficacy of the letter; they encouraged the growth of superstition and themselves led lives which Christianity would regard as immoral.

At the appearance of an "iris" in heaven (March 673), we are told that all flesh shuddered and declared that the end of the world was come.[1] Every one believed in the prediction of future events, and the Empire was overrun with impostors, unconscious or deliberate, who gratified the desire of men to believe in supernatural revelations. A monk who dabbled in astrology and a Cappadocian abbot foretold to Leontius the Isaurian his future elevation. Another Cappadocian prophesied to Justinian II his restoration. Philippicus dreamed that he would be Emperor,—his dream, that his head was overshadowed by an eagle, reminds us of the legend of the Emperor Marcian,— and on that account Apsimar banished him. The story of the ass-driver Conon (said to be the original name of Leo III), who resting in the noonday heat under the shade of oaks, hard by a fountain and a chapel of St. Theodore, was accosted by two Jews endowed with magic powers and acquainted with the secrets of futurity, and was apprised by them that he was one day to be the lord of the Roman world, illustrates not only the general credulity, but the superstitious horror with which Jews were regarded at this time by Christians. They were thought to be direct emissaries of the devil.[2] One of the minor aims of the Quinisext Council was to uproot the remains of Jewish perversity, and one of its acts ordains that no Christian is to have any dealings with the Jews, to take unleavened bread, to receive medicine from them, or to bathe with them. One of the measures of Leo III, scarcely in harmony with the

---

[1] Theoph. 6164 A.M. ʼἔφριξε πᾶσα σάρξ, ἐν μηνὶ Μαρτίῳ Δύστρῳ, ὥστε λέγειν πάντας ὅτι συντέλειά ἐστιν. Theophanes obtained this notice from a chronicle which used the Macedonian names of the months. From the same source he received the date of Muaviah's death (6171 A.M. μηνὶ ʼΑρτεμισίῳ ς΄). The

Macedonian months are used in the *Chronicon Paschale* of Alexandria, and it seems probable that Theophanes' source was a continuation of it, now lost.

[2] The same two Jews were said to have wheedled Caliph Yezid I. into adopting iconoclastic measures by promising him a long reign.

legend, was the compulsory conversion of all Hebrews in the Empire.

An incident that took place during the siege of Pergamus by the Arabs in 717 A.D. shows the depths of depravity to which superstition was impelling humanity. The inhabitants of that city, in order to fight with more effect against the besiegers, took a pregnant girl who was approaching the time of her first delivery, and having cut in pieces both her and her unborn infant, boiled the fragments in a pot of water. The soldiers then dipped the gauntlets of their right hands in this concoction, believing that the blows of their weapons would be surer and stronger after the horrible anointment. In spite of these enlightened precautions, Pergamus was taken, but it is characteristic of the age that those who condemned the act ascribed the success of the Saracens to it, and affirmed that the hands of the soldiers were unable to hold a sword on account of the defilement. This incident is worthy to be placed beside the sacrifice of the maid-servant at the tomb of the Empress Eudocia, just one hundred years before.[1]

The tragedy of Pergamus was of course suggested and instigated by one of the numerous soothsayers or hekatontarchs, who infested the Empire and were denunciated by the Quinisext Council. *Hekatontarch* was the name in use for old people who had obtained a reputation for occult lore; perhaps it was so applied in jocular reference to the extreme age of these wizards, just as the word centurion might be used as an intentional "mistake" for centenarian.

The increase of ecclesiastical influence in the Empire is one of the most striking features of the seventh century; and as the dignitaries of the Church readily acquiesced in the growth of superstition, to which they were themselves inclined, the prospect of reform seemed almost hopeless, as it would be necessary to carry it out in spite of the institution with which the spiritual life of the age was interwoven. The Isaurian Emperors in the eighth century undertook the task, but the obloquy which has ever been attached to their names among the orthodox shows how much the undertaking cost them.

We have already met indications of the way in which ecclesiastical influences had penetrated secular and political life,[2]

[1] *See* above, p. 212.   [2] *Ib.* p. 309.

and as an illustration of the same circumstance it may be appropriate to quote the coronation oath, which, we may certainly conclude, was used in the seventh century, if not before.[1] The new Emperor used to recite the oath in the great church of St. Sophia.

The declaration began with the creed, " I believe in one God the Father Almighty, etc.," and then proceeded thus: "Moreover I accept and confess and confirm the apostolic and divine traditions, and the ordinances and formulae of the six ecumenical synods [2] and the occasional local synods; also the privileges and usages of the most Holy Great Church of God. Moreover I confirm and accept all the dogmas that were laid down and sanctified by our most Holy Fathers in various places, rightly and canonically and blamelessly. In the same manner I promise to abide and continually to prove myself a faithful and true servant and son of the Holy Church; moreover to be her defender and champion, and to be kind and humane to my subjects, as is meet and right, and to abstain from bloodshed and mutilations [3] and such like, as far as may be, and to countenance all truth and justice. And whatsoever things the Holy Fathers rejected and anathematised, I do myself also reject and anathematise, and I believe with all my mind and soul and heart in the aforesaid holy symbolum of faith. And all these things I promise to keep before the face of the Holy Catholic and Apostolic Church of God. Dated . . . month, . . . o'clock, . . . indiction, . . . year."

The Emperor handed this document to the Patriarch with the following formula :—

" I, . . . the Roman Emperor and Sovereign faithful in Christ, the God, having signed this with my own hand, do hand it over to my supremely holy lord and ecumenical Patriarch, Sir [4] . . ., and, along with him, to the divine and sacred Synod."

We shall have occasion in another place to notice that the

---

[1] Codinus, *de Offic.* cap. 17, gives it in the form used after 787 A.D., as seven ecumenical synods are mentioned. But there is no reason to suppose that any change was made at the coronation of Nicephorus I. (or of any subsequent Emperor) save the substitution of seven for six. It is possible that the form may be as old as the fifth century, though it seems hardly likely that it was composed for the coronation of Leo I.

[2] I have substituted six for seven, so as to give the form in which the oath was taken by Justinian II.

[3] This clause smacks of the seventh century, and was probably introduced after the dethronement of some cruel Emperor (Justinian II? or perhaps Phocas).　[4] κύρῳ.

Emperor and the Patriarch were regarded as the two pillars of the Roman constitution, and that harmony between them was the essential condition of the prosperity of the Empire.

Sunk though Constantinople was at this period as regards learning and education, it was still the centre of European culture; thither young men still, though not so frequently as in preceding centuries, repaired from western lands to learn Greek and theology. The Empire was generally regarded as the greatest power and the centre of light in Europe; and Pope Agatho, in a letter to Constantine IV (680 A.D.), writes that it was the expressed wish of a synod assembled at Rome that the Empire, wherein is the chair of St. Peter which the other barbarians revere, should for Peter's sake have the primacy over the other peoples. But the diffusion of culture and the interchange of ideas were hindered and rendered difficult by the slowness of communication between East and West.[1] This infrequency of intercourse not only withheld advantages from the West, but reacted unfavourably on the Empire itself. Similar effects were produced by the decrease of communication between the various parts of the Roman dominions in the East. Provinces became isolated, and the better classes of their inhabitants became more and more provincial. At the sixth Council Theodore of Melitene called himself apologetically a provincial, χωρικός; and in fact there was no part of Europe, except perhaps Constantinople, to which the name might not be applied from a wider point of view. Pope Agatho complained that theological study had completely decayed, and indeed become quite impossible in Italy owing to the vicinity of the Lombards. A certain knowledge of Greek, however, was still prevalent; there were Greek monasteries at Rome; and it is probable that while the monotheletic controversy agitated the East many orthodox inhabitants of Thrace and Asia may have betaken themselves to Rome. But there is one point on which it may be well to insist; there must

---

[1] For example, the death of a Pope was not known at Constantinople four months after the event. Pope Donus died on 11th April 678, and the Emperor wrote a letter to him dated 12th August 678. His successor, Agatho, had been elected on 27th June. (*See* Mansi, xi. 195 ; Hefele, *Conciliengeschichte*, iii. 226, 227). At the same time it must be remembered that Mediterranean commerce was almost entirely in the hands of the Greek subjects of the Empire.

have been constant if not considerable intercourse between Italy and Greece, including Macedonia and Thessalonica, during the seventh century and up to the year 733 A.D., inasmuch as the Balkan peninsula, except Thrace, was under the ecclesiastical jurisdiction of the bishops of Rome.

It is a strain on our credulity to accept the remark that in western Europe during the seventh century Greek was studied more in the remote island of Ireland than elsewhere.[1] At Trim, indeed, there was a church called "the church of the Greeks," but we can only smile when we are told by a recent writer that "the Celtic monastery of Bangor became a potent focus of Hellenism." In other countries certainly we meet Greek scholars, such as they were, of more distinction than any Irish monk. Into England a knowledge of Greek was introduced by the great Theodorus of Tarsus,[2] archbishop of Canterbury, and Hadrian, an African abbot. They landed on Saxon shores in the year 669, four years before the birth of Bede. Theodore had studied at Athens ; he was profoundly learned in Greek and Latin literature, secular as well as sacred, and with his companion he formed a school in which the chief subjects were mathematics, astronomy, metrical laws, and church doctrines. Writing sixty years later, Bede, himself a Greek scholar, says, " There live even to-day pupils of these men who know Latin and Greek as their own native tongue. Never were times more happy since the arrival of the Angles in Britain." Letters flourished under the prosperous reign of Ina, king of Wessex, who invited two learned men to come from Athens in order to instruct St. Aldhelm in the Greek tongue. In Spain, Isidorus of Seville is the only

[1] I have consulted on this subject a valuable and convenient little book of seventy pages, in which M. l'abbé Tougard, of Rouen, has collected from the *Patrologia Latina* of Migne the evidences as to the knowledge of Greek in western Europe in the Middle Ages.

[2] Born 602, arrived at Rome 667. The best account of Theodore (for whose activity the *Hist. Ecc.* of Bede is our chief authority) has been written by the (present) bishop of Oxford in the *Dict. of Christ. Biography*. He writes : " It is difficult if not impossible to overstate the debt which England, Europe, and christian civilisation owes [sic] to the work of Theodore. He was the real organiser of the administrative system of the English Church, and in that work laid the foundation of English national unity. He brought the learning and culture of the eastern Empire into the West, and, with the aid of Hadrian and Benedict Biscop, established schools from which the scholars and missionaries of the following century went out to rekindle the light of christian culture in France and the recently converted parts of Germany, and thus, as has been said already, proved a most important link between ancient and modern life."

prominent scholar acquainted with Greek. As for Gaul, a bishop of Rouen mentions certain Greek authors, including Plato, Homer, Menander, and Herodotus,[1] who, he considers, are studied with too much diligence.

To return to the Empire after our digression to western Europe, it is observable that just as the influence of the Church was waxing in the State, so the influence of the monks was waxing in the Church. The monks painted pictures and maintained art, but they also maintained bigotry and superstition, and were the archenemies of spiritual reform. Along with intellectual weakness, dissolute manners also prevailed, and the misdemeanour of ecclesiastics as well as of laymen had become such a public scandal that the express object of the Quinisext Council was to regenerate morality and restore the strictness of the old regulations, which had fallen into abeyance. The acts of this council possess considerable interest, as almost the only extant document bearing on the manners and customs of the age.

It was generally agreed that the church discipline at Constantinople was far milder than the discipline enforced in the Churches which looked up to the bishop of Rome, especially in regard to the restrictions imposed on marriage. The aim of the Quinisext Council was to blend the strictness of Old Rome with the mildness of New Rome. It was enacted that no man could be admitted to an ordination who, after his baptism, had committed the enormity of marrying twice, or of keeping a concubine, or of marrying a woman who suffered from the disadvantage of being a widow, a divorced wife, an adulteress, a slave, or an actress. Of clerical persons, only readers and cantors (members of the choir) are by the new rules allowed to marry; no clergyman is allowed to harbour a woman in his house, and clergymen as well as laymen are forbidden, on pain of deposition from office and excommunication, to have intercourse with consecrated women. The special enactments in regard to all these matters naturally lead us to conclude that the forbidden acts were frequent occurrences in the see of Constantinople.[2]

---

[1] Also Pythagoras, Aristotle, Lysias, Demosthenes, Democritus. At the end of the seventh century St. Arculphus, a French bishop, visited Damascus, Alexandria, and Constantinople; he had a knowledge of Hebrew as well as of Greek.

[2] It is worth noticing that there are

On the same principle we might suppose that the Byzantine Church often blushed for such scandals as clergymen bathing along with women, or even keeping brothels; and doubtless the smuggling of females into male monasteries was no uncommon event. A married man who became a clergyman was not compelled to put away his wife unless he became a bishop; but it appears that at this time bishops were suspected of maintaining conjugal relations with their former wives, for it is ordained that the wife of a newly consecrated bishop must be removed to a *tolerably distant* cloister. Many improprieties of other kinds had also crept in. Some clergymen seem to have been small capitalists and to have lent out money on usury. It was a common event for clerks to sanctify by their presence theatrical spectacles and horse-races; nor did they disdain to witness the licentious amusements and coarse festivities—survivals of paganism—with which marriages were still celebrated, for a significant clause directs clergymen and monks to leave a wedding party when the games begin. Some were indecent enough to lay aside their clerical garb in the privacy of their houses or on a journey. Anchorets or hermits, whom it became to wear their hair short, used with long hair and unsuitable dress to seek the distractions of cities and converse with the "people of the world." It is found necessary by the Trullan Council to lay down strict injunctions that nuns shall not leave their cloisters save with the special permission and benediction of the abbess, and in the company of old sisters; moreover, that they shall in no case spend a night beyond the walls; a similar rule is to apply to monks. It was usual for ladies who were taking the veil to appear at the altar decked out in gold and jewels, and in the presence of a congregation which might divide its admiration between their splendour and their piety, exchange the glittering apparel for a black garment. The prudence of the council directed that this practice, as suggesting that the novices had left the world unwillingly, should be discontinued.

Many ancient customs, relics from the pagan world,[1] still

no clauses against so-called "unnatural crime" in the acts of the Quinisext, whence we might conclude it had become less common than it was in the days of Justinian. A contemporary council at Toledo in Spain found it necessary to legislate against such vices.

[1] The people of Maina in the south

lingered on and offended the stricter members of the Church. Some old feasts were not yet extinct, such as the feast of the kalends, the feasts of Bota in honour of Pan, and Brumalia in honour of Bacchus. Women danced in public; and when men arrayed themselves as women, and women appeared in masculine apparel, it might be thought that sex was indecently confused. The old comic, satyric, and tragic masks were still worn at dramatic representations; mimic performances, accompanied by ballet-dances, were enacted in the old style. At the gathering in of the vintage the god Dionysius was still invoked. Another heathen custom, which had withstood the assaults of time and religion, was that of illuminating fires in front of houses and shops at the time of the new moon and leaping over the flames; the more pious Christians compared such acts to that of the godless Manasses. All these survivals of pagan times were strictly prohibited by the council of 692; in fact, one of the express objects of that assembly was to wipe away any vestiges of paganism that still remained. The use of a pagan oath was forbidden on pain of excommunication. Some superficial forms of superstition are also branded as worthy of punishment. Soothsayers, men who lead round bears and other beasts for show, " to the hurt of simpletons," and sell tufts of their hair as amulets, men who profess to set nativities or work enchantments, are threatened with penalties of considerable severity. Yet notwithstanding this authoritative disapprobation of such occult arts, Emperors and probably Patriarchs believed in the prognostics of soothsayers and astrologers. Another ordinance of the council was that false tales of martyrs should be burned.

From general prohibitions, which do not especially concern the clergy, we cannot draw many conclusions in regard to the morality of the age. In all ages men gamble with dice; in all ages women use medicaments to procure abortion; in all ages women plait and adorn their hair to seduce; in all ages obscene pictures delight the vulgar or the prurient. It is noteworthy that the Quinisext Synod found it necessary to enjoin that copies of the Old or the New Testament, or of the writings of the Fathers, should not be destroyed or cut up, or

of the Peloponnesus were still pagans (Hellenes), and were not converted till the end of the ninth century.

sold to others—for example, to perfumers—for such purposes, except the book were so eaten by moths as to be utterly useless. Other clauses ordained that no tavern, confectioner's shop, or booth should be erected in the immediate vicinity of a place of worship; and that the garrulity of women should cease during the celebration of divine service. Law students were expressly forbidden to adopt any pagan custom, to appear at the theatre, or to wear foreign clothes; it would seem that they affected some outlandish garb—oriental or Slavonic?—just as turbulent youths in the fifth and sixth centuries used to dress themselves like Goths or Huns. I have already mentioned the hostile attitude of the Quinisext Council to Jews.

Whatever may have been the prevailing morality, it must be acknowledged that the Emperors themselves set a good example. The sovereigns of the Heraclian dynasty seem to to have led exceptionally irreproachable, almost severe lives, for even against the unpopular and heterodox Constans and the tyrannical Justinian no charges of sensual extravagance have ever been brought. A heterodox Christian in exalted position, like Constans, must be indeed of stainless character if his orthodox countrymen cast no stones of calumny.

The rise of the Paulician sect in the seventh century is worthy of observation. Its founder was a certain Constantine of Manalis in Commagene (near Samosata), and his doctrine may be described as a *christian dualism*. Trained up in a dualistic faith, which was probably Manichaean, he became acquainted with the New Testament, and conceived the idea of blending the theory of two independent principles with the doctrines of Christianity. His admiration for the apostle Paul led him to adopt the spiritual name of Silvanus, and in 660 A.D. he founded his new community at Cibossa in Armenia. His tenets were not distinguished by the public or the government from those of the Manichaeans, and the laws against Manichaeism were put in force against Paulicianism. Silvanus was executed in 687 by imperial order, but Simeon, who had been sent to carry out the execution, was converted himself, and succeeded Silvanus as the leader of the sect under the name of Titus. The doctrine spread in Asia Minor, and its chief centre was Phanaroea in Helenopontus. Although the doctrine of the Paulicians was a dualism like the doctrine of Manes, there were many differences between the two systems. For example, the creation of the world was attributed by Manes to God, whereas the Paulicians ascribed it to the evil principle, or Demiurge, and drew the corollary that the body was the work of the devil. Their doctrines were expressed in mystical language which would have been appreciated by William Blake.[1]

Like the monophysites, the Paulicians were strongly opposed to the worship of the Mother of Christ, and entertained but small veneration for the cross. For them Mary was merely a human agent and the wood merely a material instrument, and their wisdom or audacity refused to see in either the one or the other any religious value or import. In this spirit they approach the Hussites of Bohemia, the Vaudois of the Alps, and other free religious sects who in later days rebelled against the yoke of the Church. And in fact it may be considered almost certain that the Paulicians of Asia Minor were the forefathers of these heretics who prepared the way for the Reformation. For colonies of Paulicians were settled in Thrace in the eighth century by Constantine V, and in the tenth century by John Tzimiskes. The heresy penetrated into Bulgaria and thence into central Europe. Of the Paulician sects may be mentioned the Bogomiles, the Sclavoni, the Athingani.[2]

The derivation of the doctrines of the Albigenses and the Vaudois from the tenets of the Paulicians is a subject on which much has been written, and the reader will find some interesting pages on the subject in Hallam's *Middle Ages* as well as in Gibbon. But what interests us here is not the later propagation of the doctrines, but the circumstance that the new faith made its appearance not long before the birth of the great iconoclast Leo the Isaurian, whose religious movement was animated in some respects by the same spirit. Notably the opposition to Mariolatry and to undue respect for relics

---

[1] On the Paulicians I have consulted Schmidt's article in Herzog and Pflitt. As an example of their mystical style, the following sentence (from a letter of Sergius) may be quoted: ἡ πρώτη πορνεία ἦν ἐκ τοῦ Ἀδὰμ περικείμεθα εὐεργεσία ἐστίν· ἡ δὲ δευτέρα μείζων πορνεία ἐστὶ περὶ ἧς λέγει· ὁ πορνεύων εἰς τὸ ἴδιον σῶμα ἁμαρτάνει. The *own body* seems to refer to the Paulician sect. For literature on the Paulicians, *see* the excellent article in the *Dict. of Christ. Biography* by Rev. M. B. Cowell.

[2] The connection of *Athingani* (ἀ-θιγγάνειν) with *Tsiganes*, *Zigeuner* ("gypsies") seems improbable.

and symbols was common to the Paulicians and the iconoclasts. The significance of this resemblance appears when we remember that the founder of the Paulician sect was born in Commagene, and that the inaugurator of iconoclasm was, if not born at Germanicia, closely connected with it. Aversion to symbolism and concomitant superstitions seems to have been in the spirit of the sturdy highlanders of the Taurus mountains.

BOOK VI

THE HOUSE OF LEO THE ISAURIA

CHAPTER I

THE REPULSE OF THE SARACENS[1]

On the 25th of March 717 Leo the Isaurian entered Constantinople by the Golden Gate, and rode along the great street which led thence to the acropolis in triumphal procession.

Five months were granted to Leo for organising the Empire and preparing Byzantium to undergo a siege before the arrival of the Saracens on the shores of the Propontis. How far the arrangements which the prudence of Anastasius II had made for meeting an apprehended attack of the unbelievers were still available we are not informed.

With an army of 80,000 men, Moslemah marched across Asia Minor and took the city of Pergamus on his way; he crossed the Hellespont at Abydos, reduced some Thracian forts on the Propontis, and on the 15th of August encamped before the city, which he surrounded with a ditch and a breastwork of huge uncemented stones. Sixteen days later, on the 1st of September,[2] Suleiman arrived with a fleet, consisting of eighteen hundred great warships and fast sailers.

The first object of the admiral was to cut off the city from communication either with the Euxine or with the Propontis

---

[1] Our Greek authorities for the siege are Theophanes, 6209, 6210 A.M., and Nicephorus (ed. de Boor), pp. 52-55. For the Saracen account I have, as usual, depended on Weil (*Geschichte der Chalifen*, i. 565 *sqq.*) For the period comprised in this Book, Finlay (*History of Greece*, vol. ii.) is extremely valuable; he sympathises throughout with the Isaurian Emperors. Schlosser's work, *Geschichte der bilderstürmenden Kaiser des oströmischen Reichs*, is still worth consulting. Maimbourg's *L'histoire des iconoclastes* has a psychological interest as an essay in bigotry.

[2] The Arabic writers place the siege a year earlier, 716-717. Theophanes describes the siege under 6209 A.M. = 716-717; because the siege began in August, he is led to anticipate the events of the following (first) indiction. Theoph. calls Suleiman the πρωτοσύμβουλος.

and Aegean. Accordingly, having remained quiet for a space of two days between Magnaura and Kyklobios,[1] he took advantage of an opportune south wind, and while one division of his squadron sailed to places on the Asiatic shore, named after Eutropius and Anthemius, which commanded the southern entry to the Bosphorus, other ships steered northward to occupy the entrance to the Euxine from the castle of Galata to the extremity of the straits. The weighty ships of burden, defended each by 100 soldiers, sailed in the rear of the line; unwieldy by the freight which they carried, and obliged to steer against the current, they progressed slowly. The watchful eyes of Leo, who perhaps stood on the Pharos in the palace observing the operations of the enemy, perceived the situation. He caused ships which were in readiness to be launched, and, going on board himself, burned twenty of the transport vessels with the redoubtable marine or " Roman " fire. This success encouraged the citizens, and filled the enemy with terror of "the very drastic operation of the moist fire."[2]   On that same night the Emperor caused the chain which closed the Golden Horn to be removed with pretended secrecy, and the Saracens, supposing that some cunning snare was being prepared, avoided the place and moored in the haven of Sosthenion, or at the islands called " Sharp " and " Flat."[3]

A long and unusually severe winter was passed by the army and navy of the Arabs in a dreary blockade. The fall of snow was so great and the frost lasted so long that the solid earth was not seen for a hundred days, and many men and other animals perished. It was the besiegers and not the besieged who suffered from these inclemencies ; the Byzantines were more accustomed than natives of Syria, Egypt, or Arabia to cold and frost, and were better provided with means to defy them. The death of the admiral Suleiman [4] was another misfortune for the Saracens. But with spring new hope and new reinforcements came. Sophiam, with a great armament and

[1] According to Theophanes, Magnaura was west of the city, on the Propontis (353, 27, ed. de Boor), while Kyklobios was a promontory (*ib.*) close to the Golden Gate, with a round castle, Strongylon Kastellion (448, 18).

[2] τὴν τοῦ ὑγροῦ πυρὸς ἐγνωκότες δραστικωτάτην ἐνέργειαν (Theoph.) Nice-

phorus (not Theophanes) mentions the number of ships burnt (p. 53).

[3] ἕτεραι δὲ μέχρι τῆς 'Οξείας καὶ Πλατείας νήσου λαυρίζουσαι ἀπηνέχθησαν (Theoph.) τῷ λιμένι τῷ καλουμένῳ Σωσθενίῳ (Nic.) λαυρίζω doubtless means to rush violently, as though it were λαβρίζω from λάβρος.

[4] On 8th October (Theoph.)

supplies of food and arms, was sent from Egypt; and his arrival was soon followed by that of Yezid with a large number of transports from Africa. These transports, afraid to approach the Bosphorus on account of the deadly "Roman fire," moored at Satyrus, Bryas, and Kartalimen, harbours on the Bithynian coast.

Both the fleet of Sophiam, which drew up at Kalos Agros, "Fair Farm," in the Bosphorus, and the fleet of Yezid contained many Egyptian Christians. By a previously concerted agreement these men, who liked not their Mohammedan lords, detached on a certain night little boats[1] from the ships and rowed to the city, shouting "Long live the Emperor!" The information which these deserters supplied to Leo was doubtless useful. He straightway sent vessels, fitted with the various appliances[2] for hurling Roman fire, to consume the transport ships, and the fire-vessels triumphantly returned laden with booty. It must be assumed that they only burned a few ships, and that the crews of the rest fled or surrendered. This important success, so discouraging to the Saracens, could not have been obtained so easily and so soon but for the desertion of the Egyptian Greeks, whose natural instinct led them to take the right side on one of the most critical occasions for the decision of the greatest question of history.

The besiegers were not only assisted by the reinforcements of men and provisions sent over seas; they were also supported by an army under Merdasan, who, entering Asia Minor by the Cilician gates, traversed Cappadocia and Phrygia by the well-known routes and arrived in the neighbourhood of Nicomedia and Nicaea. Hovering on the coast of the Bosphorus and the Propontis,—the peratic coast, as it was called by the Byzantines, —he was able to prevent Roman boats, sent across the straits, from obtaining supplies. But the army of Merdasan was as luckless as the armament of Sophiam. It was surprised by foot-soldiers under the command of some Roman officers, who concealed themselves "like Mardaites" in an ambush, and, falling suddenly upon the Saracens, cut many to pieces and utterly routed the rest. Thus the peratic coast was made free for the Byzantine boats (*chelandia*); and the fishes which

---

[1] τοὺς τῶν κατηνῶν σανδάλους (Theophanes). σανδάλους is explained by Ni- cephorus' less colloquial λέμβους (p. 54).

[2] σίφωνας πυρσοφόρους (Theoph.)

they caught, along with those taken by nets or rods suspended from the walls or on the adjacent islets, kept the city adequately provisioned. In the meantime famine prevailed among the Arab hosts, and became so terrible that, according to the probably exaggerated account of a Greek historian, they were obliged to feed on a pulp, which they cooked in ovens, consisting of the flesh of dead men mingled with their own excrement. This deadly substitute for nutrition produced a plague, which increased the misery and the death rate.

The final blow to this unfortunate expedition was struck by the Bulgarians,[1] who came from the north and slew, it is said, twenty-two thousand Saracens. It is interesting to see the not yet slavised and not yet christianised Bulgarians, who led however many Slaves to war, fighting for Christendom at this great crisis against the Mohammedan Arabs. They knew not then that the nation which they were organising would in future days have to struggle long for freedom against the yet more barbarous Mohammedan Turks.

On the 15th of August 718 A.D., after a siege of just twelve months,[2] the remnant of the Saracen expedition, despairing of a cause which the skill and fortune of their enemies had baffled, and which nature herself seemed to have condemned, departed on their homeward journey. But even then they had not been sufficiently discomfited. The land forces reached Syria in safety, but the fleet met with calamities similar to those which befell the squadron that had besieged New Rome in the reign of Constantine IV. Before the ships had passed through the Dardanelles a tempest scattered them; but this was little compared with the storm of thunder and lightning (" burning hail ") which caught them in the Aegean and destroyed all save ten vessels. Of these ten, five were captured by the Romans and five returned to tell the story in Syria.[3]

Regarding this terrible discomfiture of the archenemies of

---

[1] This is mentioned by the Mohammedan historians, who call the Bulgarians *Burdyan*. They called the Slavonic lands north-west and west of Byzantium *Sakalibe*. See Weil, i. 569.

[2] The exact date, 15th August 717 to 15th August 718, looks suspicious, and the statement of Nicephorus that the siege lasted thirteen months increases our doubts (p. 53). As Nicephorus fixes 15th August as the end of the siege, he must have thought it began on 15th July.

[3] Of an army of 180,000, only 30,000 (land army) returned, according to Arab sources. Paul the Deacon, the Lombard historian, makes the number of those who died 300,000 ! By the time numbers reached Italy, they were beyond recognition.

Christendom, and essentially, if not superficially, of civilisation, we cannot doubt that Theophanes the chronicler, in his pious reflections on the supernatural protection of the christian Empire, merely repeated the feelings, not only of Roman, but of European Christians. At this time New Rome, not Old Rome, was the great bulwark of christian Europe, and if New Rome had fallen it might have gone hard with the civilised world. The year 718 A.D. is really an ecumenical date, of far greater importance than such a date as 338 B.C. when Greece succumbed to Macedon on the field of Chaeronea, and of equal importance with such dates as 332 B.C. when an oriental empire fell, or 451 A.D. which marked the repulse of the Huns. The expedition which Muaviah had sent against Constantinople nearly fifty years before was not so tremendous or so formidable, for neither was it conceived on such a great scale, nor was the Saracen empire in the days of the fourth Constantine so extensive and powerful as in the days of the third Leo. The expedition led by Moslemah was, we may say, the great culmination of Omeyyad ambition; from this time forward the Omeyyad dynasty declined in the East, and the caliphs little thought that a recent conquest in the extreme West was destined to be the sole possession of their posterity at a period not far distant.

Asia Minor, however, during the eighth century was as much exposed as ever to the inroads of the Moslem, who entered by the Cilician gates and plundered in one year Cappadocia, in another year "Asia" or Opsikion. For six or seven years indeed after the calamity of the great expedition of 718, Romania had rest. The Caliph Hischam, who succeeded to the throne in 724, devoted his attention to erecting palaces, constructing roads, aqueducts, and gardens, and improving the internal condition of his empire. But in 726 the invasions began again, and were repeated almost every year during Leo's reign under the generals Suleiman and Muaviah.[1] Caesarea in Cappadocia was taken, Nicaea was hard pressed. A general decline in agriculture was the inevitable result of such conditions.

---

[1] In 726 and 730 Cappadocia was invaded, and in 732 the enemy advanced as far as Paphlagonia; in 727 Nicaea was besieged; in 734 and 737 "Asia" was invaded; in 736 and 738 "Romania" was attacked, without specification of parts.

In the last year of Leo (739)[1] the Saracens undertook an expedition on a larger scale than usual. An army was collected numbering 90,000 men, and placed under the command of four generals. One of these proceeded with 10,000 to the western part of the Taurus peninsula and plundered in "Asia"; Suleiman, with 60,000, confined himself to the districts of Cappadocia; while the other two generals, Malik and Sid Albattal, at the head of 20,000 cavalry, advanced in a north-westerly direction through the Anatolic theme. At Acroinon, a place south of Dorylaeum and near the frontiers of the Opsikian and Anatolic districts, the Emperor Leo and his son Constantine joined battle and completely defeated the Saracens. The battle of Acroinon is especially famous, because Abd Allah Albattal, said to be the prototype of the hero of the Spanish legends of the Cid, perished on the field, and his grave is still shown. The other division of the Mohammedan army, which plundered the Aegean coast and Cappadocia, returned to Syria in safety with numerous captives.

We need not pursue all the details of the hostilities between the Empire and the caliphate in the reign of Constantine V, Leo's son and successor. On the whole, the Empire was successful. The Cibyraiot fleet baffled an attempt of the Saracens in 746 to take possession of the island of Cyprus, which had been reconquered, we know not at what time, by the Romans since the days of Justinian II. The Saracen fleet was utterly destroyed. Constantine had invaded Commagene and northern Syria in the preceding year, taking advantage of the civil wars which convulsed the caliphate, and had captured the reputed birthplace of his father, Germanicia, whose inhabitants,[2] chiefly Syrian monophysites, he transferred to Byzantium and other places in Thrace, where they could be recognised sixty years later by their heretical religious opinions. In 751 he took Melitene and Theodosiopolis, and carried away prisoners from Armenia. The domestic struggles of the Saracens and their wars with the Turks prevented them from

---

[1] The Mohammedan authorities place the expedition in 739, thus supporting the revision of the chronology of the period which I have adopted. Cf. Weil, i. 638.

[2] Theophanes states that Constantine found kinsfolk of his mother in Germanicia and settled them in Byzantium (6237 A.M.) If Leo's wife was a native of Germanicia, the statement that Leo "the Isaurian" was born there may be explained.

attacking Romania with serious effect, but Germanicia and Melitene were recovered some years afterwards, and on two occasions defeats were inflicted on Byzantine armies.[1] It may be noticed that the practice of interchanging captives began to become usual at this time, and thus, as Finlay remarks, the commercial view of prisoners as saleable articles introduced humanity into the usages of war.

In the year 750 Damascus was taken by the Abbasids [2]; the last Omeyyad caliph, Mervan II, fled to Egypt and was there slain in a church; and Abd Allah, called Al Saffah ("the Bloodshedder"), became the Commander of the Faithful. This change of dynasty led to the formation of two rival Saracen powers; for after a struggle in Spain the power there remained with the Omeyyad faction, and the Omeyyad emirs of Cordova, though they did not at first assume the title of caliph, asserted and maintained complete independence of the caliphs of the East.[3]

---

[1] In 759 Paul, the general of the Armeniakoi, was defeated near the Melas. In 771 the cavalry themes were routed at Isaurian Syke, which was besieged by a Saracen army and by a fleet. The Anatolic, Armeniac, Bucellarian, and Cibyraiot forces had been united against the foe. In 772 the Saracens carried off 5000 captives, but were defeated by the Mopsuestians, who surprised them as they were returning.

[2] Abbas was the uncle of Mohammed.

[3] At the beginning of the eighth century some expeditions were undertaken by the Saracens against Sicily, but they were of no importance; see Amari, *Storia dei Musulmani di Sicilia,* i. cap. vii.

THE mere elevation of Leo did not immediately quench the embers of anarchy, although it allayed the flames, and, as soon as the danger from the Mohammedans had passed by, uneasy spirits formed a conspiracy against the man who had delivered them from jeopardy. Anastasius, or, to give him once more his private name, Artemius, who was living at Thessalonica, still nourished hopes of regaining, as Justinian had regained, the throne from which he had fallen, and for this purpose he entered into communications with several important ministers who were not loyally disposed to the new aristocratic government. Sisinnius Rendaces, a patrician who had been sent to Bulgaria by Leo to negotiate an alliance against the Saracens, promised the ex-Emperor to induce the Bulgarian monarch Terbel to undertake his cause. Isoes the count of Opsikion, Theoctistus the chief secretary of state, Nicetas Xylinites the *magister officiorum*, and Nicetas Anthrax, the commissioner of the fortifications, secretly favoured the pretensions of Artemius, who had also the support of the archbishop of Thessalonica. The treason was disclosed to Leo in good time, and he promptly seized those conspirators who were at Byzantium. Theoctistus and Xylinites were decapitated; others were mutilated and banished.

Meanwhile the persuasions of Sisinnius had been effective with the Bulgarians, and Artemius, accompanied by the arch-

---

[1] Our main authorities are still Nicephorus and Theophanes, except for the legal reforms, which have come down to us in the original *Ecloga*. For the *Ecloga*, Zachariä's *Geschichte des griechisch-römischen Rechts* (ed. 2, 1877) is invaluable.

bishop and Sisinnius with a Bulgarian army, was advancing to Heraclea, while rough Slavonic sea crafts coasted along beside them. But the inhabitants of Byzantium had not forgotten who had saved them from the jaws of the infidel, and when the Bulgarians discovered that the popular feeling for Leo was pronounced and unmistakable, they hearkened to that monarch's proposals and surrendered the pretender whom they had come to support. Leo executed Artemius and the archbishop of Thessalonica in the Kynegion; as for Sisinnius, the Bulgarians had sent his head to the Emperor, presumably because he was too brave to allow himself to be taken alive. Horse-races were celebrated in the hippodrome in honour of the suppression of the conspiracy, and the heads of the rebels were exposed on poles.

While Leo punished his adversaries he rewarded his supporters. To Artavasdos,[1] the general of the Armeniac district, who had supported him against Theodosius, he gave his daughter Anna in marriage and made him general of the Opsikian theme. The fruit of this marriage was two sons, who also obtained distinguished posts while they were still young. Nicephorus, the elder, received a high command on the Thracian frontier, and Nicetas was made general of the Armeniacs.

The joy of Leo at the discomfiture of the Saracens was increased by the birth of a son. The boy was baptized by the Patriarch Germanus under the name of Constantine; his mother Maria was crowned Augusta at the same time in the chamber of Augusteus, and the new Empress did not forget to distribute the "consular donation" (25th December 718).[2] Almost a year and a half later (25th March 720), just after the suppression of Artemius' conspiracy, the young Constantine was crowned Emperor by the Patriarch Germanus in the tribunal of the Nineteen Accubiti.[3]   At the age of fourteen or fifteen (732) Constantine was betrothed to Irene, the daughter of the khan of the Khazars, who were generally on friendly

---

[1] 'Αρταύασδος (Theoph. ed. de Boor), 'Αρτάβαςος (Niceph.)

[2] The MSS. of Theoph. have 'Οκτωβρίου, but M. de Boor is doubtless right in emending Δεκεμβρίου, after Anastasius. Maria scattered the donation, ὑπατεία, from the church to the gate Chalke. Theophanes, perhaps in his youth, heard a description of the ceremonies from the mouths of old men.

[3] Theoph. 6212 A.M. (=719-720), Niceph. p. 57. M. Paspatis (*op. cit.* p. 227 *sqq.*) has essayed to determine the position in the palace of the chamber known as τὸ τριβουνάλιον τῶν ιθ' ἀκουβίτων (said by Codinus to have been built by Constantine I.)   He places it in the palace of Daphne, north of the Octagon.

terms with the Roman Empire and on hostile terms with the Saracen caliphate.[1] This was the second time that a Khazar princess became a Roman Empress.

Besides the conspiracy of Artemius, a revolt in Sicily troubled the peace of Leo. Sergius, the general of that province, threw off his allegiance and caused one of his staff, Basil, son of Gregory Onomagulus, to be saluted Emperor under the title of Tiberius. This happened while the Saracens were besieging Constantinople; the western provinces deemed it a good opportunity to rebel against the government. Leo appointed Paul the Patrician, on whose loyalty and military skill he could rely, stratêgos of Sicily, and sent him to quell the revolt, supplying him with letters to the governors of the western parts and a *sacra* or imperial manifesto to the army. The soldiers returned to their allegiance immediately, Sergius fled to the duchy of Beneventum,[2] and the heads of Basil and the other chief conspirators were sent, swathed in cloth or linen,[3] to Leo.

Thus, about four years after his accession, having won immortal fame by repelling the great expedition of the enemies of Europe, having quelled conspiracies in the East and in the West, having begotten a son to succeed him, Leo might feel himself secure on his throne, and begin to address himself to the great work of his life.

This work was no less than the regeneration of the Roman Empire. While the twenty years of anarchy, from a political point of view, represent the culmination of the struggle between the autocratic and aristocratic elements in the State; from spiritual, social, and moral points of view they represent a low stage in a long decline. These years were the darkest point of the dark ages in southern Europe. As we already observed, society was sunk in ignorance, and the surest sign of this ignorance was the gross superstition that prevailed. There was a dearth of writers; no books were written, except perhaps tracts on the monotheletic controversy.[4] Education,

---

[1] For example, in 728 the Khazars invaded Media and Armenia, annihilated a Saracen army, and thoroughly frightened Islam.

[2] Afterwards, despairing of his safety, he gave himself up to Paul, on condition that his life should be spared.

[3] φουσκιάσας (Theoph.)

[4] I must, however, limit this statement by mentioning that the Chronicle of John Malalas of Antioch, preserved in an imperfect state, was perhaps

affected with the deadly disease of superstition, must have been in a sorry condition. The law schools had degenerated, and with them the knowledge of jurisprudence. This circumstance directly affected the administration of justice and undermined the very foundations of society.

What gave the reforming spirit of Leo its peculiar complexion was the fact that he did not content himself with renovating each branch of the administration separately, but attempted to cut away the root of the evil. He improved the discipline and efficiency of the army, he restored the majesty of law and justice, he reformed the police control, and he attended assiduously to the financial and commercial interests of the Empire; but he did much more than this. He essayed to eradicate the prevailing superstition by the iconoclastic policy, which has made him so famous or notorious; and, even if he failed and the Empire could not endure to have such a vital sore removed, the results show that a new spirit of order and improvement was breathed into Roman society. An account of his iconoclastic measures will be given in another chapter, and we shall now proceed to consider his secular reforms, of which we have but scanty records. Such departments of history as this are neglected by monastic chroniclers; and unfortunately the Isaurian Emperors were regarded with such hatred by their successors on account of their religious policy that none of their laws were incorporated in the great ninth-century Code of Basil I. and Leo VI.

Roman law, like the Latin language, was no longer understood in the Empire, which was tending more and more to become entirely Greek, now that it had lost Syria in the south, Africa in the west, and the northern provinces of the Haemus peninsula. Thus the nominal law of the Empire was practically in abeyance in the provinces, and while

composed about this time. It. is a work, however, that will not redeem the age from the charge of ignorance and superstition. The date of John Malalas is a well-known *crux historica*. The circumstance that Malalas is referred to in the third oration against Iconoclasm of John of Damascus fixes a posterior limit; while a passage in the Chronicle about the Bulgarians has been adduced as internal evidence that it was composed after 680, the date of the foundation of the Bulgarian kingdom (ed. Bonn, p. 97); *see* Sotiriadis, *Johannes von Antiochia*, p. 105. Malalas (like George Hamartolus) had the honour of being translated into Old Bulgarian, probably by the Presbyter Gregory in the reign of the great Tsar Simeon. For this translation, *see* Haupt, *Ueber die altslavische Uebersetzung des Joh. Mal.* Hermes xv.

on the one hand old local customs superseded the forgotten law, on the other hand a wide room was left for the good pleasure or arbitrary opinion of judges, uncontrolled by a written, accessible, and intelligible code. If the judges had been a class of lawyers independent of the civil administration, their ignorance might not have been so fatal to justice and equity, although there was still the certain danger that fear or bribery would often corrupt them. But, as the provincial governors were often the judges, and cases were constantly occurring in which the interests of the governor or his friends were at stake, there was no guarantee for the distribution of justice when the written laws were inaccessible and therefore practically obsolete.

Leo met the imperative need of his subjects by preparing a handbook in Greek for popular use, containing a short compendium of the most important laws on the chief relations of life. It was entitled an *Ecloga*,[1] and was not published until the last year of Leo's reign (740), but doubtless several years were spent on its preparation, which involved long preliminary studies. The preface shows the spirit in which it was undertaken; and I may quote parts of this proem as an original document illustrating the intellectual atmosphere of the eighth century.

"The Lord and Maker of the universe, our God, who created man and granted him the privilege of free will (αὐτεξουσιότης), and gave unto him a law (in the words of prophecy) to help him, made known thereby all things which ought to be done by him and all things which ought not to be done: to the intent that he should aim at the former as things that provide salvation,[2] and avoid the latter as things that

---

[1] The full title is—"A compendious selection (*ecloga*) of the laws, made by the wise Emperors Leo and Constantine, from the Institutes and the Digesta and the Codex and the Novels of the great Justinian; and an improvement thereof in the direction of humanity (εἰς τὸ φιλανθρωπότερον); edited in the month of March, ninth indiction, year of the world 6248." It is fortunate that this encheiridion, as it is sometimes called, has survived in spite of the bigoted endeavours of later Emperors to destroy every monument of the activity of the great iconoclasts. It was published by Leunclavius in the 2d vol. of his *Juris Graeco-Romani*, etc., but has been more recently published and thoroughly commented on by Zachariä. Bishop Stubbs remarks (*Constitutional History of England*, i. p. 214), "The very fact of the issue of a code illustrates the progress of legislative power in assimilating old customs or enacting provisions of general authority." The Ecloga is not a code so much as a handbook; but it marks a crisis in the Empire, as a legislator's recognition of altered conditions.

[2] πρόξενα σωτηρίας — as it were, official entertainers of salvation.

cause punishment.   And not one of those who keep His commandments or who—save the mark !—disregard His statutes,
shall fail to receive the appropriate recompense for his deeds.
For it was God who declared both these things aforetime ; and
the power of His words, charged with immutability and meting
to the work of each man its deserts, shall not (in the words of
the Gospel) pass away. . . .

"Whence, busied with such cares, and watching with sleepless mind the discovery of those things which please God and
are conducive to the public interests, preferring Justice to all
things terrestrial, as the provider of things celestial and as
being, by the power of Him who is worshipped in her, sharper
than any sword against foes ; knowing, moreover, that the
laws enacted by previous Emperors have been written in many
books, and being aware that the sense thereof is to some
difficult to understand, to others absolutely unintelligible, and
especially to those who do not reside in this our imperial city,
protected of God ; we have called Nicetas, the most illustrious
Patrician, our quaestor, and the most illustrious Patricians
Nicetas and Marinus, and our most illustrious consulars and
comptrollers (ἀντιγραφεῖς), and others who have the fear of
God, and we have ordered that all their books should be
collected in our palace.[1]   And having examined all with careful attention, going through both the contents of those books
and our own new enactments, we considered it right that the
decisions in many cases and the laws of contract and the
respective penalties of crimes should be repeated more lucidly
and minutely, in order to a eusynoptic knowledge of the force
of such pious laws and to facility in deciding matters clearly,
and to a just prosecution of the guilty, and to the restraint
and correction of those who have a natural propensity to evil-
doing.

"But those who have been appointed to administer the law,
we do exhort and command to abstain from all human passions ; and from a sound understanding to bring forth the
sentences of true justice, and neither to despise the poor nor
to permit a powerful transgressor to go unconvicted. . . .

---

[1] Many of these books were doubtless records of precedents and customs.
The Ecloga probably contains little new
legislation, and the appendices to it
(military, agricultural, and maritime),
to be spoken of hereafter, are merely
registers of customs.

"Let those, and those only, who participate in sense and reason and know clearly what true justice is, exercise straight vision in their judgments and without passion assign to each his deserts. For so also our Lord Jesus Christ, the power and wisdom of God, giveth unto them far more abundantly the knowledge of justice and revealeth those things that are hard to discover, who also made Solomon truly wise, when he sought out justice, and granted him the privilege of successfully hitting the mark in the sentence pronounced to the two women in the matter of the child. . . .

" It is just to abstain from all taking of presents. For it has been written, ' Woe unto them who justify the unrighteous for the sake of gifts and declining the paths of the humble take away from him the right of the just man. Their root will be as ash and their flower will come up as dust, because they did not wish to fulfil the law of the Lord.' Presents and gifts blind the eyes of the wise. Therefore, being solicitous to put an end to such wicked gain, we have determined to provide from our Patrimony (σακέλλιον) salaries for the most illustrious quaestor, for the comptrollers, and for all the officials employed in administering justice, to the intent that they may receive nothing whatever from any person whatever who is tried before them ; in order that what is said by the prophet may not be fulfilled in us, ' he sold justice for money,' and that we may not incur the indignation of God, as transgressors of his commandments."

This preface shows clearly the decline that had taken place both in legal knowledge and in the administration of justice, and also the earnest purpose of reform that animated Leo. But what especially strikes one who is accustomed to the language of Gaius or Tribonian is the ecclesiastical note which characterises both the preface and other parts of the Ecloga. The point of view of the old Roman jurists had been almost completely lost, and the spirit of Roman law had been transformed in the religious atmosphere of Christendom.[1] Men tried now to base jurisprudence on revelation, and to justify laws by verses of scripture. The judgment of Solomon became a sort of commonplace which pious lawyers quoted for

---

[1] The christian point of view is of course often manifested in the consti- tutions of Justinian, but not as affecting legal principles.

edification; while in the proceedings of law courts the venerable and mystic Romans, Titus and Seius, were deposed in favour of the scriptural worthies Peter and Paul. As a further illustration of this change we may note that, in the first title of the treatise which is before us, law is defined to be "the discovery of God" as well as a political or social compact. In the second title, where the duties and functions of the Emperor are set forth, it is explained that it devolves upon him to maintain (1) all things laid down in scripture, (2) all the enactments of the seven holy synods, (3) the Roman laws. It is stated moreover to be highly important that he should hold correct theological opinions, and the orthodox doctrine is defined.

All this harmonises with the general theory of the constitution of the Empire, which is enunciated in terms that expressly affirm the preponderance of the ecclesiastical element. The constitution of the State is compared to the organism of a man (in the third title), and the Emperor and the Patriarch are declared to be the two chief parts. Consequently, as the well-being of a body depends on the unison of the chief organs, the peace and happiness, both bodily and ghostly, of the subjects depend on the union and harmony of the Patriarch and the Emperor.[1] In point of fact, though not in name, the Roman Empire of Leo III, or the Eastern Roman Empire of Basil I., was as much a *Holy* Roman Empire as the Western Empire of the Othos.

The Ecloga gives a short account of the duties of the Emperor himself, of the Patriarch, of the prefect of the city, of the quaestor, and of the provincial governors, and supplies us here with some interesting information.[2] The true aim of the Emperor is stated to be the conferring of benefits, while his special objects are (1) to preserve the strength which his Empire has, (2) to recover lost dominions by sleepless care, (3) to make fresh acquisitions by wisdom and just triumphs. In interpreting the laws he must regard the custom of the State as a clue, and if he errs, should err on the side of clemency.

---

[1] Nevertheless the Emperor, not the Patriarch, is the representative of St. Peter in the East, as the Pope is in the West; and this apostolic mission is alluded to in the Preface to the Ecloga thus: God "has ordered us to feed his flock, like Peter the chief of the apostles." It will be seen below, cap. iv., that Pope Gregory II recognised this position of the Emperor.

[2] In cap. xiii. below, this information will be utilised.

From the functions of the various members of the imperial government the treatise passes first to personal law, then to obligations and actions, and finally to public law (criminal and military). Thus *real* law is almost entirely omitted, and even the important subject of *servitudes* is not mentioned; whence it is evident that in this department it was considered expedient to allow local customs to continue.

The great interest of the Ecloga is the clear view which it gives us of the tendencies of Roman law as they developed under the christian influences of the Middle Ages without reference to past legislation. This medieval development was cut short in the ninth century by the return to Justinianean law, which was inaugurated by the first Basil and carried out by the sixth Leo.[1] It is especially instructive to compare the Ecloga with the Code of Justinian on the subject of marriage and divorce. The influence of Christianity on the legal conception of the conjugal relation was, as Zachariä remarks, small up to the time of Justinian; and it was the Isaurian Emperors who really introduced a christian legislation on the subject.[2] The following points are worthy of note: (1) Justinian permitted concubinage, while Leo and Constantine ordained that every concubine was to be considered a wife. (2) The Ecloga sternly institutes punishments for fornication, which the laxer law of earlier days had regarded as a venial immorality, to be dealt with by the Church. (3) The Ecloga required the consent of both parents to the marriage of their child, while the older law recognised only the father. In this point Basil returned to the rule of Justinian. (4) The marriage of Christians with Jews had been forbidden by Justinian, but not the marriage of Christians with heretics. The Ecloga assumes the latter

---

[1] Zachariä von Lingenthal (*Gesch. des gr.-röm. Rechts*, Preface, p. v.) observes the analogy in the development of private law between the East and the West. "Auch bei den Byzantinern lässt sich eine mittelalterliche Rechtsbildung (im vii. bis ix. Jahrhundert) unterscheiden, welche durch die Restauration des Justinianeischen Rechts wie später im Abendlande durch die Reception desselben unterbrochen und durchkreuzt wird." On the other hand, in regard to constitutional law there is not an analogy but a contrast; western kings and princes have very limited sovereign rights at first, but gradually win full rights, whereas the eastern Emperor starts with full power, which becomes gradually reduced. There is also an obvious difference in the relations of State and Church. The contrast between the practical legislation of the iconoclasts and the anachronistic resuscitation of traditions by the Macedonian Emperors is neatly put by Skabalonovitch, *Vizantyskoe Gosudarstvo*, p. 241.

[2] Zachariä, *ib.* p. 37.

relation, which had been condemned by the Quinisext Council, to be illegal. (5) The Ecloga forbade the marriage of cousins to the sixth or even seventh degree.[1] In regard to divorce, the contrast of the earlier and the later legislation is striking.[2] The general principle of Justinian and his lawyers was that all contracts and agreements made by men are dissoluble by the consent of both parties; and an arrangement *ne liceat divertere* was invalid. Hence divorces could take place by private agreement without the intervention of a court. But instead of the secular and rational principle underlying the legislation of Justinian, the Ecloga adopts the religious principle that man and wife are one flesh, and refuses to permit divorce except in four cases, namely: (1) if the wife commit adultery, (2) if the husband be proved to be impotent, (3) if either spouse circulate calumnies which endanger the life of the other, (4) if either spouse be afflicted with leprosy. It appears that adultery on the part of the husband was not a valid cause for divorce. Many avoided this stringent law by acting as sponsors to their own children and thus incapacitating themselves from further intercourse with their spouses, but in the year 780 Leo IV strictly forbade this artifice for annulling the marriage bond. In the Basilica, however, the older and laxer law is restored. In regard to a third marriage, the Ecloga affects to regard such an act as inconceivable, and it was definitely forbidden by Irene in 800.[3]

The *patria potestas* is another matter in which the Justinianean and Isaurian attitudes notably differ. Long before Justinian, the power of the father over the person and property of his children had been growing weaker; it had become easy to obtain emancipation; and practically, though not theoretically, the maternal had become equal to the paternal influence in guiding the life of the son. But here Justinian preserved the letter of the old law and did not bring the theory into accord with practice; the father still retains his old rights over his

[1] It may be noted that the Ecloga enacted that the marriage contract should be regularly written δι' ἐγγράφου προικῴου συμβολαίου; only in case of poverty it might be made δι' εὐλογίας(benediction) or ἐπὶ φίλων (Zachariä, *Gesch. des gr.-röm. Rechts*, p. 51). The word εὐλογία came to mean the marriage ceremony.

[2] Zachariä, *ib.* p. 55 *sqq.*
[3] In regard to the common property of married people (the *dos* and the *propter nuptias donatio*), the Ecloga gives more rights in case of one survivor than the Codex. Here again we see the principle of the *unity* of the spouses (*ib.* p. 67).

son's person and property; and the son is only permitted to have the independent disposal of his *castrense peculium*. The Ecloga here adapts the law to the fact and sets aside the old Roman conception of the *patria potestas*. Equal duties or rights are assigned to both the mother and the father, and thus as long as either parent is alive no guardian[1] is requisite. The personal consequences of the *patria potestas* disappear, and though the management of the son's property is still in the hands of the parents, this is considered not so much a legal right as a parental care for the interests of the children.

The publication of the Ecloga was accompanied by three special codes embodying and sanctioning the customs which regulated military, agricultural, and maritime affairs. The Maritime Code (Νόμος Ναυτικός), known as the Rhodian laws, Rhodes having been in old days a centre of ocean traffic, shows us that in the eighth century mercantile trade by sea was carried on by companies.[2]   The Mediterranean was infested by Slavonic and Saracen pirates, and sea commerce was so dangerous that merchants and skippers could not undertake it except on condition that the risk should be common. Thus the Isaurian Emperors lay down the law that in case of ship or cargo being injured by an accident for which no one can be blamed, the loss is to be borne jointly by the skipper, the owner of the freight, and the travellers.[3]

The Agricultural Code (Νόμος Γεωργικός)[4] leads us to consider the important question as to the changes which had taken place in the agricultural population and in the institution of serfdom since the fifth century. A great but silent revolution had been accomplished in the intervening ages, so gradual that it has been left unnoticed by the writers whose works have come down to us, but deducible with absolute certainty from a comparison of the legislation of the eighth with the legislation of the fourth, fifth, and sixth centuries. The institution of the

---

[1] The Isaurian Emperors adapted the principle of guardianship to ecclesiastical institutions, for in case the parents made no arrangement before death the care of the children was to be entrusted to some religious house such as an ὀρφανοτροφεῖον. Here the Basilica returned to the law of Justinian (Zachariä, *Gesch. des gr.-röm. Rechts*, p. 100). It may be further noted that in the Ecloga the old distinction of *hereditas* and *bonorum possessio* disappears (*ib.* p. 165).

[2] *Ib.* p. 294.

[3] *Ib.* p. 295. These subsidiary codes, if they were not issued contemporaneously with the Ecloga, certainly appeared soon after it.

[4] It was a system of police regulations for the country (*ib.* p. 234 *sqq.*)

colonate has been slowly undermined, and by the age of the iconoclasts has completely disappeared; in the Agricultural Code there is no mention of the *adscripticii*[1]; and we find no cultivators fastened to the soil by the chains of law. Peasants of two kinds are mentioned, and both classes are in every sense free. There are (1) peasants who are allowed by a proprietor[2] to settle on his land and cultivate it, but they can leave it when they like, though they are obliged to compensate the proprietor for any loss accruing to him from their untimely departure. As rent for the land these tenants paid the landlord a tithe of the produce ($\mu o \rho \tau \acute{\eta}$),[3] and hence they were called $\mu o \rho \tau \acute{\iota} \tau a \iota$. There are (2) free communes of peasants, who possess land in common, which they divide among the members. Each member ($\kappa o \iota \nu \omega \nu \acute{o} s$) farms the land either himself or with the help of slaves; or even rents it or part of it to some other person on condition of receiving a percentage of the profits.

When we proceed to inquire how this change[4] in the economical condition of the provinces came about, and how serfdom disappeared, we are reduced to speculation. It is clear that the explanation of these facts must lie partly in changes in the national character and partly in the external history of the Empire. Now a great change had taken place in the population, both in the European and in the Asiatic provinces, since the middle of the sixth century. The north-western regions of Asia Minor as well as the Balkan peninsula had been filled with Slavonic settlers; while the other provinces of Asia— Syria had been lost—were colonised by the free Mardaites and in the east by Armenians. The new settlers were not accustomed to the colonate and the system which enchained the son to the

---

[1] Zachariä, *Gesch. des gr.-röm. Rechts*, p. 241. Cf. above, vol. i. p. 29, where I pointed out that M. Fustel de Coulanges is mistaken on this point.

[2] Called $\chi \omega \rho o \delta \acute{o} \tau \eta s$ (Leunclavius, *Jur. Gr.-Rom.* ii. p. 258).

[3] A tithe was the usual, but not invariable rent. Sometimes no less than half the produce went to the landlord ($\dot{\epsilon} \phi \eta \mu \iota \sigma \epsilon \acute{\iota} a$), Leunclavius, *ib.* The tithe system is thus recognised, $\mu o \rho \tau \acute{\iota} o \upsilon$ $\mu \acute{\epsilon} \rho o s$ $\delta \epsilon \mu \acute{a} \tau \iota a$ (*fasciculi*) $\dot{\epsilon} \nu \nu \acute{\epsilon} a$ $\chi \omega \rho o \delta \acute{o} \tau o \upsilon$ $\delta \grave{\epsilon}$ $\mu \acute{\epsilon} \rho o s$ $\delta \epsilon \mu \acute{a} \tau \iota o \nu$ $\ddot{\epsilon} \nu$.

[4] For this discussion I must acknowledge my debt to the work of N.

Skabalonovitch (already referred to), *Vizantyskoe Gosudarstvo i Tserkov v xi. Věkě.* In the fifth chapter the author sets forth most lucidly the nature of the change and its causes; and the importance of the Slavonic element in bringing about the change is naturally not neglected by a Russian scholar. It is strange that Finlay did not grasp the fact of this change or the importance of the $N \acute{o} \mu o s$ $\Gamma \epsilon \omega \rho \gamma \iota \kappa \acute{o} s$. The decline of "predial slavery" did not escape him, but he did not see that the colonate was a thing of the past. (Cf. Finlay, ii. p. 220.)

profession of the father; and the Roman Emperors, who were straining every nerve to beat back Persians or Avars or Saracens, were not injudicious enough to force the colonate upon them. Moreover, during the Persian and Saracen invasions the colons were doubtless called upon, if not for offensive, at least for defensive military service, and the continuance of this abnormal state of things must have led to practical changes in their position.   When new cultivators were settled in a district, the condition of the old cultivators who had lived under the colon system must have been gradually assimilated to that of the new settlers.   But, in addition to this, the invasions of the Avars, Slaves, and Bulgarians in Europe, and of the Persians and Saracens in Asia, had depopulated wholly or partially many districts.   The peasants were either slain, or led captive, or compelled to flee to other provinces.   In the last case, the general confusion occasioned by constant invasions secured the fugitives from being recalled to their old state of serfdom; and we may conjecture that when captives were redeemed from an enemy those who had been serfs were allowed to settle, on new conditions, in the provinces.

Thus the continuous invasions from the middle of the sixth century to the end of the seventh operated both directly and indirectly in the abolition of the colonate—directly by removing the serfs, indirectly by changing the character of the population. Now the latter change has a peculiarity which throws further light on the problem before us.

The most important new element in the population was the Slavonic.   One point of difference between the Slaves and the Germans was that the Slaves had no institution corresponding to the German *laeti*.   The Slaves had slaves, but they had no free cultivators attached to the soil.   Now the development of the Roman colonate in its later stages was closely connected with the settlement of Germans in the Empire; and the success of the system was certainly due partly to the fact that the Germans, familiar with the notion of *laeti*, readily adapted themselves to the institution of the *coloni*.[1]   "But the institution which was signified in the Byzantine Empire by the word ἐναπόγραφοι was strange to the spirit of the Slavonic race; the Slaves did not understand it and could not reconcile themselves

---

[1] This is justly insisted on by Skabalonovitch, *op. cit.* pp. 239, 240.

to it. A direct result of the intrusion and settlement of the Slaves was the abolition of this institution; the tie connecting the peasants and the soil was broken, the peasants ceased to be serfs and received the right of free movement from place to place." [1] The new Slavonic settlements reacted on the condition of the colons and *adscripticii.*

The hypothesis that the Slaves were mainly influential in bringing about this change is confirmed by the existence of peasant communities, attested by the Agricultural Code of the Isaurian sovereigns. Besides the new class of free tenants " there appeared peasant communities which were organised by Slaves in the provinces occupied by them, according to Slavonic custom, and which, it may be, were borrowed from the Slaves by peasants of other nationalities subject to the Byzantine Empire." [2]

It thus appears that while the Roman institution of the colonate worked out a natural development among the Teutonic nations of the West, it ceased to exist in the Roman Empire itself, where new conditions were to lead to a great struggle, in the ninth and following centuries, between the rich and the poor proprietors. The colonate did not arise again in the East, and references to this system in the Basilica are anachronisms, having no application to contemporary society, but merely repeated from the Code of Justinian.

As the iconodulic chroniclers did not know, or did not care to tell of Leo's beneficial reforms, we are left in the dark as to the details. The successes gained during his own reign against the Saracens, the successes gained by his son Constantine against the Bulgarians, indicate that he restored the relaxed discipline and improved the efficiency of the military forces.[3] If he did not extend the frontiers of the diminished Empire, he made it firm and compact from Haemus to Taurus. He also improved the police control both in the city and in the

---

[1] I translate from Skabalonovitch, p. 240.   [2] *Ib.*

[3] The strictness of military discipline enforced by the Isaurians may be learned from the νόμος στρατιωτικός. The law (Leunclavius, p. 249) that men condemned for adultery were not allowed to serve is worthy of notice; and also the law that a soldier conniving at the adultery of his wife should be cashiered. Soldiers were not allowed to busy themselves with agriculture or merchandise, nor to be agents or sureties for others. Traitorous desertion was punished with horrible deaths by burning or crucifixion (*ib.* p. 255).

provinces; but on this subject we may speak more conveniently in another place. During the years of anarchy brigandage had flourished in the highlands of Thrace and doubtless also in the highlands of Asia Minor. To Constantine V is due the credit of suppressing the bands of scamars which infested Thrace and were recruited by peasants whose lands had been wasted by Bulgarians or drained by heavy taxation.[1] A notorious chief of one of these robber bands was made an example by an inhuman punishment; his extremities were amputated and he was dissected alive by surgeons.

It is certain that the financial condition of the Empire was not satisfactory when Leo ascended the throne. At the time of Philippicus' succession,[2] after the death of Justinian Rhinotmetos, the treasury was full, but the voluptuous upstart spent in a short season the greater part of the treasures. The expenses incurred by Anastasius in preparing for, and by Leo in undergoing, a long siege were probably considerable, and the revenue proceeding from direct taxation must have been appreciably affected by the circumstance that Asia Minor had been so long exposed to annual invasions, which injured the agricultural prosperity of the country. It may be concluded that Leo was anxious to improve the revenues, and that his fiscal measures were not likely to be lenient. For six or seven years Asia Minor suffered little from the Saracens and had time to recover its productiveness (719-726); then the Emperor saw good to increase the burden suddenly.

The manner in which he carried out this measure was peculiar, if I am right in interpreting a curious aberration in the chronology of the time. I believe that Leo caused the taxes which would regularly have been paid in two years to be paid in one year, and that for this purpose he adopted the original idea of altering the calendar.[3] The official mode of reckoning was by indictions; thus the year current from 1st September 726 to 1st September 727 was the tenth indiction. Leo threw two indictions into one, or, in other words,

---

[1] Cf. Finlay, ii. p. 54.

[2] *See* Zonaras, Bk. xiv. cap. 26 : σώρους χρημάτων ἐκ τῶν παλαιοτέρων θησαυρισθέντας αὐτοκρατόρων ἐν τοῖς βασιλείοις εὑρών, κ.τ.λ.

[3] My reasons for departing from the received chronology will be found in the Note at the end of this chapter. I would observe that my rectification of the chronology and my conjecture as to the cause of the error are quite independent of each other. The conjecture may be wrong, but that will not affect the question of the actual dates.

omitted one indiction, either the eleventh or the twelfth (probably the eleventh), and then exacted the double tribute. Thus the year current from the end of 728 to the end of 729 was called in the official records the thirteenth indiction, whereas according to the natural reckoning it should have been the twelfth. The consequence of this has been that the chroniclers, who took their dates from the public records and were not aware that an indiction had been suppressed, have misled modern historians, who, when they perceived that the indictions and the years of the world did not correspond, assumed that the indictions were right and the years of the world wrong. Nearly fifty years later, shortly before the death of Constantine V, the alteration was cancelled and the right reckoning restored by counting two years as one indiction. But for fifty years of the eighth century all the received dates are wrong by a year. Leo III, for example, reigned a year less than is generally supposed, and his son Constantine V a year longer.

In 732 Leo ordained that a register should be kept of the male children born in the Empire, a measure which his religious enemies held up to odium.[1] In the same year he increased the capitation tax in Sicily and Calabria, and ordained that a sum of three and a half talents of gold, which was annually paid to the patrimony of the Apostles at Old Rome, should be paid to the treasury.

A great earthquake which occurred in October 739 may be recorded here, because it gave rise to a new tax. Some of the oldest monuments in the city were thrown down by the shock, the statue of Constantine the Great, at the gate of Attalus ; the statue and sculptured column of Arcadius ; the statue of Theodosius I., over the Golden Gate, and the church of Irene, close to St. Sophia. The land walls of the city were also subverted ; and in order to repair the fortifications Leo increased the taxes by one-twelfth, or a *miliarision* in a *nomisma*.[2]

From Leo's time forward it was the habit of the Emperor to pay more direct personal attention to the finances than before,[3] so that the officer called *logothetes* was rather the

---

[1] Theoph. 6224 A.M., who compares Leo to Pharaoh.

[2] Miliarision (1s. ½d.) = one-twelfth of a nomisma (12s. 6d.) = two keratia ; hence the tax was called dikeraton. Finlay is severe upon Leo for this mea-

sure, but it is difficult to judge of the circumstances of the case.

[3] Finlay notices this, and attributes the innovation to Leo—wrongly, as I try to show.

imperial secretary in fiscal matters than a responsible minister, while the Emperor was himself chancellor of the exchequer. This, however, was a matter of practice and not of statute, and the relation between the logothete and the sovereign varied according to the judgment or character of the latter. Active princes like Leo and his son might take the direction of the fisc altogether into their own hands, and leave to their logothetes little more than routine work; while indolent monarchs like Michael III, or delicate monarchs like Leo IV, might surrender a large proportion of the financial administration into the grand accountant's hand. I am not confident, however, that this change was first introduced by Leo; I am rather inclined to believe that it dated from the reign of Constans, one of whose characteristics was the habit of doing things himself. His grandfather Heraclius was called upon to solve serious financial difficulties at the beginning of his reign, and must have exercised a careful personal supervision over the fisc and the " count of sacred largesses." Now before the end of the seventh century we find that this name has become obsolete, and that our historians, whose language generally echoes that of their sources, use the term logothete (τοῦ γενικοῦ).[1] It seems not improbable that the change of name was concurrent with the change in the functions of the office, and that the autocratic and independent Constans managed the affairs of the exchequer himself, and transformed the count of sacred largesses into a secretary, who received the name λογοθέτης τοῦ γενικοῦ. As the new office was almost equivalent to a private secretariate, it becomes intelligible that Theodotus, a monk, held it under Justinian II, just as freedmen held such posts in the early Empire.

---

[1] On the financial officers, *see* above, p. 324 note 2.

NOTE on the CHRONOLOGY of the EIGHTH CENTURY

FROM the year 727 A.D. to 774 A.D. the indictions and the *anni mundi* in the Chronicle of Theophanes do not correspond. The question is, are his indictions or his *anni mundi* right? Chronologists and historians (Baronius, Pagi, Muralt, Finlay, Schlosser, Hopf, Hefele, etc.) have invariably accepted his indictions and rejected his *anni mundi*. For example, the death of Leo III took place in the ninth indiction, which should have been current from 1st September 740 to 1st September 741; and thus historians place it in June 741. On the other hand, the same authority states that the same event happened in 6232 A.M., current 1st September 739 to 1st September 740; and this date, in opposition to the received doctrine, I hold to be correct.

(1) The first question to be determined is, whether the discrepancy is merely due to an oversight on the part of Theophanes himself. Now on this point we fortunately possess a piece of incontestable documentary evidence in the title of the Ecloga (quoted above, p. 412), where that handbook is stated to have been issued ἐν μηνὶ μαρτίῳ ἰνδ. θ´ ἔτει ἀπὸ κτίσεως κόσμου ςσμη´, "in the month of March, ninth indiction, 6248 A.M." In the date of the month and indiction all the MSS. are at one; in the year of the world the later MSS. have several variants, but the three oldest MSS. agree in the date which I have printed. Now 6248 of the era of Constantinople corresponds to 6232 of the era of Antioch (or rather of Panodorus the Egyptian), which was used by Theophanes, that is 739-740 A.D.; whereas the ninth indiction, as we have seen, corresponds to the year 740-741. Thus it appears that in the official date of a contemporary record we find the same discrepancy that we find in Theophanes. The conclusion is that the discrepancy has some deeper cause than the error of an individual chronographer.[1]

---

[1] On this discrepancy in the date of the Ecloga, *see* Heimbach, "Griechisch-römisches Recht," in *Ersch und Gruber*, p. 215. He assumes that Leo changed the *anni mundi*: "man darf . . . behaupten dass diese Abweichung von der gewöhnlichen Weltära auf officiellem Wege veranlasst worden sei."

(2) The next problem is, was it the indictions or the *anni mundi* that were tampered with in the eighth century? was an indiction left out, or was a year of the world counted twice over? Now one of the most valuable tests of chronological data are the certain calculations of astronomy, and in this case we can fortunately appeal to this impartial arbitrator, as a solar eclipse which took place in a year of the period with which we are concerned is recorded by Theophanes. Under 6252 A.M., corresponding to the fourteenth indiction, he states that an eclipse took place on Friday, 15th August, at four o'clock in the afternoon. According to the received chronology, which accepts the indictions and rejects the *anni mundi*, the eclipse took place in 761. Now in 761 a total eclipse of the sun did take place, but it was only visible in Asia, and the date was Wednesday, 5th August (*L'art de vérifier les dates, depuis la naiss. de N. S.* vol. i. ed. 1783, p. 66). Theophanes cannot have referred to this. On the other hand, there was an annular eclipse on 15th August 760 (= 6252 A.M.), visible at three in the afternoon in Europe and Africa (*ib.*); and the 15th August in 760 fell on Friday. Thus astronomy proves that the *annus mundi* is right and the indiction wrong. And this is what we might have expected *a priori.* It is more likely that the official system of reckoning was modified than that a temporary practice prevailed of placing the creation of the world 5510 instead of 5509 years B.C.

Another point connected with the same year 760 confirms this conclusion. Theophanes notices that Easter 6252 fell on 6th April, but that some celebrated it on 13th April. Now, Easter actually fell on 6th April in 760, and not in 761.

(3) I must now notice some points that apparently make against this conclusion. In five cases besides those mentioned, Theophanes, in stating the day of the month, adds the day of the week. (*a*) 6232 = ninth indiction, he makes 26th October fall on Wednesday. According to the received date this year was 740, according to my theory 739. Adding together 3, the *concurrent* of 739, and 2, the *régulier solaire* of October, we find that in that year 1st October fell on (2 + 3 = 5) Thursday, and therefore 26th October on Monday; whereas in 740 (a leap year) 1st October was Saturday and 26th October Wednesday. (*b*) 6235 A.M., twelfth indiction. Valid was slain on the fifth day of the week, 16th April. This suits 744, the received date (*concur.* = 3, *rég.* = 1 ∴ 1st April = Wednesday, 16th April = Thursday). (*c*) 6254 A.M. = first indiction, 30th June = Thursday, which suits 763, not 762. (*d*) 6260 A.M. = seventh indiction, 1st April = Saturday, which suits 769, not 768.

These four cases seem inconsistent with my theory and favourable to the received doctrine. Another case still remains. (*e*) 6221 A.M. = thirteenth indiction, 7th January = Tuesday. This suits

NOTE *CHRONOLOGY OF THE EIGHTH CENTURY* 427

neither 729, my date, nor 730, the received date. In 729 (*concur.* 5
+ *rég.* 2 = 7; hence 1st January = Saturday) 7th January = Friday,
in 730 7th January = Saturday (Hefele proposes to read ιζ' = 17,
which would suit 730). In this case, on either theory Theophanes
is wrong, and I think we may infer that the mistake is due to his
own calculation. I suspect that in many instances his authorities
supplied only the day of the month, and that he reckoned the day
of the week himself. This at least seems a case of mis-reckoning.

If this be so, we can explain *a, b, c, d.* Suppose that Theophanes
was writing his Chronicle in the year 800 (= eighth indiction), and
wished to find out on what day of the week the 1st of April fell in
768 = 6260 A.M. = seventh indiction. Knowing that in the present
year, 800, 1st April was Thursday, he might reckon back to the
year 768, taking leap years into account; and in doing this it
would be very natural for him to count by indictions. He might
thus conclude that from April 768 to April 800 there were thirty-
one years (8 + 15 + 8 = 31), whereas there were really thirty-two
(800 – 768 = 32). This mistake would be due to not understanding
that the twelfth indiction was spread out over two years, 6265 and
6266 (September 772 to September 774); and it is clear from his
Chronicle that he had not grasped this curious fact. Hence
Theophanes, wishing to calculate for 768, would have really calculated for 769.

In any case, I submit that the little phalanx *a, b, c, d* is not strong
enough to contend against the solar eclipse, combined with the date
of Easter 760, and supported by the antecedent probability that
the indictions were more likely to be modified than the years of the
world, which had no reference to practical questions. If any
ecclesiastical theorist had induced the Roman world for half the
eighth century to adopt a new era, we should certainly have heard
of it; whereas a change in the indictions made for fiscal purposes
(if the conjecture I put forward in the foregoing chapter be well
founded) belongs to that class of things which chroniclers either do
not know or do not deign to tell.

In investigating this question I naturally turned to Muralt, but
derived little assistance. His book makes us regret that Clinton
did not go further than 641. It is on the edit. of George Hamartolus rather than on the *Essai de Chronographie byzantine* that
Muralt's fame will rest.

CHAPTER III

THE ICONOCLASTIC MOVEMENT

THE historical import of the iconoclastic controversy, as I conceive it, did not consist in the mere definite point at issue concerning the worship or reverence paid to sacred pictures, but rather in the fact that the movement represented a great reaction against the gross superstition which hung as a cloud over Christendom. The adoration of pictures tends to become a most degraded form of superstition, as uneducated minds fail to distinguish between the sign and the thing signified; and it naturally leads to other forms of credulity. There were many pictures which, in the belief of men, had descended from heaven, and were not made with hands; and not only the populace but even a Pope believed in the power of *icons* to work miracles. Thus picture-worship was selected by Leo the Isaurian as the main point of attack. But what especially interests us and concerns history is, not the details of the controversy itself, but the fact that Leo III, Constantine V, and their party were animated by a spirit of rationalism, in the same sense that Luther was animated by a spirit of rationalism. They were opponents, not only of iconolatry, but also of Mariolatry[1]; they did not believe in the intercession of saints, they abhorred reliques which were supposed to possess

[1] Cf., for instance, Theoph. p. 406 (ed. de Boor). For this and the following chapter, beside Theophanes, we have the acts of the seventh Ecumenical Council in Greek (Mansi, xii. 951 *sqq.* and xiii. 1-821), and also the essays against iconoclasm by John of Damascus; in Latin the most important source is the *Liber Pontificalis*. On the iconoclastic controversy ecclesiastical students may be interested to read the *Antirrhetica* of the Patriarch Nicephorus, published by Cardinal Pitra in the 1st vol. of his *Spicilegium Solesmense*. Nicephorus was perhaps the ablest supporter of image-worship.

magic potency. They were, moreover, especially Constantine V, the sworn foes of monks, whom they justly regarded as the mainstays of superstition and mental degradation; for although the monks of south-eastern Europe were on the whole more pious and chaste than their brethren in the West, and although some of them were learned men, the large majority were ignorant, narrow-minded, and obstinate.

At first sight it might be thought that these purists, who preferred that the walls of their churches should be unadorned by rich pictures and mosaics, and who, in their zeal, destroyed valuable works of art and persecuted their opponents, were fanatical zealots and somewhat rude pietists, like the Puritans of the seventeenth century in England.[1] This comparison, however, would be a wholly misleading one. The Isaurian Emperors and their Amorian successors were not opposed by any means to the pomps and vanities of the world. On the contrary, one of their rational principles was that many things which the monks called pomps and vanities were really only innocent and not unbecoming amusements. The Emperor Theophilus, who persecuted image-worship in the ninth century, was one of the gayest and most brilliant monarchs that ever reigned at Byzantium; in fact, we may say that he introduced a new period of oriental splendour. In the reign of Constantine V the palace was constantly a scene of frivolity and festivity. The iconoclasts were not the apostles of puritanism; they were the apostles of rationalism, and the opponents of extreme austerity.

While, from a historical point of view, iconoclasm was a great reaction, from a dogmatic point of view it was not new; it was connected with old controversies. The objection of the iconoclasts to represent Christ in art was simply a corollary to the doctrine of the monophysites; and the opposition of the Isaurians to Mariolatry was a thoroughly monophysitic feature. The monotheletism of the seventh century was a connecting

---

[1] M. Lenormant (*La Grande-Grèce*, t. ii. p. 386) speaks of the movement as "la tentative d'une sorte de calvinisme anticipé." It would have been more just to say Lutheranism. M. Lenormant is not fair to the iconoclasts —we might say that he regards them from a South-Italian bias. He justly ridicules "a scholar known by his ardent radicalism" for upholding the thesis that the work of Leo and Constantine was an anticipation of the French Revolution. Yet the thesis has this much truth, that Leo and Constantine waged war against superstition and in the interests of reason and education.

link between monophysitism and iconoclasm; but there were two new influences which affected the eighth-century movement and gave it a peculiar character, namely the Paulician doctrines and the Mohammedan religion.

It is a great misfortune that no historical or other works composed by iconoclasts (with the exception of the Ecloga, which does not deal with iconoclasm) are extant, and that we derive all our knowledge of the movement from the accounts of their antagonists, the iconodules, who, with malevolent bigotry, misrepresented their motives, exaggerated their faults, and calumniated their moral character. The hatred against the iconoclasts was so great in subsequent ages that all their works have perished except the Ecloga, which was preserved by accident, probably because it was wrongly attributed to Leo VI and Constantine VII.

It was in the year 725 that Leo first began to put forward his objections to the worship of images.[1] Several stories were current as to the influences which caused Leo to assume this position. At the seventh general Council, which condemned iconoclasm in 787, a monk named Johannes stated that Leo had communicated with the Saracen caliph Yezid, through the mediation of Constantine, bishop of Nacolia, and had at his suggestion waged war against pictures. Yezid had in his dominions issued a decree against pictures some years before, by the persuasions of a Jew of Laodicea.[2]

Whatever truth or falsehood may lie in these stories, there

---

[1] In 306 A.D. the council of Elvira (canon 36) expressed itself unfavourable to images, but that was before the use of art in christian buildings had begun to prevail. The early history of the attitude of the Church to images belongs to the department of ecclesiastical history; a good account of it will be found in Prof. Stokes' article on "Iconoclastae" in *Dict. Christ. Biogr.*, which is especially valuable as pointing out the connection between iconoclasm and the earlier heresies of monotheletism and monophysitism (after Combefis' *Hist. Monothel.*), but he does not give sufficient weight to the influence of Islamism and Paulicianism.

[2] Pope Gregory II said that Theodosius of Ephesus was Leo's secret adviser; he was one of his chief supporters. A certain Beser, a christian captive in Syria, infected with the doctrines of the Arabs ($\pi o\iota\omega\theta\acute{e}\nu\tau a$ $\tau o\hat{\iota}s$ $A\rho\acute{a}\beta\omega\nu$ $\delta\acute{o}\gamma\mu a\sigma\iota\nu$), is mentioned by Theophanes as a friend of Leo. The later legend is that two Jews had met Leo or Conon, while young and obscure, travelling to seek his fortune. They predicted that he would become Emperor, and begged him to banish idolatry. There is another legend that Yezid was influenced by two Jews, who held out to him false promises of worldly prosperity (cf. Theoph. 6215 A.M.) These legends illustrate well the detestation and horror in which Jews were held by Roman Christians. *See* Mansi, xiii. 197.

is no doubt that the Mohammedan religion, which was freer from superstition and materialism than a degraded Christianity, exercised considerable influence on the religious doctrine of the iconoclasts; and that it could do this all the more readily on account of the kinship of the worship of Allah to the worship of Jehovah, and the connection of Judaism with Christianity. Neither of the great Semitic religions permitted the use of images and pictures in its service, and this austerity maintained a less sensual conception of God.   Hence it was a common reproach, levelled against Leo and Constantine, that they were imbued with Arabic ideas.[1]   Here too lies the meaning of the nickname Kopronymos, which was fastened to Constantine.   We need not necessarily reject the tale, which our historian [2] professes to have had on unimpeachable testimony, that perfidious nature played the child an indecent trick at the moment of his immersion in the font; but the point of the name is illustrated by the word "magarise," which soon acquired an unsavoury sense.   And it was not only in the condemnation of picture-worship that the religion of these Emperors had a flavour of Islamism and Judaism; they were fain to degrade the Virgin and the saints from an almost divine eminence, and their doctrine tended towards an Arianism which verged on monotheism.   Yet they were by no means favourers of the Jews.   Four years after his accession, Leo attempted to compel all the Jews in the Empire to be baptized; possibly he thought that they might leaven the Church with a new spirit.   At the same time he tried to force the Montanists [3] to embrace the orthodox creed; but they were so devoted to their faith that, sooner than yield, they assembled in a building, and, having set it on fire, perished in the flames.[4]

But the resemblances of iconoclasm to Paulicianism appear to me more important than its points of contact with Mohammedanism.   When we remember that the home of the Paulician doctrine was in Commagene, and that Leo III, if not born

---

[1] For example, Leo is called by Theophanes σαρακηνόφρων, and said to be Ἀραβικῷ φρονήματι κρατυνόμενος.   It should not be forgotten that Omar is said to have written a dogmatic epistle to Leo to convert him to Islam.   On the other hand, it has been said that Leo's policy was designed to convert the Saracens to Christianity.

[2] Theophanes.

[3] Montanism has been described as "Irvingism and the Salvation Army combined, confusing mere carnal and physical excitement with the pure motions of divine charity," by Prof. G. T. Stokes in a paper on the "Ancient Churches of Africa," 1887.

[4] Theoph. 6214 A.M.

at Germanicia, was closely connected with those regions, it seems natural to suppose that he or his parents inhaled among the Paulicians a spirit of antagonism to Mariolatry and superstition. Moreover, Leo afterwards stamped with his approval the heresy which his predecessors had persecuted. He summoned a certain Paulician named Gegnaesius to New Rome,[1] and caused him to be tried before the Patriarch Germanus. Gegnaesius was honourably acquitted of the charges which "slanderers" had brought against him, and Leo sent him back to his home with a written safe-conduct to protect him against future persecution.[2]

Leo issued his first decree against the worship of images in 726.[3] The purport of this decree was not, as is often stated, that pictures should be hung higher in the churches, in order that people should not adore them and kiss them; it commanded that they should be totally abolished.[4] One of the first acts in the execution of this edict, the destruction of a specially revered image of the Saviour above the palace gate of Chalke, caused a riot. An old legend was connected with this image, and it was called Antiphonetes.[5] The officers who were breaking or taking down the image were attacked and killed by enraged women; and Leo was obliged to proceed to strong measures in order to enforce his decree. It must not be supposed, however, that he had recourse to harsh extremes with the lower classes of the people; his enemies tell us expressly that his anger fell on those who were conspicuous

---

[1] Gegnaesius was the son of Paul, an Armenian, and bore the spiritual name of Timothy. He lived at Episparis, but spent the last years of his life (after his acquittal) at Mananalis in Commagene, the cradle of the doctrine. See Photius, *contra Manichaeos*, Bk. i. (ed. Migne), vol. ii. pp. 54, 56; and Petrus Siculus, *Historia Manichaeorum*. It is strange that Finlay does not mention the affair of Gegnaesius.

[2] Photius, *ib.* p. 56: τύπον ἔγγραφον πᾶσαν αὐτῷ διδόντα τὴν ἄδειαν οἴκοι τε διατρίβειν καὶ τὰ αὐτοῦ ἀνεπηρεαστῶς πράττειν καὶ μηδὲν ἔτι τῶν συκοφαντῶν δεδιέναι τὰς γλώσσας.

[3] Historians attribute a superstitious motive to Leo. In the summer of 726 the sea between the islands of Thera and Therasia was agitated, vapours

were exhaled from the waters, became dense by degrees, and, finally petrified by ignition, formed an addition to the island of Hiera, which had itself been thrown up in 196 B.C. Pumice-stones were showered as far as Asia Minor, Lesbos, Abydos. (On small islands which have been since formed by similar eruptions, *see* Mr. Tozer's note, Finlay, ii. p. 43.) Leo was said to have attributed this phenomenon to the prevalence of idolatry.

[4] Hefele has made this clear. The mistake was due to misdating the first letter of Pope Gregory (Mansi, xii. 959).

[5] That is, surety (cf. the expression ἀντιφώνησον ἡμᾶς in prayers). A panegyric on the image has been published by Combefis in his *Historia Monothel.*

by their birth and education. When those whom he expected, on account of their position, to join him in his enlightened campaign against superstition, refused to do so, he attempted to coerce them. But Leo, although he was determined to carry through his reforms, was not as intolerant or violent as his son Constantine, and did not go beyond petty persecutions. At that age of the world it was impossible for any religious movement, rationalistic or other, to avoid the tendency to intolerance; and no one seemed to imagine that intolerance was inconsistent with enlightenment.

We must touch here on the subject of education, for the policy of Leo in this respect has been made a ground of serious accusations against him. Theophanes, the monk, states that he exterminated the educational establishments and put an end to the pious system of instruction which had prevailed since the time of Constantine the Great.[1] In other later sources, George the Sinner and Zonaras,[2] we find a curious statement. There was an imperial institution between St. Sophia and the palace walls, near the place called the Bronze Bazaar (Chalkoprateia). This academy contained a large library of both sacred and profane rolls, and was the residence of a personage entitled the Ecumenical Doctor (*Didaskalos*), who was assisted by twelve learned men. It was, in fact, a college with a provost or master and twelve fellows. They were fed at the public expense, and gave instruction in arts and theology. The Emperor used to consult them on political matters, and they enjoyed a high reputation at Constantinople. Leo thought that if he could gain over to his side the representatives of learning and education, the victory would be easily won; but he failed. The conservative spirit that generally exists in universities and bodies of learned men is sufficient to explain their opposition to the Emperor's radical reforms; but the dark atmosphere of superstition that had prevailed so long and the mists of theological prejudice had probably obscured their reason. I do not suggest this because they upheld the cause of pictures; really learned and relatively

[1] τὰ παιδευτήρια σβεσθῆναι, κ.τ.λ. 6218 A.M.

[2] Zonaras, vol. iii. p. 340; Georgios Hamartolus (ed. Muralt). p. 634. M. Sathas identifies this imperial institution with the university of Constantinople, but this is doubtful; and it has been supposed that the "Ecumenical Doctor" was a foundation of Maurice, who patronised learning and was fond of things ecumenical.

enlightened men, like John of Damascus, were earnest antagonists of iconoclasm. But if it be true (and there seems no
reason to doubt) that Leo disendowed the college, ejected the
Ecumenical Doctor and the twelve fellows, and perhaps removed the library to the precincts of the palace, it is clear
that he considered the institution a nursery of superstition.
So much truth, I believe, underlies the outrageous and absurd
slander which was circulated in later times to shed obloquy on
the reformer's name. It is narrated by Zonaras and George
Hamartolus that, having failed in many discussions to win over
the learned men, he surrounded the imperial house, as their
college was called, at night with heaps of inflammable wood,
and burned the building down with professors, library, and all.
If there were no direct evidence against this story, it would be
incredible in Leo, who never proceeded to extreme persecution
with any individual; it would be incredible even in Constantine,
though he did not hesitate at executions. But the silence of
the orthodox historians Theophanes and Nicephorus, who bitterly
hated the memory of the iconoclast, is absolutely conclusive.
Yet the existence of such a gross calumny is instructive, and
shows us with what circumspection and distrust we must accept
all statements of the friends of pictures regarding their opponents.

When we combine the brief statement of Theophanes,
quoted above, that Leo put an end to "pious education" and
shut up educational institutions, with this later notice touching the Ecumenical Doctor and the imperial house, it is plain
that the Emperor's reforms extended to education. But nothing could be less critical and less equitable than to repeat,
as some modern historians have done,[1] the adverse statements
of his enemies, that in a spirit of bigotry he quenched education and threw the Greek world into a slough of ignorance and
darkness, from which it did not begin to rise until the reign of
Constantine Porphyrogennetos, and did not finally recover until
the days of Michael Psellus in the eleventh century. Such an
assertion is absurd. The fact is that education in the Roman
Empire had been enveloped in darkness since the middle of
the seventh century, and that, but for the new spirit which
the iconoclastic reaction introduced, south-eastern Europe and
Asia Minor would have walked in the same path of ignorance

[1] *See* M. Sathas, *Bib. Gr. Med. Aev.* vol. iv. Pref. p. xliii.

and corruption as western Europe during the succeeding centuries. That Leo, the knight-errant against superstition, should have taken measures to exterminate liberal education, is a charge too ludicrous to entertain. But it is sufficiently refuted by facts recorded in Ignatius' *Life of Nicephorus*, or in the *Life of Theodore of Studion*,[1] where we are told that these learned divines received an excellent secular education in grammar, language, science, and philosophy. There was, in fact, a large number of educated and learned men at the end of the eighth century, and there was not a single educated man of eminence at the beginning of the eighth century.[2] The iconoclast movement intervened, and by the inductive method of difference we are justified in attributing the improvement to its salutary influence. And yet we are told that iconoclastic bigotry quenched liberal education.

What Leo really did in the matter of education is indicated by the words of Theophanes. He suppressed the schools of theology, which were doubtless hotbeds of superstition and bigotry, and that is what Theophanes means by the extinction of " pious education." The imperial house, from being originally an institution for the maintenance of both secular and sacred knowledge, had probably degenerated into a theological seminary, where all subjects were touched with the deadly breath of superstition and every branch of learning was obscured by religious irrelevancies. By disestablishing such an institution Leo was cutting at the very root of the evils against which he was contesting; and we may feel sure that the abolition of the Ecumenical Doctor and his twelve coadjutors was no loss to the cause of education, but rather a gain.

It was easy to deal with the Ecumenical Doctor, but it was not quite so easy to deal with the Ecumenical Patriarch. Germanus refused to support Leo's policy, and Leo determined to depose him, as the importance of the Patriarch in the Empire made his co-operation highly desirable and his opposition extremely formidable. A suspicious story is told,[3] that one

---

[1] On the course of education as illustrated by these sources, *see* p. 519.

[2] I do not count Johannes Chrysorroas of Damascus, the opponent of iconoclasm, because he was not an imperial subject.

[3] Theophanes, 6221 A.M. Germanus was a very old man (about ninety) at this time. His contributions to the controversy are two letters, one to John of Synnada and one to Thomas of Claudiopolis.

day, as the Emperor and Germanus were discussing the controverted subject, the latter remarked that pictures would be destroyed, but not in Leo's reign. "In whose reign, then?" demanded Leo. "In the reign of Conon," was the reply. "My name is really Conon," said the Emperor. "God forbid," ejaculated Germanus, "that the evil should be accomplished now in your reign! For he who fulfils it is the precursor of Antichrist and the subverter of the mystery of the incarnation." At this Leo was angry, and Germanus reminded him of the covenant which he had made before his coronation, not to shake or change the apostolic and divinely transmitted canons of the Church.

On the 7th of January 729[1] Leo summoned a conclave or *silentium* in the tribunal of the Nineteen Accubiti for the purpose of condemning iconolatry, and invited Germanus to attend it. Germanus replied by resigning his office, and as he laid down his episcopal surplice or *ômophorion*, he said, "If I am Jonah, cast me into the sea." The principle on which he based his opposition to Leo was that he could not introduce innovations without the authority of an Ecumenical Council. Germanus was deposed, and Anastasius, the Patriarch's *syncellus*, who had taken Leo's side in the controversy, was elected in his stead (22d January), and immediately issued a manifesto, which was important in that it gave ecclesiastical authority to Leo's policy. Pope Gregory II refused to recognise the elevation of the new Patriarch; but we must postpone to another

---

[1] Theoph. 6221 A.M. In the Life of Nicetas Hegumenos (*Acta Sanctorum*, April iii.), the deposition of Germanus and elevation of Anastasius are thus mentioned (p. 260): *fugitque nido veneranda hirundo quae vernam ecclesiae tranquillitatem dulcisono sonabat garritu Dominica festa condecorans; et in locum ejus inductus est deformis corvus hians et absonum crocitans*, etc. The deposition of Germanus is mentioned in the second oration of John of Damascus in behalf of image-worship, but the accession of Anastasius is not mentioned. This seems to fix the date of that work to the first (or second, as news travelled slowly) month of 729. Prof. Stokes (article on "Leo III" in *Dict. Christ. Biogr.*) bases an argument on this circumstance in support of Hefele's interpretation of the edict of 726, but of course on the assumption of the received chronology. My correction of the chronology strengthens his argument, which is this: "The second [oration of John] was published because of the difficulty experienced by the faithful in getting copies of the first. That first *Apology* . . . must have taken a considerable time to get into circulation. . . . This will throw its composition back at least to the year 728." But the first oration presupposes an edict ordaining the destruction of images, and therefore Hefele's view is necessary. According to my chronology, the first oration will be thrown back into the year 727 on the same grounds.

chapter an account of the important results which the iconoclastic edict produced in Italy.

I may mention in this place the revolt that broke out in
Greece in the year 727, although we cannot believe that it was
entirely caused by the religious policy of Leo. We may rather
suppose that oppressive taxation was the deepest cause,[1] and
that orthodox ardour against the iconoclast only hurried the
catastrophe. At the same time it must be admitted that we
can assign rough geographical limits to the distribution of
iconolatry and iconoclasm, and that Greece was devotedly
attached to pictures, central and southern Asia Minor being
the home of the heretics.

Theophanes says that the Helladikoi and the inhabitants
of the Cyclades rebelled against Leo and proclaimed one Cosmas
Emperor. This passage is the *locus classicus* for the word
Helladikoi, which is usually explained as a contemptuous
expression for the inhabitants of Greece proper—that is, for
the Greeks who dwelled between Mount Olympus and Cape
Taenarum. There is, however, not the least ground for the
supposition that the word is charged with a contemptuous or
scornful implication[2]; nor, on the other hand, is it probable that
it includes the Peloponnesus; perhaps it does not even include
the inhabitants of north-western Greece. When Leontius was
appointed stratêgos of Hellas by Justinian, Hellas was a definite
geographical district not coincident with Hellas in the modern
sense any more than it was coincident with Hellas in the
ancient sense. The medieval district or theme of Hellas[3] did
not include the Peloponnesus; it included Attica, Boeotia,
Phocis, and Thessaly; it may possibly at first have also included the western regions of Epirus, Acarnania, and Aetolia,
which in the tenth century formed the theme of Nicopolis, but
it is just as likely that the theme of Nicopolis was independent
from the beginning. The word Helladikoi was the natural
name to use, primarily of the soldiers, and then generally

---

[1] If the severe taxation which I de-
duce from the change in the numbering
of the indictions was imposed 1st September 726, it will help to explain the
revolt of spring 727. The revolt is
narrated by both Nicephorus and
Theophanes (6218 A.M.)

[2] Finlay, ii. 37, "the scornful expression."

[3] At this time (eighth century) Hellas
and the Peloponnesus seem to have been
turms, governed by turmarchs, who
were subordinate to a stratêgos generally known as the stratêgos of Hellas.
It is impossible to decide whether the
stratêgos of Hellas was simply the old
proconsul of Achaia with a new title,
or an entirely new institution.

of the inhabitants of the military district of Hellas, on the
analogy of the names Armeniakoi and Anatolikoi.[1]

Thus the district of Hellas combined with the Cyclades,
which belonged to a separate jurisdiction, and the armament of
the rebels arrived at Constantinople under the command of
Agallianus, the turmarch of Hellas, on the 18th of April 727.
With the help of marine fire, the imperial fleet found no difficulty in routing the insurgents; Agallianus leaped into the sea
in full armour when he saw that the cause was desperate;
Cosmas and one other leader were beheaded. It is probable
that Leo did not push his iconoclastic policy to extremes in
Greece, especially after this rebellion; in the same way we
shall see that he did not press matters too far in southern
Italy. Nevertheless, it is not improbable that many of the
monks who sought refuge in Italy in consequence of the
iconoclastic movement were natives of Hellas and the Peloponnesus.

[1] *See* above, pp. 348 and 351.

CHAPTER IV

IMPERIAL ITALY IN THE EIGHTH CENTURY [1]

THE iconoclastic movement was destined to lead to important political results in Italy. It was destined to assist in the accomplishment of two tendencies that had been always operative, the tendency of the Roman possessions of central and northern Italy, in which there was a strong Latin element, to separate themselves from the Empire, which was becoming gradually Greek, and the tendency of southern Italy, which still retained some traces and memories of the days when it was Magna Graecia, to go a different way from the rest of the peninsula and throw in its lot with Sicily and the eastern Mediterranean. During the ninth, tenth, and eleventh centuries, while the main bulk of Italy was Latin, southern Italy was Greek. Apulia and the land of Hydrus or Otranto, which owing to a temporary Lombard occupation had lost its old appellation Calabria, and the false Calabria, which once was called Bruttii and by an accident of Roman administration obtained a fairer name,—all these were part of the Greek or " Roman" world under the name of Longobardia[2]; just as before the Roman conquest Apulia and the true Calabria and Bruttii were nationally grouped with the peoples of the

---

[1] For this chapter our authorities are the same as for the preceding, the Latin being now more important. Besides Hefele, I have consulted J. Langen's *Geschichte der römischen Kirche von Leo I. bis Nikolaus I.* (1885) ; and Dr. Döllinger's essay on "Gregory II" in his *Papstfabeln des Mittelalters.* There are good articles on "Iconoclastae" and "Leo III" in the *Dict. of Christ. Biog.* by Prof. G. T. Stokes.

[2] The theme of Longobardia was instituted in the reign of Basil I. after the conquests of Nicephorus Phocas. It included Gaeta, Naples, Amalfi, and Sorrento. It consisted of two divisions, Longobardia and Calabria.

Aegean and not with those of the Tyrrhenian Sea. The repetition of history becomes still more striking when we observe that the inhabitants of Rhegium, Croton, and Taras in the days of Hiero and Gelon, or in the days of Agathocles, saw a struggle of the same import in Sicily as took place in the days of Basil the Great or in the days of George Maniakes. In ancient times it was the struggle between the Aryan Greek and the Semitic Phoenician, in which the Romans finally intervened; in medieval times it was the struggle between the Aryan Greek or Byzantine and the Semitic Arab, in which the Normans finally intervened·; but in both cases a people who spoke Greek and a people who spoke a Semitic tongue were contesting the lordship of Sicily, and in both cases " Great Greece " was vitally interested.

  But of the history of medieval Magna Graecia, as we might call it, or Longobardia, as it was actually called from the end of the ninth century, only the first act falls within the limits of this work. The present chapter will narrate how the iconoclastic movement contributed in two ways to a new departure in Italy, consciously in one way, unconsciously in another; and how this prepared for that series of events—the fall of the exarchate, the appeal to Pipin, the overthrow of the Lombard kingdom, the new policy of the Popes—which led up to the constitution of the Western Roman Empire. The intentional innovation was the transference of the Churches of Calabria and Sicily along with that of Illyricum from the see of Old Rome to the see of New Rome ; the unintentional innovation was the colonisation of southern Italy by Greek refugees from the iconoclastic persecution. These two events had a common cause, and were followed by a common effect, but they may be treated separately ; and we naturally begin by considering the somewhat entangled history of the affairs that took place in Italy between the year 726, when the edict against images was issued, and the year 732 (according to received chronology 733), when the ecclesiastical innovation mentioned above was carried out.

  It must not be supposed that the revolt of the exarchate was first or solely caused by the iconoclastic edict of Leo. Before the news of that measure had reached Ravenna or Rome, Pope Gregory II had lent his countenance to a general opposition of the imperial Italian subjects to an extraordinary taxation.[1] He supported the inhabitants of Rome in their refusal to obey the imperial governor; and duke Basil was driven from the city and compelled to become a monk. About the same time Liutprand, king of the Lombards, invaded the exarchate and took Classe, but failed to take Ravenna,[2] while Narnia was lost to the Lombards of Spoleto.

Then the news of the destruction of the mystic image of Christ, called the Antiphonetes, horrified the pious or super-stitious souls of the Latins. The rumour was a vaunt-courier of the edict itself,[3] which soon arrived, along with instructions to the civil officers and a letter to the Pope (727). The feel-ing of dissatisfaction with the government which had before prevailed became now undisguised animosity, and all the cities of the exarchate rebelled. The imperial officials were killed or expelled, and each district elected a duke for itself. The idea was even conceived of electing an Emperor in Italy and escorting him in triumph to New Rome. Exhilaratus, duke of Naples, who tried to enforce obedience to the edict, was lynched, and in Rome the feeling was so high, owing perhaps to the idea that the Pope's life was in danger, that an army was despatched from Ravenna to quell the recalcitrant spirit in its central seat. But King Liutprand, who from his palace in Pavia was watching for an opportunity to extend his dominion, which he perhaps hoped to make conterminous with Italy, assumed the position of a supporter of the Pope and Latin orthodoxy against the imperial heretic, and entered into communication with the rebels. At his instance the Lombards

---

[1] Cf. Theoph. 6217 A.M. Lib. Pont., *censum in provincia ponere praepedicbat.* It must have been extraordinary, as Döllinger (*op. cit.* 152 *sqq.*) and Hefele point out (cf. Langen, *op. cit.* p. 613). Pope Gregory II would not have en-couraged resistance to the regular dues. He always showed himself anxious to pacify a downright rebellion; but for him, says Paulus Diaconus, a rival Em-peror would have been proclaimed. The question is between the credibility of Theophanes on the one hand and the "Papstbuch" and Paul the Deacon on the other; and I think we must follow Döllinger in preferring Italian witnesses on an Italian matter. I have found

here, as elsewhere, Hefele's *Concilien-geschichte* a valuable guide, and I may notice that J. Langen of Bonn, in his work mentioned above, follows Hefele in the main as to the order of events.

[2] It is sometimes stated that he actually took Ravenna, but F. Hirsch has shown that he only took Classe (*Das Herzogthum Benevent,* p. 34). Cf. Paul. Diac. vi. 49.

[3] The early arrival of this news is proved by a passage in the first letter of Gregory to Leo. Foreigners (Franks, Vandals, Goths, Moors, also Romans) had seen the act of desecration and noised it abroad in the West.

of Spoleto and Tuscany surprised the army which was marching from Ravenna to Rome at Ponte Salario—the bridge which Totila destroyed and Narses restored—and prevented its further progress.

Ravenna meanwhile was rent with discord, some supporting the Emperor and others declaring for the cause of rebellion, or, as they loved to say, for the Pope. The latter faction, whose zeal was doubtless stimulated by private agents of Liutprand, prevailed, killed Paul the exarch, expelled his successor Eutychius,[1] and enabled the Lombard king to gain possession of the strong city [2] of the marshes, which Lombard kings had so long coveted in vain, and he himself had failed to take a year before. The cities of the Pentapolis, Rimini, Fano, Pesaro, Ancona, and Umana, the Roman cities of Aemilia, and the city of Auximum invited Liutprand to occupy them with garrisons, and some time later Sutri was taken by the Lombards of Tuscany.

Eutychius, the successor of Paul, had fled to Venice when he found the insurgent faction too strong for him. The duchy of Venice was theoretically, like Rome and Naples, under the government of the exarch, but practically independent, since the citizens had begun to elect their own dukes in the year 697. It was, however, still attached to the Empire, and a letter of Pope Gregory to his friend duke Ursus brought to Ravenna a Venetian army, with whose help Eutychius expelled the Lombards from the city of the exarchs. This assistance rendered by Venice to Ravenna was an anticipation of the succour that she was to lend her against the Spaniards in the fifteenth and sixteenth centuries.

As to the dates of these events we are left by our authorities in uncertainty; the very order of their occurrence is confused. But they clearly occupied a considerable time, and meanwhile Pope Gregory had taken up a decided position and exerted himself actively against iconoclasm,[3] while he took care not to encourage the rejection of Leo's civil authority and

---

[1] The disturbed state of Ravenna must have lasted for a considerable time before the Lombard occupation, as the news of Paul's death had time to reach Constantinople, and Eutychius had time to come to Ravenna. For these events, see Anastasius, *Vita Gregor. II* (Migne, *Patr. Lat.* vol.

127, p. 981).

[2] Hirsch, *ib.* First letter of Gregory to Leo (Mansi, xii. 969); Paul. Diac. vi. 54.

[3] The Pope condemns absolute *worship* of images (λατρευτικῶς) while he approves of their relative adoration (σχετικῶς προσκυνεῖν).

disapproved of the idea of creating a rival Emperor in Italy.[1]
I say a rival Emperor in Italy; but I must explain clearly
that there was no idea afloat of disconnecting Italy from
the government of New Rome or creating a second Roman
Empire; the contemporary biographer of Gregory II states
expressly that Italy thought of electing an Emperor and *leading
him to Constantinople.* The idea of the Roman Imperator and
New Rome were still indissolubly connected in men's minds.
Three extant letters of Gregory, one to the Patriarch Germanus
and two to the Emperor Leo,[2] are important documents for the
iconoclastic controversy, and show us the position of Gregory.
Like John of Damascus, who wrote in Syria against the
enemies of image-worship, Gregory asserted that the Emperor
had no right to interfere in the question of ecclesiastical doctrines. Leo had laid claim to priestly functions in virtue of
his imperial station, and had written "I am an Emperor and a
priest."[3]   In answer to this, Gregory admitted that Constantine
the Great, Valentinian I., Theodosius the Great, and Constantine IV were really both priests and Emperors,—because they
were orthodox; but he denied it in the case of Leo, and
insisted on the essential difference between ecclesiastical and
temporal jurisdiction. In defending picture-worship he chiefly
appealed to the authority of the Fathers, but also pointed out
that it had a certain educational use for the masses; and he
accused Leo of having diverted the people from a wholesome
interest in pictures and "occupied them with idle talk, harp-
playing, cymbals, flutes, and such trivialities."[4]

---

[1] "Cognita vero imperatoris nequi-
tia omnis Italia consilium iniit ut sibi
eligerent imperatorem et *Constantinopolim ducerent.* Sed compescuit tale
consilium pontifex, *sperans conver-
sionem principis*" (Anastas. *Vit. Greg.*
p. 979). Gregory did not despair of
the conversion of the Emperor. In
Tuscany at the *Castrum Manturianense*
a tyrant or "seducer" (*quidam
seductor*) named Tiberius Petasius obtained a following and was called emperor, but the movement was only local
and was promptly suppressed (*ib.* 983).
[2] The two letters to Leo were found
(in the sixteenth century) by Fronton
Le Duc in the library of the cardinal of
Lorraine. The first was evidently
written in 727 immediately after the

receipt of Leo's, which was written in
726 (ninth indiction). *See* Hefele, iii. p.
373, who has clearly demonstrated the
true date, as I have observed above.
The letter to Germanus will be found
in Mansi, xiii. 91.
[3] βασιλεὺς καὶ ἱερεύς εἰμι (quoted in
the second letter of Gregory, Mansi, xii.
976). Gregory admits in principle the
claim of the Emperors to be considered
pontiffs—successors of St. Peter; but
by heterodoxy of course an Emperor
forfeits his claim. The difference, I
suppose, between an Emperor and a
Pope is that an Emperor can be heterodox, while a Pope is incapable of
heresy.
[4] ἠσχόλησας αὐτοὺς (τοὺς ταπεινοὺς
λαούς) εἰς ἀργολογίας καὶ ὕθλους καὶ

Having held a council in Rome (727), which condemned iconoclasm, Gregory anathematised the enemies of pictures—expressly mentioning Paul the exarch of Ravenna, but not extending the ban to the Emperor. Leo threatened to treat him as Constans had treated Martin; but the Pope felt secure, with the Lombards and western Christendom to support him, and plainly told the Emperor of New Rome that the Church of Old Rome was the great bulwark of the Empire in Italy against the Lombards. At the same time, it was not the policy of the Popes to favour the extension of Lombard domination in Italy; although the presence of such domination to a certain degree was useful to them as a check on the imperial power. The history of Italy has shown that a double, treble, or multiple political rule has tended to exalt the papal power, and a single rule has tended to depress it; effects which might have been predicted. Accordingly, whether the Popes of the period were on friendly or hostile terms with the Emperors, they regarded with disfavour Lombard aggressions on imperial territory. Yet Lombard aggressions at this time began to turn out to the advantage of the Roman see; for the moral influence of the Popes induced the Lombard kings to present as a donation to the successors of St. Peter what they had taken away from the successors of Constantine. Thus the letters of Gregory II persuaded Liutprand to hand over to him the strong town of Sutrium (south of Viterbo), shortly after it had been captured by the Tuscan Lombards.

Eutychius had not been long restored to his residence at Ravenna when a new and curious political combination, re-versing the usual relations of Italian politics, surprised the peninsula for a moment. The exarch Eutychius and King Liutprand formed a league against the Pope and the dukes of Beneventum and Spoletium,[1] who had allied themselves to win back from Liutprand the cities of the exarchate.

I must remind the reader of the position of the dukes of Beneventum and Spoletium. They enjoyed an almost complete immunity from the interference of the Lombard kings,

---

κιθάρας καὶ κροτάλιά τε καὶ αὐλούς καὶ λήρους καὶ ἀντὶ εὐχαριστίας καὶ δοξολογίας εἰς μύθους αὐτοὺς ἐνέβαλες.

[1] Anastas. *V. Greg. Eutychius patricius et Liutprandus rex inierunt con-*

silium nefarium, etc. For this affair, see Hirsch, *op. cit.* p. 35. Langen remarks (*op. cit.* p. 610), "Charactere wie Liutprand, Gregor, Leo konnten unmöglich mit einander in Frieden leben."

who dwelled far away in the north at Pavia, and were separated from them by the hostile territory of the exarchate. These duchies were in fact, throughout the seventh century and until the reign of Liutprand, independent principalities. The dukes appointed their own civil officers, and there was no royal domain, at least in Beneventum, to give the king a pretext to interfere. Thus it was to their interest that the exarchate should continue to exist, and that a strip of Roman territory should separate their dominions from the dominion of the king. This was especially desirable when the throne was filled by a vigorous ruler like Liutprand, who aimed at reducing all Italy under his sway, and first of all at bringing into a state of dependence the duchies of his own nationality.

The action of the dukes, Transmund of Spoletium and Romuald II of Beneventum, in allying themselves with the Pope against himself, decided Liutprand to exact their homage and allegiance. At the same time he felt a grudge against the Pope for his share in compassing the recovery of Ravenna, notwithstanding the donation of Sutrium. The exarch, in spite of the Pope's recent assistance, was bound to assert the imperial authority which the Pope had allowed to be defied in Rome. And thus this remarkable league came into existence.

Liutprand did not find it necessary to advance farther than Spoletium, nor was he obliged to make use of force to constrain the dukes to his allegiance. They both met him at Spoletium and acknowledged his suzerainty. He then proceeded to Rome and joined the exarch, who was besieging the city; but his arrival was the means of deliverance for the Pope. Furnished with the pomp and solemnities of his office, Gregory went forth into the camp of the Lombards, and by the influence of his personality moulded the will of the susceptible king, who, laying his arms at the feet of the pontiff, yielded to his wishes and induced the exarch to acquiesce in a peace favourable to Rome.

Soon after this Gregory II died[1] and was succeeded by Gregory III, whose election is remarkable for the circumstance

---

[1] According to my chronology, Gregory II died in 730 and the council was held 1st November 730; received date 731. *III Idus Feb.* of the fourteenth indiction is the date in Anastasius for Gregory's death.

that he was the last bishop of Old Rome for whose consecration the consent of the Emperor who resided at New Rome was asked. The third Gregory opposed iconoclasm, like his predecessor,[1] and in his pontificate the struggle came to an end as far as Italy was concerned. A council of ninety-three bishops assembled at Rome and excommunicated the iconoclasts; and in reply Leo sent a naval armament[2] of Cibyraiot seamen under the command of Manes to arrest the Pope on the charge of treason and bring him to Constantinople, as Martin had been treated eighty years before by Constans. The expedition never reached Rome, but the details of its failure are not clear. It appears that the armament was scattered by a storm in the Adriatic, and that the Greek troops were not over eager to carry out the Emperor's wishes.

At this juncture Leo came to the important conclusion that he would no longer oppose the Pope's ecclesiastical power in the dominions of the exarchate, but would translate the ecclesiastical jurisdiction of Sicily and Calabria, as well as of the dioceses of Illyricum, from the bishop of Rome to the Patriarch of Constantinople. The jurisdiction of Calabria meant the jurisdiction of the metropolitan Churches of Rhegium and Severiana and Hydrus (Otranto). All the bishoprics of the Bruttian peninsula were included in the two metropolitan provinces of Rhegium and Severiana, a town probably as old as the age of Pliny, now called by a name which it obtained in the tenth century, Santa Severina, and famous as the natal place of Pope Zacharias.

The effect of this act of Leo, which went far to decide the medieval history of southern Italy, was to bring the boundary between the ecclesiastical dominions of New Rome and Old Rome into coincidence with the boundary between the Greek and the Latin nationalities. In other words, it laid the basis of the distinction between the Greek and the Latin Churches. The only part of the Empire in which the Pope now possessed authority was the exarchate, including Rome, Ravenna, and Venice. The geographical position of Naples, intermediate between Rome and the extremities of Italy, determined that its sympathies should be drawn in two directions; in religious

---

[1] Gregory III sent three messengers to Leo, but they were all imprisoned.
[2] Theoph. 6225 A.M.

matters it inclined towards Old Rome, in political matters it was tenacious of its loyalty to New Rome.

The fact that the execution of such a thorough innovation as the detachment of south Italy from Rome was attended with no difficulty or opposition, may at first seem surprising. To explain it we are led to consider the other important, though indirect, result of iconoclasm, which was mentioned at the beginning of this chapter, namely the second Greek colonisation of southern Italy in the eighth century A.D., whereby it became a Greek land for four centuries, just as it had been a Greek land before the Roman conquest.

In the crypt of the cathedral of San Sabino at Bari an old discoloured Greek madonna is shown to visitors, which the inhabitants of Bari believe to be the celebrated Hodêgêtria, a picture supposed to have been executed by the hands of St. Luke himself. It was said to have come from Constantinople in one of the ships of the fleet of Manes (autumn 731), a fugitive from the sacrilegious hands of Leo. It had been originally presented to the princess Pulcheria and had been kept in the church of Hodêgos at Constantinople as a possession of priceless and talismanic value, and had sometimes been carried into battle to ensure victory. Regarded with a superstitious reverence above other pictures, it was a special stumbling-block to reason in the eyes of Leo the Isaurian, who decided that it should be burnt, in spite of its antiquity and historical associations; but two monks were sufficiently bold and cunning to convey it to one of the ships about to set sail for Italy, and store it away secretly and safely. When the tempest arose in the Adriatic "above the vessel in which this miraculous image was hidden, an angel descended from heaven under the form of a young man of the greatest beauty, who restored confidence to the terror-stricken crew, and seizing the helm guided the vessel safe and sound into the port of Bari, on the first Tuesday in March."[1] The inhabitants of Bari claim that they still possess this holy picture, now nearly two thousand years old. But the Greek inhabitants of Constantin-

[1] From the Synaxarion of the Greek church of Bari, translated by Lenormant, *op. cit.* vol. ii. p. 388. I am indebted to this valuable book, which sets forth clearly the truth about the Greek recolonisation of southern Italy (as first demonstrated by M. Zambellis), for many hints on the history of the Calabrian and Bruttian towns.

ople contend that they have the work of St. Luke, also miraculously preserved from the wrath of the iconoclasts, in a church of Blachernae.

This legend, as M. Lenormant elegantly remarks, may be taken " as a poetical symbol of the transplanting of Hellenism to Italy by orthodox refugees." In the eighth century it was decided that central and northern Italy were to be Latinised and pass out of the sphere of direct Greek influences, while southern Italy was to be Hellenised and detach itself in religion, nationality, and language from the Latin and German [1] world. This change, which knitted the south portion of the peninsula more closely to the eastern Mediterranean, was rendered possible by the indirect and unintentional consequence of iconoclasm, the emigration of an immense number of monks and laymen, who hoped in the recesses of Calabria and Bruttii, beyond the reach of Leo's arm, to be able to adore pictures and relics without fear. The number of orthodox Greeks— priests, monks, and laymen—who escaped from the East to southern Italy in the reigns of Leo and Constantine has been set at 50,000. It was really, as has been pointed out, a new Greek colonisation, which may be compared to the old Greek colonisation fourteen or fifteen hundred years before, and which explains such facts as that Squillace was a purely Latin town in the sixth century in the days of Cassiodorus, and a purely Greek town in the tenth century. Besides Bari, many other towns, such as Barletta in Apulia, Otranto, Amalfi, and Salerno, pretend to possess old Greek pictures brought from the East by iconodulic refugees.

The firm opposition which his religious reforms excited in the West prevented Leo, who was politically far-sighted, from pressing matters to extremes. He saw the danger of alienating the inhabitants in provinces, which without their co-operation might at any moment become the prey of the king of the Lombards or of the duke of Beneventum. He also apprehended clearly that northern Italy and Rome were more alien to the rest of the Empire than were southern Italy and Sicily. Under these circumstances, his policy was to draw in the less alien districts still closer, and allow the rest to remain as they were. But it necessarily resulted that the closer connection of the

---

[1] Teutonic elements were, however, to be introduced by the Normans.

one with the Empire caused the other to drift more and more away. The special mode, I conceive, in which this tendency operated, was the exclusion of the Pope from all jurisdiction in the eastern part of the Empire; his authority was confined to Latin-speaking districts. He was thus driven as it were into the arms of the German powers, in whose dominions his authority was still accepted as supreme; whereas in the Empire, with whose traditions his office was so closely associated, his influence was practically inoperative, except in a few provinces held by a precarious tenure, and the domains of the see of St. Peter had been confiscated by the temporal power.

Thus the great influx of Greeks, especially monks and priests, who were firmly attached to the Greek liturgy and forms of worship, explains the ease with which southern Italy was alienated from Old Rome. Leo, as I said, was judicious enough not to attempt to enforce his iconoclastic edicts in these regions, which seem to have enjoyed in the eighth century an almost unique period of material prosperity combined with spiritual peace, for which, however, a severe Nemesis in the shape of the "unnameable" Saracens was destined to overtake them in the ninth.

CHAPTER V

CONSTANTINE V [1]

SOON after the death of Leo, which occurred on the 18th June 740,[2] the elements of opposition to his government, which had smouldered during his lifetime, began to flame forth against his son Constantine, who was imbued with his father's ideas and inclined to carry them to further extremes. There were two distinct interests involved, which became blended in a common feeling of hostility to the Isaurian dynasty, the interest of the aristocratic class who maintained the old quarrel with imperial autocracy, and the interest of the orthodox friends of images. It was a favourable opportunity for an ambitious man to utilise the general discontent of large and influential circles before the new sovereign had securely established himself on the throne. Nor was the opportunity lost. Artavasdos, who had supported Leo at the time of his accession and married his daughter Anna, was not deterred by the ties of relationship from determining to oust his brother-in-law. He was count of Opsikion, and had two sons to support him, Nicephorus and Nicetas, of whom one held a command in Thrace, while the other was general of the Armeniac theme. The Armeniac troops were devoted to him; but the Anatolic and Thracesian themes were faithful in their allegiance to the son of Leo.

It was in June 741 that Constantine crossed over to Asia

---

[1] Our sources for this chapter are still Nicephorus and Theophanes. Nicephorus' history deserts us at the year 768. It seems to have been written before the conquest of the Avars by Charles the Great in 796, cf. p. 34, Παννωνίᾳ τῇ νῦν ὑπὸ 'Αβάροις κειμένῃ.

[2] Theoph. 6232 A.M. (τέθνηκε Λέων σὺν τῷ ψυχικῷ καὶ τὸν σωματικὸν θάνατον). The received date is 741, which, if the indictions had not been tampered with, would correspond to the ninth indiction (τῆς θ' ἰνδικτιῶνος). See above, p. 425.

Minor in order to conduct a campaign against the Saracens, and pitched his camp at a place called Krasos in Phrygia. He sent an order to Artavasdos, who with the Opsikian troops occupied the plain of Dorylaeum (near the borders of the Anatolic theme), to join him. Artavasdos, however, was already coming; he had assumed imperial rank, and he put to death the Emperor's messenger Bisêr, a patrician. Constantine had barely time to escape to Amorium in the Anatolic theme, where he was sure of personal safety and a loyal reception. The Anatolic troops swore to fight to the death for him, and were joined by the Thracesians under the command of Sisinnius.

Meanwhile Theophanes[1] Monôtios ("One Ear"), who had been left by Constantine as a sort of viceroy at Byzantium, declared for Artavasdos, and at his suggestion proclaimed publicly that Constantine was dead. Artavasdos was accepted as the new Emperor, his son Nicephorus with the Thracian army occupied the city, and the officials who remained loyal to the Isaurian family were displaced. The basis on which the usurper proposed to establish his power and secure popularity was the revival of picture-worship, and no time was lost in restoring pictures in the churches. The Patriarch Anastasius is said to have deserted his iconoclastic colours and to have publicly asserted that Constantine did not believe in the divinity of Christ. Anastasius probably found it necessary to temporise, but we must remember that his conduct is reported by writers who sympathised with his ecclesiastical opponents.

Constantine advanced with his army to Chrysopolis (Scutari), but no action took place, and he returned to Amorium, where he wintered. In the spring of 742 two battles were fought, in both of which Constantine was victorious and displayed his military skill. He first defeated Artavasdos, who was devastating the Thracesian provinces, at Sardis; and then marching in a north-easterly direction, met Nicetas, who was advancing with the Armeniac troops and Armenian auxiliaries,[2] and routed him utterly at Modrine in the Bucellarian theme. He next proceeded, supported by the Cibyraiot fleet, to besiege

---

[1] This Theophanes is called by the historian Theophanes, 6233 A.M., μάγιστρον ἐκ προσώπου, which shows that the office of *magister militum* *in praesenti* still existed.

[2] They were commanded by Tiridates, a cousin of Artavasdos.

Constantinople, where Artavasdos, having fled from the field of Sardis, had shut himself up. The city, unprepared to stand a siege and blockaded by land and sea, was soon reduced to straits of distress,[1] and it was necessary to relieve the pressure by tacitly allowing a large number of the non-fighting inhabitants to escape. All these were received kindly in the camp of Constantine, and many persons of high position, to whom Artavasdos would not have deemed it safe to grant permission to leave the city, stole out secretly in the disguise of women or monks.

Nicetas meanwhile had collected new forces since his defeat at Modrine, and now advanced to the relief of his father. Constantine met him at Nicomedia and defeated him a second time, taking him prisoner, as well as Marcellinus, the archbishop of Gangra, whom he beheaded. After this discomfiture Artavasdos, who had doubtless been holding out in expectation of succour from his son, fled to Nicaea, and having there collected a few soldiers, took refuge in the fortress of Puzane, where he was captured by a battalion of Constantine's army. At the spectacle in the hippodrome which celebrated Constantine's restoration to Byzantium, Artavasdos and his two sons were exposed to the view of the populace and then thrown into prison. Some time afterwards the general of the Thracesians, Sisinnius, who had stood by the Emperor in his difficulties, was convicted or suspected of treasonable plotting, and was deprived of his eyesight. It is possible that this plot was a scheme for the elevation of Artavasdos, as the eyes of Artavasdos [2] and his sons were also put out immediately afterwards.

The troubles that beset Constantine on his accession were a true augury of a stormy and uneasy reign; but the ability which he had displayed in overcoming the difficulties, also boded that his energy and skill would hold the joints of the

---

[1] The famine was so great that a bushel (modius) of barley was sold for 10, a bushel of pulse for 19, a bushel of millet or lupines for 8 nomismata respectively. 5 lbs. (litrai) of oil cost a nomisma, a pint of wine (ξέστης, *i.e.* *sextarius*) cost a semission. The Cibyraiot ships were kept at bay by the fireships, which lay in the imperial arsenal at the disposal of Artavasdos.

[2] On the influence of Armenians and Asiatics in the Empire, *see* Finlay, ii. pp. 200, 201; cf. Bardanes, Artavasdos, Alexius Mouselé (790), Bardan (rebelled against Nicephorus I.), Arsaber (father-in-law of Leo V).

time together. Although it was a time of uneasiness, it was
not a time of rottenness, like the reign of Phocas or the reign
of Apsimar; the policy of Leo had reformed the State.   But
the very tendency to reform had created an uneasy surging
movement in the Empire.   This tendency did not consist
merely in the conscious endeavours and definite activity of the
Emperor and those who sympathised with his spirit of rational
enlightenment.   All these conscious endeavours and activities
were themselves the result of a general tendency to change,
which was latently at work among the inhabitants of the
eastern Mediterranean in the eighth century.   I already touched
on this subject in speaking of the pestilence which raged in
the reign of Justinian, and put forward the conjecture that
plagues on a great scale spread at periods when the organisms
of a people are involved in a precarious condition of transfor-
mation or decay, and may be peculiarly susceptible to noxious
external influences.   The plague itself contributes to the formation of a new world by clearing away an effete population
and making room for new settlers, while only the fittest of the
old inhabitants survive its ravages.

A great plague of this kind broke out in the reign of Constantine and desolated large portions of the Roman dominions.
It originated in Syria (744) and spread thence to Constantinople,
not, however, by way of Asia Minor, but in a circular direction,
travelling through Egypt, Africa, Sicily, and Calabria, and
passing thence to Greece and the Archipelago.   It is interesting to note this course, for it shows that the plague followed
lines of commercial traffic.   Had Syria still belonged to the
Roman Empire the pestilence would doubtless have traversed
Asia Minor and so reached the Bosphorus, as in the days of
Justinian; but there was now little intercourse by land between Asia Minor and Syria, as a chronic state of hostility
prevailed between the caliphate and the Empire and the trade
of the two states was carried on by sea.

The following account of this pestilence is given by Theophanes, who was born about the time of its prevalence :—

" A pestilential death, beginning in Sicily and Calabria,
advancing like fire to Monobasia [1] (*i.e.* Monembasia) and Hellas

---

[1] In the biography of St. Wilibald,   by his kinswoman, a nun of Heiden-
bishop of Eichstädt (741-786), written   heim, we find the following statement ·

and the adjacent islands, spread throughout the whole of the four-teenth indiction (744-745), chastising the impious Constantine and restraining the mad violence against holy churches and sacred pictures; yet he remained incorrigible, like Pharaoh of old. And this plague of *bubo* (swelling in the groin) reached the imperial city in the fifteenth indiction (745-746); and then, suddenly and without visible cause, many crosses of olive oil began to appear on the garments of men and on the sacred cloths of the church (St. Sophia). Hence men were seized with sorrow and great despondency, in perplexity at such a sign; and the divine wrath, destroying and not sparing, over-took not only the inhabitants of the city but those who dwelled round about it. Moreover, many saw apparitions, and, having fallen into ecstasy, they fancied that they were communing with certain strange, as it seemed, and hideous faces, and that they addressed them as friends and discoursed with them, and noting what they said, declared it unto others. And they saw the same forms entering their houses and slaying some of the household, and wounding others with swords. But most of the things which the forms told them fell out, as they afterwards beheld.

" And in the spring of the first indiction (747) the pesti-lence spread to a greater extent, and in summer its flame culminated to such a height that whole houses were entirely shut up, and those on whom the office devolved could not bury their dead. In the embarrassment of the circumstances, the plan was conceived of carrying out the dead on saddled animals, on whose backs were placed frameworks of planks. In the same way they placed the corpses above one another in waggons. And when all the burying-grounds in the city and suburbs had been filled, and also the dry cisterns and tanks, and very many vineyards had been dug up, the gardens too within the old walls were used for the purpose of burying human bodies, and even thus the need was hardly met."

inde navigantes venerunt ultra mare Adriaticum ad urbem Monafasiam in Slavinica terra, *et inde navigantes in insulam nomine Choo dimittebant Corinthios in sinistra parte.* The journey of St. Wilibald to the East took place be-tween 723 and 728, so it would appear that at that time the Slaves dwelled in the Peloponnesus, though of course they did not hold Monembasia. Hopf, how-ever, discredits the statement, and em-phasises the geographical ignorance of the authoress. But we have seen that there is no reason to assume that there were not considerable Slavonic settle-ments in the Peloponnesus as early as the seventh century (*see* the statement of Isidore, above, p. 280). Hopf in the Graeco-Slavonic controversy is almost as much an *advocate* as Fallmerayer.

Towards the end of 747 the violence of the disease abated. Constantinople was depopulated after the black year, and while his orthodox enemies were making the most of the misfortune as a direct visitation on the iconoclasts, whom they regarded as no better than Jews, Constantine began to take measures for repopulating the capital. For this purpose he transplanted families on a large scale from Greece and the islands to Constantinople. The effect of this act was to leave room in the Greek peninsula, already depopulated by the plague, for the Slaves, who began to press southward in greater numbers than ever, and complete the process of Slavising large districts of Hellas and the Peloponnesus,[1] in which there was a considerable Slavonic element already. Two tribes, called Ezerites and Melings, established themselves on Mount Taygetus, and long remained independent.

The question suggests itself, how far the Slaves who had been settling in Greece as early as the second half of the sixth century were interfused with the native Greek population. On this subject we have little or no evidence, but we may be

---

[1] Our authority is the celebrated notice of Constantine Porphyrogennetos (*de Them.* ii. 6), ἐσθλαβώθη δὲ πᾶσα ἡ χώρα καὶ γέγονε βάρβαρος, of which Fallmerayer made so much for his Slavonic theory. We know not what basis Constantine had for his statement, but there is no reason to doubt it ; and it is quite impossible to explain away (as M. Sathas and others have attempted to do) the word ἐσθλαβώθη. The pronunciation Sthlaves was a Greek softening of Sclaves. But at the same time πᾶσα must not be pressed, it is evidently an exaggeration ; and we must not, with Fallmerayer, draw any conclusions as to the large towns, which continued to be Hellenic. Constantine illustrates his assertion by a witticism of the grammarian Euphemius (in the tenth century), who described the face of Nicetas, a conceited Peloponnesian, as γαρασδοειδὴς ὄψις ἐσθλαβωμένη. Hopf explains γαρασδοειδής as "cunning" (*verschmitztes, Gr. Gesch.* p. 96) ; Banduri rendered it by γερορτοειδής ; while Finlay emended it to γαδαροειδής, "asslike" (ii. p. 305). But the emendation, though ingenious, carries no conviction ; why should the intelligible γαδαρο- (mod. Gk. γαΐδαρος = ass) have become the difficult γαρασδο- ? It is clear that

γαρασδο- is not Greek, and from the context we might be inclined to conclude that it contains some special Slavonic allusion. I conjecture that the Greeks applied the term Γαρασδοι or Γαραζοι to the inhabitants of Slavonic town-settlements—"men of a *gârad*" (or town). This Slavonic word (Church. Slav. *grad*, Russ. *górod*) is familiar from such names as Novgorod, Belgrad. The use of the word by the Slaves who settled in Greece is proved by three towns called Gardíki in Greece, one in Messenia and two in Thessaly. *Gardíki* is a diminutive form, cf. Russ. *gorodók*. Γαρασδοι was probably applied to the Slaves of some special gârad (or gardíki), well known to the contemporaries of Constantine VII. According to this conjecture we might translate the verse,

" A Slavonised and Garaditish face."

The numerous Slavonic names of places in modern Greece are an important confirmation of Constantine's assertion ; they have been treated of in the essay of Miklosich, *Die slavischen Elemente im Neugriechischen.* I may add that our English Slavonic scholar Mr. Morfill holds the view that Greece was Slavised, see *Early Slavonic Literature.*

justified in speculating that the infusion took place rapidly, and that the Slaves who settled in Greece between the dates 570 and 640 were gradually and easily converted to Christianity. It is at least remarkable that we hear of no intestine conflicts in Greece, nor yet of a mission for the conversion of the Slavonic settlers there. It is inviting to compare the infusion of the Slaves with the Greeks to the speedy amalgamation of the Danes, who invaded England in the ninth century, with the Angles. "The Danish Odo, Oskytel, and Oswald were archbishops in less than a century after Halfdane had divided Northumbria"[1]; and just in the same way the Slavonian Nicetas became Patriarch of New Rome in the reign of Constantine V. We may pursue the parallel further, and compare the later Danish migrations of the eleventh century to the later Slavonic migration of the eighth century, of which we have just spoken. It was against these new immigrants, not yet amalgamated with the inhabitants, that the expedition of Stauracius was directed in 783.

Thus the plague was fruitful in far-reaching changes. On the one hand, an immense number of the inhabitants of Greece, who kept up many old Hellenic traditions, were either exterminated or transferred to a new place, where they came under new influences. On the other hand, a vast portion of the inhabitants of Byzantium, who maintained a certain Roman character and many Roman traditions amid all their half-Hellenic half-oriental ways, had been carried off by the plague, and were replaced by pure Greeks who had not inherited the effects of Roman influence, but, on the other hand, had been affected by intercourse with the Slaves. A double process went on in Byzantium; the new Greek settlers were Byzantinised, and at the same time Byzantium was Hellenised more completely than before. This was an important step in the direction of becoming a Greek nationality, to which goal the Roman Empire was steadily tending.

But we must especially emphasise the fact that these changes mark the final separation of the Empire from the ancient world and its assumption of a completely medieval

---

[1] Stubbs, *Constitutional History*, i. p. 219. The rapid amalgamation of Slavonic settlers in more northern regions of the Illyric peninsula is indicated by the position of Belisarius, if I am right in interpreting his name as Slavonic (White Dawn).

character. The removal of the Greeks from Greece cut off the dim survivals of the ancient Hellenic spirit; the depopulation of partly-Roman New Rome cut off the dim survivals of the ancient Roman spirit. All the elements that define the Middle Ages operated henceforward unstifled and unmodified. In the middle of the sixth century, the time of the plague in Justinian's reign, we left the ancient world and entered the outer gate of the medieval city[1]; in the reign of Heraclius, after the conquest of Persia, we passed an inner gate[2]; but the innermost gate is not reached till the eighth century; and the plague in the reign of Constantine marks the new departure. The ninth century and the twelfth are far more homogeneous than the sixth and the eighth.

Neither Constantine nor his father Leo took pains to commemorate their reigns by costly buildings, as did other less patriotic Emperors when the public purse could but ill afford the expense. Constantine, however, executed one solid and useful public work. The aqueduct of Valens had been destroyed by the Avars when they besieged Constantinople in the reign of Heraclius, and had never been restored since. The consequence was that the city was not well supplied with water, and when there was a drought in 766, the want of a duct to bring water from the hills was painfully felt. The Emperor immediately set about the restoration of the old aqueduct, which involved a large outlay. He collected skilled workmen from various parts of the Empire: a thousand masons and two thousand plasterers or cement-workers from Pontus and from Asia (that is, the western coast lands of Asia Minor); five thousand labourers and two hundred potters from Thrace; five hundred *ostrakarioi* or pottery-workers from Greece and the Aegean islands.[3]

Constantine was said to be avaricious, and one writer calls him a " Christ-hating new Midas." This accusation seems

---

[1] *See* vol. i. p. 399.

[2] *See* above, p. 246. It may be well to state that I use the conventional terms *ancient*, *medieval*, and *modern* as a convenient way of marking certain broad distinctions, but without attaching any intrinsic value to arbitrary lines of division.

[3] Both κεραμοποιοί and ὀστρακάριοι mean potters. The latter, I suppose, made the earthenware pipes (which Vitruvius considered better than leaden, as the water that passed was purer), and the former were the brickmakers. *See* Theophanes, 6258 A.M. = 765-766.

to be chiefly founded on a curious and unjustifiable economic
measure, which, whether designedly or not, had the effect of
benefiting the non-productive portion of the community at the
expense of the productive. He withheld the imperial revenue
from circulation, and this at once cheapened all articles of
food. The farmers and corn-growers were forced to sell their
products at absurdly small prices; so that the money received
was hardly sufficient to pay the taxes, which were not diminished and were exacted in coin. Meanwhile the non-agricul-
tural classes, the buyers, were jubilant, attributing the low
prices to plenteous crops, instead of to the true cause, scarcity
of the medium of exchange. This affair is an interesting para-
graph in the history of political economy.[1]

Constantine married three times. By his first wife, Irene,
the daughter of the khan of the Khazars, he had one son Leo
(nicknamed " the Khazar "), who succeeded him. His second
wife, Maria, died childless in 751. He then married Eudocia,
who bore him five sons, Christophorus, Nicephorus, Nicetas,
Anthimus, and Eudocimus. The eldest son, Leo, married an
accomplished and ambitious Athenian lady named Irene in
768. The second and third sons were raised to the rank of
Caesar and the fourth and fifth to the rank of nobilissimus in
768; the youngest, Eudocimus, was not made a nobilissimus
until the reign of his half-brother Leo.[2]

---

[1] On the great wealth of society at
this period, *see* Finlay, ii. 213. Our direct
evidence for the amount of specie in circulation in the Roman Empire concerns
the reign of Theophilus rather than the
eighth century; but it is certain that
the Empire kept the west of Europe
supplied with gold coins.

[2] Constantine had a daughter named
Anthusa by his third wife. She was
called after a nun, a friend and protégée
of her mother. " The princess Anthusa

was distinguished for her benevolence
and piety; she is said to have founded
one of the first orphan asylums established in the christian world; and her
orthodox devotion to pictures obtained
for her a place among the saints of the
Greek Church, an honour granted also
to her godmother and teacher " (Finlay,
ii. p. 68). The intimate relations of
the nun Anthusa to the imperial family
shows Constantine's domestic mildness.

ISAURIAN DYNASTY

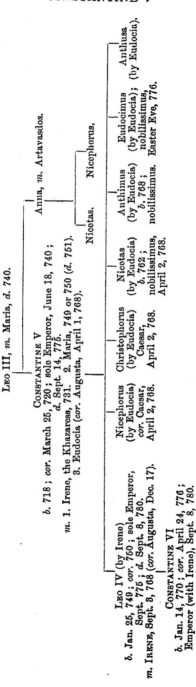

CHAPTER VI

CONSTANTINE was an apt pupil of his father Leo in the lessons of autocratic government and the assertion of imperial supremacy in ecclesiastical affairs. But in the matter of iconoclasm his little finger was thicker than his father's loins, and he detested so intensely the superstition and stupidity which were fostered by the monks that he ended by persecuting them with a sort of passionate bitterness. As monasticism was one of the most radical elements of medieval Christendom, Constantine's opposition may appear vain and untimely [2]; nevertheless, he was not altogether beating the air. For, although persecution is always impolitic, the attitude of the iconoclasts was the expression of a new and healthy spirit, and we should not blame them much if they fell into the error of intolerance, whose entire eradication can be looked for only after a long education of the human race. And when we read the accounts of the persecutions we must remember that they emanate from Constantine's opponents, and that no sources written in the iconoclastic interest are extant. It will not be necessary to enter here into the details of the "martyrdoms,"

---

[1] For this chapter my chief Greek authorities are the Chronography of Theophanes ; the Acts of the seventh Ecumenical (second Nicene) Council, Mansi, vols. xii. and xiii.; the Life of St. Andreas of Crete (*Acta Sanctorum*, Oct. viii.); *Vita Stephani Junioris* (published 1688 A.D. in the *Analecta Graeca* of the Benedictines). A pamphlet against Constantine V, falsely ascribed to John of Damascus, is contained in the *Cod. Reg.* 2428—a codex written by Leo Cinnamus in the year sψπδ′=6784, who transcribed it from a codex written in sσξζ′ = 6267 (5̄17 years before)=758 A.D. Migne has included this in his edition of John Damascenus.

[2] I shall point out further on that Constantine's policy was actuated by economic motives as well as by hatred of superstition.

which find a fitter place in works on ecclesiastical history ; our attention is directed rather to the general spirit of the rationalistic movement.

Constantine not only condemned picture-worship and hated monachism, but his orthodoxy in theological doctrine was extremely doubtful, and in some respects his moral principles were decidedly far from austere.   Thereby he laid himself open to the attacks of his opponents, who made him out to be almost a pagan in creed and a Minotaur or a Cyclops in manners.

The stories that are told to illustrate his tendency to Nestorianism, or even to Arianism, have probably a basis of fact, and both Leo and Constantine may have been secretly inclined to a unitarian system as a purer form of religion.   In any case, Constantine won the reputation of being addicted to free theological speculation.   He forbade the prefixion of the epithet *saint* to the names of men ; he would not permit any one to speak of St. Peter, but only of the apostle Peter.   He bantered his courtiers unsparingly when they displayed traits of superstition or an inclination to practise austerities, which he deemed unjustified by reason.   If one of his nobles slipped and fell in his presence and happened to employ such an expression as " Virgin, help me," he was exposed to the Emperor's smiles or sneers.   If a minister was in the habit of attending church services with a pious and punctilious regularity, or complied with such a custom as the keeping of a sacred vigil, the Emperor laughed him to scorn.   Even an over-scrupulous care in avoiding profane language was held up to ridicule by this enemy of all that savoured of superstition.

Constantine recoiled in horror from the austerity as well as from the superstition of monasticism, and he held a merry, perhaps ribald court, which gave his enemies welcome material for charges against him.   His palace was the scene of banqueting, music, and dancing ; he was not prudish in conversation ; he was fond of the companionship of handsome young men.   His ecclesiastical opponents circulated mysterious stories of secret orgies ; and a tale was told, which may be true or false, that a youth named Strategius, whose intimacy Constantine courted with peculiar ardour, communicated the dangerous secret to a third person, and was on that account put to death by the Emperor.[1]

Both Leo and Constantine, while they deprived the people of sacred pictures, desired to substitute other things, not for their edification, but rather for their amusement. Pope Gregory accused Leo of endeavouring to replace images[2] by harps, cymbals, and flutes, as means of popular enjoyment; perhaps Leo organised public concerts. Constantine was fond of music; the attention which he paid to harp-playing is one of the charges brought against him; and it was he who sent to Pipin the first "organ" that ever reached western Europe. Theatrical entertainments, to which the Quinisext Synod had assumed an uncompromisingly hostile attitude, were in favour with the iconoclasts[3]; nor did their reprobation of sacred and seductive pictures by any means imply hostility to the art of painting as an art. For example, when the walls of St. Maria in Blachernae were stripped (after the synod of 753 A.D.) of pictures which illustrated the history of Christ, they were covered instead with paintings of landscapes,—trees and birds and fruits. How beautiful such ornamentation may have been we can fancy from the exquisite mosaics preserved in the church of St. George at Salonica; but the author of the *Life of Stephanus* describes St. Maria as transformed into an aviary and a fruit market. The Patriarch's palace was adorned with "Satanic" representations of hunting scenes, horse-races, and similar subjects. Hence we cannot take literally the condemnations of painting in itself which are recorded to have been uttered by the synod of 753.

This synod, which condemned image-worship as contrary to Christianity, was held at Constantinople, and consisted of 338

[1] Constantine has been accused, among other things, of intercourse with demons, of delighting in effeminate practices (μαλακίαι), and of a strange hankering after the excrement of horses (whence, it is said, he was called "Kaballinos"). In regard to Constantine's character, it is as stupid of Walch, his admirer, to make hazardous assertions about his chastity as it is irrelevant of his detractors to dwell on the statements that impugn his morality in sexual relations. It is well worthy of note that in this respect the fame of Leo III has not been even breathed upon by the most virulent of his foes.

[2] See above, p. 443.

[3] For example, John of Damascus, in a letter to Constantine V, mentioned several of that Emperor's followers as fond of theatrical shows, as we are told in the *Vita Stephani Junioris*. He called the iconoclastic bishops κοιλιοδούλους τε καὶ γαστρόφρονας; he called Constantine himself αἱρεσχελῇ(?) καὶ Μάμωθ εἰκονοκαύστην τε καὶ μισάγιον. The reading αἱρεσχελῇ is uncertain; it is rendered in the Latin translation *haereticam blateronem*, as if αἱρεσερεσχελῇ.

members, but was not attended by representatives from Rome, Alexandria, Antioch, or Jerusalem, so that it had no just claim to be styled ecumenical.[1] The Patriarch Anastasius had died of a foul disease in the preceding year, and as no one had been elected in his place, Theodosius, bishop of Ephesus and son of the Emperor Apsimar, presided at the council. Soon afterwards the patriarchal chair was filled by Constantinos, bishop of Sylaeum, who was presented to the people in the church at Blachernae by the Emperor himself, with the words, "Long live the ecumenical Patriarch." A few days afterwards, accompanied by the new Patriarch and the bishop of Ephesus, Constantine declared aloud his heretical doctrine in the Augusteum (Forum of Constantine).

After the synod, coercive measures were taken to carry out its resolutions. It would seem that for almost ten years after Constantine's victory over Artavasdos he had abstained from active proceedings against the adoration of pictures, waiting until he should feel himself securely established on the throne, and that consequently the churches which Leo had purified were once more adorned with sacred paintings and images. The monks, moreover, had taken advantage of the lull to propagate the orthodox doctrine and encourage the forbidden practices ; nor did they cease after the synod to agitate against the Emperor and the Patriarch. But for several years wars and other affairs prevented Constantine from pushing coercion to extremes and suppressing by violent measures the refractory monks who, from the aspect of Caesaropapism, were no better than rebels.

But in 761 the persecution began, and among the many monks who were put to death or maltreated six stand out conspicuously, as the Greek Church commemorates the anni-

---

[1] In the preceding year preparatory synods were held in the provinces. The Patriarchs of Alexandria, Antioch, and Jerusalem declared themselves in favour of image-worship. Notwithstanding the fact that the see of Constantinople stood alone, the council of 753 styled itself the seventh Ecumenical Council. It condemned images of Christ and images of the saints on different grounds ; the former (and here we see the approximation to monophysitism), because Christ's nature being divine, is ἀκατάληπτος, incomprehensible, and ἀπερίγραφος, not circumscribable, and therefore must not be represented circumscribed by the limits of a figure in space ; the latter (to which this reasoning would not apply), because all images and idols in religious worship savoured of heathen usage. It must be specially noted that the synod enjoined that rich churches were not to be plundered or injured on the pretence of iconoclasm.

versaries of their martyrdoms. Peter Kalybites,[1] who had called Constantine a new Valens and a new Julian,—he probably detested an Arian even more than a pagan,—was flogged to death in the circus of St. Mamas in Blachernae on the 16th of May. John of Monagria suffered two months later. The year 766 was signalised by the executions of Paul of Crete and Andreas of Crete. Another Paul underwent martyrdom in 771 (8th July). But of all the victims the most celebrated and influential was the abbot Stephanus, whose death is commemorated on the 28th day of November ; the year in which he suffered cannot be fixed with positive certainty, as the statements of our authorities are contradictory. Stephanus lived the austere life of an anchoret in a cell on Mount Auxentius in Bithynia, and when Constantine began (about the year 760 or 761) to suppress monks and monasteries, not only the monks of Bithynia, but those of Constantinople and the country round about, betook themselves to the secluded mountain and lived under the guidance of the abbot. It was said that false witnesses were suborned by the Emperor to bring charges against this powerful opponent, and that a noble widow, Anna, the spiritual daughter of Stephanus, was accused by her slave of having indulged in carnal conversation with the abbot, and was whipped in the vain hope of extorting a confession (about September 762). When this charge failed, Stephanus was accused of having transgressed the Emperor's edict that no monk should take in a novice, and of having tried to seduce a young court page into embracing monastic life under his guidance. Of course the biographer of the martyr represents this charge as false, but we cannot accept his colouring of the story without reservation, and must regard it as at least quite possible that the complaints of the page had some foundation.[2]

---

[1] Theophanes erroneously calls him Andreas Kalybites, while conversely he calls Andreas of Crete Peter Stylites. *See* the article of the Bollandists, "de Andrea Cretensi dicto in crisi," *Acta Sanctorum*, Oct. vol. viii. (1853). John, the abbot of Monagria, is commemorated on 4th June ; Paul of Crete on 17th March ; Andreas of Crete on 20th October. Hefele and the Bollandists place the martyrdom of the two last in 767. According to my chronology the date is 760, which corresponds partly

to 6258 A.M. and partly to 6259 A.M.

[2] The charges against Stephanus (according to the Patriarch Nicephorus) were that "he deceives many, teaching them to despise present glory and houses and kindred, and to leave the imperial court and adopt the monastic life" ; and Nicephorus, so far from hinting that the charges are false, considers the alleged conduct part of the monk's piety. Stephanus' proselytising habits were just what made him so obnoxious to the Emperor.

At all events, the Emperor's representations of the matter in Constantinople created a current of popular excitement against the monks, and Constantine no longer hesitated to send soldiers to Mount Auxentius with orders to pull down the monastery and the church, which were built at a lower point on the mountain than the cell of the abbot,[1] to disperse all the monks, and to conduct Stephanus to the island of Proconnesus. He was allowed to remain there in exile for a space of two years, but as crowds of monks congregated to him and he continued to preach the doctrine of image-worship with unflagging energy, he was at length removed in fetters to Constantinople (764) and flung into the praetorian prison (*praetorium*) with 342 monks, who were condemned to suffer various penalties and indignities—some losing their eyes, some having their ears or noses slit, while the beards of others were tarred and burnt. Stephanus was condemned to death, and stoned or hewed to pieces in the street.[2]

Soon after he had removed from his way the zealous and noxious Stephanus, the Emperor adopted the measure of exacting an oath from all his subjects that they would not worship pictures. About the same time he induced the Patriarch Constantinos to relax the severity of manners affected by ecclesiastics, to abandon the habit of eschewing meat, to join in good fellowship at the imperial table, and to assist at musical entertainments. The Patriarch thus became, in the eyes of the monks, no better than a worldly reveller.

When he had returned from his unfortunate expedition against Bulgaria (765), Constantine entertained the populace and held the monks up to ridicule by a curious exhibition. He caused a large number of monks to walk up and down the hippodrome, each holding a harlot, or, according to some accounts, a nun, by the hand, spat upon and jeered by all the people. As for the monasteries, which were numerous, he had either caused them to be pulled down, as those of Calli-

---

[1] The cell was situated under the highest peak of the mountain.

[2] The body of Stephanus was thrown into a place called "the tombs of Pelagius" (or Pelagioi), where pagans and suicides were buried. The exact name is not clear, for the MSS. of Nicephorus in one place read ἐν τοῖς καλουμένοις τάφοις τῶν Πελαγίου (p. 72, ed. de Boor) and in another place (p. 75) τοὺς τῶν Πελαγίων καλουμένους τάφους (so Theoph. p. 674). I am inclined to think that the original name was τὰ Πελαγίου, and that it afterwards became corrupted to the plural.

stratus and Dion, or converted them into barracks for soldiers like that of Dalmatus.

Hitherto the campaign against monachism had been chiefly confined to Byzantium and regions in the vicinity on either side of the Propontis; but in 766 Constantine appointed staunch and unflinching iconoclasts, men after his own heart, to governorships in the Asiatic provinces, and commanded them to abolish pictures and coerce monks. Michael Lachanodrakon was made governor of the Thracesian, Michael of Melissene of the Anatolic, and Manes of the Bucellarian theme. Who can describe, cries the chronicler, the evils which these men did in the provinces? But we hear no details until the end of the year 769 or the beginning of 770, when Lachanodrakon assembled all the monks and nuns of the Thracesian theme in a plain called Tzukanisterion ("Pologround"), and bade them immediately marry under pain of being transported to Cyprus. Many, most probably, yielded, but some chose the penalty. Subsequently the same governor attacked the monasteries, committed all the patristic books, monastic manuals, and sacred relics to the flames, and sent to the Emperor a welcome sum of money obtained by selling the costly consecrated vessels. The Emperor wrote him a letter of warm thanks, and said, "I have found a man after my own heart." Not a monk was left in the Thracesian theme, and it is said that Lachanodrakon anointed the beards of some with a mixture of oil and wax and set fire to them; but these are the stories of opponents.

I may here draw attention to another aspect of Constantine's war against the monks, and point out that economical considerations as well as the desire of uprooting superstition evidently influenced his policy. In a society where the danger was depopulation, not over-population, the monastic system was distinctly an evil. A few monasteries scattered here and there might have been not only innocuous but highly beneficial; but in the Roman Empire cloisters multiplied every year, and a sort of mania seems to have seized the wealthier classes in the eighth century to found monasteries and retire to their seclusion. The consequence was that an unduly large proportion of the population, men who should have been productive and reproductive citizens, led a life of sterility and inactivity, saving as they thought their own souls, utterly regardless of the State.   The progress of this individualism was fraught with peril for the Empire, which was always surrounded by enemies and needed the active co-operation of every subject for its preservation ; and I believe that this was one of the deepest causes which led to the decline of the Eastern Empire.   For after the iconoclastic movement had died out, the monastic spirit increased more and more, and almost every man who was in receipt of a respectable income saved money in order to endow a monastery before he died ; while it was a common occurrence that ministers or governors embraced the spiritual life ere they had passed their prime.

Constantine V could not be blind to this aspect of the monastic system, nor could he fail to see that it stood in direct antagonism to the interests of the State.   It is recorded that he always became angry if he heard that any of his courtiers or officers entertained the intention of retiring to a cloister ; and the statement not only indicates the Emperor's attitude but also illustrates the fact that persons of rank frequently sought the seclusion of cells.   The measure of compelling monks to marry proves, I think, that a desire to redress the evil of depopulation, as well as the motive of eradicating superstition, determined Constantine's policy.   It may be added that the enormous ravages which the great pestilence made among the inhabitants of the Empire rendered the population question more important and pressing than ever. If we once realise that not merely ecclesiastical differences of opinion, but social and political problems of the greatest magnitude, were involved in Constantine's conflict with monasticism, we shall be more able to comprehend and ready to make allowances for the unrelenting severity with which he suppressed men like Stephanus, who, though personally amiable and well-meaning, exerted all their power and influence to maintain a system which, as he plainly saw, was undermining and ruining the Empire.[1]   One might almost say that the

---

[1] In regard to the method adopted by Constantine in secularising the lands of monasteries and religious houses, we have no certain historical evidence ; but it seems at least probable that he put into practice the *charistic* system, which was so notable a feature in the eleventh century.   At all events, it is well worthy of notice that John, a Patriarch of Antioch, in his

spirit of Constantine's policy anticipated the famous paradox of Gibbon that the virtues of the clergy are more dangerous to society than their vices.

Before concluding this chapter I must mention the fate of the Patriarch Constantinos, of which the causes are somewhat obscure. A conspiracy was formed against Constantine in August 765, shortly after his disastrous expedition to Bulgaria, by a number of men of high rank, including Antiochus, who had filled the posts of governor of Sicily and *logothete of the course*[1]; Constantine Podopagurus, who was in office as logothete of the course, and his brother Strategius, the domesticus of the imperial guards; David, count of Opsikion; Theophylactus, governor of Thrace. Constantine and Strategius were beheaded, others were blinded. But the most remarkable circumstance was that the iconoclastic Patriarch Constan-

---

Oratio in donationes monasteriorum Laicis factos, traces this system to the iconoclastic Emperors, especially Constantine V. (*See* Cotelerius, *Ecclesiae Graecae Monumenta*, i. 168, 169). The *charistic* system, as it may be called, corresponded to the benefice system of the West, and consisted in making over lands as a present, διὰ χαριστικῆς, without any contract or written conditions. The lands were consequently not alienated, and if the charistikiar (as the receiver of the benefice was called) did not satisfy the possessor or fulfil his verbal conditions, the possessor might resume possession when he liked. This practice was very common in the eleventh century in the case of monasteries, but there is no evidence that it was employed in the case of secular landed property. M. Skabalonovitch gives a long and interesting account of the system in his *Vizantyskoe Gosudarstvo i Tserkov v* xi. *Vĕkĕ*, p. 253 *sqq.* He identifies this system with the system of *beneficia* or *precaria* (*prekarno-benefitsialnaya sistema*), of whose existence in the fifth century we have evidence in Salvian and the Code of Justinian, and which was in full force in Gaul under the Merovingians. Among the Franks the two chief sources of feudalism were (1) benefices of two kinds, and (2) commendations. The charistic system and the πρόνοιαι

(imperial gifts, resumable at pleasure) of the eleventh century are the analogues of one form of the western *beneficia*; and we have proofs that the other form of benefice also existed at the beginning of the tenth century. Poor landowners gave (τρόπῳ δωρεᾶς) their property to richer lords for the sake of the protection and patronage of the latter, as we learn from constitutions of Romanus. In this practice there were the germs of a mild feudalism, and it is interesting to observe that the Emperors endeavoured to counteract the tendency. The expression δωρεά, which is also applied to the charistic custom, leads Skabalonovitch (p. 262) to bring the two customs into close connection. The second form of benefices in the West may be traced back to the *patrocinia majorum* of Salvian, but it would be hazardous to argue that the custom was prevalent in the East before the ninth century. The two forms are explained by Stubbs, *Constitutional History*, i. 275. The other element of feudalism, *commendation*, "may have had a Gallic or Celtic origin" (*ib.* 276); it never appeared in the East. It need hardly be said that Byzantine centralisation never permitted anything like "grants of immunity."

[1] λογοθέτης τοῦ δρόμου, who superintended the *cursus publicus*. See *post*, p. 471.

tinos[1] was suspected of being an accomplice; or else the Emperor was angry with him for some other reason, and framed against him a false charge of participation in the conspiracy. The historians say that some of his own servants were suborned to declare that their master had conferred treasonably with Podopagurus. Accordingly Constantinos was banished to Hieria, and Nicetas, a Slavonian and of course an iconoclast, was elected in his stead. A year later (6th October 766) Constantinos, who had in the meantime been transferred from Hieria to Prince's island, was brought to Constantinople. He was first beaten so severely that he could not walk, and then carried in a litter to St. Sophia, where an imperial secretary read out a list of the accusations which had been preferred against him, accompanying the recitation of each item with a blow in the face, to the delectation of the new Patriarch Nicetas, who looked on. He was then beaten backwards out of the church; and on the following day, sitting on an ass, with his face turned to its tail, was exposed in the hippodrome to the spits and mocks of the people. He was beheaded in the Kynegion, his head was exposed in the Milion, and his body was dragged by ropes along the streets to "the place of Pelagius," the barathrum of Byzantium.

Unfortunately we know nothing of the crimes or misdemeanours which the imperial secretary read in the solea of St. Sophia, and it is not a little surprising to find the Emperor treating thus an iconoclastic Patriarch, whom he had at first regarded with marked favour. If I may hazard a conjecture, perhaps Constantinos, while he agreed with the Emperor in his hatred of image-worship, did not agree with him in his hatred of monks, and did not approve of his thoroughgoing policy, which aimed at the extirpation of the monastic system. I am inclined to think that in this respect the iconoclastic clergy were not at one with the supporters of Constantine's policy against monachism, and that this difference may have occasioned a breach between the Patriarch and the Emperor.

[1] Like Finlay, I call this Constantine *Constantinos* to distinguish him from the Emperor.

CHAPTER VII

BULGARIA

THE Bulgarian monarch Terbel, who had restored Justinian II to the throne, and in return for that service obtained the rank of a Roman Caesar, who had afterwards attacked the Saracens as they besieged Constantinople, and in the following year espoused for a moment the cause of the ex-Emperor Anastasius, died in 720, after a reign of twenty years, during which the Bulgarian kingdom had been on terms of almost unbroken peace with the Roman Empire.[1] Forty-three years passed, during which two princes, both fameless and one nameless, ruled the Bulgarians; then in 753 Kormisoš usurped the royal power, and a period of disturbances set in.

As the Bulgarians were in the habit of making inroads on Thrace, Constantine took measures to secure the frontier by establishing strong fortresses, and planting, as settlers in the northern parts of Thrace, the Syrian and Armenian inhabitants of towns in Asia, which he conquered from the Saracens. At this juncture (755) Kormisoš sent a message to Constantine demanding the payment of tribute, that the Emperor's refusal might be an excuse for invading the Empire. According to one

---

[1] A treaty, fixing the boundaries and determining commercial relations, was concluded in the brief reign of Theodosius III. We learn this fact incidentally from a notice of Theophanes when he is dealing with Crumn and Nicephorus I., 6305 A.M. τὰς ἐπὶ Θεοδοσίου τοῦ Ἀδραμυτηνοῦ στοιχηθείσας καὶ Γερμανοῦ τοῦ πατριάρχου σπονδὰς πρὸς Κορμέσιον τὸν κατ' ἐκεῖνο καιροῦ κύριον Βουλγαρίας· αἴ τοὺς ὅρους περιεῖχον ἀπὸ Μηλεωνῶν τῆς Θράκης, ἐσθῆτάς τε καὶ κόκκινα δέρματα ἕως τιμῆς λ' λιτρῶν χρυσίον . . . τοὺς δὲ ἐμπορευομένους εἰς ἑκατέρας χώρας διὰ σιγιλλίων καὶ σφραγίδων συνίστασθαι, τοῖς δὲ σφραγῖδας μὴ ἔχουσιν ἀφαιρεῖσθαι τὰ προσόντα αὐτοῖς καὶ εἰσκομίζεσθαι τοῖς δημοσίοις λόγοις. Theophanes errs in the name of the king of Bulgaria, who was Terbel in 716, not Kormesios. Jireček (p. 140) wrongly places this treaty in 714.

historian, the Bulgarians devastated Thrace up to the Long Wall, but were then attacked and routed by the Emperor[1]; according to another, they returned to their country unharmed.[2]

In 758 Constantine proceeded to Macedonia to reduce the Slaves, whose numbers in those regions had considerably increased of late. In consequence of the ravages of the plague, there had been a very large migration of families from northern Greece and the Peloponnesus to Constantinople; and this evacuation had left room for the Slaves to press southwards, where they were fast gaining ground. The Sclavinias, as the settlements in Macedonia and Thessaly were called, were nominally tributary to the Emperor, but they were ever ready to throw off the yoke, and it was not always easy for the Emperors, occupied by Saracen or Bulgarian wars, to reduce them to submission. Constantine subjugated "the Sclavinias," and made prisoners of the refractory.

In the following year he headed an expedition against Bulgaria,[3] but when he arrived at the pass of Berégaba, somewhere between Anchialus and Varna, he was met by the enemy, and experienced a defeat, which was fatal to two important ministers, the general of the Thracesian theme and the master-general of the post (logothete of the course).[4] Three years later we find that Kormisoš is no longer king, that the Bulgarians have revolted and set up Teletz (Teletzes), a man of a bold, and some said bad, disposition. The domestic discord that prevailed at this time induced an immense number of Slaves, two hundred and eight thousand, to leave Bulgaria. They fled in their boats on the Euxine to the shelter of the Roman Empire, and Constantine settled them near the river Artana in Bithynia.

---

[1] Nicephorus, p. 66.

[2] Theophanes, 6247 A.M. Nicephorus and Theophanes are our only original authorities for this chapter. An old half-Slavonic half-Bulgarian list of Bulgarian monarchs (Jiriček, p. 139) gives us a few names.

[3] 6251 A.M., 759 A.D. Jiriček (p. 141) would identify Berégaba with either: "Nadir Derbend oder der Saumpfad von Mesembria über Eminé nach Varna." Nicephorus mentions, without date, a very successful expedition of Constantine by land and sea.

He defeated the Bulgarians in a battle at Marcellae (Marcellon?), and ravaged their country. This is not mentioned by Theophanes (or Jiriček), but from the order of the narration in Nicephorus must have taken place about 756 or 757.

[4] λογοθέτης τοῦ δρόμου. This is the earliest mention of this office, which in the sixth century belonged to the praet. prefects. It is to be presumed that the logothete of the course was created in the seventh century, when the praet. pref. of the East ceased to exist.

Teletz soon attacked Roman towns and plundered Roman territory in the neighbourhood of Mount Haemus, and Constantine prepared an expedition to chastise his insolence. On the 17th of June 762 he left the city, having previously sent by the Euxine a fleet of eight hundred transport vessels,[1] carrying twelve horses each, to meet him at Anchialus. When Teletz heard of these preparations, he collected about two thousand auxiliary troops from the neighbouring Slavonic tribes of Illyricum,[2] and secured his fortresses. The Emperor encamped in the plain of Anchialus, and on the 30th of June, when Teletz arrived with a large army, a battle was fought, lasting from eleven o'clock in the forenoon until late in the evening. The Bulgarians and Slaves were beaten back and routed by the Roman cavalry. Many were killed and many captured; the latter were carried through the streets of Constantinople on wooden planks,[3] adorning the triumph of the Emperor, who then delivered them to the populace to deal with as it willed.

The defeat of Teletz was fatal to his supremacy. The people rebelled, slew him and his ministers, and set up Sabin, the son-in-law of Kormisoś, in his stead. The new king sent to the Emperor a proposal of peace, but this policy displeased his disorderly subjects, who delighted in war. They met together in a sort of diet, called by the Greek historian *komventon* (*conventus*), and having deposed Sabin, asking him, " Is Bulgaria to be enslaved to the Romans by thee ? " they elected Baian (Paganos).[4] Sabin fled to Constantine, who espoused his cause ; and the Emperor found some means to seize the wives and relations of the Bulgarian nobles who had led the opposi-

---

[1] Theophanes says 2000.

[2] ἔχων εἰς συμμαχίαν καὶ Σκλαβηνῶν οὐκ ὀλίγα πλήθη (Nic.) These cannot have been his subjects, and were presumably his western or south-western neighbours. Theoph. say he obtained two thousand troops from neighbouring nations.

[3] ξυλοπανδούροις (Theoph.)

[4] Theophanes calls him Pagános, but his true name, Baian, is known from the old Bulgarian catalogue, already referred to. The name Baian was familiar to the Greek historian ; it was a common name of Hunnic sovereigns. We cannot, therefore, suppose that the corruption was due to Theophanes. I suspect that the Slaves (or

Vlachs ?) gave this king the name of Pagán, " heathen," as a sort of play on Baïan. The Latin word *paganus* had passed into the Slavonic tongues, apparently in Pannonia, and Constantine Porphyrogennetos actually regarded it as a Slavonic word. The Byzantines, hearing the king called Pagan by the Slaves, adopted the name. It has, however, been suggested that Pagan and Sabinus were sprung from the Roman population of the Balkan lands —in fact, that they were Roumans or Vlachians. If so, their reigns were an anticipation of the Vlacho-Bulgarian empire of later days. It is noteworthy that Nicephorus distinguishes *Baïan* and *Kampagános*.

tion against Sabin. The possession of these hostages rendered the Bulgarians desirous of peace,[1] but Constantine apparently declined at first, and made an ineffectual expedition against their country, which they were able to protect by occupying in good time the passes of Mount Haemus. After this (762) the Emperor consented to grant an audience to Baian and his bolyars, whom he received in the presence of Sabin, and, having reproached them for their rebellious behaviour, made a treaty with them.

Thrace suffered not only from the inroads of the northern kingdom, but also from the pillaging expeditions of independent Slaves and the brigandage of mountain outlaws. About this time Constantine captured a chief of the Slovene tribe of the Severs, nominally dependent on Bulgaria, who had inflicted many evils on Thrace.[2] He also captured Christianus, an apostate Christian, who had "magarised" or turned Mohammedan and commanded a band of scamars. I have already mentioned the horrible punishment which this man suffered.[3]

We hear not what became of Baian, but he was succeeded by Omar, who represented the interests of Sabin, and was opposed by Toktu, Baian's brother.[4] Constantine invaded Bulgaria to suppress Toktu, who, supported by the majority of the Bulgarians, had driven Omar from the land; and, finding the passes undefended, he advanced as far as the river Tundža,[5] plundering the villages. In the woods on the banks of the Danube, Toktu was captured and slain. The Roman invasion wrought terrible mischief to Bulgaria, which, as is specially stated, offered a spectacle of devastated fields and burnt hamlets.

Constantine followed up this success by organising another expedition on a larger scale in the following year. Two thousand six hundred transport ships were prepared; troops were assembled from their various stations for a simultaneous attack

---

[1] These details are narrated by Nicephorus, who places these events in the first indiction, that is, according to the official reckoning of the time, 6254 A.M. (=761-762). Theophanes, on the other hand, places them in 6256 (=764). I prefer to follow Nicephorus; and place the expedition of Constantine in the third indiction, as noted by Nicephorus, identifying it with the expedition noted by Theophanes under 6256.

[2] Theoph. 6256 A.M. τὸν Σεβέρων ἄρχοντα Σκλαβοῦνον (so de Boor).

[3] Ib. See above, p. 422.

[4] Nicephorus calls Toktos Baian's brother, and immediately afterwards speaks of Toktos and Baian's brother as two distinct persons. The position of Omar, as Sabin's representative, is not clear. He is mentioned as reigning forty days in the Slavonic list of Bulgarian monarchs.

[5] De Boor, however (with Anastasius), reads ἕως τοῦ Τζίκας instead of ἕως Τούνζας.

on Bulgaria by land and by sea. But a north wind blew hard and wrecked the ships as they were sailing to Anchialus. The crews were drowned, and by the Emperor's orders the bodies were fished up with hooks and received christian burial (765).

Before Constantine's next Bulgarian expedition King Telerig [1] had ascended the throne, and his measures for the defence of his kingdom were so efficient that in the year 773 Constantine, who had arrived with a land army and a naval armament,[2] abandoned the idea of hostilities and concluded a written treaty, each party undertaking not to attack the other.[3] This was in May or June. In October of the same year Constantine, who had friends and emissaries [4] in Telerig's dominions, was informed by them that the king was sending an army of twelve thousand men to enslave the Slavonic land of Berzetia [5] and remove the inhabitants to Bulgaria. Promptness and secrecy were necessary to anticipate this invasion ; and, as Bulgarian ambassadors were then present at Constantinople, the Emperor pretended that the preparations which he set on foot were for war against the Saracens. To keep up this pretence he caused some troops to cross over to Asia ; but as soon as the ambassadors had departed he assembled in Thrace an army of eighty thousand, consisting of garrison soldiers collected from all the themes, of the Thracesian regiments, and of the Optimati who were settled in Pontus. At Lithosoria he completely surprised the unsuspecting army of the enemy, gained a great victory, and returned with abundant booty.[6] In 774 he again embarked a large squadron of cavalry, but at Mesembria the ships were wellnigh wrecked by a storm and the expedition returned without having effected its object. The success that generally attended Constantine in his

[1] Theophanes (6266 A.M.), Τελέριγος ; also called Tzerig.

[2] Theophanes mentions 'Ρούσια χελάνδια, and Finlay notes the passage as containing the first mention of the Russians in Byzantine history (ii. 87). But de Boor, though he prints 'Ρούσια sic, takes ρούσια χ. in his index as red boats.

[3] The Bulgarians sent to Constantine a bolyar (βοιλᾶν) καὶ Τζιγάτον (so de Boor). It seems to me probable that this word should be written with a small initial, as its collocation with βοιλᾶν demands and as one MS. confirms. I take it for a Bulgarian word meaning "warrior," and identical with the

Tartar *djiguit*, used by Circassians and Cossacks.

[4] τῶν κρυπτῶν φίλων αὐτοῦ (Theoph.)

[5] Βερζετία, in Macedonia. The Berzétai took part in the siege of Salonica in 676. At the present time Brzaci or Brsjaci live in Macedonia about Prilêp, Veles, Bitol, and in the district of Tikveš (Jiriček, p. 119).

[6] October, twelfth indiction, but the preceding May was also in twelfth indiction, as one indiction was spread over two years (*see* p. 423). Thus the date of the campaign is end of 773, or beginning of 6266 A.M. The dates in Finlay and Jiriček require correction.

Bulgarian campaigns was greatly promoted by the presence of his agents in Bulgaria, who, keeping him well informed concerning the state of the country and the intentions of the monarch, enabled him to seize favourable opportunities. Telerig knew this, and, in order to identify the traitors, had recourse to a stratagem. He wrote to Constantine announcing his intention of fleeing from his realm and taking refuge in the Roman Empire, and asked him to advise him touching persons to whom he might most wisely confide his scheme. Constantine was taken in by the guile and sent to Telerig the names of his friends, whom Telerig immediately put to death.

In August 775 the Emperor, indefatigable in his hostilities against Bulgaria, headed an army and marched northward once more, but, seized with an inflammation in his legs, he was obliged to return to Arcadiopolis, whence he was brought to Selymbria,[1] and a few days later died in the vessel that was conveying him to Constantinople.

In the reign of his successor Leo IV, Telerig carried out in earnest the intention which he had falsely professed to Constantine and fled from his kingdom to the Roman Emperor, at whose court he was baptized, created a Patrician, and married to a Roman princess. Cardam succeeded Telerig, and in his reign the Romans were on the whole unsuccessful. The general of Thrace was surprised and his army routed in the neighbourhood of the Strymon (788).[2] Two or three years later Constantine VI led a fruitless expedition against Bulgaria; the Romans and the Bulgarians fled from each other in mutual terror (April 791).

The second expedition of Constantine VI, in July 792, was attended with a calamitous defeat. Cardam with all his forces advanced to meet him, and the fair presages of false prophets induced the Emperor to give battle at a disadvantage. The Romans were utterly routed and left some of their most able officers on the field,[3] among whom was the veteran Michael Lachanodrakon, the beloved of Constantine V. The Emperor made good his escape, but the disaster almost cost him his throne, as it led to a revolt in the army.

---

[1] He sailed from Selymbria 13th of September, fourteenth indiction = 775.

[2] The general's name was Philetos. The date falls between 1st September 788 and 1st September 789.

[3] Bardas, a patrician; Nicetas and Theognostos, stratêgoi; Stephanus, a protospathar, and others are named as having fallen.

The next campaign took place in 796. Cardam sent a message to the Emperor demanding a donation of money, and threatening, in case the demand were refused, to lay waste Thrace up to the Golden Gate. The Emperor sent him back horse-dung rolled up in a napkin, with this message : " I send you the tribute that is meet for you. You are an old man, and as I don't wish you to tire yourself by coming so far, I shall go to the fort of Marcellon. God will decide the result." The peratic themes were collected for this expedition, but Cardam fled without hazarding an engagement. Here we take leave of the Bulgarian kingdom, on the eve of the accession of one of its most warlike and savage monarchs, the famous Crumn, and of the catastrophe of the Roman Emperor Nicephorus I., who was slain in battle and whose skull was used as a goblet in the palace of Peristhlaba or of Varna.

By the end of the eighth century, as we have seen, the Bulgarian kingdom had not advanced beyond its original frontiers ; but, on the other hand, the Slovenes had pressed southwards in great numbers, had Slavised the country districts in northern Greece and the Peloponnesus, and had probably increased in strength in the regions of Illyricum and Macedonia, which they had occupied before. This Slavonic movement really prepared the way for the extension of the Bulgarian power in a south-western direction, and before the end of the ninth century the southern boundary of the kingdom was the same as the northern boundary of modern Greece. The first step in this direction was the capture of Sofia, which took place in 809 ; but this lies beyond the limits of the present work.

I should not omit to mention that in the eighth century the northern parts of the Aegean Sea were rendered unsafe by the bands of Slavonian pirates who infested it. These pirates belonged to " the Sclavinias," that is, Macedonia and Thessaly. In the year 768 they carried off into bondage no less than two thousand five hundred inhabitants of Tenedos, Imbros, and Samothrace, and Constantine ransomed the captives by silken robes.[1] " No act of his reign," says Finlay, " shows so much real greatness of mind as this," because to make terms with pirates was for an Emperor to lower his dignity.

---

[1] Nic. p. 76 ; in the seventh indiction, *i.e.* 767-768.

CHAPTER VIII

LEO IV

THE short reign of Leo IV is by no means remarkable. He was an iconoclast at heart like his father; but just as his father had refrained from giving full effect to his theories for some years after his accession, so Leo at first veiled his real opinions and not only favoured the monastic order, electing monks to metropolitan sees—a practice which seems to have become prevalent by the end of the seventh century—but even pretended to be "a friend of the Mother of God," whom iconoclasts generally treated with scant respect. His generosity with the stores of money which his father had laid up gained him popularity. But before he died he laid aside the veil and imitated his father's policy against image-worship, not, however, proceeding to such violent extremes. In 780 a number of distinguished men, among them Theophanes the chamberlain, were arrested for iconodulic practices; they were flogged, tonsured,[1] led in procession through the streets, and shut up in the praetorian prison, where Theophanes died. It is noteworthy that the Slavonic Patriarch Nicetas died (6th February 780) and was succeeded by the Cyprian Paul just before the persecution began; and it might be conjectured that the influence of Nicetas was exerted in the direction of tolerance, and that the newly elected Paul instigated the Emperor to renew the persecutions.

Soon after Leo's accession measures were taken, at the express desire of the imperial governors and the people, to

---

[1] This punishment (never, of course, used by Constantine V) shows that Leo did not sympathise with his father in anti-monachism.

secure the succession to his son Constantine.   Leo was probably consumptive and felt that he could not expect to live very long. On Good Friday (776 A.D.) all the governors of the themes, ministers, and persons of senatorial rank, all the soldiers present in Byzantium, the representatives of all classes of citizens, and especially of the guilds of artisans,[1] took an oath of allegiance to the child Constantine.   As Finlay observes, a more than usually popular character was given to the ceremony.   On the following day the Emperor created his brother Eudocimus (a boy who can have been little older than his own son) a nobilissimus in the chamber of the Nineteen Accubiti.   Thence he proceeded, accompanied by his son and the two Caesars and the three nobilissimi, to the church of St. Sophia, probably by way of the covered passage which connected the church with the palace.   Having changed his dress in a side room, he entered the ambo with his son and the Patriarch Nicetas ; and the people who had assembled in the church came forward in order and deposited their written oaths on the altar.   " Behold, brethren," said Leo, " I fulfil your request and give you my son for Emperor.   Behold, receive him from the Church and the hand of Christ."   The people cried in reply, " O Son of God, be our surety, that we receive from thy hand the lord Constantine as Emperor, even to protect him and die for him."   The next day was Easter Day, and at dawn the Emperor proceeded with the Patriarch to the hippodrome.   There the *antimission*,[2] a carpet which was used on ceremonial occasions, was spread out beside the Emperor's throne ; the Patriarch stood upon it and prayed ; then Leo crowned his son ; and the two Augusti proceeded to St. Sophia accompanied by the Caesars and nobilissimi.

Shortly after this ceremony a conspiracy was discovered, in which the Caesars Nicephorus and Christophorus were involved. Though the popular feeling was strongly in favour of punishing the princes, they were pardoned, but their confederates were banished to Cherson, and on them doubtless the real blame rested, as all Leo's half-brothers were weak men.

---

[1] οἱ τῶν ἔσω ταγμάτων καὶ τῶν πολιτῶν πάντων καὶ οἱ τῶν ἐργαστηριακῶν, Theophanes—who for this and the following reign is in every sense a contemporary source.   Leo IV was called " the Khazar " because his mother was a Khazar princess.

[2] Also called *antiminsion*; derived from *mensa*.   Interchange was common between νσ and σσ, cf. προκένσον for *processus*.

A considerable success was gained over the Saracens in 778. Leo organised a large expedition, 100,000 strong, for the invasion of Syria. All the Asiatic themes except the Cibyraiots took part in it; the iconoclast Lachanodrakon commanded the Thracesians, Artavasdos (an Armenian) the Anatolics, Gregory the Opsikians, Karisterotzes the Armeniacs, and Tatzates the Bucellarians. Germanicia was blockaded, but Lachanodrakon was bribed to raise the siege, and the army turned to plunder the country. The Saracen forces then arrived and experienced a severe defeat; in honour of which the generals were received on their return to Constantinople with a triumphal welcome. A number of Syrian Jacobites were led captive and settled in Thrace. In the following year a Mohammedan army invaded Asia Minor and ineffectually besieged Dorylaeum. Harassed by the Roman troops, who did not risk a general engagement, but cut off the provisions and obstructed foraging parties, they were compelled to return home. In 780 the successful siege of Sêmalûos [1] rewarded Harun's invasion of the Armeniac theme, but another army under Othman was defeated by the general of the Thracesians.

Leo IV died [2] on the 8th of September 780, and was succeeded by his wife Irene and his son Constantine, then ten years old.

---

[1] τὸ Σημαλοῦος κάστρον : Weil calls it Semabrum.

[2] Boils broke out on his head, and he succumbed to a violent fever.

CHAPTER IX

CONSTANTINE VI AND IRENE

THE record of the twenty-two years which elapsed from the death of Leo IV to the deposition of Irene (in 802) is chiefly occupied, apart from military and ecclesiastical events, with conspiracies and intrigues, the unnatural struggle of Irene[1] with her son, and the schemes of rival eunuchs. We will first note the conspiracies in which the brothers-in-law of the Empress were involved; we will pass on to the details of the tragedy which was determined by the unscrupulous ambition of Irene, and then to the intrigues which troubled the five years of her sole power after the fall of Constantine. The chapter may be concluded with a short notice of the monotonous wars with the Saracens.

All the sons of Constantine V, six in number, were men of inferior ability; Leo, who actually reigned, was probably the best of them all, notwithstanding his physical weakness. The other five were always glad to share in a treasonable conspiracy

---

[1] Irene was the second Athenian lady who married a Roman Emperor and became an Augusta; the first was the famous Athenaïs (Eudocia). It is interesting to observe that periods in which women are prominent figures in Byzantine history alternate with periods in which the Empresses are ciphers. From the beginning of the fifth century to the reign of Justin II we have a series of self-asserting Augustae in Eudoxia, Pulcheria, Eudocia, Verina, Ariadne (even Lupicina-Euphemia seems to have had a will of her own), Theodora, Sophia. Then for nearly forty years there is a break in the traditions of female imperialism; of the wives of Tiberius, Maurice, Phocas we only know the names, and the first consort of Heraclius did nothing to win publicity. Then we have Martina, whose career recalls the glories of Verina and Sophia; but her example is not followed by the spouses of Heraclius' successors. We know not even the name of the wife of Constans II; and Anastasia, Theodora, Maria, Irene, Maria, and Eudocia played as little part in political affairs as the nameless wives of the Emperors between 695 and 716. Irene made up for the deficiencies of her predecessors.

whose object was to place one of themselves on the throne; but none of them had the energy to organise a plot himself or the capacity to carry it out with a fair prospect of success. The way in which the three Caesars, Nicephorus, Christophorus, and Nicetas, and the two nobilissimi, Anthimus and Eudocimus, are always grouped together, like a company of puppets ever ready to be employed by any designing conspirator, without any initiation on their own part, is really amusing. We have already seen, in the reign of Leo, a conspiracy to elevate Nicephorus, which resulted in the exile of all the guilty persons except the Caesar himself. About six weeks after the accession of Constantine VI and Irene a similar plot was formed, of which the prime movers were probably nobles and courtiers who had supported the iconoclastic policy of Leo and his father and disliked the iconodulic proclivities of the Greek Empress-mother. Bardas an ex-governor of the Armeniac theme, Gregory the logothete of the course, Constantine the commander (domesticus) of the imperial guards, Theophylact Rangabé the admiral (drungarius) of the Dodecanese,[1] and other distinguished men were flogged, tonsured, and banished. The three Caesars and the two nobilissimi were ordained and caused to administer the sacrament on Christmas Day,[2] in order to impress on the people the fact that they had become ministers of the Church. As there was no such institution as an official gazette, these measures of informing the public were adopted.

Irene appointed Elpidius governor of Sicily in February 781. Whether he had been secretly connected with the recent conspiracy we are not told; Irene plainly had no suspicion of his disloyalty. In April news reached Constantinople that he had revolted and professed to support the claims of the late Emperor's brothers. Theophilus, a spathar or aide-de-camp, was sent to bring him back; but the Sicilians would not allow him to be arrested; so that Irene was obliged to content herself for the time with flogging and imprisoning his wife and children. The support which Elpidius found in

---

[1] This is the first occasion on which we hear of the "Twelve Islands" as a separate province.

[2] On this occasion there was a State procession, and Irene (προελθοῦσα, the technical word for procession) placed in the church the crown, set with pearls, which her husband Leo had appropriated (Theoph. 6273 A.M.)

Sicily seems to show that he was not an iconoclast, or that, if he was, he carefully disguised the fact. We may in any case be sure that he used the names of the Caesars merely as a cloak. In the following year an armament was sent against Sicily under the command of the patrician and eunuch Theodore, an energetic officer. Accompanied by the duke Nicephorus—the duke, one may conjecture, of Calabria—Elpidius immediately fled to Africa, where he was well received by the Saracens. This revolt reminds us of the Sicilian revolt at the beginning of the reign of Leo III, when Sergius fled to the Lombards, just as Elpidius fled to Africa.

For the next ten years the three Caesars and the two nobilissimi were permitted to live in an obscurity from which they were not worthy to emerge. But at length, in the year 792, when general dissatisfaction was felt with Constantine in military circles after the grievous defeat which he had suffered at the hands of the Bulgarians, through his own credulity and ineptitude, the soldiers formed the design of deposing him and elevating his uncle Nicephorus, notwithstanding the clerical status of that Caesar.[1] Constantine, seeing that the priestly garb was not a sufficient disqualification for elevation to the throne, blinded the eyes of Nicephorus and slit the tongues of the other two Caesars and of the two nobilissimi (15th August). He probably considered himself, and was generally considered, clement in not putting them to death.

For five years after this the five puppets of fortune were left in peace and confinement; but in November 797, after Constantine VI had been blinded—a retribution, his uncles probably thought, for his cruelty to themselves—and Irene had become sole sovereign, some restless persons organised a plot to set one of her brothers-in-law on the throne, and they were enabled to escape from their prison and seek refuge in St. Sophia. Aetius, the eunuch and chief favourite of the Empress, immediately repaired to the church, and the five princes, assured that no harm would befall them, followed him as readily and meekly as they had concurred in the schemes of the conspirators, and were banished to Athens. As Athens was the native city of Irene, she thought that she could rely on its loyalty. In March 799, however, a plot was formed in the Helladic

---

[1] Ex-Caesar, τὸν ἀπὸ Καισάρων (Theoph. 6284 A.M.)

theme, and an appeal was made to Akamer, the lord of the Slovenes of Belzetia,[1] to make one of the unfortunate brothers Emperor. Irene promptly suppressed the revolt, and the eyes of the conspirators were put out. It might have been expected that the Greeks, among whom the iconoclastic movement was unpopular, would have been loyal to the restorer of image-worship, all the more as she was Greek herself. We can hardly avoid suspecting that many, perhaps most, of the Helladikoi were Slaves. In Greece there were multitudes of Slaves who were theoretically Romans and possessed lands entailing the duty of military service, as well as of Slaves who were only tributary and constantly hostile.

The struggle for sovereignty between Irene and her son broke out in the year 790, when the latter was twenty years old. As long as he was a boy and submitted implicitly to her authority, Irene was content that her own name should come second in official documents; but when he began to show signs of impatience at his own nonentity, his mother determined to affirm her authority by reversing the order of the imperial names, and afterwards even to depose her son altogether. When he was about twelve years old (782) a marriage had been arranged between him and Rotrud,[2] whom the Greeks called Erythrô, the daughter of Charles the Great, and a certain Elissaeus had gone to the court of Aachen to teach the future Empress Greek. The imagination of the boy seems to have been attracted by the idea of marrying the Frank princess, whom he never saw, and he was inconsolable when his mother broke off the match and compelled him to marry, at the age of eighteen, a lady of Paphlagonia, named Maria, for whom he never cared.

Soon after his marriage Constantine became bitterly aware of the fact that the favourites of his mother, especially the logothete Stauracius, conducted all the affairs of government quite independently of him, and that she was resolved to exclude him from all share in sovereignty as long as she lived. The

[1] Theoph. 6291 A.M. ὁ τῶν Σκλαυινῶν τῆς Βελζητίας ἄρχων νυχθεὶς ὑπὸ τῶν Ἑλλαδικῶν. Is Belzetia the same as Berzetia?

[2] The Poeta Saxo writes of Rotrud (Rhuotrodis)—

hanc et Graecorum luxerunt ditia regna
quod non hac tali digna forent domina.

See Theophanes, 6274 A.M.

circumstance that no one ever thought of presenting a petition to him, all repairing with their grievances or requests to Stauracius, was humiliating.   It was the interest of the courtiers to foster the jealousy and widen the breach between the mother and son.   The eunuchs and creatures of Irene, knowing how to play on her unscrupulous ambition, flattered her into the hope of being sole sovereign.   Stauracius, a patrician and a eunuch, was at this time the most powerful minister.   He held the office of logothete of the course, or post, and had won laurels by reducing the rebellious Slaves of Macedonia, northern Greece, and the Peloponnesus, and compelling them to pay tribute (783 A.D.)[1]   At another time he had been employed in negotiating with the Saracen caliph, and it was he who superintended the disbanding of the refractory guards, who had rioted in the cause of iconoclasm and prevented the meeting of a synod (786).

The intimate friends of the Emperor were few.   Three are especially mentioned—Theodore Camulianus, Peter the *magister officiorum*, and Damanus.   Wishing to assert himself, Constantine took counsel with these and others, and a plan was formed (January or February 790) to overthrow Stauracius and banish Irene to Sicily.   But the watchful Stauracius discovered the plot in time and revealed it to his mistress, who banished some of Constantine's party to the Peloponnesus and Sicily, and punished others by confining them to their houses,[2] a mode of punishment which became frequent at Byzantium.   Her son she actually struck, and prevented him from leaving his apartments for several days.   An oath was then formulated, which all the soldiers in the Empire were required to take, to this effect: " As long as you live, we will not receive your son to reign over us."   All the troops in the city took the oath, and the regiments of Asia also acquiesced, except the Armeniacs, who refused to place the name of Irene before that of Constantine.   Then the Empress sent to them Alexius Mouselé, the drungarius of the watch, but he did not much avail her cause, as the soldiers placed their stratêgos Nicephorus in custody and replaced him by Alexius, proclaiming Constantine sole

---

[1] He brought back many spoils and captives ; thus the Slavonic territory was treated as a foreign country. He enjoyed a public triumph in January 784.

[2] ἐκάθισεν ἐν τῷ οἴκῳ.   The more usual phrase is ἀπρόϊτον ποιεῖν.

Emperor. Then the other themes, in spite of their recent oath,[1] followed the example of the Armeniacs, and elected new generals. These events took place in September, and in October all the themes, except the prime movers, the Armeniacs, who were too far away, assembled at Atrôa and demanded the presence of the Emperor. Irene, unable to resist this pressure, allowed her son to go, and the soldiers straightway proclaimed their allegiance to him and deposed her. Then Constantine sent two officers to the Armeniacs to receive a formal oath of loyalty from them. In December he returned to Constantinople and removed Irene's favourites. Stauracius was whipped, tonsured, and banished to the Armeniac theme; Aetius, also a eunuch, and many other of her confidants were likewise exiled. She was herself confined in the palace of Eleutherius, which she had built, and in which she was supposed to have concealed much money—a part of those stores of treasure which had been laid up by Constantine, her father-in-law.

A circumstance may be noticed here which seems to indicate that soon after her husband's death Irene deposed the governors of themes who had been appointed by Constantine or Leo. For we observe that the iconoclast Michael Lachanodrakon, who before the accession of Irene had been governor of the Thracesian theme, was an adherent of Constantine VI, and was one of the two officers who were sent by him to secure the allegiance of the Armeniacs. Now we are told that all the themes deposed their generals, who were evidently supporters of Irene; hence Michael Lachanodrakon can no longer have been general of the Thracesians, for, as he was a staunch supporter of Constantine, there would have been no reason for deposing him. Nor can this conclusion be escaped by saying that, while in most cases the generals were displaced by the soldiers, the Thracesian theme may have been an exception; for, had Lachanodrakon been governor of the Thracesians, he would hardly have been sent to the Armeniac theme [2] on a mission which was suitable for a spathar, or for an officer whose functions were unconfined to a district, but

---

[1] This is a source of much shaking of the head to the pious historian Theophanes.

[2] Along with Lachanodrakon was sent the Emperor's protospathar and bajulus (βάγυλος) John.

not for the governor of a province.   Moreover, in 792 Lachanodrakon is spoken of as the *magister* (*officiorum*).[1]

During the following year (791) Constantine, who had
inherited his grandfather's love of war, was occupied with
expeditions against the Bulgarians and Arabs, but in January
792 he was weak enough to consent to allow his mother to
be proclaimed Empress again.   Nor did he confine himself to
a mere passive consent, but when the Armeniac theme resisted
the measure he determined to enforce actively their recognition
of his mother's title.   He had summoned to Constantinople, a
short time before, Alexius, the governor of that theme, who
was suspected of aiming at usurpation; and as soon as the
Armeniacs declared their refractory spirit and demanded that
their governor should be restored to them, the Emperor imprisoned Alexius in the praetorium, having first flogged and
tonsured him, according to the custom of the time.   After the
Bulgarian expedition, which ended disastrously and led to a
plot which was wellnigh fatal to Constantine, Alexius was subjected to the severe penalty of losing his eyesight.   When the
Armeniacs heard of this, they were greatly enraged, and retaliated
by blinding Theodore Camulianus, who had succeeded Alexius
as their general.   Then Constantine sent against them an
army commanded by Constantine Artaseras and Chrysocheres,
the general of the Bucellarian theme; but the Armeniacs were
victorious in a battle, and blinded the two generals.[2]   Nothing
was left for Constantine but to go forth and punish those wicked
servants himself.   The treachery of the Armenian auxiliaries
secured him an easy victory.[3]   Three of the instigators of the
rebellion were put to death, one of whom was the bishop of
Sinope[4]; the rest were mulcted by fines or total confiscation.
One thousand were led in chains to Constantinople and conducted through the Blachern gate, as an example to men,
each of them bearing on his face an inscription tattooed in
black ink, "Armeniac conspirator."   They were then banished
to Sicily and other islands.

---

[1] Theoph. 6284 A.M.   Or does μάγιστρος here mean *magister in praesenti*
(ἐκ προσώπου)?

[2] November 792.

[3] 27th May 793.   The Armenians
expected rewards for their treachery (or

loyalty) but received none, and consequently gave up the fort of Kamachon
to the Arabs.

[4] The other two were Andronicus
and   Theophilus,   both   turmarchs,
doubtless friends of Alexius, who had
perhaps appointed them.

The ensuing year was uneventful, but on the 3d of January 795 a new act of the imperial drama was opened by the divorce of Maria, Constantine's unwished-for consort, who then retired to a nunnery. The Emperor's affections had been for some time bestowed on Theodote, a maid of honour, and he crowned her Augusta and married her before the end of the year. This marriage, as his first wife was still alive, created a great scandal among strict orthodox Christians, and some said that his mother Irene had instigated him to divorce Maria and marry Theodote in order that he might incur public odium and that she might win a chance of resuming the reins of government. The Patriarch Tarasius refused to perform the ceremony, but he countenanced the imperial sin, inasmuch as he did not excommunicate either the Emperor or the abbot Joseph, who officiated at the nuptials. Chief among those who openly expressed their indignation at what seemed to them an unblushing act of adultery, were the abbot Plato and his monks. He had founded a monastic retreat in his estate at Saccudion in Bithynia, and lived there a quiet but influential life. He repudiated the conduct of Tarasius and refused communion with him. Bardanes, the commander (domesticus) of the scholarii, and Johannes, count of Opsikion, were immediately despatched to Saccudion; Plato was taken to Constantinople and imprisoned in a room in the palace (adjoining the chapel of St. Michael), and his flock of monks, conspicuous among whom was his nephew Theodore, were banished to Thessalonica.[1] It was a welcome opportunity for Irene to embrace the cause of the monks, and place Constantine's conduct in the worst light.

Constantine and his mother visited Prusa in autumn 796 for the sake of the hot baths, which made it a place of resort. While they were there, the welcome news arrived that a son[2] was born to Constantine, who immediately galloped off to the city with his staff and attendants. Irene took advantage of his absence to beguile the military officers with gifts and pro-

---

[1] Theoph. 6288 A.M. Theodore, in a letter to his uncle Plato, describes the journey to Thessalonica (Migne, *Patr. Gr.* vol. 99). His account will be found in brief in Finlay, who took it at second hand from Schlosser. But Finlay does not note the interesting point that the person whom he calls the governor of Thessalonica is the praetorian prefect of Illyricum (ἔπαρχος), whose former wide sphere has dwindled down to the local mayoralty of Salonica. An account of Plato and his life at Saccudion will be found in Theodore's panegyric on him.

[2] He was named Leo ; born 7th Oct. 796, died 1st May 797.

mises, and persuade them to undertake to place the imperial
power in her sole hands.   She was almost as successful as she
could have wished ; she drew all men unto her by flatteries.
The intrigues of Irene's supporters rendered ineffectual an
expedition against the Saracens which the Emperor headed
himself in the following spring ; it was important to prevent
him from acquiring popularity by winning military glory.   At
length in June (797) it was decided to strike the final blow.
As Constantine was proceeding from a spectacle in the hippodrome to the church of St. Mamas in Blachernae, he was
attacked by troops bribed to kill him, but he escaped to the
imperial boat (chelandion), which conveyed him to the Asiatic
coast.   He intended to flee to the Anatolic theme, where the
Isaurian Emperors were always befriended, but unfortunately
he was accompanied by false friends who were really attached
to his mother.   A letter from Irene, who threatened to disclose
their treason to her son unless they acted promptly, decided
their wavering resolution ; they seized Constantine and hurried
him back to Constantinople.   Arriving early in the morning,
they shut him up in the palace in the Purple Chamber, in
which he had been born, and at the ninth hour (15th August)
put out his eyes in a brutal manner, intentionally calculated to
cause his death.[1]   The superstitious observed the coincidence
that on the same day five years before Constantine's uncles
had been blinded by his orders, and saw therein a supernatural
retribution.   It was also said that a miraculous darkness prevailed for more than two weeks.

Irene had now attained her wish and was sole sovereign of
the Empire.   Her court became the scene of quarrels between
her eunuchs Stauracius and Aetius, each of whom desired, not
to be an Emperor—for a eunuch on the throne would not
have been tolerated—but to be an emperor-maker and to secure
the succession for a friend of his own.   These favourites had
probably been allowed to return[2] from their banishment in

---

[1] Constantine, however, as it appears, did not die; he lived till the
reign of Michael the Stammerer, as is
expressly affirmed by the (tenth-century) author of the Chronicle from Leo V
to Michael III in *Contin. Theoph.* The
words of Theophanes are (6289 A.M.)
ἐκτυφλοῦσιν αὐτὸν δεινῶς καὶ ἀνιατῶς πρὸς
τὸ ἀποθανεῖν αὐτὸν, γνώμῃ τῆς μητρὸς

αὐτοῦ καὶ τῶν συμβούλων αὐτῆς, which
imply that he died.   *See* Schlosser,
*Geschichte der bilderstürmenden Kaiser
des oströmischen Reichs*, p. 327 sqq.
[2] Thus we find Stauracius actively
engaged in bringing about the fall of
Constantine.   It was he who contrived
the scheme which rendered Constantine's campaign in 796 futile.

792, when Irene resumed her position as Augusta. Their quarrels must have made her life uneasy, but Stauracius seems to have been the prime favourite until May 799,[1] when she fell sick, and the eunuchs, seeing an immediate prospect of her decease, schemed and strove more than ever. Aetius obtained for a while the ear of the Empress, accused his rival of aiming at power, and made her believe that he was the cause of all the factions and discords that prevailed. Irene scolded and threatened Stauracius, but he was able to win her confidence again and turn her against Aetius. She was the plaything of her favourites.

In the following February Stauracius organised a definite conspiracy against the throne, enlisting the guards (scholarii and excubitores) in his interest by bribes. His conduct was so suspicious that Irene held a *silention* in the " room of Justin- ian" to examine the matter, and the curious order was issued that no military persons should hold converse with Stauracius.[2] He did not live long after this. He was afflicted with a spit- ting of blood, which the doctors knew must soon prove fatal; nevertheless, until the day of his death (in June 800) the flatterers and clients who frequented his house, like those of other great men, including the doctors themselves, wizards and monks ("unmonkish" or spurious monks they are called by the historian), continued to assure him that he suffered only from a slight indisposition, and that he was destined to live and reign. It would appear from this that Stauracius actually dreamed of ascending the throne himself, and exhibit- ing to a horrified world the unheard-of monstrosity of a eunuch wielding the sceptre of Augustus and Constantine. While he was suffering from the fatal disease, he was occupied with planting and fostering a conspiracy in Cappadocia, which was intended to bring about the violent overthrow of Aetius, who now occupied his own place in the confidence of Irene. Two days after his death the explosion for which he had laid the train broke out, but it was promptly extinguished and the

---

[1] On Monday of Paschal week 799 it is noticed that Irene went forth from the palace in a golden car drawn by four white horses and driven by four patricians (Bardanes, governor of the Thracesians ; Nicetas, the domesticus of the scholarii, a friend of Aetius ; Constantine Boïlas ; and Sisinnius, general of Thrace). The hypateia (consular donative) was generously doled.

[2] He was, if I may be permitted to use a phrase of modern slang, to be "sent to Coventry" by the army.

conspirators were punished.   Henceforward, until her fall two years later, Aetius was the prime minister of the Empress, a position which in later times became a recognised office, its holder being called ὁ παραδυναστεύων.[1]   The extent of Aetius' power may be estimated by the fact that the Opsikian and Anatolic themes were placed together under his sole command.

At this time Charles the Great, shortly after his coronation (25th December 800 A.D.), conceived the idea of uniting together the Teutonic Roman Empire and the Greek Roman Empire by a marriage with Irene.   If this had taken place it would have brought about for a moment one European Roman Empire, somewhat resembling in geographical extent the old Roman Empire of Constantine the Great, and it would have added a new map to our historical atlases.   But it could not have had any permanent duration ; the marriage of countries and peoples so ill assorted must have been followed by a speedy divorce.   As it was, this second design of an alliance of the Isaurian with the Karlingian house was thwarted by the influence of Aetius, who was bent on securing the throne for his relation Nicetas, the captain of the guards.

But the patricians and lords could not long be patient of the powerful eunuch's insolence, and they determined to anticipate his designs by dethroning Irene and electing an Emperor from among themselves.   Nicephorus, the chancellor of the exchequer or " general logothete," was chosen, and on the last day of October 802, as Irene was suffering from indisposition and residing in her mansion of Eleutherius, the conspirators proceeded to the palace gate of Chalke and knocked for admission.   They informed the porter (*papas*) that they were sent by the Empress to make arrangements for the proclamation and coronation of Nicephorus, as she wished to forestall and thwart the ambitious plans of Aetius.   The palace officials did not hesitate to believe their statements and admit them, as they were all well-known men of the highest position.   Having obtained possession of the palace, they collected a crowd of people in the Augusteum and proclaimed Nicephorus Emperor before the break of day, having

---

[1] Zonaras actually uses this word of Aetius—" the man who has power at court."   In many respects these ministers may be compared to the justiciars of English history.

taken the precaution of surrounding the house of Irene with soldiers. Then they transferred her to the great palace, and Nicephorus was crowned in St. Sophia—the first Augustus crowned there who cannot be called " the Roman Emperor " unreservedly, but must be called " the eastern Roman Emperor." [1]

On the following day the new monarch paid a visit to Irene, who had accepted her fall with a quiet dignity, and only asked to be allowed to continue to live in her private house. Nicephorus promised to grant her request if she disclosed to him the secret stores of treasure which she was generally known to have concealed. She agreed, but when the Emperor had obtained the desired information he failed to fulfil his promise, and banished her first to " Prince's island," where she had built a monastery, and afterwards to Lesbos, where she died.

We must now notice briefly the wearisome wars with the Saracens, which possess little interest, as our sources give us no details. In 781 Mahdi's general, Abd Elkebir, led an army against Asia Minor, but, by Irene's orders, the strength of all the themes was concentrated at the frontier, consisting of from eighty to a hundred thousand men,[2] under the command of Johannes, the sacellarius, and the Arabs were utterly defeated at Mêlon.

In the following year, 782, the Romans were not so successful. Harun, the son of the caliph, and Rabia Ibn Junus invaded Asia Minor with an army of a hundred thousand, which they divided into three parts. Harun marched to Chrysopolis ; Ibn Junus, whom Theophanes calls Bunusus (Bonosus), laid siege to Nacolia; and Jahja the Barmecide (in Theophanes, Burniché) entered the Thracesian theme, where he fought a battle with the able general Michael Lachanodrakon at Darênon and lost fifteen thousand men. The treachery of Tatzates, the general of the Bucellarian theme, brought about a peace disadvantageous to the Roman Empire. Tatzates was jealous of the influence of Stauracius,

---

[1] *See* below, cap. xi.

[2] Arabic sources give 80,000, Byzantine 100,000 as the number. According to the former, Michael Lachanodrakon and an Armenian named Taridon commanded the Romans. The troops were sent to the frontier in June (Theoph. 6273 A.M.) Cf. Weil, ii. 98.

the confidential minister of the Empress ; and he received rich rewards for going over to the Saracens with his troops.   Irene was forced to treat for peace—Theodore's expedition against the rebel Elpidius in Sicily had reduced the number of available fighting men—and the Roman delegates [1] foolishly entered the Saracen camp without the precaution of an interchange of hostages.   The Saracens perfidiously seized them, and Irene was obliged to pay 70,000 dinars yearly for a peace which was to last for a term of three years.

Mahdi died in 785.   His son Hadi enjoyed the sovereign power for a year,[2] and was succeeded in September 786 by his brother, the famous Harun, "undeservedly called Arraschid, the Just." [3]   Soon after his accession, Harun took measures for strengthening his north-western frontier.   The fortresses which defended it had hitherto been part of the large province of Mesopotamia ; Harun formed them into a separate government.   He also strengthened the fortifications of Tarsus, and sent thither a large colony of Mohammedans.   His armies invaded Romania almost every year,[4] and in 790 his fleet endangered a Roman island, either Cyprus or Crete. On this occasion the armament of the Cibyraiots and the armament of the Aegean islands co-operated against him, and in a naval battle the general of the Cibyraiots, Theophilus, was taken prisoner.   Harun would have not only granted him his life but raised him to high honours if he had consented to embrace Islam, but he refused on any terms and was executed. This incident shows that their religion really meant much to the Byzantine nobles.   We are not told whether Elpidius, the recreant ex-governor of Sicily, became a Mohammedan ; he is said to have taken part in an invasion of Asia Minor.

[1] Stauracius himself was one of them.

[2] Arab authors relate that in Hadi's reign the Greeks destroyed the fortress of Hadath, but were repelled by Mayuf, who then made depredations in Romania (Weil, ii. 123).

[3] Weil, ii. 127.

[4] The following is a list of these tedious campaigns and expeditions :—

789. Romania invaded ; Romans severely defeated and their captains slain.
790. Naval expedition of Arabs against Cyprus (Theoph.) or Crete (Arab sources).

791. Campaign led by Constantine VI ; he advances to Tarsus, but does nothing notable.
795. Second campaign led by Constantine VI.   He gains a victory at Anusan.
796. The Arabs penetrate to Amorium, but gain no success.
797. Third campaign of Constantine ; rendered ineffectual by treachery of his mother's friends.   A frontier fortress (named Safssaf) taken by Arabs led by the caliph himself.
798. Romania invaded ; Arabs penetrate to Ephesus.   Cappadocia and Galatia devastated.   The Opsikians experienced a severe defeat.   Peace for four years, for which Romans pay a tribute.
801. The third son of Harun (Kasim) threatened Asia Minor.

A peace was concluded at the end of the year 798, by the terms of which the Romans were to pay a tribute, as in the peace with Mahdi ; but the cessation of hostilities was welcome to Harun himself, for he was troubled by the invasion of the Khazars, who harassed Armenia and relieved the Roman Empire by diverting and dividing the Saracen forces, just as in old days the White Huns and Turks used to divert the Sassanid monarchs from their wars on the Euphrates.

CHAPTER X

THE Empress Irene, as might be expected from her Greek origin, was devotedly attached to the worship of images, and earnestly desired its restoration. But although the supreme power centred in her on her husband's death, as her son Constantine was too young yet to be more than a nominal Emperor, she was for several years unable to accomplish her design of reversing the acts of the three latest Emperors. This delay was caused by the strong iconoclastic spirit that prevailed among the soldiers as well as the officers in the army; as the Empire was at war with the Saracens, and the tributary Slaves of Macedonia were refractory, it would have been dangerous to run the risk of exciting an intestine conflict by agitating prematurely the burning question. At the same time, there is no doubt that complete tolerance was secured to the adorers of images from the beginning of the reign of Constantine and Irene, and pictures were restored to churches by a consent that was generally understood if it was not expressly declared. When peace had been made with the Abbasids, and the Slaves had been brought back to their allegiance, the field was free for settling the ecclesiastical question; and just then a new feature was given to the situation by the resignation of the Patriarch Paul and the succession of Tarasius.

The resignation of Paul[1] was attended by circumstances advantageous to the reactionary policy. In August 784 he fell sick, and, conscience-smitten for his iconoclastic views, which he suddenly discovered to be false and impious, he

[1] Theoph. 6276 A.M.

resigned his office and exchanged the palace of the Patriarch for a cell in the monastery of Florus.   When Irene, who had not anticipated such an event, learned the tidings, she visited the new monk, and heard with pleasure his acknowledgment of error.   "Would," he said, "that I had not sat on the sacerdotal chair of the Church of God, for this Church is in rebellion,[1] and severed from the other Catholic chairs (of Christendom), and subject to a ban"!   Then Irene sent to Paul's bedside a number of senators and nobles who were inclined to iconoclasm, in order that the influence of his repentance might induce them to mend their ways and support the official restitution of image-worship.

An assembly was convoked in the palace of Magnaura for the election of a new Patriarch, and the secretary Tarasius, a layman, was elected by a large majority.   Irene, remarking that the imperial choice had already fallen on him, but that he had declined the honour, asked him to speak for himself. Tarasius, having dwelt on his own unworthiness, stated that the chief reason which caused him to hesitate was the great schism which separated the Church of Constantinople from the other Churches of Christendom, and urged the re-establishment of ecclesiastical unity.[2]   Although dissentient voices were heard, the speech of Tarasius was received with general acclamation; and on Christmas Day 784 he was consecrated Patriarch.   It is evident that the proceedings in the Magnaura were due to a prearranged plan between Tarasius and Irene.

It was almost a year later that Pope Hadrian received two communications from Constantinople, brought to him by a Byzantine priest, who was escorted by a Sicilian bishop.[3]   One of these was the enthronistic or inaugural manifesto of Tarasius[4]; the other was a *divalis sacra* or imperial letter from Constantine and Irene, wherein the Pope was asked to fix a time for the convocation of an Ecumenical

---

[1] τυραννουμένης; the word implies that the schismatic Patriarchs are really usurpers or "tyrants."

[2] Tarasius' speech is given at length by Theophanes.   As it comes within the province of ecclesiastical rather than of political history, I have not reproduced it.

[3] The bishop of Catana.   It was at first intended that the bishop of Leontini should be the bearer.

[4] Tarasius sent copies of this to the sees of Alexandria, Antioch, and Jerusalem, but owing to the jealousy of the Arabs they never reached the Patriarchs. Some eastern monks, however, took upon themselves to write answers to the manifesto.   The *divalis sacra* is printed in Mansi, xii. 984.

Council at Constantinople to decide on the question of image-worship. This letter was dated 29th August 785,[1] and Hadrian replied to it on 27th October, so that the transmission was effected in a relatively short time. In his reply Hadrian rejoices over the imperial orthodoxy, and expresses his expectation that Constantine will be a second Constantine the Great and that Irene will prove a new Helena, while he insists that one essential condition of the realisation of such hopes is the recognition of the spiritual sovereignty of the chair of St. Peter. Having defended picture-worship at some length, he promises to send legates to an Ecumenical Council, and demands a *pia sacra* (in accordance with ancient custom) signed by the Emperor and Empress, the Senate and the Patriarch, to the effect that no pressure or constraint will be brought to bear on the representatives of Rome. Returning again to the interests of the Roman see, he demands the restoration of the *patrimonia Petri*, which the iconoclastic Emperors had confiscated; he revives the old complaint that the epithet "ecumenical" was appended to the name of the Byzantine Patriarch; and he censures the election of a layman and ex-soldier to the patriarchal chair. He concludes by promising that if the Emperor of Constantinople follow the guidance of the head of the christian Church he will be victorious over his barbarian foes, just as Charles, king of the Franks and Lombards and Patrician of Rome, his son and spiritual fellow-father, *spiritualis compater*,[2] had conquered the barbarians of the West, because he treated the Pope with veneration. Hadrian also wrote a letter to Tarasius in which complaints about his election were judiciously balanced with expressions of joy at his orthodox opinions.[3]

When the delegates arrived at Constantinople for the council, in August 786, the imperial court was absent at some town in Thrace, and the interval of delay was spent by the iconoclastic bishops and their supporters in organising plots for the prevention of the intended synod. When the Emperor and Empress returned, the 17th day of August was arranged for the first session, and the church of the Apostles was

---

[1] The best authorities agree that *ind.* viii. should be read for *ind.* vii. in the passage of Anastasius (*see* Hefele).

[2] A reference to the fact that he had baptized a son of Charles 781 A.D.

[3] The letters of Hadrian to the Emperor and the Patriarch will be found in Mansi, xii. 1056, 1057.

selected as the place of assembly. On the 16th the imperial guards and other soldiers[1] collected in the precincts of the church and made a hostile demonstration; and on the following day, although the session was allowed to begin, the soldiers rushed into the church in the middle of the proceedings, to the delight of the iconoclastic bishops, and threatened to slay all present. The remonstrances of the ministers whom the Empress sent to pacify them did not avail, and no course was open but the dissolution of the assembly.

The triumph of the iconoclastic party, who cried "We have conquered," was not of long duration. By a dexterous stratagem Irene paralysed the military opposition. She pretended to make preparations for a campaign against the Saracens, and with her whole court proceeded to Malagina in Thrace (September 786). In the meantime Asiatic (peratic) troops occupied Constantinople; a new corps of guards was formed, and the iconoclastic regiments were obliged to give up their arms, and disbanded. In the following May a new synod was convoked, and the papal legates, who had reached Sicily, returned to New Rome. On the 24th of September the first session was held, not, however, at Constantinople, but at Nicaea, memorable as the scene of the first great council of the Church. The Emperor and Empress were not present, but were represented by Petronas, a patrician, and Johannes, imperial ostiarius and logothete.[2] At the first sessions several iconoclastic bishops, who had repented like Paul, stood forward and owned their errors. At the seventh sitting (5th or 6th October) the definition (ὅρος) of doctrine was drawn up; after a summary repetition of the chief points of theology established by previous Universal Councils, it is laid down that the figure of the holy cross and holy images, whether coloured or plain, whether consisting of stone or of any other material, may be represented on vessels, garments, walls, or tables, in houses or on public roads; especially figures of Christ, the Virgin, angels, or holy men: such representations, it is observed, stimulate spectators to think of the originals, and, while they must not

---

[1] *Scholarii, excubitores*, etc. (Theoph. 6278 A.M.)

[2] The number of those present was from 330 to 367. The eastern patriarchates were represented by monks, but it was clearly recognised that they were not officially empowered by the Patriarchs, who appear to have been inaccessible at this time.

be adored with that worship which is only for God ($\lambda \alpha \tau \rho \epsilon i \alpha$), deserve adoration ($\pi \rho o \sigma \kappa \dot{\nu} \nu \eta \sigma \iota \varsigma$). The council called down anathemas upon Theodosius the bishop of Ephesus, Sisinnius Pastillas, and Basilius Trikakkabos; upon the three Byzantine Patriarchs, Anastasius, Constantine, and Nicetas; moreover, upon John of Nicomedia and Constantine of Nacolia; while the names of Germanus, John of Damascus, and George of Cyprus were greeted with acclamations as the "heralds of truth."

The eighth session was held, not at Nicaea, but in the imperial palace at Constantinople, where the acts of the council were confirmed and signed [1] by Constantine and Irene. Thus the Churches of Old Rome and New Rome were again united, and the cause of iconoclasm was defeated.[2] . It was not dead, however; it revived and was powerful again, twenty-five years later, in the reign of Leo the Armenian. The image-worshippers were destined to prevail in the end, but at the same time they did not undo the work which their enemies had accomplished, the regeneration of the Empire. The suppression of pictures was only the superficial side of the great battle which Leo III and Constantine V had waged unflinchingly and ruthlessly against superstition; and it cannot be ignored that, though pictures were not destined to be suppressed, the general tone of education and morality in the Empire was better at the end of the eighth century than it had been at the beginning, and the vitality of the State was higher, just as its position among nations was more assured.

[1] With purple ink. There was a special officer called kanikleios, who was custodian of the imperial ink.

[2] At the present day the Greek Church permits the worship or veneration of pictures, but excludes statues, $\dot{\alpha} \gamma \dot{\alpha} \lambda \mu \alpha \tau \alpha$, from churches. Mr. Tozer (in his ed. of Finlay, ii. p. 165) has a note on this subject, and remarks that the change in the attitude of the Church to statues "seems to have been brought about very gradually, so much so that no trace remains to us of the steps by which it came to pass." In his *Highlands of Turkey*, i. p. 187, the same scholar notices the only statue existent in the Greek Church, namely a wooden figure of St. Clement of Rome at Ochrida. He suggests an ingenious and probable theory as to the history of this statue, which he ascribes to the age of the Slavonic apostles Cyril and Methodius.

CHAPTER XI

THE dissolution of the connection subsisting between the Popes and New Rome, which went hand in hand with the formation of a close connection between Old Rome and the Frank kingdom, was a slow process, and it is hard to define at what period the Roman see ceased to be part of the Roman Empire. I must give a brief account of the Italian complications in which this tendency revealed itself and note the steps by which it gradually led up to that great event, the coronation of a Teutonic king as Roman Emperor at Old Rome.

The chief cause which induced the Popes to look to the Franks for succour against the Lombards was the simple fact that the wars with the Saracens in the East rendered the Emperors unable to protect their outlying possessions in Italy with an adequate force. The iconoclastic heresy, which had severed the sympathy between the Roman see and the Empire, made the Popes still more ready to apply to a foreign power. But at first these applications were without effect. Gregory II could not move Charles Martel, the mayor of the palace, to intervene. In 737 or 738 (seventh indiction) another and more urgent petition for help was made by Gregory III. The Pope and the duke of Rome had harboured Transmund, the duke of Spoleto who had rebelled against King Liutprand, and they refused to surrender him. Accordingly Liutprand seized four important towns[1] and threatened Rome. But

---

[1] Orte, Amelia, Bieda, and Bomarzo (Polimartium). *See* Paul, *Hist. Lang.* vi. 56 ; Anastasius, *Vita Zachariae.* Anastasius gives the date seventh *indic-* *tione*=737-738 (*vulg.* 738-739). Besides Anastasius and Paul, the Continuatio of Fredegarius, *apud* Bouquet, *Script. rer. Gall. et Franc.* vol. v., is important

although the Pope in his straits sent to Charles Martel rich presents and the keys of the sepulchre of St. Peter,[1] thereby making him protector of the Church, the appeal was not successful. When in the following year new hostilities were undertaken by the Lombards against the exarchate and the territory of Rome, yet another message was sent to Charles, but proved equally resultless.

These wars with Liutprand were chiefly due to the policy of the Popes in espousing the cause of the dukes of Spoletium and Beneventum, who were struggling for their independence against the king. The situation was changed by the election of the Greek Zacharias (December 740) to the papal chair. He abandoned the Lombard dukes and allied himself with the Lombard king, who restored not only the four cities which he had seized, but also confiscated domains belonging to the Roman patrimony, and made a peace for twenty years with the duke of Rome. By the intervention of the Pope, he also made peace with the exarchate.[2]

Liutprand died in 743, and his nephew Hildebrand's reign of a few months was followed by the reign of Rachis, who was a friend of the Roman see. Among the Lombards there prevailed a strong spirit of hostility against the Greeks, and they were impatient of a king who, yielding to papal influence, was disinclined to prosecute the war. They unanimously deposed him (748) and elected his brother Aistulf, who acted with such rigour that two years after his election he had taken Ravenna and overthrown the exarchate (750). He then turned his arms against the duchy of Rome. Zacharias had died, and Stephen, who succeeded him in 751, applied in vain for help to the Emperor Constantine V. He then turned to Pipin, who had succeeded Charles Martel as mayor of the palace in 740, and this time the appeal was successful. The Pope went in person to Gaul and met Pipin at Ponthion; he deposed Childeric, the last of the Merovingians; he anointed Pipin of Landen king of the Franks, in order that he who possessed the royal power might also have the royal name, and

---

for Italian history of the eighth century. L. Armbrust's tract, *Die
territoriale Politik der Päpste von 500
bis 800*, has been useful to me, and
also the articles in Herzog and Pflitt

on the Popes of the eighth century.
[1] *Chron. Moissiacense*, Pertz, i. 291.
Anastasius, *Vit. Greg. III.*
[2] Hirsch, *Das Herzogthum Benevent*
p. 40.

created him a Roman Patrician.[1]   This was the first step towards a goal not yet visible, the foundation of a Western Roman Empire. If it is asked by what right Pope Stephen bestowed the title of *Patricius Romanorum* on Pipin, the answer is that he had no constitutional right. " Patrician " was a title of dignity, not of office, but legally the Emperor alone had the right to bestow it. The title had been given in former days to Odovacar, to Theodoric, to Chlodwig, and in the same way it might be given to Pipin; but it had no validity except as granted by the Emperor. Neither Pipin nor the Pope could reasonably expect that the Empire would recognise the Teutonic king as a Patrician. Nor is it likely that they thought of the title in very strict connection with the Empire.[2] What the Pope did was rather this : he took an old familiar name—a title which had always belonged to the exarch—placed it in a new combination, and gave it almost a new sense. While it still conveyed the notion of a high dignity, it came, by its union with the genitive *Romanorum*, to suggest the word *patronus* or *pater*, and indicate a relation of protection. And *Romanorum* itself is to be taken in a limited sense. The *Romani* are primarily the people of Rome and its neighbourhood; they are not the *Romaioi*.

Pipin on his part undertook to march against the Lombards, to restore to the Pope those parts of the Roman patrimony which the Lombards had seized, and place in his power the territories of the exarchate. Aistulf was soon compelled (753) to sue for peace, and he engaged to surrender to the Pope the promised lands and never aggress again. But when the Franks had returned he declined to keep his promise, and the combined forces of the northern and the Beneventan Lombards laid siege to Rome. Pipin descended a second time into Italy, and Aistulf was bound to harder conditions and constrained to pay tribute to the king of the Franks (755).

[1] As a concurrent cause in the establishment of an intimate connection between the papacy and the Frankish kingdom, we must not overlook the mission of Boniface (Winifred of England) as an apostle among the Germans. The king of the Franks was deeply interested in the lands east of the Rhine, and the foundation of a German Church under the direct inspiration of the papacy brought him into closer contact with it, the enterprise demanding a certain amount of co-operation.

[2] The only Roman duke who bore the title of *patricius* was Stephen (730-750), who was probably appointed by the Pope and not by the Emperor (Armbrust, *op. cit.* p. 93).

Thus Ravenna and (partially) the territory of the exarchate,[1] having remained four years in the possession of the Lombards, passed to the papal see by what was called the donation of Pipin. As Rome was still nominally, if not more than nominally, a city of the Empire, and the Pope still a subject of the Emperor, the act of 755 might be considered theoretically the recovery of the exarchate for New Rome; but the mode of its recovery and its new position, as well as the indifference of New Rome, rendered it in point of fact an independent papal state.

In the same year Aistulf died and was succeeded by Desiderius, the duke of Tuscany, who was at first friendly [2] and afterwards hostile to Pope Stephen. In 757 he repeated the experiment which Liutprand had tried thirty years before, an alliance with the Greeks against Pope Paul and the Lombard dukes of southern Italy. Constantine V was asked for aid—a request which shows how utterly Old Rome and New Rome were estranged; and though he could not send it, the fleet of Sicily combined with Desiderius and took Hydrus (Otranto), which henceforward remained in the hands of the Greeks. The duchy of Beneventum was reduced to dependence on the Lombard kingdom. Desiderius maintained friendly relations both with his suzerain King Pipin [3] and with Pipin's son and successor King Charles, who married the daughter of the Lombard monarch; and the Popes did not assume an attitude unfavourable to the Lombards until the accession of Hadrian in 771.

Pope Hadrian I. was a Roman of noble family and a strong antagonist of the Lombard party at Rome, which was led by Paul Afiarta. He entered into close relations with King Charles; he refused to crown the sons of Karlmann (Charles' brother), who had fled to Pavia; and he ordered the archbishop of Ravenna to imprison Afiarta. The archbishop, placing an

[1] Besides Ravenna, Cesena, Forum Livii, Forum Pompilii, Bobium, and Comiaclum (Commachio) were handed over to the Pope. Aistulf retained Imola, Faventia, Bononia, Ferraria, Adria, Gabellum; he also obtained all the cities of the Pentapolis except Ancona, and six of the Decapolis (Anastasius, *Vit. Steph.*)

[2] The Pope supported his candidature for the Lombard crown, and he promised to restore some of the cities (including Ancona and Osimo), which Aistulf had kept back (*Cod. Carolinus*, ed. Jaffé, *Ep.* xi.)

[3] An embassy from Pipin induced Desiderius to come to a peaceable understanding with the Pope about territorial boundaries (*Cod. Carol. Ep.* xix.)

unduly severe interpretation on this command, put the man to death. In consequence of these causes of discord, Desiderius plundered the territory of Rome, and Hadrian[1] wrote to his friend King Charles for help. Charles set out in September 773 and forced Desiderius to retreat to Pavia, where he seized him, and then assumed himself the crown and title of the king of the Lombards. Thence, in the guise of a deliverer, and recognised as such, he proceeded to Rome, where he celebrated Easter (774) and renewed to Pope Hadrian the grants which his father had made to Stephen.

As to this donation of Charles the Great, diverse opinions prevail. The document itself, if such a document existed, is lost, and our only authority is Anastasius' *Life of Hadrian*, wherein it is stated that Charles made over to the chair of St. Peter, not only the exarchate, but Venice, Istria, Corsica, Beneventum, and Spoleto. Such a statement sounds incredible and almost unmeaning. Some regard it as a mere falsification,[2] others defend it[3] and lay emphasis on the form of the expression *promissio donationis*. Another disputed question in regard to this donation is whether Charles reserved to himself the overlordship of the territory which he conceded to the Pope or not; here also various opinions prevail.[4]

On the whole, we may perhaps conclude that Charles confirmed the Pope in his rule over the Pentapolis and the exarchate; and that the question of overlordship did not arise at the time. It is not likely that contemporaries asked themselves distinctly the question, in what precise relation the Pope stood on the one hand to the Emperor and on the other hand to the Patrician of the Romans, or what precisely was the legal nature of the papal tenure of the lands which had been once governed by the exarchs. But in 781 (1st December) Hadrian took a step which was equivalent to a formal and final rupture of the thin bonds that bound East Rome to West Rome. He ceased to use the years of the Emperors as dates, and adopted the

---

[1] Hadrian meanwhile collected all the forces he could muster from Campania, Tuscany, the duchy of Perusia, and the Pentapolis. "Campania" of course includes Latium, and with Tuscany formed the duchy of Rome. The duchy of Perusia went with the Pentapolis.

[2] Muratori, Gregorovius, Sybel, Mar-tens, Armbrust, etc.

[3] Döllinger, Waitz, Sickel, etc.

[4] Papencordt and Niehues believe that Charles gave the Pope full sovereignty; while Gregorovius, Döllinger, and others hold that Charles retained the suzerainty. *See* Zoepffel's article on "Hadrian I." in Herzog and Pflitt's *Encyclopädie.*

formula " Under the reign of the Lord Jesus Christ, our God and Redeemer." From this time until 25th December 800 we may say that the Church of Rome held the anomalous position of not being connected with a Roman Empire.

At this period, for ten years or more (766-777), the Popes had spiritual rivals in Italy, who like themselves affected temporal dominion. These were the archbishops of Ravenna, who had always endeavoured to maintain as far as possible an independent attitude towards the Popes. Archbishop Sergius succeeded in obtaining the larger part of the exarchate, which had been nominally transferred to the Pope, and " he administered all things like an exarch," in which he was secretly encouraged by King Charles.[1] After the fall of Desiderius, Leo, the successor of Sergius, seized many new towns with impunity and attempted to extend his jurisdiction over the Pentapolis; but after his death in 777 the exarchate passed actually into papal hands.[2]

Charles and Hadrian, thus brought into more intimate relations, did not remain long on friendly terms. Charles could see under the pontifical robe that greed for territorial aggrandisement[3] which animated so many of St. Peter's later successors, and helped to bring about both the power and the corruption of the Church. For this worldly greed in a spiritual potentate the Teutonic king must have felt a contempt. Hadrian on his part found out that, if Desiderius was overthrown, he had to do with a new and far more powerful " King of the Lombards."

In 780 the general of Sicily united with the dukes of Beneventum and Spoletium against the Pope, who was compelled to send across the Alps and summon the " Patrician of the Romani" to lend aid against the Patrician of the Romaioi. He came and set things in order, and in the following year (781) he crowned his son Pipin king of Italy and his son Ludwig king of Aquitania. The new title, "King of Italy," did not mean any fresh arrangement of practical signification, but it

[1] Agnellus, *Lib. Pont.* (Mur. *S. R. I.*) *veluti exarchus omnia disponebat.*
[2] Armbrust, *op. cit.* p. 77.
[3] Thus Hadrian wished to assume the overlordship of the duchy of Spoletium, and pretended that Charles had given it to him, *quia et ipsum Spoletinum ducatum vos praesentaliter offeruistis protectori vestro*, etc. (*Cod. Carol. Ep.* lvii.) Charles, however, soon showed him that his pretension was unfounded.

marked a distinct stage in the development of the new relations into which Italy had entered. In 786 Charles appeared again in Italy to reduce to subjection Arichis, the Prince of Beneventum,—in 774 the duchy had become a principality,—and thus he became overlord of all Italy down to the borders of Calabria. But Beneventum was always practically independent of the Frank empire, and even the theoretical relation of vassaldom does not seem to have been more than transitory. On both these occasions, in 780 and in 786, new agreements advantageous to the Pope seem to have been made between Hadrian and Charles in regard to the extent of the *Patrimonium Petri.* In the last years of Hadrian's pontificate the discord which had been often manifested between him and Charles was increased, and there was a report that the latter had discussed with Offa, king of Mercia, the advisability of deposing the Pope. The ill feeling was augmented by a difference of opinion on the subject of image-worship. Pope Hadrian had thought to patronise the Emperor and Empress of New Rome; he had written them a letter in which flattery, rebuke, and concern for the patrimony of Peter were seasonably blended; and he approved of the seventh Ecumenical Council, at which his delegates were present. That council had quietly ignored the Pope's communications except so far as they bore on the matter in hand; but the Pope was not in a position to resent the rebuff. He sent a copy of its acts to the Teutonic king, who agreed with the learned men at his court in disapproving of the doctrines there set forth. The famous *libri Carolini* were composed, in which the seventh Council was spoken of with scant respect and a theory was expounded which represented a compromise between iconoclasm and image-worship. On receiving this publication the Pope threatened Charles with the ban of the Church, and the monarch replied by holding the synod of Frankfurt (794) which condemned the recent council of Nicaea. In the following year Hadrian died on Christmas Day, and was mourned by Charles, notwithstanding all their dissensions.

Immediately after his election the next Pope, Leo III, sent the keys of the sepulchre and the flag of Rome to Charles, and asked him to send some of his nobles to receive allegiance at Rome. In reply to this Charles wrote a letter full of whole-

some admonition—strange language coming from a king to a
Pope—in which the following words occur: "It is ours to
defend the Church of Christ everywhere on earth, outwardly
against the heathen and unbelievers, inwardly by the recognition of the true faith. It is yours, most holy father, with
hands raised like Moses, to support our strife, that at your
intercession by God's gracious help the christian people may
triumph over the enemies of his name, and that the name of
our Lord Jesus Christ may be glorified." These words breathe
the spirit of a holy Roman Emperor, and are a clear recognition
of the position which Pope Paul wished to assign to Pipin,
a king divinely inspired to liberate the holy catholic and
apostolic Church.

The friends of the deceased Hadrian agitated against the
new Pope, and their attempts at violence obliged Leo to flee to
France. As they preferred various charges against Leo, it was
decided that he should be tried by a court. The trial was held
at the end of the year 800, and Charles came to Rome for the
purpose of presiding. The Pope was triumphantly acquitted.

This was the moment at which the decisive act, which had
such a vast effect on European history, the coronation of Charles
the Great as *Imperator Augustus*, took place. The celebrated
passage in the Annals of Lauresheim, describing the event, runs
thus [1]:—

"And because the name of Emperor had now ceased among the
Greeks, and their Empire was possessed by a woman, it then seemed both
to Leo the Pope himself, and to all the holy fathers who were present in
the selfsame council, as well as to the rest of the christian people, that
they ought to take to be Emperor Charles king of the Franks, who held
Rome herself, where the Caesars had always been wont to sit, and all the
other regions which he ruled through Italy and Gaul and Germany ; and
inasmuch as God had given all these lands into his hand, it seemed right
that with the help of God and at the prayer of the whole christian
people he should have the name of Emperor also. Whose petition King
Charles willed not to refuse, but submitting himself with all humility to
God, and at the prayer of the priests and of the whole christian people, on
the day of the nativity of our Lord Jesus Christ he took on himself the
name of Emperor, being consecrated by the lord Pope Leo."

The consecration consisted of coronation with a golden
crown and unction with holy oil. The latter ceremony was not

[1] I have borrowed the translation of this passage from Bryce's *Holy Roman
Empire*, p. 53.

practised at New Rome; it was borrowed from the custom of the Visigoths of Spain. The Pope then adored the new Emperor and cried aloud: "To Charles the most pious Augustus, crowned of God, the great Emperor, who giveth peace, be life and victory."[1]

The various theories which have been held as to the legal basis and import of this coronation have been discussed by Mr. Bryce, and I suppose that all unprejudiced readers will concur in the justness of his conclusion. "As the act was unprecedented, so was it illegal; it was a revolt of the ancient Western capital against a daughter who had become a mistress; an exercise of the sacred right of insurrection, . . . hallowed to the eyes of the world by the sanction of Christ's representative, but founded upon no law, nor competent to create any for the future."[2] At the same time, I am inclined to think that if a contemporary had been asked for a theory of the coronation he would have interpreted it as an election of Charles by the Romans and their Republic, the Pope as the most exalted personage at Rome being their representative. No one would have looked on it as a direct consequence of Charles' conquests or as resting on the Pope's authority alone.

The most important, and also most easily misconceived, circumstance in regard to this event is that Charles was considered the successor of Constantine VI.[3] This is distinctly implied in the cause assigned by contemporary writers for Charles' coronation—"the name of Emperor had now ceased among the Greeks, and their Empire was possessed by a woman." There was an idea prevalent, which Mr. Bryce's book, it is to be hoped, has finally dispelled, that Charles posed as the successor of Romulus Augustulus, who abdicated in 476. This error was due to the false use of words. It was the habit and is still the habit to speak of the dominions ruled by Honorius and his successors as the Western Empire. This false " Western

---

[1] *See* Anastasius, *Vita Leonis*. The adoration of Charles by Leo is mentioned in the Chronicle of Moissac, published in Pertz, *Mon. Hist. Germ.* vol. i.

[2] *Holy Roman Empire*, p. 57. Mr. Bryce speaks of the "weakness and wickedness of the Byzantine princes" —an expression which is unjustifiable. They were weak in so far as they could no longer hold Italy. A discussion of the question whether the coronation was a surprise to Charles or was prearranged will be found p. 58 *sq.*

[3] "In all the annals of the time and of many succeeding centuries, the name of Constantine VI, the sixty-seventh in order from Augustus, is followed without a break by that of Charles, the sixty-eighth " (Bryce, p. 63).

Empire" was then connected in thought with the true Western Empire, the Holy Roman Empire, which was founded in 800, and whose coexistence as a rival made the name Eastern Empire for the first time applicable to the realm of the sovereigns of New Rome. Romulus Augustulus was succeeded by Zeno; and if Pope Leo had regarded Charles as the successor of Romulus he would have been obliged to regard the sovereigns whom the Popes acknowledged for three hundred years as usurpers. The fact is, that Romulus Augustulus was as much forgotten in the eighth century as any obscure name in history, and no one would have thought of making the year 476 A.D. a historical landmark.

When I call the Holy Roman Empire the true Western Empire, and the Empire of Nicephorus I. and his successors the true Eastern Empire, I use the word "true" in a sense that requires a line of explanation. The Empire whose centre was Old Rome and the Empire whose centre was New Rome claimed each to be the Roman Empire. Nicephorus and his successors logically ought not to have admitted that Charles was a Roman Emperor; and Charles and his successors ought not to have conceded the title to their rivals. From a mere legal point of view the claim of the sovereigns of New Rome was good; while that of Charles rested on a basis completely infirm. But actually the two Roman Empires coexisted, compelled to recognise each other, but quite distinct, one in the East and one in the West; so that the terms Eastern Empire and Western Empire are really applicable. It was quite otherwise, as has been already so often observed, with the Empire in the fifth century. Then there was one Roman Empire, ruled by two Emperors, who for convenience divided the territory which they governed, but at any moment this arrangement might cease and one Emperor might rule the whole. If any one speaks of a Western and an Eastern empire in the fifth century, he should write "empire" with a small initial so as to show distinctly that he uses the word in a different sense from that which it bears in the expression "Roman Empire," of which unity was an inseparable attribute.

It is hardly necessary to observe that the election of the new Roman Emperor, if it was not legally defensible, was yet as thoroughly justifiable by the actual history of the two preceding centuries as it has been justified by the history of ten succeeding centuries. For the Popes had practically assumed in the West the functions and the position of the Emperor. It was around them and their bishops that the municipalities rallied in a series of continual struggles with the Lombards ; the presence of the Emperor's delegates in Italy was becoming every year less and less effectual. It was the Popes who organised missionary enterprises to convert the heathen in the West, just as it was the Emperors who furthered similar enterprises in the East. Gregory I., in spite of the respectful tone in his letters to Maurice and Phocas, was the civil potentate in Italy. The mere fact that the Pope was the largest landed proprietor in Roman Italy concurred to give him an almost monarchical position. As the virtual sovereign then of Italy as far as it was Roman,—for even in the days of exarchs he had often been its sovereign far more truly than the exarch or the Emperor,—and as the bearer of the idea of the Roman Empire with all its traditions of civilisation, the Pope had a right, by the standard of justice, to transfer the representation of the ideas whereof he was the keeper to one who was able to realise them.

CHAPTER XII

SINCE the beginning of the fifth century, when the Roman
Empire was still conterminous with European civilisation, the
political map of Europe was never so simple as in the last few
days of the eighth and during the following centuries; and it
has never been so simple since. The smaller independent
kingdoms of the West had disappeared, partly conquered by
the Saracen, partly gathered up into the dominion of the new
Emperor of the West, and thus civilised Europe was divided
among three chief powers—the Empire of the East, the Empire
of the West, and the emirate, which afterwards became the
caliphate, of Cordova. But there was another power which,
though not at this period European, formed an important
element in the political situation; this was the caliphate,
afterwards the eastern caliphate, which included the north of
Africa. Though the Omeyyad lords of Spain at first contented
themselves with the title of emir, their dominion was not even
theoretically part of the caliphate, from which they had revolted; not only had the court of Bagdad as little authority at
Cordova as the court of Constantinople possessed at Aachen,
but the Omeyyad emirs and the Abbasid caliphs were irreconcilable foes. When the emirs at length assume the
superior title, the old caliphate becomes for historians' convenience the eastern caliphate, just as the Roman Empire
becomes the Roman Empire of the East. It may be added
that in the ninth century the eastern caliph became a
European potentate by the conquest of Sicily.

At the end of the eighth century then the political aspect of civilised Europe consisted in the existence of two christian and two mohammedan powers; a Roman Empire in the East and a Roman Empire in the West, a caliphate in the East and an independent emirate in the West. The mutual relations of these four powers were such as might be predicted, as Mr. Freeman has so often pointed out. On the one hand, rivalry existed between the two Empires, and rivalry existed between the two caliphates, if we may call the emirate a caliphate by anticipation; on the other hand, there were constant hostilities between the two eastern powers, whose frontiers coincided, and between the two western powers, whose frontiers likewise coincided. The consequence was that the Emperor of Constantinople was generally on friendly terms with the emir or caliph of Cordova, and the Emperor of Aachen was on friendly terms with the caliph of Bagdad. Two smaller and outlying states, the christian Anglo-Saxons of Britain and the heathen Bulgarians of Moesia, were independent; the former by their geographical position being more closely connected with the Western and the latter with the Eastern Empire.[1]

Such being the general aspect, we may now turn to the details, and examine the historical changes which took place during the eighth century, more especially as they affected the political geography of Europe.

The first feature that strikes us is that the two greatest powers in Europe, the Roman Empire and the Franks, were then recovering from a period of decline. The Roman Empire was renovated under the Isaurian Emperors, as the Frank kingdom was renovated under the Karlings. In both cases there had been a struggle between the monarchy and the aristocracy. In the Teutonic kingdom things went so far that the Merovingian dynasty was reduced to a simulacrum of royalty and the nobles wielded the power; while in the Roman Empire the strong but unpopular Heraclian dynasty was finally overthrown by an unmanageable aristocracy, and for a moment things went almost as far as in Gaul, when the

---

[1] Terbel was made a Caesar by Justinian II, and this act may be regarded as bringing the Bulgarian kingdom within the imperial system, somewhat as the Franks of the sixth century were connected with the Roman Empire.

throne was occupied by the insignificant Emperor Theodosius III, whose power was little more substantial than that of a Merovingian king.

It frequently happens that a period of internal reform or domestic prosperity for a state is ushered in by a successful defence against some dangerous invader.[1] We may regard the victories of Charles Martel over the Saracens in the south of Gaul as the signs or heralds of Karlingian greatness, while the far greater achievement of Leo III in repulsing the enormous forces of Muaviah from the walls of Constantinople inaugurated the epoch of Isaurian reformation. We speak intelligibly, though perhaps not quite philosophically, if we say that, but for the Karlings in the eighth century, there would never have been Emperors crowned at Old Rome to rival the Emperors crowned at New Rome; or that, but for the Isaurian sovereigns, the old Roman Empire would not have continued to exist in the south-east beside the new Roman Empire of the West. It is hard for us to imagine that the Saracens might ever have settled permanently in Gaul and spread northwards, perhaps even to the English Channel, and that Paris, like Arles, might have been once a Saracen city; we cannot but suppose that, even had they extended their power farther than Septimania and maintained it for a longer period than forty years, they would have been driven back from Gaul many centuries sooner than they were actually driven back from Spain. But it is easy to imagine, on the other hand, that the Mohammedan Arabs might have occupied permanently the south-eastern corner of Europe seven centuries sooner than it was blighted by the presence of the Mohammedan Turks.

While the greater powers increased, the smaller powers diminished. The kingdom of the Visigoths was conquered by Tarik and Musa (711-713 A.D.), including Septimania,[2] or Gothia, as the portion that remained to the Visigoths of their Gallic possessions, which had once extended to the Loire,[3]

---

[1] Compare the well-known instances of the Danish invasion of England, Punic invasion of Italy, Persian invasion of Greece.

[2] The colonists in southern Gaul in the time of Julius Caesar were named after legions; Narbo was the colony of the Decimani, Arausio (Orange) of the Secundani, Arelate of the Sextani,

Baeterrae of the Septimani. The name Septimania survived. For these colonies, *see* Mommsen, *History of Rome* (Eng. Trans.), vol. iv. p. 542.

[3] At this point the Goths disappear from history, but the Gothic name and tongue were preserved by the Tetraxite Goths of the Crimea, who survived till the tenth century. In 1562 a Belgian

was sometimes called. The kingdom of the Lombards, which under Liutprand had seemed likely to rise to greatness, was overthrown by the Franks and became a group of Frank provinces, destined afterwards to become a separate kingdom under the suzerainty of the Teutonic Roman Emperor.

The frontiers of the Frank power advanced in four different directions. (1) To the south they were extended by the acquisition of the Lombard territories, Austria, Neustria, Tuscia, and the duchies of Friuli and Spoleto, and by the subjection of the exarchate. (2) To the south-west the Visigothic province of Septimania was added to Frank Gaul; but it was not won directly from the Visigoths, just as the exarchate was not won directly from the Greeks. Septimania became first a Saracen and then a Frank province, just as the exarchate passed into the hands of the Lombards before it passed to the Franks. The Lombards weakened the Greeks in northern Italy as the Saracens weakened the Goths in southern Gaul, and in both cases the Franks profited. (3) To the north-east lands were conquered from the heathen waste of central Europe by the victories of Charles over the Saxons in 772 and the following years; while (4) to the south-east the kingdom of the Avars in Pannonia was conquered by the same monarch (796 A.D.), whose power also extended into the Slavonic lands of Carinthia and Istria.[1]

When we speak, however, of a Cisalpine dominion of the Franks, we are not speaking quite strictly, and must make two modifications. Although the power of Charles in Italy practically amounted to a Cisalpine dominion of the Franks, Charles did not hold either his Lombard conquests or the exarchate in the capacity of king of the Franks. He assumed the title of king of the Lombards, and thus, from a theoretical aspect, the kingdom of the Lombards did not disappear in the eighth century, but continued to exist under sovereigns who were also kings beyond the Alps. As for the exarchate, it was under the direct control of the Popes, by virtue of the donation

traveller, Busbek, met at Constantinople two Gothic ambassadors from the Crimea, and wrote down words of their language which are genuine Gothic words. (*See* Mr. Bradley, *The Goths*, p. 363.)

[1] As a result of this Frank domination Sirmium received the name Frankochorion, and the name of the mountain, Fruška Gora=Frankenberg, still preserves the memory of the episode. *See* Jiriček, *op. cit.* p. 144.

of Pipin, which Charles the Great confirmed; and thus it was as Roman Emperor and not as king of the Franks, it was by right of his coronation and not by right of his conquest, that Charles could claim dominion over the patrimony of St. Peter.

The memory of the Lombard power, which endured in Italy as an independent kingdom for two hundred years, is perpetuated by the name Lombardy,[1] which is still used to designate the land which was called Neustria, and part of what was called Austria. In the same way the name Romagna still survives, a memorial of the exarchate and the rule of the Greek Romans in Italy. Perhaps no geographical appellation is more suggestive of the fortunes of the Roman name than Italian Romania—not even that of Asiatic Romania, the Seljuk kingdom of Roum. A tract of country, within a few days' march from Rome herself by the Flaminian road, receives the name of Rome, but not until that name has first travelled to Constantinople and thence returned, after two and a half centuries, to Ravenna and the adjacent districts. Thus the only part of Italy that is called by a name derived from Rome, received that name, not from Old Rome on the Tiber, but from New Rome on the Bosphorus.

The overthrow of the Lombard kingdom did not carry with it the extinction of all independent Lombard power in the peninsula. The duchy of Beneventum, which since its foundation had been practically independent of the royal government at Pavia, until the energetic action of Liutprand in the eighth century brought for a moment the dukes of Beneventum and Spoletium into nominal subjection, was never incorporated in the dominions of the Karlings, although at first its lords were compelled to recognise the conqueror of Lombardy as their suzerain (786 A.D.) But the immediate consequences of the Frank conquests were agreeable to the duke. He at once assumed the title of prince, and henceforward we must speak of the principality, instead of the duchy, of Beneventum. He might reasonably anticipate that there would be less danger of interference with his independence from the new Transalpine than from the old Cisalpine lords of northern Italy.

---

[1] The name Garda for Lake Benacus is perhaps another reminiscence of the Lombard dominion.

One state in northern Italy, which was theoretically part of the exarchate though before the end of the seventh century it was practically independent, never passed under Frankish rule, the duchy of Venice. Venice continued to be nominally subject to the Emperor of Constantinople, and, for some centuries to come, must be considered as an outlying post of the Eastern Empire in northern Italy. The policy of the city of St. Mark was to maintain her independence by playing off the Emperor of the East against the Emperor of the West, and thus she carved out a peculiar history of her own. The republic of the lagoons was quite distinct in character from all other Italian cities; there was not much occidental flavour about it, and yet it cannot be quite called a Byzantine city. Its spirit, well symbolised in the church of St. Mark, was so unique that it can only be designated by the word " Venetian "; nevertheless, of the elements which composed the Venetian type the Byzantine element preponderated. We may say that the Venetians formed an intermediate stage between the western European nations and the Byzantines, just as the Byzantine world itself formed an intermediate stage between the Orient and the Occident. It was the Byzantine character of Venice that determined the peculiar part she played at the time of the Fourth Crusade and under the dynasty of the Palaeologi.

While in the West it was the tendency of smaller kingdoms to disappear, because the power of Francia increased, in the south-east a new kingdom had been established before the Isaurian sovereigns regenerated the Empire. There would be little use in considering whether, supposing the Bulgarians had not crossed the Danube in the reign of Constantine IV, but had waited until the eighth century to press southwards, Leo III or Constantine V would have been strong enough to prevent them. It is certain that these Emperors did not consider it feasible to drive the intruders out; they contented themselves with hindering further aggression and preserving the frontier of Mount Haemus. The expeditions of Constantine V aimed at weakening the power rather than at effecting the conquest of the Bulgarian kingdom.[1]

[1] It was mentioned before that the population of the Thraco - Illyrian peninsula was Latin - speaking in the fifth and sixth centuries. From this population are descended the Vlachians in their various homes both north and south of the Danube. North of the Danube indeed there probably

We have already considered at length the import of the foundation of the Holy Roman Empire and the new attitude assumed by the papacy in the eighth century, and it has been observed that without a comprehension of these events modern history is unintelligible.   It is interesting to compare the offices which the new Empire in the north-west and the old Empire in the south-east respectively performed.   In many respects their functions were similar.   They were both forced to play a part in the decision of the " eternal question " ; while the eastern Emperor defended Mount Taurus against the eastern caliphate, the western Emperor held the Pyrenees against the western caliphate ; and it devolved upon both Emperors to keep the heathen of central Europe at bay, the Magyars (before they became Christians) and the Patzinaks. Both Emperors ruled over Slaves ; the western Emperor over the Slaves in Pannonia, the eastern Emperor over the Slaves in Macedonia and Greece ; and in both cases the Slaves proved an alien and troublesome element.[1]

Both Empires were the champions of order in Europe ; both Old and New Rome were ranged for civilisation against barbarism.   But there is a broad contrast between them.   The part played by the Eastern Empire may be described as negative, while the part played by the Western Empire was positive.   The Eastern Empire protected Europe against the inroads of Asiatic barbarism, while the Western Empire extended Christianity and order in central Europe.   The Eastern Empire conserved and in many respects refined ancient civilisation ; the Western Empire learned of the Eastern, and

---

survived in Walachia and Moldavia a layer of Roman population, though Roesler would have it that when Aurelian abandoned Trajan's Dacia, it was entirely evacuated by the Romans ; but this layer cannot have been large, and Pič has not disproved that it was a medieval immigration of cis-Danubian Vlachs that rendered a "Roumania" possible. "Great Walachia" in Thessaly was formed by a southward movement of these Illyrian Romans, who were probably pressed into the highlands of Pindus and the promontories of Acarnania by the Slaves. But there remained for many centuries a considerable Vlachian population in Bulgaria itself.

[1] The absence of royalty is a feature of primitive Slavonic societies, and it is interesting to observe that the Slaves derived their names for emperor and king from the Eastern and Western Roman Empires respectively. Καῖσαρ, *Caesar*, became (perhaps through a Frank medium) Tsesar, and then, by the omission of one of two similar syllables, Tsar ; while *korol, kral*, "king," perpetuates the christian name of the founder of the Western Empire, Karl the Great. Doubts have been thrown on this derivation of Tsar (Czar), but *tsesarstvo*, "kingdom," in Matthew xiii. 24 establishes it.

developed what it learned in new directions. In Russia indeed New Rome played a more positive part than elsewhere, but its influence there was spiritual rather than political. Thus the Holy Roman Empire has in some respects more resemblance than the Eastern Empire to the old pagan Roman Empire. I do not mean the more superficial circumstances that the centre of both was Italian Rome, and that in both Latin was the official language; I mean the essential circumstance that they performed similar offices for Europe; for just as the pagan Roman Empire civilised Gaul, the Holy Roman Empire civilised central Europe. The Eastern Empire, on the other hand, had the function of the ancient Greeks rather than that of the ancient Romans—spiritual rather than temporal dominion; it was the great permanent fixture which remained until western Europe was prepared to take the torch for ever and march with certain footsteps in new paths of development.

CHAPTER XIII

THE endeavours of the Isaurian monarchs to renovate the
Empire bore such fruits as were possible at a period when
the horizon of the human spirit was determined by a series
of ecclesiastical formulae. Whereas at the beginning of the
century there was no distinguished writer, no man of pre-
eminent learning within the limits of the Empire, there was at
the close of the century quite a large group of literary men, who
had studied a great many subjects and could write very good
Greek. There was George the Syncellus, who wrote a history
or chronicle of the world and carried it down as far as Diocletian; there was his friend Theophanes [1] the monk, who continued the chronicle where George ended and carried it down
to his own times; there was Theodore the abbot of Studion,
who has left works which form a good-sized volume [2]; there
was the learned Nicephorus, who, at first a secretary, afterwards became Patriarch and wrote a short history of the
Empire from the accession of Heraclius to the middle of the
reign of Constantine V [3]; there was Tarasius, who enjoyed also

---

[1] The reader may have formed some
notion of the language of Theophanes,
who wrote in the vulgar tongue, from
the short quotations from him inter-
spersed in the notes of this volume.
His chronicle, however, is written in
better Greek than that of John Malalas;
Theophanes would not have used such
a form as ἔβαλα from βάλλω, although
he has the isolated aorist ἀνεπάη ("he
died"), formed from ἀναπαύω, just as
classical ἐκάην is formed from καυ-
(καύσω, pres. καίω). The recent edition
of Theophanes by C. de Boor is ad-
mirable.

[2] Edited by Migne in the *Patrol.
Graec.* vol. 99.

[3] Also a short Χρονογραφικόν (lists
of emperors, empresses, patriarchs,
popes, etc.) His anti - iconoclastic
works have been mentioned. His
style, like that of Theodore Studita,
forms a contrast to that of Theophanes;
he avoids all colloquial expressions,
introduces such words as ἀσηκρῆτις with
an explanation (p. 49, ed. de Boor),

a secular education and was suddenly promoted to the highest ecclesiastical dignity; and there was the abbot Plato, who, though he did not write himself, perhaps exercised to some extent a literary as well as a monastic influence. Besides these, John Lekanomantis, a learned man of science, who had an evil repute for occult lore in the days of Leo the Armenian, must at this time have been receiving his education.

A few glimpses of the usual course of education are afforded to us in the lives of certain of the famous ecclesiastics just mentioned, which were in some cases written by eminent contemporaries.[1] Children were sent at an early age to an elementary teacher or *grammatistes*, who gave them what was called an " eisagogic " or " propaedentic " training. Theodore of Studion was taught by a grammatistes for no less than seven years. It probably often happened that parents who had the requisite leisure and knowledge taught their children at home ; and from the fact that Theoctiste, Theodore's mother, was uneducated *because she was an orphan,* and was obliged to teach herself after her marriage, it might be inferred that women received only home instruction. The elementary training was followed by a higher or university course[2] in philology (" grammar "), dialectic, and rhetoric ; some also studied mathematics and music.[3] The study of philology doubtless consisted in a careful reading of literary works and perhaps the practice of composition in Hellenistic style,[4] which was so different from the spoken language that for writing in it—as well (for example) as Theodore of Studion could write—a diligent course of study was necessary. We are told that Theodore objected to the elegance and emptiness of the rhetors,—but it is not

---

etc. When Mr. Freeman marked a period of writers, like Theophanes and Constantine VII, intervening between the earlier period of stylists, like Procopius and Agathias, and the later period of stylists, like (Psellus and) Anna Comnena, he should have added that throughout the middle period there were some writers who were careful to avoid colloquialisms ; *see* his most interesting article, " Some Points in the History of later Greek," *Hellenic Journal,* vol. iii.

[1] The Life of Theophanes was written by Theodore of Studion ; the Life of Nicephorus by Ignatius the Patriarch. These lives have been recently published by M. de Boor in his editions of Theophanes and Nicephorus.

[2] This course was generally called ἡ θύραθεν παιδεία, "secular education" ; esoteric studies were no longer philosophical, but theological.

[3] For example, Nicephorus. An interesting account of studies in logic and philosophy as prosecuted at the period will be found in the *Vita Nicephori,* ed. de Boor, p. 150.

[4] ἐξελληνίζειν γλῶσσαν καὶ γραμματικήν.

quite clear whether the rhetors of the past or rhetors of his own day are referred to.

Theodore had studied poetry, and composed sacred poems which were popular and widely circulated. A curious story is told which indicates their wide diffusion. There was a certain man in Sardinia who was very fond of these verses, especially of the Triodia composed for the season of Lent. One day he entertained in his house some monks who were pupils of Gregory of Syracuse, and when he began to descant on his favourite literature they turned the poems into ridicule as provincial and bad. The easily impressed host veered round to the opinion of his guests; but that night Theodore himself appeared, to take vengeance on his admirer for his faithlessness, and caused him to be whipped. This is only one of many miracles which were connected with St. Theodore.[1]

We must notice here a celebrated Greek writer of the eighth century, who was not, however, a subject of the Empire, the Syrian John of Damascus.[2] His father held an administrative post under the Omeyyad caliphs, and possessed considerable landed property in Palestine and Judaea. He spent a large amount of his money in redeeming christian captives, and if any of them wished to remain in the country he bestowed on them small farms on his own estates. On one occasion he had the good fortune to purchase a monk of Italy, probably of Calabria, named Cosmas, whom the Arab pirates had brought from over seas to the slave market of Damascus, and he installed him as teacher of his son Johannes. Cosmas was learned in philosophy as well as in theology, and intimately acquainted with the writings of both Aristotle and Plato. The pupil profited by this instruction, and was considered in his day such a master of style that he was called Chrysorroas. He is chiefly known to the historians by his essays against the iconoclastic

---

[1] The author of the first *Vita Theodori* says that the tales of the miracles were told (1) by Theodore's friend Leo, (2) by Sophronius.

[2] The Life of John Damascenus was written by Johannes, bishop of Jerusalem, probably him who lived in the reign of Nicephorus Phocas, and was burned by the Saracens. For the views on ethics held by the scholar of Damascus I may refer the curious to the first vol. of W. Gass's *Geschichte der christlichen Ethik*, p. 218 sqq., and there is an important work by J. Langen entitled *Johannes von Damaskus* (1879). One of John's most important works is the πηγὴ γνώσεως (*Fons Scientiae*), in which he professes to cull and present to the reader the best things in Greek philosophy, and, moreover, discusses heresies and gives an exposition of the orthodox faith (ed. Migne, vol. i. pp. 5, 21 *sqq.*)

movement, which, however, are a very small portion of his works.

With the exception of the iconoclastic movement itself, which, although suggested by the Mohammedan doctrine, had many points of originality, there were no new ideas in the eighth century. The only eccentricity that I can find is the theory of Virgilius (condemned by Pope Zacharias), who not only believed in the existence of the Antipodes, but held that a race of men dwelled there who were not descended from Adam and for whom no Redeemer had died.

All that Leo and Constantine had done against superstition and monasticism did not touch the foundations of religious belief; their policy affected only the accidents of Christianity. They could not rouse up thought from the dead level and monotony to which it is condemned when its envelope is a stereotyped creed, anything different therefrom being incredible, almost unimaginable. They could not even remove the blight of superstition from the more educated classes, though their efforts were attended with some success. It was seriously believed that Leo IV died from boils on his head, a direct visitation from heaven because he had worn a crown which had been dedicated in St. Sophia. It was gravely asserted that the eyes of Constantine VI were put out on the 15th August because five years before he had put out the eyes of his uncles on that day, the coincidence of date indicating the retributive justice. It might be conjectured that the enemies who blinded him chose that very day on purpose, in order that the general public might look upon the crime as a punishment ordered by heaven, but in any case it is an example of superstition.[1]

The discord in Church and State created by the marriage of Constantine VI with Theodote, the maid of honour, is instructive. It disclosed the difference between monks like Plato and Theodore, and men of the world like Tarasius and Nicephorus, who had led a secular life at first and entered the

---

[1] The mention of superstition reminds me of the story told in the "Vita Tarasii" (*Acta Sanct.* Feb. xxiii.) of a case which came before George, Tarasius' father, who was a judge. Poor women were accused of killing sucking infants by penetrating through windows or even shut doors. Here we have the survival of the very ancient belief in the hobgoblin Gello, who is mentioned in a fragment of Sappho. George acquitted the accused, and the Emperor Constantine V, the enemy of all superstition, approved.

Church almost by accident. The austerity of the former was thoroughly honest, and justified by the letter and spirit of the religious canons; and Theodore alleges, in proof of the gravity of the Emperor's transgression, that the imperial example was infectious, and that governors of provinces—the Gothic governor of Bosporus is especially mentioned—began to imitate it securely. On the other hand, the tolerance of Tarasius, who, though he did not venture to perform the matrimonial ceremony, gave a tacit consent, is characteristic; and, I venture to say, it was an unconscious result of the rationalistic and anti-monastic spirit diffused by the two great Isaurian Emperors. In fact, I believe that the very election of Tarasius, a layman and at one time a military officer, to the patriarchal chair would never have been possible but for the views disseminated by those two Emperors, who deprecated over-strictness and condemned the superlative punctiliousness of monks. In the eyes of the Pope the election of such a Patriarch was doubtless a clear indication of the general demoralisation of the Empire.

The lenient manner in which the orthodox treat the Empress Irene is also worthy of note. They never forget that she led the reaction against iconoclasm and brought about the seventh Ecumenical Synod; and if her son after his questionable marriage is no longer a new Constantine the Great, Irene, in spite of all her questionable conduct towards her son, is always a new Helena.[1] The ethical judgment of the contemporary historians is perverted by a prejudice; the virtue of orthodoxy covers a multitude of vices; and the fact that Irene took the part of the monks against her son, although her motive was clearly to serve her own worldly ends, is imputed to her credit. She was a beautiful and accomplished woman who could beguile hearts, and we certainly do not expect writers to enlarge on the thesis that she was an unnatural mother; but it is amusing that the struggle between her and her son should be set down altogether to the account of the devil.

[1] I select at hazard Ignatius' words of laudation (*V. Niceph.* p. 146), τὸ κραταιόφρον ἐκεῖνο καὶ θεοφόρητον γύναιον: where γύναιον has somewhat the same nuance as our "creature." In the second vol. of Migne's ed. of the works of John of Damascus there is a certain *Letter to Theophilus* (falsely ascribed to John), probably written by the bishops of the East, and giving a short sketch of the history of iconoclasm. In it Irene is spoken of as a new Helena; she and her son are called a rose and lily among thorns.

The great attraction which monastic life possessed for men of the highest rank in the eighth century—the tendency, which Constantine V so vigorously combated, to found monasteries and retire from a public career—has been already noticed. Women as well as men were sometimes carried away by this desire ; for example, Theoctiste, the mother of Theodore Studita, became a nun in middle life, to the surprise and consternation of her friends and of the Empress herself, who wondered that a lady in such a good social position [1] should abandon the world. She was, however, an impulsive woman, and I think we may conclude that it was not fashionable among ladies of rank to get them to a nunnery.

The parents of Theoctiste and Plato were victims of the great plague, and the children were left orphans at an early age. Plato was trained to be a notary and was employed as a secretary by a relation who held the important office of general logothete. But he soon embraced monastic life, and became the abbot or hegumenos of the monastery of Saccudion, situated beside Mount Olympus on the coast of Bithynia.[2] At the time of the general synod of Nicaea he visited Constantinople and stayed with his sister Theoctiste, who had married Photinus, a minister of rank. The spiritual personality of Plato influenced so profoundly not only his nephews but his brother-in-law and sister, that they all determined to enter immediately upon the more excellent way of life. So Photinus and Theoctiste (to the surprise of her fashionable friends), along with their family, including a girl and three boys, of whom one was the famous Theodore, left Constantinople together and settled in a country retreat which belonged to them, named Boskytion. This domain, not far from the monastery of Saccudion, was enclosed at one end by a crescent of trees, and overlooked a pleasant breezy plain which stretched below ; an expanse of transparent water enhanced its delights. But, best of all in the eyes of its inhabitants, it afforded " quiet to those who dwelled in it, to be alone with God and at rest from the senses." Here Theodore became a monk and engaged in hard agricultural work, like a common farm labourer, not,

---

[1] Her niece Theodote was the maid of honour whom Constantine married.

[2] It is related that Plato not only excluded women from his monastery, but banished even female animals.

however, neglecting his studies.[1]   We are told that he was very zealous to reform monastic corruption, and this desire was doubtless felt by many men of his rank,[2] who became monks from purely disinterested motives, and led blameless lives. Such men, of high breeding and good education, must have produced incalculable effects by their example and influence in keeping personal morality at a relatively high point; and it cannot be denied that in this way the political decay involved in the monastic system was to some extent neutralised. When Theodore in later years was appointed abbot of the monastery of Studion (whence he derived his distinctive name Studites), he introduced the practice of mechanical work among the brethren; every one learned a trade; some were builders, some weavers, some bronzesmiths, some ropemakers, others shoemakers.   Many new houses, organised on a similar system, were founded throughout the Empire by Studite monks.

Perhaps no one was more austere, no one more uncompromisingly militant against the instincts of the senses, than the monk and historian Theophanes,[3] who, while the other ecclesiastics proceeded to the council of Nicaea on splendid horses and in fine array, rode thither on an ass, clothed in a hair garment.   He was one of those divine men, says his friend and biographer Theodore, the example of whose lives, like stars appearing after a storm to sea-tossed merchants, bring men safe to port.   He had a considerable fortune, which he spent on charitable works, and a kinsman who did not wish that the property should leave the family complained of the matter to Leo IV.   The Emperor threatened Theophanes with the loss

---

[1] His favourite author was St. Basil, and he especially delighted in Basil's book on monasticism.

[2] The senate in the eighth century had much the same functions as in the fifth. Its activities, like those of the Anglo-Saxon witenagemot, depended much on the character of the Emperor. They were generally limited to formalities, attending ceremonies, etc.; but in crises the senate had a constitutional right to act, as in the case of the deposition of Heraclonas and Martina. It is uncertain whether the judicial functions assigned to the senate by Justinian were still

exercised by it in the eighth century. M. Lécrivain writes (*Le Sénat Romain depuis Dioclétien*, 1888, p. 224), "Ici, comme à Rome on devine plutôt qu'on ne saisit sur le fait l'action du sénat; les textes ne la montrent guère que pour les élections impériales et les affaires réligieuses." To what extent the Emperors, *e.g.* Leo III and his son, were wont to consult the senate we cannot even guess.

[3] Son of Isaac and Theodote. When he was three years old his father died. He was a member of the corps of stratores in the reign of Leo IV, and afterwards received the dignity of spathar.

of his eyes if he persisted in his irrational unworldliness, and sent him on business to Cyzicus, in order to entangle him if possible in the things of this life. But the deaths of both the Emperor and the dissatisfied relation soon relieved Theophanes from such vexatious constraint, and he retired with his wife to the island Kalonnesos, where he built a monastery. The wife of this saint was wife only in name, and the description of the wedding night is curious and edifying. He treated his bride to a discourse on the spiritual necessity of unsullied purity; they agreed that they would never contaminate themselves by physical union; and the lady remained for ever a maiden, νύμφη τ' ἄνυμφος παρθένος τ' ἀπάρθενος. At the moment when they undertook the chaste engagement they were aware of a savour of sweet spices which filled the whole house, a miraculous token vouchsafed of celestial approval; this touch reminds us of the mystic odours in the legend of the Holy Grail.

It has been already remarked that Constantinople was becoming ever more and more a Greek city, and that its Greek character was greatly increased by the consequences of the plague. At the same time, its streets swarmed with numbers of wholly Graecised, half Graecised, or utterly barbarous foreigners, especially Armenians and Slavonians.[1] The importance of the Armenian element is indicated by the number of Armenians who held governorships in the Empire ; for example, Artavasdos, the son-in-law of Leo III, was an Armenian.[2] A Slavonic clergyman, Nicetas, was made Patriarch, and in the early part of the ninth century Thomas the Slavonian was one of the most powerful men of the time and wellnigh ascended the throne. A story is told, by a late writer, of the Patriarch Nicetas, that when reading a chapter of the New Testament he pronounced the name Ματθαῖου as if it were a quadrisyllable, Ματθάϊου. When some one present corrected

[1] There were also doubtless a good many Jews, but by the law (cf. *Ecloga*, title 9) Hellenes, Jews, and heretics were disqualified from civil and military service.

[2] The Emperor Philippicus was an Armenian, and at the beginning of the ninth century an Armenian, Leo V, ascended the throne. *See* above, p. 452.

There seem to have been many Armenian colonies in Thrace, as is proved by numerous Armenian inscriptions discovered there by M. A. Dumont, cf. Rambaud, *L'empire grec au dixième siècle*, p. 147 (also Mr. Tozer's note on Finlay, ii. 228). Armenian origin has been claimed for Basil I., but it seems more likely that he was a Slave.

him he indignantly cried, "Don't be silly; my soul utterly abhors diphthongs and triphthongs."[1]

If newspapers had been published at Constantinople in the eighth century, columns of court news and columns of church news would have occupied most space. Almost every week, and often more than once a week, there would have been a description of some elaborate ceremonial procession. It would be tedious to go into the details of these ceremonies,[2] which come within the scope of archaeology rather than of history, and we may go on to glance at the functions of the prefect of the city and the quaestor,[3] the two officials who had most to do with the police control and maintenance of order in Constantinople, and whose names remind us of the continuity of Roman history.

Next to the Emperor himself, the prefect of the city was the greatest man in Byzantium. He was the supreme judge, not only inside the walls, but for one hundred miles beyond them. Let us enter his court and see what sort of cases used to come before him. At one time it was a slave—it must not be thought that Christianity had entirely blotted out slavery[4]— who had taken refuge in a church and pleaded that he had paid the money for his freedom and had not been emancipated; at another time it was a poor patron who claimed to receive support from his former slaves, who had been manumitted. The prefect was often obliged to "teach" ($\sigma\omega\phi\rhoo\nu\acute{\iota}\zeta\epsilon\iota\nu$) by threats or flogging freedmen who ventured to treat with contumely or scant courtesy their patrons, or patrons' wives or children; if a freedman went to the length of informing or conspiring against his old master, he was beaten with clubs and tonsured, his freedom was cancelled, and he was handed over to his patron. Probably one of the commonest misdemeanours was the malversation by guardians of their wards' property.

---

[1] Glycas, p. 284.

[2] Our main source for the court ceremonies is the treatise of Constantine Porphyrogennetos, *de Caerimoniis*.

[3] Their duties are described in the *Ecloga*.

[4] The *Ecloga* proves that slaves were still numerous and slavery a recognised institution, although tending to disappear, cf. Finlay, ii. 220, 221. Finlay quotes a passage from Theodore Studita, "as a proof of the improved philanthropy of enlightened men during the iconoclast period": "A monk ought not to possess a slave, neither for his own service, nor for the service of his monastery, nor for the culture of its lands ; for a slave is a man made after the image of God." Theodore adds, however, "and this, like marriage, is only allowable to those living a secular life."

It was considered a crime to hire out a slave for prostitution, on the principle apparently of preventing, not cruelty to animals, but the corruption of human souls; and the prefect was supposed to interfere. It devolved upon the prefect to provide for fair dealings in the exchange and for fair prices in the meat market; and it was his duty also to preserve discipline in the streets and at the public games, for which purpose he had soldiers under him. He possessed the power of excluding any individual from the city or from any part of it, from trading in it or from attending a show, from practising a profession in it, and he could impose all these disabilities either temporarily or permanently. Thus the office of prefect still combined judicial with executive functions.

Some, however, of the duties which in a modern state, where there is a strict police control, would be discharged by that department, devolved, not upon the prefect, but upon the quaestor. For the quaestor had power over all strangers sojourning in the city, whencesoever they came and of whatsoever sex or profession they were,—even over clerks, monks, and nuns. It was his business to inquire who each was, whence he came, and what he wanted, and to take care that if he sought redress he should obtain it, in order that he might return as soon as possible to his home. For provincials were not allowed to stay in the capital or visit it whenever they liked; they were only tolerated there when they sought redress for injury or had a petition to present to the Emperor.[1]

The general law laid down by Justinian[2] was that if the quaestor found any one within the walls of Byzantium who was neither gaining his livelihood by a trade or profession nor concerned in a lawsuit, he was to be sent out of the city, if he were not a native; if he were a native and an able-bodied

---

[1] Farmers were especially discouraged from leaving their farms and coming to the city; yet they were often obliged to come when their lords refused to pay what they owed them for produce. Whenever the unjust lords tried to take advantage of the law's delays and thereby detain the plaintiffs in the capital, the quaestor was entitled to use short and severe measures, and dispense with legal formalities. The position of the farmers, γεωργοί, in the eighth century has been described above, p. 419. The following law from the Νόμοι Γεωργικός (Leunclavius, ii. p. 257) will show how free they were from anything like serfdom; it presents an instructive contrast to the laws about the *Colonatus* in the codes of Theodosius and Justinian. ἐὰν ἀπορήσας γεωργὸς πρὸς τὸ ἐργάζεσθαι τὸν ἴδιον ἀγρὸν καὶ ξενιτεύσῃ καὶ διαφύγῃ, οἱ τὰ δημόσια ἀπαιτούμενοι (the officers of the fisc) τρυγείτωσαν τὸν ἀγρὸν, μὴ ἔχοντες ἄδειαν ἐπανερχομένου τοῦ γεωργοῦ ζημιοῦν ἢ ζητεῖν αὐτὸν τὸ οἱονοῦν.

[2] Novel xcix. (ed. Zachariä).

man, he was to be enrolled among the public workmen, or placed in a bakery, or employed as a garden labourer, or have some other occupation assigned to him; in case he declined to work, he was to be expelled from the city. On the other hand, such as were maimed or old were to be gently dealt with. Besides these functions the quaestor had a judicial office of small scope; a certain kind of cases came before him, namely those of forgery and false coinage.

It is interesting to notice the two reasons assigned, in the eighth-century handbook of law, for the strict prevention of idleness in Constantinople. The first is that idleness leads to crime, and hence for self-protection the State is justified in discountenancing it. The second is that it is unfair that strong men should live by the consumption of the superfluity of the labour of others, because that superfluity is owed to the weak. The duty of supporting the weak is one of the christian ideas that had long since been recognised by custom, and had already penetrated into civil law.

The employments specially instanced as open to a man who wanted work are worth noting.[1] We are reminded that, besides the inevitable staff of public workmen, who, in a city like Byzantium, where fires were frequent and earthquakes not uncommon, had much to do beyond the repairs necessitated by the wear and tear of time, the State also supported multitudes of bakers, as the *panis et circenses* were a survival of antiquity that lasted long into the Middle Ages; and we are taught that the gardens, to which we sometimes meet casual references in the historians, were not the property of private citizens, but were parks for the people, kept up at the State's expense.

Little can be gleaned from our sources as to the details of the daily life of the educated lay classes. We get no glimpses into the drawing-rooms of the countesses, archontesses, or hypatesses[2]; all we can say with confidence is that religion filled a relatively large portion of daily life, and, as at all other periods, this applies especially to women. We might have

---

[1] Novel xcix. (ed. Zachariä).

[2] The wives of the officials received their husbands' titles with feminine terminations (as in Germany—Generalin, Majorin, Professorin, etc.) Letter 145 of Theodore of Studion is addressed to the "turmarchess of Hellas," to console her for the death of a son killed in war. In letter 195 we meet Eudocia, a canditatess, and in 217 the wife of the hypatos Demetrius is called hypatess (ὑπάτισσα).

conjectured with subjective certainty that the monks in their resistance to iconoclasm found firm allies in the female sex, even if we did not possess direct confirmatory evidence. Nor is it insignificant that a woman headed the reaction. But although the women, like the monks, had much to answer for in fostering and transmitting superstition, there were doubtless many enlightened mothers who could educate without tainting their children's minds.

There is evidence that weddings had still a Fescennine flavour, and the customs of licentious antiquity[1] had not been entirely abolished. But it is highly probable that there was not at this period more of that which might reasonably offend a delicate or seriously religious nature than there was at marriage festivities in the days of our ancestors not so long ago.

A few interesting traits are related about the domestic life of Theoctiste, whose acquaintance the reader has already made, by her son Theodore.[2] She was a considerate mistress to her servants; she allowed them not only bread, wine, and lard, but on feast days treated them to fresh meat, condiments, and fowl.[3] But nature had given her a quick temper, and being an orphan she had not been taught to keep it under control. Consequently she used often to fly into a passion and box the ears of her maids; but when she became cool again she would retire to her bedroom and strike her own cheeks to punish herself for her want of self-restraint. She used then to call the injured maid and ask her pardon.

The material splendours and the literary and scientific culture which had begun to distinguish the court of the Abbasid caliphs in their new city on the Tigris were well known and reported with exaggerations at Byzantium, but there is no evidence that they produced any visible influence on Byzantine life until the reign of Theophilus. Abu Djafar Manssur, the founder of Bagdad, had intended the place rather as a strong military fortress—to control Kufa on the one side and Chorasan on the other—than as a rich and luxurious capital. This caliph was miserly, even mean, in his habits, dressed

---

[1] Alluded to by Theodore Stud. in his *Funeral Oration on his Mother*; Migne, vol. 99, p. 885, μηδὲ τὸ ὄμμα   αἴρουσα εἰς τὰ θυμελικὰ παίγνια.
[2] In the *Funeral Oration*, Migne, 99, 884 *sqq*.   [3] *Ib.* p. 888.

shabbily, and was disinclined to pageantry and pomp. He did
not encourage poetry and he abhorred music; a story is told
that on one occasion, hearing a slave playing a tambourine, he
ordered the instrument to be broken on the player's head.
But he encouraged all positive sciences, history, law, grammar,
and natural science ; under him flourished Chalil the great
student of literature, and Mohammed Ibn Ishak the father of
Arabic history. It is remarkable, however, that most of the
learned men were of Persian nationality, and Chalid, the architect of Bagdad, was a Persian. The elevation of the Abbasid
dynasty and the translation of the centre of the empire to the
Tigris were accompanied by the rise of Persian influence,
which may perhaps be compared to the growth of Armenian
influence in the Roman Empire.

It was Manssur's son Mahdi, whose character in all respects
contrasted with that of his father, that originated the splendour
and luxury for which Bagdad soon became famous throughout
the world. The care for luxurious comfort may be illustrated
by the incident that ice was sent to Mecca in September
when the caliph was visiting the holy city. "The capital,
continually increasing in size," writes Weil, " soon became a
centre for all the rich and noble men of the realm ; music and
song, which in the reign of Manssur were condemned to silence,
resounded in the streets ; scholars and poets were drawn to the
court and rewarded with royal bounty ; everything was done
to support commerce and industry ; postal arrangements connected the capital with all parts of the empire ; and great
pilgrimages were organised, with a luxury and lavish munifi-
cence of which all the poor from Bagdad to Mecca profited ;
a special divan was made for the support of the blind." Thus
the reign of Mahdi was marked by a great reaction against the
stern parsimony of his father ; and the cruel Harun, the
famous hero of flattering romances, followed the example of
Mahdi in beautifying Bagdad and making his court attractive
by luxury and culture.[1]

The court of New Rome, from its foundation by Constantine,
was characterised by many oriental features derived from Persia.

---

[1] A picturesque account of Bagdad
has been written by M. A. Marrast.
This study is entitled "Bagdad sous les
Khalifes," and is published in the same
volume as " La vie byzantine au vi^e
siècle." He notices that the dancing-
girls at Bagdad corresponded to the
hetairai of Byzantium.

In dress, for example, the tiara and the skaramangion (state robe), the profuse use of ornaments, were imitated from Persian customs. In each succeeding century there was doubtless a marked increase in the distance of Byzantine life from old Greek and early christian simplicity, and in approximation to oriental richness. The rich men of Constantinople wore gold and jewels on their shoes [1]; the floors of their houses shone with glazed tiles. For the vessels of domestic use a simple and beautiful form no longer sufficed, they were overlaid with heavy gold leaf. This delight in rich and showy material naturally travelled to western Europe, which in all such matters revered Constantinople from afar, and relics at Aachen show how Byzantine ornamentation influenced art at the court of Charles. We must not think of comparing the luxury and opulence that marked daily life at Byzantium with the magnificence of old Romans, like Lucullus or the rich men described by Horace and Martial. Such colossal splendour is a thing quite distinct from the diffusion of oriental luxury on a small scale; and the houses of rich men at Constantinople in the eighth century resembled in point of opulence the mansions of wealthy merchants nowadays rather than the palaces of the old Roman aristocrats and bankers. In the first place, people were not so enormously rich; and in the second place, the spirit of the established religion seems to have had the effect of suppressing tendencies to extravagant display. Men did not think of lavishing fortunes on banquets of inordinate costliness; voluptuous carouses, celebrated in a showy and expensive manner, would have been considered a scandal and regarded as an insult to society.[2] Many unkind things were said of Constantine V because he kept a merry table, and yet we never hear it hinted that he wasted money on luxury or display.

The East was a country of fables and romances as well as

[1] We learn from the "Vita Tarasii" (*Acta. Sanct.* Feb. xxiii., p. 579) that Tarasius was obliged to correct and confine within decent limits the luxury displayed by the clergy in their dress. Garments of silk and girdles of gold seemed unseemly extravagance to a Patriarch who used to distribute clothes to the poor in a cold winter (p. 580).

[2] The reader may remember how in the reign of Philippicus the Bulgarians surprised on the shore of the Bosphorus a wedding party, provided with rich paraphernalia for feasting, γάμους τε ἐνουσίους καὶ δαψιλεστάτους ἀρίστους (wedding breakfast) μετὰ ποικίλου καὶ λοιπῆς ἀποσκευῆς (Theoph. 6204 A.M.) ἀργυρον ὡς πλεῖστον καὶ σκεύη οὐκ ὀλίγα (Niceph. p. 48). Here there was nothing extraordinary.

of material splendour, and here we come to an important field in which it influenced Europe. Novels and stories composed by individuals are in their nature an ephemeral branch of literature; and of the numbers that were disseminated in the Middle Ages comparatively few have survived. We have many tales in Italian or French, which came from Byzantine and ultimately from oriental sources, but of which neither the oriental original nor the Byzantine intermediate form remain. These stories reached the West in various ways, by southern Italy, by the exarchate while it lasted, and by Venice. The caliphate of Cordova in later times was a centre for their diffusion. But in this place we need not pursue a subject on which we have no direct evidence at such an early date, and I shall merely speak of the story of Barlaam and Josaphat, which doubtless reached Europe in the eighth century, even if it was not written in Greek by John of Damascus, as is usually stated. The tale underwent four translations or adaptations. The Indian original was rendered into Pehlevi, the Pehlevi into Syriac, the Syriac into Greek, and the Greek into Latin; whence German and French versions of the story were composed.

No one can read *Barlaam and Josaphat* without being struck by the resemblance which it bears to the life of Buddha. The heathen father of Josaphat in vain takes every precaution to hinder the decree of destiny or providence that his son was to become a Christian, and Barlaam converts the young prince, whose soul, being "naturally christian," was easily determined to abjure the things of this world and aspire to the ideal of monasticism. The discourses of Barlaam, which convince the prince of the new doctrine, are rich in oriental similes and metaphors, but the exposition seems to have been worked up anew and adapted for the Byzantine world by the Greek monk John, of the monastery of St. Saba, who brought the " edifying story " (ἱστορία ψυχωφελής) from India to the Holy City.[1] The note of the whole tale is the contrast between the

---

[1] The heading is: ἐκ τῆς ἐνδοτέρας τῶν Αἰθιόπων χώρας τῆς 'Ινδῶν λεγομένης πρὸς τὴν ἀγίαν πόλιν μετενεχθεῖσα διὰ 'Ιωάννου μοναχοῦ ἀνδρὸς τιμίου καὶ ἐναρέτου μονῆς τοῦ ἀγίου Σάβα· ἐν ᾗ ὁ βίος Βαρλαὰμ καὶ 'Ιωσὰφ τῶν ἀοιδίμων μακαρίων. In an article in the *Contemporary Review*, July 1870, Max Müller pointed out the resemblances of this story with the life of Buddha, as told in the *Lalita Vistara*.

world and the spirit,—the transitory and the abiding. The world is as a city where a new king is elected every year, and at the end of that term, when he is at the height of enjoyment and expects to reign for ever, the citizens dethrone him and banish him naked to a distant island. The wise man will follow the example of that rare king, who prudently thought of the future, and during his year's reign caused the treasures of the palace to be conveyed to the island of exile, so that when he was sent thither his wants were well supplied. But nothing in this vein is so striking as the allegory of the man suspended in the pit — a picture of medieval grotesqueness that might have been painted by Albrecht Dürer. A man fleeing from an unicorn which pursues him, stumbles into a pit, but rescues himself from falling into its depths by grasping a tree, which grew on the margin, and supporting his feet on a jutting ledge. But when he looked downward he saw a fiery terror in the shape of a dragon, eager to devour him; and at the roots of the tree he saw a black and a white mouse gnawing, whence he knew that his support must soon give way and precipitate him into the jaws of the monster. And from the ledge on which his feet rested he saw the heads of four asps peeping forth. Then turning his face from these horrors and looking upwards he saw a drop of sweet honey distilling from the tree, and a longing for the sweetness so possessed him that the things below were soon clean out of mind. The unicorn from which the man runs is death; the pit is the world; and the tree is the space of man's life. The white and black mouse which nibble at the roots of the tree are day and night; while the four asps represent the four unstable elements of which the human organism is built. The drop of honey is the pleasantness of the sweets of this world; the fiery dragon is the fearful belly of hell.[1]

An attempt was made, at the suggestion of the idolater Theudas (who afterwards burned his magic books, like Cyprian), to turn away Josaphat from his ascetic unworldliness by the temptation of beautiful and alluring women. As with Buddha, this stratagem was ineffectual; Josaphat was forearmed by a dream, which transported his imagination to a pleasant plain and a city, where he saw all the fascinations of beauty

---

[1] John of Damascus, vol. iii. ed. Migne (*Patrologia*), p. 976.

and pleasure, and, as his spirit was yielding to the seductions, he was removed thence to dark and dolorous places, where the young women seemed fouler than corruption.[1] In contrast with the asceticism of Barlaam and Josaphat is the temperament of the king, Josaphat's father, who held the bright pagan view of life, which accepts cheerfully and securely "this sweet light and the pleasant things which the gods gave to delight us."[2]

[1] John of Damascus, vol. iii. ed. Migne (*Patrologia*), p. 1149.
[2] *Ib.* pp. 1089, 1091.

CHAPTER XIV

CONCLUSION

AT the beginning of the period treated in this work the universal dominion of Rome was passing away. We have seen the Empire dismembered; we have seen how it came to pass that the West was taken and the East was left; and we have traced the history of nearly four centuries in which the Roman Empire, no longer a universal mistress, was administered by great legislators, great warriors, and great reformers, who ruled in the New Rome on the Bosphorus and were called by the same title as Octavian and Trajan.

If the idea of the Roman Empire before it was dismembered was universal dominion, if its function was to rule the peoples, *regere imperio populos*, what was its function, it may be asked, when it no longer represented that idea of universal dominion?

The answer is that the Roman Empire was the material and moral support, the political and spiritual bulwark of European Christendom; it represented the principle of cosmos. It was not enough, as some have thought,—as M. Guizot seems to have thought,—for the Roman Empire at the height of its greatness to give once for all a principle of order to the "wild nations." The author and giver of the principle could not be discarded; like the God of Descartes, the Roman Empire was the preserver as well as the initiator of civilisation. The view of the historical Anaxagoras, who attempts to explain European development by a prime impulse communicated once for all by the Roman Empire ere it retreated from the shores of western Europe, and who regards the "Romaic" Empire (if he does not call it by some more disparaging name) as a superannuated and decrepit survival, is a view which can as little satisfy the true student of history as the view, which represented Nous as the prime arranger of the elements of the world and then laid it aside as unnecessary, could satisfy the true philosopher. The Roman Empire was not, as many would have it, discarded as superannuated when its western provinces were lost; its existence could not have been dispensed with; its obliteration would have been fatal to the cause of civilisation. The "wild nations" had not yet learned more than the alphabet of their lesson; and if they disdained a mistress in the sense of a queen, *domina*, they required a mistress in the sense of a teacher, *magistra*, for a long time yet.

In the first place, the later Roman Empire was the bulwark of Europe against the oriental danger; Maurice and Heraclius,[1] Constantine IV and Leo the Isaurian were the successors of Themistocles and Africanus. The idea of European Christendom, at once Teutonic and Roman, making common cause against the peoples of Asia, who, if their progress had been unresisted, would have made the world stand still, first appeared clearly when Aetius and Theodoric fought together against the champion of desolation on the Mauriac Plain. But from that time forward it was destined that the Romans should perform alone the work of defending Europe; and until the days of the crusades, the German nations did not combine with the Empire against the common foe. Nor did the Teutons, by themselves, achieve any success of ecumenical importance against non-Aryan races. I may be reminded that Charles the Great exterminated the Avars; but that was after they had ceased to be really dangerous. When there existed a truly formidable Avar monarchy it was the Roman Empire that bore the brunt; and yet while most people who read history know of the Avar war of Charles, how few there are who have ever heard of Priscus, the general who so bravely warred against the Avars in the reign of Maurice. I may be reminded that Charles Martel won a great name by victories

---

[1] We do not associate the name of Justinian, like that of Heraclius, with the defence of Christendom against the Persians; for Justinian was not a hero, a warrior, or a deliverer. But we must not undervalue what Justinian did. While he was carrying out his great projects in the West, he successfully defended, both by arms and by diplomacy, the eastern frontier against the greatest monarch who ever sat on the throne of the Sassanids. I think this great historical fact is often lost sight of.

in southern Gaul over the Saracens; yet those successes sink into insignificance by the side of the achievement of his contemporary, the third Leo, who held the gate of eastern Europe against all the forces which the Saracen power, then at its height, could muster. Every one knows about the exploits of the Frank; it is almost incredible how little is known of the Roman Emperor's defence of the greatest city of christian Europe, in the quarter where the real danger lay. What should we say of the knowledge of one who was acquainted with the victory of the western Greeks over the Punic invaders of Sicily, and had never heard of the battle which was fought by the eastern Greeks at Salamis? The same remarks might be made of the earlier siege of New Rome in the days of Constantine IV, when the armies and the armaments of Muaviah were driven back and the nations of the West acknowledged the greatness of the Roman Emperor.

In later centuries the chivalry of western Europe went forth against the Moslem; but the crusades whose name is so familiar were of far less moment than that crusade against the fire-worshippers which was fought and won long before by the Emperor Heraclius, when the work was not merely to rescue the sanctuary of christian sentiment but to save the centre and bulwark of the christian world. For in the days of Heraclius Constantinople was in far greater peril than in the days of the Comneni, and its fall in the seventh century would have been a far more serious blow to the cause of European civilisation than its fall in the eleventh or the twelfth.

But, in the second place, the Empire was much more than the military guard of the Asiatic frontier; it not only defended but also kept alive the traditions of Greek and Roman culture. We cannot over-estimate the importance of the presence of a highly civilised state for a system of nations which were as yet only beginning to be civilised. The constant intercourse of the Empire with Italy, which until the eleventh century was partly imperial, and with southern Gaul and Spain, had an incalculable influence on the development of the West. Venice, which contributed so much to the growth of western culture,[1]

---

[1] It may be noticed especially that the art of enamelling was carried from Byzantium to Limoges through Venice; Labarte, *Handbook of the Arts of the Middle Age and Renaissance* (Eng. Trans.), p. 142.

was for a long time actually, and for a much longer time nominally, a city of the Roman Empire, and learned what it taught from Byzantium. The Byzantine was the mother of the Italian school of painting, as Greece in old days had been the mistress of Rome in the fine arts; and the Byzantine style of architecture has had perhaps a wider influence than any other. It was to New Rome that Teutonic kings applied when they needed men of learning, and thither students from western countries, who desired a university education, repaired. Nor should Englishmen forget that the man who contributed more than any other individual to the making of the English Church, both by ecclesiastical organisation and by the training of the clergy, was one born in Cilicia and educated at Athens, one who in his youth had rejoiced in the glories of Heraclius and lamented over the first conquests of the Saracen invaders,—the great Theodore of Tarsus. It was, moreover, in the lands ruled by New Rome that old Hellenic culture and the monuments of Hellenic literature were preserved, as in a secure storehouse, to be given at length to the "wild nations" when they had been sufficiently tamed. And in their taming New Rome herself played an indispensable part. The Justinianean law, which still interpenetrates European civilisation, was a product of New Rome.

In the third place, the Roman Empire for many centuries entirely maintained European commerce. This was a circumstance of the greatest importance; but unfortunately it is one of those facts concerning which contemporary historians did not think of leaving records to posterity. The fact that the coins of the Roman Emperors were used throughout Europe in the Middle Ages speaks for itself. To Finlay belongs the credit of having pointed out the extent of the commercial activity of Greeks in the Middle Ages; yet even still the old error is prevalent which regards the Saracens as commanding the commerce of the Mediterranean.[1] The mere circumstance that the law of the Mohammedans forbade the lending of money on interest gave the Greeks a considerable advantage.[2]

---

[1] For example, in a lecture of Dr. R. von Scala, *über die wichtigsten Beziehungen des Orientes zum Occidente in Mittelalter und Neuzeit* (Wien, 1887).

[2] Finlay, *History of Greece*, vol. ii. p. 212. We may say with Finlay that in the seventh, eighth, and following centuries " Constantinople was as much superior to every city in the civilised world, in wealth and commerce, as London now is to other European capitals " (*ib.*)

In the fourth place, the Roman Empire preserved a great idea which influenced the whole course of western European history down to the present day—the idea of the Roman Empire itself. If we look at the ecumenical event of 800 A.D. from a wide point of view, it really resolves itself into this: New Rome bestowed upon the western nations a great idea, which moulded and ordered their future history; she gave back to Old Rome the idea which Old Rome had bestowed upon her five centuries before. In point of actual fact, of course, the title of Emperor was usurped; but the immediate accidents of the transaction do not alter the general truth, that but for the preservation of the Roman Empire and the integrity of New Rome there would have been no Western Roman Empire; if Constantinople and the Empire had fallen, the imperial idea would have been lost in the whirl of the "wild nations." It is to New Rome that Europeans really owe thanks for the establishment of the principle and the system which brought law and order into the political relations of the West.

Of the incalculable services which the Roman Empire continued to perform for Europe and Christendom after the year 800 A.D. it does not devolve upon me to speak here; the diffusion of culture and Christianity among the southern and eastern Slaves, the missions of St. Methodius and St. Cyril, all that Russia owes to New Rome, belong to the history of the "Eastern Roman Empire," as it may fairly be called.

From the fifth century, when Rome on the Tiber ceased to be an imperial capital, until the fifteenth, when Rome on the Bosphorus fell, the Empire continued to represent the principle of civilisation; for a great part of that time it was the bulwark of Europe. Philosophers know that change is inconceivable without a principle of permanence, and cosmos impossible without an idea; and historians must recognise that the development of the German nations in the West, by which from a state of almost primitive barbarity they attained so soon to a highly complex civilisation, was rendered possible by the presence of the Roman Empire in their midst. Such was the function of the Roman Empire in Europe; it represented the principle of stability, and was a perpetual link between the present and the past—a permanent background, we might say, in a theatre of changes and commotions. With the name of

Rome, whether borne by Romani or by Romaioi, were indissolubly joined the ideas of law and culture (*civilitas*), and in the days of the Othos or of the Karlings, as in the days of Alaric, the true Roman Empire deserved and commanded the respect of the wild peoples ;

discite vesanae Romam non temnere gentes.

INDEX

---

[1] τὸ Ἀρξάμων (Theophylactus), τὸ Ἄρξαμων (Theophanes). The defeat of Leontius (*see* vol. ii. p. 199) took place at Arxamûn according to our texts of Theophanes, but one MS. gives Ἀρξαμοῦν and Anastasius has Ardamum. There can be no doubt that the scene of Leontius' defeat was close to the scene of Philippicus' victory.

---

[1] Called Black Bulgaria by the Bulgarians
of Moesia, who called their own kingdom
White Bulgaria. *White*, like *great*, was used
of the most important country; the original
settlement on the Volga was superseded, as it
were, by the settlement on the Danube.

---

[1] The ancient name of Drster or Silistria has many forms — Dorostolon, Dorostolos, Dorystolon, Durostorum, Dorostena, etc.

---

[1] I differ from Ducange (*Constantinopolis Christiana;* cf. the plan in Spruner's atlas) as to the site of Hebdomon. He places it near Blachernae, and thinks that the pro-

montory of Hebdomon was on the Golden Horn ; while I place the promontory on the Propontis, not far from the Golden Gate and Kyklobios. Cf. vol. ii. pp. 205, 310. It seems to me that the passage of John of Antioch, referred to on p. 205, and the passage of Theophanes, on p. 402, are decisive for the sites of Hebdomon and Magnaura.

---

[1] Šafarik's identification with Mankala has been abandoned. Küstenǵe corresponds to Constantiana, a little north of Tomi.

---

1 Zeuss held that Tudunus is not a proper name, but a title of a Khazar governor of Cherson, and appeals to a passage in Einhard (*Die Deutschen und die Nachbarstämme*, p. 739).

2 P

---

[1] Zaldaba in John of Antioch (fr. 214 e), Zaldapa in Procopius (*de Aed.* p. 308) and Theophylactus. The MSS. of Theophanes have Zardapa and Zandapa.

THE END

Printed by R. & R. CLARK, *Edinburgh*

254770

Made in the USA